# The Modernized Anti-Sicilians

## Volume 2
## Moscow Variation & Sidelines

Ravi Haria

First edition 2023 by Thinkers Publishing


All sales or enquiries should be directed to Thinkers Publishing, 9850 Landegem, Belgium.

Email: info@thinkerspublishing.com
Website: www.thinkerspublishing.com

**Managing Editor:** Adrien Demuth

**Assistant Editor:** Daniël Vanheirzeele

**Proofreading:** Conor O'Donnell

**Software:** Hub van de Laar

**Cover Design:** Kimberley Rubio

**Graphic Artist:** Philippe Tonnard

**Production:** BESTinGraphics

**ISBN:** 9789464201871
D/2023/13732/6

# The Modernized Anti-Sicilians

# Volume 2
# Moscow Variation & Sidelines

Ravi Haria

Thinkers Publishing 2023

Thinkers Publishing

# Key to Symbols

| | |
|---|---|
| ! | a good move |
| ? | a weak move |
| !! | an excellent move |
| ?? | a blunder |
| !? | an interesting move |
| ?! | a dubious move |
| □ | only move |
| N | novelty |
| ⟳ | lead in development |
| ⨀ | zugzwang |
| = | equality |
| ∞ | unclear position |
| =/∞ | with compensation for the sacrificed material |
| ⩲ | White stands slightly better |
| ⩱ | Black stands slightly better |
| ± | White has a serious advantage |
| ∓ | Black has a serious advantage |
| +− | White has a decisive advantage |
| −+ | Black has a decisive advantage |
| → | with an attack |
| ↑ | with initiative |
| ⇆ | with counterplay |
| ∆ | with the idea of |
| ⌓ | better is |
| ≤ | worse is |
| + | check |
| # | mate |

# Table of Contents

# Preface

This second and final volume of my Anti-Sicilian series covers our approach for all alternatives to 2...♘c6. The choice against 2...d6 was obvious. The Moscow variation is the only critical alternative to 3.d4 that has caused any concerns for Black – by developing with a tempo, we force Black to make an immediate decision on move 3 and wait for the right moment to open the position.

Whilst in the Rossolimo book I tried to achieve an objective advantage against every line, my choices in the Moscow were mainly selected by their ability to create practical difficulties for the opponent. Naturally, it is not possible to find an advantage in every variation but I have ensured to add many detailed explanations to guide plans and aid understanding in the various positions we'll encounter.

Against 3...♘d7, I analyse two distinct options – either castling immediately with the aim of breaking in the centre with c2-c3 and d2-d4, or first playing 4.a4 and denying Black their typical counterplay on the queenside. Against the solid 3...♗d7, I offer two choices of achieving central control. 5.c4 aims for a more positional Maroczy structure, whereas the alternative 5.0-0 transforms the position into a French advanced-type structure, where we develop interesting chances on the kingside. We already discussed 3...♘c6 in the first volume from the move order 2...♘c6 3.♗b5 d6, but I've analysed a second option – 6.h3 instead of 6.c3. The point is to limit Black's piece activity by suppressing the scope of the c8-bishop.

It was a bit harder to choose between 3.c3 or 3.g3 against 2...e6 – so I analysed both! The former transposes to an Alapin where my recommendations generally revolve around generating an attack against Black's king – this is even attempted in the more 'positional' lines after 3...d5 4.exd5 ♕xd5. The latter aims for a slower build-up before striking in the centre with d2-d4. Particular attention is given to Black's attempts to generate immediate activity with a ...d7-d5 push, and I think my analysis here makes Black's path to equality extremely narrow.

Finally, I thought it was important to also consider the less popular second moves (2...g6, 2...a6, and 2...♘f6). In particular, I examined both 3.c3 and 3.c4 against 2...g6. The latter transposes to an Accelerated Dragon, which I can justify including in an Anti-Sicilian book as I believe it's correct to enter an 'Open-Sicilian' type position if it benefits us. This approach has been emphasised across both volumes and it is made especially clear in the chapter against 2...g6.

On a personal note, in the two years since I published the first volume I have graduated from university, attained the Grandmaster title, represented England at the World Cup, European Teams', and Olympiad, and started a new job. I hope this somewhat justifies the delay in releasing this second volume – and for the few readers of this book, I hope the wait has been worth it. Theory has moved on from two years ago and it will continue to change, but I'm confident that this Anti-Sicilian series will provide a strong lifetime repertoire, and a foundation to respond to future theoretical developments.

My thanks to Kimberley Rubio for her generosity and skill in designing an amazing cover; Conor O'Donnell and Adrien Demuth for their extensive help and patience in editing and finalising this publication; my friends without whom this series would have been completed a lot faster; and as always my parents, simply for everything they do.

Ravi Haria
London, February 2023.

# Introduction

The Sicilian Defence has historically been Black's most popular weapon against 1.e4. Its prestige is grounded on a combative nature and fighting approach; Black isn't just playing for equality, but rather seeks to acquire counter-attacking chances straight from the opening. In response, the prevalence of Anti-Sicilians (alternatives to 3.d4) propagated due to their value in reducing the effectiveness of Black's counterplay. In this series, I aim to provide the foundation of a repertoire which seeks to retain the core values of Anti-Sicilians. Namely, I have consistently attempted to create endless practical difficulties for Black, whilst wisely waiting for the right moment to open the position and generate a dangerous initiative.

For too long, Anti-Sicilian rhetoric has centred on the logic of simplicity, geared towards reaching playable positions with easy plans while simultaneously avoiding depths of theory. The danger of this logic is the ease with which we can fall into the trap of inactivity; of mindlessly playing an opening without striving to trouble Black; of solely playing an Anti-Sicilian to avoid theory. In contrast, throughout the volumes I will advocate an active approach – with continuous underlying themes of achieving rapid development, dynamic piece play and dominant central control, with an important focus on denying Black the counterplay that they seek when choosing the Sicilian Defence.

In nearly every system against the various Sicilians, I have provided the reader with multiple options to choose from. Modern-day openings are constantly changing, and the necessity of flexibility in preparation has never been more vital. Having the ability to play different systems against the same opening is also beneficial in increasing our enjoyment of chess. Moreover, each alternative varies in style, enabling us to directly target our opponent's weaknesses – as well as concentrate on our own strengths. Obviously I can't promise that every line will ensure us an advantage. But by providing a wide variety of options, we can consistently make life difficult for Black and continue to create new and interesting ideas.

Although every variation has been checked and inspired by a combination of Leela Zero and Stockfish, the emphasis has always been on choosing the most human lines. Readers may notice that the analysis is often extensive – I felt this was often necessary in justifying my suggestions. Nevertheless, the focus in these volumes should be inspiration by the various ideas, rather than memorisation of long lines.

In tandem with textual explanations, my fundamental hope is for the reader to absorb the interconnected ideas between each variation. This will be extremely useful in responding to future developments in the Anti-Sicilian.

# Part I

# Moscow with 3...♘d7

# 4.0-0 ♘gf6

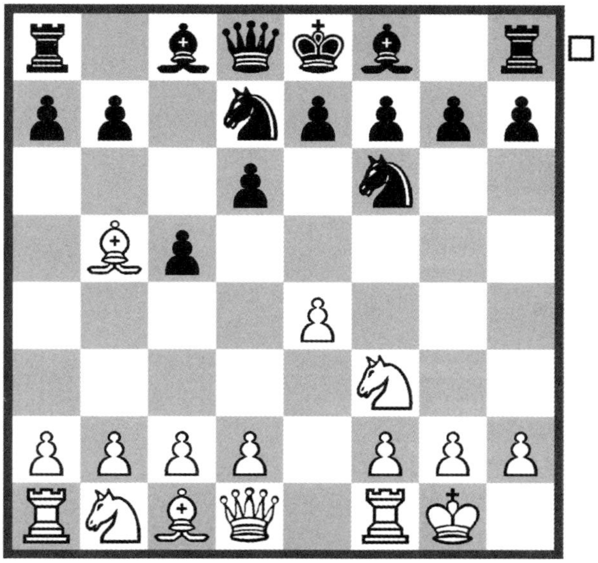

**1.e4 c5 2.♘f3 d6 3.♗b5+ ♘d7**

**4.0-0 ♘gf6**

# Chapter Guide

## Chapter 1 – 4.0-0 ♘gf6

1.e4 c5 2.♘f3 d6 3.♗b5+ ♘d7 4.0-0 ♘gf6 5.♖e1 a6 6.♗f1

## a) 6.--

**1. e4 c5 2. ♘f3 d6 3. ♗b5+ ♘d7 4. 0-0**

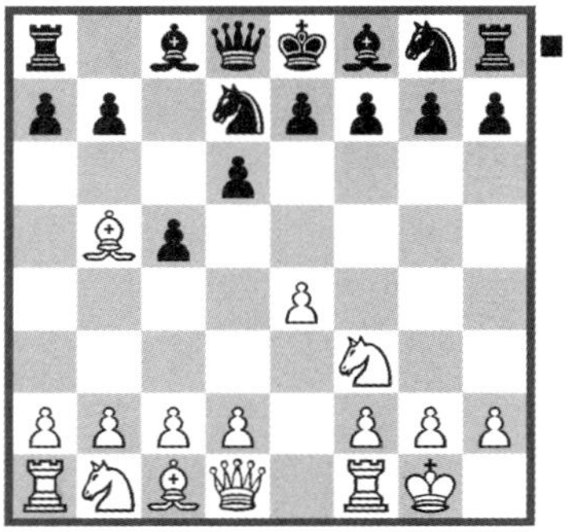

Position after: 4. 0-0

**4... ♘gf6**

By forcing us to play ♖e1, Black avoids our early c2-c3 option. However, the downside to this is our bishop is able to immediately retreat to f1 after ...a7-a6. As a result, White is essentially given an extra tempo to use in attempting to control the centre.

**5. ♖e1 a6 6. ♗f1**

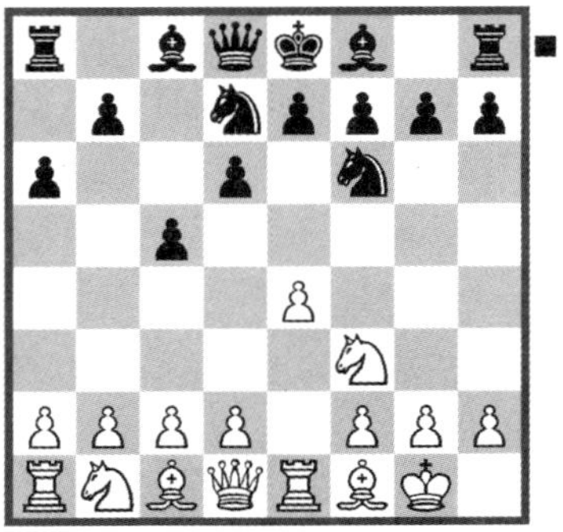

Position after: 6. ♗f1

**e6**

**A)** 6... b6 is the most popular continuation, aiming to prevent c2-c3 and d2-d4 by exerting pressure on the e4-pawn. I will illustrate how to instead continue in Maroczy style in the next subchapter.

**B)** 6... g6?! Gifting us both the centre and an initiative. 7. c3 ♗g7 8. d4 Hinting at e5, so for now Black has no time to push ...b5.

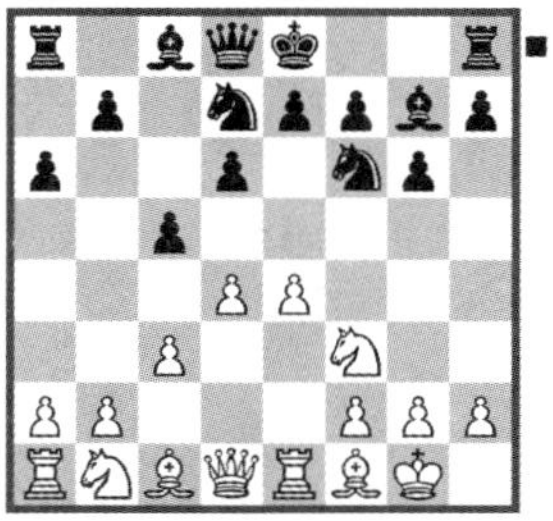

Position after: 8. d4

**B1)** 8... e5 9. dxe5 dxe5 [9... ♘xe5 10. ♘xe5 dxe5 11. ♕xd8+ When we are able to exchange queens in these structures, we should be doing very well. 11... ♔xd8 12. a4 ♗e6 13. ♘a3±] 10. a4! b6 11. ♘a3 0-0 12. ♘c4!

*(see analysis diagram next page)*

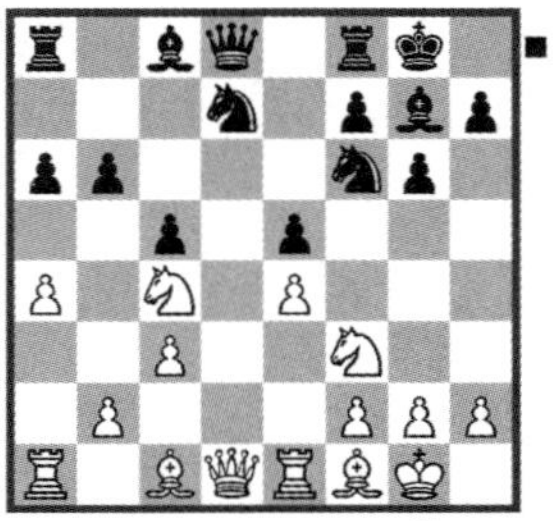
Position after: 12. ♘c4!

[I played 12. ♗g5± and went on to win a nice game in Haria – Sargissyan, Batumi 2018, but 12. ♘c4 seems even more convincing.] 12... ♗b7 [12... ♕c7 13. ♕d6!+– Forcing huge concessions.; 12... ♖e8 13. ♘d6 ♖e7 14. ♗c4+– followed by ♘g5 is overwhelming.] 13. ♘d6 ♗c6 14. ♘g5!

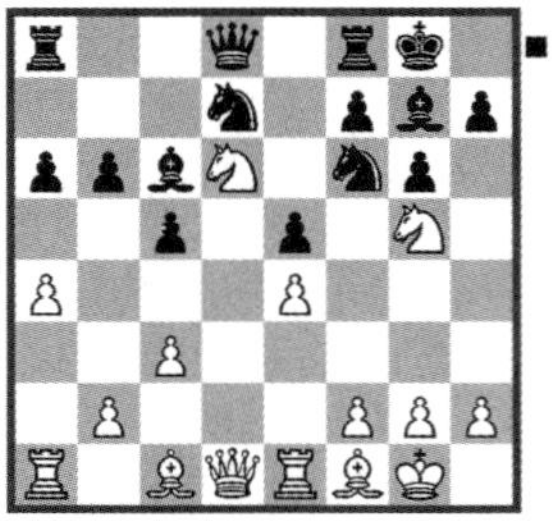
Position after: 14. ♘g5!

It's pretty much impossible for Black to defend the f7-square, e.g. 14... b5 15. ♕b3 c4 16. ♗xc4!+–.

**B2)** 8... cxd4 9. cxd4 0-0 10. a4! transposes to 8... 0-0.

**B3)** 8... ♕c7 9. e5! This move is even stronger when Black hasn't castled yet. 9... dxe5 10. dxe5 ♘g4 11. e6 fxe6

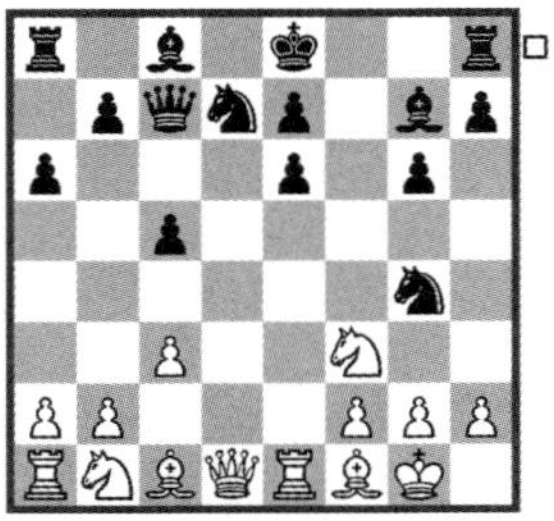
Position after: 11... fxe6

In Munoz Santana – Gruenfeld, Tromso 2014, the best continuation for White was 12. ♕a4! c4 [12... ♘ge5 13. ♘g5! ♕b6 14. ♘a3 0-0 15. ♕h4 h6 16. ♘xe6!+–] 13. ♕xc4 ♕xc4 14. ♗xc4 ♘ge5 15. ♘xe5 ♘xe5 16. ♗f1± with a very pleasant queenless middlegame.

**B4)** 8... 0-0

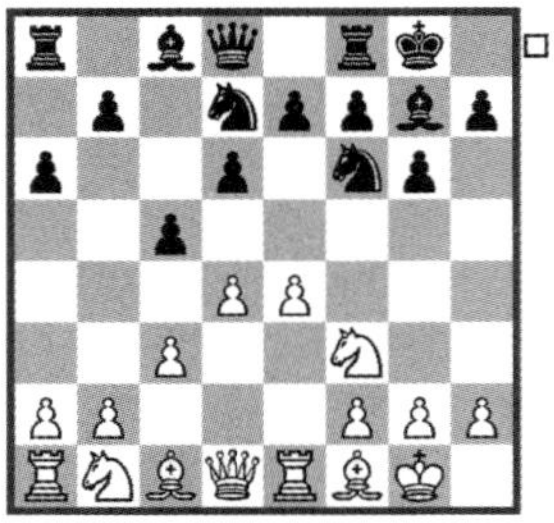
Position after: 8... 0-0

**B4.1)** 9. e5!? is always an interesting possibility:

**B4.1a)** 9... dxe5 10. dxe5 ♘g4 11. ♗f4! ♘dxe5 Black's g4-knight is trapped, so this is almost forced. Black is able to win back the piece but faces an unpleasant ending. 12. ♕xd8 ♖xd8 13. ♘xe5 ♘xe5 14. ♗xe5 ♗xe5 15. ♖xe5 ♖d1

16. f3 ♗f5 17. ♔f2 ♖xb1 18. ♖xb1 ♗xb1 19. a4! ♔f8 20. ♖xc5±

**B4.1b)** 9... ♘e8 10. a4 [10. h4!? seems logical too. 10... dxe5 11. dxe5 ♘c7 12. ♕e2 b5 13. a4 ♗b7 14. h5→] 10... cxd4 11. cxd4 dxe5 12. dxe5 ♘c7 13. ♘c3 b6

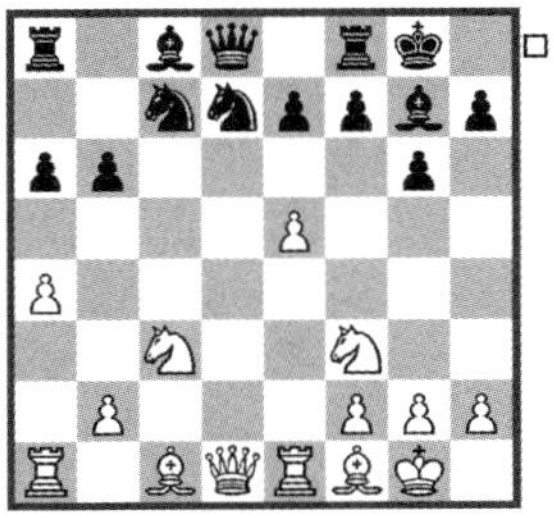

Position after: 13... b6

14. h4! Once again the position calls for an advance of the h-pawn. Things remain very complex, and there is much more that can be analysed after 9.e5. Nevertheless, it seems like a very decent option for us. 14... ♘e6 15. h5 ♗b7 16. h6 ♗h8 17. ♗e3±

**B4.2)** 9. a4! As always I'm keen to prevent Black from playing ...b7-b5.

Position after: 9. a4!

**B4.2a)** 9... b6 10. e5! An improved version of 9. e5. 10... ♘e8 11. ♗g5!

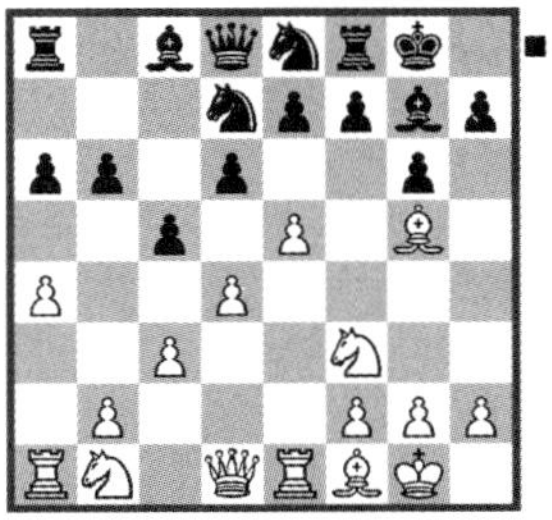

Position after: 11. ♗g5!

Threatening to capture on d6. 11... dxe5 12. ♘xe5 ♘xe5 13. dxe5 ♕c7 14. ♕e2± Again Black is left with a very passive position, and his queenside pawns risk being exposed as critical weaknesses later in the game.

**B4.2b)** 9... e5 10. dxe5 ♘xe5 11. ♘xe5 A draw was prematurely agreed in Roganovic – Sarenac, Ruma 2017. White was clearly better after the natural 11... dxe5 12. ♕xd8 ♖xd8 13. a5!±.

**B4.2c)** 9... cxd4 10. cxd4

Position after: 10. cxd4

10... e5 This central break is probably critical, but we can continue with the simple plan of creating a space advantage on the queenside. [10... b6 11. ♘c3 ♗b7 12. h3± is very pleasant too.] 11. d5 ♘c5 12. ♘fd2 a5 13. ♘c3±

**7. c3**

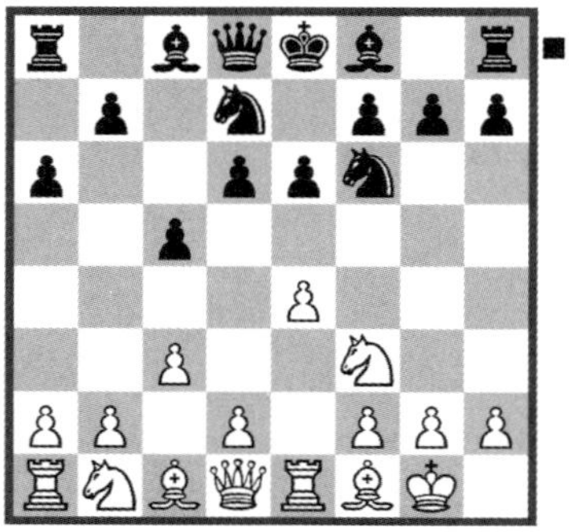

Position after: 7. c3

**7... ♗e7**

**A)** 7... ♘e5?! has been played several times but shouldn't really concern us. 8. d4 cxd4 [8... ♘xf3+ 9. ♕xf3 e5 10. dxe5 dxe5 11. ♘d2± Ricardi – Zair, Ubeda 1999.] 9. cxd4

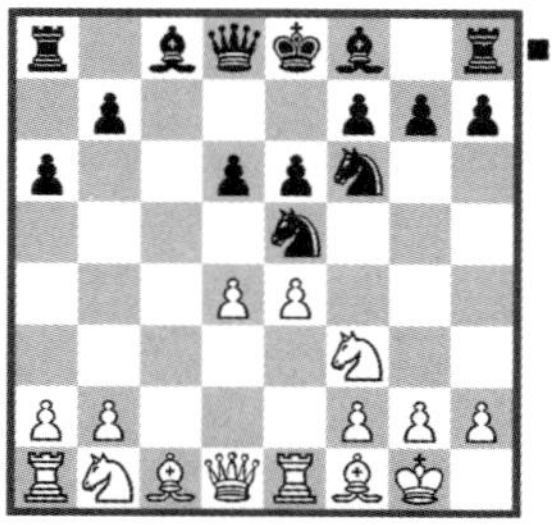

Position after: 9. cxd4

9... ♘xf3+ [9... ♘g6 10. a4 ♗e7 11. ♘c3±] 10. ♕xf3 ♗e7 This position was reached in a Garry Kasparov simultaneous game. Here it's possible for White to take over the initiative with 11. e5! dxe5 12. dxe5 ♘d5 13. ♕g3 ♔f8 14. ♖d1 ♗d7 15. ♘c3 ♘xc3 16. bxc3 ♕c7 17. h4→.

**B)** 7... b6 8. d4 ♗b7 9. d5!

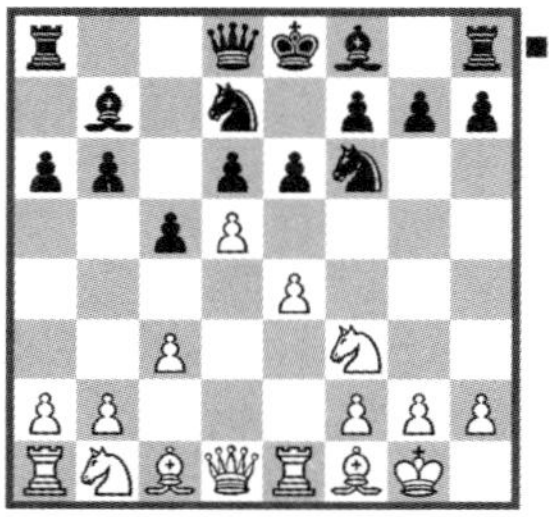

Position after: 9. d5!

Playing against the b7-bishop. White will stand clearly better in the resulting pawn structure. 9... exd5 10. exd5+ ♗e7 11. c4 0-0 12. ♘c3±

**C)** 7... b5 8. d4 ♗b7 This move order has occurred in a few top-level games, but White has a strong continuation: 9. e5! ♘d5 10. dxc5!

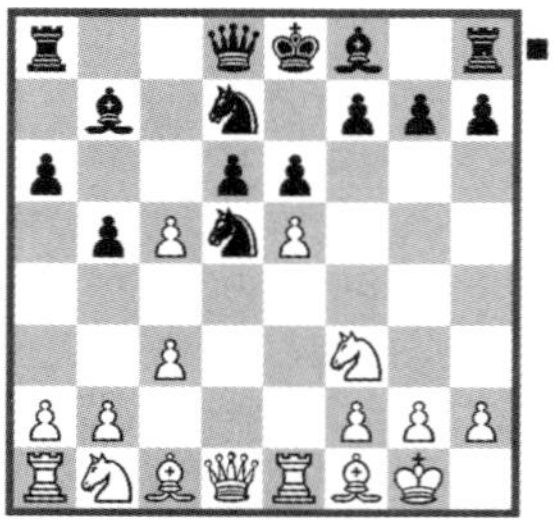

Position after: 10. dxc5!

10... dxc5 Now our simplest continuation is to take the positional approach. [10... ♘xe5 11. ♘xe5 dxe5 12. b4±; 10... ♘xc5 11. b4! ♘d7 12. a4±] 11. c4 bxc4 12. ♘fd2!±

**8. d4 cxd4**

8... 0-0 9. a4 b6 10. d5! A common idea if Black refrains from capturing on d4. 10... exd5 11. exd5 ♗b7 12. c4±

**9. cxd4**

Position after: 9. cxd4

**9... b5!**

Pretty much forced, or else Black gets way too passive. However we still have a pretty comfortable position with normal moves.

9... 0-0 10. a4± Black's position is feeling increasingly cramped.

**10. ♗d3**

10. a4 ♗b7 11. d5!? is potentially even stronger.

**10... 0-0 11. a3 ♗b7 12. h3 e5 13. ♘c3±** With a solid edge.

## b) 6...e5 7.c3 ♗e7 8.d4 --

**1. e4 c5 2. ♘f3 d6 3. ♗b5+ ♘d7 4. 0-0 ♘gf6 5. ♖e1 a6 6. ♗f1 e5**

*(see diagram opposite column)*

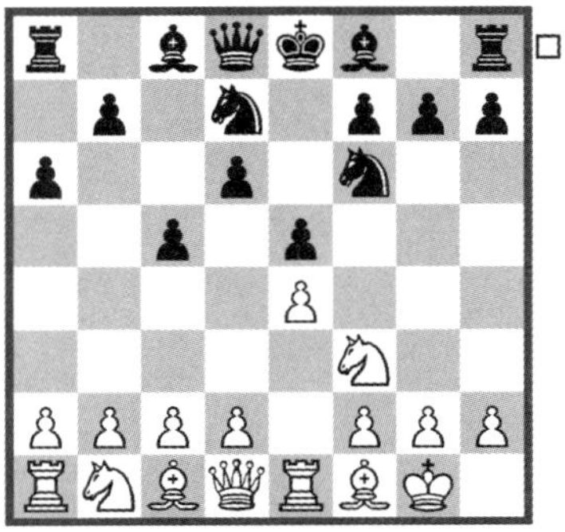

Position after: 6... e5

**7. c3 ♗e7 8. d4**

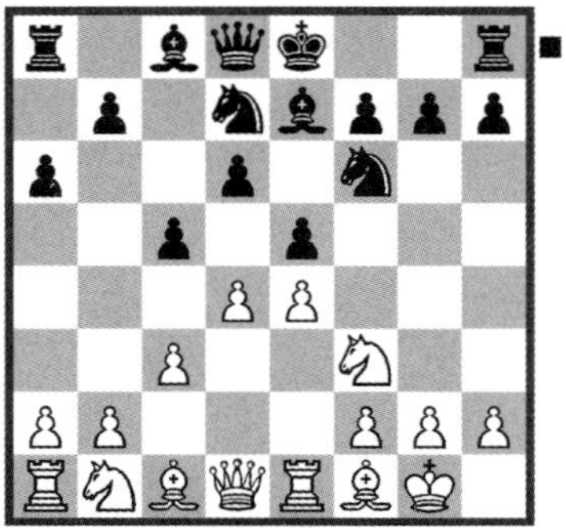

Position after: 8. d4

It's important to note that in this position we have the choice between two different plans to pursue. It's been very common to capture on e5 and try and positionally exploit Black's d5-square. However, another interesting plan is to play with d4-d5 and a2-a4. In this case, our knight will stand well on c4 and Black could face greater long-term problems with weaknesses on d6 and b6. We'll choose between these plans informed by how Black decides to arrange their forces in the meantime.

**8... ♕c7**

**A)** 8... cxd4 9. cxd4

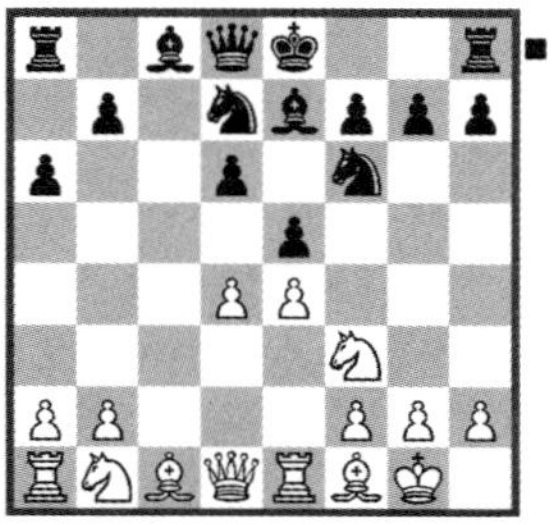

Position after: 9. cxd4

**A1)** 9... b5!? It might make sense for Black to play this before castling, but we can alter our piece set-up to maintain a good position. 10. a4 b4 11. ♗g5!

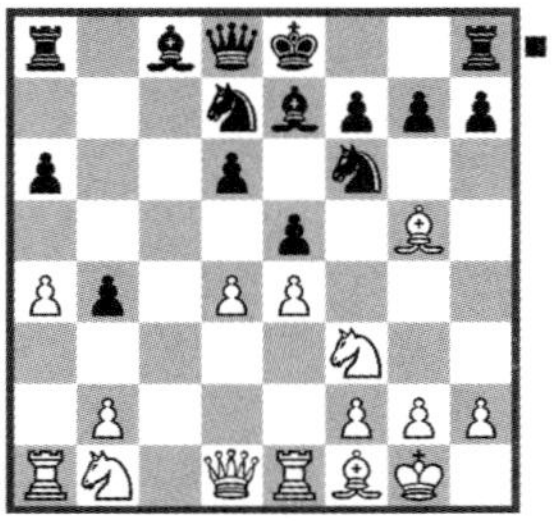

Position after: 11. ♗g5!

It's useful having a bishop here, as it often means that Black won't be able to enact a central break. 11... 0-0 12. ♘bd2 h6 13. ♗h4 ♗b7 14. a5 ♖c8 15. h3± Black still doesn't have a way to effectively break in the centre, and their queenside pawns look like they could become targets for attack.

**A2)** 9... 0-0 10. a4!

Position after: 10. a4!

We want to prevent Black from gaining space on the queenside with ... b7-b5.

**A2.1)** 10... b6 11. ♘c3 ♗b7 12. d5! Gaining this space advantage means any action on the queenside will be favourable for White. Also, the e4-d5 pawn construction is a good way to play against Black's light-squared bishop. 12... ♖c8 13. ♘d2 ♘e8 14. ♘c4±

**A2.2)** 10... d5!? Black sacrifices a pawn to gain some activity, but I don't think they'll be getting full compensation for it. 11. exd5 exd4 12. ♕xd4 ♗c5 13. ♕c4±

**A2.3)** 10... exd4 11. ♘xd4 d5 [11... ♘c5 12. ♘c3 ♖e8 13. b4 ♘e6 14. ♘f5 ♗f8 15. ♗b2± White had a great position in Bartel – Zakhartsov, Tallinn 2016.] 12. e5 ♘e4 13. f3 ♘xe5!?

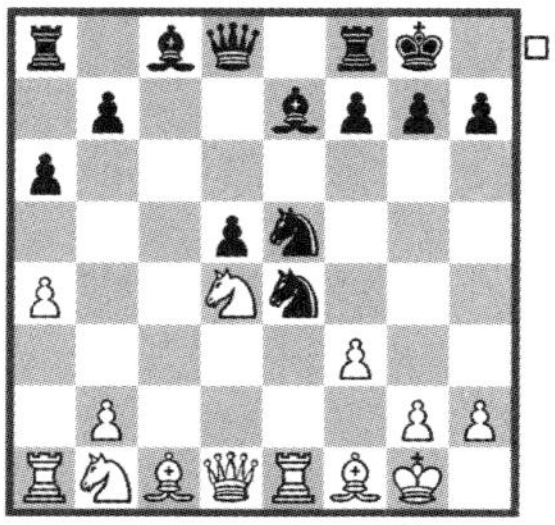

Position after: 13... ♘xe5!?

Another way that Black can sacrifice material to gain activity, but invariably I don't think that it's enough compensation. [13... ♘ec5 14. ♘f5+–] 14. fxe4 ♗c5 15. ♗e2! ♕b6 16. ♗e3 ♕xb2 17. ♘a3± Most likely followed by ♘ac2, and White has consolidated well.

**B)** 8... b6 9. a4 0-0 10. d5!±

**C)** 8... b5 9. a4 ♖b8 10. axb5 axb5 11. ♘a3 b4 In Christiansen – Anisimov, St Petersburg 2018, White missed a clever intermediate move. 12. dxe5!

Position after: 12. dxe5!

12... ♘xe5 [12... dxe5 13. cxb4 cxb4 14. ♘c4 ♕c7 15. ♗g5 0-0 16. ♖c1+–] 13. ♘xe5 dxe5 14. ♕xd8+ ♗xd8 15. ♘c4 ♗c7 16. ♗e3 bxc3 17. bxc3 ♘xe4 18. f3 ♘xc3 19. ♘xe5!

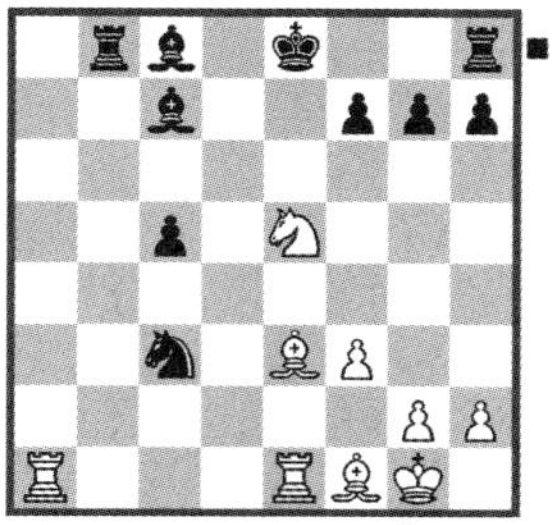

Position after: 19. ♘xe5!

19... ♗xe5 20. ♗xc5 f6 21. f4+– Despite material being pretty much balanced, White is completely winning due to the power of their bishop-pair and the activity of their rooks.

**9. a4!**

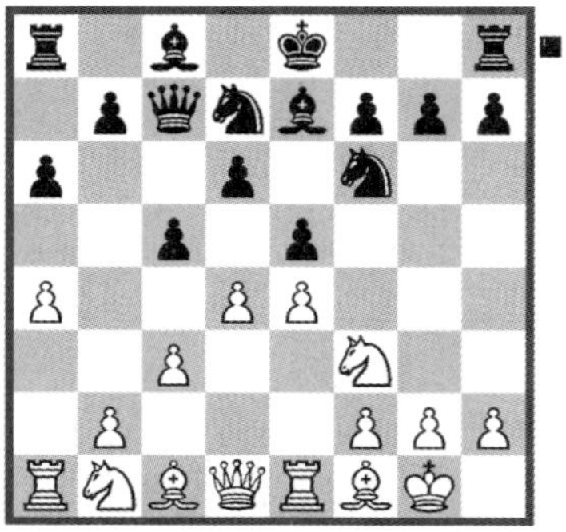
Position after: 9. a4!

In this case I prefer not to play 9. dxe5 because after 9... dxe5! 10. c4 ♘b8! Black has already protected the e5-pawn, and now the queen's knight can immediately be rerouted to c6. Even if White retains some pressure after 11. ♘c3 ♘c6 12. ♘d5 ♕d8 13. ♗e3 0-0, Black remains solid and I fear the advantage might dissipate soon.

**9... 0-0**

9... b6 10. d5! Black's queen seems misplaced on c7, and once again I really like this structure for White. 10... 0-0 11. ♘a3 ♔h8 12. b4 ♘g8 13. ♘c4 f5 14. exf5 ♖xf5 15. h4!

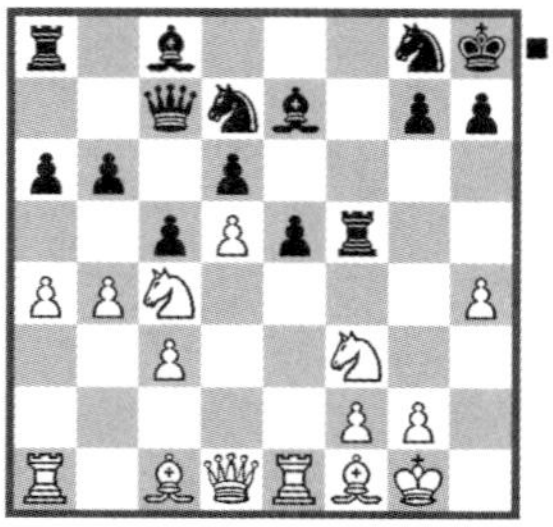
Position after: 15. h4!

We're obviously unable to play b4-b5 yet, but Black's attempts to do something on the kingside have opened up new avenues for us to explore. 15... ♗b7 16. ♘g5→

**10. d5! b6 11. ♘a3 ♗b7 12. b4 ♔h8**

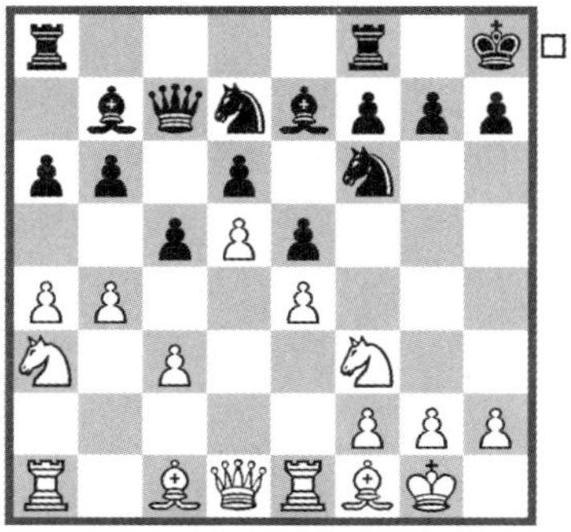
Position after: 12... ♔h8

It's probably wise for Black to prepare a kingside break, but we'll continue with the same plan of b4-b5.

**13. ♖b1! ♘g8 14. b5 a5 15. g3±**

Our knight will sit fantastically on c4, and we can begin to manoeuvre our pieces over to the kingside.

## c) 6...e5 7.c3 ♗e7 8.d4 0-0

**1. e4 c5 2. ♘f3 d6 3. ♗b5+ ♘d7 4. 0-0 ♘gf6 5. ♖e1 a6 6. ♗f1 e5 7. c3 ♗e7 8. d4 0-0**

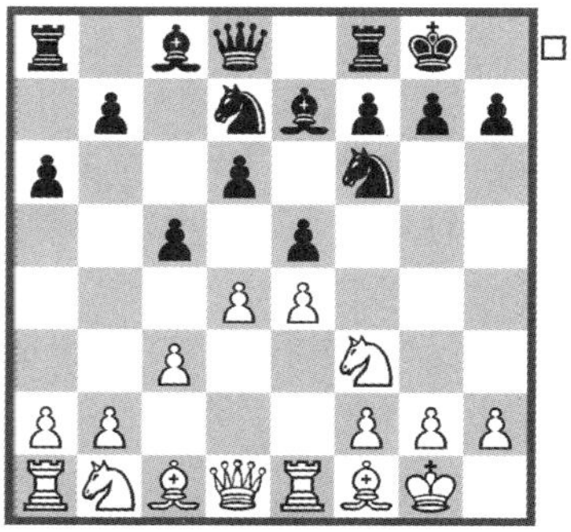

Position after: 8... 0-0

**9. dxe5**

It makes more sense to capture on e5 now compared to the line after 8...♕c7, as Black's queen stands well on that square, supporting the manoeuvre ...♘b8-c6.

9. a4!? is a flexible alternative.

**A)** 9... ♖e8 10. d5! ♘f8 11. a5 ♘g6 12. ♘bd2 ♘f4

Position after: 12... ♘f4

13. ♘c4+– White was already close to winning, and converted with ease in Ter Sahakyan – Valsecchi, A, Gjakova 2016.

**B)** 9... exd4 10. cxd4 d5 was played in Gallagher – Karthikeyan, London 2016. Here I think the best continuation was 11. e5 ♘e4 12. ♘c3!

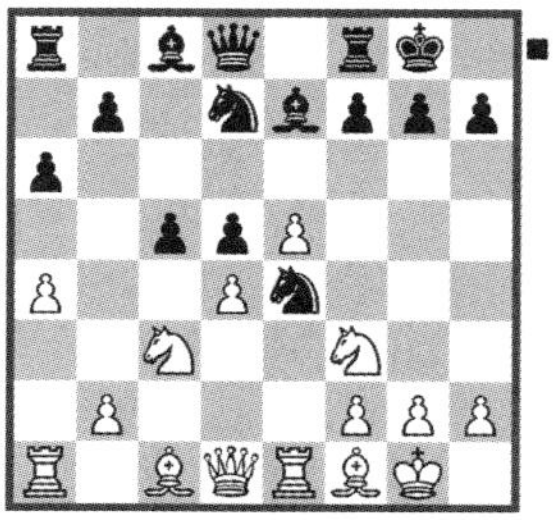

Position after: 12. ♘c3!

12... ♘xc3 13. bxc3 cxd4 [13... c4 14. g3!± Black's d5-pawn looks like it will be a weakness.] 14. ♘xd4±.

**C)** 9... b6 10. d5!

Position after: 10. d5!

The point - now Black is very passive on the queenside. The following variation is a good illustration of how to carry out our plan in these structures. 10... ♘e8 11. ♘a3 g6 12. ♗h6 ♘g7 13. ♕d2 f5 14. exf5 ♖xf5 15. ♘c4 ♗b7 16. b4 ♖c8 17. b5!

Position after: 17. b5!

It may seem weird to block the queenside like this, but actually it's an excellent positional decision. Our knight will be immovable from the c4-square, and we can focus our attention to the kingside. In the long-term, Black will always face big problems with weaknesses on b6 and d6. 17... ♖a8 18. h4!± Followed by ♘g5 with a strong initiative.

**D)** 9... cxd4 10. cxd4 transposes to 8...cxd4.

**9... ♘xe5**

9... dxe5 10. c4! White is in good shape to achieve ♘c3-d5.

**A)** 10... ♖e8 11. ♘c3 h6 In the game Haria – Eggleston, Newcastle on Tyne 2021, I chose 12.♕c2 with a comfortable game. A slightly better plan, however, was 12. a4!

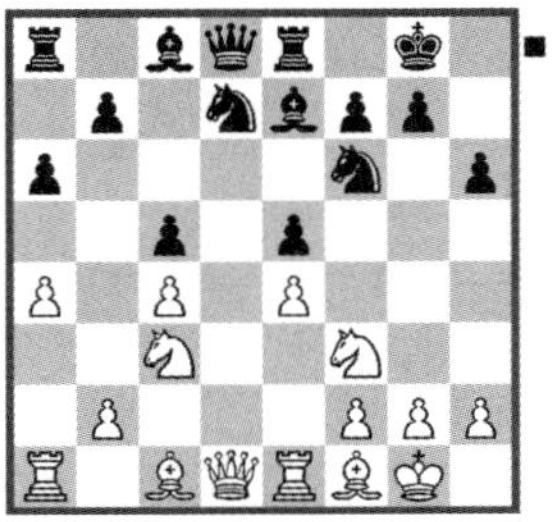

Position after: 12. a4!

12... b6 13. b3± followed by either ♗b2 or ♖a2-d2. In any case, White has numerous ideas and a very comfortable position, so there's no need to analyse any further.

**B)** 10... ♘e8 Black must try and respond accordingly by planting a knight on d4, but White can keep a large advantage with accurate play. 11. a4! ♘c7 [11... a5 12. ♖a3! ♖a6 13. ♖d3 ♖d6 14. ♖d5!±] 12. a5 ♘e6 13. ♘c3 ♘d4 14. ♘xd4! cxd4 15. ♘d5± Followed by ♗d2 and b2-b4.

**10. ♘xe5 dxe5 11. ♕xd8 ♖xd8**

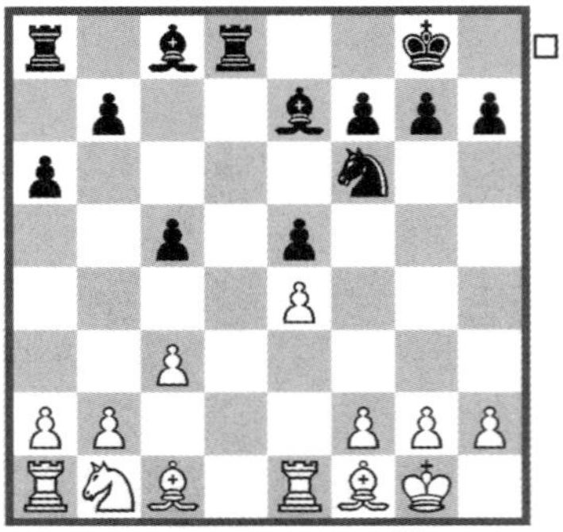

Position after: 11... ♖xd8

**12. a4!**

This ending is very pleasant for White.

**12... ♗d7**

12... ♗e6 13. ♘d2 ♘d7 14. a5±

**13. a5 ♘e8 14. ♗e3 ♖ac8 15. ♘a3 ♘d6**

In Muzychuk – Sebag, Beijing 2013, White should have continued with:

**16. ♘c4!**

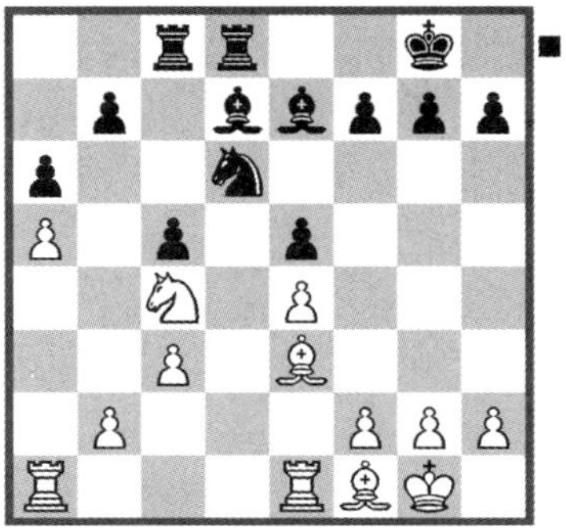

Position after: 16. ♘c4!

**16... ♘xc4**

16... ♘xe4 17. ♘xe5 ♗e6 18. ♘c4±

**17. ♗xc4 ♗c6 18. f3±**

## d) 6...b6 7.d4 cxd4 8.♘xd4 ♗b7 9.c4 --

**1. e4 c5 2. ♘f3 d6 3. ♗b5+ ♘d7 4. 0-0 ♘gf6 5. ♖e1 a6 6. ♗f1 b6**

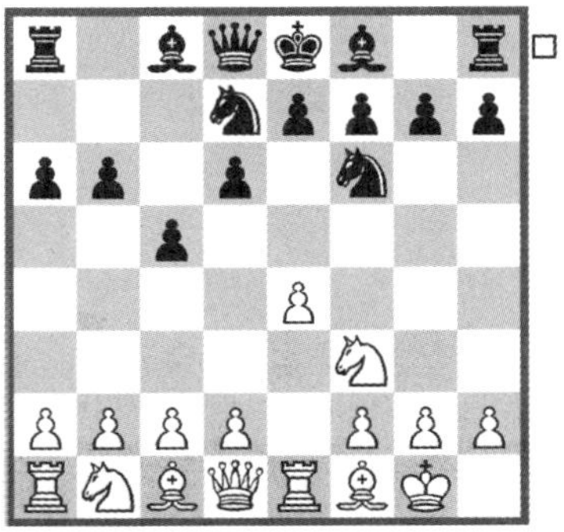

Position after: 6... b6

**7. d4!**

This subchapter will have a substantially different feel, as there are practically no forced lines but I still want to give a sense of the character of two different kinds of positions: those where Black plays ...g6, and those where they play ...e6.

**7... cxd4 8. ♘xd4 ♗b7 9. c4**

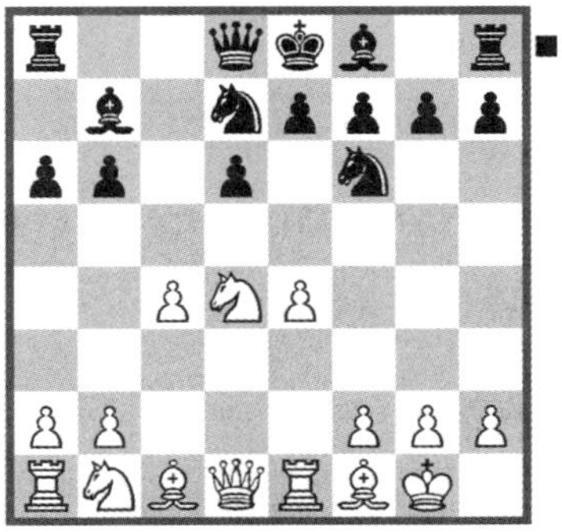

Position after: 9. c4

It's also fine to play f2-f3 first, but

there's no need as the e4-pawn isn't actually hanging here.

**9... g6**

One of the main problems with fianchettoing here is that, as we'll see in the lines after 9...e6, Black often needs to create kingside counterplay if they can't execute a central break. By playing 9...g6 Black decides to prioritise their king safety rather than play for ...h5-h4 or ...g5-g4. However, this means that it'll be harder for them to achieve the desired ... d7-d5 break and they'll also have additional weaknesses to deal with after any future ... e7-e6.

**A)** 9... ♗xe4? 10. ♘c3 ♗b7 11. ♘f5+–

**B)** 9... ♘xe4? 10. f3

Position after: 10. f3

10... e5 This is the best try, though White is doing very well. [10... ♘ef6 11. ♘f5±] 11. ♘f5 g6 12. fxe4 gxf5 13. exf5 ♖g8 14. ♘c3 ♘f6 15. ♗e3±

**10. f3 ♗g7 11. ♘c3 0-0**

*(see diagram next column)*

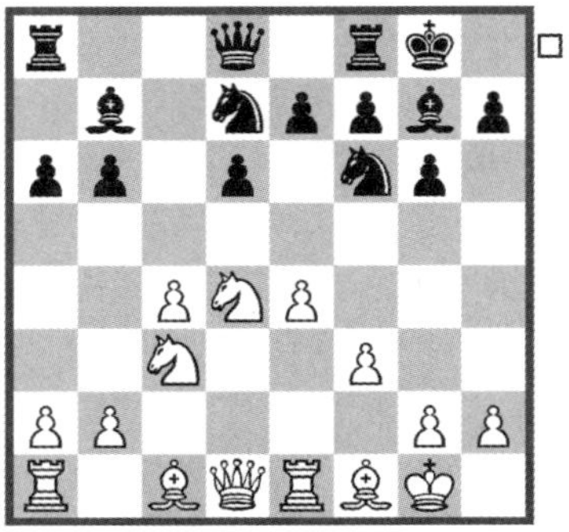

Position after: 11... 0-0

**12. ♗g5**

12. ♗e3 It's obviously possible to not tempt ...h7-h6, and instead just play ♗e3 straight away. 12... ♖c8 13. ♕d2 ♖e8 14. ♖ad1 e6 15. ♘c2 ♗f8 16. ♗h6 ♗e7 Now an improvment over Safarli – Esen, Al – Ain 2012 seems to be controlling the d5-square even more with 17. ♘e3! before continuing to play on the queenside. For example: 17... ♕c7 18. a3 ♗c6 19. b4 ♕b8

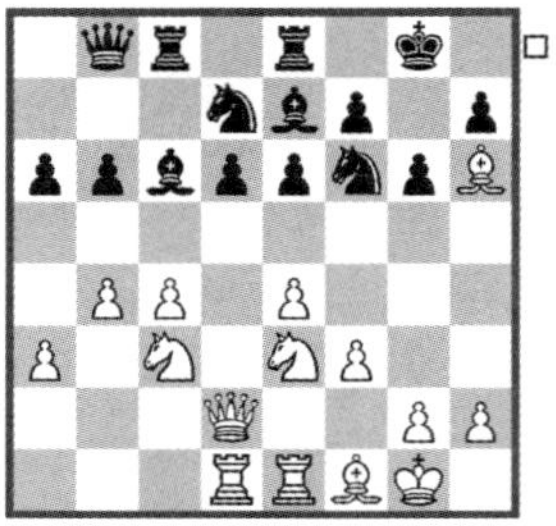

Position after: 19... ♕b8

Black is now prepared to break with ...b7-b5, as obviously ...d7-d5 is completely off the cards. However White can keep the advantage with the following line: 20. ♕d4!? [20. ♖c1 ♘e5 21. ♗e2 b5 22. cxb5 axb5 23. ♕d4 ♖ed8

24. ♔h1±] 20... b5 21. cxb5 axb5 22. a4! bxa4 23. b5 ♗a8 24. ♘xa4±

**12... ♖c8**

12... h6 13. ♗e3 will be better for White than the 12.♗e3 line due to the additional weakness provoked on h6.

**13. ♕d2 ♖e8 14. ♔h1**

14. ♖ac1!? might be even better, gearing towards queenside expansion. 14... ♕c7 15. ♖ed1 ♕b8 16. b4±

**14... ♕c7**

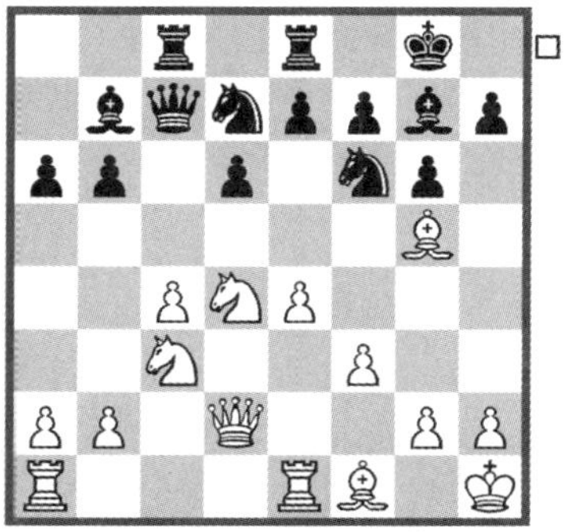

Position after: 14... ♕c7

**15. ♘d5!?**

This seems like a clever way to exploit the fact that Black has fianchettoed their bishop. If they do now kick the knight away with ...e7-e6, they'll have only succeeded in creating additional weaknesses.

**15... ♕b8 16. ♖ad1 ♗a8**

16... e6 17. ♘xf6+ ♘xf6 18. b3±

**17. b3 e6 18. ♘xf6+ ♗xf6 19. ♗xf6 ♘xf6**

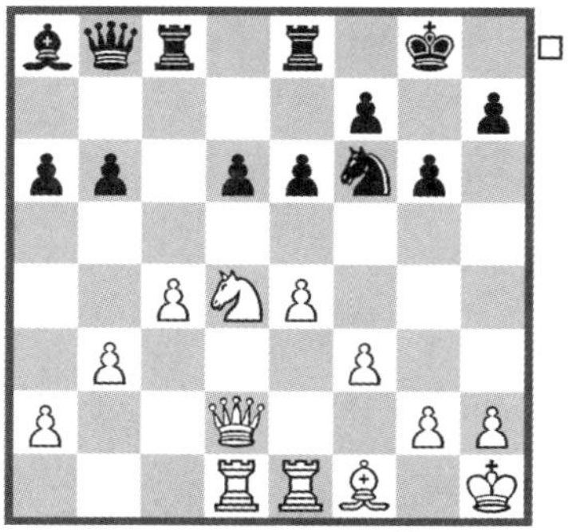

Position after: 19... ♘xf6

**20. ♘c2 ♖cd8 21. ♕d4 ♘h5 22. ♘e3±**

Black was unable to cope with the dark-squared weaknesses, and succumbed to defeat in David – Vignesh, Chennai 2015.

## e) 6...b6 7.d4 cxd4 8.♘xd4 ♗b7 9.c4 e6

**1. e4 c5 2. ♘f3 d6 3. ♗b5+ ♘d7 4. 0-0 ♘gf6 5. ♖e1 a6 6. ♗f1 b6 7. d4! cxd4 8. ♘xd4 ♗b7 9. c4 e6**

*(see diagram next page)*

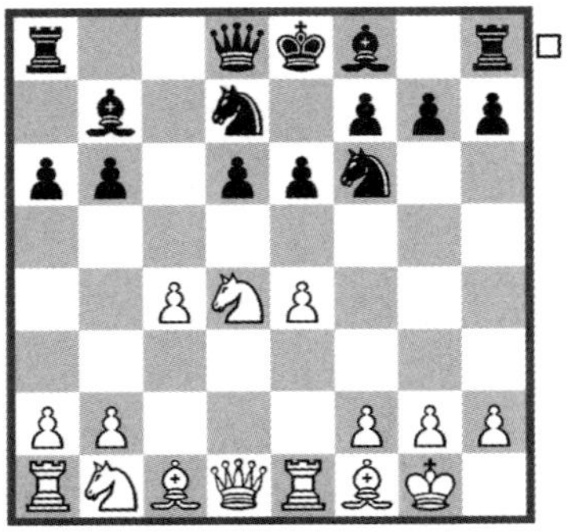

Position after: 9... e6

**10. ♘c3 ♗e7 11. f3 0-0 12. ♗e3 ♖c8 13. ♕d2 ♕c7 14. ♖ac1 ♕b8**

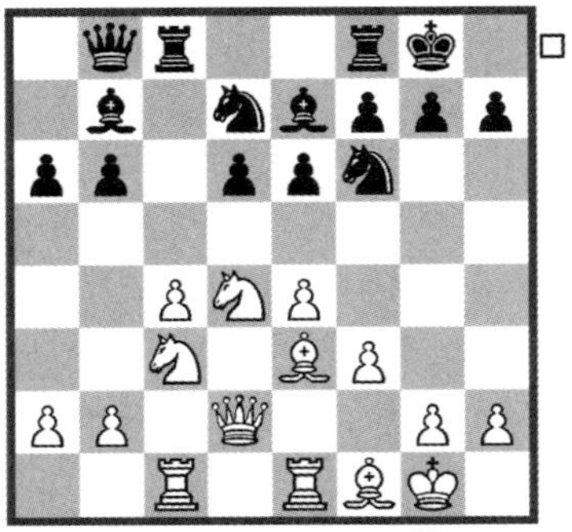

Position after: 14... ♕b8

We've reached a very typical Hedgehog structure. Actually, a lot of deviations were already possible over the last few moves, but nothing dramatically different. In the spirit of just providing some schematic notes to the stem game (Svidler – Topalov), I will first highlight a few plans for both sides here before referring to them in the variations below. It's evident from our piece placement that White should be playing on the queenside. For now it looks like a good idea to advance b4 at some point, as well as play ♘a4. (That doesn't mean the game will be positional in nature forever; the resulting positions can often become very tactical and require precise calculation.) Then, our most likely pawn break will probably be c4-c5, to open up the b- and c-files. Furthermore, if Black trades a few pieces, the d6- and b6-pawns may become targets for attack. White can also respond to Black's plan of playing ...♗d8-c7 with ♔h1 and ♗g1 to protect the h2-pawn. Black's strategy will revolve around trying to achieve a pawn break. As our light-squared bishop stands on f1, this break will almost certainly be ...d5 rather than ...b5. In most cases we'll be able to defend against ...d7-d5 effectively, either by capturing twice and targetting the resulting weakened a6-pawn, or by playing exd5 followed by c4-c5, with a positional advantage. Therefore Black will also strive to create kingside counterplay. They can do this in two ways: by pushing ...h5-h4-h3 (trying to weaken the a8-h1 diagonal), or by ...♔h8, ...♖g8 and ...g5-g4. In either case we should try and meet Black's kingside play with a quick queenside reaction; in many cases, Black will shuffle the pieces for a long time to try and arrange more fortuitous circumstances for some tactical strike.

**15. ♔h1**

15. ♘a4!? I prefer starting with this move. 15... ♖fe8 16. b4 ♗d8 17. ♔h1

**A)** 17... ♘e5 Black will often put the knight on e5 to try and induce f3-f4, which weakens our e4-pawn. On certain occasions it may be a good idea to push f3-f4 and embark on a kingside attack with f4-f5 and ♗d3, although it depends on the exact circumstances. 18. ♗g1 ♘fd7 19. ♖c2 ♗c7 20. ♖b1±

**B)** 17... ♗c7 18. ♖ed1 h5

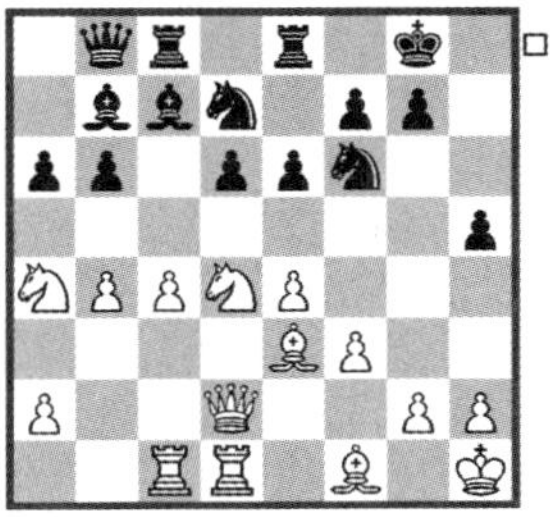
Position after: 18... h5

[18... d5?! 19. c5!±] 19. ♘b2! It's very typical to relocate the knight to d3 via the b2-square. 19... h4 [19... d5 20. exd5 exd5 21. c5±] 20. ♘d3± Now 20...h3 is well met with 21.g3. Otherwise we will consider both the potential of a queenside break - perhaps beginning with an a2-a4 push - or even the interesting prospect of placing our d3-knight on h3 to stem Black's counterplay.

**15... ♖fe8**

*(see diagram next column)*

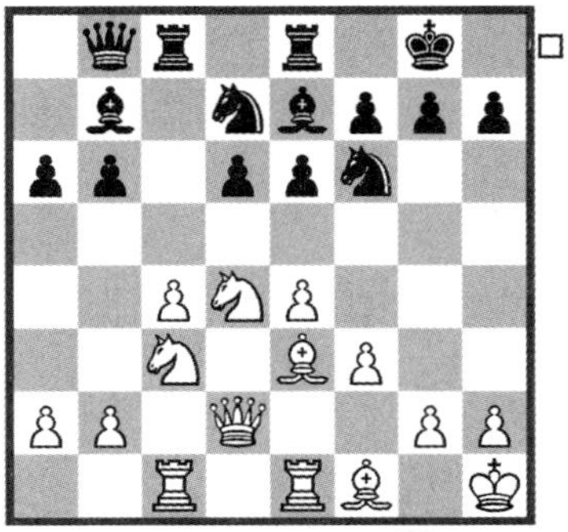
Position after: 15... ♖fe8

**16. a3?!**

This feels like a waste of time, although in such positions it's not obvious that a move is a 'waste of time'.

16. ♘a4 makes more sense, as our b2-b4 push will be supported by the queen on d2. 16... ♗d8 17. b4 h5

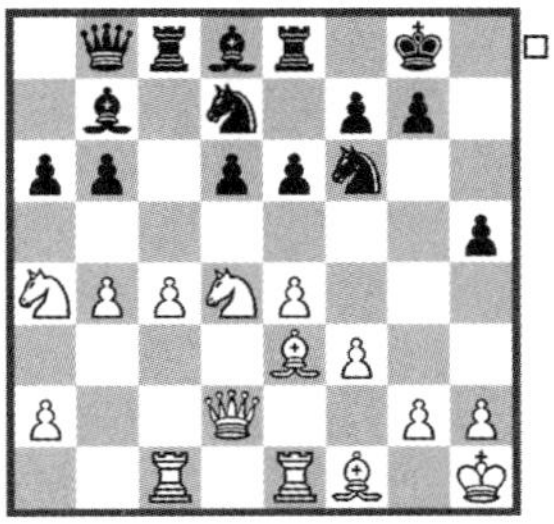
Position after: 17... h5

18. ♗f2! ♗c7 19. h3 ♘e5 20. ♕b2!?± Followed by ♖ed1 and either b4-b5 or c4-c5.

**16... ♗d8 17. ♗g1**

I would recommend only playing ♗g1 once Black plays ... ♗c7. Otherwise the bishop may stand better on e3 in response to ...h5-h4 ideas.

**17... h5!?**

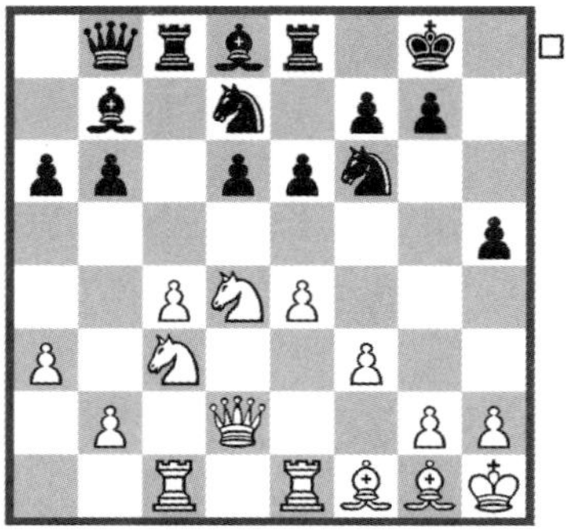

Position after: 17... h5!?

Neither central break is possible, so Topalov strives to achieve some kingside counterplay first.

17... ♗c7 18. b4 ♘e5 19. ♘a4

Position after: 19. ♘a4

19... ♘g6 [19... h5 20. c5! dxc5 21. bxc5 b5 22. ♘b6 ♖cd8 23. ♕a5!± Followed by pushing a3-a4.] 20. ♖c2 h5 21. ♘b2! As we've seen before, it's always a useful plan to reroute our a4-knight on d3. From there it stands very well, controlling central squares and supporting a future c4-c5 advance. 21... h4 22. ♘d3

Position after: 22. ♘d3

22... ♕a8 [22... h3 23. g3+–] 23. c5!? dxc5 24. bxc5 bxc5 25. ♘xc5 ♗f4 26. ♕e2±

**18. b3!**

Svidler reacts well to Black's kingside counterplay. As we are still a few moves away from creating a queenside reaction, we should actually consolidate our queenside before trying to match Black on the kingside.

If we continue to play expansively on the queenside with 18. ♘a4 h4 19. b4 ♘e5 20. ♗e3, things become unclear. [20. ♖c2 h3! achieves good counterplay. 21. gxh3 ♕a8∞] 20... h3! 21. gxh3 ♘h5⇆

**18... ♘e5**

18... ♗c7 19. ♖cd1 ♘e5 20. f4! ♘g6 21. f5 exf5 22. ♘xf5↑

**19. f4!**

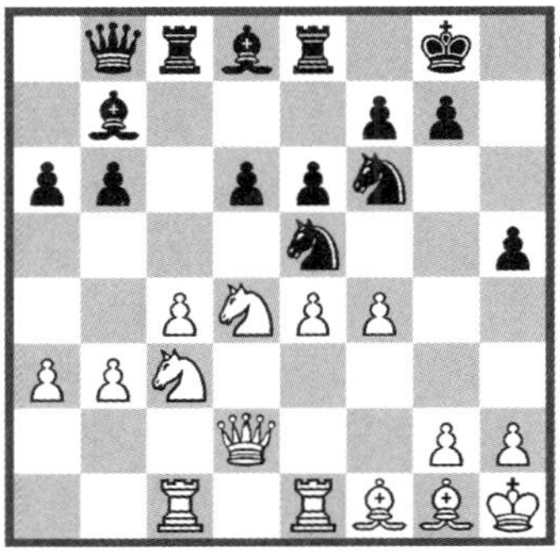
Position after: 19. f4!

**19... ♘ed7**

19... ♘g6 feels like a better try. 20. ♖cd1 ♕c7 21. f5! White should now fight back on the kingside. 21... ♘e5 22. fxe6 fxe6 23. ♘f3± White maintains superior control of the position.

**20. b4**

Now that White has better control, we can push b3-b4 to prevent ...♘c5.

**20... ♕a8 21. ♗d3 ♗e7 22. h3**

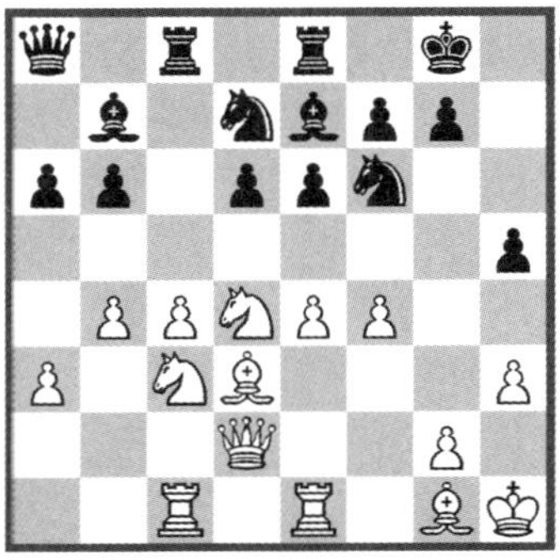
Position after: 22. h3

**22... ♖c7**

It feels like Black is struggling to find a consistent plan, whereas White's pieces are well placed for a central break.

22... h4!? The best practical option to achieve counterplay. 23. ♘f3 ♘h5 24. ♗f2 ♘g3+ 25. ♗xg3 hxg3 26. ♕e3± White still stands better, as the g3-pawn will fall. Nevertheless, Black has decent hopes of attaining counterplay

In Svidler – Topalov, Baku 2015, White missed his chance for a central break with:

**23. e5!**

23. ♖e2 h4! 24. ♗f2 ♘h5∞ was Svidler – Topalov, Baku 2015.

**23... dxe5 24. fxe5 ♘h7 25. ♗h2 ♘df8**

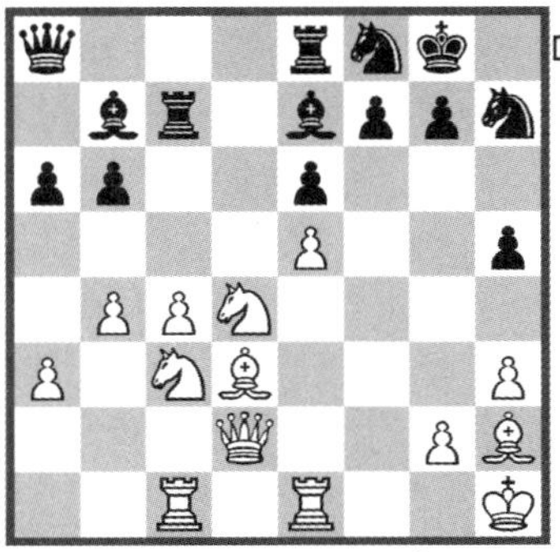
Position after: 25... ♘df8

**26. ♘e4+–**

With full control. Black is too passive and we can continue manoeuvring our pieces before jumping in with our knight do d6.

## Conclusion to Chapter 1

It is clear that if Black delays ...a7-a6 by playing 4...♘gf6, it's an open invitation for White to establish control in the centre. The critical lines in subchapters a, b, and c were when Black responded to our c2-c3 and d2-d4 advance by expanding on the queenside with ...b7-b5. It's important to note that depending on the variation, we either preemptively play a2-a4 to prevent this queenside push, or wait for Black to play ...b7-b5 before pressuring the b5-pawn with a2-a4.

Subchapters d and e showcased our alternative approach of controlling the centre, by responding to 6...b6 with d2-d4 and c2-c4. I think I effectively demonstrated our route to an advantage with the Maroczy structure. The key thing to note from the variations is how to organize our pieces, and correctly timing either a central or queenside pawn break.

# 4.0-0 a6

**1.e4 c5 2.♘f3 d6 3.♗b5+ ♘d7**

**4.0-0 a6**

# Chapter Guide

## Chapter 2 – 4.0-0 a6

1.e4 c5 2.♘f3 d6 3.♗b5+ ♘d7 4.0-0 a6 5.♗d3

## a) Early ...♘e5 Ideas

**1. e4 c5 2. ♘f3 d6 3. ♗b5+ ♘d7 4. 0-0 a6**

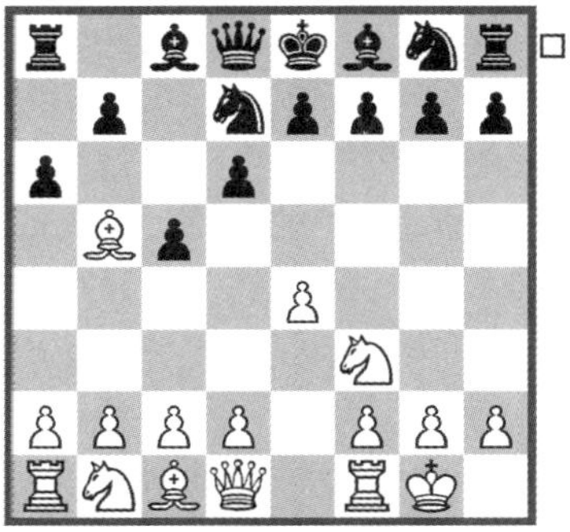

Position after: 4... a6

Not allowing us time to prepare ♖e1.

**5. ♗d3**

Black has often tried to exploit our bishop placement by playing ...♘e5, either here or after 5...♘gf6. These lines have held up okay in practice, but when we are armed with some knowledge it shouldn't be too difficult to prove an advantage.

**5... ♘gf6**

5... ♘e5?! 6. ♘xe5 dxe5 7. a4! Our set-up will involve playing b2-b3, ♗b2, ♘a3-c4 and f2-f4.

*(see analysis diagram next column)*

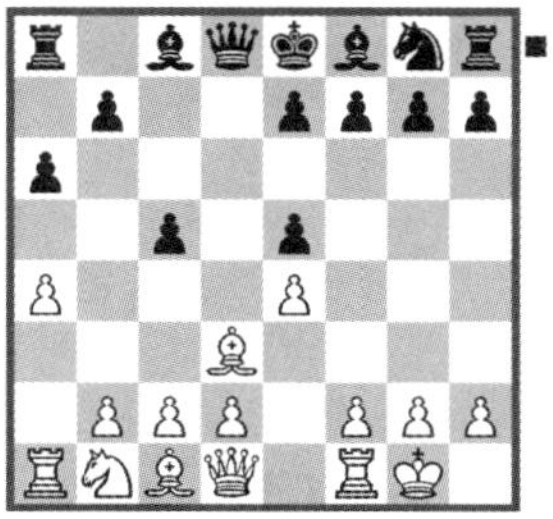

Position after: 7. a4!

7... ♘f6 [7... b6 8. ♘a3 ♗b7 9. ♘c4 f6 10. b3 ♘h6 11. ♗b2 We need to control the e5-square before pushing f2-f4. 11... ♕c7 12. ♕e2 ♘f7 13. f4 exf4 14. e5! 0-0-0 15. ♖xf4±] 8. ♘a3 ♗e6 9. ♕e2 g6 10. ♗c4

Position after: 10. ♗c4

10... ♕d6 [10... ♗d7 is more stubborn, but we can continue to play normal moves. 11. b3 ♗g7 12. ♗b2 ♕c7 13. ♗c3! 0-0 14. ♗d3 ♗e6 15. a5±] 11. ♗xe6 ♕xe6 12. a5 ♗h6

*(see analysis diagram next page)*

Position after: 12... ♗h6

A mistake but we still have an excellent position after, for example, 12... ♗g7 13. d4! ♗xc1 14. d5 ♕g4 15. ♕xg4 ♘xg4 16. ♖fxc1+– White had a positionally winning ending in Hracek – Esen, Warsaw 2013.

**6. c3**

6. ♖e1 is slightly more popular but I couldn't find anything convincing in the variation after 6... e6 7. c3 b5 8. ♗c2 c4∞.

**6... ♘e5**

This is a better attempt by Black to achieve a positional stronghold over the d4-square. We've already played c2-c3, so it's wise to change plans and continue with a different setup.

**7. ♘xe5**

7. ♗e2 ♘g6! It seems like the knight's position has massively improved, and Black won a nice game in Trent – Palliser, England 2013.

**7... dxe5**

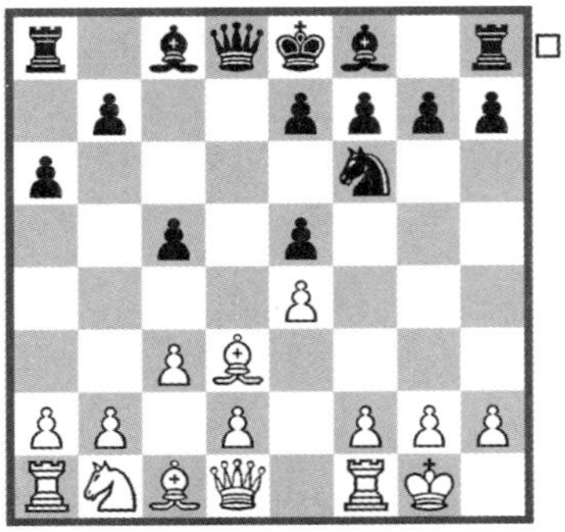
Position after: 7... dxe5

**8. ♗c2 g6 9. d3 ♗g7 10. ♗e3 ♕c7 11. a4!**

Position after: 11. a4!

I like the idea of playing on the queenside here, as Black's g7-bishop is shut out by the e5-pawn.

**11... b6**

**A)** 11... ♘g4 12. ♗d2 b6 13. b4↑

**B)** 11... a5? 12. ♘a3±

**12. b4! cxb4**

**A)** 12... 0-0 13. a5!±

**B)** 12... ♘g4 13. ♗d2 0-0 14. bxc5 bxc5

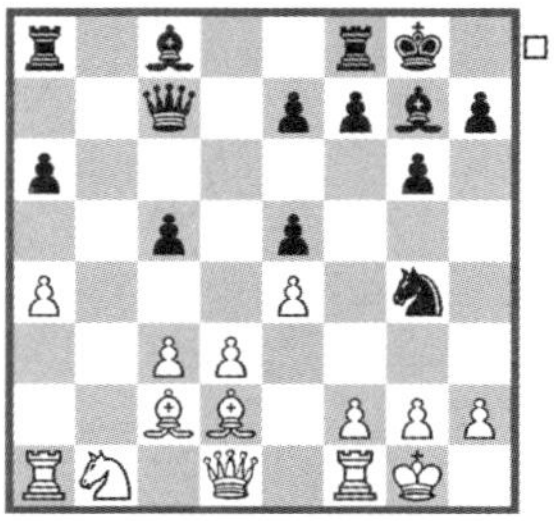

Position after: 14... bxc5

15. ♗b3! Our bishop will stand well on c4, and Black will have to contend with a weak c5-pawn for the remainder of the game.

**13. cxb4 0-0 14. ♗b3 ♘g4**

14... ♖d8 15. a5!±

**15. ♗d2 ♖d8**

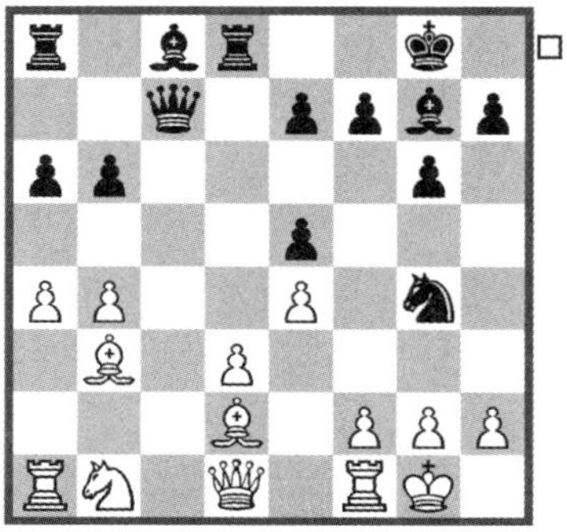

Position after: 15... ♖d8

**16. ♗c4±**

After kicking the knight away, we can continue with normal moves such as ♗e3, ♕b3 and ♘c3. The position seems very comfortable for White.

## b) 5...♘gf6 6.c3 e5 7.a4 ♗e7 8.♖e1 0-0

**1. e4 c5 2. ♘f3 d6 3. ♗b5+ ♘d7 4. 0-0 a6 5. ♗d3 ♘gf6 6. c3**

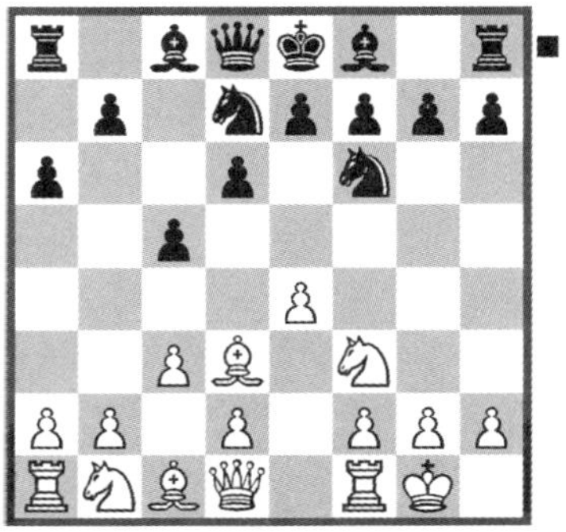

Position after: 6. c3

**6... e5**

I think this is a very underrated option. In the lines after 4...♘f6, we saw that with our bishop on f1 we were able to achieve an advantage in all lines. Here, the natural place for our bishop is on c2, but the variations illustrate that it could be misplaced on this square unless Black makes some concession first.

**7. a4!**

Controlling the b5-square before attempting to push d2-d4.

7. ♗c2 This has been the more popular

option, but I wasn't able to findanything convincing after 7... c4!∞.

**7... ♗e7 8. ♖e1**

Preparing to move the bishop to either f1 or potentially c4.

**8... 0-0 9. ♗c4!?**

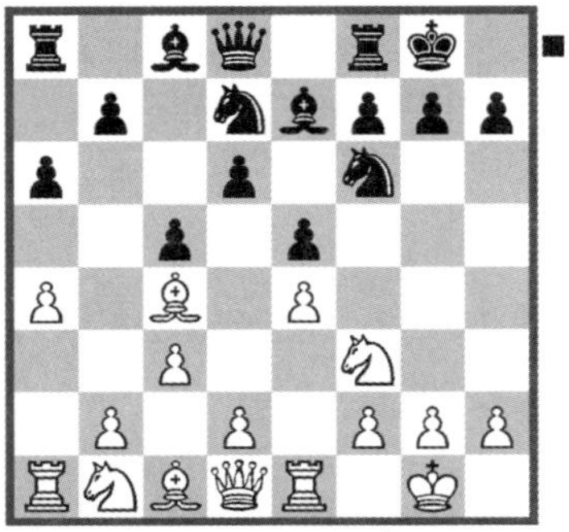
Position after: 9. ♗c4!?

This Italian-like alternative seems more appropriate to me than retreating the bishop to c2. I'm not claiming that White has a sizeable advantage, but I think it's an effective way to play against Black's setup. We're simultaneously preventing both ...b7-b5 and ... d7-d5, and our next few moves such as d2-d3, and ♘a3 are intuitive. I'll just provide a few illustrative lines.

**9... ♖b8**

**A)** 9... ♕c7 stops d2-d4, although that wasn't really our plan anyway. 10. ♘a3 h6 11. d3 ♘b6 12. ♗b3±

**B)** 9... ♘b6 10. ♗a2 d5

Position after: 10... d5

The immediate attempt to break in the centre doesn't equalise as Black suddenly has a few problems surrounding the weak e5-pawn. 11. d3! dxe4 [11... ♗g4 12. exd5 ♘bxd5 13. h3 ♗h5 14. g4 ♘xg4 15. hxg4 ♗xg4 16. ♕e2 ♖e8 17. ♘bd2+–] 12. dxe4 ♕xd1 13. ♖xd1 ♘xe4 14. ♘xe5± The main difference in this position is White's superior a2-bishop compared to Black's bishop on e7.

**C)** 9... ♘b8 This looks like the poor cousin of 8...♘b8. White can proceed in Italian style, or play 10.h3, or even break immediately: 10. d4!?

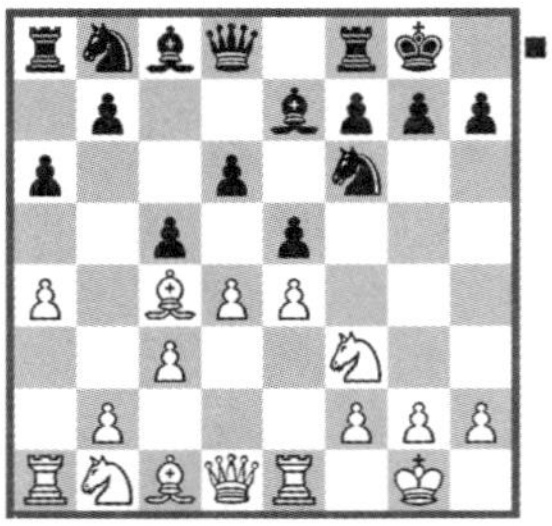
Position after: 10. d4!?

10... exd4 [10... ♗g4 11. dxc5 ♗xf3 12. ♕xf3 dxc5 13. ♘d2±; 10... cxd4 11. cxd4 ♘c6 12. h3±] 11. cxd4 ♗g4 12. dxc5 dxc5 13. ♕xd8 ♖xd8 14. ♘g5

♗h5 15. ♘c3± Our knight can re-route to f4 via h3.

**D)** The Marshall-esque 9... d5!? 10. ♗xd5 ♘xd5 11. exd5± also remains to be tested. My initial impression of it is not great, but maybe there are specific ways in which the bishop-pair can be used.

**10. ♘a3 h6 11. h3 ♘b6 12. ♗b3**

*(see diagram opposite column)*

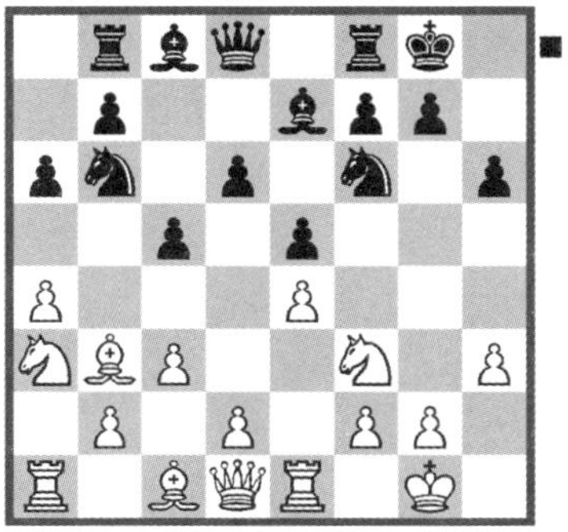

Position after: 12. ♗b3

**12... ♗e6 13. ♗xe6 fxe6 14. a5 ♘bd7 15. ♘c4±**

The game is still very complex, and I would advise the reader to analyse 9.♗c4 for themselves. However, I do think it is the best option in terms of posing as many challenges as possible for Black.

## c) 5...♘gf6 6.c3 e5 7.a4 ♗e7 8.♖e1 ♘b8

**1. e4 c5 2. ♘f3 d6 3. ♗b5+ ♘d7 4. 0-0 a6 5. ♗d3 ♘gf6 6. c3 e5 7. a4! ♗e7 8. ♖e1 ♘b8!?N**

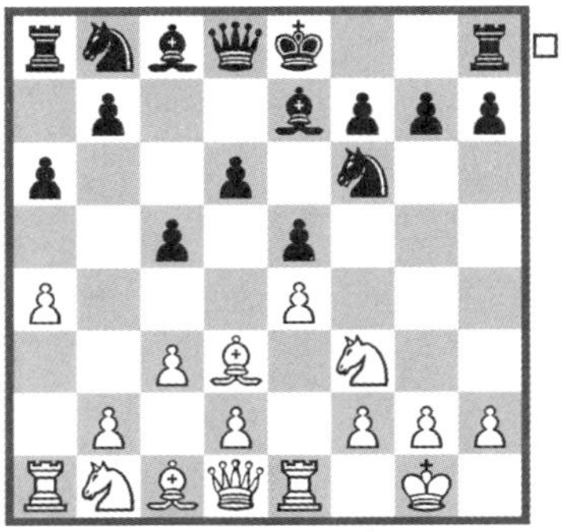

Position after: 8... ♘b8!?N

The engine's top choice, preparing for d2-d4 without wasting time castling.

**9. ♗c2**

I also checked 9. ♗c4 but wasn't terribly convinced this time due to the following variation: 9... ♘c6 10. d4 [10. d3 h6 11. ♘bd2 0-0 12. ♘f1 ♗e6= Zawadzki, S – Heberla, B Rowy 1998; 10. h3? ♘xe4∓ and only Black can be better.] 10... cxd4 11. cxd4 ♗g4 12. d5 ♘d4 13. ♘bd2 ♖c8 14. b3 b5!

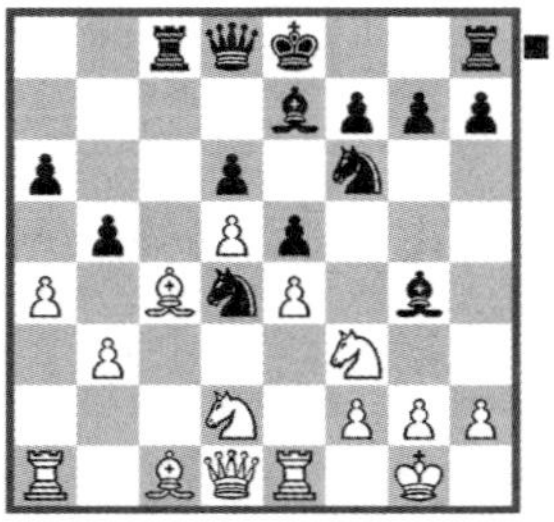

Position after: 14... b5!

15. axb5 axb5 16. ♗d3 0-0= White's position still feels easier, but any advantage is going to be quite intractable here.

**9... ♘c6**

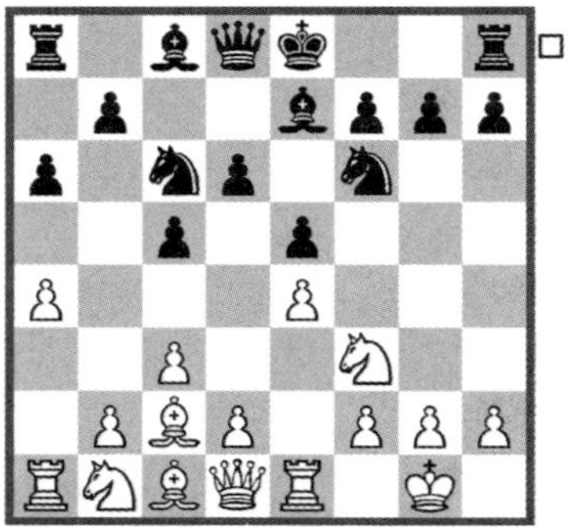

Position after: 9... ♘c6

9... ♗g4?! 10. h3 ♗h5 11. d3± Black's bishop stands badly on h5 - the simple plan of ♘bd2-f1-g3 followed by d3-d4 looks nice for White.

**10. h3!?**

Preparing the d2-d4 advance.

10. d4 poses less problems. cxd4 11. cxd4 ♗g4 12. ♗e3 exd4 13. ♗xd4 0-0 14. ♘c3 ♗xf3 15. gxf3 d5=

**10... 0-0**

The more flashy options are not holding up so well:

**A)** 10... g5?! 11. d4 cxd4 12. ♗xg5 ♖g8 13. ♗xf6 ♗xf6 14. ♔h1±

**B)** 10... ♖g8 11. d4 cxd4 12. cxd4 g5 13. d5 ♘b4 14. ♗b3 a5 15. ♘a3±

**C)** 10... ♕b6 11. ♘a3 ♗e6 12. d3± To be followed by ♘c4-e3 with an edge.

**11. d4 exd4**

11... cxd4 fails to equalise after 12. cxd4 exd4 13. ♘xd4 d5 14. ♘xc6 bxc6 15. exd5 ♘xd5 16. ♕d3 g6 17. ♗h6 ♖e8 18. ♘c3±.

**12. cxd4 d5 13. e5**

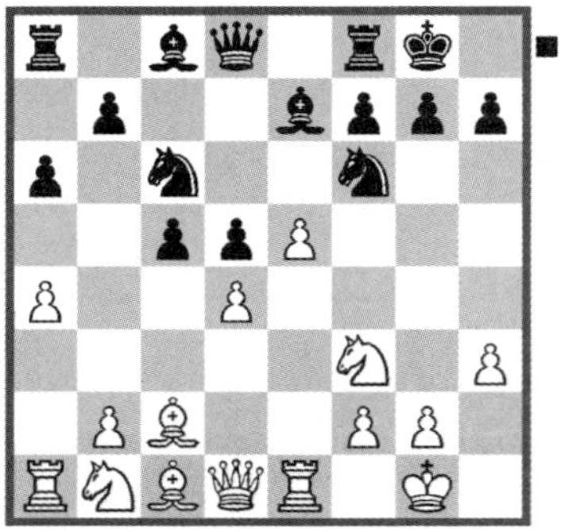

Position after: 13. e5

**13... ♘e4 14. dxc5**

Probably White's best attempt at finding an advantage here.

14. ♘c3 is an alternative. 14... ♗f5! [14... ♘xc3? 15. bxc3 cxd4 16. ♘xd4!±] 15. ♘xe4 ♗xe4 16. dxc5 ♗xc5 17. ♘g5 ♗g6!

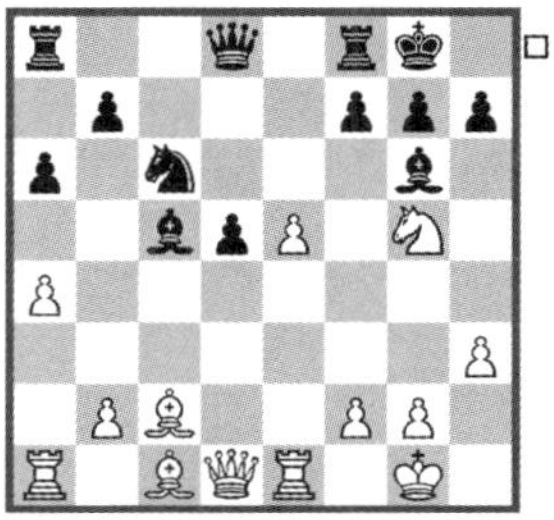
Position after: 17... ♗g6!

18. ♗xg6 fxg6! [18... hxg6 19. ♕g4→] 19. ♘f3 It feels like Black has enough counterplay here, although the position remains complicated with chances for both sides.

**14... ♘xc5!**

14... ♗xc5 15. ♗e3 ♗xe3 16. ♖xe3 ♘c5 17. ♖e2±

**15. ♗e3 ♘e6 16. ♕d3**

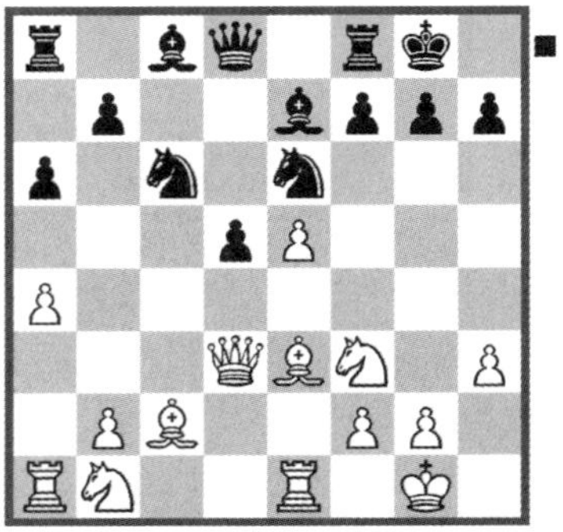
Position after: 16. ♕d3

The start of a relatively forcing line.

**16... g6 17. ♗h6 ♖e8 18. ♘c3 d4 19. ♘e4 ♘b4 20. ♕d2**

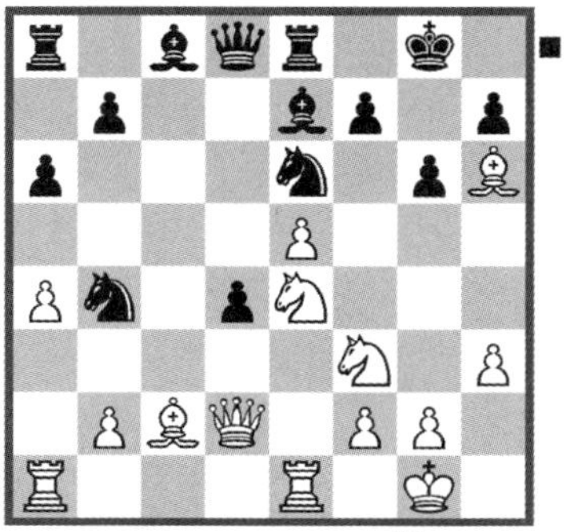
Position after: 20. ♕d2

**20... ♘xc2**

20... ♕d5 21. ♕xb4!±

**21. ♕xc2 ♗d7**

21... ♕d5 22. ♘f6+ ♗xf6 23. exf6± White definitely has the better practical chances due to Black's dark-squared weaknesses.

**22. ♖ed1 ♖c8 23. ♕d3 ♕c7 24. ♘xd4 ♕xe5 25. ♘f3**

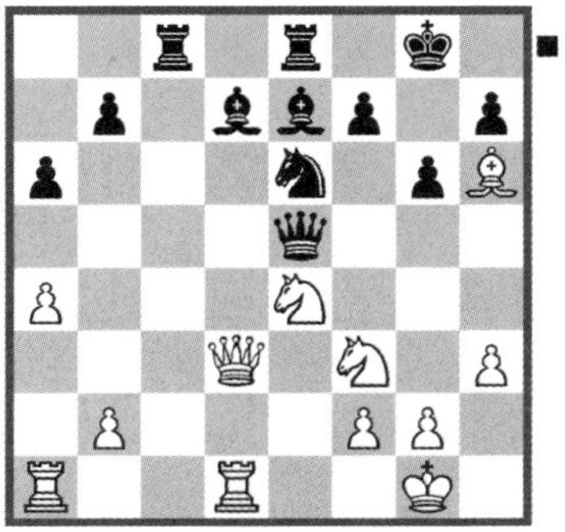
Position after: 25. ♘f3

**25... ♕b8!=**

As a result of some extremely accurate moves by Black, it looks like they've pretty much equalised. The d7-bishop is immune as our queen will get trapped.

## d) 5...♘gf6 6.c3 g6 7.♗c2 c4

**1. e4 c5 2. ♘f3 d6 3. ♗b5+ ♘d7 4. 0-0 a6 5. ♗d3 ♘gf6**

5... g6

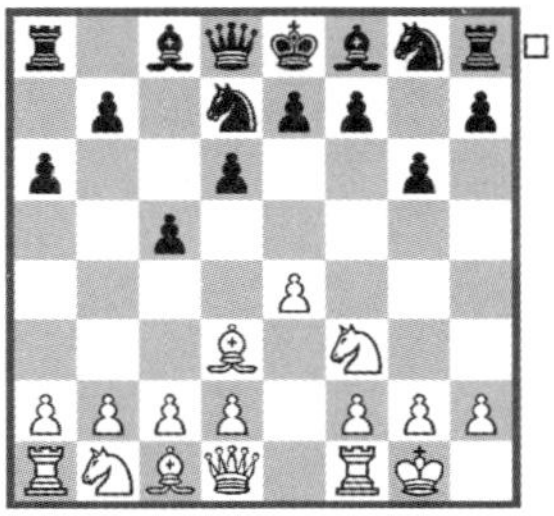

Position after: 5... g6

should also be considered without 5...♘gf6. 6. c3 ♗g7 7. ♗c2

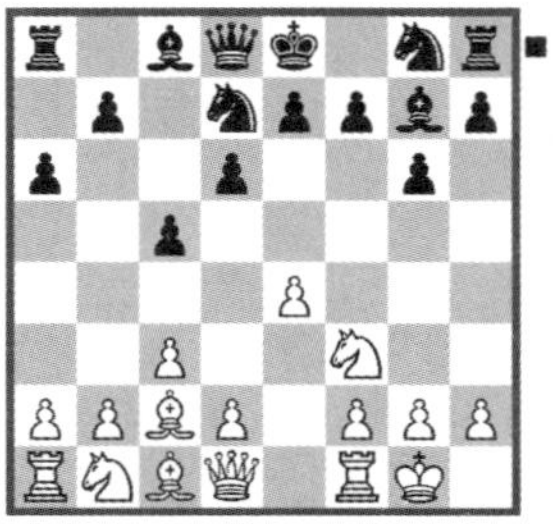

Position after: 7. ♗c2

**A)** 7... b5 One of the independent options (with 7... ♘e5!?), as it doesn't directly transpose to 5...♘gf6. 8. d4 ♗b7 9. ♖e1

**A1)** 9... ♘gf6?! is just bad. 10. e5!

Position after: 10. e5!

10... dxe5 11. dxe5 ♘g4 [11... ♘d5 12. e6 fxe6 13. ♘g5 ♘c7 14. ♕e2±] 12. e6 ♘de5 13. ♘xe5 ♘xe5 14. exf7+± Followed by ♕e2, and we have a significant advantage.

**A2)** 9... cxd4 10. cxd4 ♘gf6

Position after: 10... ♘gf6

11. ♗d2!?± Lining up a2-a4, ♗d3, and ♘a3 to put pressure on the b5-pawn. I really like White's position here. [11. e5 is also possible, although it seems unnecessarily

complicated. 11... dxe5 12. dxe5 ♘d5 13. e6 fxe6 14. ♘g5 ♘c5 15. ♘xh7 ♕d6∞ Xu – Idani, Moscow 2017.]

**B)** 7... ♘e5!? This attempt to prevent d2-d4 has been played by some very strong players. 8. ♘xe5 dxe5 Our strategy here is very similar to the early ...♘e5 lines subchapter. We essentially want to complete development while preventing Black from getting too active. 9. a4!

Position after: 9. a4!

Immediately forcing ...b7-b6. 9... b6 10. d3 ♘f6 11. h3 ♘h5 11... 0-0 Our plan remains unchanged. 12. ♗e3

**B1)** 12... a5 was seen in Niemann – Rapport, chess24.com INT 2022. Now the best continuation was 13. b4! axb4 14. cxb4 cxb4 15. ♘d2± with ♖b1 to follow.

**B2)** 12... ♕c7 is more accurate, although I still like White's position after 13. b4 cxb4 14. cxb4± followed by ♘d2, and either ♗b3-c4 or even a4-a5 immediately. There are plenty of options and Black's queenside pawns seem to be weak.

**6. c3 g6**

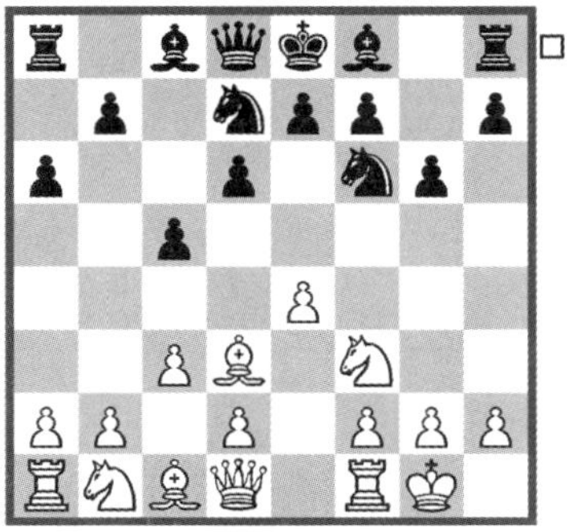

Position after: 6... g6

**7. ♗c2 c4**

Analysis demonstrates that this isn't a good option for Black after 6...g6.

**8. b3! cxb3**

8... b5 9. bxc4 bxc4 10. ♘a3 ♘b6 11. e5!

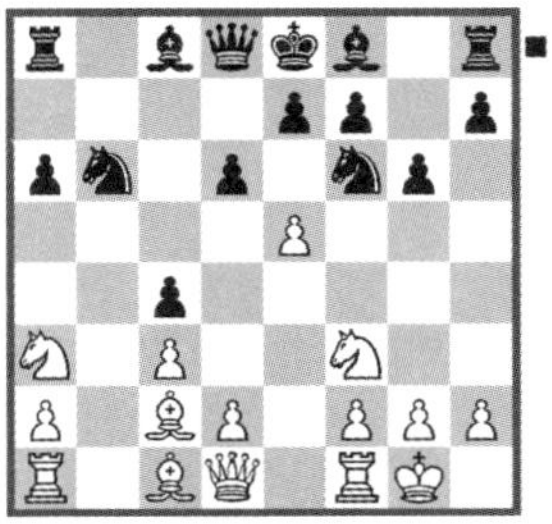

Position after: 11. e5!

11... dxe5 12. ♘xe5 ♕c7 [12... ♗e6 13. ♗a4+ ♘fd7 14. ♖b1 ♘xa4 15. ♕xa4 ♗f5 16. ♖b2±] 13. ♖b1!±

**9. axb3 b5 10. c4!**

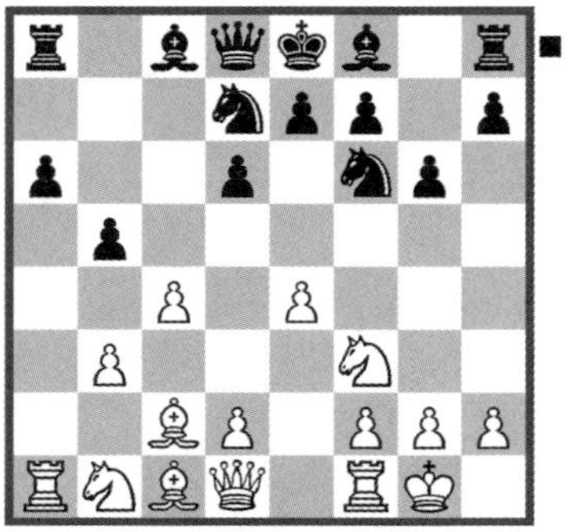

Position after: 10. c4!

**10... ♗b7**

**A)** 10... b4 11. d4 White's central pawns look pretty menacing and Black's lack of development suggests that e4-e5 is definitely on the cards. 11... ♗b7 12. ♕e1!

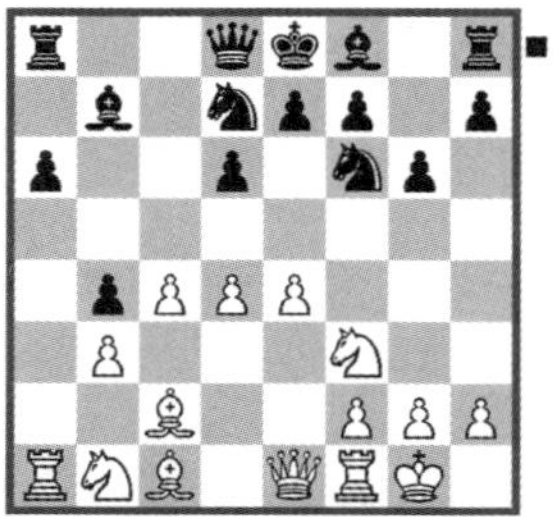

Position after: 12. ♕e1!

Taking the queen off the d-file and posing questions about the b4-pawn. 12... a5 [12... ♕b6 gives White time to build quite a large attack, starting with the tempo-gaining 13. ♘bd2 ♗g7 14. c5!±.] 13. e5 dxe5 14. dxe5 ♘h5 15. e6 fxe6 16. ♘g5 ♖a6 17. ♘xh7!

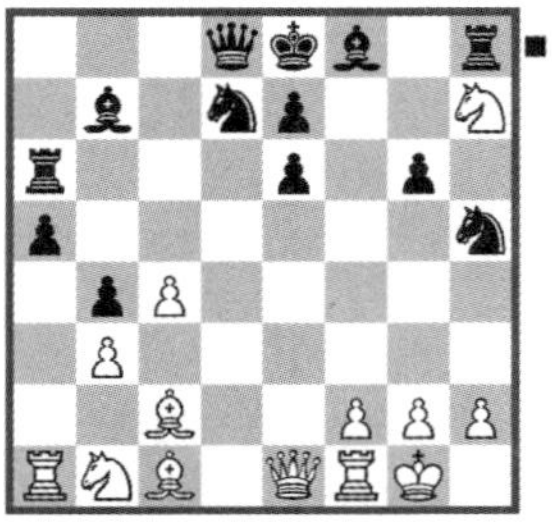

Position after: 17. ♘xh7!

17... e5 18. ♘xf8 ♖xf8 19. ♘d2±

**B)** 10... bxc4 11. bxc4 would just open up more lines for White to utilise.

**11. ♘c3 ♗g7 12. d4 0-0 13. ♗a3 ♕b6 14. ♕e2 ♖fc8 15. ♖fd1 e6**

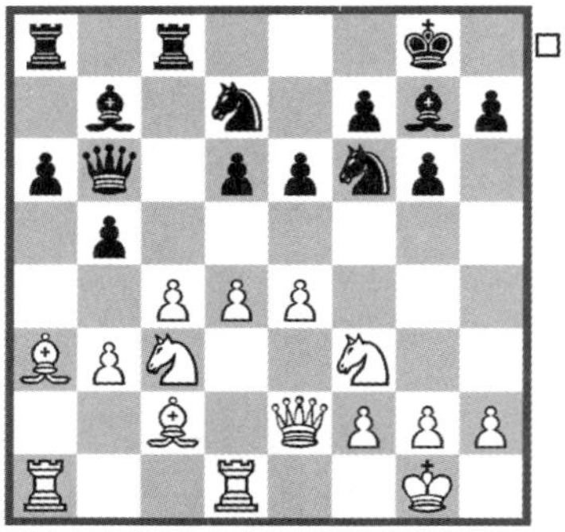

Position after: 15... e6

**16. ♗d3±**

## e) 5...♘gf6 6.c3 g6 7.♗c2 ♗g7

**1. e4 c5 2. ♘f3 d6 3. ♗b5+ ♘d7 4. 0-0 a6 5. ♗d3 ♘gf6 6. c3 g6 7. ♗c2 ♗g7**

Position after: 7... ♗g7

**8. d4 0-0**

Black chooses to brazen it out and invite e4-e5.

**A)** 8... ♕c7 is more cautious approach, stopping e4-e5.

**A1)** 9. a4!? 0-0 10. d5!

Position after: 10. d5!

As we saw in the lines after 4...♘f6, it makes a lot of sense to play this setup when Black's queen is already on c7. 10... b6 11. c4 e6 12. ♘c3 exd5 13. cxd5 ♖e8 14. h3 ♖b8 15. ♕e2± White had a very comfortable position in Caruana – Topalov, Bucharest 2012.

**A2)** 9. ♖e1 0-0 [9... cxd4 10. cxd4 0-0 11. a4±] 10. e5! The typical move when Black doesn't capture on d4. Now that our knight can't come to c3, we should find an alternative way to play for the initiative. 10... dxe5 11. dxe5 ♘g4 [11... ♘e8 12. ♗f4±] 12. e6 ♘de5 [12... fxe6 13. h3 ♘ge5 14. ♘g5±] 13. ♘xe5 ♘xe5

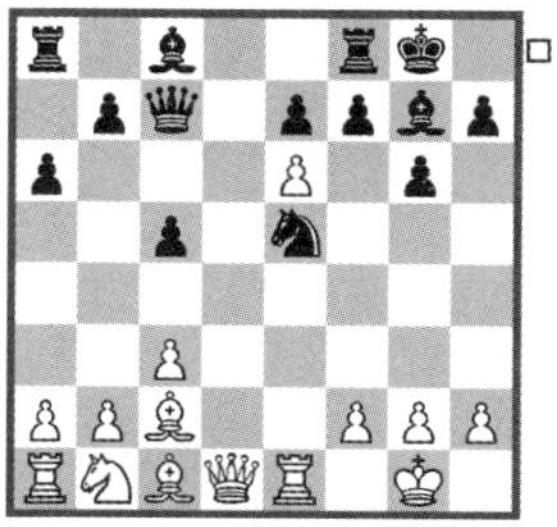

Position after: 13... ♘xe5

14. f4 ♘c6 15. exf7+ ♖xf7 16. ♗b3 e6 17. ♘d2± Irrespective of whether Black captures on f4, the forthcoming Ne4 jump will be very strong.

**B)** 8... cxd4 When Black exchanges on d4, we can continue to develop normally as our b1-knight has gained the c3-square. 9. cxd4 0-0 10. a4!

*(see diagram next page)*

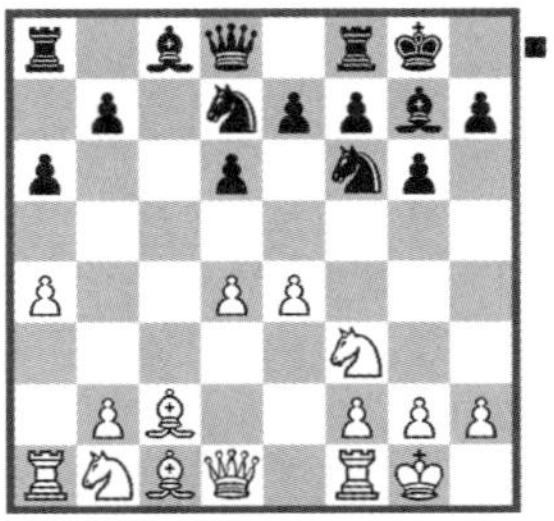

Position after: 10. a4!

10... b6 11. ♘c3 ♗b7 12. ♕e2 b5 [12... e5 13. d5±] 13. e5! It's evident that our pieces stand very well to support the e4-e5 break now. 13... dxe5 14. dxe5

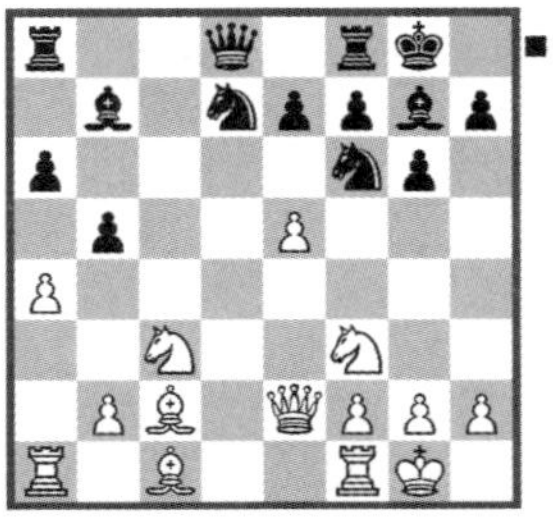

Position after: 14. dxe5

14... ♘d5 [14... ♘g4 15. e6 ♕b8 16. ♗e4±; 14... ♗xf3 Black can double our pawns but it doesn't hurt us because of our piece activity. 15. gxf3 ♘h5 16. e6 ♘e5 17. ♖d1 ♕c8 18. ♗e4±] 15. e6 ♘xc3 16. bxc3 ♗xf3 17. gxf3 ♘c5 18. exf7+

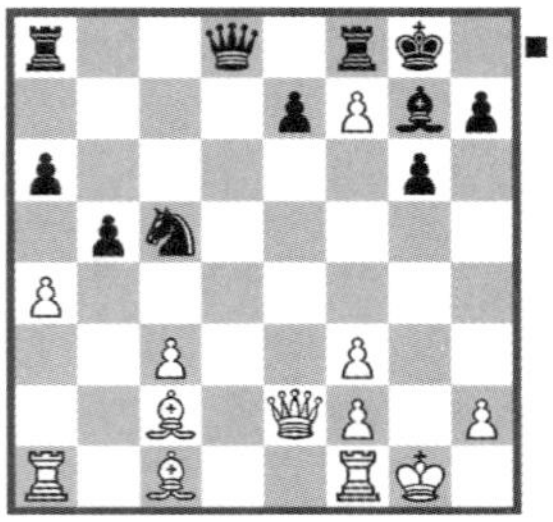

Position after: 18. exf7+

18... ♖xf7 19. axb5 axb5 20. ♖d1!± Black is forced to trade their queen for two rooks, and the resulting material imbalance very much favours White.

**9. a4!**

Stopping Black from playing ... b7-b5, and also not giving up on possible e4-e5 ideas.

9. e5!? This is definitely worth considering as an alternative.

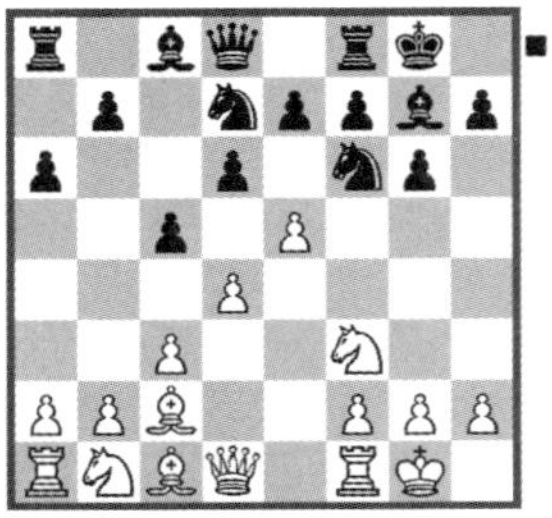

Position after: 9. e5!?

**A)** 9... dxe5 10. dxe5

**A1)** 10... ♘e8?! is dubious here as Black's structure will be damaged by force. 11. e6!

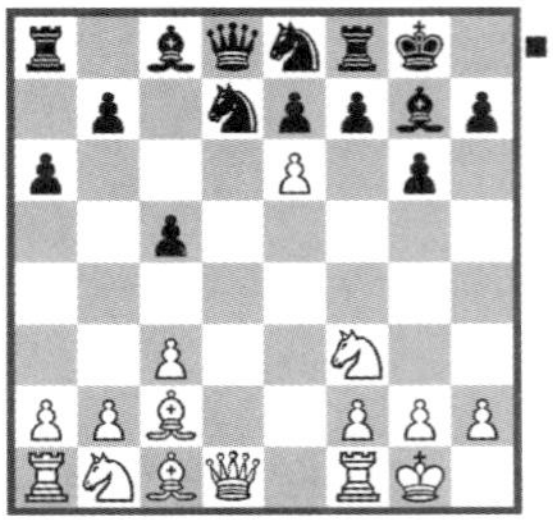

Position after: 11. e6!

11... fxe6 12. ♕e2 [12. ♘g5 also looks strong. 12...·♕b6 13. ♘a3±] 12... ♘d6 13. ♘bd2 b5 14. ♖e1 c4 [14... ♘f6 15. ♘g5±] 15. a4! There's no rush to capture on e6, and we can continue creating weaknesses for Black. 15... ♖b8 [15... ♘c5 16. axb5 ♕b6 17. ♘g5 h6 18. ♘ge4±] 16. axb5 axb5 17. ♕xe6+

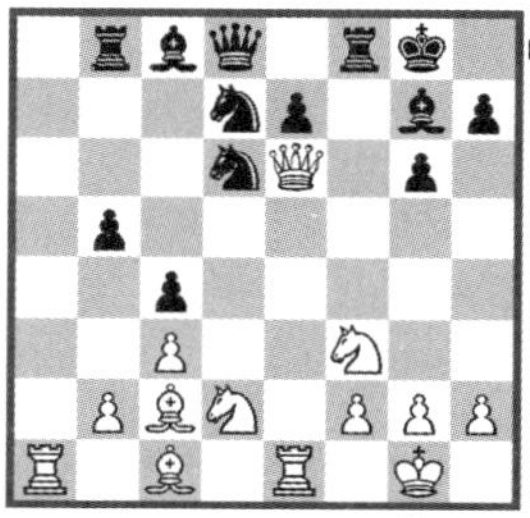

Position after: 17. ♕xe6+

17... ♔h8 [17... ♖f7 18. ♘g5 ♘e5 19. ♕d5 ♗b7 20. ♘xf7 ♗xd5 21. ♘xd8+–] 18. ♕xe7 ♕xe7 19. ♖xe7 ♘c5 20. ♘f1±

**A2)** 10... ♘g4 11. e6

**A2.1)** 11... fxe6?! Was Christiansen – Donchenko, Reykjavik 2017. Now the best continuation for White was 12. ♕e2!. The best square for the queen and White can just continue developing normally, rather than trying to win back the pawn immediately. 12... ♘de5 [12... ♘df6 13. ♘bd2±] 13. ♘g5 h6 14. ♘e4± We threaten f2-f4, and Black's kingside pawns look very weak.

**A2.2)** 11... ♘de5 Black can avoid accepting our sacrifice but their resulting pawn structure will still be slightly inferior.

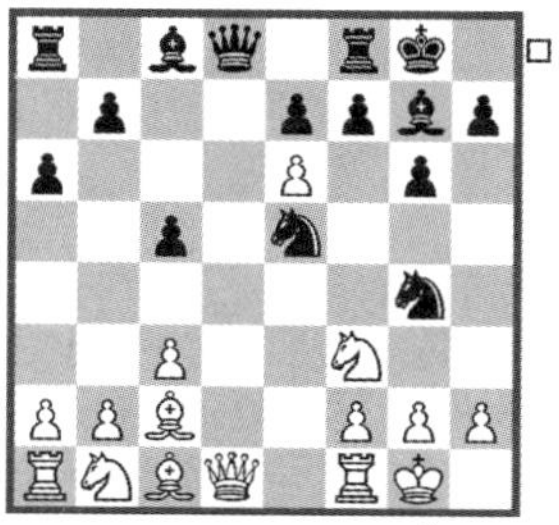

Position after: 11... ♘de5

12. exf7+ ♘xf7 13. h3 ♘f6 14. ♘bd2± With the better pieces and better pawn structure.

**B)** 9... ♘e8! 10. ♖e1 [I spent a lot of time analysing the tactical line 10. e6 fxe6 11. ♘g5 ♘c7 12. dxc5 d5 13. f4 e5

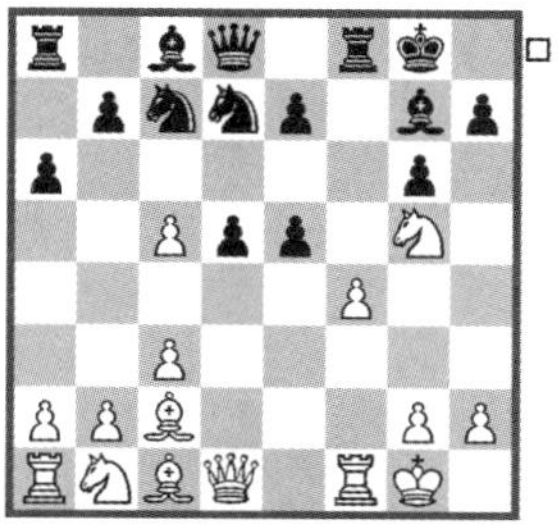

Position after: 13... e5

14. ♘xh7! but in the end decided there's no need to overcomplicate things.] 10... cxd4 [10... ♘c7 11. exd6 exd6 12. dxc5 dxc5 13. ♘bd2±] 11. e6! Otherwise Black's position is quite easy to play with moves like ...♘c7,

...b7-b5, and ...♗b7. 11... fxe6 12. cxd4

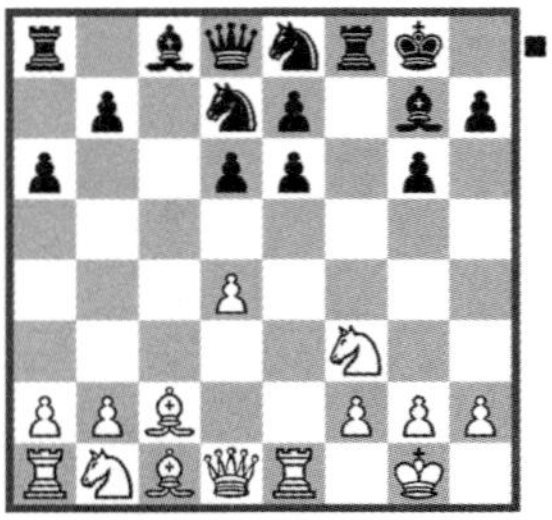
Position after: 12. cxd4

**B1)** 12... ♘c7 13. ♘c3=∞ White remains a pawn down but Black is extremely passive. A logical course of action is to keep developing and wait for the right moment to push h2-h4. I think Black's position is incredibly difficult to navigate.

**B2)** 12... ♘b8 It looks like Black's knight belongs on c6. 13. ♘c3 ♘c6 14. ♗e3 ♘b4 15. ♗b3 d5 16. ♘e5=∞ White has good compensation here but I wasn't convinced enough to have this as my mainline.

**9... b6**

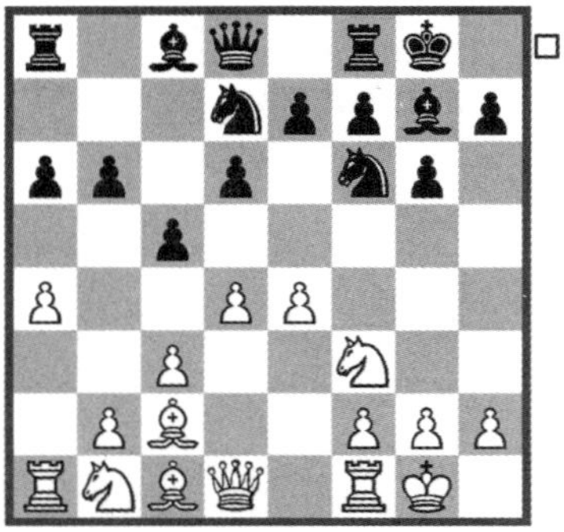
Position after: 9... b6

9... ♕c7 10. d5 transposes to Caruana – Topalov above.

**10. e5!**

Here I think we reach slightly more favourable versions of the lines seen after 9.e5.

In case of the more cautious 10. ♖e1 ♗b7 11. ♘bd2 e6= Black's position seems fine as long as they don't exchange on d4 too early.

**10... ♘e8**

10... dxe5? 11. dxe5 Now the e5-e6 push is even more effective. 11... ♘g4 12. e6

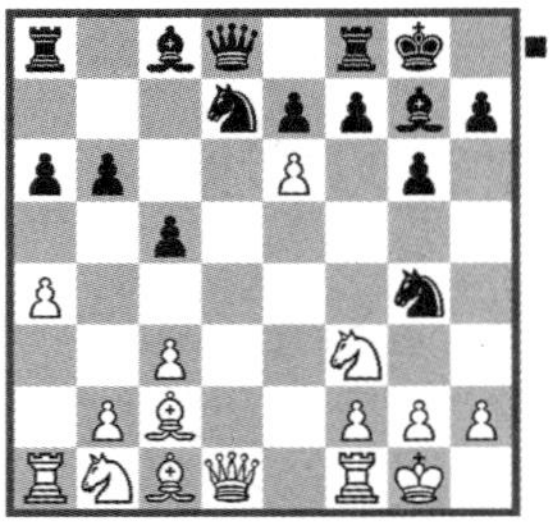
Position after: 12. e6

12... ♘de5 [12... fxe6 13. ♕e2 ♘de5 14. ♘e1!+– followed by either f2-f4 or h2-h3 is decisive.] 13. h3! ♕xd1 14. ♗xd1 ♘d3 15. exf7+ ♔h8 16. ♗g5 ♘ge5 17. ♘xe5 ♘xe5 18. ♘d2± with excellent chances in this queenless middlegame.

**11. e6!**

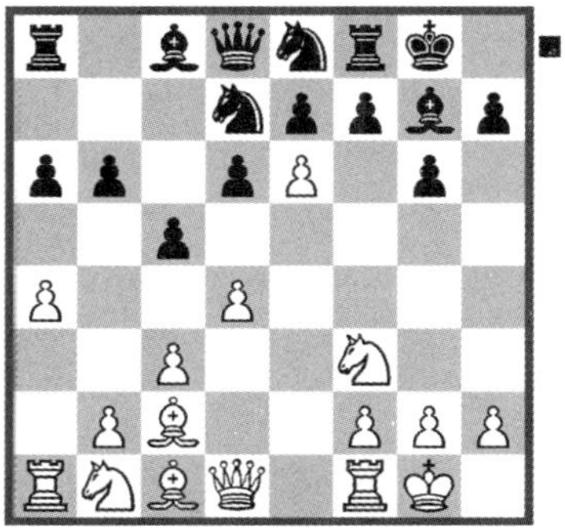

Position after: 11. e6!

**11... fxe6 12. ♘bd2**

Let's consider what we've achieved for the sacrificed pawn. Black's kingside is weakened - we immediately have ideas of h2-h4 and ♘g5. The pawn on e6 also cramps Black's pieces and although the f-file is open, Black is quite passive. I won't dive too deep into the position but we can consider a few sample variations.

**12... ♘df6**

**A)** 12... cxd4 13. cxd4 ♗b7 14. ♘g5 ♗d5 15. ♘de4!=∞ Re-routing the knight to c3.

**B)** 12... ♗b7 13. ♖e1 ♘c7 14. ♘e4→ Potentially followed up by h2-h4.

**13. ♘g5!**

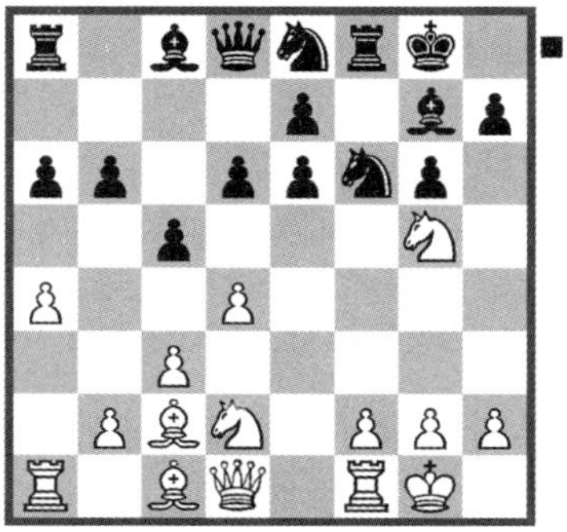

Position after: 13. ♘g5!

This is always a good location for the knight as Black never wants to push ...h7-h6. In fact, it's difficult to find a good move for Black here.

**13... ♖b8 14. ♘df3→**

Followed by ♖e1 and h2-h4 - the position is very uncomfortable for Black, and it's tough to find a way to unravel.

## f) 5...b5

**1. e4 c5 2. ♘f3 d6 3. ♗b5+ ♘d7 4. 0-0 a6 5. ♗d3**

It's slightly premature for Black to push

**5... b5**

because of the following line:

*(see diagram next page)*

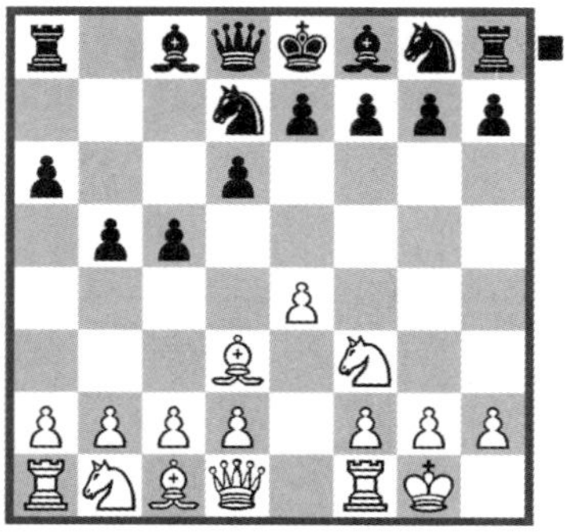

Position after: 5... b5

**6. c4!**

It looks like White has an advantage everywhere. The main point is that our development advantage is fairly large and Black is struggling to keep the position from blowing open. I'll give an overview of the various lines:

**6... ♖b8**

**A)** 6... bxc4 7. ♗xc4 ♘b6 8. ♗b3

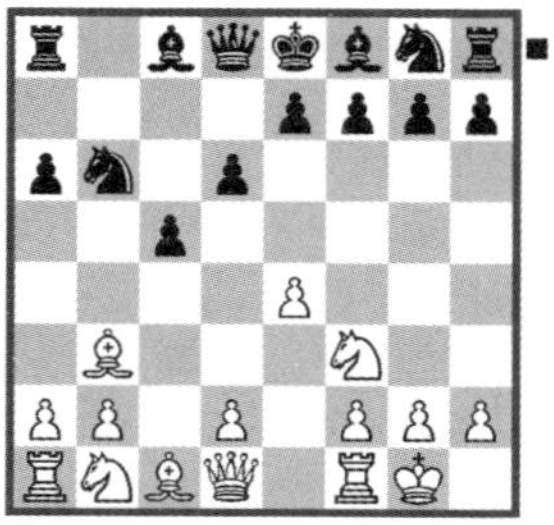

Position after: 8. ♗b3

8... ♘f6 [8... e5 It's logical for Black to prevent the centre from opening, although they've now incurred a positional weakness on d5. 9. d3 ♗e7 10. ♗d2 Threatening ♗a5. 10... a5 11. a4!± Followed by ♕e1 and ♘a3-c4.] 9. d4! ♘xe4 [9... cxd4 10. ♘xd4 e5 11. ♘c6! ♕c7 12. ♘a5 ♘xe4 13. ♗e3± with ♘d2 and ♖c1 to come – White has a strong initiative.] 10. ♖e1 d5 [10... c4 11. ♗a4+ ♘xa4 12. ♕xa4+ ♗d7 13. ♕xc4±] 11. ♘e5!

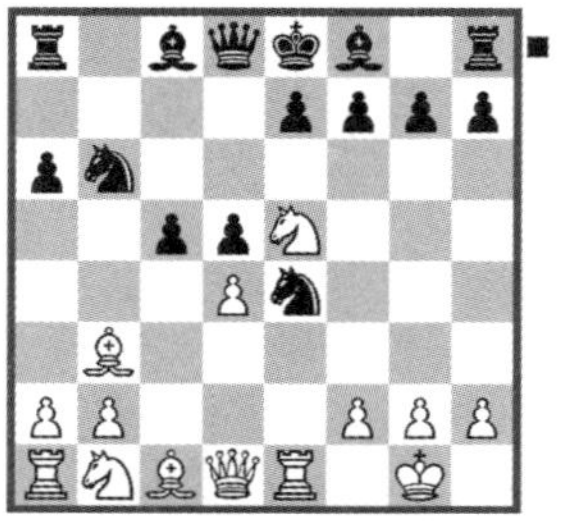

Position after: 11. ♘e5!

Despite being a pawn down, we have excellent compensation in the form of active pieces. 11... e6 12. ♘c3 ♘f6 13. ♗f4± Black will again struggle to survive.

**B)** 6... ♘e5 has also been tried here, although after 7. ♘xe5 dxe5 8. ♕f3!

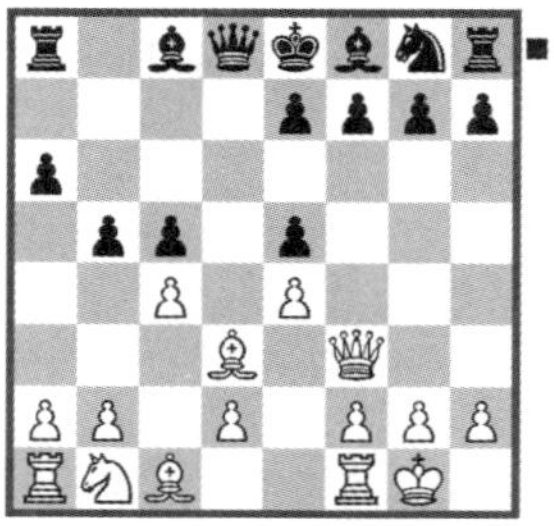

Position after: 8. ♕f3!

White has a nice position. For example: 8... b4 9. ♗c2!± Followed by a2-a3 and potentially d2-d3, ♕g3, and f2-f4. White's play is easy and intuitive.

**C)** 6... b4 7. a3 ♗b7 8. axb4 cxb4 9. ♗c2+– With d2-d4 coming, White had a superb position in Hammer – Vovk, Chess.com INT 2015.

**D)** 6... ♗b7? Exchanging the b5-pawn for the e4-pawn is too risky here: 7. cxb5 axb5 8. ♗xb5 ♗xe4 9. ♘c3 ♗b7 10. d4 cxd4 11. ♘xd4 ♘gf6 12. ♖e1 e6 13. ♗g5 It's clear that Black is busted. 13... ♗e7 14. ♗xf6!

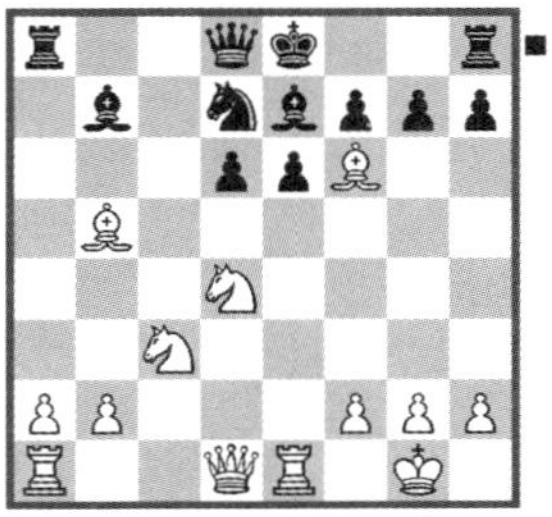

Position after: 14. ♗xf6!

14... gxf6 15. ♖xe6! ♖g8 16. ♗c6+– White won a fantastic game in Boruchovsky – Papp, Zalakaros 2015.

**7. cxb5! axb5 8. ♕e2**

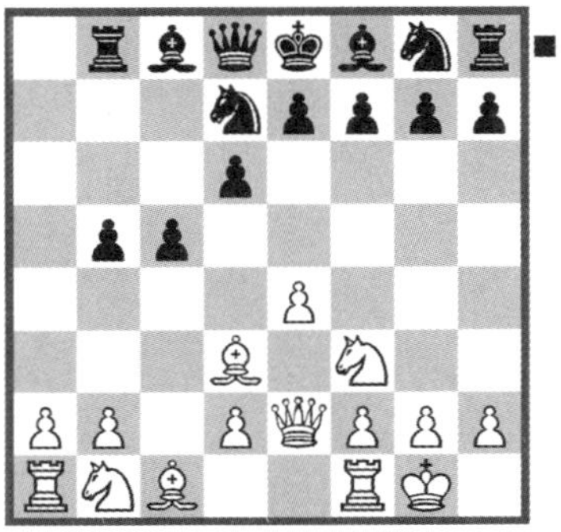

Position after: 8. ♕e2

Continuing to apply pressure on the b5-pawn.

**8... b4**

8... ♕b6 9. a3! The plan now is ♘c3, b2-b4, and ♖b1. 9... g6 10. ♘c3 ♗a6 11. b4± ♖b1 coming next looks difficult to deal with.

**9. a3! ♘gf6**

9... bxa3 10. ♗b5!

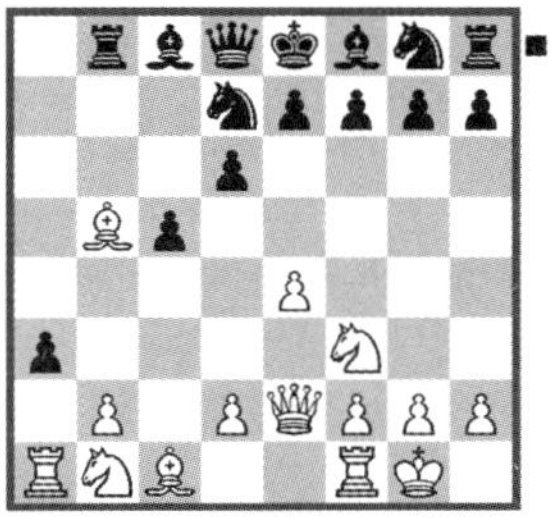

Position after: 10. ♗b5!

A very important point. 10... e5 [10... axb2 11. ♗xb2 e5 12. ♗c3+–] 11. bxa3 ♘gf6 12. ♘c3 ♗e7 13. a4± We'll continue with d2-d3 and ♘d2.

**10. axb4 ♖xb4 11. ♘c3±**

Black doesn't have a good way to deal with ♗b5 followed by ♘e1-c2. If they drop the rook back to b8 immediately we can continue with ♗c4 and d2-d4.

## g) 5...♘gf6 6.c3 -- & 6...b5 7.a4 --

**1. e4 c5 2. ♘f3 d6 3. ♗b5+ ♘d7 4. 0-0 a6 5. ♗d3 ♘gf6 6. c3**

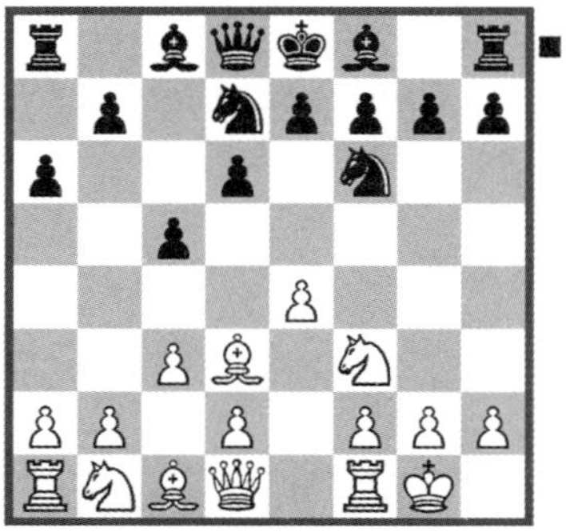

Position after: 6. c3

Prioritising central control by planning a quick ♗c2 and d2-d4.

6. ♖e1 is the alternative but I didn't like the following line: 6... e6 7. c3 b5 8. ♗c2 c4! 9. a4 ♗b7⇆ This counterplay feels like exactly what Black wants when playing the Sicilian.

**6... b5!**

The critical test of this variation. It's also the reason why I started to consider 4.a4 instead of 4. 0-0, as I felt that Black's ability to push ... b7-b5 might give too much counterplay.

6... e6 belongs in this subchapter because without following up with ...b5 next, Black's setup makes little sense. 7. ♗c2

**A)** 7... c4?! 8. a4!

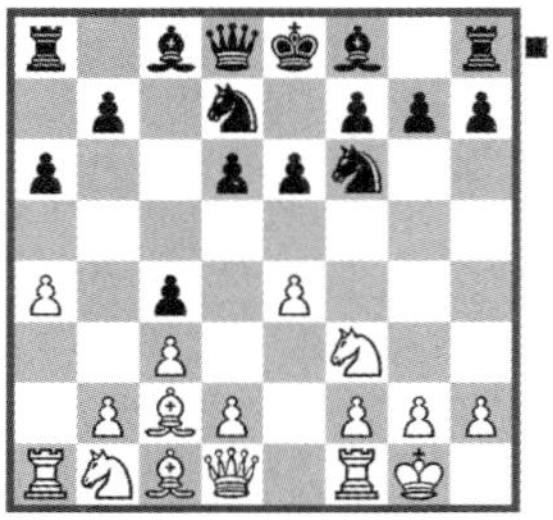

Position after: 8. a4!

Black's c4-pawn is now very weak, so they are forced to make a concession. 8... d5 9. exd5 exd5 10. ♖e1+ ♗e7 11. d4! cxd3 12. ♕xd3±

**B)** 7... ♗e7

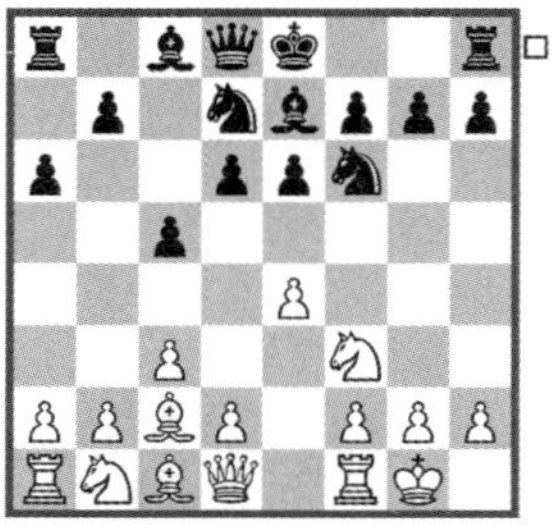

Position after: 7... ♗e7

The issue with delaying ...b7-b5 is that we can now completely prevent it. 8. a4! 0-0 9. ♖e1 b6 10. d4 ♗b7 11. ♘bd2± White basically has an improved version of the line after 7...b5 and can continue with useful moves such as ♘f1-g3 and ♗d3, whilst always considering the option of pushing e4-e5.

**C)** 7... b5 8. d4 ♗b7 9. ♖e1 ♗e7 10. a4!

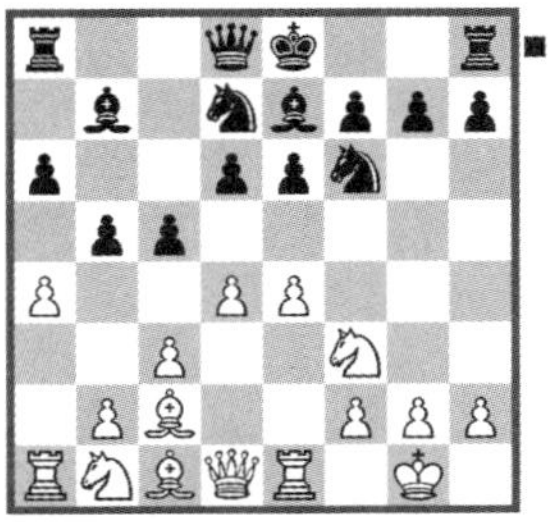
Position after: 10. a4!

10... cxd4 [10... 0-0?! 11. e5!↑ Followed by ♕d3 when it is clear we are doing well.] 11. cxd4 0-0

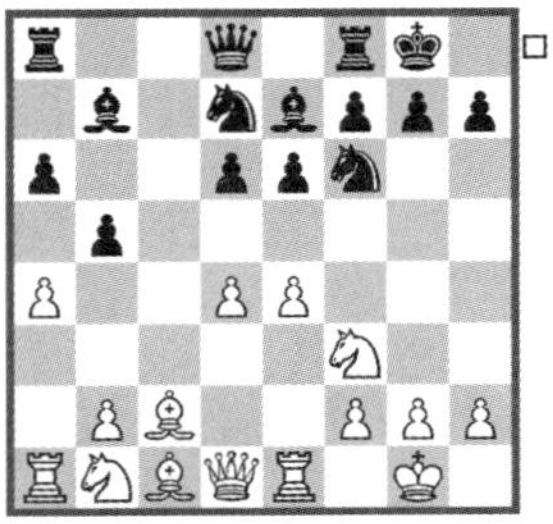
Position after: 11... 0-0

12. a5! Trying to deprive Black's pieces of squares to jump to. [12. e5 isn't good here, as after 12... dxe5 13. dxe5 ♘d5 14. ♕d3 g6∓ Black has good activity based on the fact that the c-file is open, along with the immediate threat of ...♘b4.] 12... ♖c8 13. ♘bd2± This seems very pleasant for White - we'll continue with something like ♗b1, and either ♘f1-g3 or ♘b3.

**7. a4!**

7. ♗c2 is also an option, but after 7... ♗b7 8. ♖e1 c4! I think Black has the type of unclear position that Sicilian players strive for.

**7... c4?!**

This natural-looking move is a big inaccuracy, as we can immediately target Black's queenside pawns with a quick d2-d3 push.

**A)** 7... ♗b7 is the main line, covered in the final subchapter.

**B)** 7... ♖b8?! 8. axb5 axb5 9. b4!± Followed by targetting Black's b5-pawn gives a clear edge.

**8. ♗c2 ♗b7 9. axb5 axb5 10. ♖xa8**

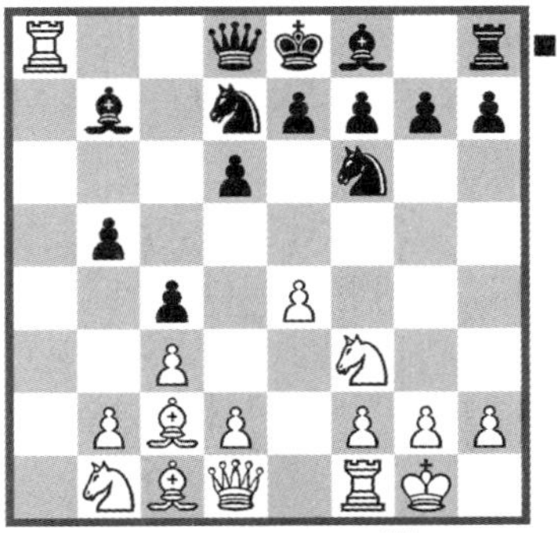
Position after: 10. ♖xa8

**10... ♗xa8!**

10... ♕xa8 11. ♘a3!

**A)** 11... ♗xe4 has been most commonly played here, but after 12. ♗xe4 ♘xe4 13. d3!+– Black's position is simply collapsing. The biggest problem is the lack of kingside development - our forthcoming queenside play will be too fast.

**B)** 11... ♘xe4 12. ♘xb5 ♕b8 13. d3 cxd3 14. ♕xd3

Position after: 14. ♕xd3

Even though material is equal, Black's lack of development is a big problem. We should keep developing and put our pieces on active squares to capitalise on the initiative. 14... e6 15. ♘bd4 ♗e7 16. ♖e1 ♘ef6 17. ♘g5!

Position after: 17. ♘g5!

17... ♗d5 18. ♕e2+– Ideas such as c3-c4, ♘f5, and even capturing on e6 are all possible. Black would be doing very well to not collapse immediately.

**11. d3! cxd3 12. ♗xd3**

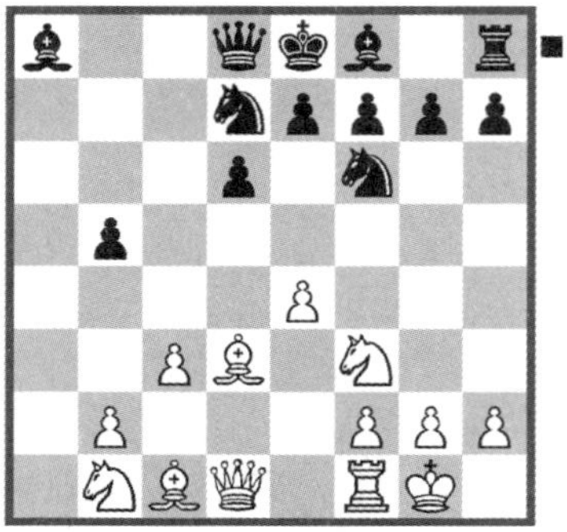

Position after: 12. ♗xd3

**12... e5!**

It is safest for Black is to prioritise kingside development.

12... ♗xe4? 13. ♗xe4 ♘xe4 14. ♖e1 ♕a8 15. ♘a3+– White had a typically strong initiative in Carlier – Smeets, Netherlands 2015.

**13. ♗xb5 ♗e7 14. ♘bd2 0-0 15. ♖e1 ♘c5**

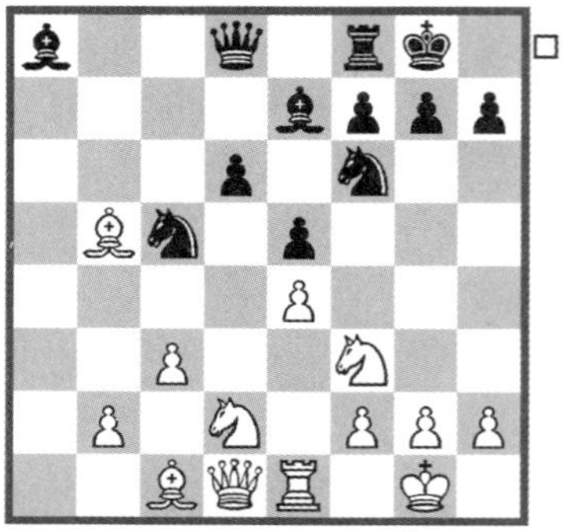

Position after: 15... ♘c5

**16. ♕c2±**

We maintain our pawn advantage.

## h) 5...♘gf6 6.c3 b5 7.a4 b4

**1. e4 c5 2. ♘f3 d6 3. ♗b5+ ♘d7 4. 0-0 a6 5. ♗d3 ♘gf6 6. c3 b5! 7. a4! b4!?**

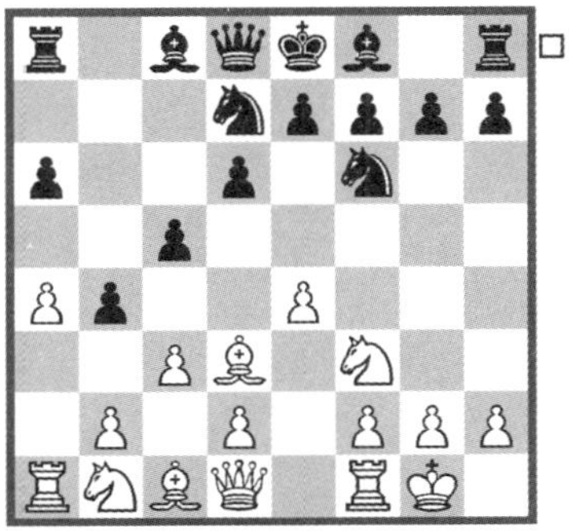

Position after: 7... b4!?

A reasonable option which has been played by some very strong players. Generally Black will opt for this move if trying to avoid the extremely tactical variation after 7...♗b7.

**8. ♗c2 ♗b7**

8... a5 doesn't really make much sense, as we can now grab the centre uncontested. 9. d4 cxd4 10. cxd4±

**9. ♖e1**

There are a few different ideas for White here. If allowed, it makes sense to push d2-d4, and take space in the centre. Generally Black will try and prevent this one way or another, in which case we can develop more slowly with d2-d3. Often, playing slowly with d2-d3 also entails an a4-a5 push, after which we can attempt to either target the weak b4-pawn or exploit the potentially open b-file. The following variations will help to illustrate these ideas.

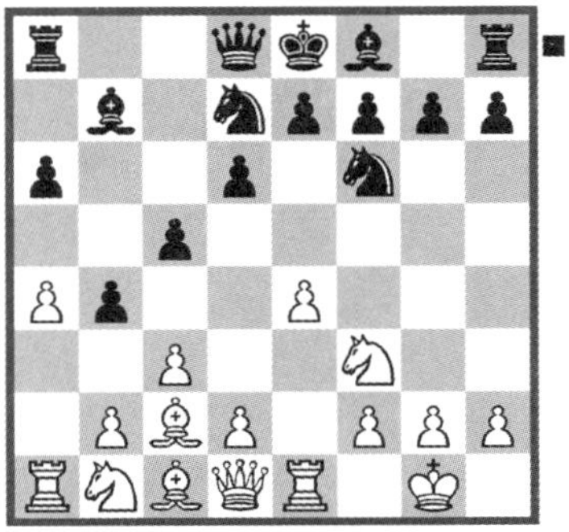

Position after: 9. ♖e1

**9... e6!?**

**A)** 9... ♖c8

**A1)** 10. d4!? is a very interesting line for the reader to explore in their own time. 10... cxd4 11. cxd4

Position after: 11. cxd4

11... ♕c7! This is Black's idea to counter our central expansion. 12. ♗d3

♘xe4∞ White has some compensation for the pawn, but I haven't been able to find anything convincing.

**A2)** 10. a5! Now we switch plans to playing slowly with d2-d3, attempting to make Black's rook look poorly placed on c8. 10... ♕c7 11. d3 bxc3 12. bxc3

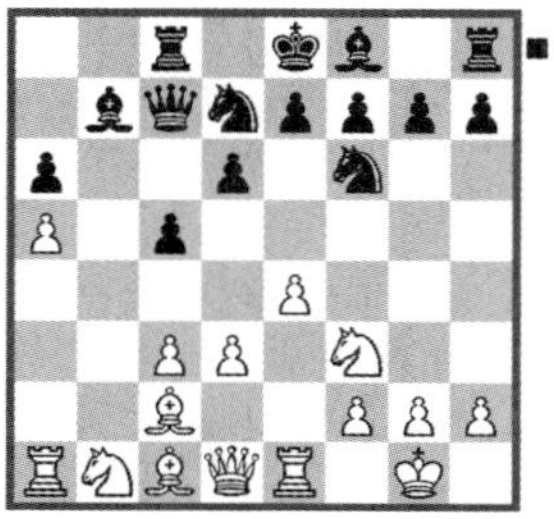

Position after: 12. bxc3

12... g6 White looks to have a pleasant game in the following line: [12... e6 13. h3 ♗e7 14. ♗f4 0-0 15. ♘bd2 ♗c6 16. ♘c4 ♗b5 In Nakamura – Grischuk, Saint Louis 2015, White's best continuation was 17. e5! dxe5 18. ♘fxe5±.] 13. ♘a3 ♗g7

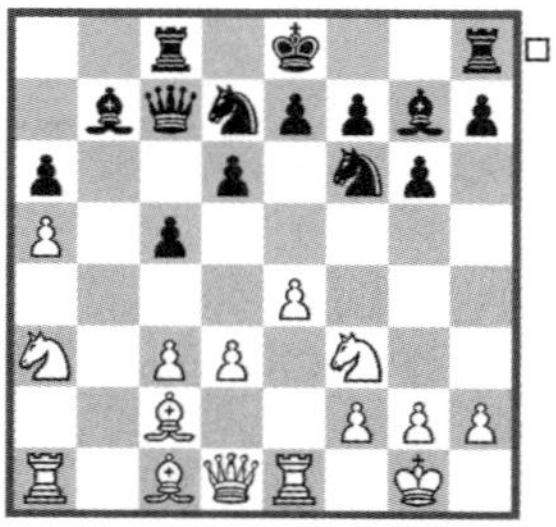

Position after: 13... ♗g7

14. ♘c4 0-0 15. ♗f4± Followed by something like ♖b1, ♕d2, and ♗a4 with easy play.

**B)** 9... ♕c7 The most popular move here. Black's idea is that the queen is better placed on c7 than the rook was on c8 in the case that we play slowly with d2-d3. However, I - well, more like Stockfish 15 - found a nice idea here. 10. d4 cxd4 11. ♘xd4!

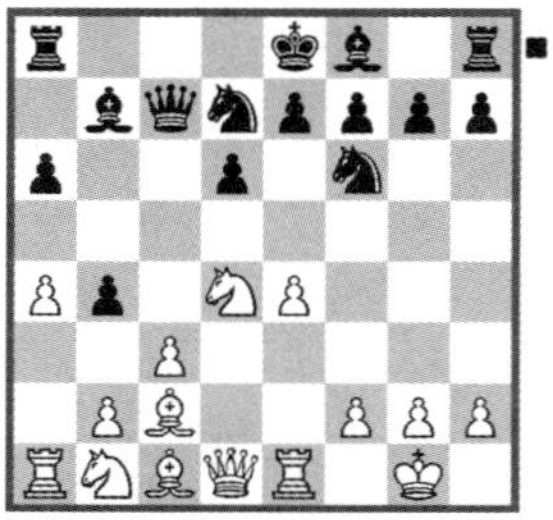

Position after: 11. ♘xd4!

Black immediately faces a problem about how to deal with the hanging b4-pawn.

**B1)** 11... e5 is the engine move in this position, but it seems very risky to play like this with Black. 12. ♘f5 d5! 13. exd5 ♘xd5 14. ♗b3 ♘7f6 15. ♕e2± Apparently castling queenside is Black's best move now, but the resulting queenless middlegame should at least present a slight advantage for White.

**B2)** 11... bxc3?! seems like a logical choice, but once we capture back on c3 with our knight it will be clear that Black's queen is misplaced on c7. 12. ♘xc3

*(see analysis diagram next page)*

Position after: 12. ♘xc3

**B2.1)** 12... e6 13. ♗b3! ♗e7 [13... ♘c5 14. ♘d5! ♘xd5 15. ♗xd5!+–] 14. ♗xe6! fxe6 15. ♘xe6+– followed by capturing on g7 and dropping the knight back to f5. Black's position is completely lost.

**B2.2)** 12... g6 13. ♘d5! ♘xd5 14. exd5 ♗g7 15. ♗b3± Black still has big problems to solve. Both the e7-pawn and the c6-square are serious weaknesses which we can attempt to capitalise upon in the near future.

**B3)** 11... ♖c8 12. ♗g5!

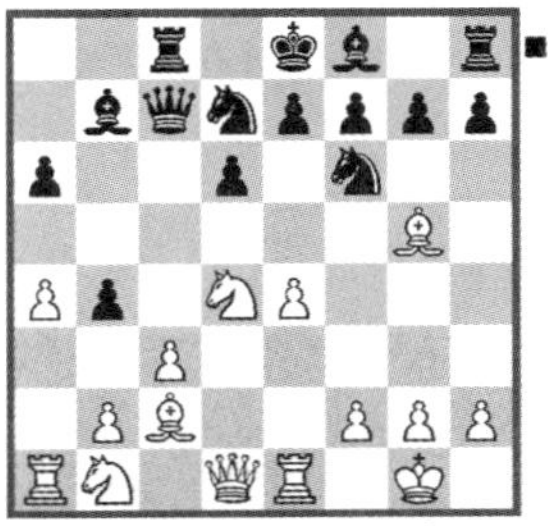

Position after: 12. ♗g5!

12... g6 [12... e6 13. ♗xf6! ♘xf6 14. a5!

Position after: 14. a5!

The point of ♗g5xf6 - our c2-bishop can now land on a4 with check. 14... ♗e7 15. ♗a4+ ♔f8 16. cxb4±] 13. ♗d3 bxc3 14. ♘xc3 ♗g7 15. ♘d5!± White is doing well once again. Importantly, Black's a6-pawn could be a big weakness in the future.

**C)** 9... g6?! 10. cxb4 cxb4 11. d4 ♗g7 12. a5 0-0 13. ♘bd2±

**10. cxb4!**

10. d4 cxd4 11. cxd4 also looks reasonable, but see the next note.

**10... cxb4 11. a5!?**

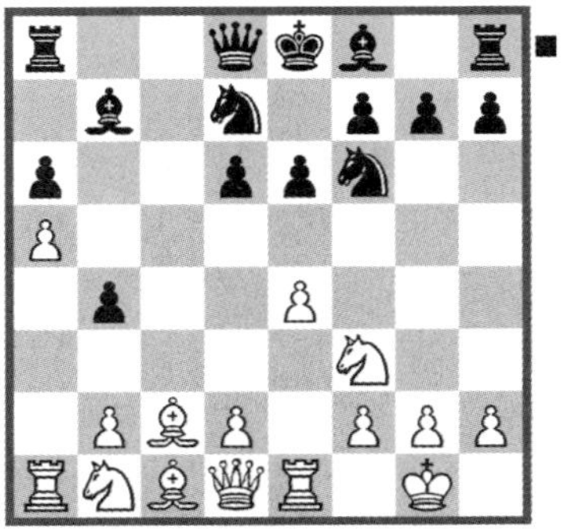

Position after: 11. a5!?

Immediately isolating Black's b4-pawn, even if this does raise the value of each move quite a bit.

Something like 11. d4 a5 12. ♘bd2 ♗e7 might be marginally more comfortable for White, but I could see this fizzling out.

**11... b3!**

After anything else White's positional advantage is evident.

**12. ♗xb3 ♗xe4**

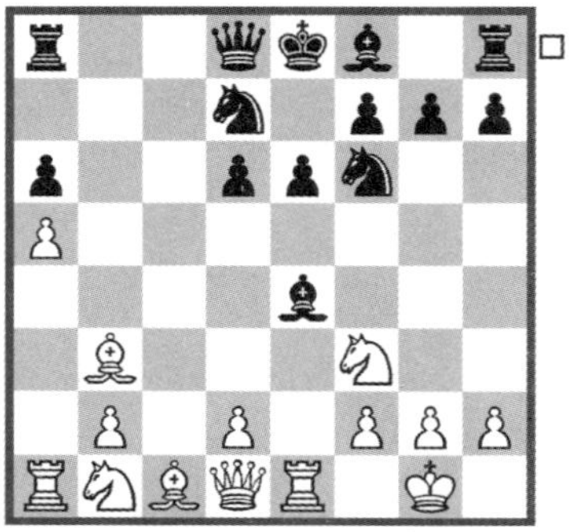

Position after: 12... ♗xe4

**13. ♘d4!**

White needs to hurry with the attack.

13. d4 allows Black to clog things up. 13... ♗e7 14. ♘c3 ♗xf3 15. ♕xf3 d5=∞

**13... ♗xb1!**

Trading some pieces and getting a pawn for the trouble.

Not something like 13... ♖b8?! 14. ♘c3 ♗a8 15. ♘xe6± when White has a huge attack.

**14. ♖xb1 ♕xa5 15. ♘xe6 fxe6 16. ♖xe6+ ♗e7 17. d4 ♖b8**

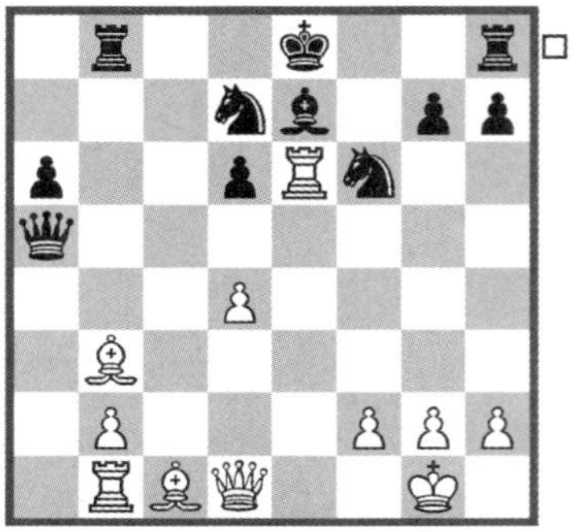

Position after: 17... ♖b8

**18. ♗f4±**

The position is still rather messy but Black has close to no chance of castling and I would argue this factor is relevant in a practical game, as well as the evaluation of around +0.5.

## i) 5...♘gf6 6.c3 b5 7.a4 ♗b7

**1. e4 c5 2. ♘f3 d6 3. ♗b5+ ♘d7 4. 0-0 a6 5. ♗d3 ♘gf6 6. c3 b5! 7. a4! ♗b7**

Position after: 7... ♗b7

The position now gets very tactical.

**8. axb5**

8. ♖e1 e6 9. ♗c2 c4! is once again a major line where I feel that Black will always be pretty happy.

**8... axb5 9. ♖xa8**

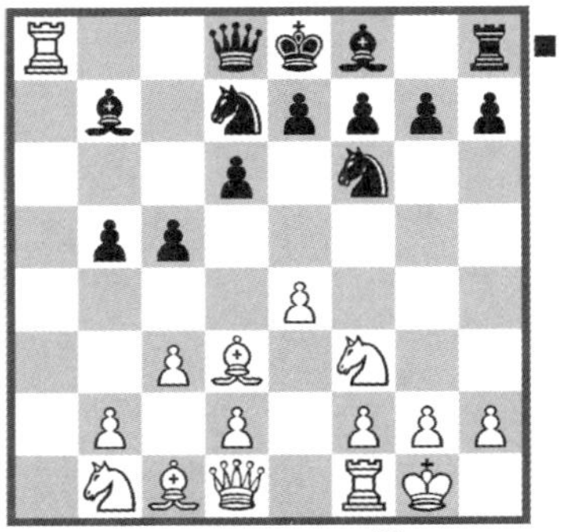

Position after: 9. ♖xa8

**9... ♕xa8!**

9... ♗xa8? 10. ♗xb5 ♗xe4 [10... ♘xe4 11. d4 cxd4 12. ♘xd4+–] 11. d4! ♗xb1 12. dxc5+– The critical difference compared to the corresponding line after 9...♕xa8 is that after 12...♗e4 here, Black doesn't control the c6-square and so we can push 13.c6.

**10. ♗xb5**

10. ♘a3!? was tested in Dubov – Saric, Riga 2021, but after 10... b4 11. ♘b5 ♕a5

Position after: 11... ♕a5

12. cxb4?! [12. ♗e2 ♘xe4∞] 12... cxb4 13. ♗c4 ♘xe4∓ White was lacking enough compensation for the pawn.

**10... ♗xe4**

10... ♘xe4? doesn't make any sense. 11. d4 cxd4 12. ♘xd4 e5 13. ♖e1! exd4 14. ♕g4 ♕c8 15. cxd4+– Followed by ♘c3. This was just one of the many ways White could have achieved a decisive advantage.

**11. d4!**

I think this is the most critical try. Certainly it's very tricky for Black if they're not adequately prepared.

11. c4!? is a surprisingly reasonable direction for White. For example: 11... e6 12. d4 [12. ♘c3 ♗xf3 13. ♕xf3 ♕xf3 14. gxf3 ♗e7=] 12... ♗xb1 13. dxc5 ♗e4 14. cxd6 ♗c6 15. ♘d4 ♗xg2 16. ♖e1 ♗xd6 17. ♘xe6∞

**11... ♗xb1**

**A)** 11... ♗xf3?! 12. ♕xf3 ♕xf3 13. gxf3 cxd4 14. ♖d1!

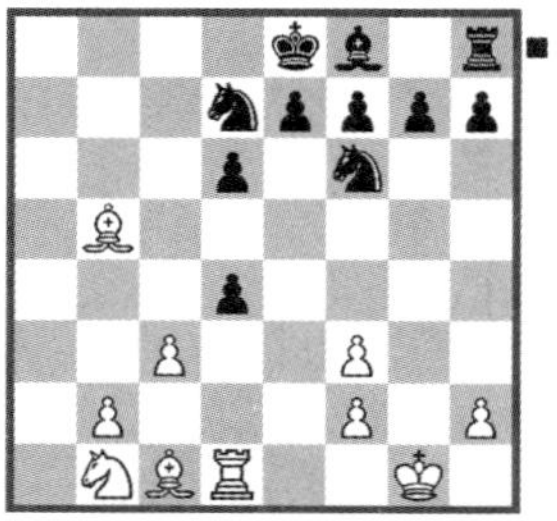

Position after: 14. ♖d1!

We want to capture back on d4 with our rook, before playing ♖a4 and ♖a7. 14... dxc3 is the only important line to check, but after 15. ♘xc3 e6 16. ♗g5 ♗e7 17. ♗xf6 gxf6 18. ♖a1+– Black is simply losing a piece.

**B)** 11... ♗c6 is another option but White is doing well after 12. c4! ♗xb5 13. cxb5 e6 14. ♘c3 ♗e7 15. ♗f4 0-0 16. dxc5 dxc5 17. ♕a1!±.

**12. dxc5 ♗e4!**

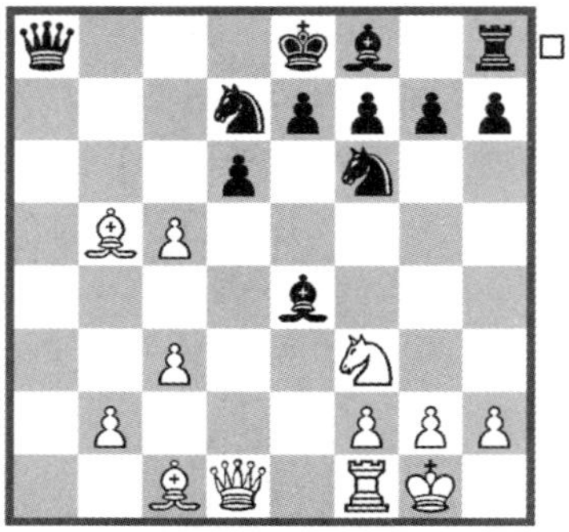

Position after: 12... ♗e4!

Preventing our c5-c6 advance.

**13. ♖e1!**

Even though we're a piece down, Black's lack of kingside development means that we can calmly develop another piece.

13. cxd6 is also interesting and delivers a more free-form game: 13... exd6 [13... ♗xf3 14. gxf3 exd6 15. ♖e1+ ♔d8 16. b4∞] 14. ♖e1 ♗e7 15. ♕e2 ♕d8 16. ♘d4∞

**13... e6!**

**A)** 13... ♗xf3? is just a bad move, as after 14. gxf3 Black will do well even to just avoid losing immediately - the king is simply far too weak. The best defence follows:

*(see analysis diagram next page)*

Position after: 14. gxf3

14... dxc5 15. ♗g5 ♕d5 16. ♗xf6 ♕xd1 17. ♖xd1 gxf6 18. ♖xd7± but this endgame clearly provides excellent winning chances for White.

**B)** 13... ♗c6?! 14. ♘d4! ♗xb5 15. ♘xb5 ♔d8 16. cxd6 exd6 17. ♗f4 ♕b7 In Muzychuk – Bodnaruk, 2019, White's best continuation was 18. ♕e2! ♘e5 19. ♗xe5 dxe5 20. ♕xe5±.

**C)** 13... e5 is a crazy computer suggestion but White is also doing well after 14. c4!

Position after: 14. c4!

14... ♗c6 15. cxd6 ♗xb5 16. ♘xe5! ♘e4 17. ♘xd7 ♗xd7 18. f3 ♕a7+ 19. ♔h1 ♗c6 20. b4!± Eventually Black will have to give one of the pieces back, and then our pawns give us slightly better chances in the resulting material imbalance.

**14. ♖xe4!**

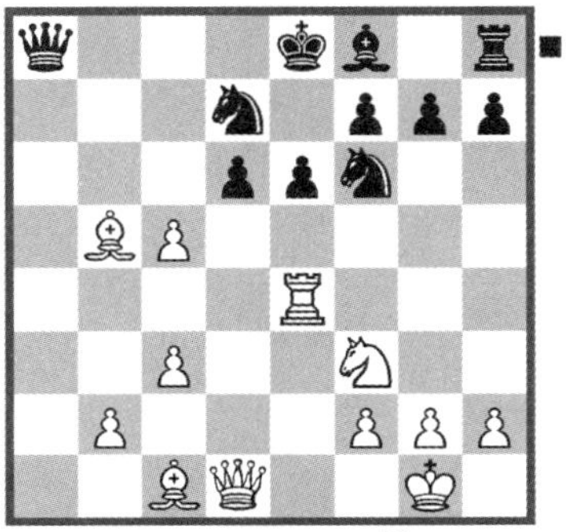

Position after: 14. ♖xe4!

Getting rid of Black's best piece.

**14... ♘xe4**

14... ♕xe4 15. c6

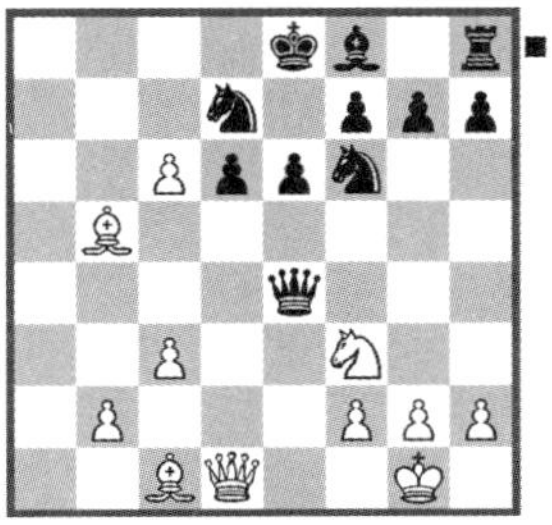

Position after: 15. c6

15... ♗e7! [15... ♘b6?! 16. c7+ ♔e7 17. ♘d4!± Followed by ♗e3, ♘c6+ and c3-c4 - in practical terms, Black's position looks horrible to defend.] 16. ♘d2

*(see analysis diagram next page)*

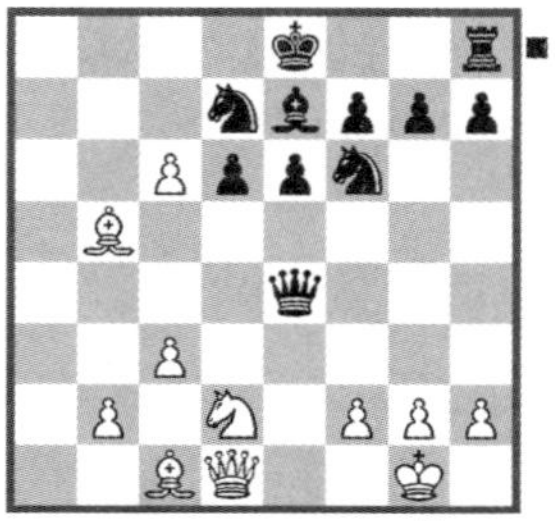

Position after: 16. ♘d2

**A)** 16... ♕f5!? The computer insists that this is fine for Black but I don't think that anyone would play this way, because our knight can now jump to d4 with a tempo. The following line provides the most practical problems for Black: 17. cxd7+ ♔f8 18. c4 g6 19. ♘b3 ♔g7 20. ♘d4 ♕e4 21. b4!

Position after: 21. b4!

21... ♖d8 22. ♘c6 ♖xd7 23. f3 ♕h4 24. ♗e3↑ Even though we're still an exchange down, Black's position is more difficult play. The simplest way for White to continue is something like ♕d2, ♗a6, and pushing the b-pawn. Of course, the engine still gives 0.00 :)

**B)** 16... ♕d5 Now that Black has defended well, it's time to try and bail out. 17. cxd7+ ♘xd7 18. ♕a4 ♕b7 19. ♗c6 ♕c7 20. ♘c4

Position after: 20. ♘c4

20... d5 [20... ♗f6 21. ♗f4 ♗e5 22. ♗xe5 dxe5 23. ♕a8+ ♔e7 24. ♕xh8 ♕xc6 25. ♘e3=; 20... ♔d8 21. ♕a8+ ♕c8 22. ♕a5+= ♔e8?

Position after: 22... ♔e8?

23. ♕a4 ♔d8 24. ♗e3+–] 21. ♘e5 ♕xe5 22. ♗xd7+ ♔d8 23. ♕a8+ ♔xd7 24. ♕a4+ ♔d8 25. ♕a8+ ♔d7 ½-½ Harikrishna – Vachier Lagrave, chess24. com INT 2020.

**15. c6**

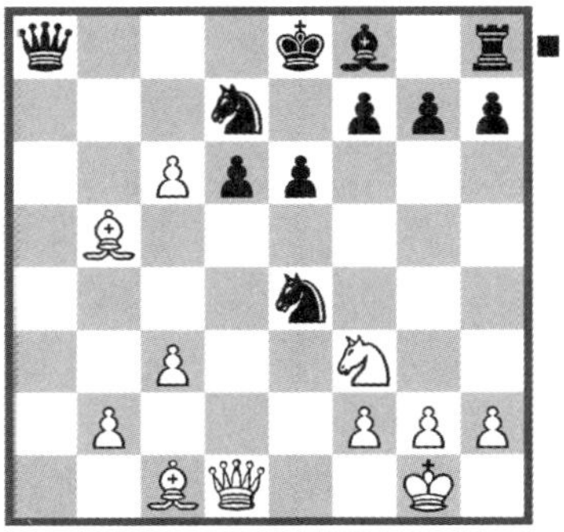

Position after: 15. c6

**15... ♘b6**

15... ♘dc5 has never been played, but Black also looks fine here. The line could continue: 16. c7+ ♔e7 17. ♘d4 ♕b7 18. c8=♕ ♕xc8 19. ♘c6+ ♔f6 20. ♕f3+ ♔g6 21. ♕g4+ ♔f6 22. ♕f4+=

**16. ♕d4 ♕a5**

**A)** 16... ♘c5 17. b4 f6 18. bxc5 dxc5 19. c7+ ♔f7 20. ♕f4 ♔g8 21. ♗d7!

Position after: 21. ♗d7!

21... ♕d5 [21... ♘xd7? 22. ♕c4 ♔f7 23. ♘d4+–] 22. ♕d2! Black can't prevent the two minor pieces vs rook material imbalance, after which White is basically playing for two results.

**B)** 16... ♘d5 is another computer suggestion but looks very risky for Black. 17. ♕xe4 ♗e7 18. ♘d4 ♘c7 19. ♗f1 ♕a1 20. ♕c2 ♗f6 21. b4=∞ I don't think White can ever be worse here.

**17. c4**

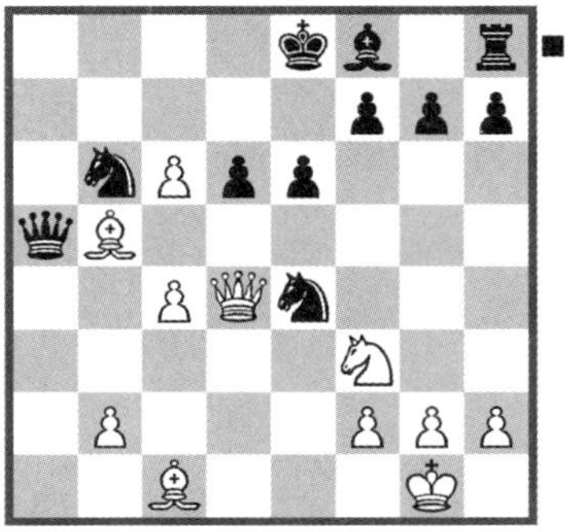

Position after: 17. c4

**17... f5!?**

**A)** 17... ♘c5? 18. b4! A very clever idea. 18... ♕xb4 19. c7+ ♔e7 20. ♕a1!+– White has full control over the position.

**B)** 17... ♕a1 18. c7+ ♔e7 19. ♕d1!

Position after: 19. ♕d1!

Threatening ♗g5+. 19... ♕a7 [19... f6? 20. ♘g5! ♘xg5 21. c5!+–] 20. c8=♘+ ♘xc8 21. ♘d4 ♕c7 22. ♘c6+ ♔e8 23.

♘b4+ ♔e7 24. ♘c6+= ½ – ½ Muzychuk – Harika, Lausanne 2020.

**18. b4! ♕a2!**

18... ♕a7 is too dangerous for Black after 19. c5 ♘c8 20. c7+ ♔e7 21. cxd6+ ♘exd6 22. ♗g5+ ♔f7 23. ♕xa7 ♘xa7 24. ♘e5+ ♔g8 25. ♗d7↑.

**19. c7+ ♔f7 20. ♕xb6 ♗e7**

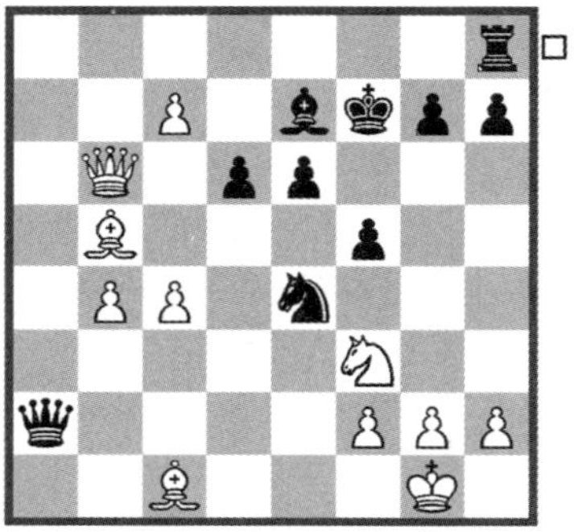

Position after: 20... ♗e7

**21. ♗d7! ♗f6 22. h4! ♕a1 23. ♕e3 ♗b2 24. ♕e1 ♔e7 25. c8=♕**

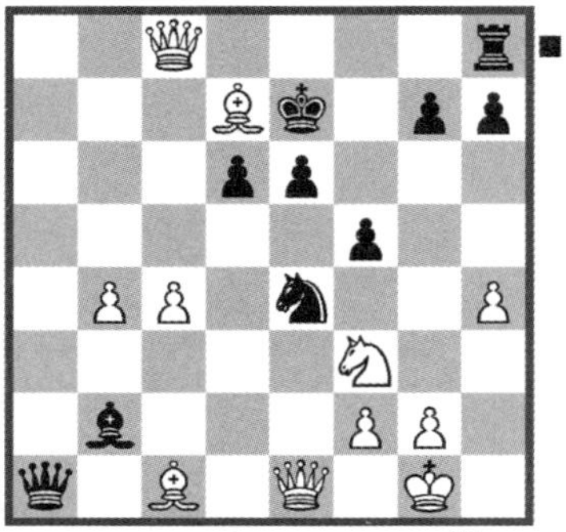

Position after: 25. c8=♕

**25... ♖xc8 26. ♗xc8 ♗xc1=**

After a forcing line the game should end in a draw.

## *Conclusion to Chapter 2*

It's clear that this subchapter is the most critical out of all the variations after 4.0-0. In all subchapters from a-h, we are either achieving an advantage or pressing for an advantage. However, our analysis in subchapter i demonstrated that Black is capable of 'forcing' equality with some accurate moves starting with 6...b5 and 7...♗b7. To this end, it is logical to play 4.0-0 against higher rated opponents who are keen to avoid this 'drawing' line – in which case we are well prepared to capitalize against all the other slightly inferior options for Black.

The next chapter will examine 4.a4, an alternative to 4.0-0, which preemptively prevents the ...b7-b5 push. This choice is more sensible if we don't want to allow any forcing lines such as those analysed in subchapter i.

# 4.a4

1.e4 c5 2.♘f3 d6 3.♗b5+ ♘d7

4.a4

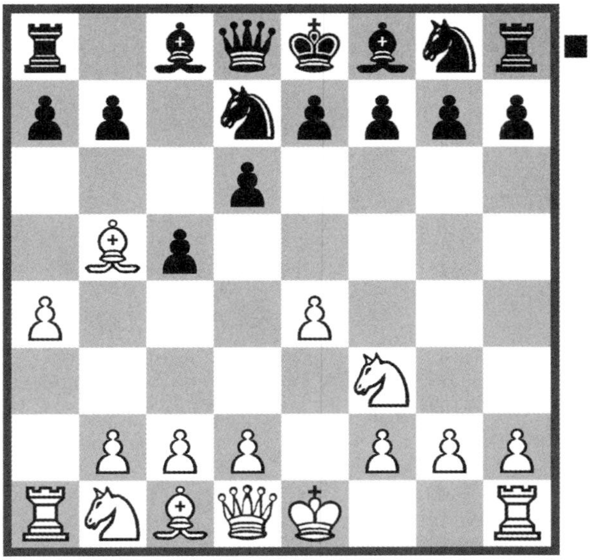

# Chapter Guide

## Chapter 3 – 4.a4

1.e4 c5 2.♘f3 d6 3.♗b5+ ♘d7 4.a4 ♘gf6 5.♘c3

## a) 5...g6 6.0-0 ♗g7 7.♖e1 0-0

**1. e4 c5 2. ♘f3 d6 3. ♗b5+ ♘d7 4. a4**

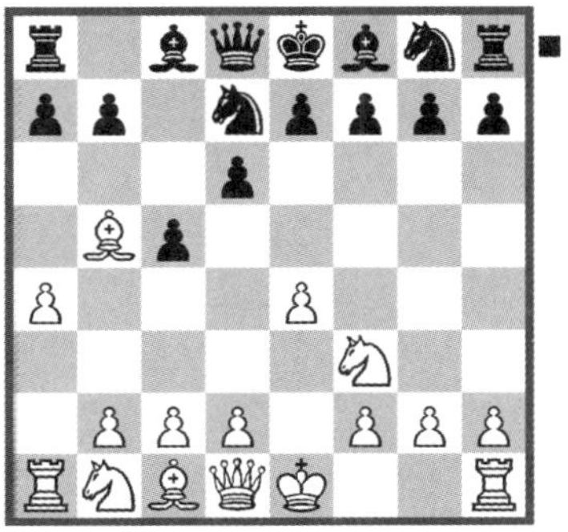

Position after: 4. a4

The point of this move is to prevent Black from achieving any active counterplay associated with an ...a7-a6 and ...b7-b5 pawn push.

**5... ♘gf6 5. ♘c3 g6**

Here we'll examine what happens if Black elects to fianchetto the dark-squared bishop, but delays playing ...a7-a6.

**6. 0-0 ♗g7**

6... a6 will transpose back to 5...a6 after 7. ♗e2, but we're also granted the additional option of 7. ♗xd7+ ♗xd7 8. e5!?.

**7. ♖e1**

7. a5 0-0 [7... a6 8. ♗e2 transposes back to 5... a6.] 8. ♖e1 a6 9. ♗f1 b5 This is a line I'm keen to avoid, as I feel like the rook on e1 and bishop on f1 are misplaced if we play the same plan of capturing on b6 and pushing d2-d3. In the corresponding structure after 5...a6, we often saw ideas revolving around ♘d2, f2-f4 and ♗f3. With our rook on e1 and bishop on f1, it seems as though our future plans are a bit more unclear.

**7... 0-0**

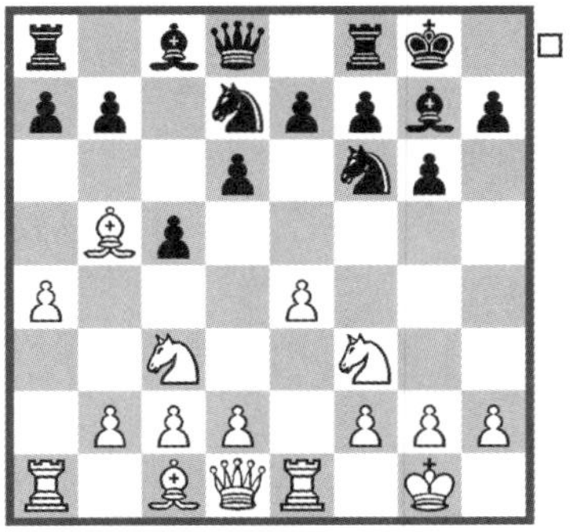

Position after: 7... 0-0

**8. d4!**

Instead of further pushing the a-pawn, I'd prefer to transform into an Open Sicilian type of position and claim that Black's knight on d7, along with our pawn on a4, are hindering Black's development.

**8... cxd4 9. ♘xd4 a6**

Black isn't forced to play this, but we're dropping the bishop back to f1 regardless and generally Black wants to control the b5-square to play moves like ...♕c7.

**10. ♗f1**

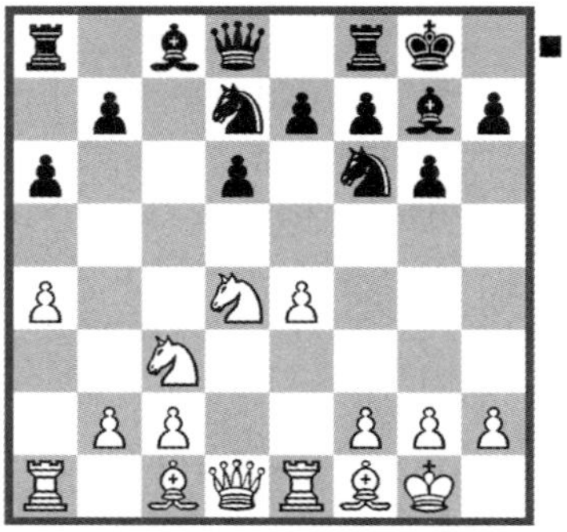

Position after: 10. ♗f1

**10... ♕c7**

It makes the most sense to keep the knight on d7 before playing ...b7-b6. However we now have ideas to highlight the drawback of 10...♕c7.

**A)** 10... ♘c5 11. h3 ♗d7 12. ♖a3!

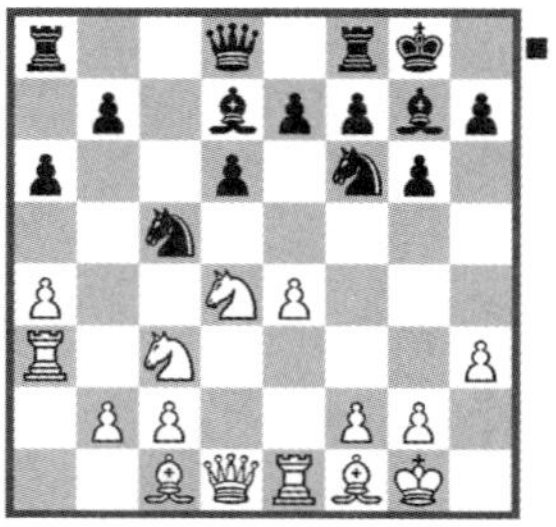

Position after: 12. ♖a3!

Preparing b2-b4 and ♘d5. 12... ♖e8 13. b4 ♘e6 14. ♘xe6 ♗xe6 15. ♘d5±

**B)** 10... ♖e8 Black is now able to play ...b7-b6 without having to worry about ♘c6, so we should react accordingly. 11. a5!

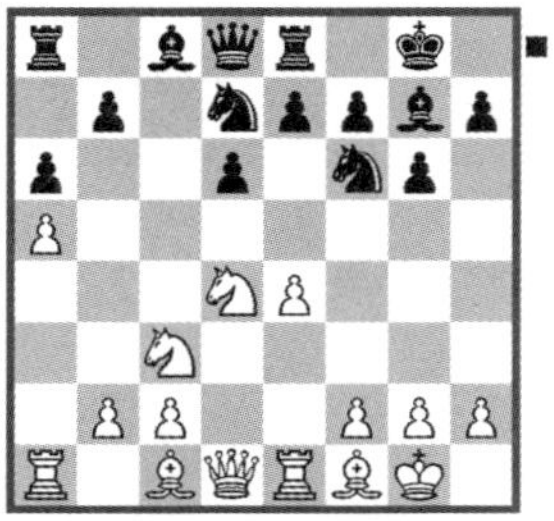

Position after: 11. a5!

11... b6 Black should play this anyway to enable queenside development, but it looks like White keeps a small advantage. [11... e5 12. ♘b3 ♕c7 13. ♗e3 b5 14. axb6 ♘xb6 15. h3±] An example line may continue: 12. axb6 ♕xb6 13. ♘b3 ♘e5 14. h3 a5 15. ♗e3 ♕c7 16. f4!

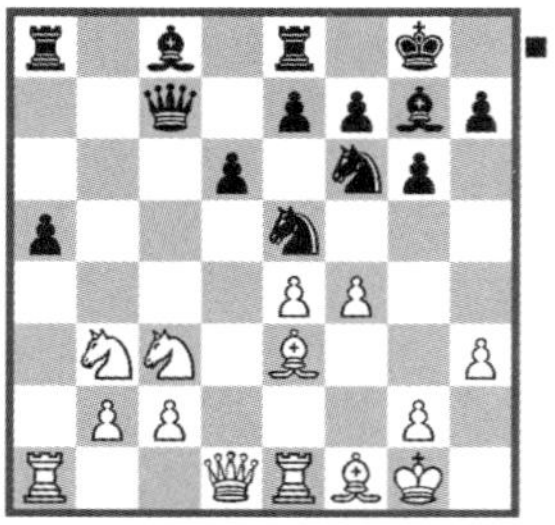

Position after: 16. f4!

16... ♘c6 17. ♘d5 ♕b7 18. ♗f2 ♗e6 19. ♖a4!±

**C)** 10... ♘e5 11. h3 Black can choose to play ... ♘c6 immediately, or prepare it with ... ♗d7.

**C1)** 11... ♘c6 12. ♘b3 b6 In this case Black prevents us from playing a4-a5 and controlling the b6-square. Nevertheless, our position looks pretty comfortable. For example: 13. ♗g5 h6 [13... ♗b7 14. ♘d5±] 14. ♗e3 ♗b7 15. ♕d2 ♔h7 16. ♖ad1± It seems like Black's b6-pawn will be a long-term weakness.

**C2)** 11... ♗d7 12. a5

**C2.1)** 12... ♘c6 13. ♘b3!

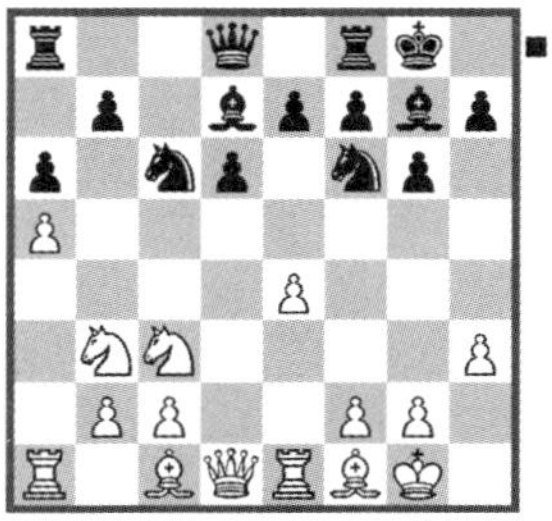

Position after: 13. ♘b3!

By retaining as many pieces on the board as possible, we can hope to cramp the Black position and aim to exploit the b6-square. 13... ♖c8 14. ♗e3 ♘e5 15. ♗d4 ♘c4 16. ♗xc4 ♖xc4 17. ♘d5± This time we do exchange pieces, as Black's light-squared bishop typically struggles against our knight.

**C2.2)** 12... ♖c8 13. ♘d5!

*(see analysis diagram next column)*

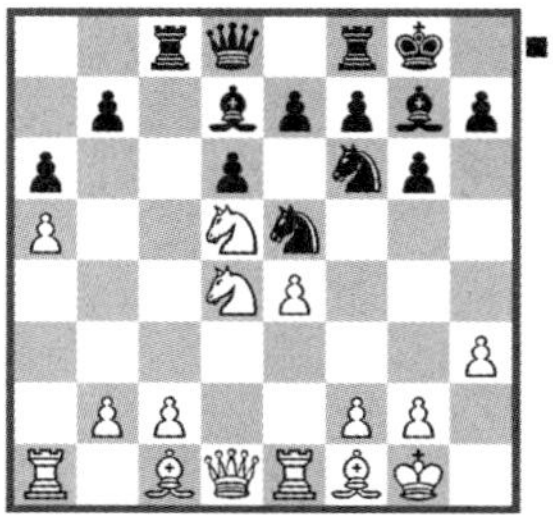

Position after: 13. ♘d5!

13... ♘xd5 14. exd5 ♖c5 15. ♘b3 ♖c8 16. c3± I'm not claiming that White has a big advantage, but our position feels easier to play - especially considering Black's weakness on b6.

**11. h3**

A useful preparatory move.

**11... ♖e8**

Black should defend the e7-pawn before playing ... b7-b6.

11... b6 12. ♘d5! ♘xd5 13. exd5 ♖e8 14. ♖a3!

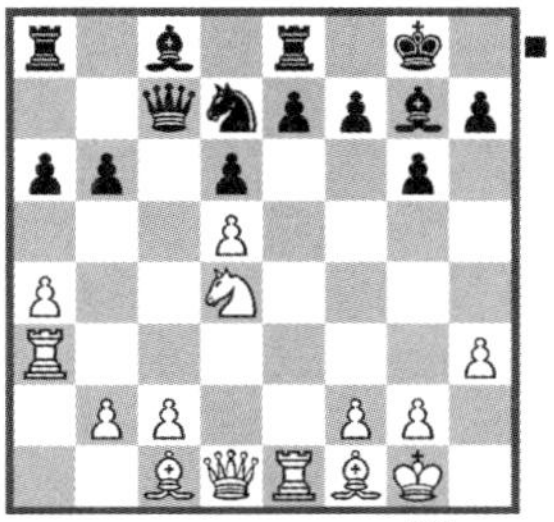

Position after: 14. ♖a3!

The c6-square is a real problem for Black now. 14... ♗b7 [14... ♘e5 15. ♖c3 ♕b7 16. g4!± with either ♗g2 or f2-f4 to come next.] 15. c4±

**12. ♘d5**

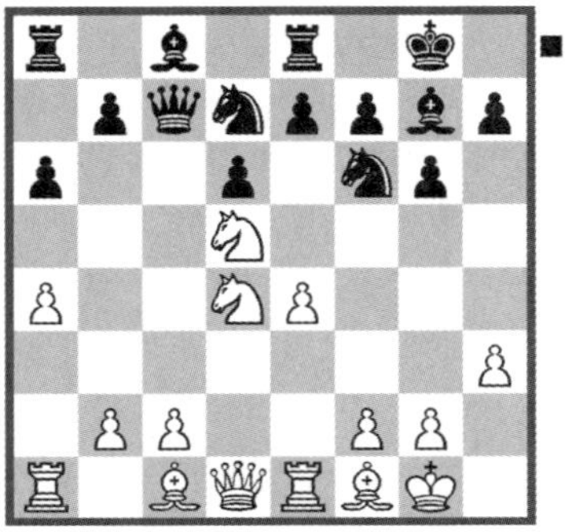

Position after: 12. ♘d5

**A)** 12. ♖a3!? A typical example of the resources at our disposal. The rook will be well placed to control the c-file from the c3-square after the forthcoming ♘d5.

**B)** 12. a5 is also logical, e.g. 12... b5 13. axb6 ♘xb6 14. ♘b3±.

**12... ♘xd5 13. exd5 ♘b6 14. ♘f3 ♗d7 15. c3±**

We maintain good pressure along the e-file, and Black's pieces struggle for any activity.

## b) 5...g6 6.0-0 ♗g7 7.♖e1 a6

**1. e4 c5 2. ♘f3 d6 3. ♗b5+ ♘d7 4. a4 ♘gf6 5. ♘c3 g6 6. 0-0 ♗g7 7. ♖e1 a6**

Position after: 7... a6

**8. ♗f1 b6!**

I had originally given up on this line, thinking that Black had zero problems. That was until my close friend and mentor Marcus 'crème de la' Harvey showed me there are still plenty of resources for White.

8... 0-0 9. d4 will transpose to 7... 0-0.

**9. d4 cxd4 10. ♕xd4!**

Usually when we recapture with the queen on d4, it means we next want to push e4-e5 immediately.

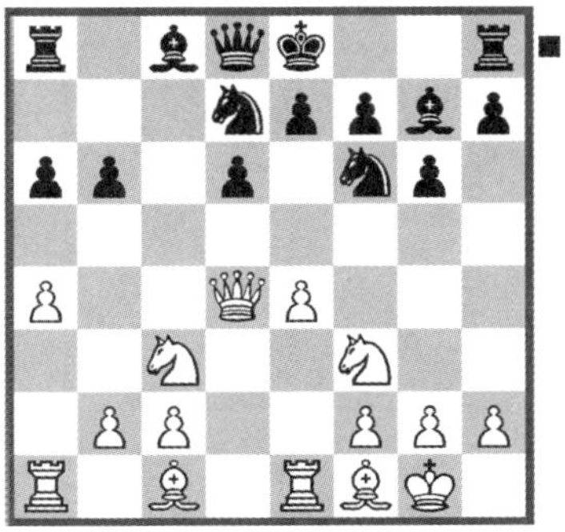

Position after: 10. ♕xd4!

**10... ♗b7**

10... 0-0 11. e5 Black is forced to capture on e5, as any knight move will be met with ♕e4 which is extremely favourable for White. 11... dxe5 [11... ♘e8 12. ♕e4±] 12. ♘xe5± White is always, at the very least, slightly better in these structures, mainly due to the weakness of Black's b6-pawn.

**11. e5!**

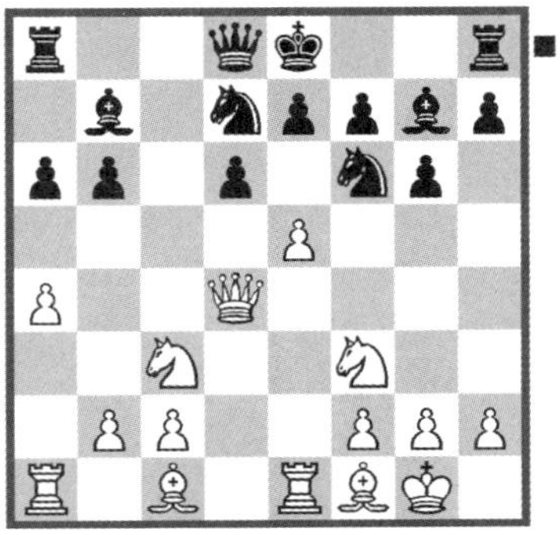

Position after: 11. e5!

Black faces a difficult choice about where to place their knight.

**11... ♘h5**

This feels like the most human move, although the position is still very dangerous for Black.

**A)** 11... dxe5?! Once again the exchange of these pawns is advantageous for White. 12. ♘xe5 ♘xe5 [12... 0-0 13. ♗f4 e6 14. ♘xd7 ♘xd7 15. ♕e3±] 13. ♕xe5 ♘h5 14. ♕g5 ♗f6 15. ♕e3!

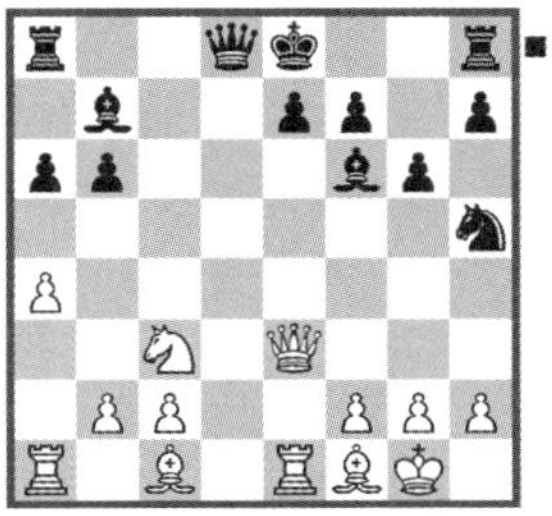

Position after: 15. ♕e3!

15... 0-0 16. ♖a3!±

**B)** 11... ♘g8 12. ♕f4! dxe5 13. ♘xe5 ♘xe5 14. ♖xe5!

Position after: 14. ♖xe5!

It's extremely dangerous for Black to accept the exchange sacrifice here.

**B1)** 14... ♗xe5?! 15. ♕xe5 ♘f6 [15... f6 16. ♕e6!+–] 16. ♗h6 White's position is extremely easy to play.

[16. ♗g5 is possibly even stronger.] 16... ♖g8 17. ♖d1 ♘d7 18. ♕e3± To be followed by moves like ♖d4 and ♘e4, gradually increasing the pressure on Black's position.

**B2)** 14... ♘f6 15. ♖e1 0-0 16. ♕b4± With ♗e3 coming next, White's position is clearly very pleasant here too.

**B3)** 14... ♘h6 15. ♖e1 0-0 16. ♗d3± Followed by ♗e3 and possibly ♕g3. White is once again slightly better due to Black's weak queenside pawns.

**C)** Importantly, 11... ♗xf3 is refuted by 12. exd6! ♗b7 13. ♖xe7+ ♔f8 14. ♗c4 ♘d5 15. ♗h6!+–.

**12. ♕b4!**

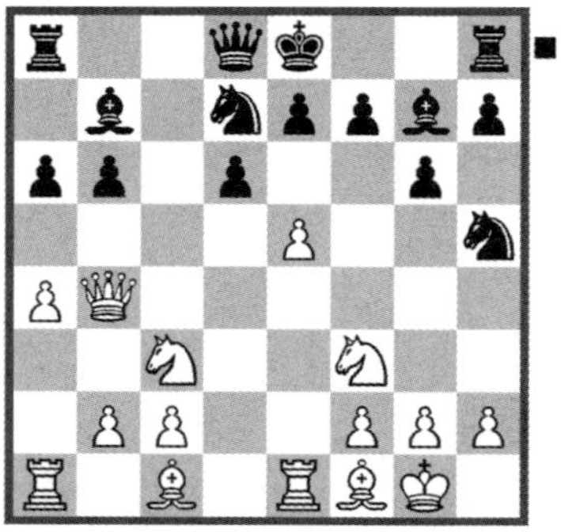

Position after: 12. ♕b4!

**12... dxe5**

12... ♘xe5 13. ♘xe5 ♗xe5 [13... dxe5 14. ♗e3±] 14. a5! b5 15. ♗h6 Suddenly Nxb5 is a serious threat.

Position after: 15. ♗h6

**A)** 15... ♕c7 16. f4! ♗xc3 [16... ♗g7? 17. ♗xg7 ♘xg7 18. ♗xb5+ axb5 19. ♘xb5 ♕c5+ 20. ♕xc5 dxc5 21. ♘d6++–; 16... ♗f6 17. ♗xb5+!] 17. bxc3↑ Followed by c3-c4 and Black's position is extremely close to crumbling.

**B)** 15... ♗g7 16. ♗xg7 ♘xg7 17. ♘xb5! axb5 18. ♗xb5+ ♔f8 19. a6 ♗c8 20. ♗c6 ♖xa6 21. ♖xa6 ♗xa6 22. ♖a1± We will win the piece back and retain good chances in the endgame with our favourable minor piece and passed b-pawn.

**13. ♖d1!**

We have excellent compensation for the pawn. The text move has a number of ideas: pushing a4-a5 and capturing on b5, controlling the d-file, and potentially landing a knight on d5.

**13... 0-0**

13... ♗c6 Attempting to control the b5-square. Here we can continue to increase the pressure on Black's position with the aggressive 14. ♘g5! 0-0 15.

♗c4 threatening to capture twice on f7 followed by ♕c4+. 15... ♕e8 16. ♘d5!

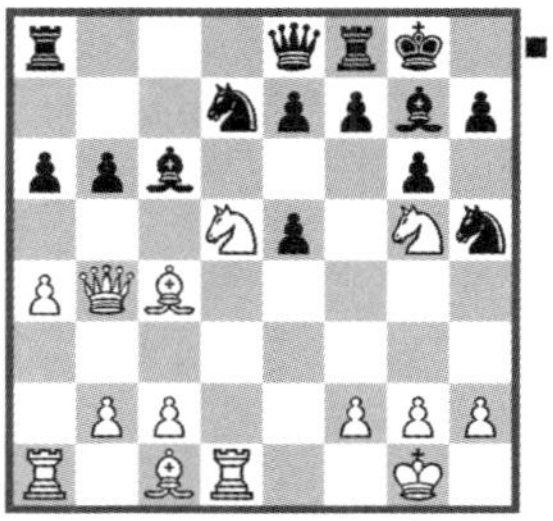

Position after: 16. ♘d5!

16... ♗xd5 17. ♗xd5 ♖d8 [17... ♖c8 18. ♘e6! fxe6 19. ♗xe6+ ♔h8 20. ♗xd7 ♕f7 21. ♕xb6 ♖xc2 22. ♗e6!±] 18. ♗e3 ♘hf6 19. ♗f3⩱∞ The engine still insists on 0.00, but this only demonstrates that White has full compensation for the pawn.

**14. a5 b5**

14... ♗c6 15. axb6 ♕xb6 16. ♕xb6 ♘xb6 17. ♖a5!± We're more interested in capturing the e5-pawn.

**15. ♘xb5!**

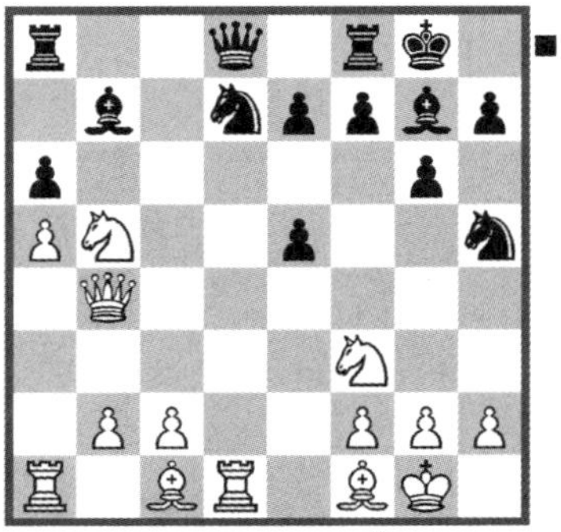

Position after: 15. ♘xb5!

**15... ♗xf3**

15... axb5 16. ♗xb5 ♗c8!? [16... ♘hf6 17. ♗xd7 ♗xf3 18. gxf3 would simply transpose to the mainline.] 17. ♗g5 ♗f6 18. ♕a4 ♗xg5 19. ♗xd7

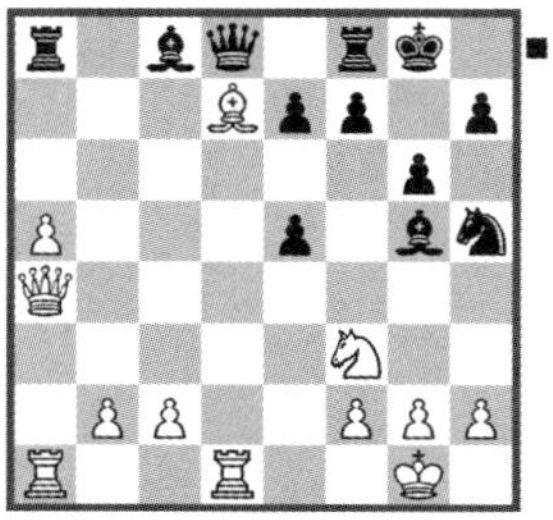

Position after: 19. ♗xd7

19... ♗c1!!= An amazing resource which I don't think any human would find over the board.

**16. gxf3 axb5 17. ♗xb5 ♘hf6 18. ♗xd7**

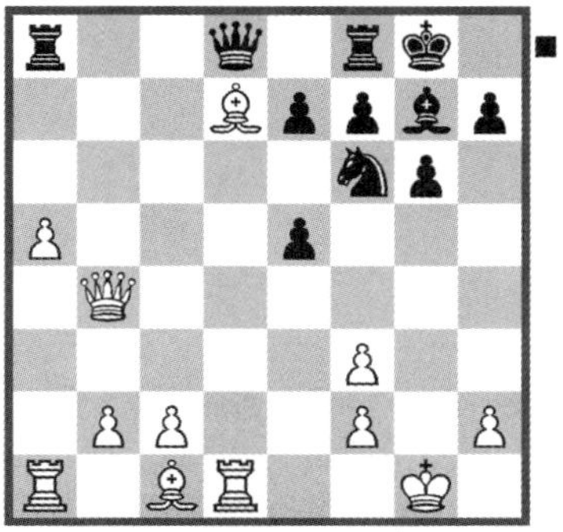

Position after: 18. ♗xd7

**18... ♖a7!**

18... ♘xd7? 19. ♕b5+– 19...♖a7 is now met strongly with ♗e3, after which White is completely winning.

**19. a6 ♖xd7 20. ♖xd7 ♕xd7 21. a7 ♕d1+ 22. ♔g2**

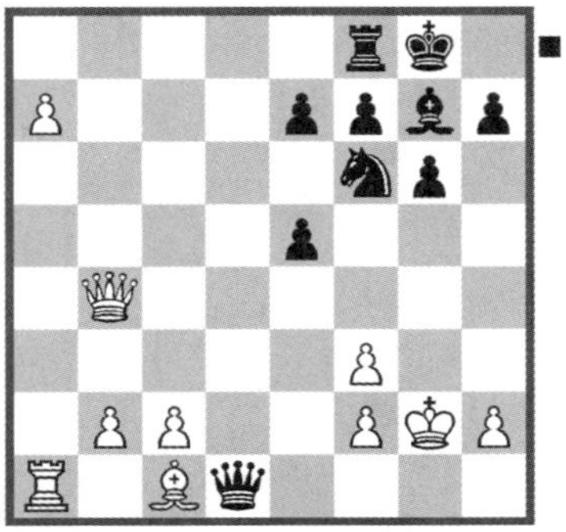

Position after: 22. ♔g2

**22... e4!=**

Black is able to force a perpetual here, but only after navigating through an extremely tricky path.

## c) 5...a6 6.♗e2 6...g6

**1. e4 c5 2. ♘f3 d6 3. ♗b5+ ♘d7 4. a4 ♘gf6 5. ♘c3 a6**

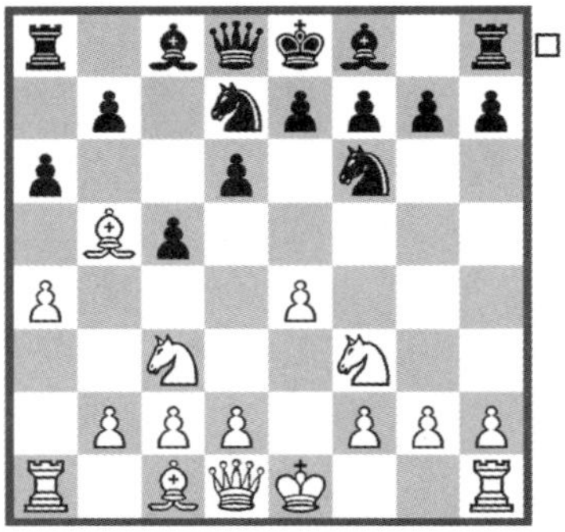

Position after: 5... a6

5... g6 will be analysed in the next subchapter.

**6. ♗e2 g6**

The recommendation of Anish Giri in his Najdorf Chessable Course.

**7. 0-0 ♗g7**

7... b6?! Black doesn't have enough time to prevent the a4-a5 push. 8. d4 cxd4 9. ♕xd4!N

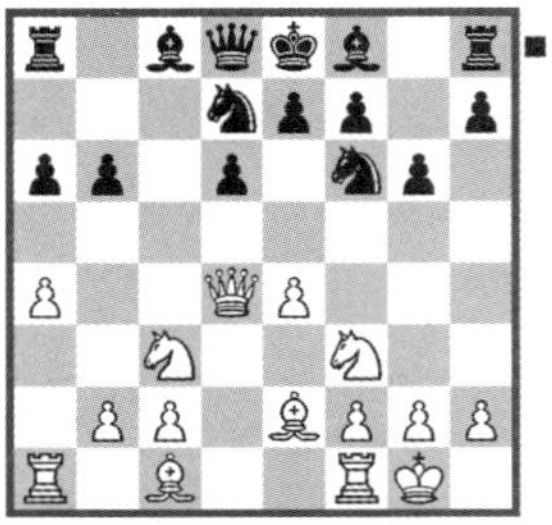

Position after: 9. ♕xd4!N

Threatening e4-e5, after which White achieves a strong initiative. 9... ♗g7 10. e5 dxe5 11. ♘xe5 ♘xe5 12. ♕xe5 0-0 13. ♖d1 ♕e8 14. ♕c7± As we'll encounter in numerous lines after 4. a4, Black's issues stem from the weak queenside pawns.

**8. a5**

**A)** The problem with the immediate 8. d4 cxd4 9. ♘xd4 is that Black can start with 9... b6!= [9. ♕xd4 also doesn't cause Black any issues after the simple 9... 0-0=].

**B)** 8. ♖e1 would be a good move if Black were to respond 8... 0-0, after which we have the option of 9.d4!. Unfortunately Black has the immediate 8... b6! which seems to equalise very easily. In the next subchapter, with the bishop standing on f1, we have more resources in this corresponding position after 9. d4.

**8... 0-0**

**A)** 8... e5?! has been played a few times by relatively strong players, but it seems like White achieves a nice advantage with 9. d3 0-0 10. ♘d2!

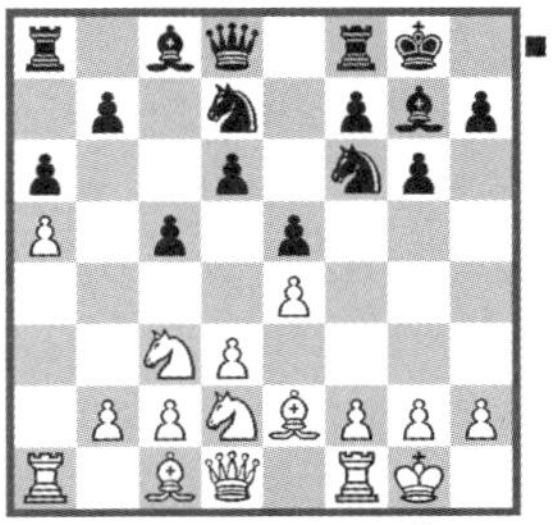

Position after: 10. ♘d2!

10... b5 11. axb6 ♘xb6 12. ♘c4!± This is basically a really nice version of similar positions reached after 8... 0-0 and 9...b6.

**B)** 8... b5 will most likely transpose to the line after 8... 0-0 and 9...b5.

**9. d3**

Anticipating Black's b-pawn push, after which our f3-knight can relocate to the queenside via the d2-square. It's important to note that with our bishop on e2 we should leave our rook on f1, anticipating future ideas of ♘d2 and f2-f4.

9. d4 For a while I was convinced that White was able to achieve a pleasant position with this move, until the engine pointed out that Black can equalise with the immediate 9... b5!=.

Position after: 9. d3

**9... b6**

**A)** 9... ♘b8 is the second most popular move. It's a logical knight manoeuvre targetting our weak a5-pawn, so we need to respond actively. 10. e5! [10. d4!? is also definitely worthy of consideration.]

**A1)** 10... dxe5?! 11. ♘xe5 ♗e6 12. ♗f3±

**A2)** 10... ♘h5?! 11. exd6 exd6 12. ♘d2! ♘f4 13. ♗f3± Followed by ♘c4 and ♘d5. White has full control over the position.

**A3)** 10... ♘g4?! 11. exd6 exd6 12. ♗g5!

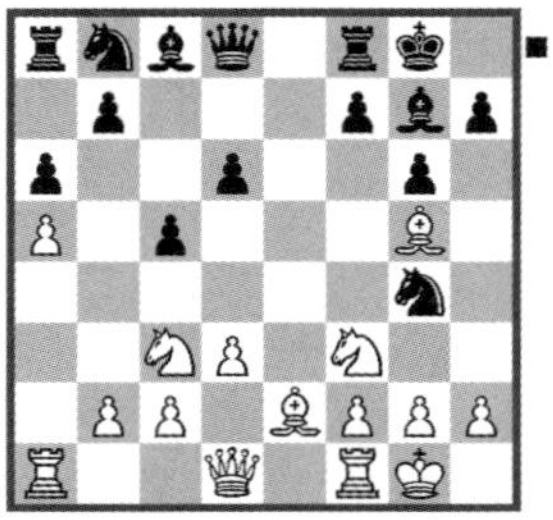

Position after: 12. ♗g5!

12... ♗f6 13. ♕d2± Black has already created a lot of weaknesses in their position, and we can continue with simple moves such as ♖fe1, ♘d5, and h2-h3 to build up the advantage.

**A4)** 10... ♘e8N Pretty much Black's only move, though remarkably it has never been played. 11. exd6 ♘xd6 [11... exd6 12. d4!±] 12. ♘e4!

**A4.1)** 12... ♘xe4 The exchange of knights leads to a really pleasant position for White, e.g. 13. dxe4 ♕c7 [13... ♘c6?! 14. ♕xd8 ♖xd8 15. c3±] 14. c3 ♘c6 15. ♕a4 ♗d7 16. ♕a3±.

**A4.2)** 12... ♘d7 13. c3± It's clear that White has, at the very least, a small advantage. Our pawn on a5 plays an important role in constricting Black's minor pieces.

**B)** 9... b5 will obviously transpose to 9... b6 after we capture en passant.

**C)** 9... e6 doesn't really solve Black's space issue - and allows us to develop with tempi. 10. ♗f4

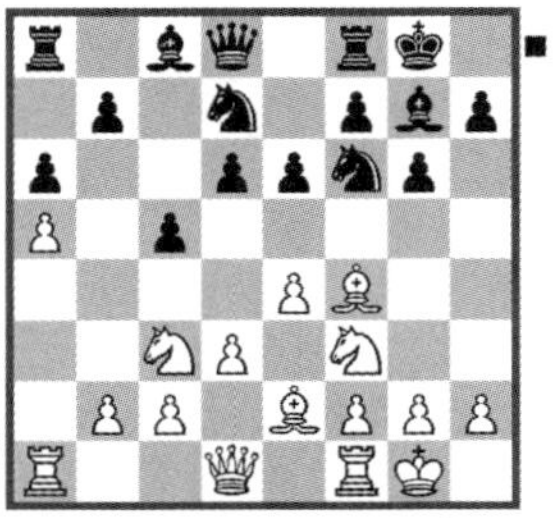

Position after: 10. ♗f4

**C1)** 10... e5 11. ♗e3 b5 12. axb6 ♘xb6 13. ♘d2± Followed by f2-f4 and/or ♘c4 exerting some pressure.

**C2)** 10... d5?! is the obvious continuation, but we are doing well after 11. ♘d2! threatening e4-e5. 11... b5 12. axb6 ♘xb6 13. ♘b3± With a better pawn structure and, importantly, control of the a5-square.

**C3)** 10... ♕c7 11. ♕c1± Black is kind of stuck. The push ...b7-b5 has to be played at some point - but it will be hugely inferior to the mainline after 9...b6.

**10. axb6**

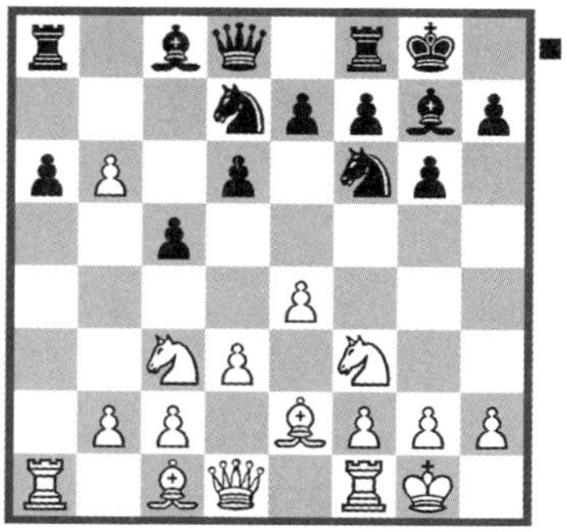

Position after: 10. axb6

An interesting moment to pause. The computer suggests that the position is objectively equal, but clearly each side has their own ideas. We will try to claim that Black's isolated a-pawn has the potential to be a future weakness, and our continuing development will most likely involve some combination of ♗f4, ♕d2, ♖a3, and doubling on the a-file. In turn, Black will try to claim that their future activity down the b-file is more important. The following variations will hopefully give you some intuition about the various plans that we have in this seemingly-slow position.

**10... a5**

Black doesn't need to rush to capture on b6, and can still decide whether to play ...♕xb6 or ...♘xb6. As demonstrated in the line after 10...♗b7, they have good reason in wanting to prevent a knight landing on the a5-square.

**A)** 10... ♕xb6 11. ♘d2! Aiming to transfer the knight to c4 with a tempo. 11... ♘e5 12. ♔h1 ♗b7 13. f4 ♘c6 14. ♘c4± Potentially followed by ♗f3, ♘e2, and an f-pawn push. 14... ♕c7 15. ♗f3 ♘d4 16. ♘a5±

**B)** 10... ♘xb6 11. ♗e3 ♗b7 12. ♕d2 a5

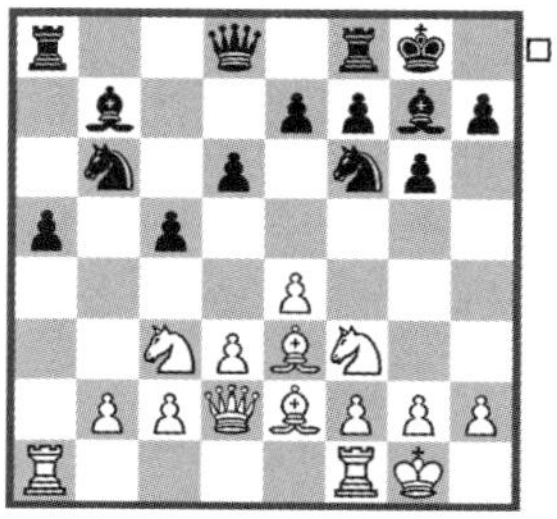

Position after: 12... a5

13. ♖a3!? The position remains equal, but I think the position is practically easier to play with White. We have ideas of both ♗h6 and ♖fa1, and Black constantly has to keep tabs on the isolated a-pawn.

**C)** 10... ♗b7?! This innocuous-looking move is an error, owing to the fact that we can rapidly transfer our f3-knight to the a5-square. 11. ♘d2 [Black's structure is too weak to break in the centre with 11...d5? After 12. ♘a4! I was already close to winning in Haria - Willow, Stafford 2022.] 11... ♘xb6 12. ♘b3 ♕c7 [12... ♖b8 13. ♗e3 ♕c7 14. ♕d2 ♖fe8 15. ♘a5 ♗a8 16. ♗f4±] 13. ♘a5± White had excellent control over the position in Robson – Shankland, Saint Louis 2021.

**11. e5!?**

I think this poses the greatest practical problems for Black. We attempt to capitalise on their weakened pawn structure, given they still need to waste time recapturing on b6.

11. ♗f4 followed by ♕d2 also seems entirely reasonable.

**11... dxe5**

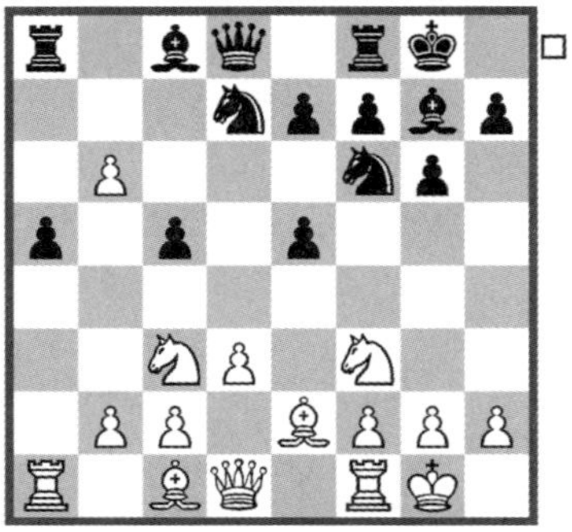

Position after: 11... dxe5

**A)** 11... ♘e8? 12. exd6 exd6 13. ♗g5! ♗f6 14. ♗h6 ♗g7 15. ♗xg7 ♘xg7 16. ♕d2±

**B)** 11... ♘xe5? 12. ♘xe5 dxe5 13. ♘a4±

**12. ♘d2 ♕xb6!**

Black needs to retain the knight on d7 to protect the weak c5- and e5-pawns.

**A)** 12... ♗b7 is another suggestion by the computer but I don't think any human would play this way. The line continues: 13. ♘c4 ♘d5 14. ♗d2 ♘f4 15. ♗xf4 exf4 16. ♘a4 ♗d5 17. ♗f3 e6 18. ♖a3!± White's position just seems really pleasant here, and Black still hasn't solved the problem of the b6-pawn.

**B)** 12... ♘xb6 13. ♗f3 ♖a7 14. ♘b3±

**13. ♗f3 ♗b7 14. ♘c4 ♕c7 15. ♗xb7 ♕xb7 16. ♖xa5 ♖xa5 17. ♘xa5**

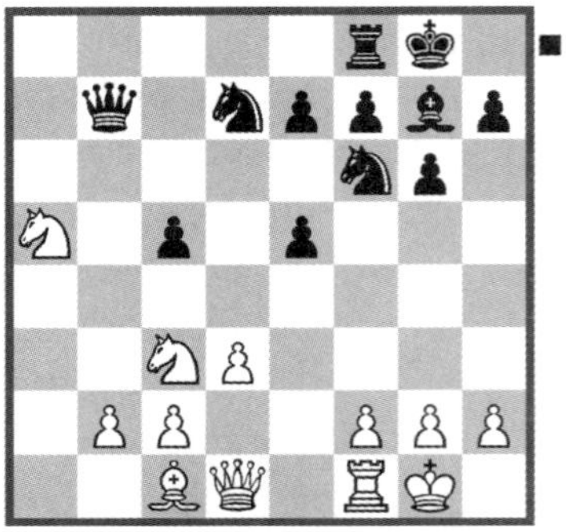

Position after: 17. ♘xa5

**17... ♕b4!=**

Aiming to trade off one of the weak pawns with either ...c5-c4 or ... e5-e4. Black is just about okay here, although the game can of course continue for a while.

## d) 5...a6 6.♗e2 e6 7.0-0 -- & 7...b6 8.d4 cxd4 9.♕xd4 ♗e7

**1. e4 c5 2. ♘f3 d6 3. ♗b5+ ♘d7 4. a4 ♘gf6 5. ♘c3 a6**

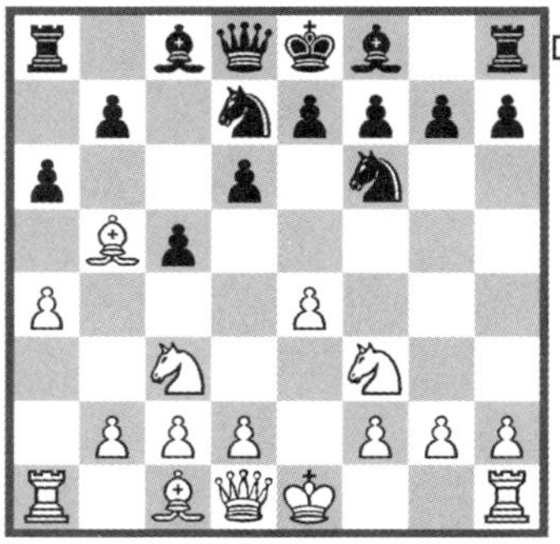

Position after: 5... a6

5... e6 Our approach won't differ even if Black delays ...a7-a6. 6. 0-0 ♗e7 7. d4 cxd4 [7... a6 8. dxc5!±] 8. ♕xd4!

Position after: 8. ♕xd4!

When Black sets up with ...e7-e6, we usually recapture on d4 with the queen so that we can re-route our f3-knight to c4 via d2. 8... 0-0 [8... a6 9. ♗e2 will transpose to 5...a6.] 9. a5! We'll continue to examine what happens if Black doesn't want to play ...a7-a6. 9... ♕c7 10. ♗e3 ♖d8

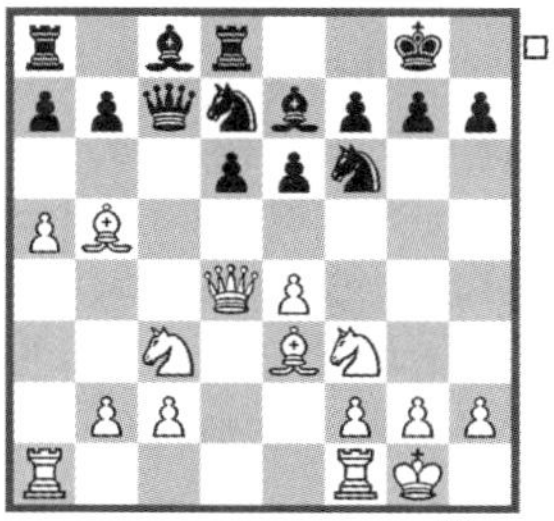

Position after: 10... ♖d8

11. ♖fd1 [11. ♕c4!? ♕xc4 12. ♗xc4 ♘b8 13. ♖fd1 ♘c6 14. h3 ♗d7 15. ♗b3±] 11... ♘b8 12. h3 ♘c6 13. ♕c4± Black's position is extremely passive.

**6. ♗e2 e6**

Instead, 6...b6 and 6...e5 will be analysed later.

**7. 0-0**

7. a5 would be an inaccuracy, as Black can equalise with the immediate 7... d5! 8. exd5 [8. e5 ♘g8! 9. d4 ♘e7∞] 8... exd5 9. d4

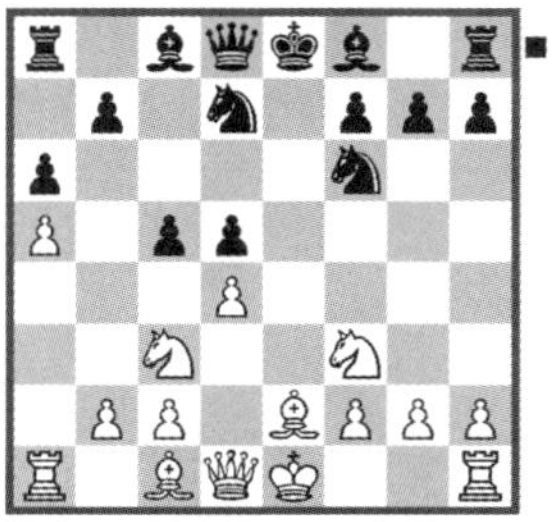

Position after: 9. d4

9... h6! when Black doesn't have any real problems.

**7... b6**

The most popular decision here, avoiding getting cramped by a4-a5. The downside for Black is that the resulting Open Sicilian type positions will give White the opportunity to target the seemingly-weak queenside pawns. My analysis shows that Black's only chance to maintain equality is to play as actively as possible.

**A)** 7... ♗e7 doesn't really change anything compared to the line after 9...♗e7. We'll still transform the position into an Open Sicilian structure. If Black then chooses to push ...b7-b6, it will most likely transpose back to 7...b6. If not, their position will remain cramped and we will always have the option to push a4-a5 if we so wish. I will give a few sample variations here. 8. d4 cxd4 9. ♕xd4

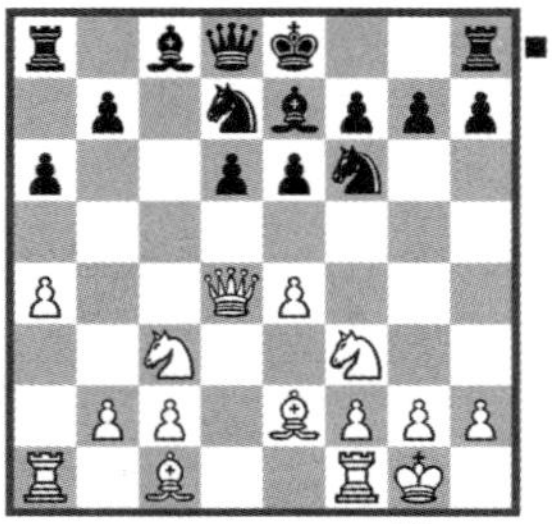

Position after: 9. ♕xd4

9... 0-0 [9... ♕c7 10. ♗e3 ♘e5 11. ♘xe5 dxe5 12. ♕c4! ♕xc4 13. ♗xc4 ♗d7 14. ♗d3!± Planning to re-route the c3-knight to c4 via b1.] 10. ♖d1 ♕c7 11. ♗e3 ♘g4 Otherwise 11... b6 would just transpose back to 7...b6. 12. ♗g5 ♘gf6 13. a5!± Black's position remains cramped.

**B)** 7... d5 8. exd5 exd5 9. d4± looks pretty pleasant for White - a big improvement on the line after 7.a5 d5.

**8. d4! cxd4 9. ♕xd4 ♗e7**

9... ♗b7 will be analysed in the next subchapter.

**10. ♖d1**

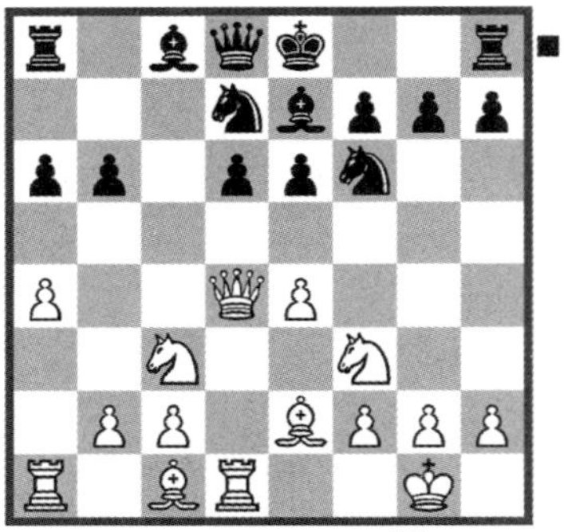

Position after: 10. ♖d1

White has two main ideas: either breaking in the centre with e4-e5, or re-routing our f3-knight to c4.

**10... ♕c7**

If Black prevents e4-e5, we have time to re-route our f3-knight to c4.

10... ♗b7 If Black chooses to delay playing ...♕c7, they give us the option of playing e4-e5. 11. e5! [11. ♗e3 is also possible but I don't really see a reason not to play 11.e5.] 11... ♗xf3 12. exd6 ♗xe2 13. dxe7 ♕xe7 14. ♘xe2 0-0 15. b3± White had a very pleasant position in Bosiocic – Volokitin, Batumi 2019. As always, Black's problems stem from their weak queenside pawns.

**11. ♗e3 0-0 12. ♘d2**

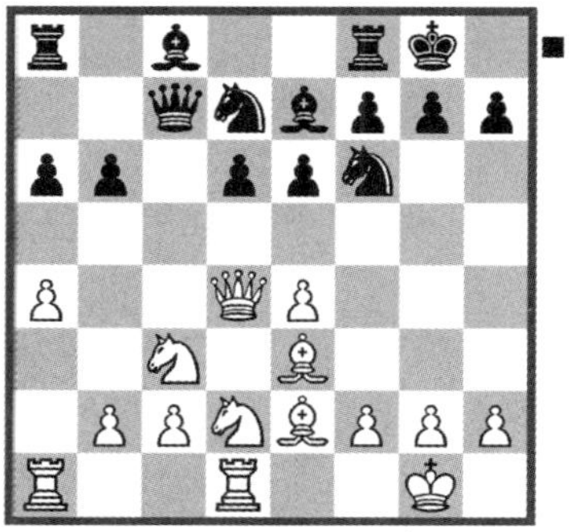

Position after: 12. ♘d2

**12... ♗b7**

12... ♘c5 13. ♘c4! A general rule is that trading our e4-pawn for Black's b6-pawn is beneficial for White. 13... e5 14. ♕d2

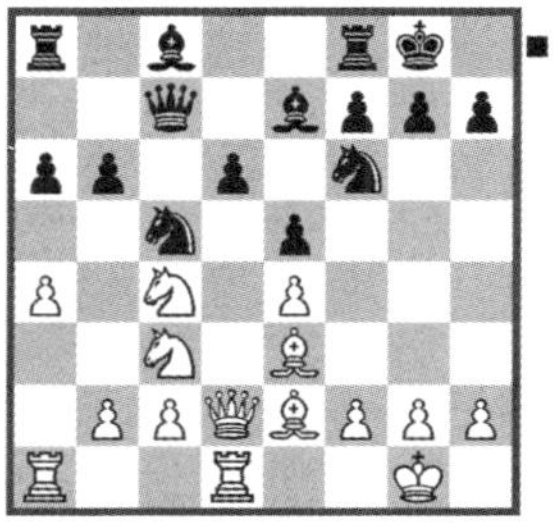

Position after: 14. ♕d2

14... ♘cxe4 [14... ♗e6 15. ♘d5 ♗xd5 16. exd5 a5 Black needed to prevent the b2-b4 push, but now their light-squares will remain extremely weak. 17. f3± White has full control over the position, with ideas such as ♘a3-b5.] 15. ♘xe4 ♘xe4 16. ♕b4 ♗e6 17. ♘xb6 ♕b7 18. f3 ♘f6 19. a5 d5 20. ♕e1! Black will face continual pressure on their a6-pawn. 20... ♖ad8 21. ♕f1±

**13. ♘c4**

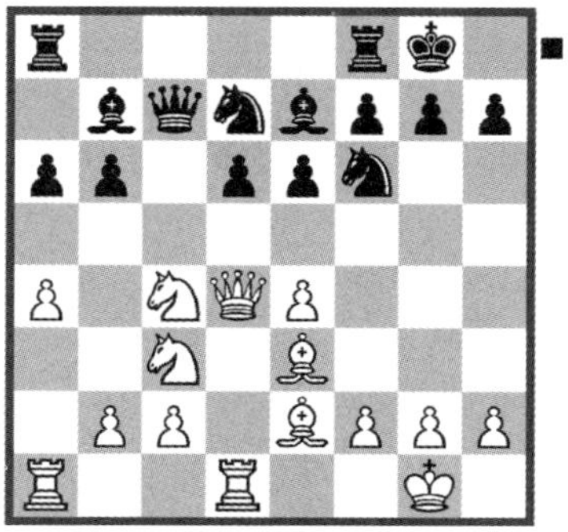

Position after: 13. ♘c4

**13... d5**

The most critical move, but White is able to retain an advantage.

**A)** 13... ♖ad8 Once again Black should usually avoid exchanging off their b6-pawn for our e4-pawn, as they will then struggle to hold on to the a-pawn. 14. ♘xb6 ♘c5 15. a5 ♘fxe4 16. ♘xe4 ♘xe4 17. f3 ♘f6 18. b4!±

**B)** 13... e5 was played against me by Falko Bindrich in the European Hybrid World Cup qualifier. As I only needed to draw the game to win the match, I chose the safe 14.♕d2, but even stronger is 14. ♕d3!

Position after: 14. ♕d3!

14... ♘c5 [14... ♖fd8 15. a5 b5 16. ♘b6±; 14... ♖ad8 15. ♗f3± Followed by ♕e2 and White has full control over the important d5-square. Pressure can then be further exerted by moves like a4-a5 and ♘b6.] 15. ♗xc5 dxc5 16. ♕f3!± followed by ♘e3.

**14. exd5 ♘xd5 15. ♘xd5 ♗xd5 16. ♗f4**

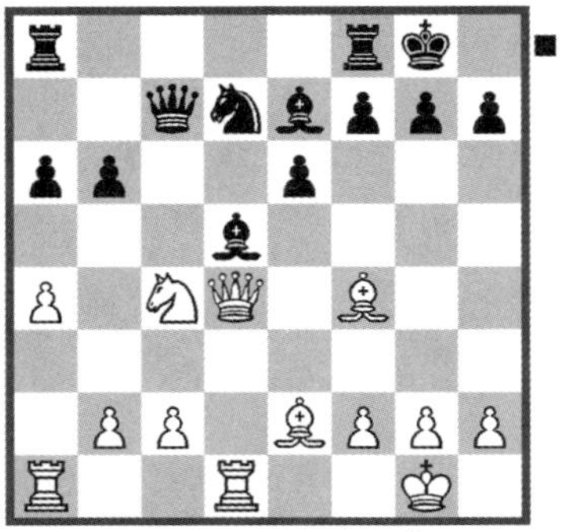
Position after: 16. ♗f4

**16... ♕b7**

**A)** 16... ♕c5 Endgames are always favourable for White due to the weakness of Black's queenside pawns. The following line illustrates one way we can target these pawns. 17. ♕xc5 ♗xc5 18. ♘e3 ♗c6 19. a5 b5 20. c4!

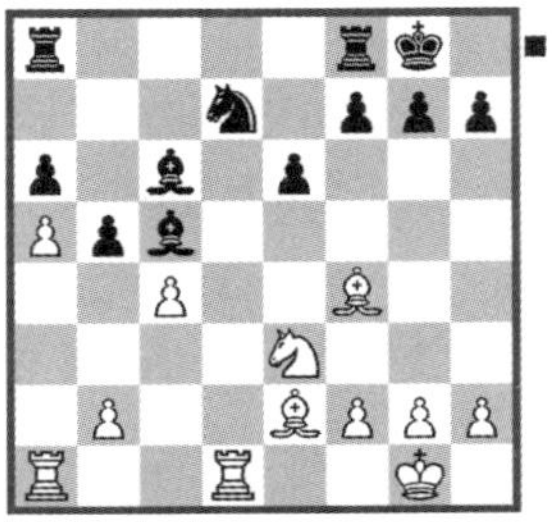
Position after: 20. c4!

20... b4 21. ♗d6 ♖fc8 22. ♘c2! b3 23. ♘b4± It's difficult for Black to avoid the queenside pawns dropping off.

**B)** 16... ♕c6 I think we're pretty happy if Black gives us the bishop pair advantage. 17. ♘e3 ♘f6 18. ♘xd5 ♘xd5 19. ♗e5±

**C)** 16... ♕a7 17. a5

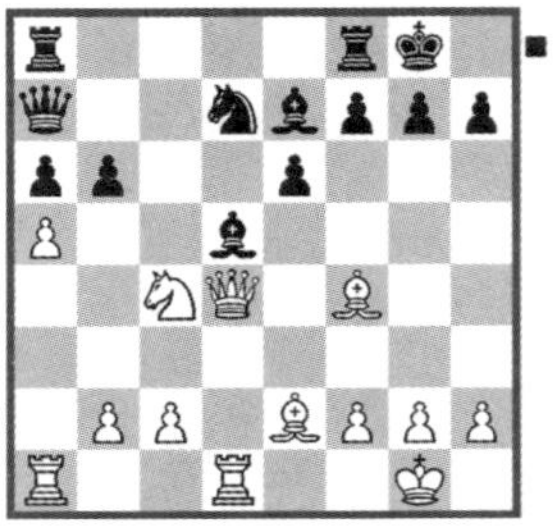
Position after: 17. a5

17... bxa5 [17... b5 18. ♕xa7 ♖xa7 19. ♘b6±] 18. ♕xa7 ♖xa7 19. ♘e3±

**17. ♘d6! ♕a7**

17... ♗xd6 18. ♗xd6 ♖fc8 19. ♖a3!± was already close to winning in Carlsen – Wei, chess24.com INT 2020.

**18. ♕e3!±**

Black isn't forced to give up the bishop pair, but our knight sits really nicely on d6 and we can begin to think about advancing our queenside pawns.

## e) 5...a6 6.♗e2 e6 7.0-0 b6 8.d4 cxd4 9.♕xd4 ♗b7 10.♖d4 ♕c7 11. ♗e3 ♘g4 12.♗g5 --

**1. e4 c5 2. ♘f3 d6 3. ♗b5+ ♘d7 4. a4 ♘gf6 5. ♘c3 a6 6. ♗e2 e67. 0-0 b6 8. d4! cxd4 9. ♕xd4 ♗b7!**

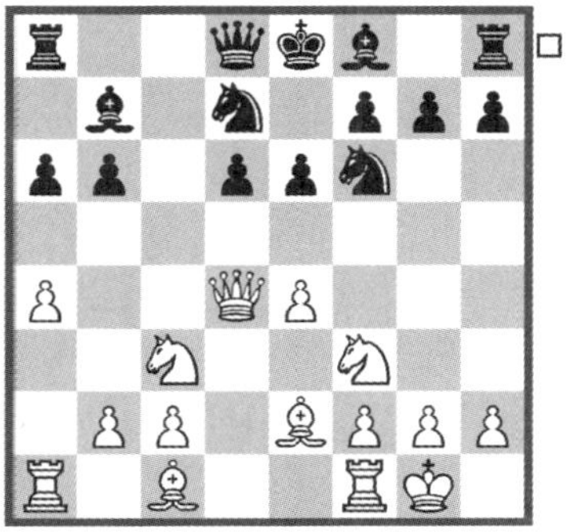

Position after: 9... ♗b7!

The point of delaying the development of the f8-bishop is demonstrated on Black's 11th move.

**10. ♖d1 ♕c7**

10... ♗e7 11. ♗e3 transposes to 9...♗e7.

**11. ♗e3**

11. ♗g5!? An interesting alternative, trying to play against Black's 11...♘g4 idea in the mainline. I'll present a shortened form of my analysis here. 11... ♗e7 [11... h6 12. ♗h4 ♗e7 13. ♗g3!

Position after: 13. ♗g3!

13... e5 14. ♕e3± This is actually exactly the same position as the one we reach in the mainline after 11.♗e3.] 12. ♘d2

Position after: 12. ♘d2

**A)** 12... 0-0 13. ♘c4 ♖ad8 [13... ♖fd8 14. ♗xf6! gxf6 15. ♔h1±

Followed by f2-f4. If Black plays ...♖ac8, we can always consider capturing on d6.] 14. ♗xf6!? gxf6 15. ♖d2±

**B)** 12... h6 13. ♗e3 0-0 14. ♘c4 d5 15. exd5 ♘xd5 16. ♘xd5 ♗xd5 17. ♗f4 ♕c5 18. ♘e3±

**11... ♘g4!**

Black is able to annoy our bishop because the g7-pawn is still defended.

**A)** 11... ♗e7 transposes to our mainline after 9...♗e7. 12. ♘d2

**A1)** 12... d5?! was played in Carlsen – Duda, chess24. com INT 2021. The game ended in a draw after 13. exd5

Position after: 13. exd5

13... ♘xd5? [13... ♗c5 is more testing, but White retains an advantage with 14. ♕h4 ♗xe3 15. dxe6! ♗xf2+ 16. ♕xf2 fxe6 17. ♕e3±.] 14. ♘xd5 ♗xd5 Here Carlsen rejected the obvious 15. ♕xg7 which is simply winning for White after something like 15... ♗f6 16. ♕h6 ♕xc2 17. ♗f3+–. Black's king is just far too weak.

**A2)** 12... 0-0 transposes to the mainline after 9...♗e7.

**B)** 11... e5?! This was played in Edouard – Eggleston, 4NCL 2018. Here White missed a nice opportunity to exchange queens, which would make it very difficult for Black to defend their queenside weaknesses. 12. ♕c4!

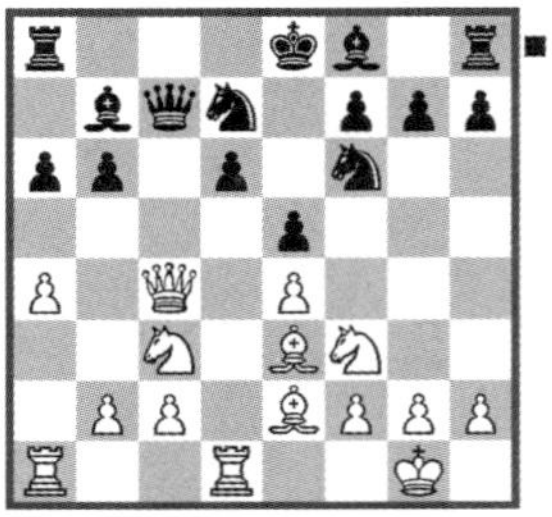
Position after: 12. ♕c4!

12... ♕xc4 13. ♗xc4 ♖c8 [13... ♘xe4 14. ♘xe4 ♗xe4 15. ♗xf7+ ♔xf7 16. ♘g5+ ♔e7 17. ♘xe4±] 14. b3 ♗e7 15. ♘d2 ♘g4 16. ♘f1±

**12. ♗g5**

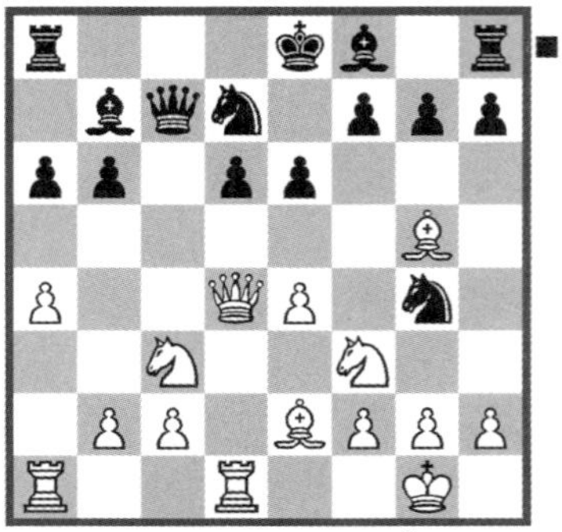
Position after: 12. ♗g5

Black's only logical plan here is to re-route the g4-knight to e5 - but they are not forced to do this immediately.

**12... ♖c8**

This has been played in two high-level games.

12... ♘ge5 It's also sensible for Black to immediately embark on this plan. I analysed this position for a long time and eventually concluded that capturing on e5 was White's best hope for achieving an advantage.

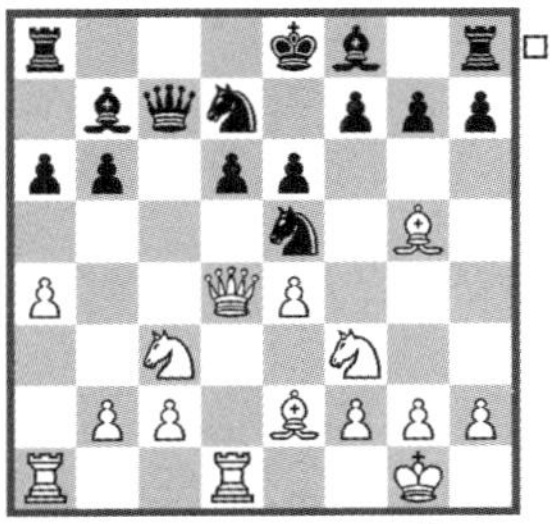

Position after: 12... ♘ge5

**A)** 13. ♕d2!?

An alternative way to play, although it might end up transposing to 13.♘xe5 anyway. 13... ♘xf3+ [13... h6 14. ♘xe5 dxe5 15. ♗e3 transposes to 13.♘xe5.] 14. ♗xf3 h6 15. ♗h4 ♘e5 16. ♗e2 ♗e7 17. ♗xe7 ♔xe7 18. f4 ♘d7 19. ♕e1 ♖hd8 20. ♖d4±

**B)** 13. ♘xe5! The most accurate. 13... dxe5 A very thematic and typical idea. White should now focus their attention on targeting Black's queenside pawns. [13... ♘xe5?! doesn't make any sense. 14. ♗e3 ♘d7 15. ♖a3±] 14. ♕d2 Provoking weaknesses in Black's position.

Position after: 14. ♕d2

**B1)** 14... ♗c5 15. ♗h5!

**B1.1)** 15... ♘f8 16. b4!

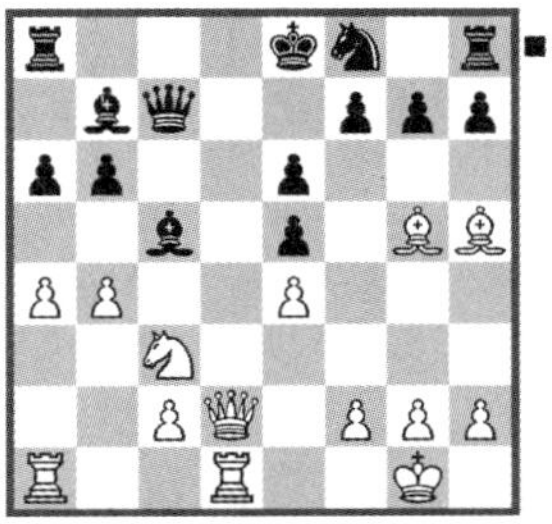

Position after: 16. b4!

16... ♗d4 [16... ♗xb4? 17. ♘b5+−] 17. ♖a3± Followed by ♘e2.

**B1.2)** 15... g6 16. ♗e2 ♗d4 17. ♗e3! ♗xc3 18. bxc3 ♗xe4 19. h4↑ White has excellent compensation for the pawn.

**B2)** 14... h6 15. ♗e3 ♗e7 [15... ♗c5 16. ♗xc5 ♘xc5 17. ♕d6 ♖c8 18. f3±; 15... ♘c5 16. f3 ♗e7 17.

b4±] 16. f3 ♖d8 [16... ♖c8 17. ♘b1! The knight will relocate to c4 via the a3-square.] 17. ♘a2!± This time our idea is to trade queens on c3, after which White should have the better chances due to Black's weak queenside pawns.

**13. ♗h4!**

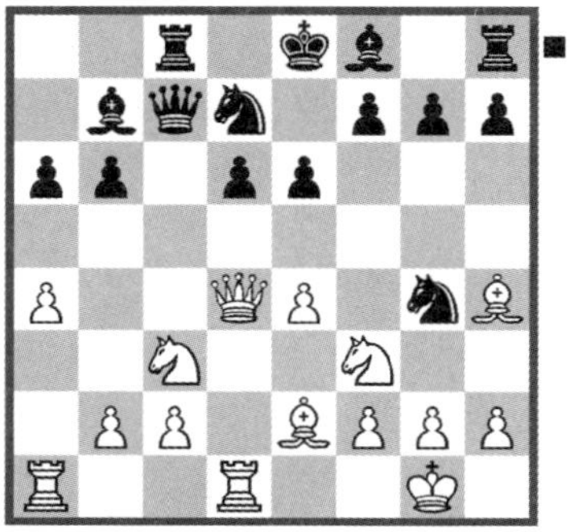

Position after: 13. ♗h4!

A useful prophylactic move.

**13... h6**

**A)** 13... ♘gf6?! In So – Carlsen, lichess.org INT 2020, White missed a nice continuation: 14. ♗g3! Forcing Black to make a big concession. 14... e5 15. ♕e3 ♗e7 16. ♘d2 h6 [16... ♘c5 17. ♗h4!+– followed by ♗xf6 with a decisive positional advantage.] 17. ♘c4 0-0 18. ♗h4±

**B)** 13... ♘ge5 14. ♕d2! Here the queen stands well on d2 for a specific reason. 14... ♘c4 15. ♗xc4 ♕xc4 16. ♗g3 e5 17. ♘xe5+–

**14. h3 ♘ge5**

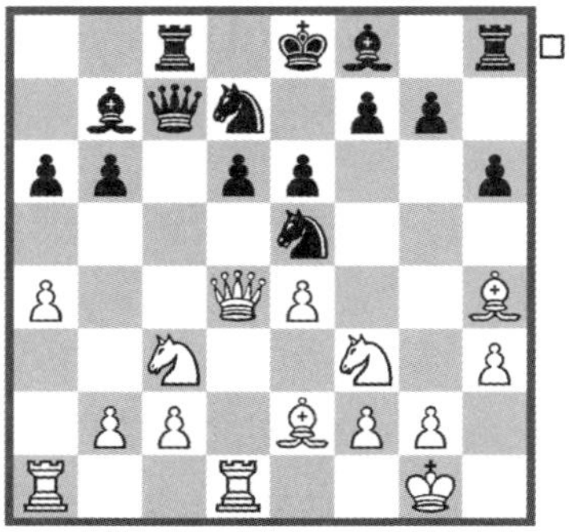

Position after: 14... ♘ge5

**15. ♕e3**

It makes sense to put the queen on e3 in order to prepare for a future doubling of rooks on the d-file.

**A)** 15. ♕d2 ♘xf3+ 16. ♗xf3 ♘e5 17. ♗e2 ♗e7=

**B)** 15. ♗g3 is also perfectly viable, followed by doubling rooks on the d-file.

**15... ♘c4**

Following the plan of re-routing the knight, although Black's lack of kingside development now encourages us to play actively.

**A)** 15... ♕c5 In Topalov – Kotronias, Gibraltar 2020, the best continuation for White was 16. ♕xc5! ♖xc5 17. ♘xe5 dxe5 18. f3±.

**B)** 15... ♘xf3+ 16. gxf3!?± Ensuring the e4-pawn is permanently protected.

We'll follow up with either ♖d2 or ♖d4.

**16. ♗xc4 ♕xc4 17. ♗g3**

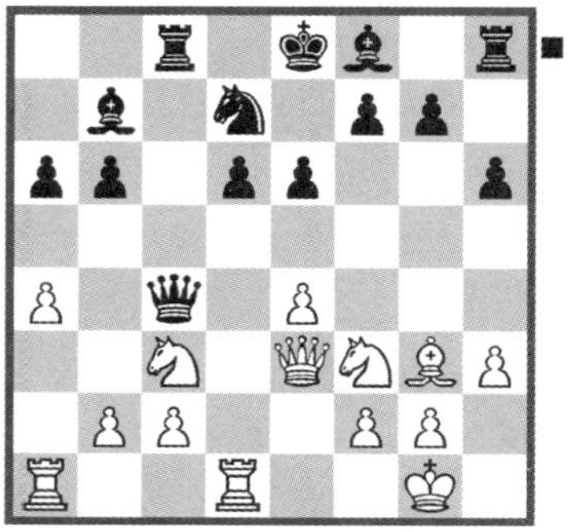

Position after: 17. ♗g3

**17... e5**

17... ♕c6 18. ♕d2!±

**18. ♘d2 ♕b4**

18... ♕c5 19. ♕d3!± with ♘f1-e3 to come next.

**19. a5!**

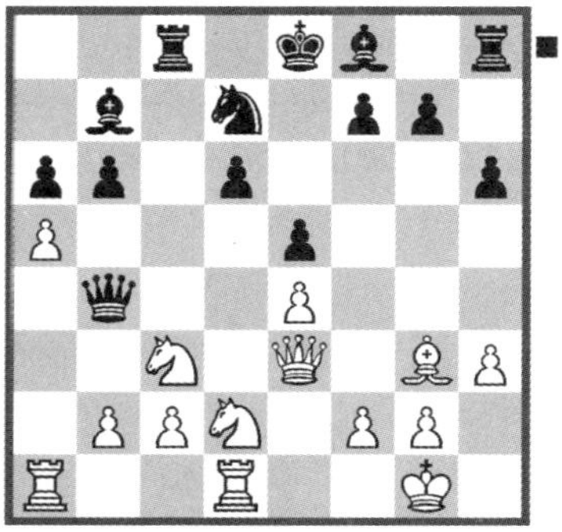

Position after: 19. a5!

**19... ♗e7**

**A)** 19... ♕xb2 20. ♘a4 ♕xc2 21. ♘xb6 ♖c3 22. ♕e1 ♘xb6 23. axb6 ♗e7 24. h4!

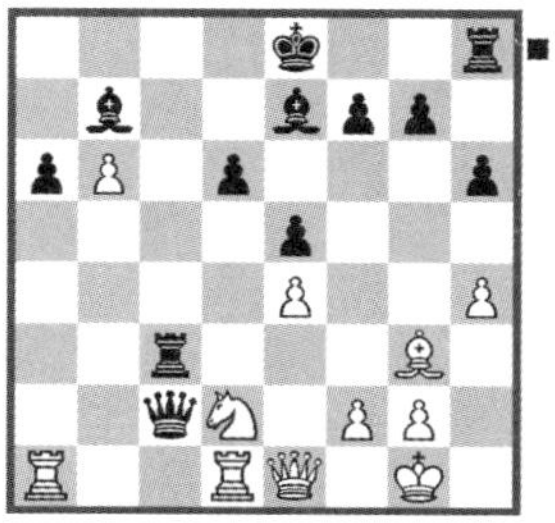

Position after: 24. h4!

Black's position is becoming increasingly difficult to play, e.g. 24... ♖c5 [24... 0-0? 25. ♖dc1 ♕d3 26. ♖xc3 ♕xc3 27. ♖c1 ♕d4 28. ♖c7+–] 25. f3!↑ followed by ♗f2 and ♘f1.

**B)** 19... b5? 20. ♕a7! ♖b8 21. ♘d5+–

**C)** 19... bxa5 20. ♘b3±

**20. ♘b3 b5**

20... ♘c5! It looks like Black is equalising with this move. 21. axb6 ♘xb3 22. cxb3 ♕xb3 23. ♘d5 ♕xe3 24. ♘xe3 ♖c6 25. f3 ♖xb6 26. ♘c4 ♖b5 27. ♘xd6+ ♗xd6 28. ♖xd6=

**21. ♕a7 ♖b8 22. ♘d5!**

*(see diagram next page)*

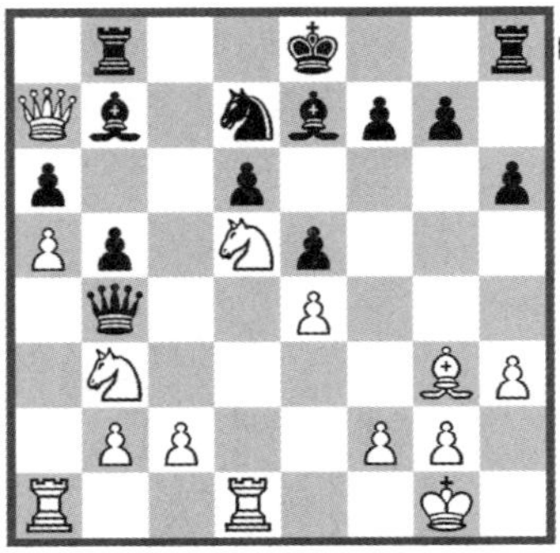

Position after: 22. ♘d5!

**22... ♕xe4 23. f3 ♕xc2 24. ♘d4!**

The start of a forcing line which results in an advantageous endgame for White.

**24... ♕c5**

24... exd4 25. ♘xe7 ♔xe7 26. ♗xd6+ ♔xd6 27. ♕xd4++–

**25. ♕xc5 dxc5 26. ♘f5 ♗xd5 27. ♖xd5 g6 28. ♘g7+**

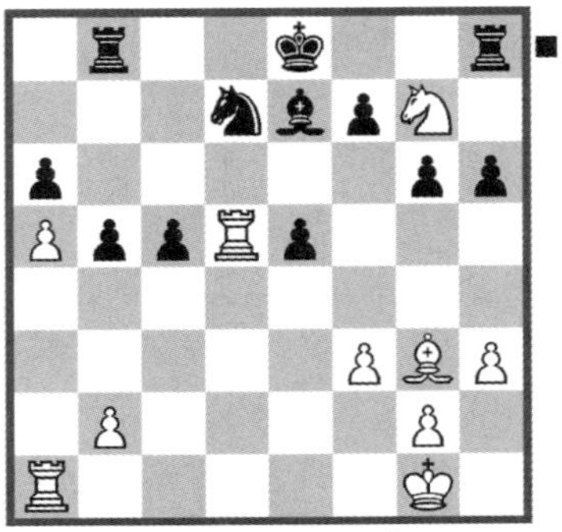

Position after: 28. ♘g7+

**28... ♔d8 29. ♗xe5 ♖b7 30. ♘f5 f6 31. ♘d6 ♘xe5 32. ♘xb7+ ♔c7 33. f4 ♘c4 34. ♖e1 ♔xb7 35. ♖d7+ ♔c6 36. ♖dxe7±**

I would recommend that readers investigate this endgame with an engine if they want to gain a better understanding of the path to victory.

## f) 5...a6 6.♗e2 e6 7.0-0 b6 8.d4 cxd4 9.♕xd4 ♗b7 10.♖d4 ♕c7 11. ♗e3 ♘g4 12.♗g5 h6

**1. e4 c5 2. ♘f3 d6 3. ♗b5+ ♘d7 4. a4 ♘gf6 5. ♘c3 a6 6. ♗e2 e6 7. 0-0 b6 8. d4! cxd4 9. ♕xd4 ♗b7! 10. ♖d1 ♕c7 11. ♗e3 ♘g4! 12. ♗g5 h6**

*(see diagram opposite column)*

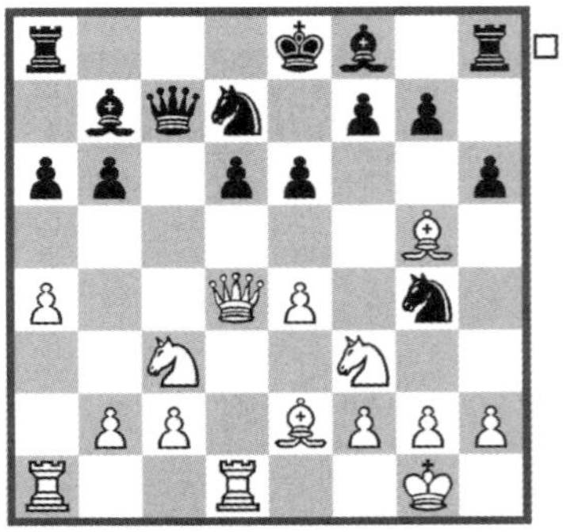

Position after: 12... h6

**13. ♗h4 ♘ge5**

The benefit of playing this after 12...h6 is that our bishop is arguably less well placed on h4.

**14. ♕e3!**

Out of all the options, this is my preference. As we will see, capturing on e5 doesn't make too much sense as the bishop on h4 will be misplaced. Instead the point of 14.♕e3 is to simply double rooks on the d-file.

**A)** 14. ♘xe5 dxe5 15. ♕d2 [15. ♕c4 ♕xc4 16. ♗xc4 ♖c8 17. ♗d3 ♗c5∓ Carlsen – Nepomniachtchi, chess24.com 2020.] 15... ♗c5∞ Black doesn't have any problems here, as our h4-bishop is misplaced.

**B)** 14. ♖d2 g5!

Position after: 14... g5!

15. ♗g3 g4 16. ♘xe5 dxe5 Hitting our queen with a tempo - thus a worse version of the corresponding line after 14.♕e3. 17. ♕d3 ♗e7∞

**C)** 14. h3!?

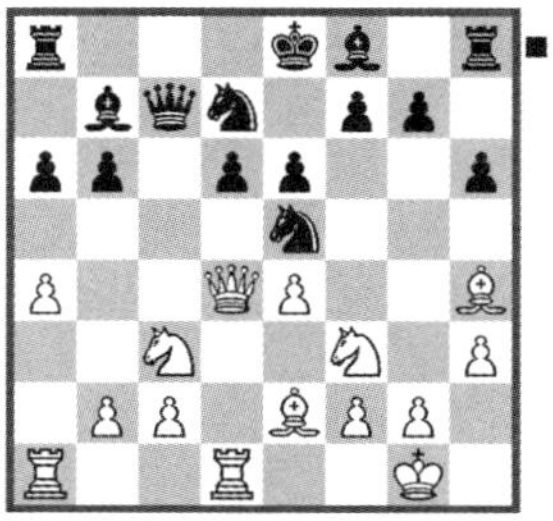

Position after: 14. h3!?

My original idea, aiming to prevent the ...g5-g4 advance. 14... ♗e7 [14... g5 is a bit too ambitious from Black. 15. ♗g3 ♗e7 16. ♖d2 h5 17. ♖ad1 ♘xf3+ 18. ♗xf3 ♘e5 19. ♗e2±; 14... ♖c8 transposes to 12...♖c8.] 15. ♗xe7 ♔xe7 16. ♕e3 Followed by doubling rooks on the d-file.

**14... ♘g4**

**A)** 14... ♗e7?! 15. ♗xe7 ♔xe7 16. ♖d4±

**B)** 14... g5 15. ♗g3 ♗e7 16. ♖d4±

**15. ♕d2**

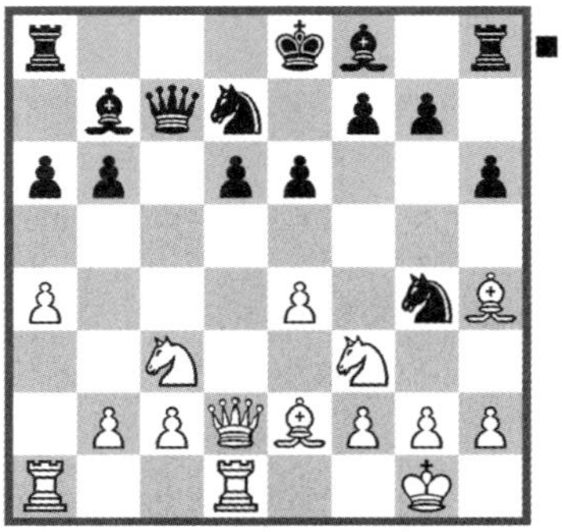

Position after: 15. ♕d2

**15... ♘gf6**

**A)** 15... ♗e7 16. a5! ♘gf6 17. axb6 ♕xb6

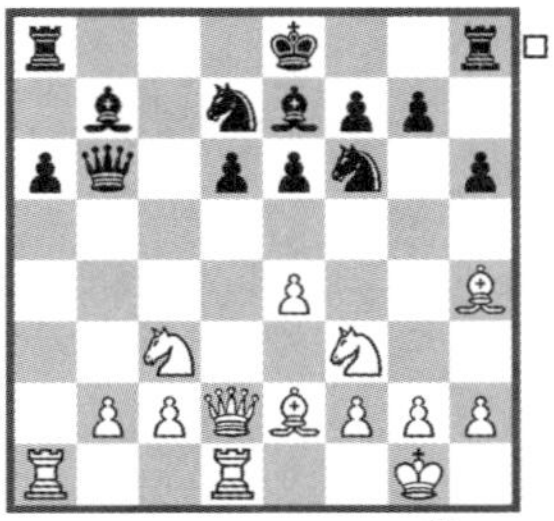

Position after: 17... ♕xb6

18. ♕d4!± The resulting queenless middlegame offers White good chances. If Black declines the trade, we can continue exerting pressure with something like ♘d2-c4.

**B)** 15... ♘ge5 In Fecker – Baenziger, Magglingen 2021, White's best continuation was 16. ♘xe5 dxe5 17. a5!

Position after: 17. a5!

Once again, 17... bxa5 can be met with 18.♖xa5. 17... b5 18. f3± The possibility of ♘xb5 hangs in the air, but White is also doing well with simple moves such as bringing the bishop back to f2.

**16. ♕d4!**

A weird sort of triangulation, but this is the best way to defend the e4-pawn.

**16... ♗e7 17. ♗g3 e5 18. ♕e3**

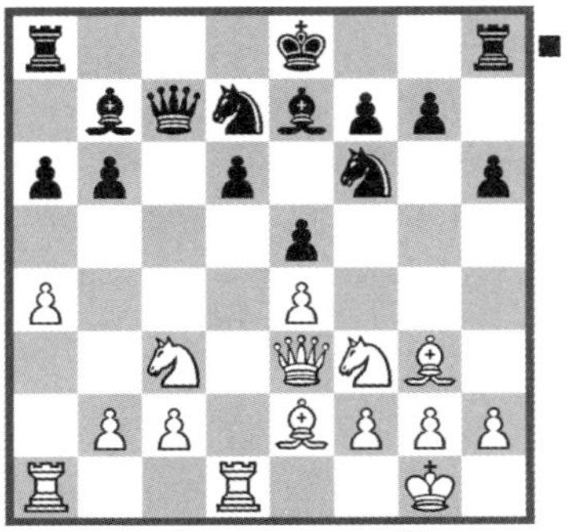

Position after: 18. ♕e3

**18... 0-0**

18... ♘c5 19. ♘d2 0-0 20. f3!± Followed by ♘c4 and b2-b4.

**19. ♘h4! ♘c5 20. ♗d3±**

This feels like a sensible place to stop. If Black captures on d3 we can capture back with the c-pawn and use the c-file for one of the rooks. Otherwise ♘f5 will most likely be our next move.

20. f3 feels more natural, but the engine finds a nice resource for Black. 20... g6! 21. ♕xh6 ♘e6⇆ With the nasty threat of ... ♘g4.

## g) 5...a6 6.♗e2 -- & 6...b6 7.d4 cxd4 8.♕xd4 e5 9.♕e3 ♗b7 10.0-0 ♗e7 11.♘d2 ♕c7

**1. e4 c5 2. ♘f3 d6 3. ♗b5+ ♘d7 4. a4 ♘gf6 5. ♘c3 a6 6. ♗e2**

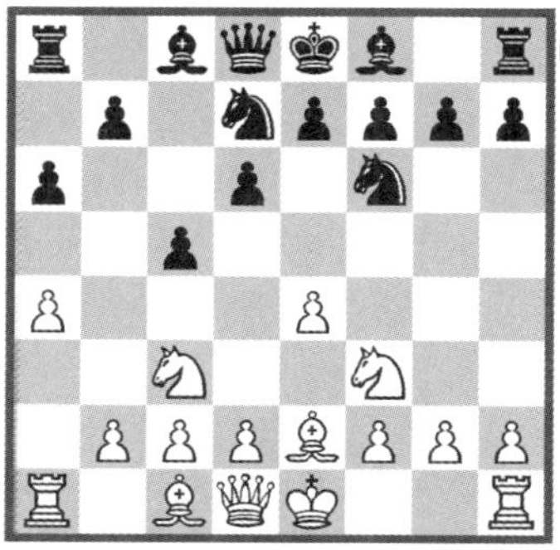

Position after: 6. ♗e2

We've seen in the ...g6 lines and ...e6 lines that White is able to gain some sustained pressure if we're allowed to break with d2-d4. Although Black may have a claim to equality, in general those positions can be slightly uncomfortable for them. Therefore the most critical continuations for Black are when they directly challenge the centre with ...e7-e5. They can either do this immediately, or wait for us to play d2-d4 before capturing and attacking our recapturing piece with ...e7-e5.

**6... b6**

**A)** 6... e5 Here White has a choice of either keeping the bishop on e2 or moving it to its more natural position on c4.

**A1)** 7. d3 ♗e7 8. ♘d2

Position after: 8. ♘d2

8... ♘b8 [8... ♘f8 9. ♘c4 ♘e6 10. 0-0 0-0 11. a5± White had a comfortable edge in Burke – Grinberg, Charlotte 2019.] 9. ♘c4 ♘c6 10. f4!±

**A2)** 7. ♗c4!? ♗e7 8. d3

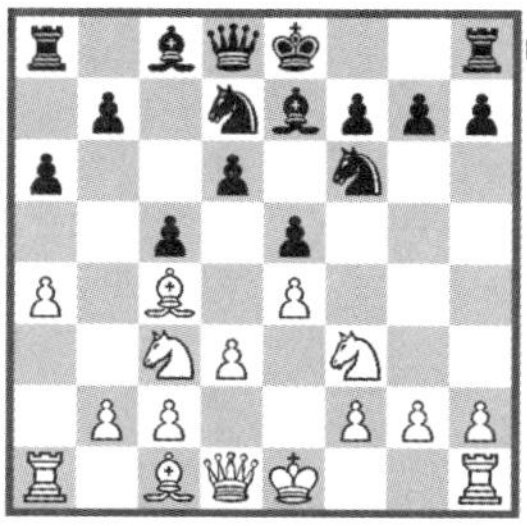

Position after: 8. d3

8... 0-0 [8... ♘b6 9. ♗a2 ♗e6 10. ♗xe6 fxe6 11. ♘g5 ♕d7 12. a5 ♘c8 13. ♕f3+– ♕h3 on the next move will win the e6-pawn.] 9. 0-0 ♘b8 [9... ♖b8 10. a5 b5 11. axb6 ♘xb6 12. ♗b3± Followed by ♘d2-c4.] 10. ♗g5 The position resembles an Italian game, and it seems that White has a slight edge here. 10... ♘c6 11. ♗xf6 ♗xf6 12. ♘d5 g6 13. c3±

**B)** 6... ♕a5!?N

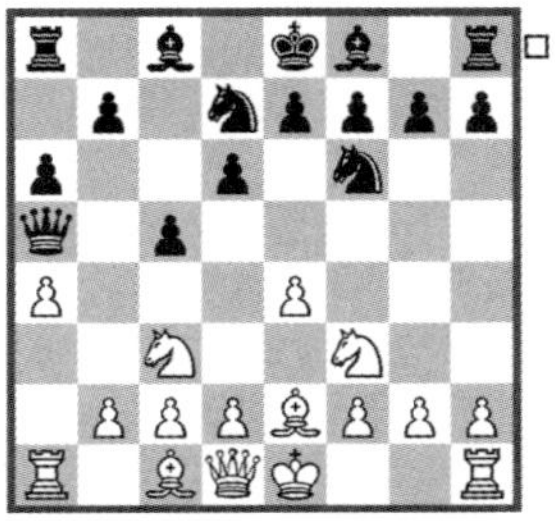

Position after: 6... ♕a5!?N

This attempt to play ...b7-b5 hasn't been tried yet, and seems like an interesting idea. 7. 0-0 [It didn't feel right to play 7. ♖b1 and I couldn't find a convincing way to play after 7... e6 8. 0-0 ♗e7 9. d4 cxd4 10. ♕xd4 ♘e5!=.] 7... b5 8. d4!

Position after: 8. d4!

It feels like this is the critical test of Black's play. I will just give a shortened form of my analysis, as it might not be a necessary variation to spend too much time on.

**B1)** 8... ♗b7? 9. e5 cxd4 [9... b4 10. exf6 bxc3 11. fxg7 ♗xg7 12. bxc3±] 10. ♕xd4 dxe5 11. ♘xe5+–

**B2)** 8... b4 9. ♘d5 ♘xe4 10. ♗c4!

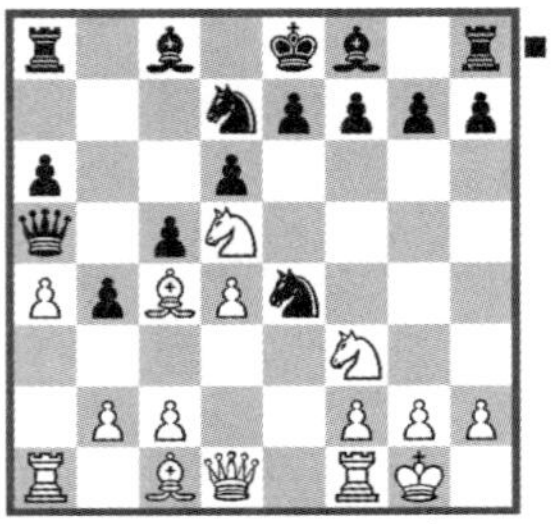

Position after: 10. ♗c4!

A very strong pawn sacrifice, after which Black has to be careful not to crumble immediately. 10... ♗b7 [10... e6 11. ♕e2! ♘ef6 12. ♘xf6+ ♘xf6 13. d5 e5 14. ♘xe5! dxe5 15. ♕xe5+ ♔d8 16. d6+–] 11. ♖e1 ♘df6 [11... cxd4 12. c3! The start of a forcing line. 12... ♕c5 13. ♖xe4 ♕xc4 14. ♖xd4 ♕c8 15. cxb4 e6 16. ♕e1!± Black will struggle to complete kingside development without making some kind of a concession.] 12. ♘xf6+ ♘xf6 13. c3!

Position after: 13. c3!

Once again we attempt to open up the position. 13... e6 14. d5 e5 15. ♗f4! Preparing to sacrifice on e5. 15... ♘d7 16. cxb4 ♕xb4 17. ♕e2 ♗e7 18. ♖a3!

*(see analysis diagram next page)*

Position after: 18. ♖a3!

18... ♘b6 19. ♘xe5 dxe5 20. ♕xe5 0-0 21. ♖g3+–

**7. d4 cxd4 8. ♕xd4 e5**

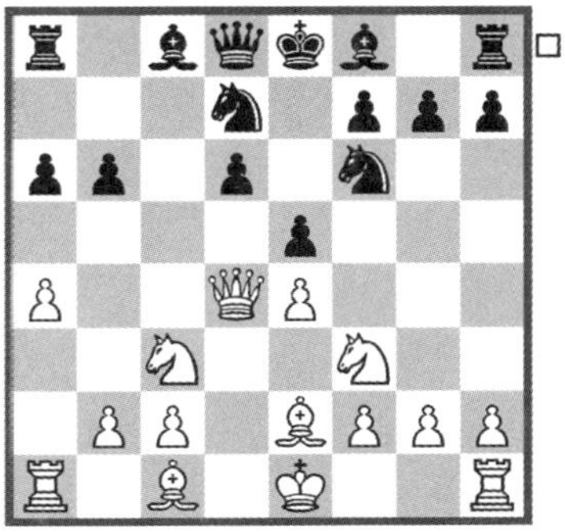

Position after: 8... e5

**9. ♕e3**

Quite an unusual square for the queen to stand on, but right now it does a good job of facilitating ♘d2-c4 whilst protecting the e4-pawn. In general, the position revolves around control of the e4- and d5-squares. Our plan is quite simple: we'll try to control the centre with moves such as 0-0, ♖d1, ♘d2, ♗f3, and perhaps b2-b3 and ♗a3. If Black allows us to gain control of the centre, it will be really difficult for them to gain any activity - and the weak a6- and b6-pawns will be future targets. Therefore Black will respond with moves like ...♗b7, ...♕c7, ...♗e7, ...0-0, ...♖ac8, ...♖ad8, and at some point either ...♘c5-e6 or, as we'll often encounter, a sudden capture on e4. The variations in the rest of the chapter might appear slightly convoluted but I'll try to keep it as digestible as possible.

**9... ♗b7 10. 0-0 ♗e7 11. ♘d2!**

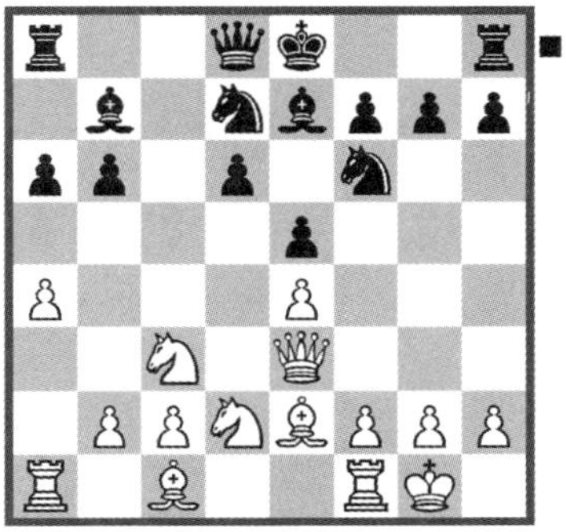

Position after: 11. ♘d2!

**11... ♕c7**

Previously I had this as my mainline but I actually think it's a slight inaccuracy, as we can alter our setup to prevent Black from having the ability to play the annoying ...♘xe4 idea that we'll encounter numerous times in the line after 11...0-0.

11... ♘c5 12. ♘c4! A common theme is that it's always beneficial for White when we trade our e4-pawn for Black's b6-pawn. In the long-run, Black's pawn on a6 will be very vulnerable.

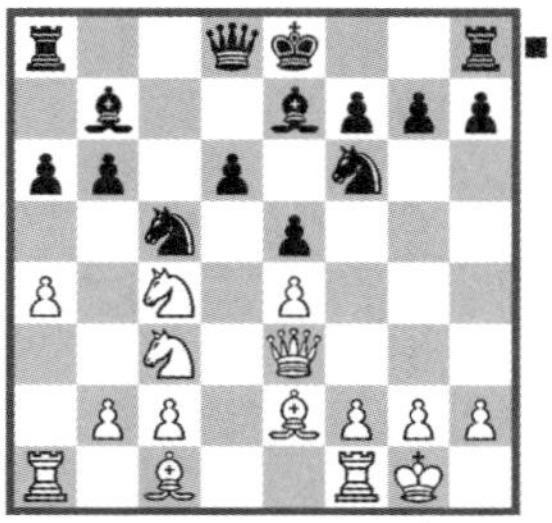
Position after: 12. ♘c4!

12... ♘cxe4 [12... ♕c7 13. b4! ♘cxe4 14. ♘xe4 ♘xe4 15. ♕xb6±] 13. ♘xe4 ♘xe4 14. ♕xb6±

**12. b3!**

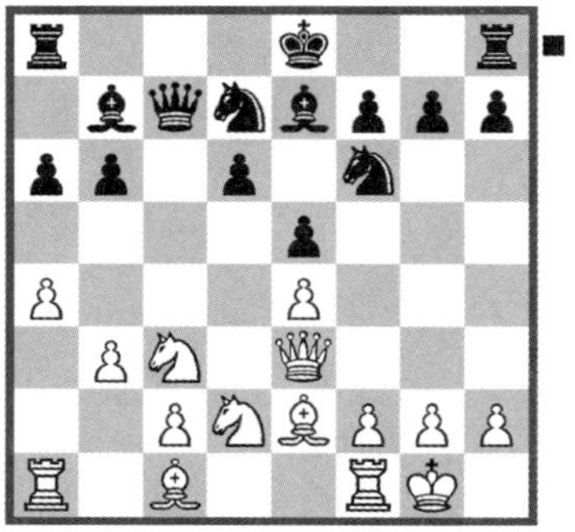
Position after: 12. b3!

I don't know how important it is to memorise all the variations in this subchapter, but I think playing through the lines will be really helpful in giving you a general feel about the different plans for both sides.

**12... ♘c5**

**A)** 12... 0-0 13. ♗a3!

*(see analysis diagram next column)*

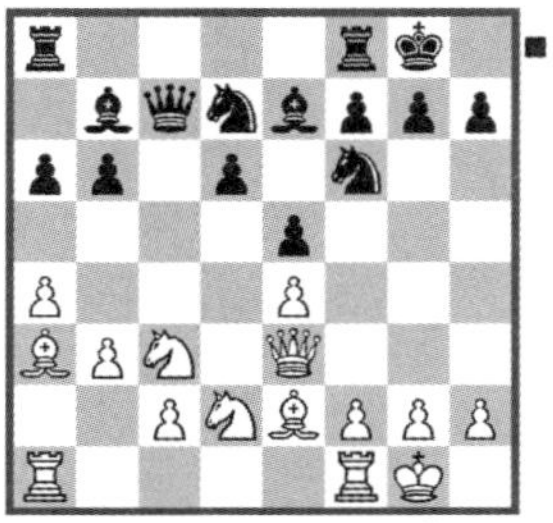
Position after: 13. ♗a3!

13... ♖ad8 [13... ♖ac8 14. ♘c4 ♘c5 15. ♗f3 transposes to 12...♘c5.; 13... ♖fd8 14. ♘c4 ♘c5 15. ♖fd1 transposes to 11... 0-0 in the 13...♖fd8 line - see next subchapter.] 14. ♖ad1 ♘c5 15. ♗xc5! This is the point of playing b2-b3 and ♗a3 so quickly. We can now make use of the fact that our knight still sits on d2, and try to target the a6-pawn. 15... dxc5 16. ♗d3!

Position after: 16. ♗d3!

16... ♖d7 17. ♕e2 ♖fd8 18. ♘f3 Now Black is pretty much forced to make a big concession, after which we certainly have a positional advantage. 18... a5 19. ♘d2±

**B)** 12... ♖c8 13. ♘c4 ♘c5 14. ♗f3 0-0 15. ♗a3 This position is analysed after 12...♘c5.

**13. ♘c4!**

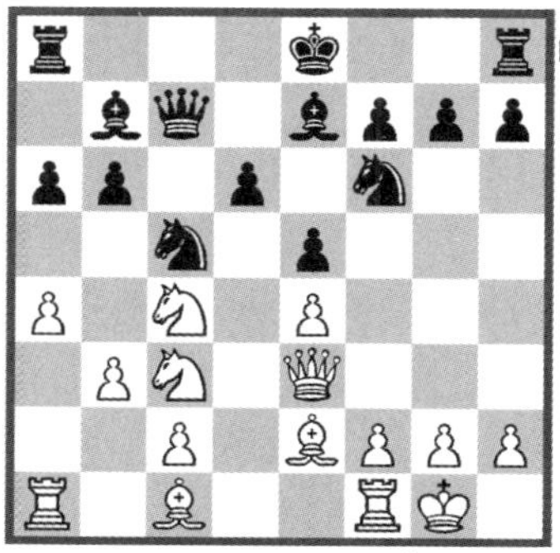

Position after: 13. ♘c4!

Preventing Black from establishing a knight on d4 via the e6-square.

**13... 0-0**

**A)** 13... ♖c8 14. ♗f3! It's important to note that Black was threatening to capture on e4. [14. ♗a3?! ♘fxe4 15. ♘xe4 ♘xe4 16. ♕xb6 ♕xb6 17. ♘xb6 ♖xc2=] 14... 0-0 15. ♗a3 transposes to 13... 0-0.

**B)** 13... ♘fxe4 As usual, the exchange of the e4- and b6-pawns is beneficial for White. 14. ♘xe4

Position after: 14. ♘xe4

14... ♘xe4 [14... ♗xe4 15. b4 d5 16. ♘d2 ♘d7 17. ♘xe4 dxe4 18. ♕xe4 0-0 19. ♗b2 ♗d6 20. a5±] 15. ♕xb6±

**14. ♗a3!**

Position after: 14. ♗a3!

As the variations will demonstrate, Black doesn't have a clear route to equality. With our bishop on a3, there isn't a point where they can effectively capture on e4, and we can respond well to ...d6-d5 breaks.

**14... ♖ad8**

**A)** 14... ♖ac8 15. ♗f3

Protecting the e4-pawn.

**A1)** 15... h6 16. ♖ad1 ♖fd8 17. ♗b4! Black is struggling to find a decent move or plan here.

*(see analysis diagram next page)*

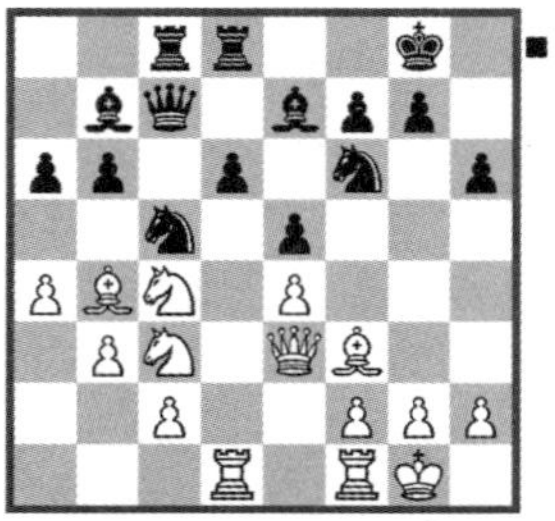

Position after: 17. ♗b4!

17... ♘fxe4 The following line is quite forcing but White will emerge with an advantageous endgame: [17... ♗f8 18. ♖fe1 ♗a8 19. h4±] 18. ♘xe4 ♘xe4 19. ♗xe4 ♗xe4 20. ♕xe4 d5 21. ♖xd5 ♗xb4 22. ♖fd1 b5 23. axb5 axb5 24. ♘xe5 ♖xd5 25. ♖xd5 ♗d6 26. ♖xb5 ♕xc2 27. ♕xc2 ♖xc2 28. g3±

**A2)** 15... ♖fd8 16. ♖ad1 ♘e6 17. ♗b4!

Position after: 17. ♗b4!

Protecting the knight on c3, and thus attacking the b6-pawn. 17... ♘d4 18. ♖xd4! A typical idea which is nearly always favourable for White. 18... exd4 19. ♕xd4 ♘d7 20. ♘d5 ♗xd5 21. ♕xd5 ♘f6 22. ♕d2±

**A3)** 15... ♘e6 16. ♖ad1 ♖fd8 17. ♗b4 Potentially preparing an a4-a5 push. 17... ♘d4 18. ♖xd4!

Position after: 18. ♖xd4!

A very thematic exchange sacrifice – White simply extends their control over the centre. 18... exd4 19. ♕xd4± It will be tough for Black to protect the b6-pawn - e.g. 19... ♘d7 is met with 20.♗g4.

**B)** 14... ♖fd8 15. ♖fd1

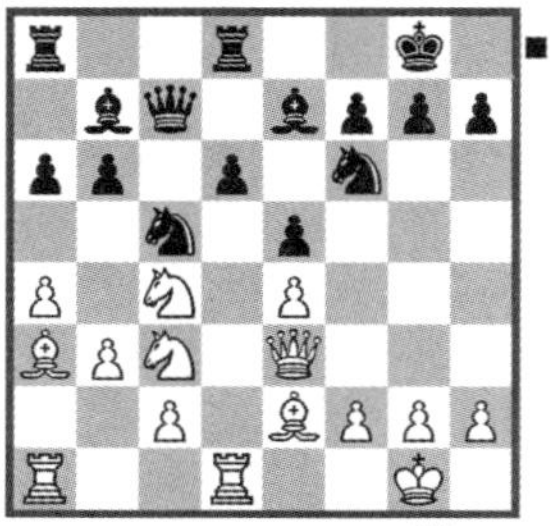

Position after: 15. ♖fd1

The capture on e4 is once again possible, but in general the resulting endings should always be favourable for White.

**B1)** 15... ♘fxe4 16. ♘xe4 ♘xe4 17. ♕xb6 ♕xb6 18. ♘xb6

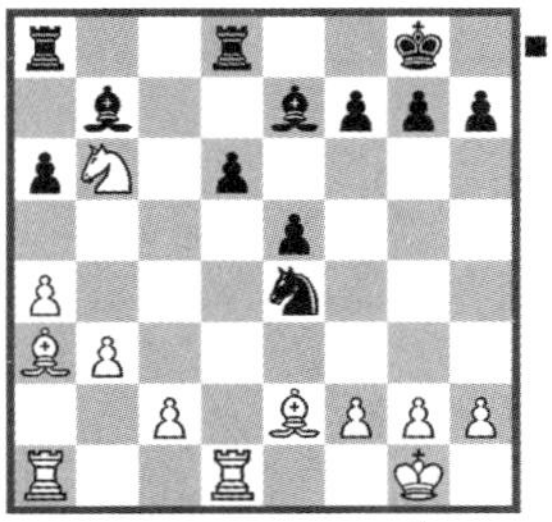
Position after: 18. ♘xb6

18... ♘c3! The most testing move. [18... ♖ab8?! 19. ♗b4 ♗g5 20. ♗c4±] 19. ♖e1 ♘xe2+ 20. ♖xe2 ♖ab8 21. a5

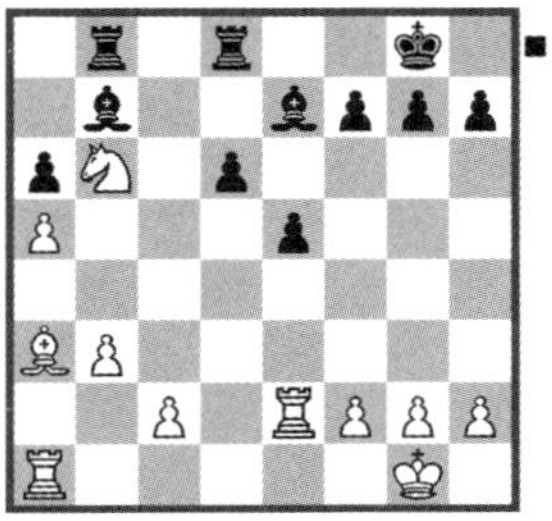
Position after: 21. a5

White's knight is really good on b6, basically constricting Black's pieces. Black now wants to push ...d6-d5 but this requires preparation. 21... ♗f6 [21... f6 22. ♖e3!± hinting at ♖c3 is pleasant.] 22. ♗b2! Prophylaxis against the ...d6-d5 push. 22... ♖e8 [22... ♗e7 23. ♖d1 f6 24. ♗a3 ♔f7 25. ♖ed2 ♔e6 26. c4±] 23. ♖d1 ♖e6 24. c4±

**B2)** 15... ♘cxe4 16. ♘xe4 ♗xe4 17. ♘xb6 ♖ab8 18. a5 ♕b7 19. ♗f3! This is a much-improved version of the ending after 15...♘fxe4.

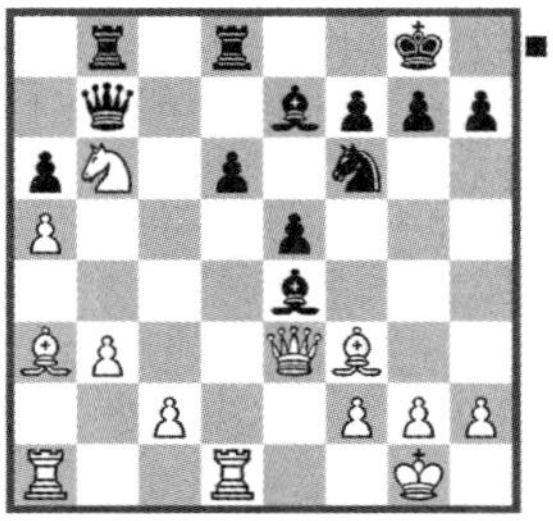
Position after: 19. ♗f3!

19... ♗xf3 20. ♕xf3 ♕xf3 21. gxf3±

**B3)** 15... ♖e8 16. f3 ♖ad8 17. b4! ♘cd7 18. ♖ab1+– Next will come b4-b5.

**B4)** 15... ♖ac8 16. a5! Finally, this is a direct transposition into the main-line of the subchapter j)

**15. ♗f3 ♖fe8**

15... d5 is logical but it doesn't quite equalise. 16. exd5 e4 17. ♗e2 ♘xd5 18. ♘xd5 ♗xd5 19. ♕g3!±

**16. ♖fd1**

Position after: 16. ♖fd1

We can slowly improve our position, while Black lacks a clear plan.

**16... h6 17. h3 ♗f8 18. ♖d2**

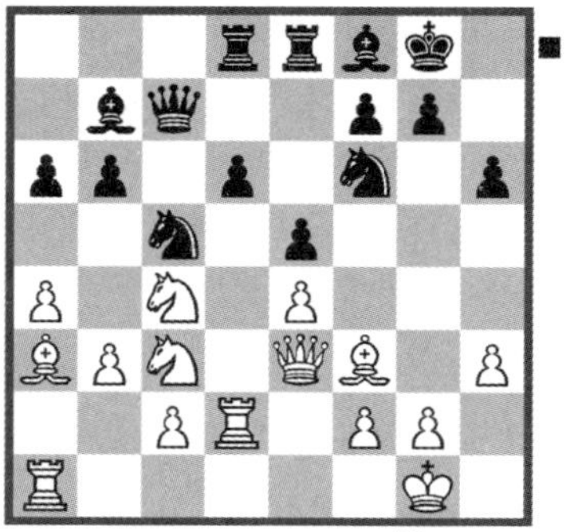

Position after: 18. ♖d2

Black has pretty much improved all of their pieces as much as they can, whereas we can still develop new threats such as ♖ad1 followed by capturing on c5. Therefore this is the critical moment to check if Black has an equalising shot.

**18... d5**

18... ♘xa4!? 19. ♘xa4 b5 20. ♘ab6 bxc4 21. ♘xc4 d5 22. exd5 ♘xd5 23. ♗xd5 ♗xd5 24. ♗d6!

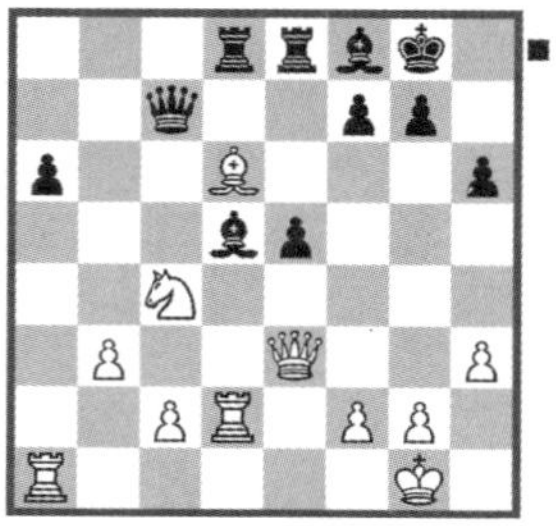

Position after: 24. ♗d6!

24... ♗xd6 25. ♖xd5 e4 26. ♖ad1±

**19. ♘xd5 ♗xd5 20. exd5 e4**

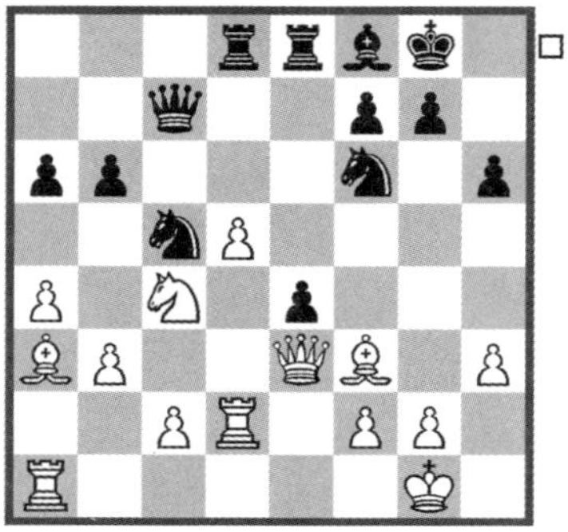

Position after: 20... e4

The start of a tactical line.

**21. d6! ♖xd6!**

21... ♗xd6 22. ♖xd6 ♖xd6 23. ♘xd6 ♕xd6 24. ♗e2+–

**22. ♖xd6 exf3 23. ♕f4 ♖e4 24. ♕h2 ♗xd6 25. ♕xd6 ♕xd6 26. ♘xd6 ♖e5**

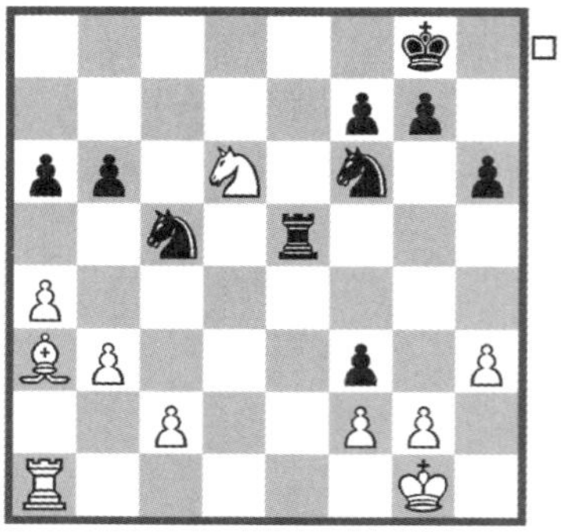

Position after: 26... ♖e5

White is slightly better in this ending

**27. a5 b5 28. gxf3±.**

## h) 5...a6 6.♗e2 b6 7.d4 cxd4 8.♕xd4 e5 9.♕e3 ♗b7 10.0-0 ♗e7 11.♘d2 0-0 12.♖d1 ♕c7 13.b3 ♘c5 14.♗b2 --

**1. e4 c5 2. ♘f3 d6 3. ♗b5+ ♘d7 4. a4 ♘gf6 5. ♘c3 a6 6. ♗e2 b6 7. d4 cxd4 8. ♕xd4 e5 9. ♕e3 ♗b7 10. 0-0 ♗e7 11. ♘d2! 0-0**

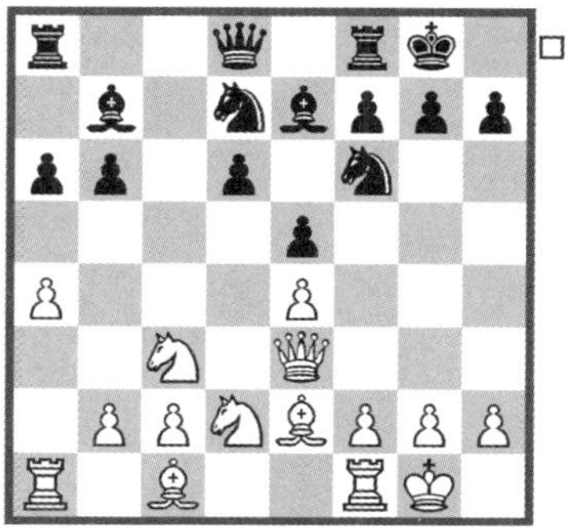

Position after: 11... 0-0

**12. ♖d1**

12. b3 ♘c5!

Position after: 12... ♘c5!

This is actually a really important move for Black. They can't waste time bringing the knight to d4 or else we have time to play ♗a3, ♘c4 and ♖ad1, before capturing on d4 under favourable circumstances. 13. ♗b2 [13. ♗a3 ♘e6∞ Followed by ...♘d4 and ...♖c8 with unclear play.; 13. ♘c4?! ♘fxe4 14. ♘xe4 ♗xe4 15. b4 d5 16. ♘d2 ♗g5!∓ This is the key difference when comparing why 12. b3 is so strong after 11...♕c7, compared to 11... 0-0.] 13... ♘e6= Black has good counterplay here.

Position after: 12. ♖d1

**12... ♕c7**

In this position there are two alternatives, both of which we will analyse deeply. Although Black can equalise in both variations, our main goal is to create as many practical problems for them as possible.

**A)** 12... ♖c8 13. ♘c4 ♕c7 14. b4!

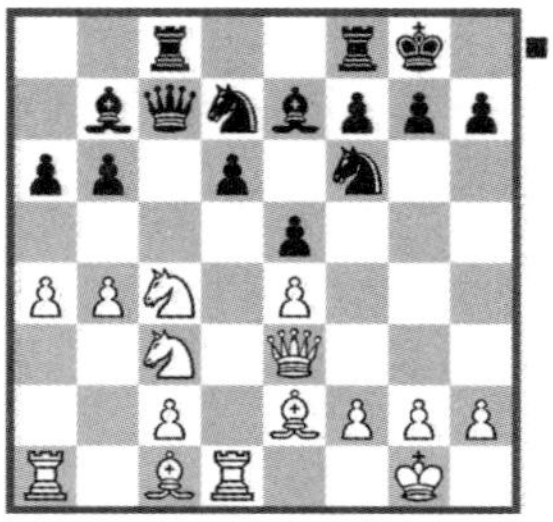

Position after: 14. b4!

This is already very comfortable for White, as Black will find it difficult to get their d7-knight into the game, or to achieve the desired ...d6-d5 break. It's important to remember the different moments where we can and can't push b2-b4. 14... ♖fd8 [14... ♘xe4 15. ♘xe4 d5 16. ♕h3! Obviously this move wouldn't be possible if one of Black's rooks stood on d8. Black's knight must go to b8, and then their pieces will be very uncoordinated. 16... ♘b8 17. ♘g5 ♗xg5 18. ♗xg5 dxc4 19. ♗g4+–] 15. ♗a3 [The immediate 15. ♗b2 gives Black the option of 15... ♘xe4 16. ♘xe4 d5∞.] 15... ♘f8 [15... ♘xe4? 16. ♘xe4 d5 17. b5!

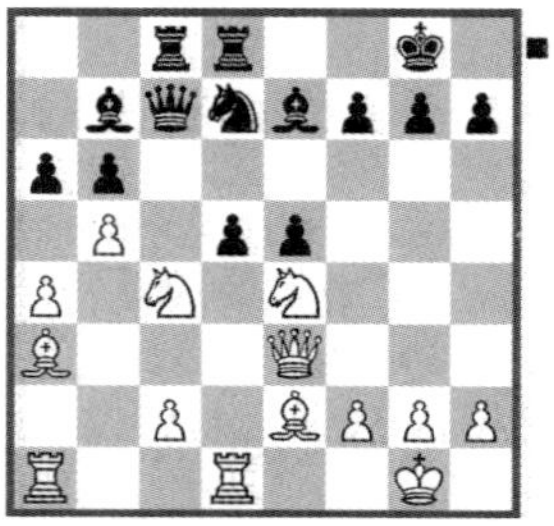

Position after: 17. b5!

17... ♗xa3 18. ♕xa3 dxe4 19. ♘d6 ♖b8 20. ♗c4+–] 16. ♗b2!

Position after: 16. ♗b2!

16... ♘8d7 [16... ♘e6 17. ♘xb6+–] 17. ♕f3!± Our queen has done her job on e3, and now we plan to play ♘e3.

**B)** 12... ♘c5 13. ♘c4!? Persisting with the claim that it's a good idea to exchange off our e4-pawn for Black's b6-pawn. If Black doesn't capture on e4 now, we'll play f2-f3 and their c5-knight will have to retreat to d7. [13. f3 also seems pleasant, e.g. 13... ♘e6 14. ♘b3±.] 13... ♘cxe4 14. ♘xb6 [14. ♘xe4?! ♗xe4 15. c3 d5∓] 14... ♘xc3 15. bxc3 Although we have doubled-pawns, Black will still face a long term problem regarding the a6-pawn. In the meantime, our doubled pawns can do a good job in suppressing Black's central pawns. 15... ♖b8 16. a5!

Position after: 16. a5!

16... ♖e8 17. c4!±

**13. b3**

13. ♘c4 will be examined in the next subchapter.

**13... ♘c5**

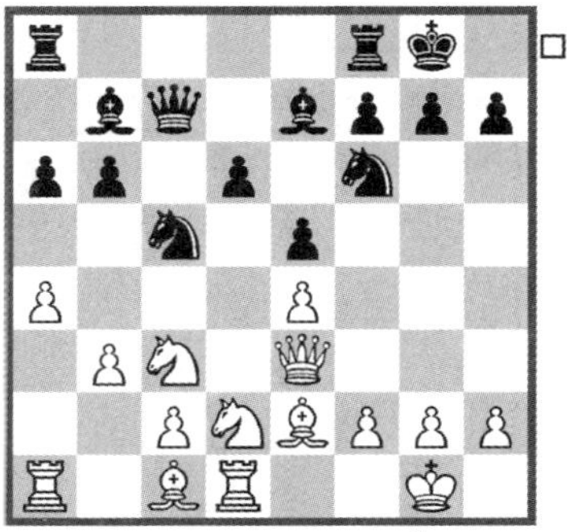

Position after: 13... ♘c5

13... ♖ac8 14. ♘c4 ♘c5 15. ♗f3± transposes to the advantageous lines after 11...♕c7, as we are able to play ♗a3 immediately (as well as considering other options such as a4-a5).

**14. ♗b2**

14. ♗a3!? It's quite interesting to examine what happens if we try to transpose to the lines after 11...♕c7 - essentially, if we are able to make it work, the bishop does stand better on a3 than b2.

**A)** 14... ♖ac8 15. ♗f3

*(see analysis diagram next column)*

Position after: 15. ♗f3

15... ♘e6 [15... ♖fd8 16. ♘c4 transposes to 11...♕c7.; 15... h6 If Black plays a random waiting move, we just continue with normal developing moves. 16. ♘c4 ♘e6 17. ♗b2! ♘d7 18. ♘d5 ♗xd5 19. ♖xd5±] 16. ♘c4 ♘d4 17. ♖xd4 exd4 18. ♕xd4

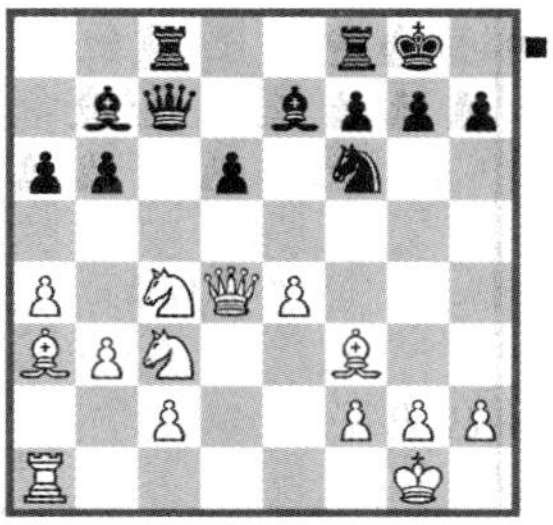

Position after: 18. ♕xd4

Another example of the exchange sacrifice. The computer says 0.00, but I think the position is slightly easier to play for White. 18... ♘d7 [18... ♖fd8 19. ♖d1 ♘d7 20. ♗g4!±] 19. ♘d5 It makes sense to claim the bishop pair here. 19... ♗xd5 20. ♕xd5 ♘e5 21. ♗e2 b5! If Black doesn't play actively, we will quickly be able to take control of the position.

*(see analysis diagram next page)*

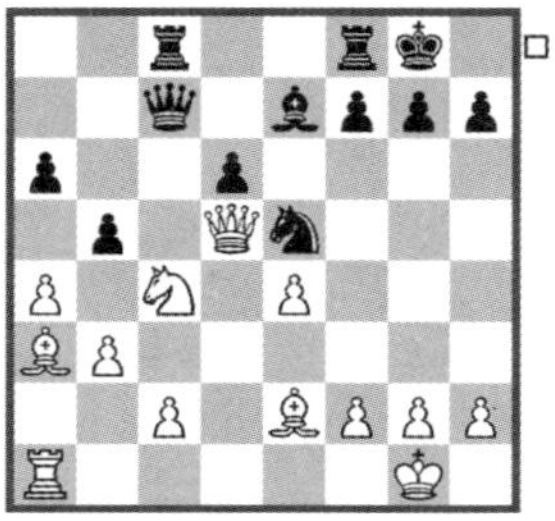

Position after: 21... b5!

22. axb5 axb5 23. ♕xb5 ♖a8 24. ♗b2 ♖xa1+ 25. ♗xa1 ♗f6 26. g3⩱ We have two pawns for the exchange, although the position is really difficult to evaluate. I guess it's worth a punt though!

**B)** 14... ♖fd8 15. ♘c4 transposes to the previous sub-chapter. [15. ♗xc5!? dxc5 16. ♗c4± Followed with ♕e2, ♘f1-e3, and f2-f3. We dominate the d5-square.]

**C)** 14... ♘e6 The critical test. 15. ♘c4

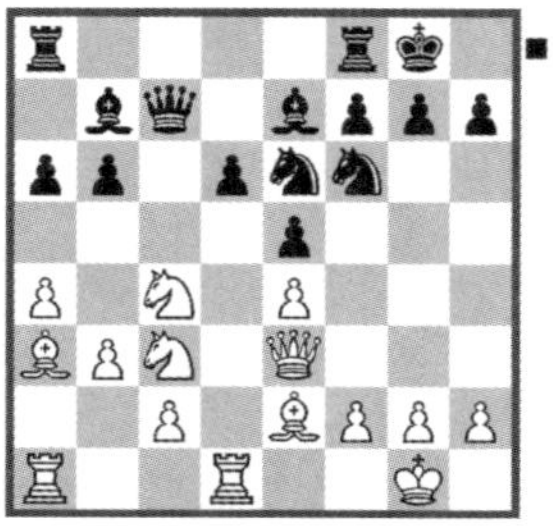

Position after: 15. ♘c4

**C1)** 15... ♖ac8 16. ♗xd6! [16. ♖xd6!?] 16... ♗xd6 17. ♘xd6 ♕xc3 18. ♕xc3 ♖xc3 19. ♘xb7±

**C2)** 15... ♘d4 16. ♖xd4 exd4 17. ♕xd4 b5! Without this move we would definitely be better, continuing with ♖d1 on the next move. 18. ♘b6 [18. axb5 Black gets a lot of activity if we accept the pawn. 18... axb5 19. ♘xb5 ♕d8 with dynamic play.]

**C2.1)** 18... ♖ae8 The engine move, hoping to ramp up the tactical elements of the position. 19. axb5 ♘xe4! 20. ♘cd5 ♗xd5 21. ♘xd5 ♘c3!

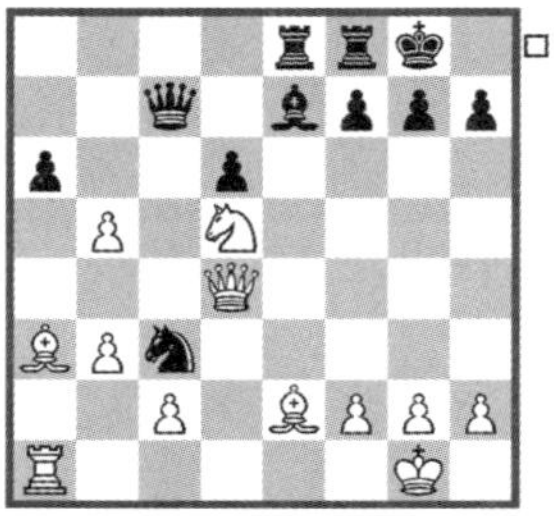

Position after: 21... ♘c3!

22. ♕xc3 ♕xc3 23. ♘xc3 ♗f6 Eventually we realise the point of ...♖ae8! I think Black is completely fine here, because at the very least, they can play the following variation: 24. ♔f1 ♗xc3 25. ♖c1 axb5 26. ♗xd6 b4! 27. ♗xf8 ♔xf8=.

**C2.2)** 18... ♖ab8 19. a5 Black is very passive, but after some normal developing moves they shouldn't be worse. 19... ♖fe8 20. ♗d3 ♗f8 21. h3 It's again really difficult to judge – Stockfish gives

0.00 and Leela gives -0.03. It seems like this 17...b5 move is really important, or else we would definitely be doing well.

**14... ♖ad8**

**A)** 14... ♘e6 15. ♘c4 ♘d4 16. ♖xd4!

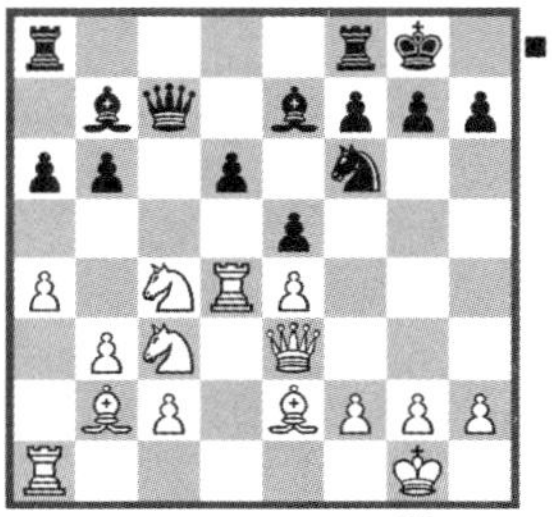

Position after: 16. ♖xd4!

This is an extremely favourable version of the exchange sacrifice for us. 16... exd4 17. ♕xd4 ♕c5 18. ♕xc5 bxc5 19. f3±

**B)** 14... ♖ac8 This is very similar to other positions we've analysed and, naturally, we play the same way. 15. ♗f3 ♖fd8 16. ♘c4 ♗f8 17. h4!? h6 18. g3 ♗c6 19. a5!

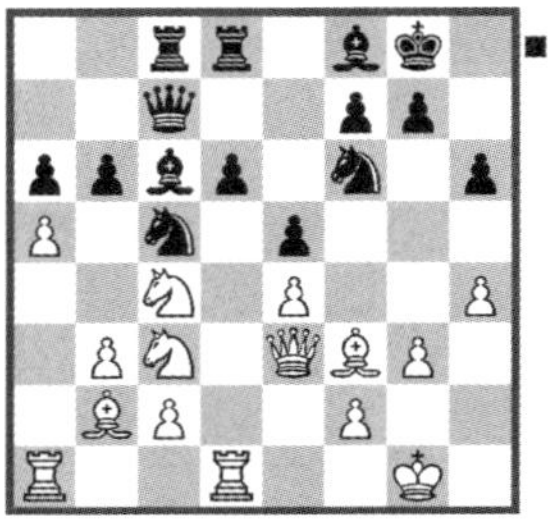

Position after: 19. a5!

19... b5 20. ♘b6 ♖b8 21. ♘cd5 ♗xd5 22. ♘xd5 ♘xd5 23. ♖xd5±

**C)** 14... ♖fd8 15. b4! ♘cd7 16. ♘c4±

**15. ♗f3 ♖fe8 16. ♘c4 ♗f8**

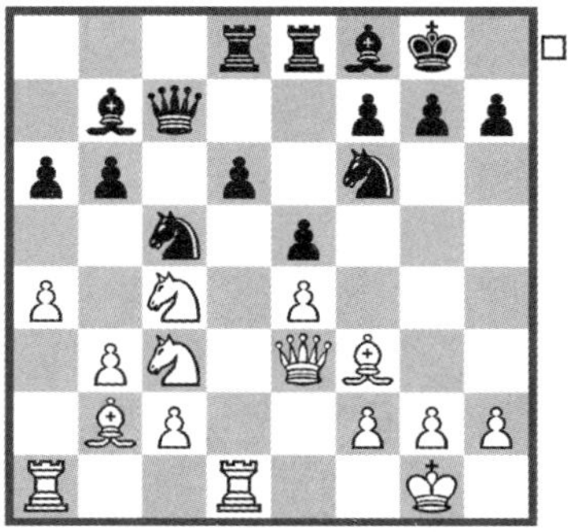

Position after: 16... ♗f8

**17. ♗a3!**

It doesn't really matter that we've wasted a tempo playing ♗b2 and then ♗a3 - as the following critical variations will demonstrate.

**17... ♘xa4**

17... d5 18. ♘xd5 ♗xd5 19. exd5 e4 20. d6!± This time the tactics work well in our favour.

**18. ♘xa4 b5 19. ♘xd6 ♗xd6 20. ♗xd6 ♖xd6 21. ♖xd6 ♕xd6 22. ♘c5±**

## i) 5...a6 6.♗e2 b6 7.d4 cxd4 8.♕xd4 e5 9.♕e3 ♗b7 10.0-0 ♗e7 11.♘d2 0-0 12.♖d1 ♕c7 13.b3 ♘c5 14.♗b2 h6

**1. e4 c5 2. ♘f3 d6 3. ♗b5+ ♘d7 4. a4 ♘gf6 5. ♘c3 a6 6. ♗e2 b6 7. d4 cxd4 8. ♕xd4 e5 9. ♕e3 ♗b7 10. 0-0 ♗e7 11. ♘d2! 0-0 12. ♖d1 ♕c7 13. b3 ♘c5 14. ♗b2 h6!**

Position after: 14... h6!

**15. b4**

15. ♗f1!? ♖fe8 16. b4 ♘e6 17. ♘c4 ♘d4 18. ♖xd4 The start of a forcing line where Black can hold equality by playing consistently active moves. 18... ♘g4! 19. ♕d3 exd4 20. ♕xd4 ♗f6 21. ♕xb6 ♕b8 22. h3 d5! 23. ♘d6 ♖d8∞

**15... ♘cxe4!**

15... ♘e6 16. ♘c4 ♘d7 17. ♘d5 ♗xd5 18. exd5 ♗g5 19. ♕g3 ♘f4 20. ♗f1±

**16. ♘dxe4 ♘xe4 17. ♘xe4 ♕xc2 18. ♘c3**

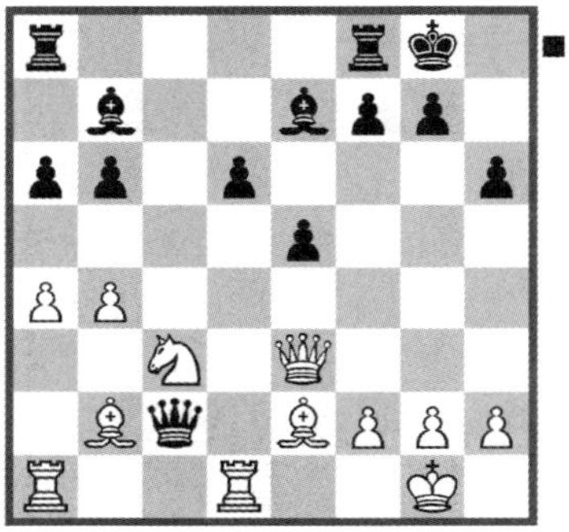

Position after: 18. ♘c3

**18... ♗g5!**

The point of Black's 14...h6 now becomes clear.

18... ♕xb2? 19. ♖db1 ♕c2 20. ♗d3 ♕xc3 21. ♗h7+ ♔xh7 22. ♕xc3±

**19. ♕xb6**

19. ♕h3!? An alternative way to try to achieve an advantage.

**A)** 19... ♖ac8!? 20. ♖ab1 ♖xc3 21. ♗xc3 ♕xe2 22. ♖xd6 ♗xg2! 23. ♕xg2 ♕c2 24. ♕f1 ♕xc3 25. ♕d3

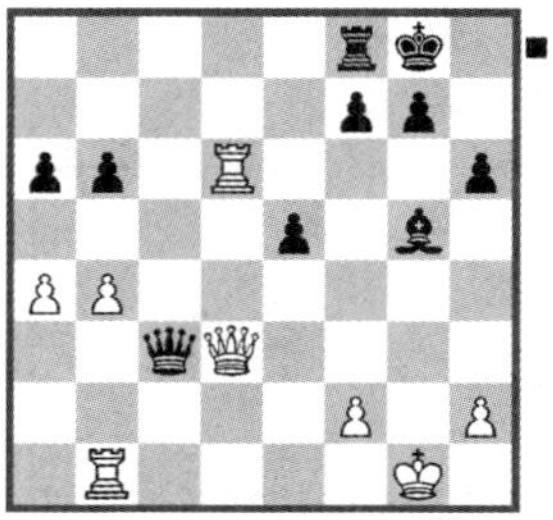

Position after: 25. ♕d3

Another position that is difficult to evaluate, but it seems like Black has to be very accurate here. 25... ♕c8! [25... ♕c7 26. ♖d1±] 26. h3 [26. ♖d1 ♕g4+ 27. ♕g3 ♕xb4=] 26... ♗e7 27. ♖xb6 ♖d8 28. ♕g3 ♕c2 29. ♖e1 ♕xa4=

**B)** 19... ♕xb2 20. ♖ab1 ♕a3 21. ♗c4 Black can't avoid losing their queen, and the resulting material imbalance is another interesting one to judge. 21... ♗c8 22. ♕g3

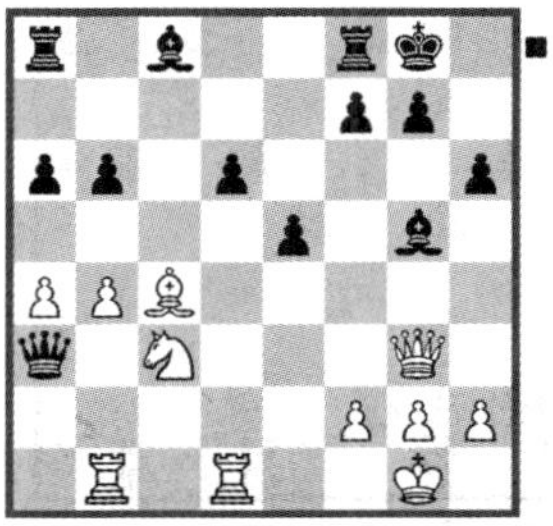

Position after: 22. ♕g3

**B1)** 22... ♗e6 23. ♖b3 ♕xb3 24. ♗xb3 ♗xb3 25. ♖xd6 b5 26. a5 ♗e6 [26... ♗e7 27. ♖xh6+–] 27. ♕xe5 ♗e7 28. ♖xe6! fxe6 29. ♕e4±

**B2)** 22... ♗f4 23. ♕d3 ♗f5 24. ♕xf5 ♕xc3 25. ♕e4± Despite being two pawns down, White is still the one pressing, due to the light square dominance and the precarious position of Black's queen.

**B3)** 22... ♗h4! Black should kick the queen away from g3 before embarking on the material exchange. 23. ♕e3 ♗e6 24. ♖b3 ♕xb3 25. ♗xb3 ♗xb3 26. ♖xd6 b5 27. axb5 [27. a5 ♗e7=] 27... axb5 28. h3∞

**19... ♕xb2 20. ♕xb7 ♕xc3 21. ♖ab1**

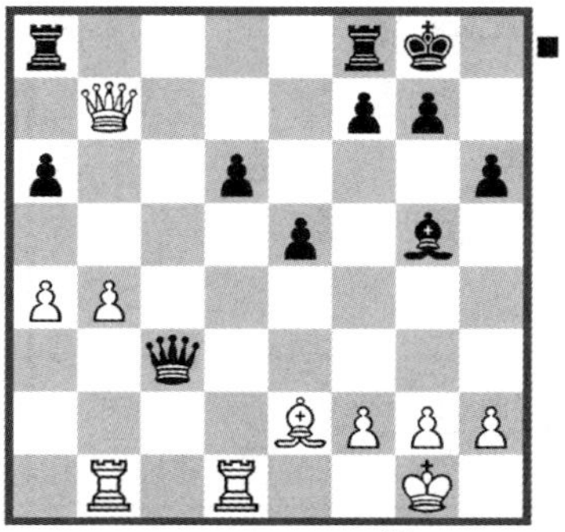

Position after: 21. ♖ab1

**21... ♕c2**

21... d5!? Perhaps the simplest way for Black to equalise here. 22. ♕xd5 ♖fd8 23. ♕c5 ♕xc5 24. bxc5 ♖xd1+ 25. ♖xd1 ♖c8 26. ♖d5 ♗e7 27. ♖xe5 ♔f8 28. ♗xa6 ♖xc5= We can still press in this ending but it's also pretty close to a draw.

**22. ♗d3 ♕xa4 23. h4 ♗f6 24. ♕e4**

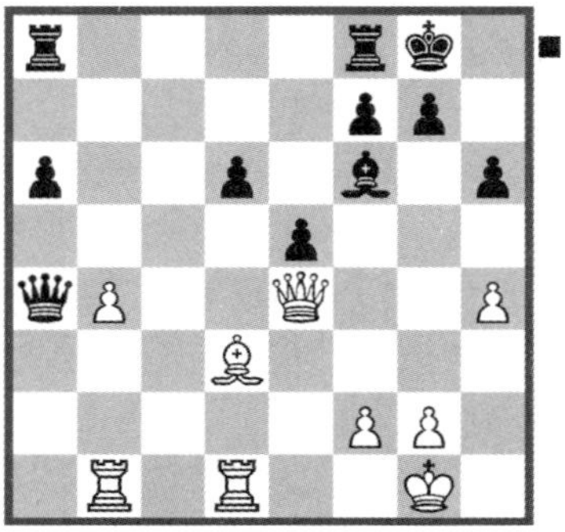

Position after: 24. ♕e4

**24... g6**

24... ♖fd8 This looks a little risky, and I guess it's unlikely to happen in a game - but worth checking anyway, as the computer says it's fine for Black. 25. ♖a1 ♕d7 26. b5! d5 27. ♕h7+ ♔f8 28. bxa6

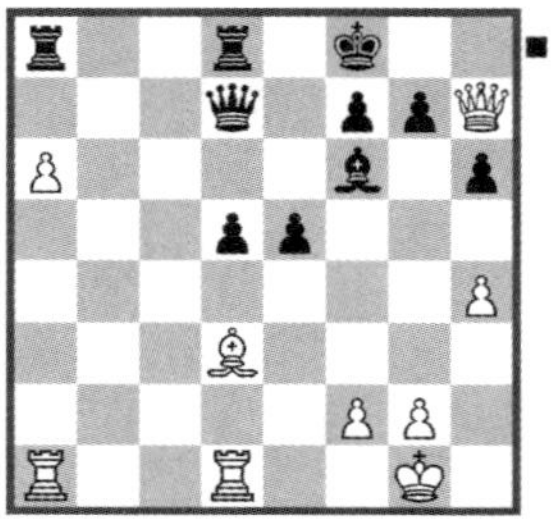

Position after: 28. bxa6

28... e4 [28... ♔e7!? 29. ♖ab1 ♖a7 30. ♖b4 ♕c6= It's difficult to see how to make progress here.] 29. ♖ab1! exd3 30. ♖b7 ♖xa6 31. ♖xd7 ♖xd7 32. ♖xd3 d4=

**25. h5**

Black needs to respond actively to ensure they aren't worse, despite being two pawns up.

**25... d5!**

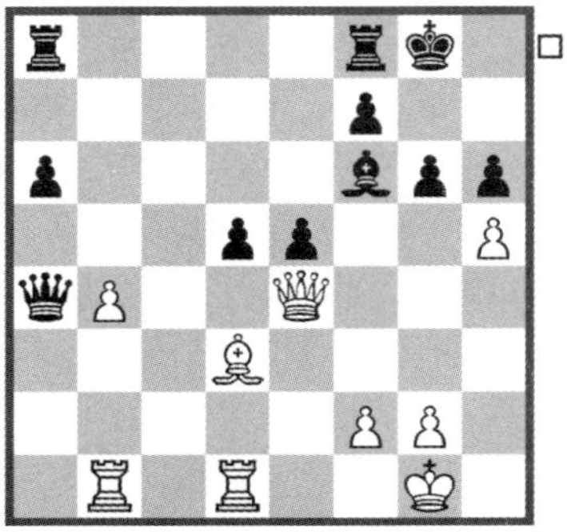

Position after: 25... d5!

**26. ♕xd5 ♖ad8 27. ♕f3 ♔g7**

27... e4 28. ♗xe4 ♖xd1+ 29. ♖xd1 gxh5= It looks slightly dodgy but Black is fine here too.

**28. hxg6 fxg6 29. ♕e4 ♕e8**

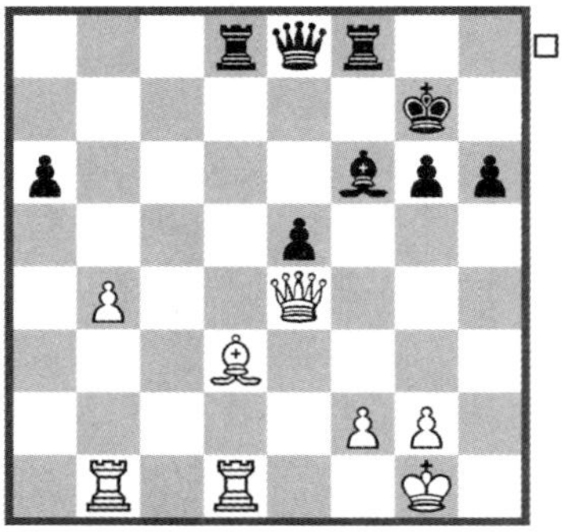

Position after: 29... ♕e8

**30. ♗xa6**

This is possibly the line where White has the best practical chances, because of Black's weak kingside pawns and our passed b-pawn. Despite this, the numerous options Black has along the way means that 14...h6 followed by an eventual...♘xe4 is a really clever way to equalise. Therefore it's worth analysing 13.♘c4, the benefit of which is that Black finds it harder to achieve simplification.

## j) 5...a6 6.♗e2 b6 7.d4 cxd4 8.♕xd4 e5 9.♕e3 ♗b7 10.0-0 ♗e7 11.♘d2 0-0 12.♖d1 ♕c7 13.♘c4 --

**1. e4 c5 2. ♘f3 d6 3. ♗b5+ ♘d7 4. a4 ♘gf6 5. ♘c3 a6 6. ♗e2 b6 7. d4 cxd4 8. ♕xd4 ♗b7 9. 0-0 e5**

Position after: 9... e5

**10. ♕e3 ♗e7 11. ♘d2 0-0 12. ♖d1 ♕c7 13. ♘c4**

Position after: 13. ♘c4

**13... ♖fd8**

**A)** It's too early to play 13... ♘c5 because after 14. f3 we immediately threaten to kick the knight back with b2-b4.

Position after: 14. f3

**A1)** 14... ♘cxe4 Fails to work despite the potential tactics associated with the g1-a7 diagonal, as Black is simply exchanging off their b6-pawn for the e4-pawn. 15. ♘xe4 ♗xe4 16. ♕xb6 ♕xb6+ 17. ♘xb6 ♖ab8 18. a5± I had a significant advantage in Haria – Raja, Delhi 2019.

**A2)** 14... ♖fd8 15. b4

*(see analysis diagram next page)*

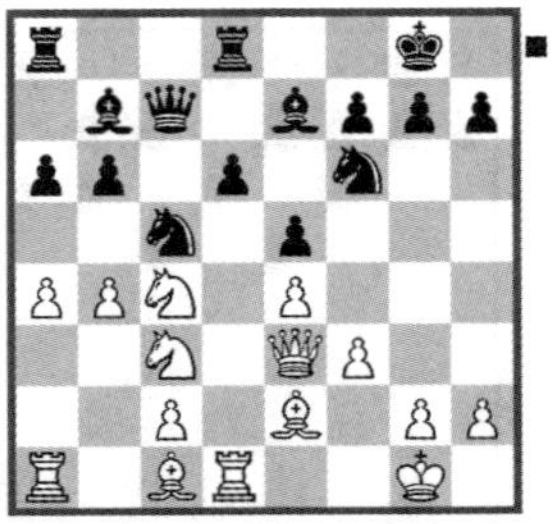

Position after: 15. b4

15... d5 The only way to keep things relatively complicated, but White keeps the advantage with accurate play. [After 15... ♘cd7 16. ♗a3 ♖ab8 17. b5!

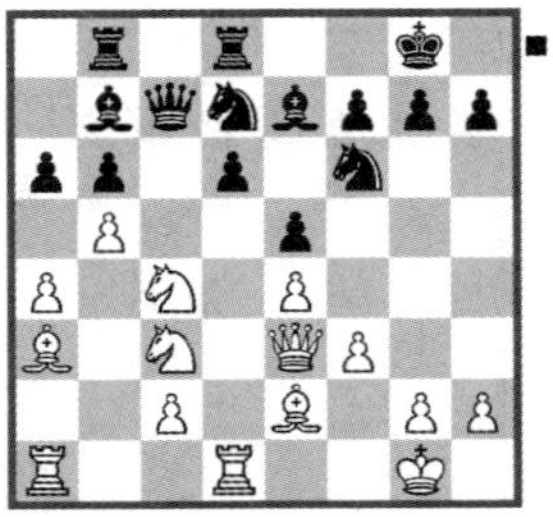

Position after: 17. b5!

17... ♘c5 18. ♗xc5 dxc5 White was completely winning in Giri – Salem, St Petersburg 2018. 19. ♖xd8+ ♖xd8 20. a5+–] 16. exd5 ♘xd5 17. ♘xd5 ♗xd5

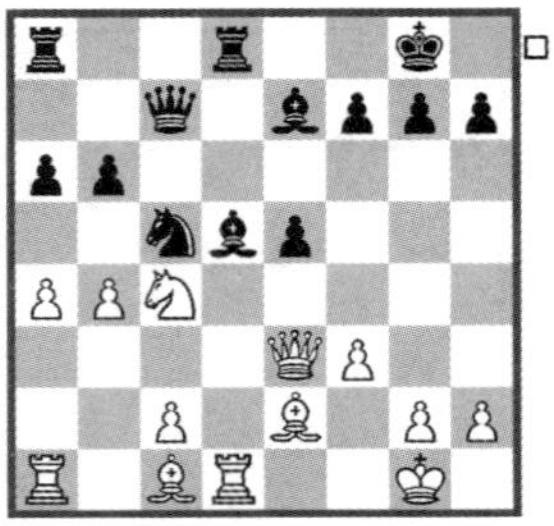

Position after: 17... ♗xd5

White has two interesting options here.

**A2.1)** 18. ♗b2!? ♘xa4 19. ♗xe5 ♕c6 20. ♗xg7 ♕e6 21. ♖xa4 ♔xg7 22. ♖xd5!

Position after: 22. ♖xd5!

22... ♕xd5 23. ♘xb6 ♕c6 24. ♕xe7! The point of White's play. We've sacrificed an exchange, but have significantly better practical chances due to Black's weakened king. 24... ♕xb6+ 25. ♔f1 ♖e8 26. ♕g5+ ♔f8 27. ♗d3⩱∞

**A2.2)** 18. ♕xe5 ♕b7 19. ♗b2 ♘e6 20. ♕f5 ♗xb4 Black wins the pawn back but our pieces are well placed to continue with a kingside approach. 21. ♔h1 ♗f8 [21... ♗c5 22. ♘e5→] 22. ♘e3 g6 23. ♕h3

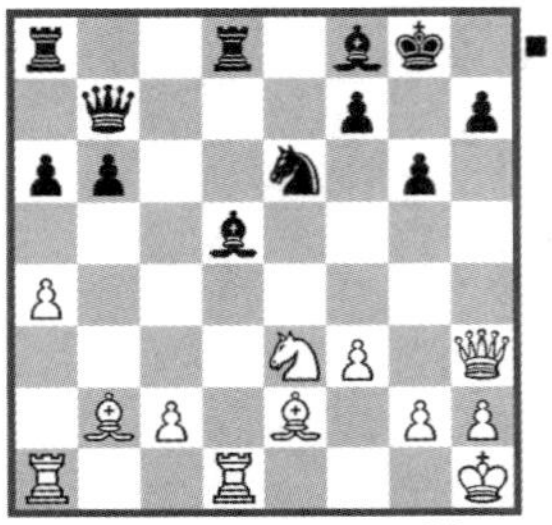

Position after: 23. ♕h3

23... h5 Black has to make a series of forced moves to keep White's pieces at bay, but it's clear that White still has the better chances. [23... ♗g7 24. ♗xg7 ♔xg7 25. ♕h4 f6 26. ♘g4±] 24. ♕h4 ♗e7 [24... ♗g7 25. ♗xg7 ♔xg7 26. f4±] 25. ♕e1 ♗f8 26. ♘xd5 ♖xd5 27. ♗c4 ♖xd1 28. ♖xd1±

**B)** 13... ♖fe8 14. b3

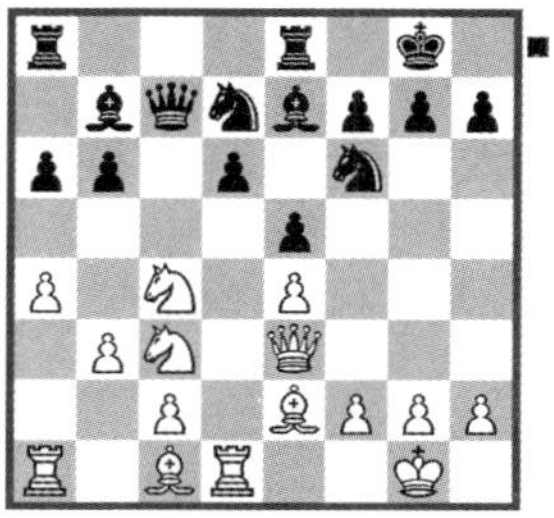
Position after: 14. b3

Deploying our bishop to a3 looks natural and keeps Black under pressure. [14. b4?! ♘xe4 15. ♘xe4 d5 16. ♕h3 ♘f8∞ illustrates the point of ...♖fe8.] 14... ♘c5 [14... ♖ad8 15. ♗a3 ♘c5 16. ♗f3± We can slowly improve, while Black lacks a clear plan.; 14... ♘xe4 15. ♘xe4 d5 16. ♗a3! ♗xa3 17. ♖xa3 dxe4 18. ♖aa1± White will be winning at least one pawn back after the simple plan of doubling rooks on the d-file.] 15. ♗a3

**B1)** 15... ♖ad8 16. ♗f3 [16. f3 d5!∓] 16... ♗f8 17. h3± White has a pleasant advantage and should continue by doubling rooks on the d-file. It's always important to constantly calculate Black's options of ...d7-d5 or ...♘xe4.

**B2)** 15... ♖ac8 16. f3! ♖ed8 [16... d5 17. exd5+–] 17. ♔h1± In this case Black is pretty much a move down on the mainline.

**C)** 13... ♖ac8 14. b4! This has already been seen in subchapter h), variation 12...♖ac8

**14. b3**

14. b4 ♘xe4 15. ♘xe4 d5∓

**14... ♘c5**

14... ♖ac8 15. ♗a3 ♘c5 transposes to the mainline.

**15. ♗a3**

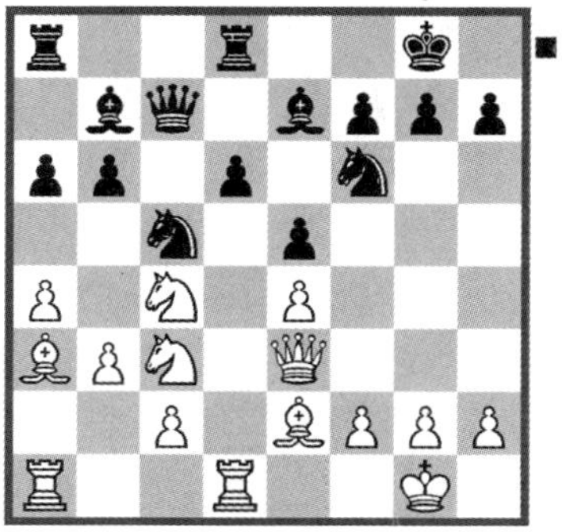
Position after: 15. ♗a3

The capture on e4 is once again possible, but in general the resulting endings should always be favourable for White.

**15... ♖ac8**

**A)** 15... ♘fxe4 16. ♘xe4 ♘xe4 17. ♕xb6 ♕xb6 18. ♘xb6

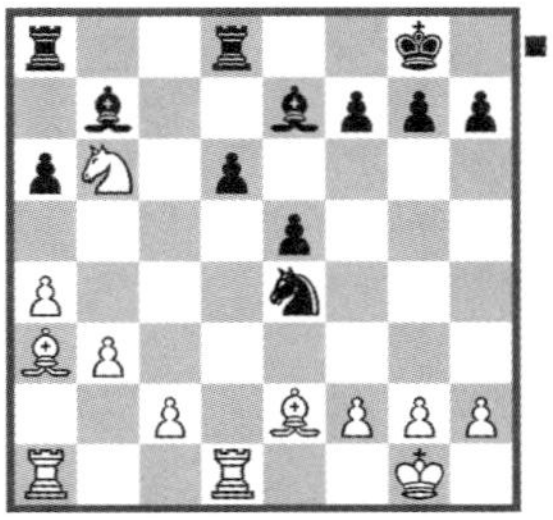

Position after: 18. ♘xb6

18... ♘c3 [18... ♖ab8 19. ♗b4 ♗g5 20. ♗c4±] 19. ♖e1 ♘xe2+ 20. ♖xe2 ♖ab8 21. a5

**A1)** 21... f6 22. ♖e3 ♖e8 [22... ♔f7 23. ♖c3±] 23. ♖d1±

**A2)** 21... ♗f6 22. ♗b2!

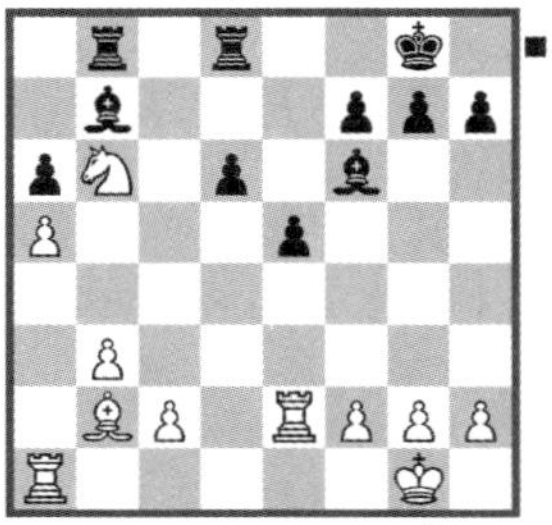

Position after: 22. ♗b2!

22... ♖e8 [22... ♗e7 23. ♖d1 f6 24. ♗a3 ♔f7 25. ♖ed2 ♔e6 26. c4±] 23. ♖d1 ♖e6 24. c4±

**B)** 15... ♘cxe4 16. ♘xe4 ♗xe4 17. ♘xb6 ♖ab8 18. a5 ♕b7 19. ♗f3 ♗xf3 20. ♕xf3 ♕xf3 21. gxf3±

**16. a5! b5 17. ♘b6 ♖b8 18. ♘cd5**

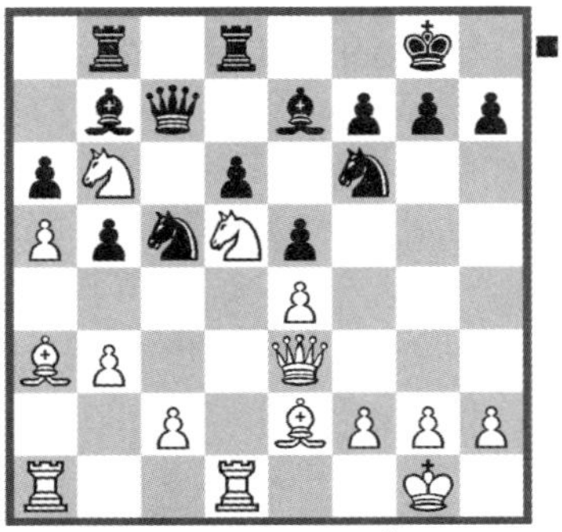

Position after: 18. ♘cd5

**18... ♗xd5**

18... ♘xd5 19. exd5 Black will struggle with our queenside majority 19... h6 20. b4 ♗g5 21. ♕h3 ♘d7 22. c4! ♘xb6 23. axb6 ♕xb6 24. c5 ♕c7 25. c6±

**19. exd5 ♘cd7**

19... ♕b7 20. c4 bxc4 21. ♗xc4 ♘cd7 22. ♘xd7 ♖xd7 23. ♕e2 ♖a8 24. b4±

**20. ♗b4!**

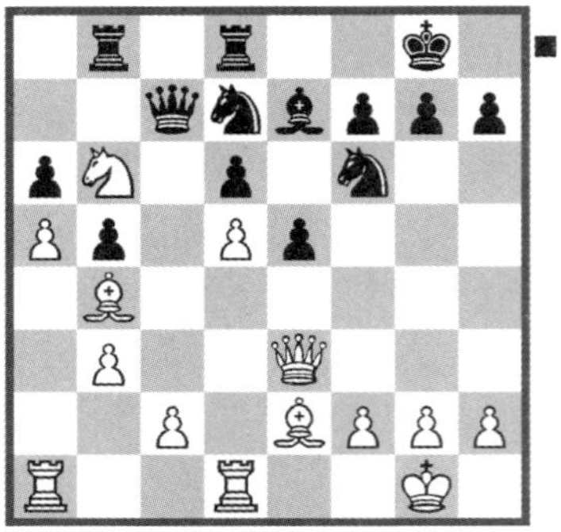

Position after: 20. ♗b4!

The strongest option. If Black decides to capture on c2, their queen will be exiled from the queenside.

**20... ♕xc2**

A) 20... ♖e8 21. ♘xd7 ♘xd7 22. ♖ac1±

B) 20... ♘xb6 21. axb6 ♕b7 22. c4 bxc4 23. bxc4±

C) 20... ♕b7 21. c4 bxc4 22. ♗xc4 ♘xb6 23. axb6 ♖a8 24. ♗d3 ♖db8 25. ♗a5 ♗d8 26. ♖ac1

**21. ♖ac1 ♕f5 22. ♖c7 ♘xb6 23. axb6 ♖d7 24. g4!**

Position after: 24. g4!

**24... ♘xg4**

24... ♕g6 25. f4! exf4 26. ♕xf4 ♖xc7 27. bxc7 ♖c8 28. ♗d3 ♕xg4+ 29. ♕xg4 ♘xg4 30. ♗f5+–

**25. ♕f3 ♕xf3 26. ♗xf3 ♘f6 27. ♖dc1 ♖xc7 28. bxc7 ♖c8 29. ♗a5 g6**

Position after: 29... g6

**30. ♖c6+–**

## k) 5...a6 6.♗e2 b6 7.d4 cxd4 8.♕xd4 e5 9.♕e3 ♗b7 10.0-0 ♗e7 11.♘d2 0-0 12.♖d1 ♕c7 13.♘c4 ♖ad8

**1. e4 c5 2. ♘f3 d6 3. ♗b5+ ♘d7 4. a4 ♘gf6 5. ♘c3 a6 6. ♗e2 b6 7. d4 cxd4 8. ♕xd4 ♗b7 9. 0-0 e5 10. ♕e3 ♗e7 11. ♘d2 0-0 12. ♖d1 ♕c7 13. ♘c4 ♖ad8!**

Black has a bunch of different rook moves, but this is the only way for Black to equalise - based on tactics associated with capturing on e4.

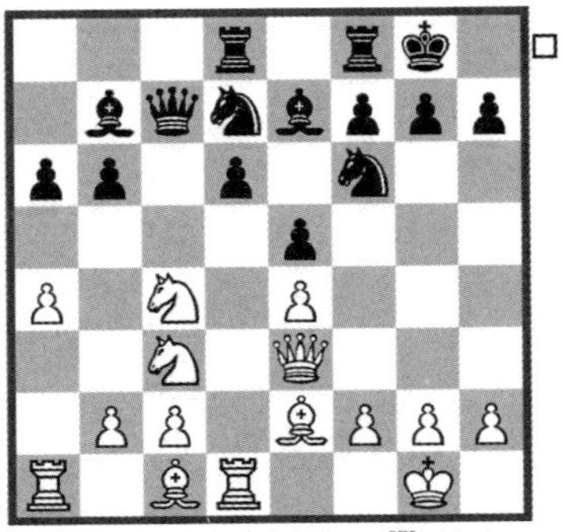

Position after: 13... ♖ad8!

**14. ♗f1N**

After a lot of analysis, this looks like White's best option to play for the win. The plan is simple - to retreat our queen to e2, before developing the c1-bishop. Black will find it difficult to achieve counterplay, as their position is quite passive.

**A)** 14. b3 This is the more cautious attempt, which doesn't prevent Black from pursuing an equalising e4-capture. 14... ♘c5

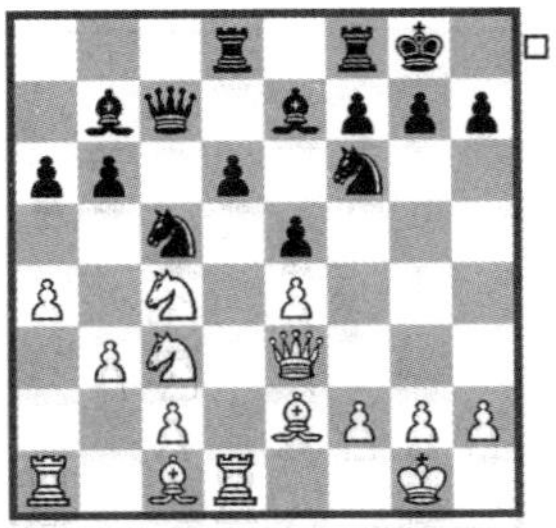

Position after: 14... ♘c5

**A1)** 15. ♗a3 ♘fxe4 One of the only moments where it makes sense for Black to exchange these pawns. The rook isn't hanging on a8, and they are well placed to start pushing the central pawns at some moment. 16. ♘xe4 ♘xe4 17. ♕xb6 ♕xb6 18. ♘xb6 ♘c3 19. ♖e1 ♖fe8!∞ Followed by ... d6-d5 with good play in the centre.

**A2)** 15. ♗f3 ♘cxe4 16. ♘xe4 ♗xe4!

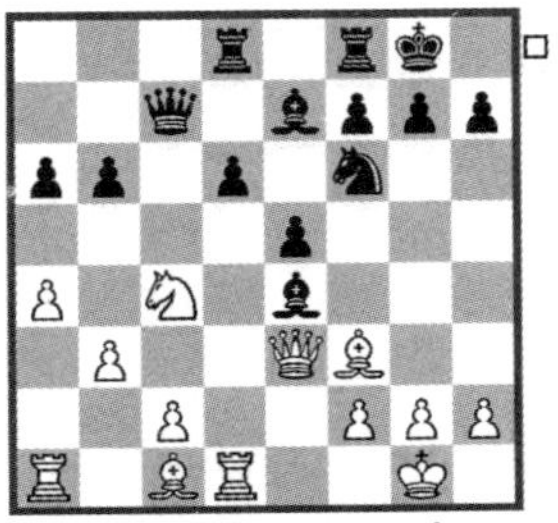

Position after: 16... ♗xe4!

17. ♗xe4 d5= Valenzuela Gomez – Papadiamandis, Sitges 2020.

**B)** 14. f3 d5–+

**C)** 14. b4

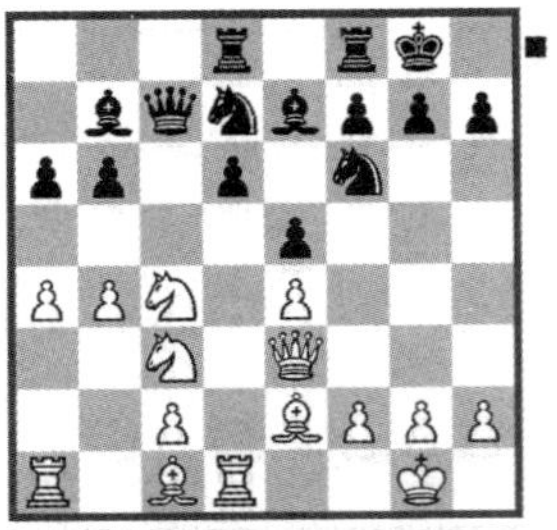

Position after: 14. b4

14... ♘xe4! I should mention that this line is a great choice for White if you are content with a draw. If Black doesn't capture on e4, they stand considerably worse. [14... d5 15. ♘xd5 ♘xd5 16.

exd5 ♗xb4 17. ♕g3 ♔h8 18. ♗a3±] 15. ♘xe4 ♗xe4 [15... d5 16. ♕g3 dxc4 17. ♗h6±] 16. ♕xe4 d5!

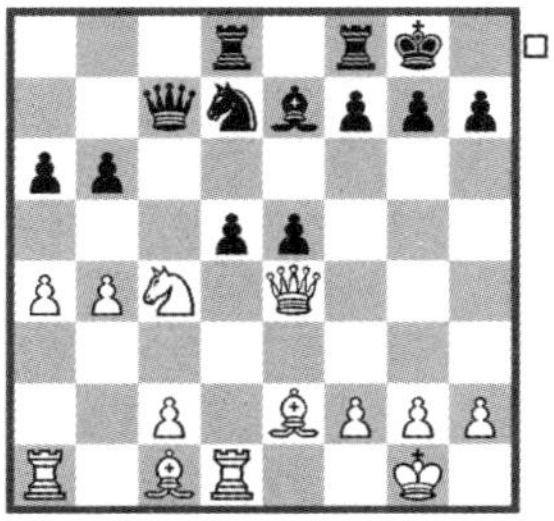

Position after: 16... d5!

17. ♕xd5 [17. ♕f3!? This temporary pawn sacrifice might be a better 'winning attempt'. 17... dxc4 18. b5! axb5 19. axb5 ♘f6 20. ♖xd8 ♖xd8 21. ♕c6 ♕b8 22. ♗b2] 17... ♘f6 18. ♕xe5 ♖xd1– 19. ♗xd1 ♕xc4 20. ♗e2 ♕xc2= Accurate play from Black has resulted in an ending which they should hold. 21. ♕b2 ♕xb2 22. ♗xb2=

**14... ♘c5**

As usual, the capture on e4 is the most critical variation.

**A)** 14... ♖fe8 15. ♕e2

Position after: 15. ♕e2

**A1)** 15... ♘xe4 16. ♘xe4 d5 17. ♗g5!

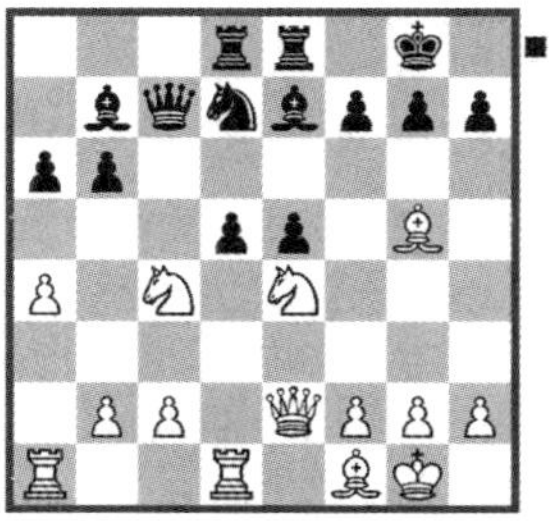

Position after: 17. ♗g5!

17... dxc4 [17... f6 18. ♗e3 dxe4 19. a5 b5 20. ♘b6 ♘c5 21. b4 ♘e6 22. c4 ♘d4 23. ♕a2 bxc4 24. ♖ac1↑ Once again the knight on b6 is fantastic in constricting Black's piece activity.; 17... dxe4 18. ♗xe7 ♖xe7 19. ♕d2± The pin is really difficult for Black to deal with.] 18. ♗xe7 ♖xe7 19. ♘d6 ♘c5 20. ♘xb7 ♘xb7 21. ♖xd8+± Followed by capturing on c4, and White is a touch better.

**A2)** 15... h6?! 16. ♘e3!

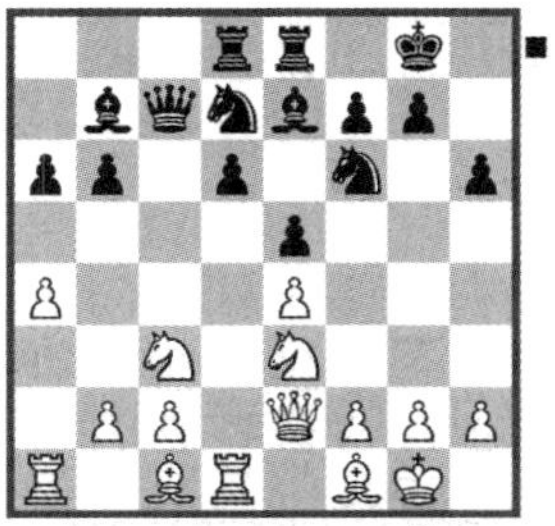

Position after: 16. ♘e3!

Another idea behind retreating the queen to e2. 16... ♘xe4 17. ♘cd5 ♕c5 [17... ♕b8 18. ♘xe7+ ♖xe7 19. ♘f5 ♖e6 20. ♕g4 g6 21. ♘xh6+

♔g7 22. ♘f5+ ♔g8 23. ♘g3±] 18. f3 ♘ef6 19. b4 ♕c6 20. b5 axb5 21. axb5 ♕c8 22. ♘xe7+ ♖xe7 23. ♖xd6±

**A3)** 15... ♘c5 16. ♗e3!

Position after: 16. ♗e3!

The e4-pawn still doesn't hang due to the weakness on b6. 16... d5 [16... h6 17. ♘d5 ♘xd5 18. exd5 f5 19. a5!

Position after: 19. a5!

Our queenside pressure is more important than any Black kingside counterplay. 19... b5 20. ♘b6 ♖f8 21. f3!± Followed by pushing b2-b4 and c2-c4.] 17. exd5 ♘xd5 18. ♘xd5 ♗xd5 19. a5 b5 20. ♘b6 ♗c6 21. ♖ac1± Once we break through on the queenside with c2-c4, Black will find the position really difficult to navigate.

**B)** 14... ♘xe4?! 15. ♘xe4 d5 16. ♕g3! g6 17. ♗h6 ♖fe8 18. ♘ed2 dxc4 19. ♘xc4± with sustained pressure.

**15. b4**

15. ♘d5!? ♘xd5 16. exd5 a5! The critical move, after which Black has pretty good play with the forthcoming ...f7-f5. [16... f5 17. b4 f4 18. ♕f3 ♘d7

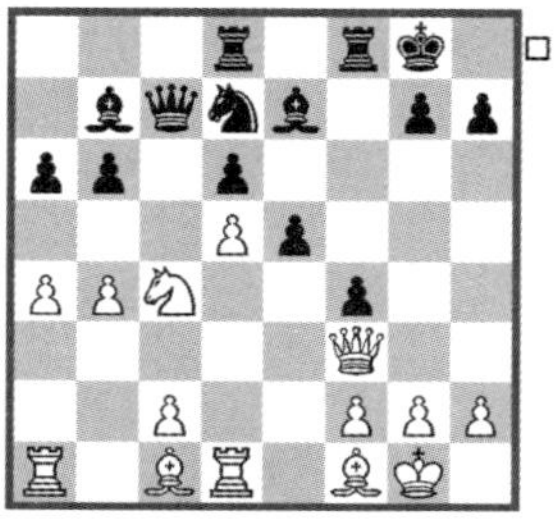

Position after: 18... ♘d7

19. ♖a2!± with the idea of ♘d2-e4, and potentially c2-c4.] 17. b4 axb4 18. ♕e1 ♗a6 19. ♕xb4 ♗xc4 20. ♕xc4 ♖a8 21. ♗e3 f5⇆

**15... ♘cxe4 16. ♘xe4 ♘xe4**

16... ♗xe4?! 17. ♕xb6 ♕c8 18. ♗d2±

**17. ♕xb6**

This is probably the critical position in the line after 13.♘c4. Black has two options - to either trade or keep the queens on. To be totally honest, I found it quite difficult to make sense of a lot of the variations here. It seems like 14.♗f1 is White's best option if you want to avoid immediate liquidation -

but as you'll encounter, the resulting positions can get quite murky.

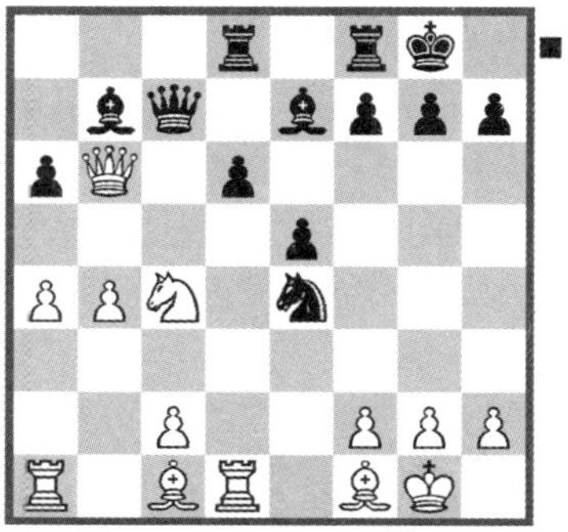
Position after: 17. ♕xb6

**17... ♕c8**

17... ♕xb6 18. ♘xb6 d5 Another difficult position to judge. Black has the advantage of strong central pawns, but their a6-pawn will always be a weakness, and our flank pawns also look more dangerous in terms of being able to advance. 19. ♗a3 ♘c3 20. ♖e1

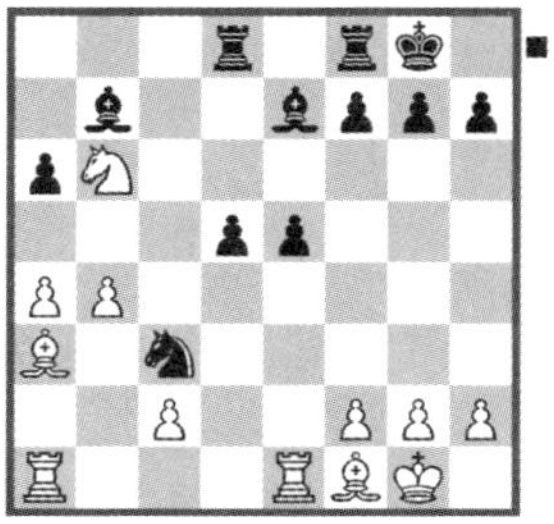
Position after: 20. ♖e1

**A)** 20... ♗f6!? 21. b5 a5 22. ♗c1! [22. ♗xf8 ♔xf8 Black has a fantastic position here, with central pawns and the bishop pair.] 22... e4 23. ♖a3± I still think Black has to be more careful than White here - our next move is ♗d2, which looks quite hard to meet.

**B)** 20... ♗d6 21. b5 axb5 22. axb5 f6 23. ♘a4 ♘xa4 24. ♗xd6 ♖xd6

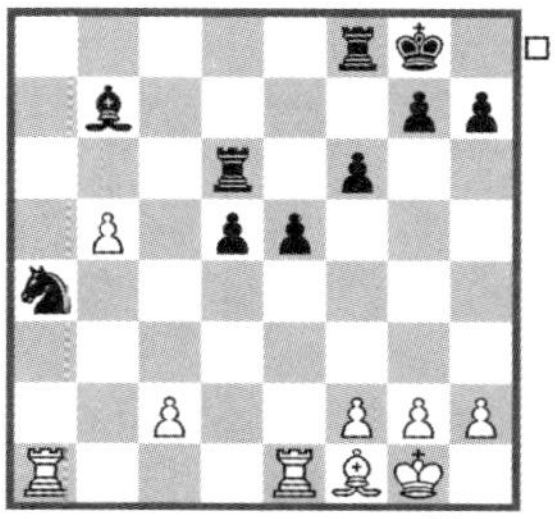
Position after: 24... ♖xd6

25. ♖xa4 Followed by c2-c4. Again the position is completely equal of course, but our passed pawn offers us a glimmer of hope.

**C)** 20... ♖fe8 21. ♖e3!

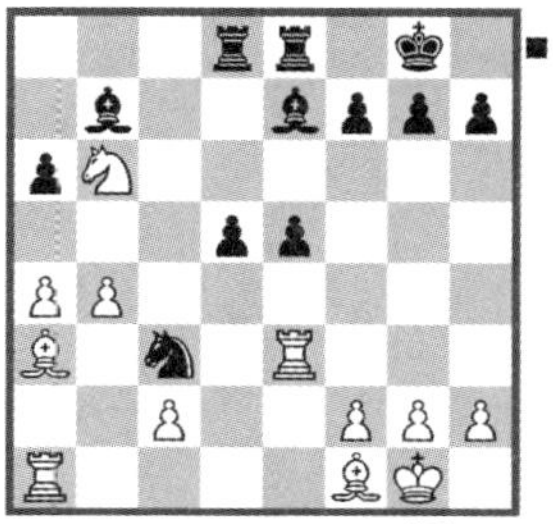
Position after: 21. ♖e3!

[21. ♖xe5 ♗f6 22. ♖xe8+ ♖xe8 23. ♖c1 ♗d4 24. ♘d7 ♘e2+⇆] 21... ♘e4 22. b5 ♗xa3 23. ♖exa3 a5 24. ♖d1 We reach another complex position, which in all honesty looks difficult for both sides.

**18. ♗e3 d5!**

I think this is the best way for Black to play - to give up the e5-pawn, rather than a6. They gain a lot more activity this way.

18... f5 19. ♘a5 ♗a8 20. ♕xa6

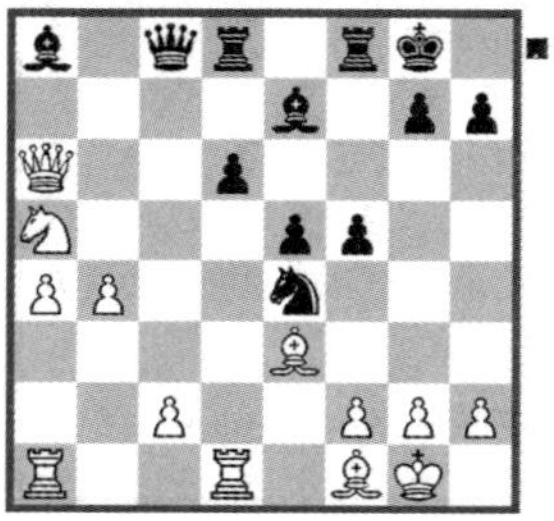

Position after: 20. ♕xa6

It looks very difficult for Black to hold equality if they gives us the a6-pawn. 20... d5 [20... f4 The following line is quite forcing: 21. ♗b6 ♕xa6 22. ♗xa6 ♖b8 23. ♗c7 ♖xb4 24. f3!

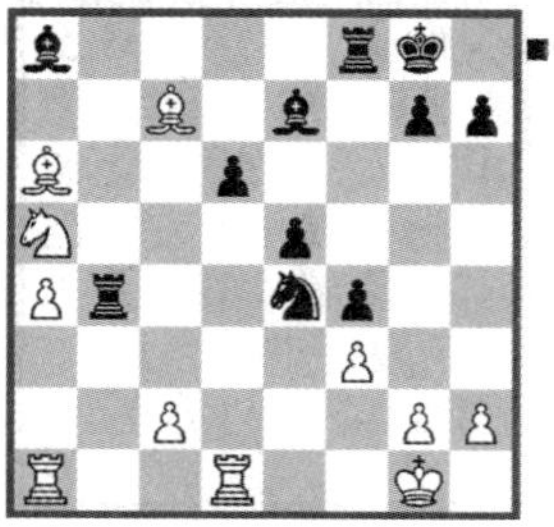

Position after: 24. f3!

24... ♘c3 25. ♗xd6 ♗xd6 26. ♖xd6 ♖xa4 27. ♖xa4 ♘xa4 28. ♘b3 g6 29. ♖e6±] 21. b5! We don't mind doubling the a-pawns, as this will open the b-file for us - and the a6-pawn will be really annoying for Black to deal with.

*(see analysis diagram next column)*

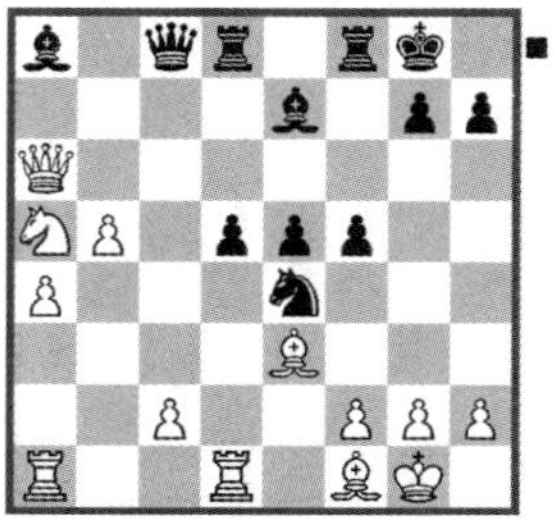

Position after: 21. b5!

**A)** 21... ♗b4 22. ♕xc8 ♖xc8 23. ♘b3 d4 24. ♗d2 ♘xd2 25. ♘xd2 ♖xc2 26. ♘f3 ♗xf3 27. gxf3 ♗a5 28. ♖ac1± Black will still have to play accurately to hold a draw.

**B)** 21... ♕xa6 22. bxa6 d4 23. ♗c1 ♘c3 24. ♖e1 e4 25. ♗d2 ♖c8 26. ♘c4 ♘d5 27. ♖eb1±

**C)** 21... d4 22. ♕xc8! ♖xc8 23. ♗c1 ♖xc2 24. ♘c4 ♘xf2 25. ♖d2 ♖xd2 26. ♗xd2 ♘e4 27. ♗c1 ♗c5

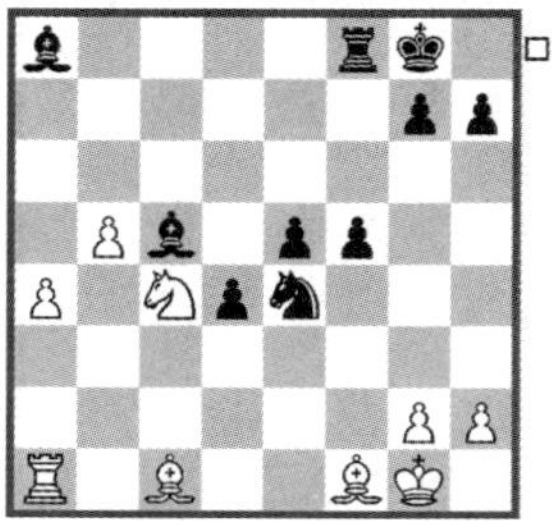

Position after: 27... ♗c5

28. ♗a3↑ Our flank pawns are quicker than Black's central pawns.

**D)** 21... f4 22. ♕xc8 ♖xc8 23. ♗a7 There are numerous computer variations which show that Black can hold equality. I don't know how helpful it is to analyse each of them, but generally Black has to play very actively.

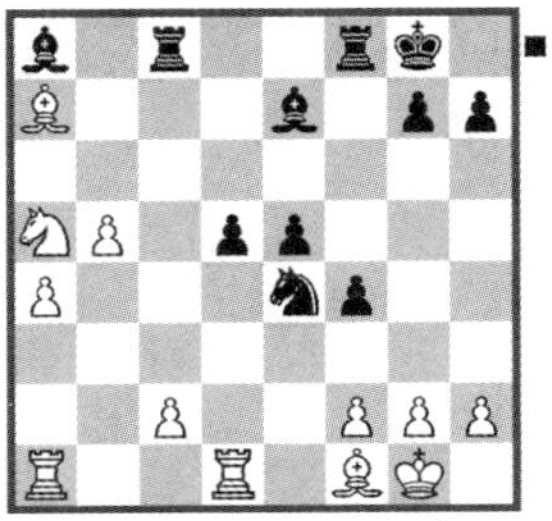
Position after: 23. ♗a7

23... ♗b4! [23... ♖f7 24. b6 ♗c5 25. b7 ♗xb7 26. ♗xc5 ♖xc5 27. ♘xb7 ♖xb7 28. a5 ♖a7 29. a6±] 24. ♘b3 f3! 25. ♖d3 [25. a5!? d4 26. a6 ♘xf2! 27. ♔xf2 fxg2+ 28. ♔g1 ♖xf1+ 29. ♖xf1 gxf1=♕+ 30. ♔xf1 ♗d5⇆] 25... d4!

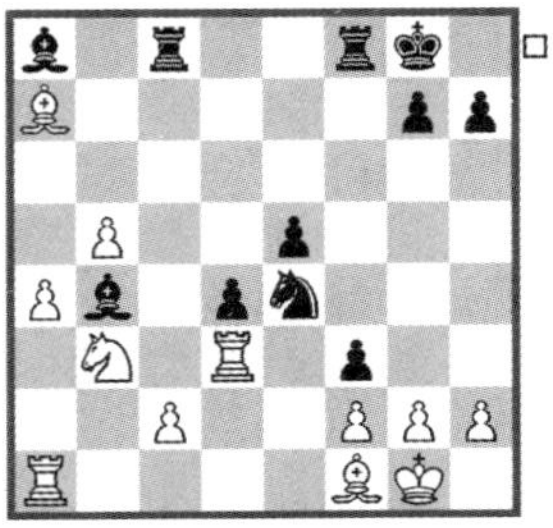
Position after: 25... d4!

[25... fxg2 26. ♗xg2 ♖xc2 27. ♗xe4 dxe4 28. ♖dd1 e3 29. ♗xe3 ♗f3 30. ♖dc1 ♖b2 31. ♖ab1 ♖a2 32. a5± There are still chances for White to press here.] 26. ♖xf3 ♖xf3 27. gxf3 ♘g5 28. ♗g2 ♖xc2= The combination of Black's active pieces and passed d-pawn means White can't be better.

**19. ♘xe5 ♗f6 20. f4**

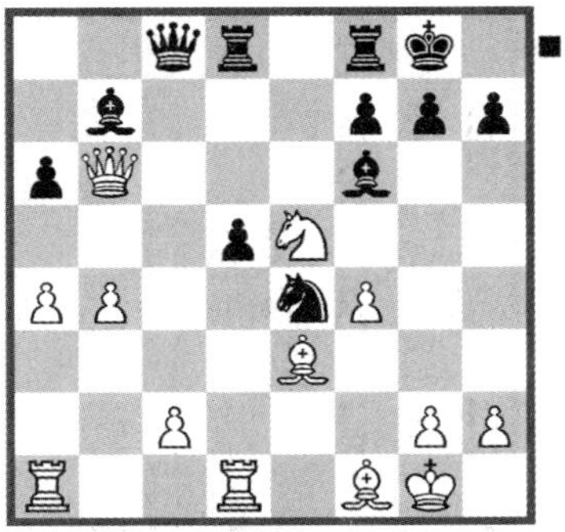
Position after: 20. f4

**20... g5!**

20... ♖fe8 This also looks reasonable for Black, although I'm not certain that it completely equalises. 21. b5 axb5 22. axb5 ♖d6 23. ♕a7 g5!

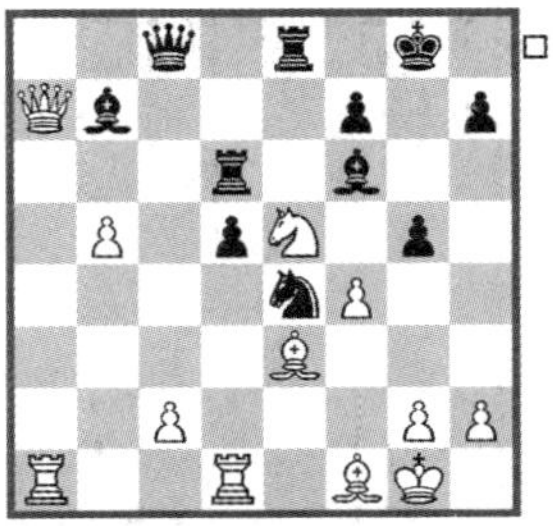
Position after: 23... g5!

24. ♗d4 gxf4 25. ♘f3 ♗xd4+ 26. ♕xd4 ♖g6 27. ♖e1 ♕g4 28. ♖a3∞

**21. ♗d3 gxf4**

**A)** 21... ♖d6 22. ♕d4± White is close to consolidating the pawn here.

**B)** 21... ♗g7!? 22. b5 gxf4 23. ♗xf4 ♖d6 24. ♕e3 ♖e6 25. ♖a3!↑

**22. ♗xf4 ♕f5 23. ♖f1 ♗xe5 24. ♗xe5 ♕xe5 25. ♕xb7 ♖d6 26. ♗xe4 dxe4**

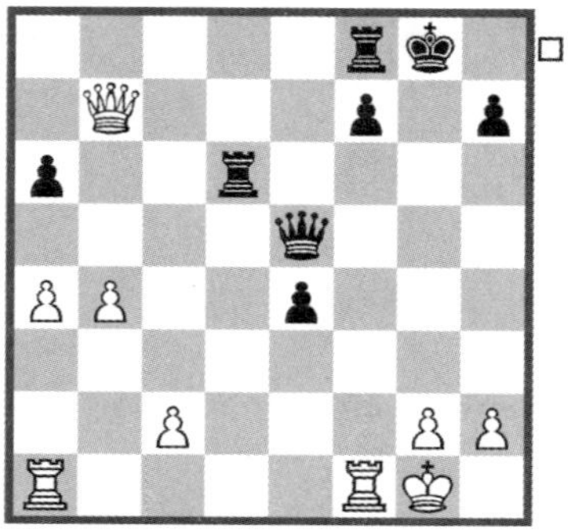

Position after: 26... dxe4

**27. ♖ae1±**

I think it's fair to suggest that White still has a small edge when we compare the king safety of both sides.

## Conclusion to Chapter 3

This chapter has been an excellent demonstration of one of our key ideas in the Anti-Sicilian: delaying opening up the position until Black's pieces are poorly placed to cope with the d2-d4 pawn break. In nearly every subchapter, I explore the option of transitioning into an Open Sicilian-type position, but only after forcing Black's knight to d7 and reducing queenside counterplay by playing the prophylactic 4.a4. A key theme which consequently emerges is Black's weak queenside pawns on a6 and b6.

While this chapter does contain a large amount of analysis in response to Black's various options, it is possible to make some common observations about our plans. In subchapters a-c where Black develops their dark-squared bishop to g7, we decide whether or not to open the centre based on Black's timing of ...a7-a6. In subchapters d-f, we examine the development plan ...e7-e6 and ...b7-b6, and quickly realise that Black's biggest problem often revolves around the weak d6-pawn.

The remaining subchapters are arguably the most critical – Black plays aggressively in the centre with ...e7-e5. The focus in this chapter generally revolves around control of the d5-square and our ability to exert pressure on Black's weak queenside pawns. It is clear that Black's only path to equality involves tricky tactics associated with sacrificing on e4. Even still, I have provided many different options – all with the aim of creating difficulties for Black, and which make the line beginning with 4.a4 extremely tough for Black to prepare for and handle in a practical game.

# Part II

# Moscow with 3...♗d7

# 4...♘xd7

1.e4 c5 2.♘f3 d6 3.♗b5+ ♗d7

4.♗xd7 ♘xd7

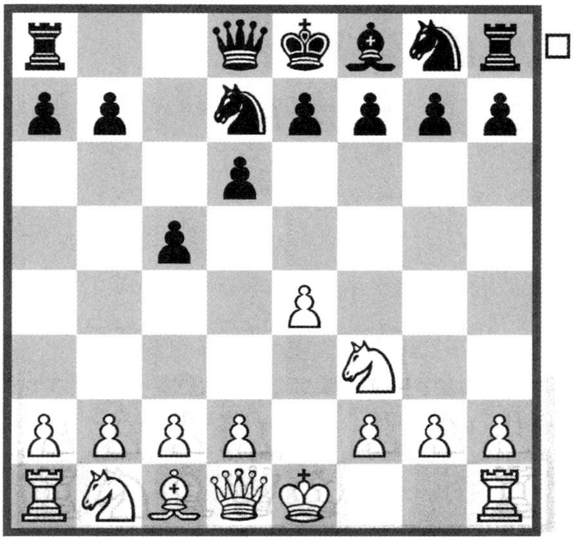

# Chapter Guide

## Chapter 4 – 4...♘xd7

1.e4 c5 2.♘f3 d6 3.♗b5+ ♘d7 4.♗xd7 ♘xd7 5.0-0 ♘fg6 6.♕e2

## a) 6...g6

**1. e4 c5 2. ♘f3 d6 3. ♗b5+ ♗d7 4. ♗xd7+ ♘xd7**

Black claims that the queen is better placed on d8, from where it can jump to a5 in the future.

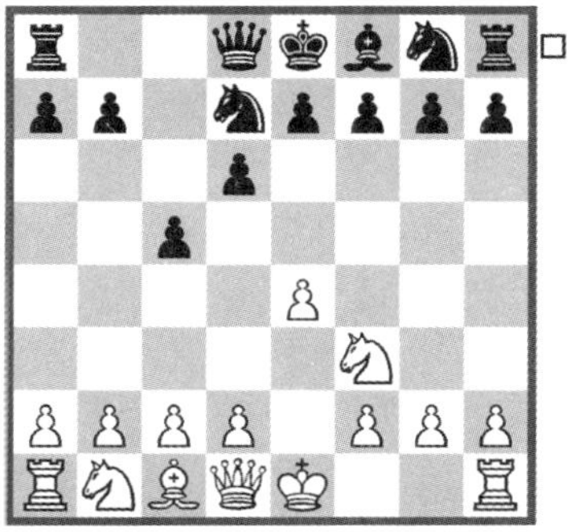

Position after: 4... ♘xd7

**5. 0-0 ♘gf6 6. ♕e2**

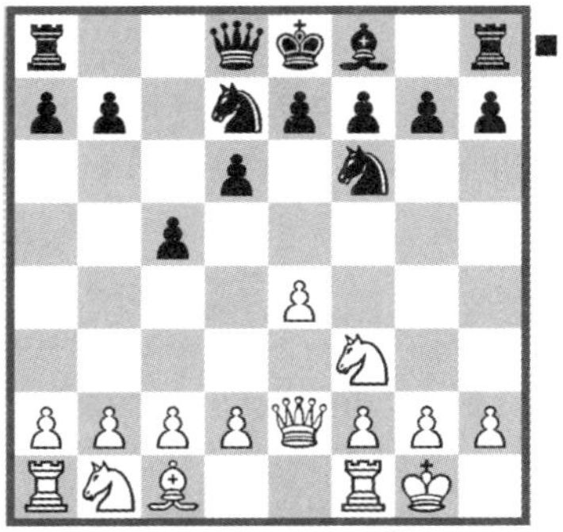

Position after: 6. ♕e2

**6... g6?!**

This is less accurate if we haven't played c2-c4 yet, as now we have a different option.

6... ♕c7!? Similarly to 6...♖c8, which we'll see next, Black postpones kingside development in the hope to determine our setup first. However the drawback compared to 6...♖c8 is that Black's queen is probably misplaced on c7. I like the idea of continuing with our plan of achieving a Maroczy structure and attempting to land our c3-knight on d5 at the right moment. 7. c4 g6 8. ♘c3 ♗g7 9. d4 cxd4 10. ♘xd4 a6 11. ♖d1 0-0

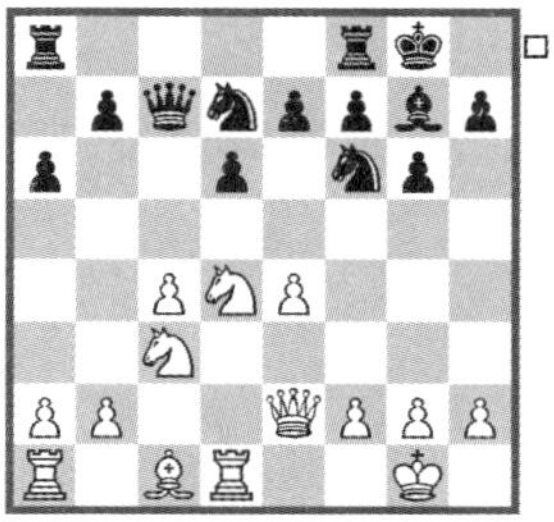

Position after: 11... 0-0

12. b3± Followed by ♗b2. Black can't really push ...b7-b5, as it would be met by ♘d5 and a pawn recapture, highlighting the new big hole on c6.

**7. c3!**

Black would love to be able to challenge in the centre with ...e7-e6 and ...d6-d5 now (as shown after 6...♖c8), but doing so would create too many weaknesses.

**7... ♗g7**

7... ♗h6 8. d4 ♗xc1 9. ♖xc1 0-0 10. ♖d1±

**8. d4**

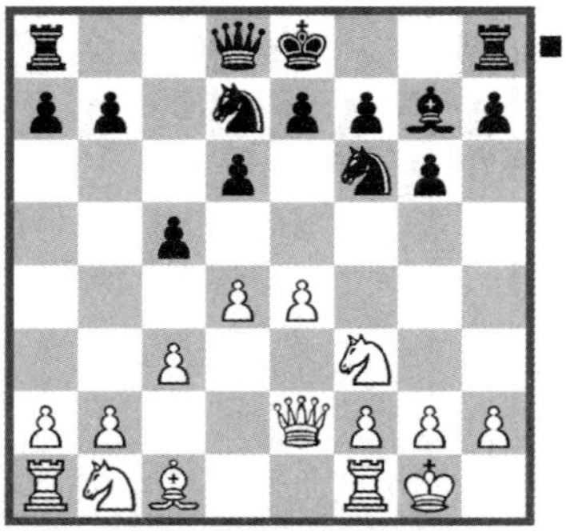

Position after: 8. d4

**8... cxd4**

**A)** 8... 0-0?! 9. e5 ♘d5 10. e6 ♘7b6 11. dxc5 dxc5 12. exf7+ ♖xf7 13. ♘g5 ♖f6 14. a4±

**B)** 8... d5?! It's way too dangerous and naive for Black to challenge in the centre here. 9. e5 ♘e4 10. c4!

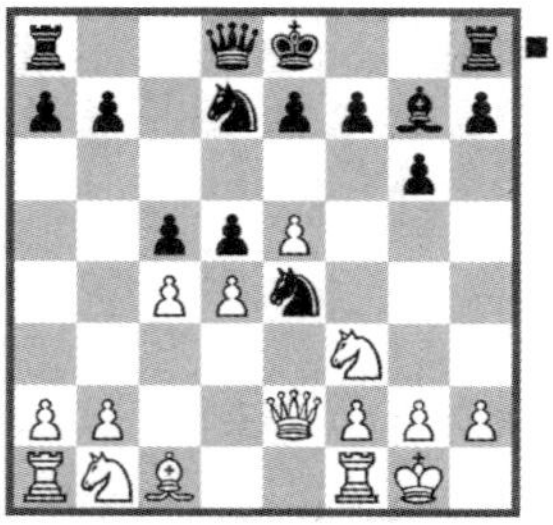

Position after: 10. c4!

10... e6 11. cxd5 exd5 12. ♘c3 ♘xc3 13. bxc3 0-0 14. ♖b1 b6 15. ♘g5± Concretely threatening e5-e6, as well as other aggressive ideas like ♕f3-h3 and f2-f4.

**C)** 8... ♕b6 is the engine's suggestion, but even here it's easy enough for White to acquire a pleasant edge. 9. ♖e1! 0-0 10. e5 dxe5 [10... ♘d5 11. e6+–] 11. dxe5 ♘d5 12. ♖d1 ♕c6 13. c4 ♘c7 14. ♘c3± Followed by ♗f4 and h2-h4 with a nice space advantage and harmonious pieces.

**9. cxd4 d5**

9... 0-0 10. ♘c3± [10. e5?! dxe5 11. dxe5 ♘d5 12. e6 ♘c5=]

**10. e5 ♘e4 11. ♕b5!**

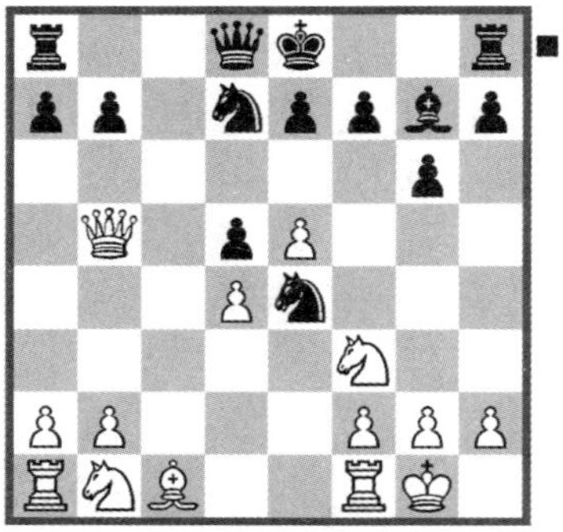

Position after: 11. ♕b5!

Winning a pawn by force.

**11... e6 12. ♕xb7±**

## b) 6...♖c8

**1. e4 c5 2. ♘f3 d6 3. ♗b5+ ♗d7 4. ♗xd7+ ♘xd7 5. 0-0 ♘gf6 6. ♕e2 ♖c8**

The rook is ideally placed to meet our forthcoming d2-d4 break. Black is waiting for us to commit to either c2-c3 or c2-c4, before deciding whether to develop the dark-squared bishop to g7 or via ...e7-e6.

Position after: 6... ♖c8

**7. c3 e6**

Now that we're committing to a c3-d4 setup, Black can alter their plan and instead challenge the centre with ...e7-e6 and ...d6-d5.

7... ♕c7 8. d4 cxd4 9. cxd4

**A)** 9... d5? 10. e5 ♘e4 11. ♘bd2 ♕c2 [11... ♘xd2 12. ♗xd2 e6 13. ♖ac1 ♕b8 14. ♖xc8+ ♕xc8 15. ♖c1 ♕b8 16. ♕b5±] 12. ♘e1 ♕c6 13. ♘b3 ♕g6 14. ♕b5 ♖c7 15. ♕xd5+– Ghinda – Miles, Dortmund 1979.

**B)** 9... ♕xc1? 10. ♖xc1 ♖xc1+ 11. ♘e1 g6 12. g3!

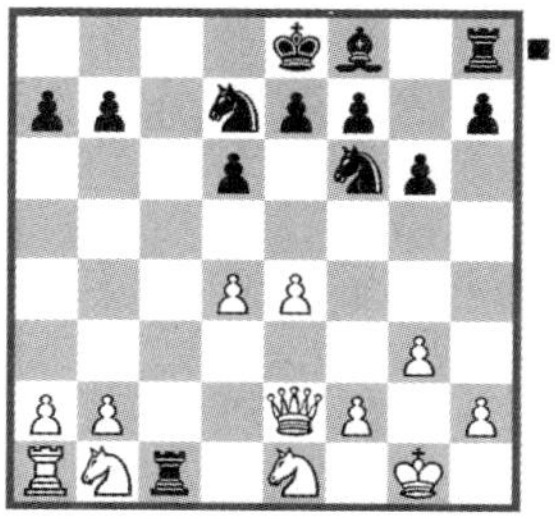

Position after: 12. g3!

12... ♗h6 13. ♔g2 0-0 14. ♘d3±

**C)** 9... ♕c4 The point of 7...♕c7 – Black attempts to trade queens. Happily for us, this fails to achieve equality. 10. ♕xc4! The simplest continuation. White should have an advantage in this queenless middlegame. 10... ♖xc4 11. ♘c3

**C1)** 11... g6 12. ♖d1 ♗g7 13. h3 e6 [13... 0-0 14. e5+–] 14. ♗e3± Followed by ♖ac1 and ♘d2 with easy play.

**C2)** 11... e6 12. ♖e1 Here Black struggles to deal with our constant threat of simply pushing e4-e5. 12... h6 [12... ♗e7 13. e5!

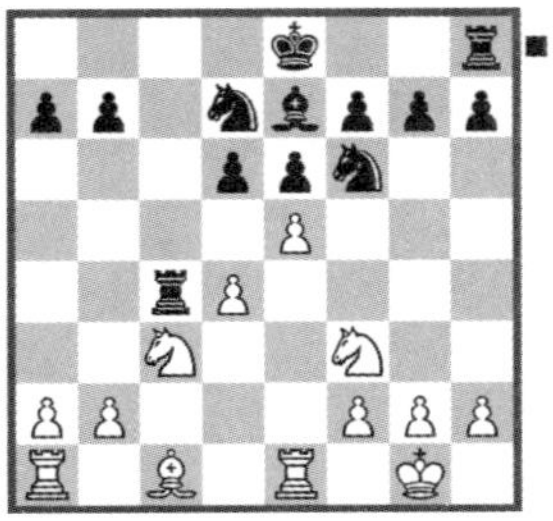

Position after: 13. e5!

13... dxe5 14. dxe5 ♘g4 15. h3 ♘h6 16. g4±] 13. ♗e3 ♗e7 14. e5! ♘g4 15. ♗d2 dxe5 16. dxe5 h5 17. h3 ♘h6 18. ♖ac1± Followed by ♘b5.

**8. d4 cxd4**

8... ♗e7 doesn't work quite as well here. 9. e5 dxe5 10. dxe5 ♘d5 11. c4 ♘b4 12. ♖d1 0-0 13. ♘c3± Black's rook is misplaced on c8, and White has an initiative.

**9. cxd4 d5 10. e5**

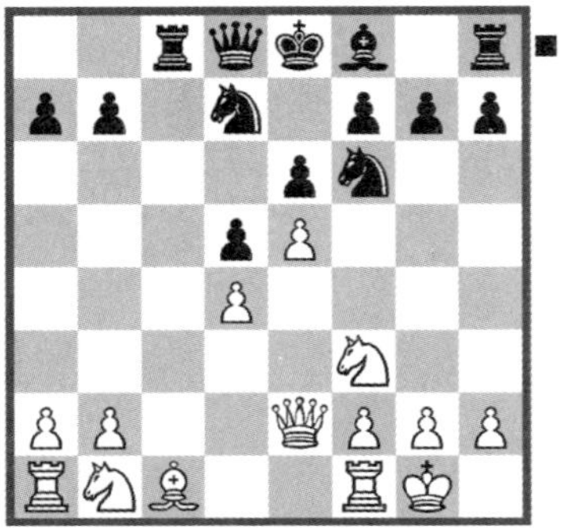

Position after: 10. e5

**10... ♘g8**

10... ♘e4?! Black's knight will end up misplaced, and they will likely have to make further concessions on the king-side. 11. ♗e3

Position after: 11. ♗e3

**A)** 11... ♘b6 12. ♘e1 ♘c4 [12... f5 13. f3 ♘g5 14. b3 ♘f7 15. ♘d3 ♘d7 16. ♘d2± Mamedov – Ivanchuk, Kocaeli 2017.] 13. ♘d3 ♘xe3 14. ♕xe3 h6 15. f3 ♘g5 16. ♘c3 ♗e7

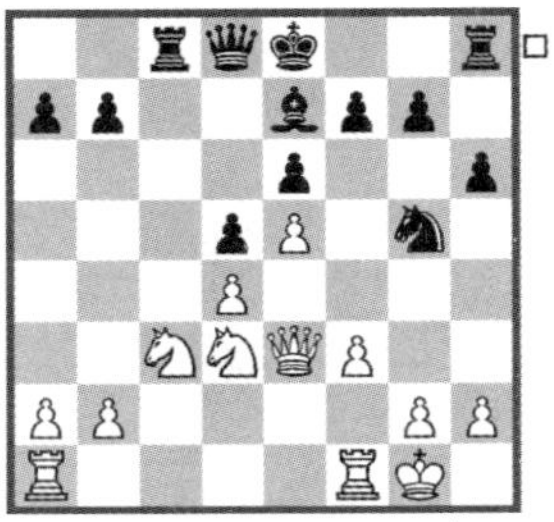

Position after: 16... ♗e7

17. h4! Dominating our opponent's pieces is more important than winning a pawn. [17. f4 ♘e4 18. ♘xe4 dxe4 19. ♘f2 0-0 20. ♘xe4±] 17... ♘h7 18. g3 0-0 19. f4±

**B)** 11... ♗e7 12. ♘e1 h6 [12... f5 13. ♘d3 0-0 14. f3 ♘g5 15. ♘c3 ♘f7 16. ♖ac1 ♖e8 17. ♖c2±] 13. f3 ♘g5 14. ♘c3 0-0 15. ♘d3 ♘b8 16. a3!

*(see analysis diagram next page)*

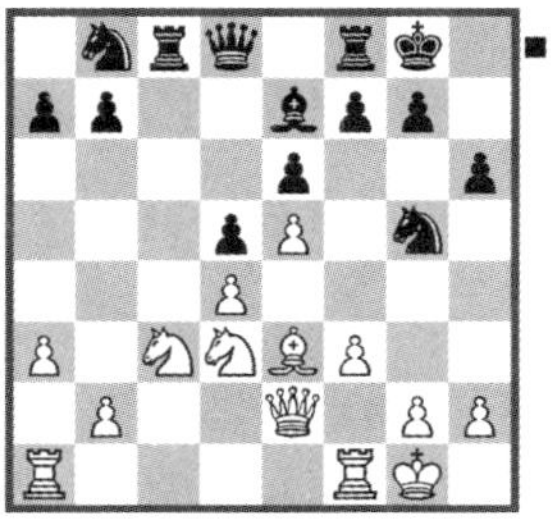

Position after: 16. a3!

This is always useful to prevent a future ...♘b4 or ...♗b4. 16... ♘c6 17. ♔h1 ♕b6 18. ♗f2±

**11. ♘c3 ♘e7**

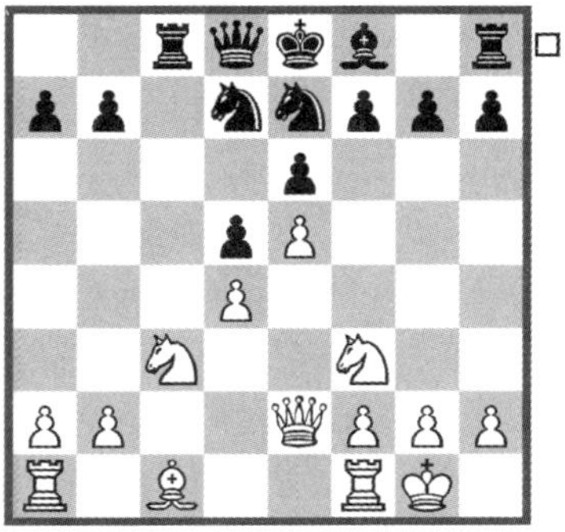

Position after: 11... ♘e7

**12. ♖d1!**

I like this option as it's the most flexible, although 12.h4 also looks good. This position is quite similar to our subchapter on 5. 0-0 after 4...♕xd7, which we well see next. Despite Black having an optically pleasant position, the exchange of the light-squared bishops makes it difficult for them to deal with our simple plan of pushing the h-pawn and pressing on both sides of the board. The lines will demonstrate that we constantly pose threats on both the queenside and kingside. An important idea is the rook lift to d3. I don't think it's hugely important to memorise too many variations, instead focusing on the various ideas we have at our disposal.

**A)** 12. ♗g5 is the most obvious move, but it doesn't pose Black a huge amount of practical difficulty. 12... a6 13. ♕d3 h6 14. ♗d2 ♘c6 15. ♘e2 ♗b4 16. ♖ac1 ♗xd2 17. ♕xd2 0-0=

**B)** 12. h4!?

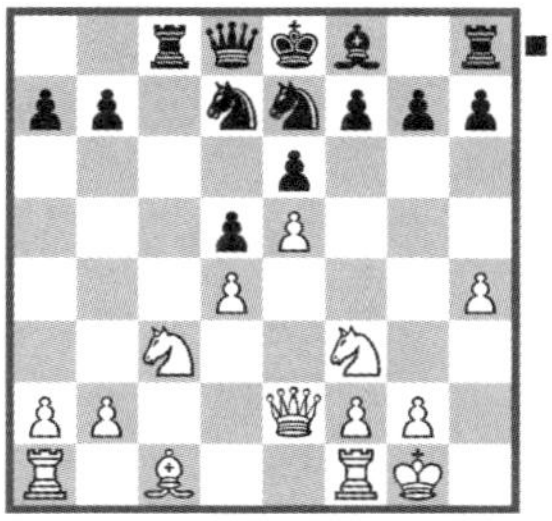

Position after: 12. h4!?

**B1)** 12... ♘f5?! 13. ♗g5 ♗e7 14. ♘b5! [14. ♕d3 Praggnanandhaa – Moussard, London 2019.] 14... a6 15. g4! h6 16. ♗xe7 ♕xe7 17. gxf5 axb5 18. ♖fc1 0-0 19. ♕xb5±

**B2)** 12... ♘c6 13. g3 ♗e7 14. ♔g2 0-0 [14... ♕b6 15. ♗e3 0-0 16. ♖ac1±] 15. ♗f4± The general plan in these types of positions is to play on both sides of the board – Black will always have to be wary of the kingside.

**12... ♘c6**

**A)** 12... ♘f5 13. ♗g5 ♗e7 [13... ♕b6 14. ♖ac1+–] 14. ♗xe7 ♕xe7 15. ♕d3 White has too many threats, as the following variation demonstrates: 15... ♘b6 16. ♘b5 a6 17. g4!

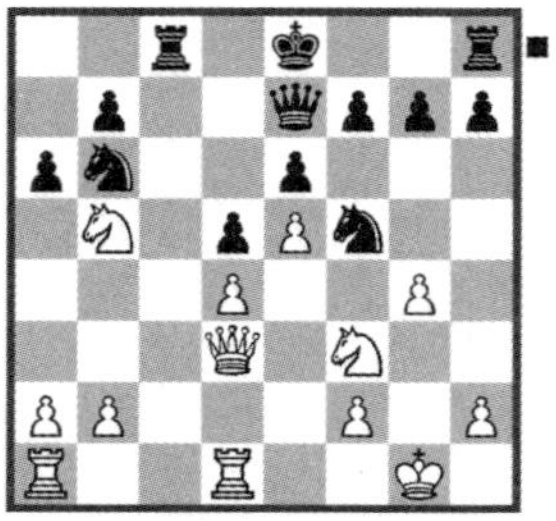

Position after: 17. g4!

17... 0-0 18. ♘a7! ♖a8 19. gxf5 ♖xa7 20. ♔h1→

**B)** 12... h6 13. ♖d3! A really thematic idea – using the rook on the 3rd rank – which is highly effective here.

**B1)** 13... ♘c6 14. ♘e1!

Position after: 14. ♘e1!

14... ♗e7 15. ♕g4 g6 16. ♗d2 ♕b6 17. ♕d1 ♔f8 18. ♘e2 ♔g7 We've played a couple of odd moves, but now it becomes clear why. 19. ♖b3!±

Black will continually find it difficult to deal with our possible threats on both the kingside and queenside.

**B2)** 13... ♘f5 14. a3! Once again restricting the possibility of ...♗b4. 14... ♘b8 15. g4! ♘h4 16. ♘xh4 ♕xh4 17. ♖g3 ♘c6 18. ♗e3 ♕d8 19. f4→

**13. ♘e1!**

Clearing the path for the queen to jump to g4.

**13... ♕b6 14. ♗e3 ♗e7 15. ♖ab1 0-0 16. ♕g4 ♖fd8**

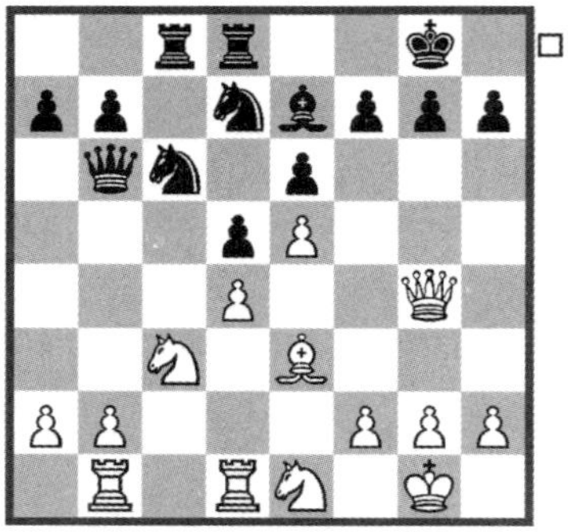

Position after: 16... ♖fd8

**17. h4→**

It feels really difficult for Black to come up with a viable plan. On the other hand, we can happily continue with logical moves such as a2-a3, ♘c2, f2-f4, and h4-h5 to further build up our position.

## c) 6...e6 7.c3 & 7.d4 cxd4 8.♘xd4 --

**1. e4 c5 2. ♘f3 d6 3. ♗b5+ ♗d7 4. ♗xd7+ ♘xd7 5. 0-0**

The logical alternative, 5. c4, would offer Black a few more options such as 5... ♘e5, so it makes more sense to delay this plan.

**5... ♘gf6 6. ♕e2 e6**

Position after: 6... e6

**7. d4**

Given that Black has put their knight on d7 rather than c6, it's an opportune moment to transition to a Maroczy structure.

7. c3!? Even though Black is relatively better equipped to meet the c3-d4 push since they've played ...e7-e6 rather than ...g7-g6, this is still a perfectly viable possibility for White. 7... ♗e7 8. d4

*(see analysis diagram next column)*

Position after: 8. d4

**A)** 8... cxd4 makes no sense, as our knight can happily jump to c3 now. 9. cxd4 d5 The critical option, or else we emerge with a pleasant advantage after 9... 0-0 10.♘c3. 10. e5 ♘e4 11. ♘e1!, threatening to trap Black's knight. 11... ♕b6 12. ♗e3 f6 13. f3 ♘g5 14. ♘d3 0-0 15. ♗f2!± Followed by moves like ♘c3, ♖ac1, ♖fd1, and either f3-f4 or h2-h4. The biggest problem for Black is that their minor pieces are incredibly uncoordinated.

**B)** 8... 0-0! 9. e5 [9. ♖d1 cxd4 10. cxd4 b5!∞ Kovalev – Sarana, Chess.com INT 2022.]

**B1)** 9... dxe5 It feels like White can start dreaming of an edge in this line. 10. dxe5 ♘d5 11. a3! [11. c4 is the obvious choice. 11... ♘b4 12. ♘c3 ♘c6 13. ♖d1 Followed by ♗f4, h2-h4, and potentially ♘e4-d6. The engine still insists on 0.00, but it feels like White is on the more comfortable side of equality.]

11... ♕a5! enabling the d5-knight to re-route to c6. [11... ♘b8 12. c4 ♘b6 13. ♘c3 ♘c6 14. ♖d1 ♕c8 15. ♗f4± Followed by ♘b5-d6.] 12. ♗d2!

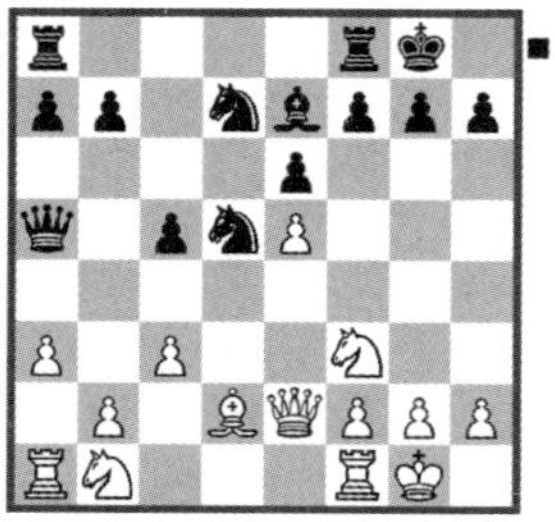

Position after: 12. ♗d2!

12... ♖fd8 [12... c4!? is an interesting pawn sacrifice but I don't see anyone playing this in a practical game. 13. ♕xc4 ♖fc8 14. ♕e2 ♕a6!

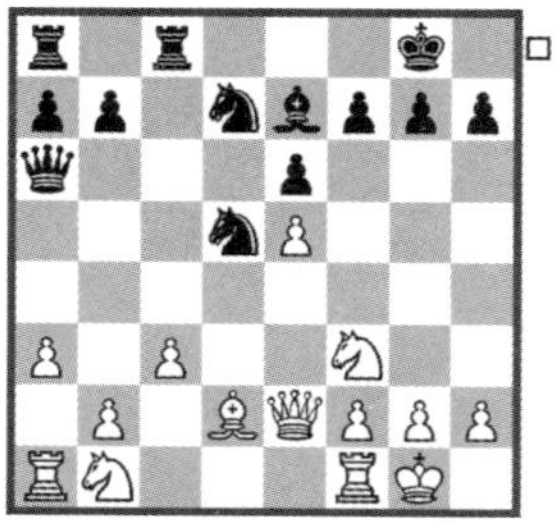

Position after: 14... ♕a6!

15. ♖e1 Black still needs to prove compensation for the pawn.] 13. c4 ♕a6 [13... ♘b4 14. ♘c3 ♘c6 15. ♘d5 Demonstrating the point of 12.♗d2. 15... ♕a4 16. ♘xe7+ ♘xe7 17. ♗g5 ♖e8 18. ♗xe7 ♖xe7 19. ♘g5!±] 14. h4↑ White has a much easier game.

**B2)** 9... ♘e8! 10. ♖d1 cxd4 11. cxd4 ♘c7 12. ♘c3 ♘b6= The game is balanced, but one potentially promising idea for White might be ♕e4-g4 and ♖d3. Meanwhile Black will stick the c7-knight on d5 and attempt to put pressure on the c-file. Regardless, Black will have had to find a couple of accurate moves to reach this position, which is still perfectly playable for both sides.

**7... cxd4 8. ♘xd4**

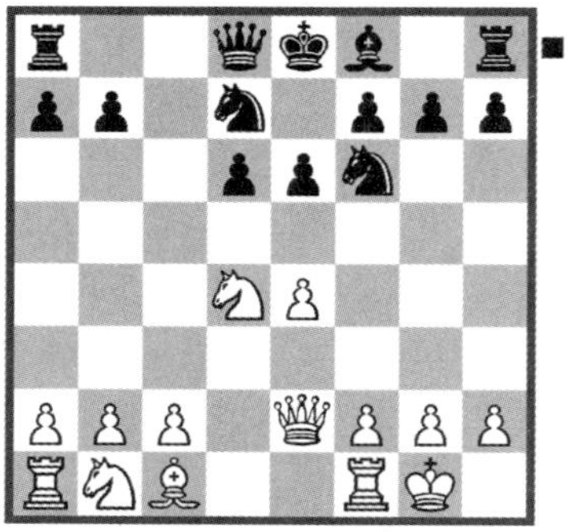

Position after: 8. ♘xd4

Black usually has two possible plans to respond to our Maroczy structure - either fianchettoing the bishop, or playing with ...♗e7. I think generally it's more important focusing on ideas, rather than exact move orders.

**8... a6**

Here we'll examine Black's attempts to fianchetto the dark-squared bishop. In general I don't think we need to know too much about these positions. I think the simplest plan is to put our bishop on b2, and rooks on c1 and d1. The prevailing issue for Black is that the d6-pawn will be a long-term weakness.

**A)** 8... ♖c8 would transpose to any of the other Black alternatives on move 8 after 9. c4.

**B)** 8... d5?! 9. exd5 ♘xd5 10. ♘xe6! fxe6 11. ♕xe6+ ♘e7 12. ♖d1±

**9. c4 ♖c8**

9... g6 This could transpose to 9...♖c8, however I think White has additional options here since Black has basically committed to putting the bishop on g7 already. For example: 10. ♘c3 ♗g7 11. ♘f3!

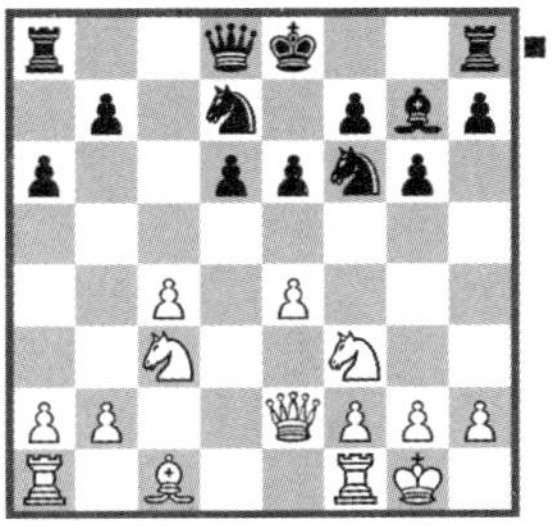

Position after: 11. ♘f3!

11... 0-0 12. ♗f4 ♕c7 13. ♖fd1 ♘e8 14. ♖ac1±

**10. b3**

10. ♘c3 ♕a5! 11. ♗e3 ♗e7 Ideally we'd have our dark-squared bishop on b2 here.

**10... g6 11. ♗b2 ♗g7 12. ♘c3 0-0 13. ♖fd1**

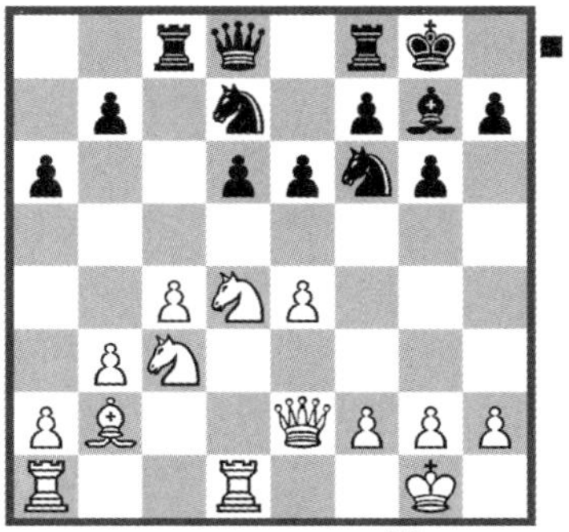

Position after: 13. ♖fd1

**13... ♖e8**

Preparing a ...d6-d5 push.

13... ♕a5 14. ♖ac1± Followed by simple chess, slowly improving our position. Black will always face problems with the d6-pawn, while we continue with moves like h2-h3, ♗a1, ♖c2-d2, etc.

**14. ♖ab1!**

14. ♖ac1 d5 15. e5 ♘h5 16. ♘f3 ♘xe5 17. ♘xe5 ♘f4 18. ♕e3 ♕g5 19. g3 ♗xe5 20. h4 ♕f5∞ The critical point is that gxf4 here isn't possible as the rook on c1 would hang.

**14... d5**

Against other moves, we can consolidate with h2-h3 and ♘f3, before bringing the b-rook to c1.

**15. e5 ♘h5**

Position after: 15... ♘h5

**16. ♘f3 ♘xe5 17. ♘xe5 ♘f4 18. ♕e3 ♕g5 19. g3 ♗xe5 20. h4 ♘h3+ 21. ♔g2 ♕f5**

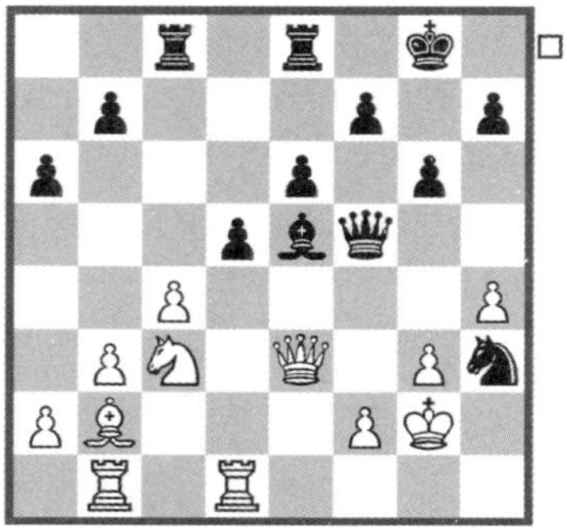

Position after: 21... ♕f5

**22. f3!±**

Most likely followed by ♘e2 or ♕d3. Black will eventually be forced to sacrifice the h3-knight, and never gains anywhere close to full compensation for the piece.

## d) 6...e6 7.c3 & 7.d4 cxd4 8.♘xd4 ♗e7

**1. e4 c5 2. ♘f3 d6 3. ♗b5+ ♗d7 4. ♗xd7+ ♘xd7 5. 0-0 ♘gf6 6. ♕e2 e6 7. d4 cxd4 8. ♘xd4 ♗e7**

Position after: 8... ♗e7

Now that Black has declined to fianchetto the bishop, the simplest way of playing the position is to put the c1-bishop on b2 and go for a kingside attack.

**9. c4 0-0 10. ♘c3**

10. b3?! d5!=

**10... a6**

**A)** 10... ♕a5 This prevents us from playing b2-b3 and ♗b2 but also wastes time for Black, and isn't too concerning for us. 11. ♗d2

*(see analysis diagram next page)*

Position after: 11. ♗d2

11... ♕c7 [11... ♖fc8 12. ♘d5 ♕d8 13. ♘xe7+ ♕xe7 14. b3± Martinez Alcantara – Sarana, Chess.com INT 2022.] 12. b3 a6 13. ♖ad1 ♖ac8 14. ♔h1±

**B)** 10... ♖c8 11. b3 [11. ♗e3 is also logical if we want to keep more pieces on the board.] 11... d5

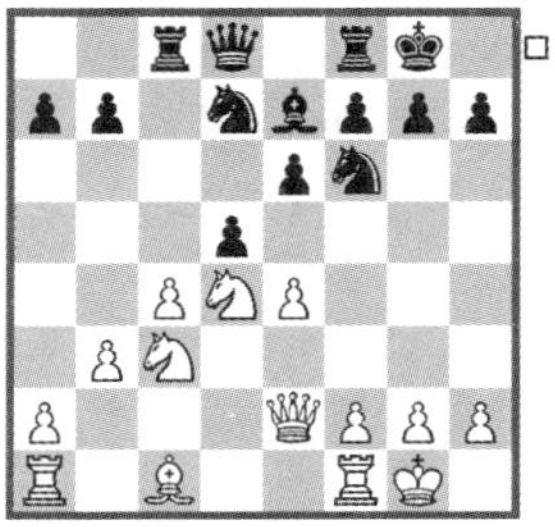
Position after: 11... d5

Black's attempt to equalise, but the resulting endgame still offers us good chances. [11... a6 12. ♗b2 will be very similar to positions after 10...a6.] 12. exd5 exd5 13. ♘xd5 ♘xd5 14. cxd5 ♖e8 15. ♗e3 ♘f6 16. ♘f5 ♕xd5 17. ♘xe7+ ♖xe7 18. ♖fd1 ♕e4 19. ♕d3± Since we have kept both pairs of rooks on the board and have a superior minor-piece, there is a long way to go before Black makes a draw.

**11. b3**

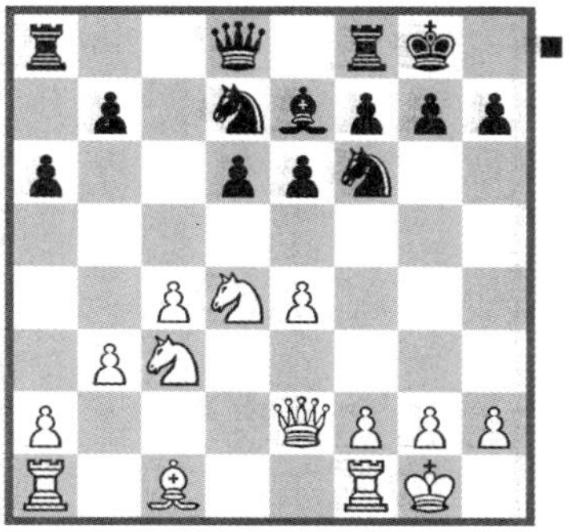
Position after: 11. b3

**11... ♖e8**

11... ♖c8 12. ♗b2 ♕a5 Another attempt by Black to hamper our kingside plans, this time by attempting to trade queens. 13. ♖ad1

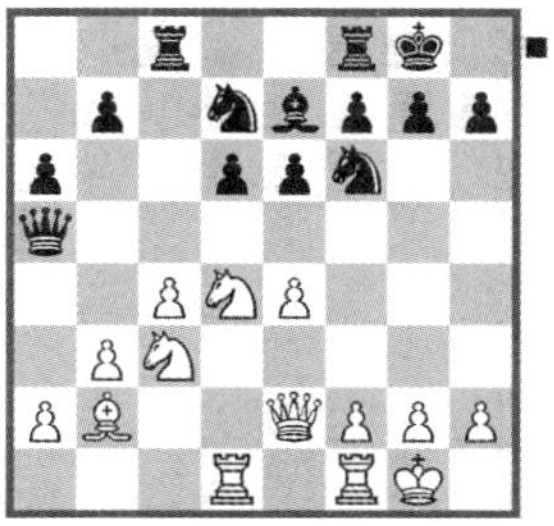
Position after: 13. ♖ad1

Since we're planning a kingside attack, it's logical to leave the f1-rook where it is.

**A)** 13... b5? 14. cxb5 ♖xc3 15. ♕e1+–

**B)** 13... ♕h5 This is completely different from the 8...♕a5 line. 14. ♕xh5! It's also completely fine to keep the queens on the board, but with so many pieces on the board we can continue our kingside attack in the queenless middlegame regardless. 14... ♘xh5 15. g3 ♖fe8 16. f4 ♗f8 17. ♘f3± Followed by e4-e5 with a strong initiative.

**C)** 13... ♖fe8 14. f4!

Position after: 14. f4!

**C1)** 14... b5 leads to several forcing lines, where White is always emerging with an advantage. 15. cxb5! ♖xc3 16. ♕e1 ♘xe4 [16... ♖ec8 17. ♗xc3 ♕xc3 18. ♕xc3 ♖xc3 19. ♖c1+–] 17. ♖f3!

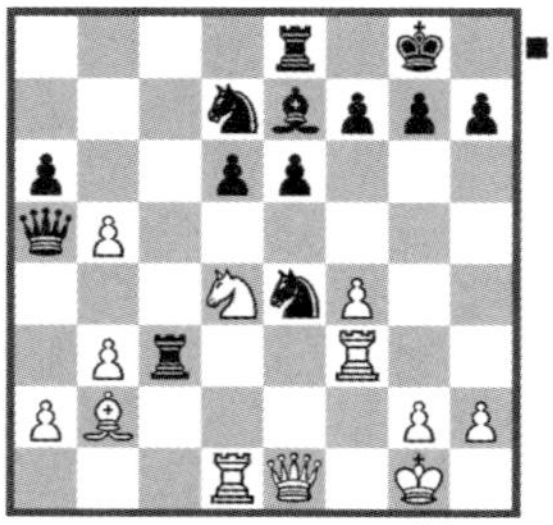

Position after: 17. ♖f3!

17... axb5 [17... e5 18. ♗xc3 ♘xc3 19. ♕xc3 ♕xc3 20. ♖xc3 exd4 21. ♖c7 ♘c5 22. b6 ♗d8 23. ♖c6±; 17... ♖ec8 18. ♕xe4 ♖3c7 19. ♘c6 ♕b6+ 20. ♗d4 ♘c5 21. ♘xe7+ ♖xe7 22. bxa6! ♕xa6 23. ♕c2±] 18. ♗xc3 ♘xc3 19. ♖xc3 d5 20. ♖c2!

Position after: 20. ♖c2!

Black has some compensation for the exchange, but after a few accurate moves the advantage should become clearer. The most important line follows: 20... ♗b4 21. ♕f2 ♗c5 22. ♖dc1! ♕b6 23. ♖xc5 ♘xc5 24. ♘e2 ♘d7 25. ♕xb6 ♘xb6 26. ♖c5±

**C2)** 14... ♗f8 15. g4! h6 16. ♔h1→ I don't think it's important to go any deeper here. We have three different pawn pushes to choose from depending on Black's moves. Otherwise, we can continue to prepare the attack with moves like ♖g1 and ♕f2.

**C3)** 14... ♕h5 15. ♕xh5! ♘xh5 16. g3 ♘hf6 17. ♖fe1± Followed by logical moves like ♖e2, ♔g2, and ♘f3. The d6-pawn is a serious weakness and our long-term target, but another interesting plan would be to advance the kingside pawns.

**12. ♗b2 ♕c7**

12... ♗f8 is the most common move but it can be well met by logical play. 13. ♖ad1 ♕a5 14. f4±.

**13. ♖ad1 ♗f8**

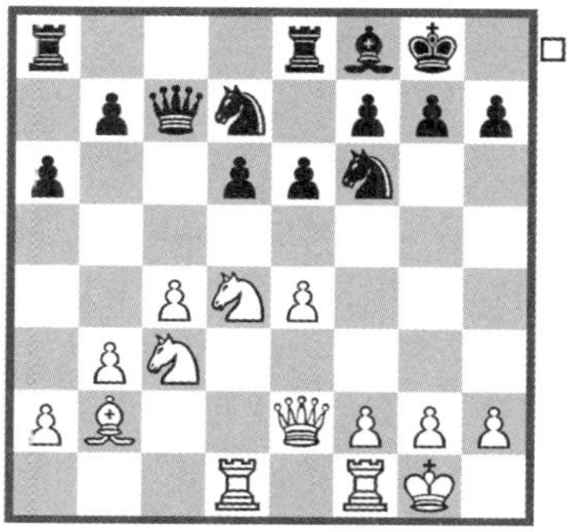

Position after: 13... ♗f8

**14. ♖fe1!?**

An important preparatory move. The point is to play ♔h1 before pushing f2-f4, whilst ensuring that ...d6-d5 can be met with ...e6-e5.

**A)** 14. ♔h1 d5!↑

**B)** 14. f4 is the most common move, but Black gains interesting counterplay with 14... b5! 15. cxb5 e5∞.

**14... ♖ad8**

**A)** 14... ♖ac8 15. ♔h1 ♘c5 16. f4±

**B)** 14... ♘e5 15. f4 ♘c6 16. ♔h1 ♘xd4 17. ♖xd4 e5 18. ♖dd1 exf4 19. ♖f1±

**15. ♔h1 g6 16. f4 ♗g7**

Position after: 16... ♗g7

**17. ♕f3±**

Now that Black has put their bishop on g7, one idea is to continue with ♘de2/♘c2 and ♗a3. Eventually we'll choose the right moment to commit to g2-g4, but we definitely don't need to rush with this plan.

## e) 6...e6 7.c3 & 7.d4 cxd4 8.♘xd4 ♕a5

**1. e4 c5 2. ♘f3 d6 3. ♗b5+ ♗d7 4. ♗xd7+ ♘xd7 5. 0-0 ♘gf6 6. ♕e2 e6 7. d4 cxd4 8. ♘xd4 ♕a5!**

This has only been played eight times, but I think it's Black's best option. The point is that the queen will switch over to h5, where it stands really well in assisting with counterplay.

**9. c4 ♖c8**

9... ♕e5 It's too risky to go pawn-hunting here. 10. ♗e3!

Position after: 10. ♗e3!

10... a6 [10... ♘xe4? 11. ♘b5±; 10... ♕xe4? 11. ♘c3 ♕e5 12. ♘db5±] 11. f3 The queen will now find herself completely misplaced. 11... ♗e7 12. ♘c3 0-0 13. g4!±

**10. ♖d1**

10. b3!? I chose to sacrifice a pawn when I encountered this line over the board. It's an interesting option as Black has to play carefully in order to maintain the balance. 10... ♕e5 11. ♗e3

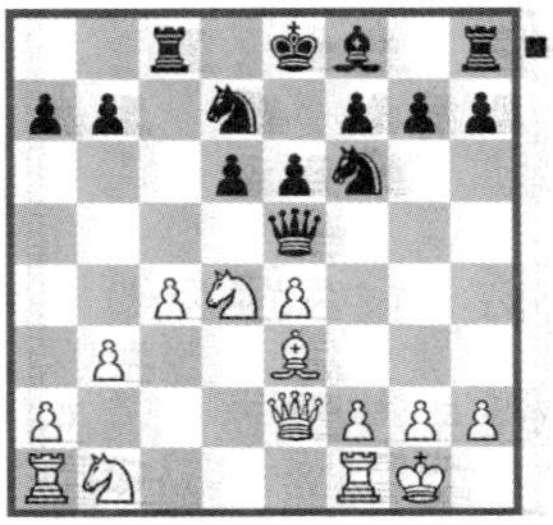

Position after: 11. ♗e3

11... ♕xe4 [11... ♘xe4 12. f4 ♕a5 13. ♘d2! ♘xd2 14. ♗xd2 ♕b6 15. ♗e3 d5 16. cxd5 ♗c5 17. dxe6 fxe6 18. ♖ad1±] 12. ♘c3

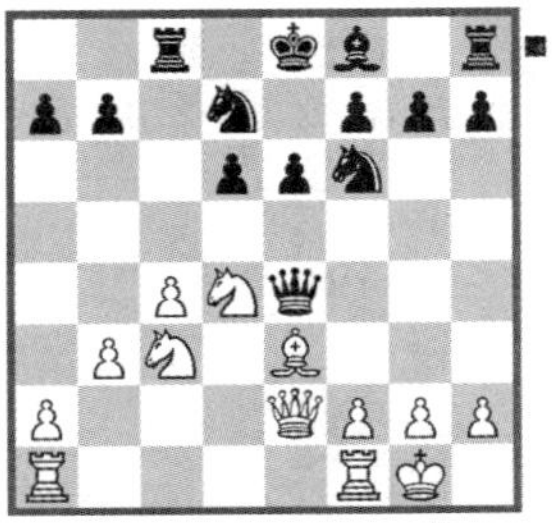

Position after: 12. ♘c3

**A)** 12... ♕e5 also looks logical. 13. ♖ac1 a6 [13... ♗e7 14. ♕f3 ♖b8 15. ♘db5 a6 16. ♗f4 ♕c5 17. ♘a4 ♘e5 18. ♕e2 ♕c6 19. ♘xd6+ ♗xd6 20. ♗xe5±] 14. g4!? Capitalising on Black's lack of development. The immediate threat is f2-f4 and g4-g5, when Black is getting overwhelmed by our pawn storm.

**A1)** 14... g5!? is also suggested by Stockfish, but after 15. b4! ♘e4 16. ♘xe4 ♕xe4 17. f3 ♕e5 18. ♕d2 ♗g7 19. ♘b3⩱ it feels like we have very real compensation. At the very least, we can repeat with ♗d4-e3.

**A2)** 14... h6? 15. f4 ♕a5 16. g5+– Next comes g5-g6, and Black is completely lost.

**A3)** 14... ♘e4 The most human reaction. 15. ♘d5!

Position after: 15. ♘d5!

15... exd5 16. f4 ♕f6 [16... ♕e7 17. ♘f5 followed by ♗d4 looks way too dangerous for Black.] 17. cxd5 ♔d8 18. ♖xc8+ ♔xc8 19. b4→ There's no point analysing this position in more depth – I know which side I'd rather be playing.

**B)** 12... ♕g6 This might be the safest move – Black will follow up with ...d6-d5 regardless of what we play. 13. ♖ad1 d5 14. ♗f4!?

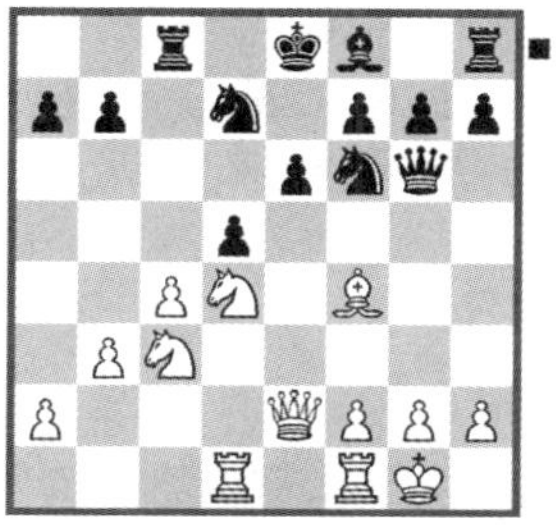

Position after: 14. ♗f4!?

14... ♕h5! [14... dxc4? 15. ♘xe6 fxe6 16. ♕xe6+ ♗e7 17. ♘b5→] 15. ♘xd5 ♕xe2 16. ♘xf6+ ♘xf6 17. ♘xe2=

**C)** 12... ♕g4

**C1)** 13. f3 looks like it might be most accurate: 13... ♕g6 [13... ♕h5 14. g4! ♕a5 15. ♖ac1↑] 14. ♖ad1 a6 15. f4 ♕h5 16. ♕xh5 ♘xh5 17. g4 ♘hf6 18. g5 ♘h5 19. f5⩱ White has great compensation for the pawn.

**C2)** 13. ♕d2 was my choice when I faced this over the board. 13... ♗e7?! [13... a6 was necessary, after which 14. ♖ae1 ♗e7 15. f4⩱ followed by f4-f5 looks very tricky for Black to deal with.] 14. ♘db5!

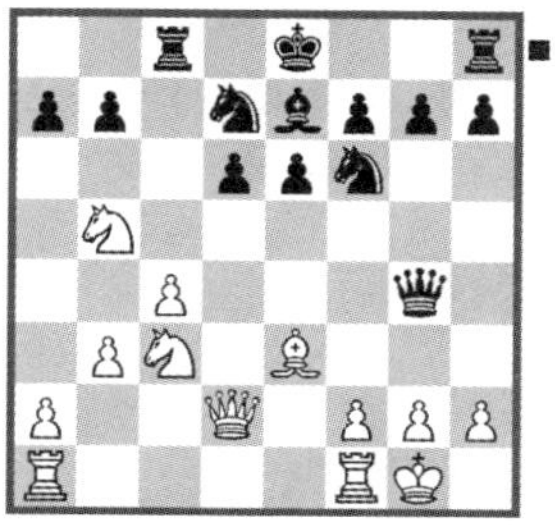

Position after: 14. ♘db5!

14... 0-0 15. ♘xa7 ♖a8 16. ♘ab5± I was already comfortably better in Haria – Roberson, Newcastle on Tyne 2021.

**10... a6**

10... ♕h5?! was played Xiong – Ter Sahakyan, Riga 2021, but White didn't capitalise on Black's failure to play 10...a6. 11. ♕xh5! ♘xh5 12. ♘b5 ♖xc4 13. ♘xa7!

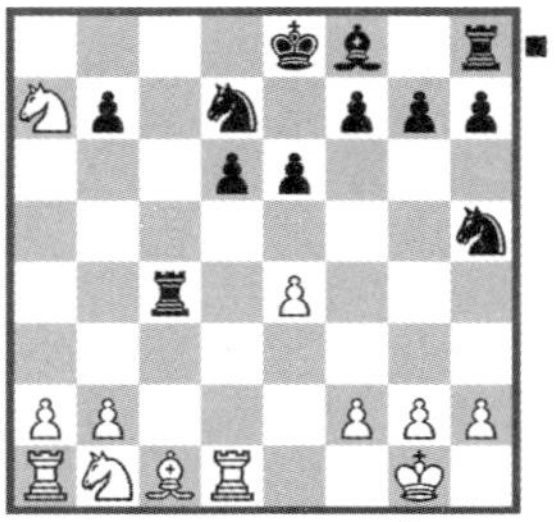

Position after: 13. ♘xa7!

13... ♖xe4 [13... ♗e7 14. ♗e3!± followed by ♘d2 gives White an edge.] 14. ♘c3 ♖c4 15. ♘cb5!↑ Followed by ♗e3, b2-b3, and ♖c1. We also have the option to take on d6 if Black lets us, although it probably makes more sense to keep developing and claim the c-file regardless.

**11. b3 ♗e7**

11... ♕h5 12. f3 ♗e7 13. ♗b2 transposes to 11...♗e7.

**12. ♗b2 ♕h5**

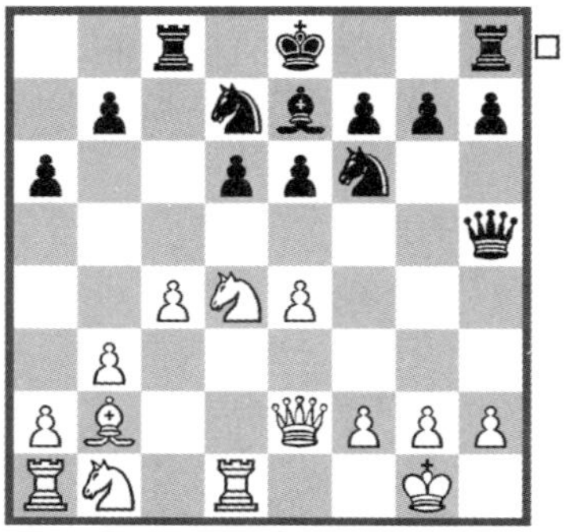

Position after: 12... ♕h5

Here White has to decide whether to exchange queens or not. I think the evaluation in both lines is the same: White will have a very small edge, but Black is extremely solid.

**13. f3**

13. ♕xh5 ♘xh5 14. ♘e2 ♘hf6 15. ♘bc3 To be honest I don't see any issues for Black here. In both correspondence games which have reached this position, Black has opted for a plan involving pushing the kingside pawns. 15... g5! 16. h3 h5∞ Biedermann – Jonsson, ICCF email 2019. Even though I said that Black doesn't have any problems objectively, it doesn't mean that this isn't playable for White. An obvious plan here would be f2-f3, ♔f2, doubling the rooks on the d-file, and manoeuvring the e2-knight to e3. In a practical game it feels like White is only playing for two results, although one of those results is obviously way more likely than the other. The benefit of this line is that compared to 13. f3, Black doesn't have an obvious ...d6-d5 equaliser.

**13... 0-0 14. ♘c3**

Black's plan is now to re-route the d7-knight to g6.

**14... ♘e5**

14... ♖fe8 15. ♖ac1 ♘f8 16. ♗a3 ♘g6 transposes to 14...♘e5.

**15. ♖ac1**

We're still making logical developing moves but as the following variations will show, it's pretty difficult to stop Black equalising with ...d6-d5 at the right moment.

15. f4 is possible but Black is solid enough after 15... ♕xe2 16. ♘dxe2 ♘ed7 17. ♗a3 ♘c5=.

**15... ♖fe8**

Position after: 15... ♖fe8

**16. ♗a3**

16. ♕f1!? looks a bit outlandish but it's an interesting way to play against the ...d6-d5 break. 16... ♘g6 17. ♔h1 d5 18. g4! ♕h4 19. exd5∞ This is a line for the reader to investigate further – Black's plan of ... ♗d6-f4 feels like enough compensation for the pawn.

**16... ♘g6 17. ♕d2 d5!**

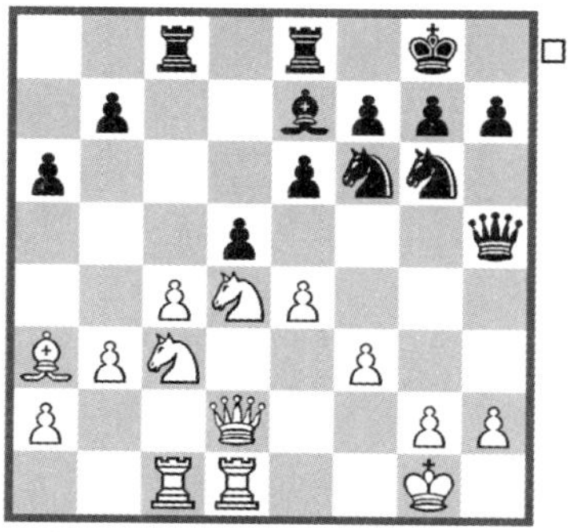

Position after: 17... d5!

**18. ♗xe7 ♘xe7 19. cxd5 exd5 20. exd5 ♘exd5=**

## Conclusion to Chapter 4

One of the reasons why this book was delayed was the inability to find anything tangible against 8... ♕a5. Naturally we can't hope for an advantage everywhere with 3.♗b5+, but this line in particular seems to completely neutralise our efforts. However the availability of the alternatives 7.c3, 10.b3, and 13. ♕xh5 makes me confident that we have enough variety to choose from against this line.

# 4...♕xd7

1.e4 c5 2.♘f3 d6 3.♗b5+ ♗d7

4.♗xd7 ♕xd7

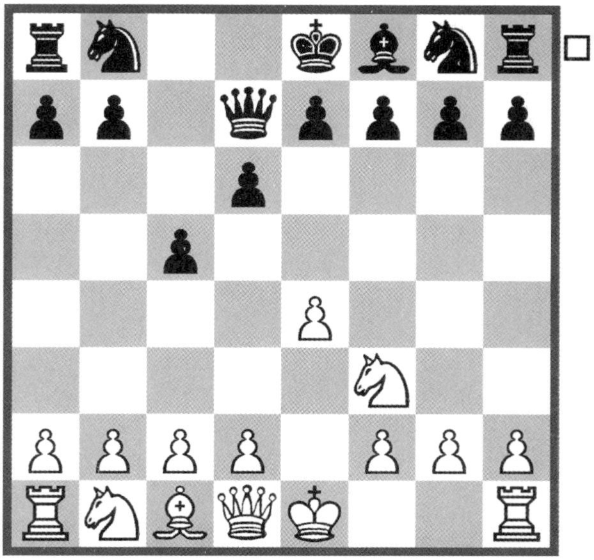

# Chapter Guide

## Chapter 5 – 4...♕xd7

1.e4 c5 2.♘f3 d6 3.♗b5+ ♗d7 4.♗xd7 ♕xd7

## a) 5.c4 --

**1. e4 c5 2. ♘f3 d6 3. ♗b5+ ♗d7 4. ♗xd7+ ♕xd7 5. c4**

Playing for a Maroczy structure has generally been viewed as White's best attempt to try and gain an advantage out of the opening in this line.

**5... ♘c6**

5... ♕g4?! This move is even worse than after 5... ♘c6, as we're able to castle and gain great compensation for the pawn. 6. 0-0 ♕xe4 7. d4

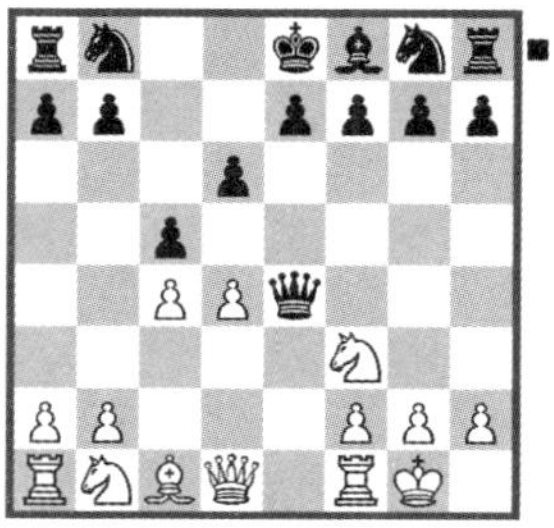

Position after: 7. d4

**A)** 7... cxd4 8. ♘xd4 ♘c6 [8... ♘f6 9. ♘c3 ♕g4 10. ♕a4+ ♕d7 11. ♘db5 ♘c6 12. ♖e1+– Next move will be ♗g5 or ♘d5 with overwhelming threats.] 9. ♘b5 0-0-0 [9... ♖c8 10. ♖e1+–] 10. ♗e3 ♔b8 11. ♘d2+– Our queenside attack will be unstoppable.

**B)** 7... ♕c6 8. ♘c3 ♘d7 9. ♖e1 ♘gf6 10. ♗f4 cxd4 11. ♘b5 e5 12. ♘fxd4 ♕b6 13. ♘f5+–

**6. d4 ♕g4?!**

This has been played many times, but engines prove that the attempt to grab a pawn is dubious.

**A)** 6... cxd4 7. ♘xd4 g6 8. ♘c3 ♗g7 9. ♗e3 ♘f6 will transpose to our mainline.

**B)** 6... e5 is also suggested by the engine, but White is definitely slightly better in the following line: 7. d5 ♘d4 8. 0-0 ♘f6 9. ♕d3 ♗e7 10. ♘c3 0-0 11. a4!± Black can't concede the b5-square by playing 11. ..a5, so we can continue to push our a-pawn followed by a b2-b4 break at the right moment.

**7. d5! ♕xe4+ 8. ♗e3 ♘d4 9. ♕a4+**

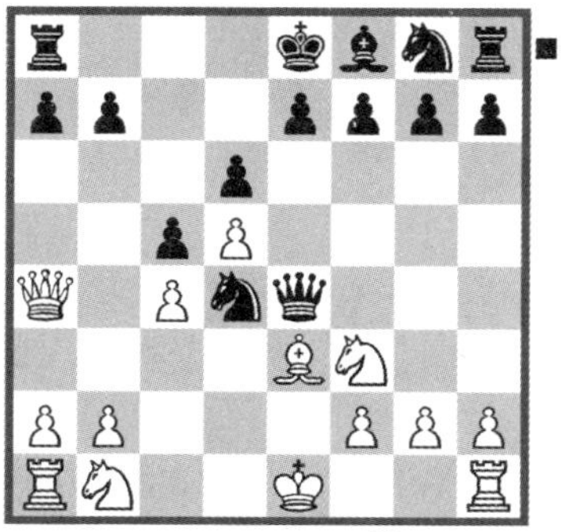

Position after: 9. ♕a4+

**9... b5**

9... ♔d8 10. ♘bd2 ♘c2+ 11. ♔e2 ♕g6 12. b4!

Position after: 12. b4!

**A)** 12... ♘xe3 13. bxc5! dxc5 [13... ♘f5 14. ♖hb1+–] 14. fxe3 ♕xg2+ 15. ♔d3 ♕g6+ 16. e4+– White's lead in development will prove to be decisive.

**B)** 12... ♘xa1 13. bxc5 ♘c2 14. ♖b1+–

**C)** 12... ♘xb4 13. ♖hb1!

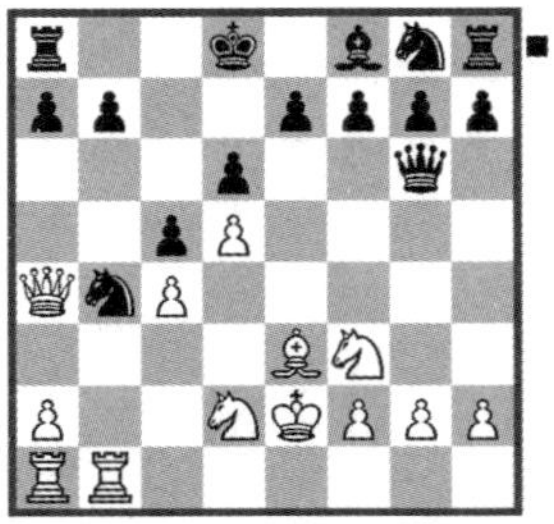

Position after: 13. ♖hb1!

13... ♘f6 [13... ♕xg2 14. a3+–] 14. ♖xb4! cxb4 15. ♕a5+ ♔c8 16. ♖c1 We can basically treat this as a position where we've castled on opposite sides to Black - and clearly our attack is much faster than theirs. 16... ♘d7 17. ♕xb4→

**10. ♕a6 ♘c2+**

10... ♖d8 11. ♘c3 ♘xf3+ 12. gxf3 ♕xf3 13. ♕c6+ ♖d7 14. ♘xb5! e6 15. ♖g1±

**11. ♔d2**

Previously 11. ♔d1 was thought to be the best move, but further analysis shows that the king belongs on d2 for some reason.

**11... ♕d3+ 12. ♔c1**

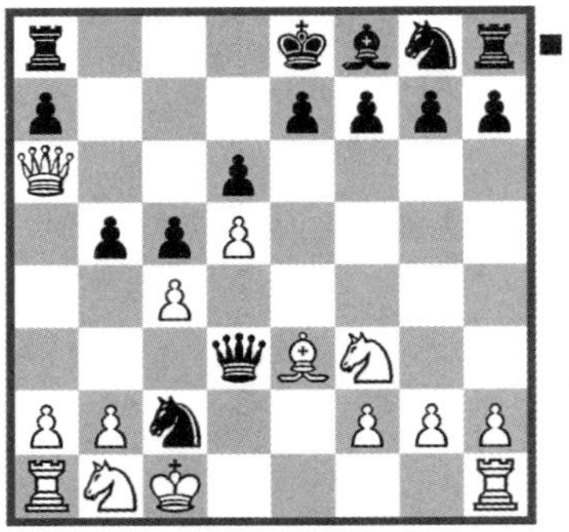

Position after: 12. ♔c1

**12... ♖b8**

12... ♖d8 13. ♖d1 ♕g6 14. ♘h4 ♕e4 15. ♕c6+ ♖d7 16. ♘c3+–

**13. ♕xa7 ♖d8 14. ♖d1 ♕f5 15. ♘h4 ♕g4 16. ♔xc2 ♕e4+ 17. ♔c1 ♕xc4+ 18. ♘c3 ♕xh4**

*(see diagram next page)*

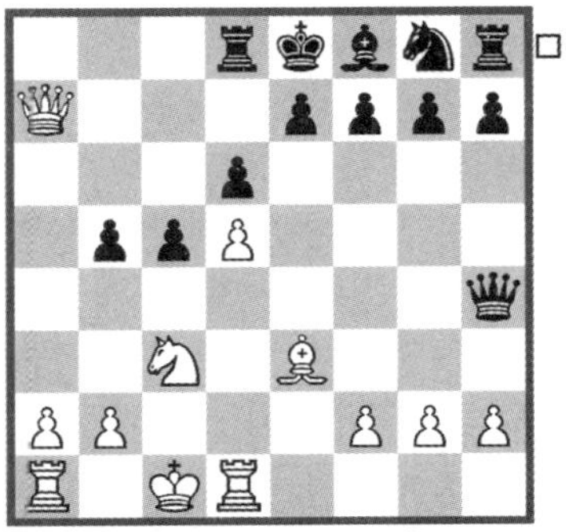

Position after: 18... ♕xh4

**19. ♕b7±**

At the end of a forcing line, White has the better chances. The b5-pawn will fall, and Black's king looks weaker than ours.

## b) 5.c4 e5 6.♘c3 ♘c6 7.0-0 ♗e7

**1. e4 c5 2. ♘f3 d6 3. ♗b5+ ♗d7 4. ♗xd7+ ♕xd7 5. c4 e5!?**

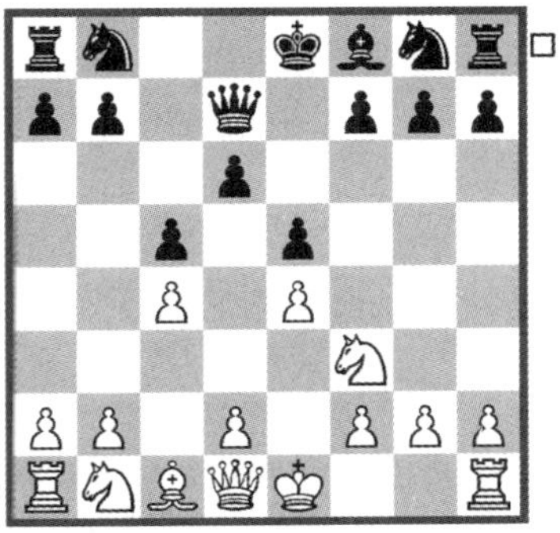

Position after: 5... e5!?

This is quite a solid setup for Black, but is mostly only used in blitz or rapid games. The main point is obvious – Black prevents us from establishing our Marcozy bind. The other idea is to break in the centre with ...f7-f5 at the right moment. On the other hand, it's clear that we already have a slight positional advantage, having exchanged off the light-squared bishops. The variations will demonstrate that our main idea is to achieve a b2-b4 break, after moves such as d2-d3, ♘c3, ♘d5, ♗d2, etc.

**6. ♘c3 ♘c6 7. 0-0 ♗e7!?**

An interesting idea which has been used by Carlsen. Black puts the bishop on d8 and develops the g8-knight to e7. The benefit of the bishop sitting on d8 is that it's arguably better placed to meet our forthcoming queenside expansion.

It's too early for the immediate 7... f5?! on account of 8. exf5 ♕xf5 9. ♖e1 ♗e7 10. ♘d5 ♕d7 11. b4!

Position after: 11. b4!

11... ♘xb4 12. ♘xb4 cxb4 13. d4±

**8. a3**

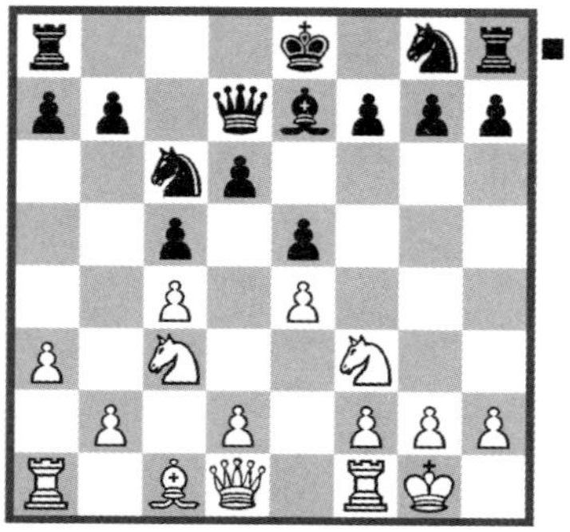

Position after: 8. a3

**8... ♗d8**

**A)** 8... f5 9. exf5 ♕xf5 10. d3 ♘f6 11. ♗g5!

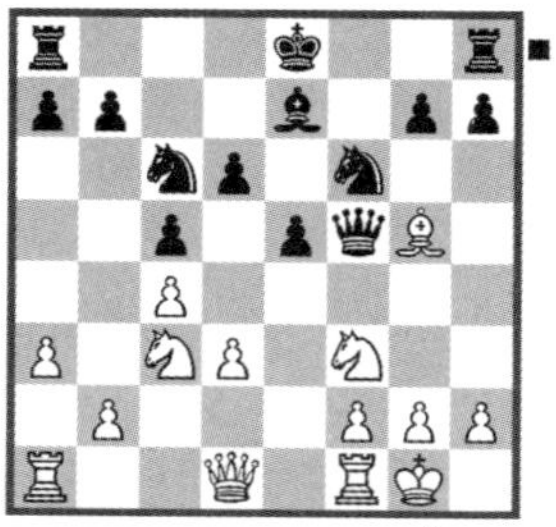

Position after: 11. ♗g5!

One example of how we want to meet the ...f7-f5 break. By exchanging on f6, we can then plant a knight on d5 and hold a nice positional edge. 11... 0-0 12. ♗xf6 ♗xf6 13. ♕e2±

**B)** 8... a5 This was played against me by Vadim Zvjaginsev via a different move-order. Here I don't think it makes sense to continue trying to push b2-b4, as Black can always capture with the c-pawn and advance ...a5-a4. Instead we can be happy that Black has weakened the b5-square, and switch our play over to the kingside. 9. d3 ♗d8 10. ♘e1!

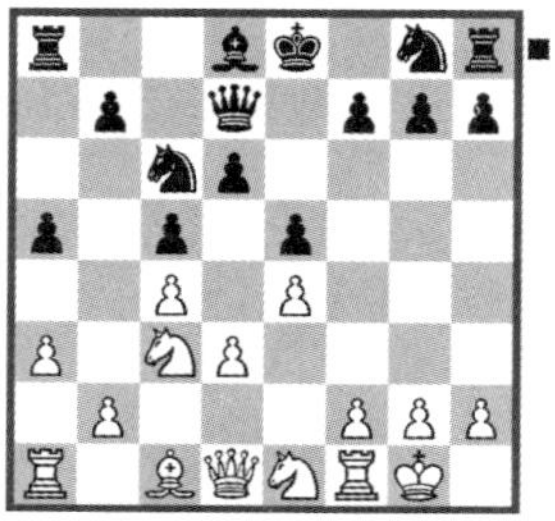

Position after: 10. ♘e1!

10... ♘ge7 11. f4± Our play on the kingside is looking promising already.

**9. b4! ♘ge7**

**A)** 9... cxb4? It's too risky for Black to accept the pawn sacrifice. 10. axb4 ♘xb4 11. ♗a3 ♘c6 12. d4+–

**B)** 9... b6 As we'll encounter throughout this sub-chapter, whenever Black elects to defend their pawn chain with ...b7-b6, we should push b4-b5 and use the b6-pawn as a hook when advancing our a-pawn. 10. d3 ♘ge7 11. b5 ♘d4 12. ♗g5! Immediately threatening to capture on e7. We're also happy to exchange dark-squared bishops, as this will further facilitate our a4-a5 advance.

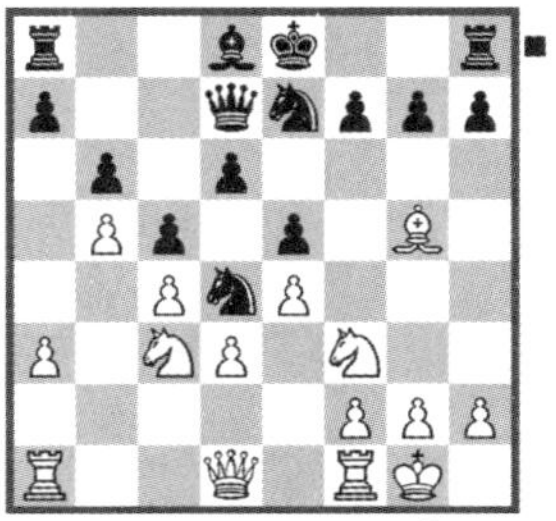

Position after: 12. ♗g5!

12... f6 13. ♗e3 0-0 [13... ♕g4 14. ♗xd4 cxd4 15. ♘d5±] 14. ♗xd4 cxd4 15. ♘a2± The problem for Black, as in many of these variations, is that they'll struggle to create an attack without creating light-squared weaknesses at some point. It's also useful that we always have the option to capture on d4.

**10. ♖b1 0-0 11. d3**

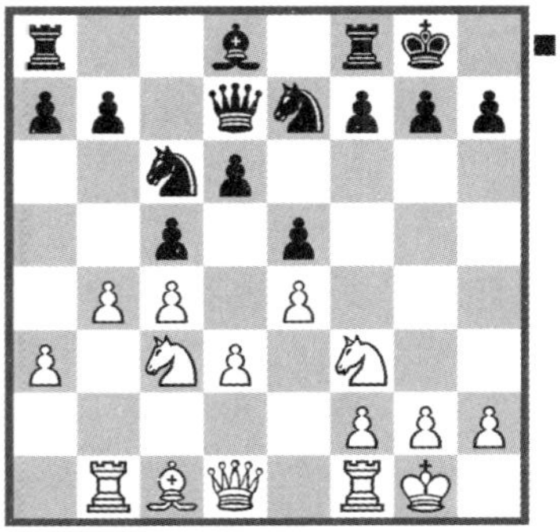

Position after: 11. d3

**11... f5**

11... b6 12. ♗g5 f6 13. ♗e3 f5 14. exf5 ♘xf5 15. ♘d2± with the idea of ♕g4.

**12. exf5 ♘xf5 13. ♕e2 ♗b6**

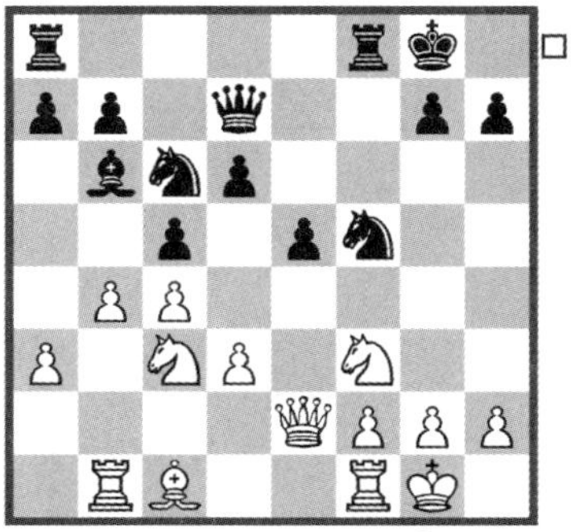

Position after: 13... ♗b6

**14. ♕e4±**

White has achieved a very pleasant position. We can continue with moves like ♗e3 and ♘d5.

## c) 5.c4 e5 6.♘c3 ♘c6 7.0-0 g6

**1. e4 c5 2. ♘f3 d6 3. ♗b5+ ♗d7 4. ♗xd7+ ♕xd7 5. c4 e5!? 6. ♘c3 ♘c6 7. 0-0 g6**

*(see diagram next page)*

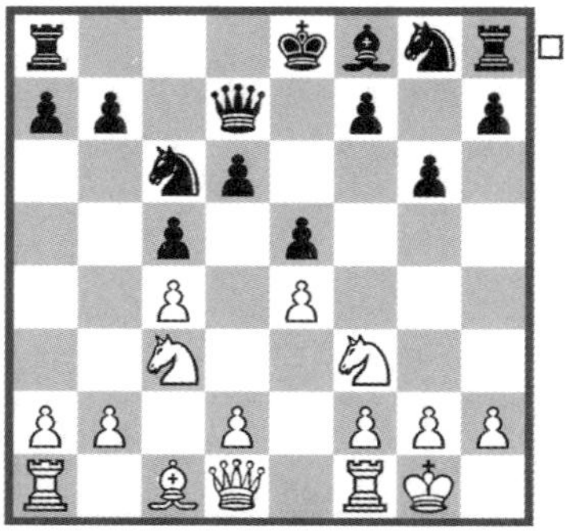

Position after: 7... g6

**8. a3 ♗g7**

8... a5? is too slow - we can just go for the b2-b4 break anyway, and Black will be in big trouble 9. ♘d5 ♖a6 10. ♖b1±

**9. b4**

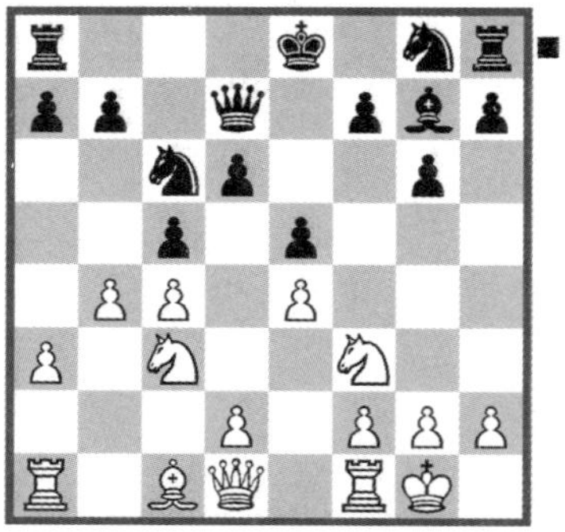

Position after: 9. b4

**9... ♘ge7**

**A)** 9... cxb4? 10. axb4 ♘xb4 11. ♗a3 ♘c6 12. ♘b5 ♗f8 13. d4+–

**B)** 9... b6 10. b5 Typically, we'll use the b6-pawn as a hook to advance a4-a5. 10... ♘d4 11. a4 ♘e7 12. d3 0-0 13. a5 bxa5 14. ♖xa5 a6 This variation is an example of how the game may continue. 15. bxa6 ♘dc6 16. ♖a4 ♘b4 17. ♗g5!

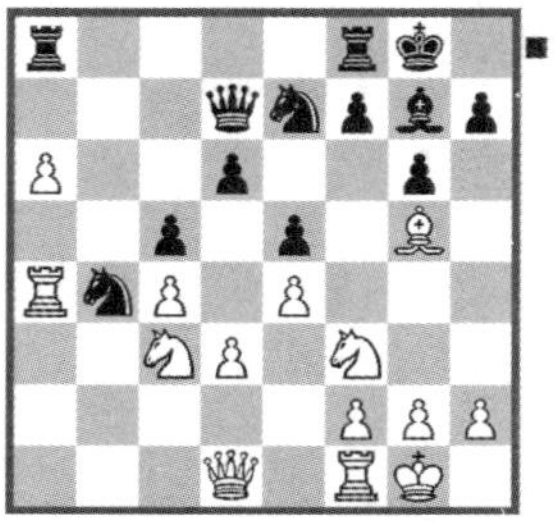

Position after: 17. ♗g5!

17... ♘ec6 [17... ♖xa6 18. ♖xa6 ♘xa6 19. ♗xe7 ♕xe7 20. ♘d5±] 18. h4! Whilst Black wastes time trying to capture the a6-pawn under the most ideal circumstances, we can set about trying to create a weakness on the kingside. 18... ♖xa6 19. ♖xa6 ♘xa6 20. h5±

**10. bxc5 dxc5 11. d3 0-0 12. ♘d5**

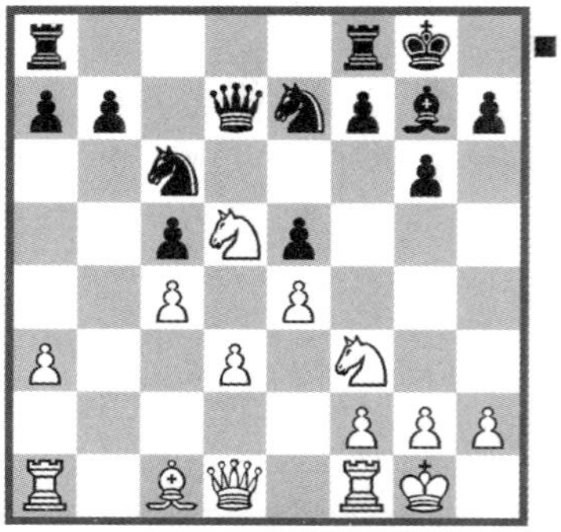

Position after: 12. ♘d5

**12... f5**

The big challenge for Black is trying to create an attack whilst also trying to minimise the extent of the existing light-squared weaknesses it will exacerbate.

**A)** 12... ♘d4?! 13. ♘xd4 exd4 14. a4± White has a superior pawn structure.

**B)** 12... h6 13. a4! The following variation is just one example of how we might continue. 13... b6 14. ♗b2 f5 15. ♖e1 ♖ae8 16. a5!

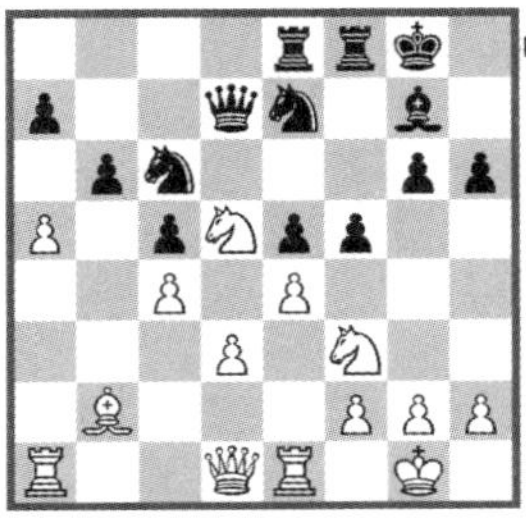

Position after: 16. a5!

16... fxe4 17. dxe4 ♘xd5 18. exd5 ♘xa5 19. ♘d2± Black's knight is completely ostracised.

**C)** 12... ♘xd5 13. cxd5 ♘d4 [13... ♘e7 14. ♗e3 b6 15. ♘d2 ♘c8 16. ♘c4 ♘d6 17. a4+– Black is positionally lost - there is no kingside attack, and we can gradually begin to prepare the a4-a5 queenside break.] 14. ♘xd4 cxd4 15. ♕b3 ♖fc8 16. ♗d2± Followed by pushing the a-pawn, perhaps in conjunction with f2-f4.

**13. a4!**

Logically we should play on the queenside.

**13... ♘xd5**

**A)** 13... f4?! 14. ♗a3 b6 15. ♗b2± Followed by ♗c3 and a4-a5.

**B)** 13... fxe4 14. dxe4 ♘d4 15. ♘xd4 exd4 16. ♕d3

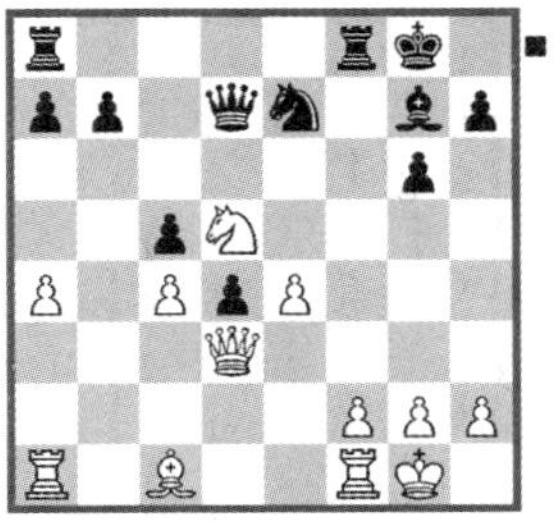

Position after: 16. ♕d3

16... ♘xd5 [16... ♘c6 17. a5 ♘e5 18. ♕b3±] 17. cxd5± It feels like our central pawns have more potential than Black's d- and c-pawns.

**C)** 13... ♖ae8 14. ♗g5!

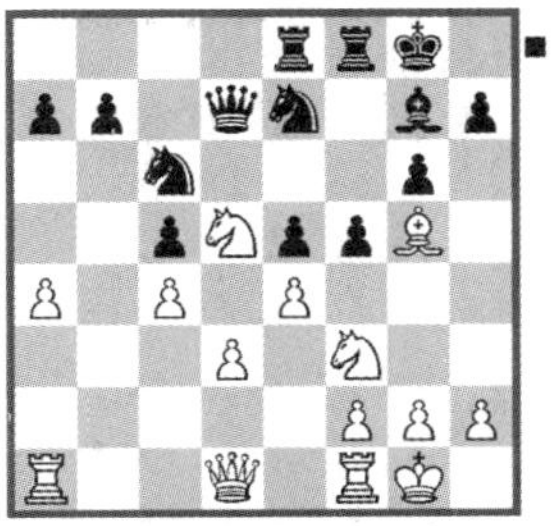

Position after: 14. ♗g5!

Taking the opportunity to exchange our dark-squared bishop for Black's e7-knight. 14... ♘xd5 15. cxd5 ♘d4 16. ♘d2!±

**14. cxd5 ♘d4 15. ♘xd4 exd4**

*(see diagram next page)*

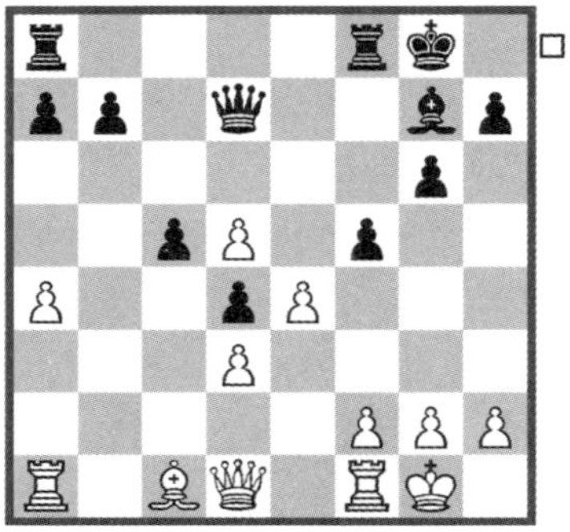

Position after: 15... exd4

**16. ♕b3±**

With a comfortable edge for White.

## d) 5.c4 ♘f6 6.♘c3 g6 7.d4 cxd4 8.♘xd4 ♗g7 9.f3 ♕c7

**1. e4 c5 2. ♘f3 d6 3. ♗b5+ ♗d7 4. ♗xd7+ ♕xd7 5. c4 ♘f6**

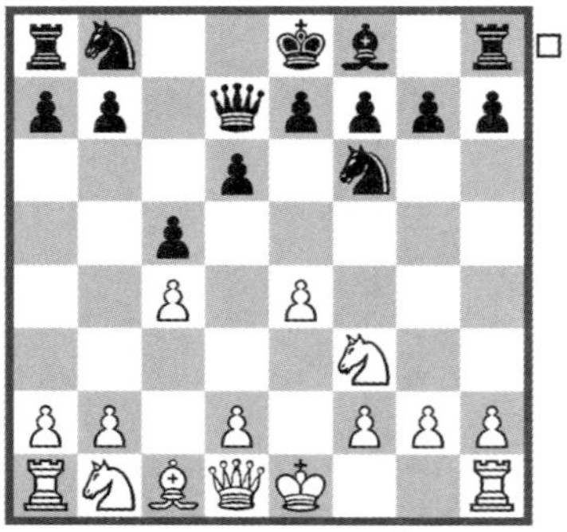

Position after: 5... ♘f6

**6. ♘c3 g6**

6... e6 Directly playing for ...e7-e6 and ...d6-d5 isn't particularly effective, and we should achieve a comfortable position with ease. 7. 0-0 ♗e7 8. d4 cxd4 9. ♘xd4 0-0 10. ♕e2

*(see diagram opposite column*

Position after: 10. ♕e2

10... ♘c6 [10... d5?! 11. cxd5 exd5 12. e5±] 11. ♗e3 The problem with Black's approach is that without a fianchettoed bishop, they are not imposing any constraints on our development. For example if Black had a bishop on g7, they would probably be able to play ...♘xe4 after we played ♕e2. But since instead we can develop freely, we should go immediately for ♖ad1 and f2-f4.

**A)** 11... d5 The immediate central break doesn't achieve equality. 12. cxd5 exd5 13. ♘xc6

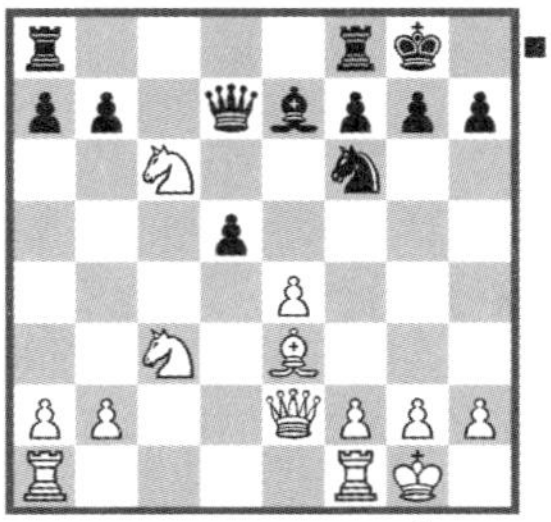

Position after: 13. ♘xc6

13... bxc6 [13... ♕xc6 14. e5 ♘e4 15. ♘b5 a6 16. ♘d4±] 14. ♖ad1± White has an easy advantage.

**B)** 11... ♖fe8 12. ♖ad1 ♖ad8 13. f4± Black's play seems pretty reactionary and we can choose the right moment to capture on c6 and play either e4-e5 or f4-f5. Another attacking possibility that seems strong is the immediate g2-g4.

**C)** 11... ♖fd8 12. ♖ad1 ♖ac8 13. f4 ♕c7 14. b3 a6 15. ♔h1 ♘d7 In Rublevsky – Klimov, Krasnoyarsk 2003, the best way to exploit Black's failure to fianchetto his dark-squared bishop was to play the immediate 16. f5!±.

**7. d4 cxd4 8. ♘xd4**

There have been many different setups attempted by White from this position, and I've experimented with ♘de2, f2-f3 and ♗g5. However, I think the setup which causes Black the greatest practical problems is with f2-f3, ♗e3 and ♖c1. Our ultimate aim should be to contain Black's breaks, and wait for the right moment to trade pieces or achieve a central or kingside pawn break.

**8... ♗g7**

8... ♕g4 The final opportunity for Black to play this move, but once again we retain an advantage with accurate play. 9. ♕a4+!

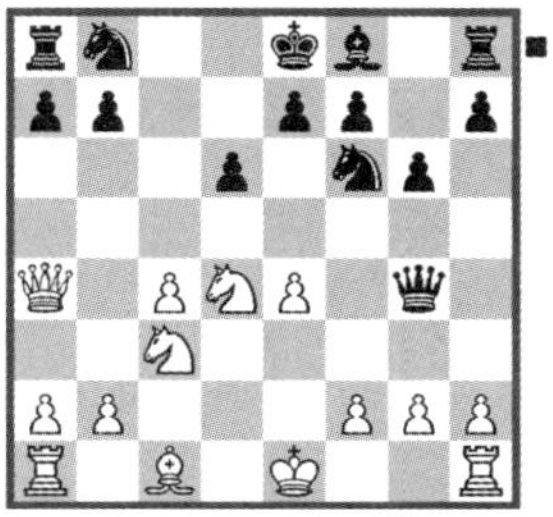

Position after: 9. ♕a4+!

**A)** 9... ♕d7 10. ♘db5! ♘a6 [10... ♘c6 11. ♘d5] 11. 0-0 ♗g7 12. ♖d1±

**B)** 9... ♘bd7 10. 0-0 ♗g7 11. f3 ♕h5 12. ♗e3 0-0 13. ♘d5! ♘xd5 [13... e6 14. ♘xf6+ ♘xf6 15. ♖ad1±] 14. exd5 This structure is typically beneficial for White. Black's e7-pawn is tied down, and their queen is out of the game. We're also not threatened by ...b7-b5 at any moment. 14... ♘c5 [14... ♘e5 15. ♕c2 a6 16. a4 ♖ac8 17. b3 ♖fe8 18. ♖ad1 ♘d7 19. a5±] 15. ♕c2 ♖ac8 16. ♕d2±

**9. f3**

**A)** 9. ♗e3?! ♘g4!

**B)** 9. 0-0?! 0-0 10. f3 ♖c8 11. b3 d5!=

**9... ♕c7**

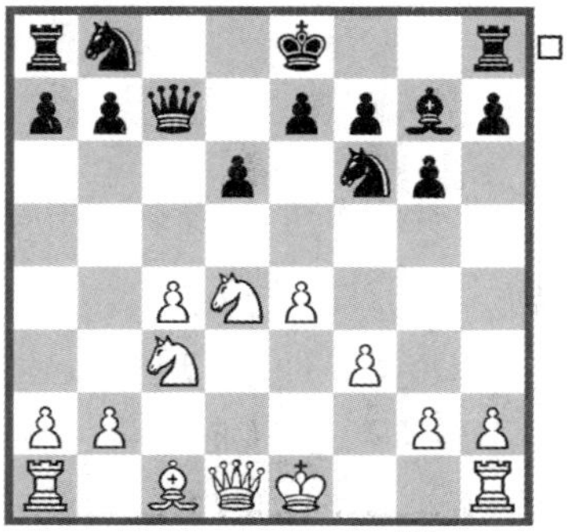

Position after: 9... ♕c7

The alternative approach to castling and playing for ...a7-a6 and ...b7-b5 is to attempt to frustrate our idea of playing ♗e3, instead forcing our dark-squared bishop to b2.

**10. b3 ♕a5 11. ♗d2**

It looks like this is objectively White's best move.

11. ♕d3 This is probably most consistent if we want to maintain the approach with ♗e3 and ♖c1 as in the mainline. 11... ♘c6 12. ♗e3

Position after: 12. ♗e3

**A)** 12... 0-0 13. 0-0 ♖ac8 14. ♖ac1 a6 In Amin – Wojtaszek, Sharjah 2017, the best way to respond to ... a7-a6 was 15. ♘xc6!

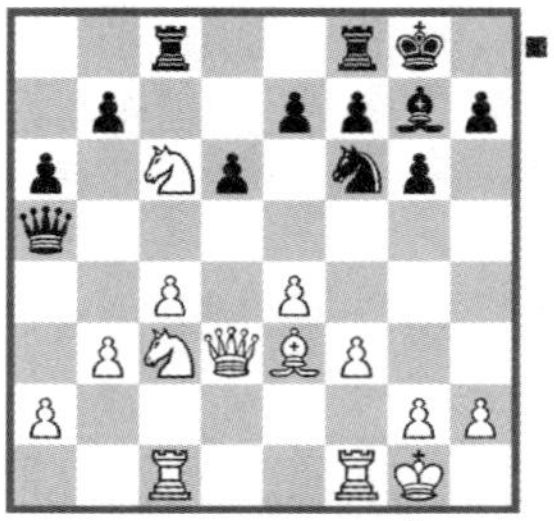

Position after: 15. ♘xc6!

15... ♖xc6 [15... bxc6 16. ♘a4 ♘d7 17. f4± We'll encounter more positions like these in our mainline.] 16. ♖fd1 ♖fc8 17. a4± White is very comfortable, and we'll always be keeping an eye out for the best moment to play ♘d5.

**B)** 12... ♘d7

**B1)** 13. 0-0-0!? This is the ambitious choice. I will give a few sample variations. 13... ♖c8 14. ♕d2 a6 15. ♔b1 b5!

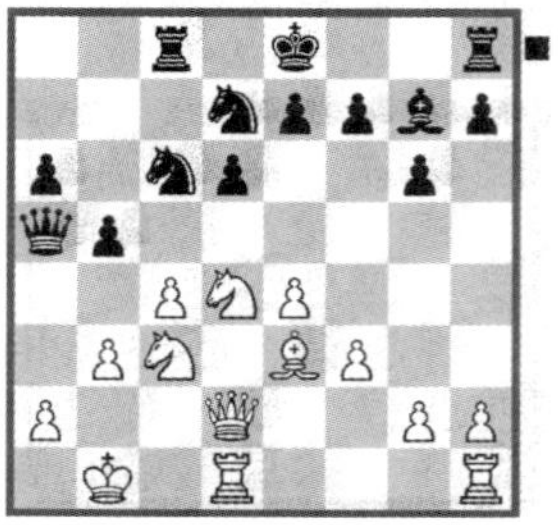

Position after: 15... b5!

16. ♘d5 ♕xd2 17. ♖xd2 bxc4 18. ♘xc6 ♖xc6 19. ♖c1 ♖c8= I think this position is probably a bit easier for Black to play than the one after 13.♖c1. Nevertheless, 13. 0-0-0 seems like a really interesting option for the reader to analyse in greater depth.

**B2)** 13. ♖c1 a6

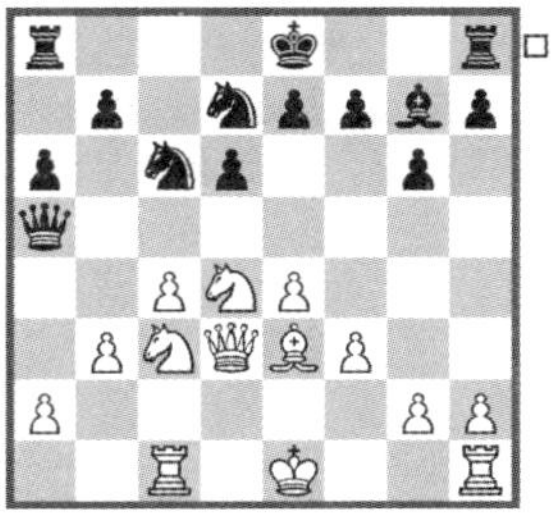

Position after: 13... a6

[13... ♘xd4 14. ♗xd4 ♗xd4 15. ♕xd4 0-0 16. 0-0 ♕b6 17. ♕xb6 ♘xb6 18. ♘d5! ♘xd5 19. exd5± This line is a good example of how we can retain an advantage even if the position liquidates.; 13... ♖c8 14. ♘de2!±; 13... ♗xd4 14. ♗xd4 ♘de5 15. ♕d2 ♘xd4 16. ♕xd4 ♕c5 17. ♕d2!± Followed by ♘a4 or ♘d5.] 14. ♕d2! We should wait for Black to castle before giving them the option to exchange queens. [14. 0-0?! ♘xd4 15. ♗xd4 ♗xd4+ 16. ♕xd4 ♕c5=; 14. ♘xc6 bxc6 15. 0-0 0-0 16. ♘a4 This was my first idea, but Black has a really annoying resource. 16... ♘c5!

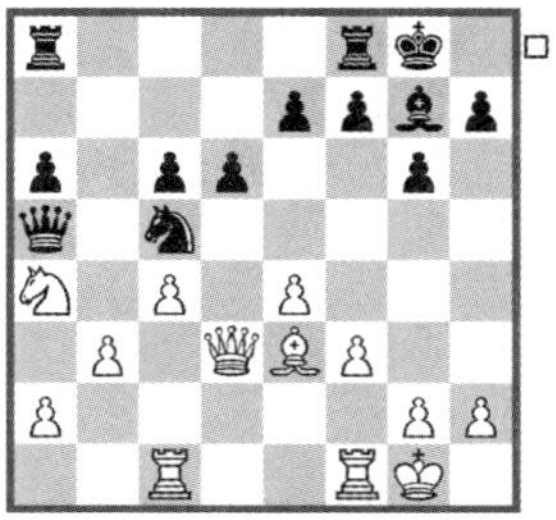

Position after: 16... ♘c5!

17. ♘xc5 dxc5 18. ♕e2 ♗d4=] 14... 0-0 [14... ♖c8 15. ♘de2!±] 15. 0-0 The position is objectively equal but as the next sub-chapter demonstrates, there are still plenty of ideas available in such positions.

**11... 0-0**

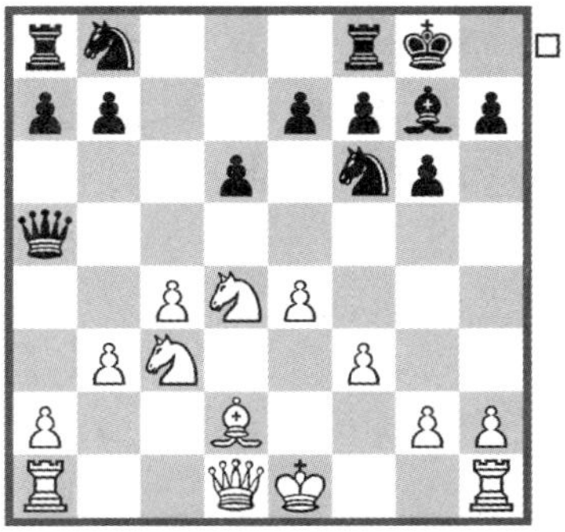

Position after: 11... 0-0

11... ♘c6 12. ♘de2! ♕b6! [12... 0-0 We have an extremely comfortable game if Black allows us to castle, e.g. 13. 0-0 ♘d7 14. ♔h1 ♘c5 15. ♘d5 ♕d8 16. ♗c3± So – Firouzja, chess24.com INT 2021.] 13. ♗g5! Planning to re-route the bishop to f2. 13... h6 [13... 0-0 14. ♕d2± Black can't prevent the bishop dropping back to e3, and has to contend with ♗h6 ideas in the future.]

14. ♗h4 0-0 15. ♕d2± Followed by ♗f2 and 0-0.

**12. ♖c1!**

**A)** 12. ♘d5 was my choice in Haria – Bacrot, Krasnaya Polyana 2021, but Black was absolutely fine after 12... ♕d8 13. ♗e3 e6=.

**B)** 12. 0-0? ♘xe4∓

**12... ♘c6**

12... a6 13. ♘ce2!± Followed by ♗e3.

**13. ♘xc6!**

Position after: 13. ♘xc6!

Transforming the structure. The bishop on d2 does a good job of securing the c3-knight, enabling us to play for a quick f3-f4 push.

13. ♘de2 Here we can't follow the same plan as after 11...♘c6, in view of the annoying 13... ♘b4!↑.

**13... bxc6 14. 0-0 ♘d7**

In Karthikeyan – Aditya, Barcelona 2021, White should have immediately gone for

**15. f4!±**

followed by ♕f3 and ♔h1.

## e) 5.c4 ♘f6 6.♘c3 g6 7.d4 cxd4 8.♘xd4 ♗g7 9.f3 0-0 10.♗e3 ♘c6 11.0-0

**1. e4 c5 2. ♘f3 d6 3. ♗b5+ ♗d7 4. ♗xd7+ ♕xd7 5. c4 ♘f6 6. ♘c3 g6 7. d4 cxd4 8. ♘xd4 ♗g7 9. f3 0-0**

*(see diagram next page)*

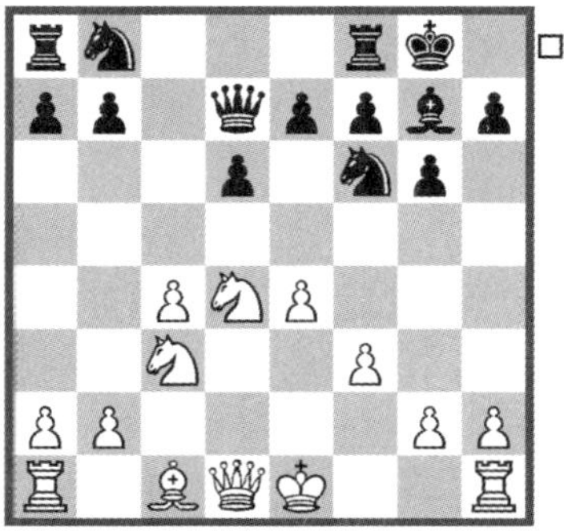

Position after: 9... 0-0

**10. ♗e3 ♘c6**

10... ♖c8 The reason for delaying castling can be demonstrated in this variation. 11. b3 e6 [11... a6 12. ♖c1±] 12. ♖c1 d5 13. e5 ♘e8 14. cxd5 exd5

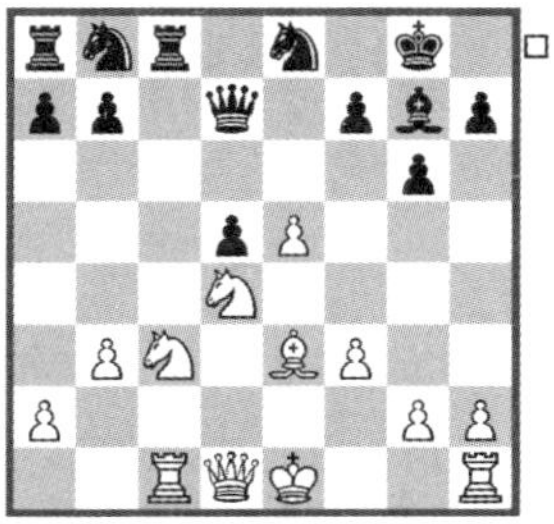

Position after: 14... exd5

15. f4!± White was already significantly better in Adams – Williams, Canterbury 2010.

**11. 0-0**

This has been the most common way to play, but I prefer 11.♖c1 because it avoids Black going down the following forcing line:

**11... a6 12. ♕d3**

This has been the most popular move for the last few years. However, Black has a nice way to basically force equality.

12. ♘xc6 ♕xc6! This is the reason why I want to start with 11.♖c1 - here Black can meet b2-b3 with ...b7-b5.

**12... ♖fc8 13. b3 b5!**

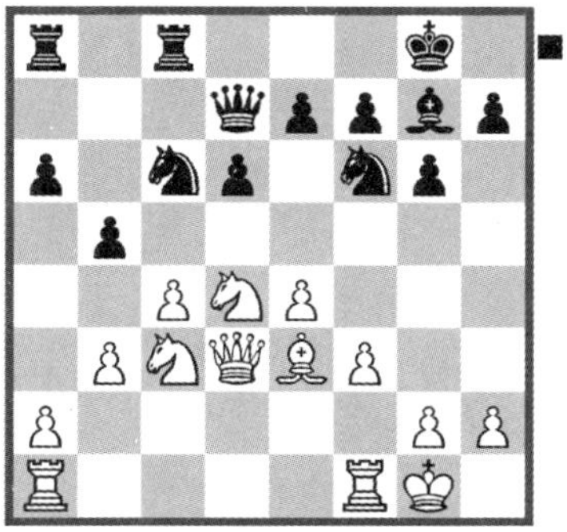

Position after: 13... b5!

**14. cxb5 ♘e5 15. ♕d2 d5! 16. ♘xd5**

16. ♘c6 ♘xc6 17. bxc6 ♖xc6 18. ♖ad1 ♖ac8 19. ♘xd5 ♘xd5 20. exd5 ♖c2= McShane – Van Foreest, Bremen 2019.

**16... ♘xd5 17. exd5 axb5 18. ♖ad1 ♕xd5 19. ♕e2 ♘c6 20. ♘xb5 ♕e6**

*(see diagram next page)*

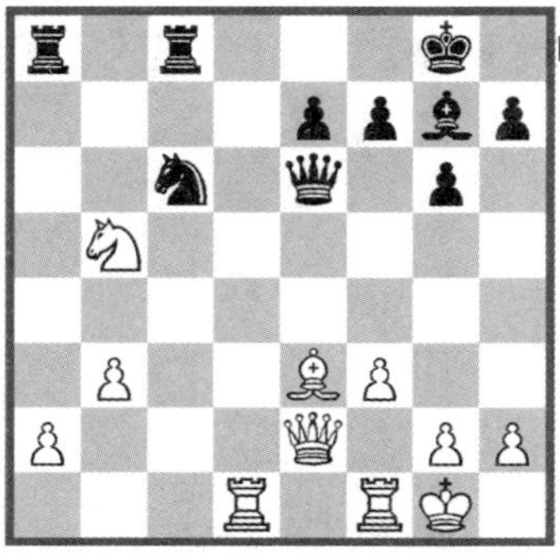

Position after: 20... ♕e6

**21. ♖fe1**

21. ♖d2 ♘b4=

**21... ♘b4 22. ♖d2 h5!=**

The computer maintains that White still has a small edge, but the reality is that our queenside pawns are simply unable to get going. All of Black's pieces are working perfectly and it is very difficult to make any progress with White. This was indeed the case in Caruana – Vachier Lagrave, 2021.

## f) 5.c4 ♘f6 6.♘c3 g6 7.d4 cxd4 8.♘xd4 ♗g7 9.f3 0-0 10.♗e3 ♘c6 11.♖c1 --

**1. e4 c5 2. ♘f3 d6 3. ♗b5+ ♗d7 4. ♗xd7+ ♕xd7 5. c4 ♘f6 6. ♘c3 g6 7. d4 cxd4 8. ♘xd4 ♗g7 9. f3 0-0 10. ♗e3 ♘c6 11. ♖c1**

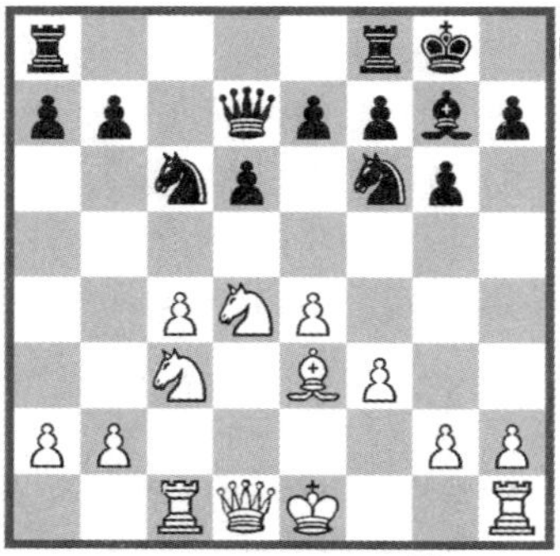

Position after: 11. ♖c1

In general it's more important to remember ideas and plans here, rather than specific variations - which probably explains the lack of depth in this subchapter. The first thing to consider is that in general, trading pieces will be good news if we can retain our space advantage. If we have more space in an ending, Black will find it difficult to prevent weaknesses from being created in their pawn structure. However when considering the trade of pieces, it really depends on the exact circumstances - and therefore it's worth calculating exact lines rather than just entering blindly into a trade. The most important thing to consider in the next few moves is that when Black plays ...a7-a6, we'll most likely want to capture on c6 (to prevent the ...♘xd4 and ...b7-b5 combination). If Black recaptures with their b-pawn, the push c4-c5 can be very effective. If Black recaptures with a major piece, we can play a2-a4, preventing ...b7-b5. The reason why we want to capture on c6 before playing a2-a4 is that Black is better placed to exploit the hole on b4 created by our advance if they have two knights on the board, rather than just one. Another logical idea for Black is to try and break in the centre with ...e7-e6 and ...d7-d5. Our general response to that will be to capture on c6 and push e4-e5 - supported by our queen on e2 or even e1. Finally, if Black isn't careful they might play ...♖fc8 followed by ...a7-a6. If this happens, ♘a4 can be a very effective move, basically winning the exchange.

**11... ♖fc8**

**A)** 11... ♖ac8 12. b3 e6 [12... a6 13. 0-0 e6 14. ♘xc6! ♖xc6 15. ♕d3±] 13. 0-0 ♖fd8 14. ♕e1!

Position after: 14. ♕e1!

A very useful motif to remember if Black tries to quickly break with ...e7-e6 and ...d6-d5. The queen stands very well here - out of the way, and able to jump to squares like h4 for example. 14... d5 15. ♘xc6 bxc6 16. e5!

*(see analysis diagram next column)*

Position after: 16. e5!

16... ♘h5 [16... ♘e8 17. ♗g5 f6 18. ♗h4±] 17. f4!± White has good control here. We threaten g2-g4, and also have the potential to jump with our knight to a4 and c5.

**B)** 11... ♖fd8 12. 0-0 e6

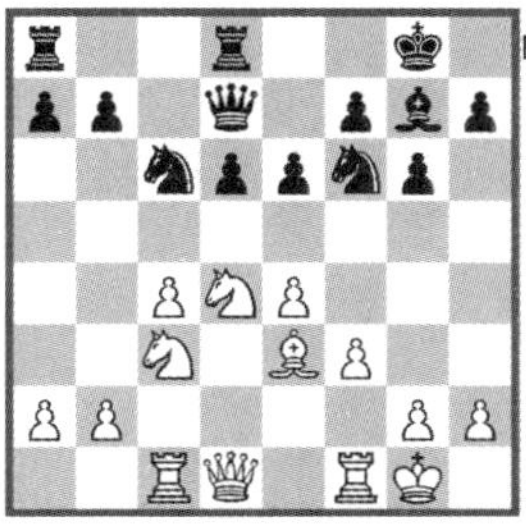
Position after: 12... e6

**B1)** I tried to play the same ♕e1 motif in two separate games, but it's not as effective here. 13. ♕e1 ♘e5! [13... d5 14. ♘xc6 bxc6 15. e5 ♘e8 16. ♗g5 ♖db8 17. ♘a4± I was slightly better in Haria – Murzin, Batumi 2018, and went on to convincingly win a nice game.] 14. ♕e2 In Haria – Kokaia, Motevideo 2017, the best continuation for Black was 14... ♖ac8 15. b3 d5! 16. cxd5 exd5

17. f4 ♘d3! 18. ♕xd3 dxe4 19. ♘xe4 ♘xe4 20. ♕xe4 ♖xc1 21. ♖xc1 ♖e8∓ and suddenly the tables have turned.

**B2)** 13. ♘xc6! bxc6 14. ♕e2 [14. ♖f2?! seems misplaced and led to a Black victory in Giri – Anand, Zurich 2016.] 14... d5 [14... ♕b7 15. ♖fd1 d5 16. e5 ♘d7 17. f4 ♖ab8 18. b3± Followed by ♘a4 – White's position is slightly preferable.] 15. e5 ♘e8 16. ♗c5 dxc4 17. f4 ♕d3 18. ♕f2±

**C)** 11... ♘xd4 12. ♗xd4 ♖fc8 13. b3 ♘h5 14. 0-0 ♗xd4+ 15. ♕xd4 ♘f6 In Carlsen – Vachier Lagrave, London 2015, White could've taken advantage of Black's premature trade of the dark-squared bishops with 16. f4!

Position after: 16. f4!

16... a6 [16... ♕c7?! 17. e5! with ♘d5 coming next.] 17. a4± We can continue slowly - for example with ♔h1, ♖ce1 and either f4-f5 or e4-e5.

**12. b3 a6**

Black wants to capture on d4 and play ...b7-b5, so we should respond accordingly.

**A)** 12... ♘xd4 13. ♗xd4 ♕d8 [13... a6? 14. ♘a4+–] 14. 0-0 a6 15. ♕d3 ♘d7 16. ♗xg7

Position after: 16. ♗xg7

16... ♔xg7 17. ♔h1!± In this case, the exchange of pieces has weakened Black's king, and we can slowly embark on a kingside attack.

**B)** 12... ♕d8 13. 0-0 ♕a5 14. ♕d3!± This is now a favourable version of the ♕d3 ideas after 11. 0-0.

**C)** 12... ♖ab8 13. 0-0 a6 14. ♘xc6! ♕xc6 15. ♕e2 ♖d8 16. ♘d5!

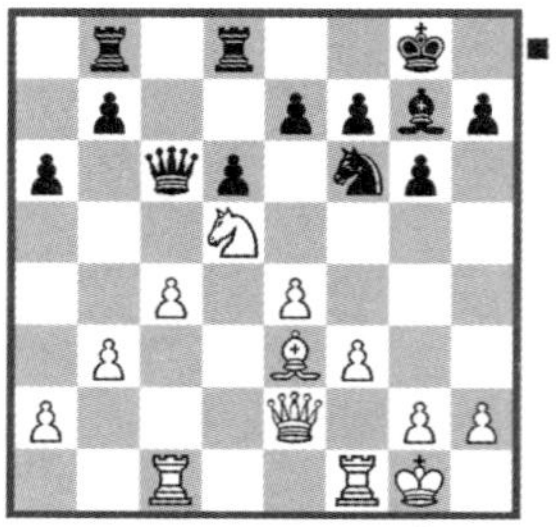

Position after: 16. ♘d5!

16... ♘xd5 17. cxd5 ♕d7 18. ♖c4

♖dc8 19. ♖fc1 I had attained a comfortable advantage in Haria – Abdulla, Newcastle 2018.

**13. ♘xc6!**

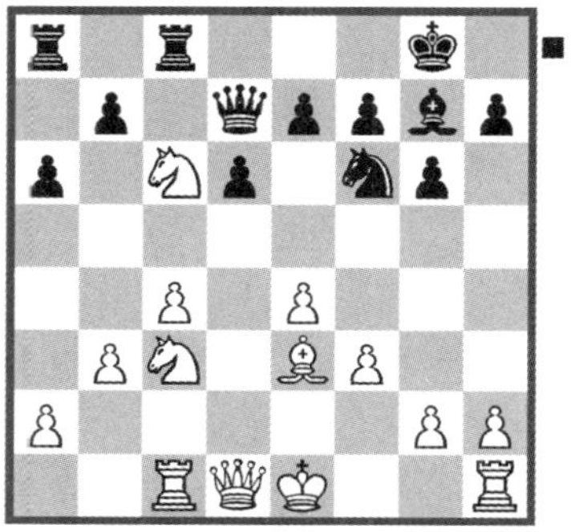

Position after: 13. ♘xc6!

**13... ♖xc6**

**A)** 13... bxc6 14. 0-0 ♕b7 15. ♘a4 ♖d8 16. ♕c2 d5?! 17. e5 ♘d7 18. f4±

**B)** 13... ♕xc6 14. 0-0 Black is still passive and unable to break out with 14... b5 because of the presence of our rook on the c-file. 15. cxb5 axb5 16. ♕e2 ♕a6 [16... b4 17. ♘d5 ♕b7 18. ♘b6 ♖xc1 19. ♖xc1±] 17. ♘xb5 ♖xc1 18. ♖xc1 ♕xa2 19. ♕xa2 ♖xa2 20. ♖c8+ ♗f8 21. ♗h6 ♘d7 22. ♘d4±

**14. a4 ♕d8 15. 0-0 ♖ac8**

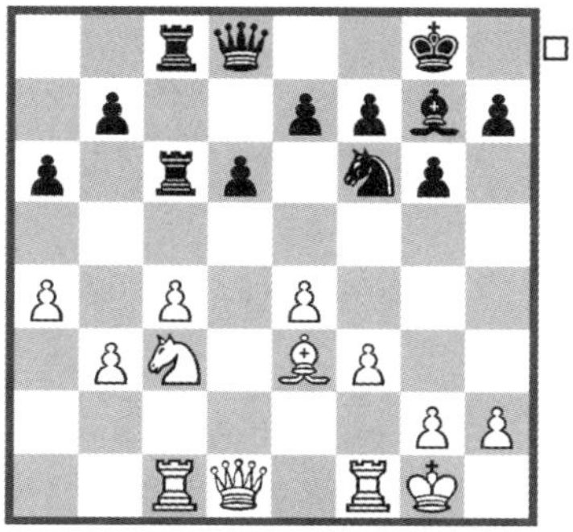

Position after: 15... ♖ac8

**16. ♘d5±**

White won a nice game in Ni Hua – Yu, China 2016.

## g) 5.c4 ♘f6 6.♘c3 g6 7.d4 cxd4 8.♘xd4 ♗g7 9.f3 0-0 10.♗e3 ♘c6 11.♖c1 a6

**1. e4 c5 2. ♘f3 d6 3. ♗b5+ ♗d7 4. ♗xd7+ ♕xd7 5. c4 ♘f6 6. ♘c3 g6 7. d4 cxd4 8. ♘xd4 ♗g7 9. f3 0-0 10. ♗e3 ♘c6 11. ♖c1 a6**

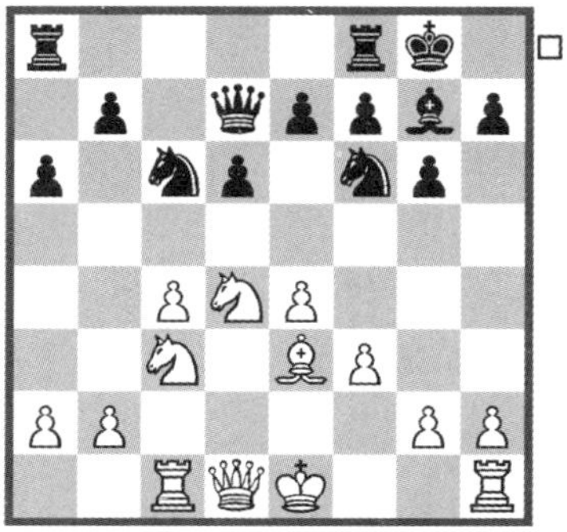

Position after: 11... a6

**12. ♘xc6!**

12. 0-0 ♘xd4 13. ♗xd4 b5=

**12... bxc6**

12... ♕xc6 Entering into the x-ray of our rook is a dangerous idea. 13. b3

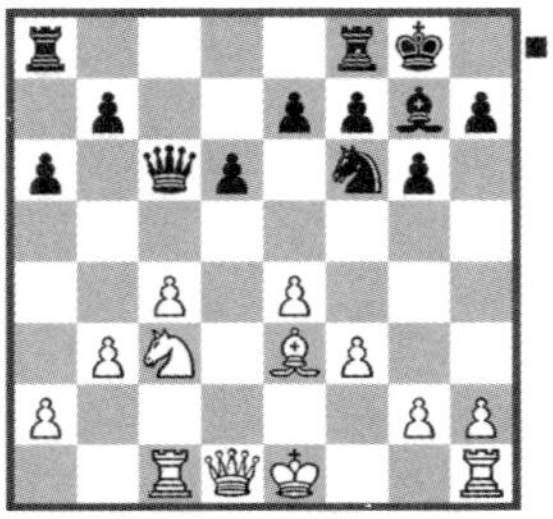

Position after: 13. b3

13... ♖ac8 [13... b5? 14. cxb5 axb5 15. ♘d5+–] 14. 0-0 ♕d7 15. ♕d2 b5 16. e5! dxe5 17. ♕xd7 ♘xd7 18. cxb5 axb5 19. ♘xb5±

**13. 0-0**

Invariably I'm not really claiming an advantage for White - just perhaps a slightly easier position to play. At the worst case, Black will find a way to forcibly equalise, but we shouldn't ever find ourselves being worse.

**13... ♖fd8**

**A)** 13... ♕c7 14. ♔h1 ♘d7 15. f4! a5 16. f5→

**B)** 13... ♕b7 14. c5!

Position after: 14. c5!

14... dxc5 15. ♘a4 ♘d7 16. ♖f2 ♖fd8 17. ♖d2 ♕c7 18. b3 ♗e5 19. h3±

**14. ♘a4 ♕b7 15. b3**

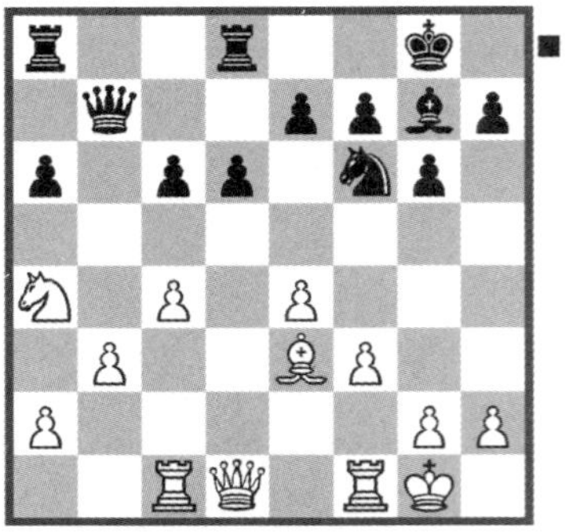

Position after: 15. b3

**15... ♘d7**

15... d5 16. ♗b6! ♖dc8 17. ♕d3 e5 18. ♗a5±

**16. ♕c2 c5 17. ♖ce1↑**

At the right moment, we'll look to continue on the kingside with f3-f4, and either e4-e5 or f4-f5.

## h) 5.0-0 Early Sidelines

**1. e4 c5 2. ♘f3 d6 3. ♗b5+ ♗d7 4. ♗xd7+ ♕xd7 5. 0-0**

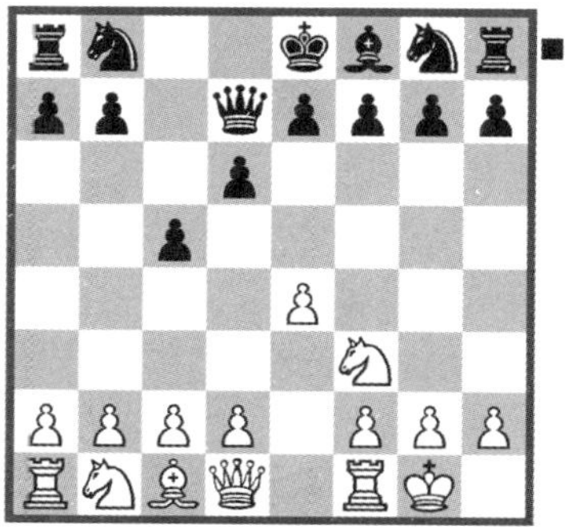

Position after: 5. 0-0

I never really thought this was a great line for White, until I saw Carlsen lose against Duda in a critical game at the World Cup. The fact that Carlsen was on the White side could have reaffirmed my initial impression, but instead it made me look more deeply at the line and I now think this can be an interesting surprise option. Instead of opting for a Maroczy structure, our plan is c2-c3 and d2-d4. This will invariably transition into a French-advanced structure when Black responds with ...d7-d5.

**5... ♘f6**

5... ♘c6 Here Black intends to meet c2-c3 with the immediate ...d7-d5 push. Delaying ...♘f6 means we won't be able to push e4-e5 with a tempo anymore. 6. c3 [6. ♕e2?! g6! 7. c3 ♗g7 8. ♖d1 e5 Black already has the better side of equality here.] 6... d5 7. exd5 Nothing else makes sense. 7... ♕xd5 8. d4

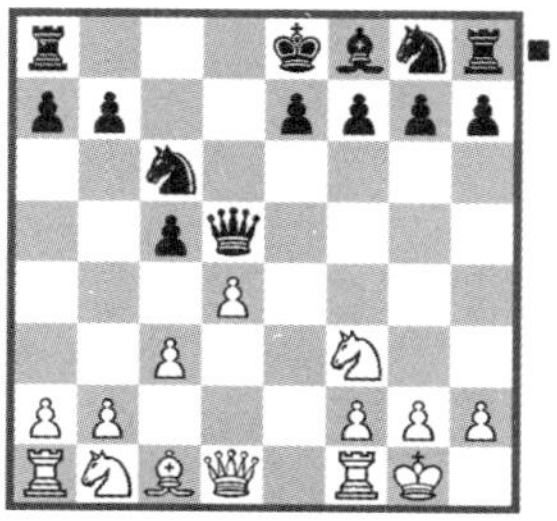

Position after: 8. d4

The position now resembles an Alapin Sicilian, and Black has to play carefully to achieve equality.

**A)** 8... ♘f6?! 9. dxc5! ♕xc5 [9... ♕xd1 10. ♖xd1 e6 11. b4 a5 12. b5 ♘d8 13. c4!± To be followed by ♘c3 giving White a great initiative.] 10. ♘a3! e6 11. ♕b3 ♕b6 Black is basically forced to ruin their queenside pawns, after which we will have a long-term advantage. 12. ♕xb6 axb6 13. ♘b5 ♖c8 14. ♗g5±

**B)** 8... ♖d8 9. ♕a4! cxd4 10. b4! Black has completely neglected their kingside development, so it makes sense to act quickly. 10... a6 11. ♘a3!± Followed by b4-b5 against pretty much anything. Black will struggle to survive here.

**C)** 8... e6 9. ♗e3

Position after: 9. ♗e3

**C1)** 9... ♘f6?! This natural move should probably lead to, at the very least, a small edge for White. 10. dxc5

**C1.1)** 10... 0-0-0 11. ♕xd5 ♘xd5 12. b4 ♗e7 In Haria – Vachier Lagrave, Germany 2022, I already had a nice advantage and the cleanest continuation was 13. ♖c1!

Position after: 13. ♖c1!

13... ♘xe3 [13... ♗f6 14. ♗g5!±] 14. fxe3 ♖d3 15. ♔f2 ♖hd8 16. ♔e2 ♗f6 17. a3±

**C1.2)** 10... ♕xd1 11. ♖xd1 ♘d5 Black's only logical option. 12. b4! Allowing Black to capture on e3 won't weaken our pawn structure. 12... a5 13. b5 ♘xe3 14. fxe3 ♘b8 15. c6! bxc6 16. c4± White has excellent practical chances here.

**C2)** 9... cxd4 10. cxd4 [10. ♘xd4 also seems reasonable, although I think Black equalises more easily here.] 10... ♘f6 11. ♘c3

Position after: 11. ♘c3

11... ♕a5 [11... ♕d6 12. ♕b3 ♕b4! transposes to 11...♕a5.; 11... ♕h5? 12. ♕b3 ♗b4 13. ♗g5!

Position after: 13. ♗g5!

13... ♗xc3 14. ♗xf6 gxf6 15. ♕xb7 0-0 16. bxc3±] 12. ♕b3 [12. a3!? also looks interesting, preventing Black's ...♕b4 idea.]

**C2.1)** 12... ♗b4 is the other logical option, but White retains an edge with the following line: 13.

♖fd1 ♘d5 [13... 0-0? 14. d5 exd5 15. ♘xd5 ♘xd5 16. ♖xd5 ♕c7 17. ♖c1±] 14. ♖ac1

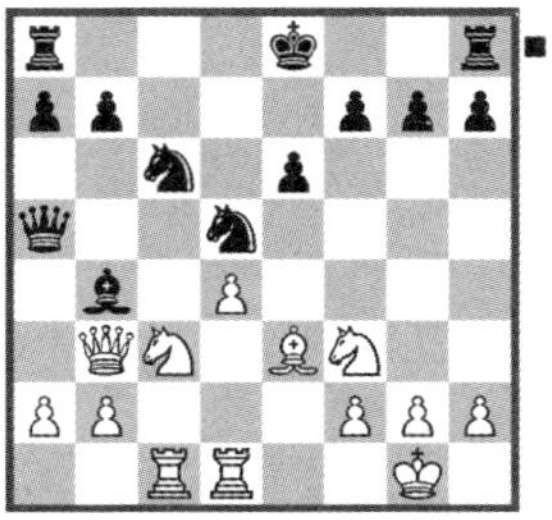
Position after: 14. ♖ac1

14... ♘xe3 [14... 0-0 15. ♘xd5 ♕xd5 16. ♖d3! Followed by a2-a3.] 15. fxe3 0-0 16. d5! exd5 17. ♘xd5 ♖ad8 18. ♔h1± The knight on d5 is a really strong piece and Black has to figure out what to do about the b7-pawn.

**C2.2)** 12... ♕b4! The only move to equalise. 13. ♘e5!? ♕xb3 14. axb3 a5!=

**6. ♕e2 ♘c6 7. c3**

Position after: 7. c3

**7... e6**

**A)** 7... e5 This can't really be a good idea considering that the light-squared bishops have already been exchanged. Also we've played c2-c3 instead of c2-c4, so Black is only temporarily preventing the d2-d4 push. 8. ♖d1! ♕g4 The only move which continues to prevent d2-d4. 9. d3 ♗e7 10. ♗g5!

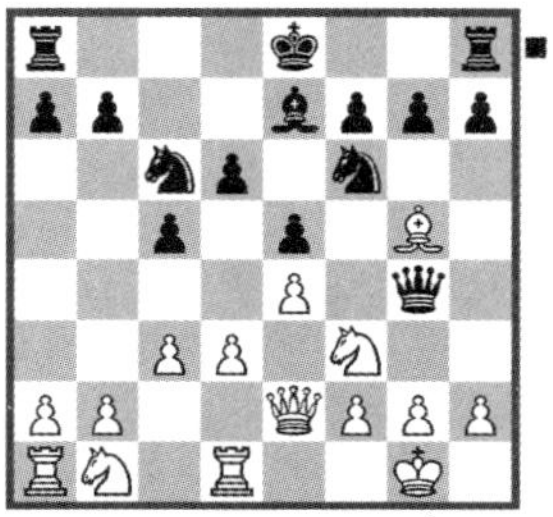
Position after: 10. ♗g5!

10... 0-0 [10... ♕e6 11. ♘a3 0-0 12. ♗xf6 ♗xf6 13. ♘c2± Followed by ♘e3 and/or queenside expansion with a2-a4 and b2-b4.] 11. ♗xf6 ♗xf6 12. d4! exd4 13. ♘xd4± We will have an extremely pleasant position regardless of whether Black elects to exchange the queens.

**B)** 7... d5?! An inferior version of the 5...♘c6 6...d5 line. Here we can push e4-e5, winning two tempi as Black has to retreat the knight to g8. 8. e5 ♘g8 9. ♘a3 The simplest continuation, bringing the knight to c2 before pushing d2-d4. The knight will play a useful defensive role on the c2-square by stemming Black's queenside counterplay. 9... e6 10. ♘c2 ♘ge7 11. d4

*(see analysis diagram next page)*

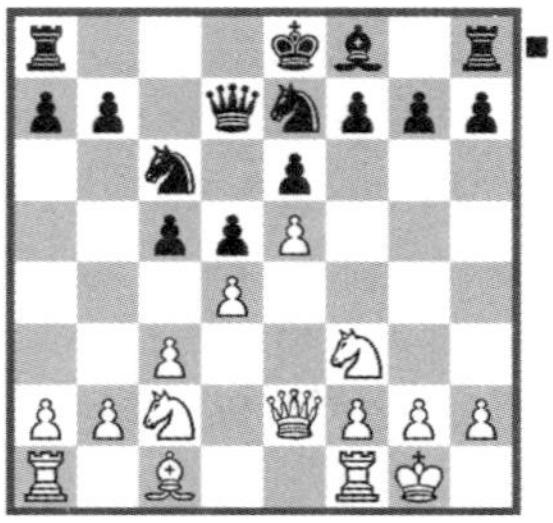

Position after: 11. d4

11... cxd4 [11... ♘f5 12. g4! ♘h6 13. ♗xh6 gxh6 14. ♔h1±] 12. cxd4 ♘f5 13. ♗d2! Bringing the bishop to c3, after which we can begin to consider queenside expansion along with the obvious plan of g2-g4. 13... a5 [13... ♖c8 14. a4 ♗e7 15. b4 ♗d8 16. ♕d3±] 14. a4!?

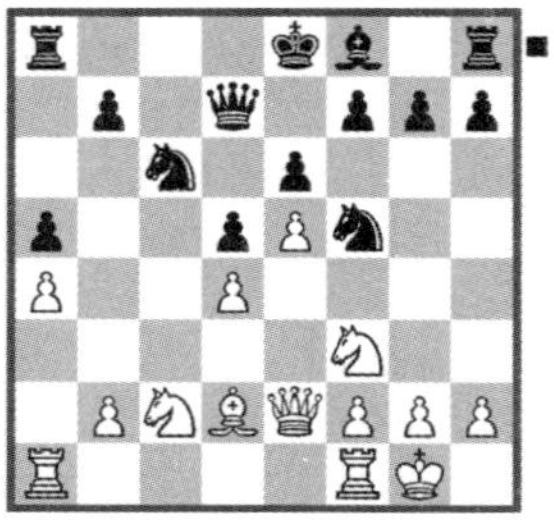

Position after: 14. a4!?

It makes sense to prevent Black from gaining space with ...a5-a4.

**B1)** 14... ♗e7 15. g4! ♘h6 [15... ♘h4 16. ♘xh4 ♗xh4 17. g5 ♘e7 18. ♘a3!± Whilst Black tries to retrieve the h4-bishop, we suddenly switch sides to attack on the queenside with ♘b5 and ♖fc1.] 16. ♘fe1!± Followed by a combination of f2-f4, ♘d3, and ♔h1. White is dominating.

**B2)** 14... ♕d8 It makes sense to want to recapture on h4 with the queen rather than the bishop. 15. ♕d3! Waiting for Black to put the bishop on e7. 15... ♗e7 [15... h6 16. h3!±] 16. g4 ♘h4 17. ♘xh4 ♗xh4 18. f4 ♕b6 19. ♔h1!↑ Preparing an f4-f5 push, maybe after further preparatory moves such as ♗c3.

**8. d4**

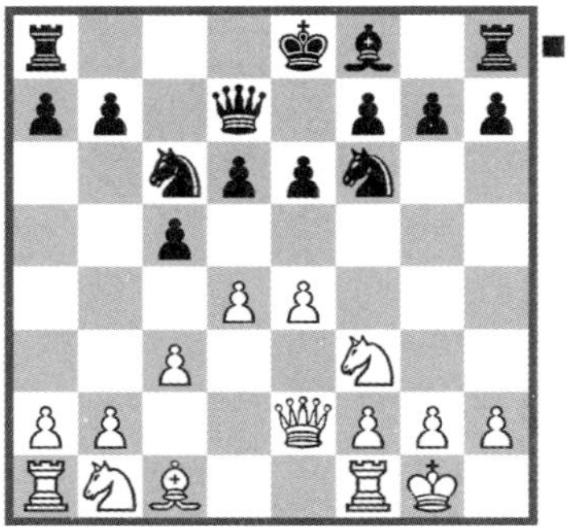

Position after: 8. d4

**8... cxd4**

**A)** 8... d5 9. e5 ♘e4 10. ♘bd2 This will undoubtedly transpose to 8...cxd4 at some point.

**B)** 8... ♗e7 9. dxc5! dxc5 10. ♖d1 We already have a slight initiative and should continue to develop actively. 10... ♕c7 11. ♘a3 a6 12. ♘c4 0-0 13. g3! b5 14. ♗f4 ♕a7 15. ♘d6± Followed by a2-a4. Our position is definitely preferable.

**9. cxd4 d5**

The critical continuation – Black can't really allow us to dominate the centre.

**10. e5 ♘g8**

An interesting alternative which has been played by a few very strong players. However it's clearly inferior to 10...♘e4, as Black just wastes more time in trying to develop their kingside.

**11. ♘c3 ♘ge7 12. ♕d3!**

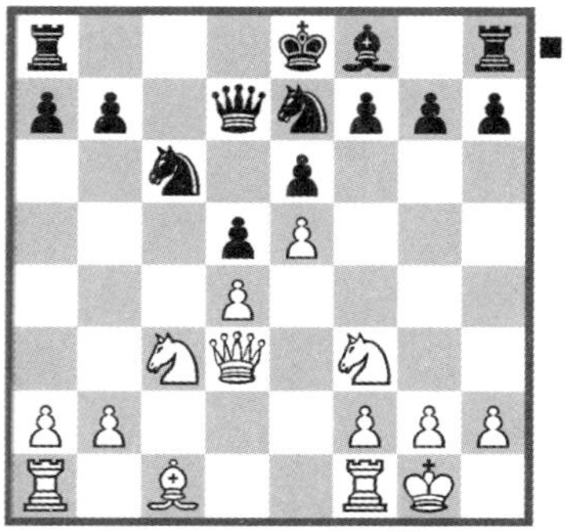

Position after: 12. ♕d3!

I think this is best - freeing the e2-square so that our c3-knight can jump to g3.

**12... ♘f5**

12... ♘g6 13. h4! This is a classic way to play against the g6-knight. The line may continue: 13... h5 14. ♘e2 ♗e7 15. g3± followed by ♗d2, ♖fc1, and expanding on the queenside. Black's g6-knight will take a while to get back into the game, and kingside castling also looks dangerous having played ...h7-h5.

**13. ♘e2 ♗e7**

13... f6 It feels a bit too dangerous for Black to open the position, given their current lack of development. 14. ♘g3 ♘xg3 [14... fxe5 15. ♘xe5 ♘xe5 16. dxe5±] 15. fxg3!↑

**14. g4! ♘h4 15. ♘xh4 ♗xh4 16. f4!**

Position after: 16. f4!

Discouraging Black from castling kingside.

**16... 0-0-0 17. ♗d2 ♔b8 18. f5!**

Continuing to expand on the kingside - our own king isn't really in any danger. Black has several choices, but I think it makes sense to focus on the most critical ones.

**18... ♗e7**

Preparing the ...f7-f6 push.

18... f6 19. ♕h3! ♗g5 20. ♗xg5 fxg5 21. ♕h5

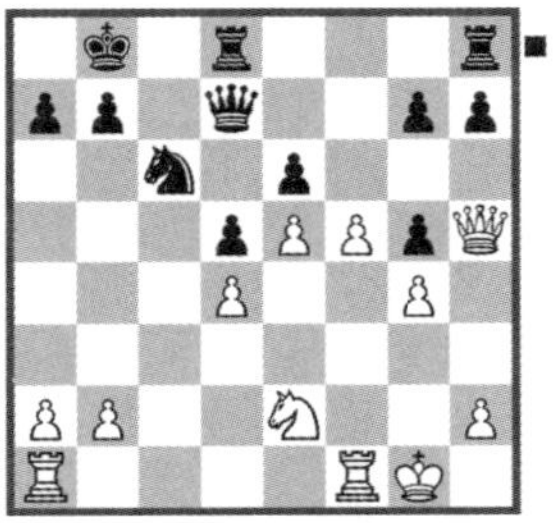

Position after: 21. ♕h5

The position is obviously a bit risky for us, but we should constantly be attempting to maximise our control of the position. 21... ♕e7 [21... g6 22. fxg6 ♕e7 23. g7! ♕xg7 24. ♖f7 ♕g8 25. ♖af1±] 22. f6 gxf6 23. exf6 ♕c7 24. ♕h6± The passed pawn on f6 is a major asset.

**19. a3 f6 20. ♘f4!**

*(see diagram next column)*

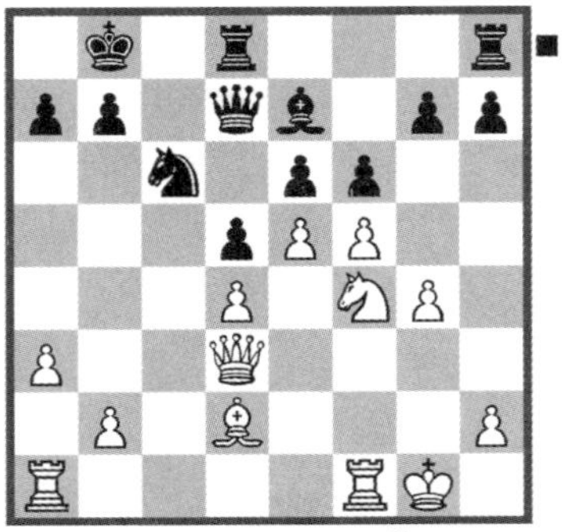

Position after: 20. ♘f4!

The line now gets forcing, but the following moves demonstrate how we can keep control even when the position becomes slightly messy.

**20... exf5 21. e6 ♕e8 22. gxf5 ♗d6 23. ♔h1⩲**

Followed by pushing our queenside pawns. Black still has real problems to solve.

## i) 5.0-0 ♘f6 6.♕e2 ♘c6 7.c3 e6 8.d4 cxd4 9.cxd4 d5 10.e5 ♘e4

**1. e4 c5 2. ♘f3 d6 3. ♗b5+ ♗d7 4. ♗xd7+ ♕xd7 5. 0-0 ♘f6 6. ♕e2 ♘c6 7. c3 e6 8. d4 cxd4 9. cxd4 d5 10. e5 ♘e4**

*(see diagram opposite column)*

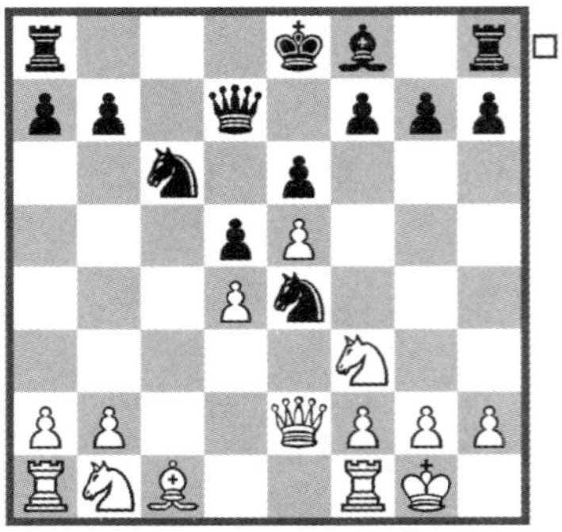

Position after: 10... ♘e4

**11. ♘bd2**

11. ♗e3 is a solid alternative, but after 11... ♗e7 12. ♘e1 f6 13. f3 ♘g5 14. ♘d3 0-0 Black's position seems fairly easy to play, and we don't have the same kingside potential that we do in the lines after 11.♘bd2.

**11... ♘xd2 12. ♗xd2**

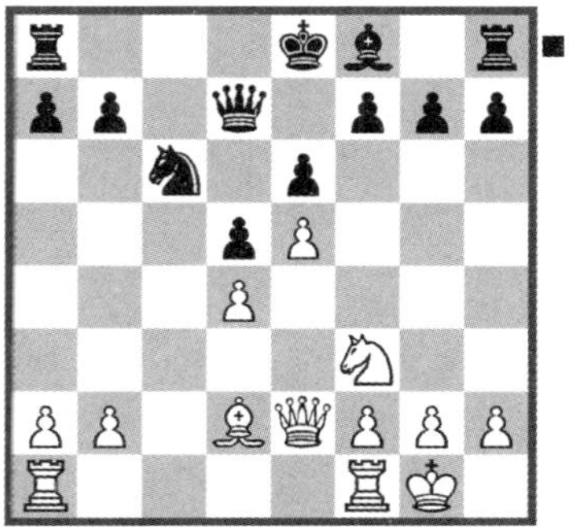

Position after: 12. ♗xd2

On first glance, the position resembles a 'good' French defence for Black, given that the light-squared bishops are exchanged. However there are a couple of things in White's favour. We have a lead in development, and the potential to play on both sides of the board. In light of this it makes sense to push our h-pawn, accompanied by either g2-g3 or even g2-g4 and ♔g2. In this way our rook can join the attack via h1, while also having the option to switch back to the c1-square if necessary. The following variations will help to demonstrate these ideas.

**12... ♗e7**

12... ♗b4 was Duda's choice, although we'll still follow the same plan as after 12...♗e7. 13. ♗f4 0-0

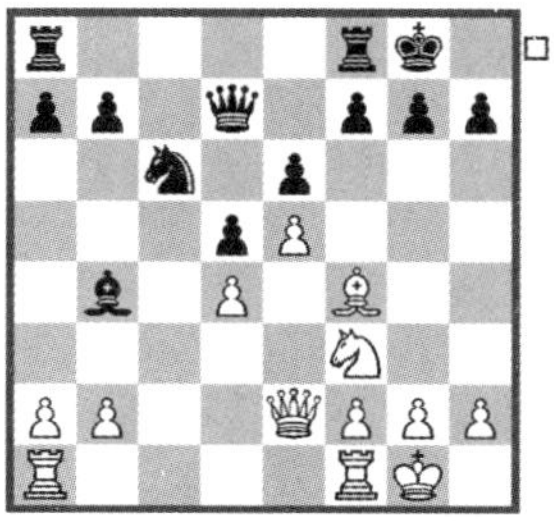

Position after: 13... 0-0

14. h4! [14. ♕d3 was the famous game Carlsen – Duda, Krasnaya Polyana 2021, but I prefer the text move.] 14... h6 [14... f6 15. exf6 ♖xf6 16. ♘e5 ♘xe5 17. ♗xe5± Followed by ♖ac1, g2-g3, and ♔g2.] 15. h5 ♖ac8 [15... a5 16. g4 a4 17. ♖ac1→] 16. ♖fd1 ♘e7 17. g4 ♕a4 18. ♖d3!

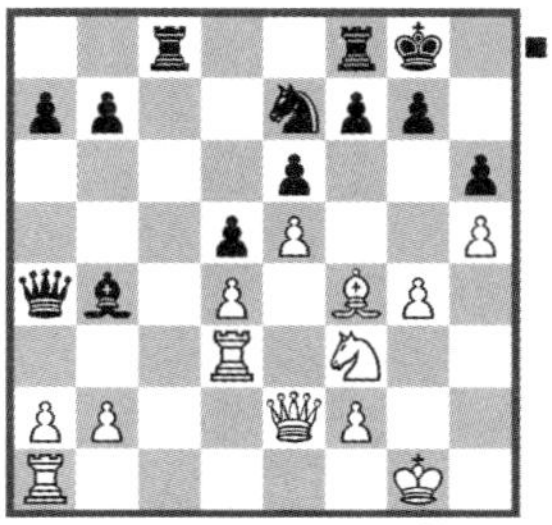

Position after: 18. ♖d3!

A thematic rook lift, gaining access to both the kingside and the queenside.

**A)** 18... ♖c2 19. ♕d1 Threatening ♘e1. 19... ♕c6 20. ♖b1± Black's control of the c-file is optically nice, but doesn't achieve anything. Meanwhile we can continue to slowly improve our position, always looking out for the right moment to push g4-g5.

**B)** 18... ♕c2 19. ♕xc2 ♖xc2 20. ♖b3 ♘c6 21. a3 ♗a5 22. ♖xb7 The computer still gives 0.00 but it feels like Black is the one who has to be more accurate here.

**13. g3! 0-0 14. ♔g2**

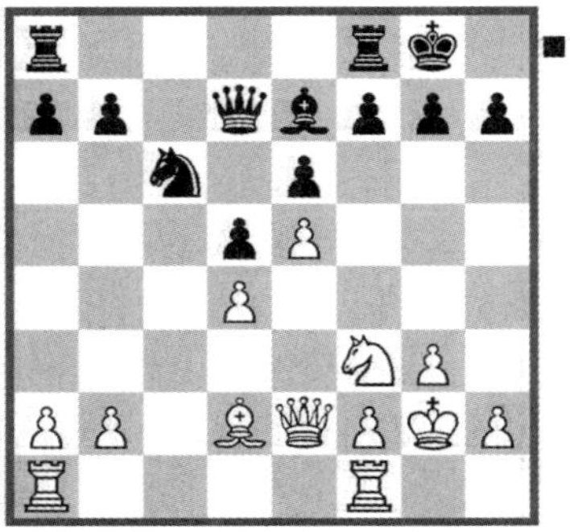

Position after: 14. ♔g2

It's suprisingly difficult for Black to deal with the simple plan of us pushing our h-pawn up the board, followed by ♖h1.

**14... ♖ac8**

**A)** 14... f6 It's likely that Black will play this break sooner rather than later. The change in structure is beneficial for White, as Black has to deal with a weak e6-pawn (and has no light-squared bishop to defend it). The following variations demonstrate various ways we can continue to exert pressure: 15. exf6

**A1)** 15... ♗xf6 16. ♗c3 ♖ae8 17. ♖fe1 ♖f7 18. ♖ad1 h6 19. ♖d3!

Position after: 19. ♖d3!

A common idea in these structures, swinging the rook to e3. 19... ♗d8 20. h4! Black's idea was to meet ♖e3 with ...♖f8, so we should make some preparatory moves before continuing to exert pressure on the e6-pawn. [20. ♖e3? was careless in Haria – Sebag, Gibraltar 2022, allowing Black to play 20... ♖ef8=.] 20... ♖f5 21. ♘h2 ♗b6 22. f4!± Potentially followed by ♘f3 and ♖e3, maintaining an edge.

**A2)** 15... ♖xf6 16. ♗f4!? ♗d6 17. ♗xd6 ♕xd6 18. ♖ad1± I think it makes sense to leave the rook on f1 here, planning to meet ...♖af8 with ♘e5. Otherwise we can think about other improving moves like h2-h4 or ♕d3 and ♖c1.

**B)** 14... a5 Black aims for queenside counterplay without risking opening the centre with ...f7-f6. 15. h4 a4 16. ♕d3!

*(see analysis diagram next page)*

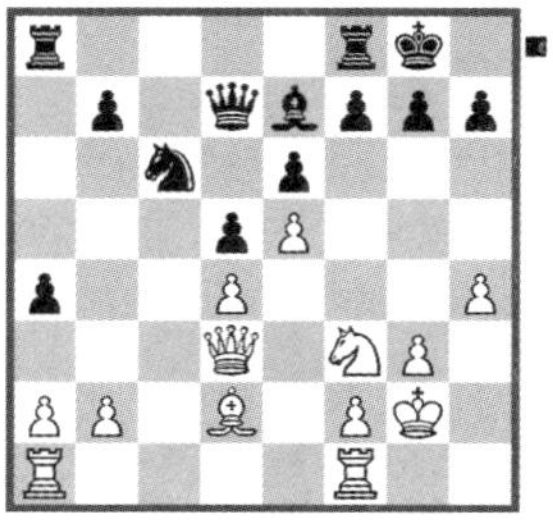

Position after: 16. ♕d3!

Eyeing up ♖h1 and ♘g5 ideas. 16... h6 [16... a3 17. b3 ♖fc8 18. ♘g5!+– This will be catastrophic for Black once the h-file gets opened up.] 17. ♖h1! Once again threatening the ♘g5 jump. 17... f6 18. exf6 ♗xf6 19. ♖ae1→

**C)** 14... ♖ae8 was played in Tari – Sjugirov, Riga 2021, preparing the ...f7-f6 break. However, after 15. h4 h6 16. ♖ad1 f6 17. exf6 ♖xf6 18. ♗f4± White maintains excellent control.

**15. h4**

Position after: 15. h4

**15... f6**

Played in all four games which have reached this position. However, the computer seems to think that White has a very comfortable advantage here.

**A)** 15... h6 16. h5 a5 17. ♖ac1 a4 18. ♖h1→ Followed by g4-g5.

**B)** 15... a5 16. h5 a4 17. h6 Black can't allow us to push our h-pawn to h6, as their king will be too cramped, and all endings will be extremely favourable for White. 17... g6 18. ♖ac1±

**16. exf6 ♗xf6 17. ♗c3 ♕f7 18. ♖ad1 ♖ce8**

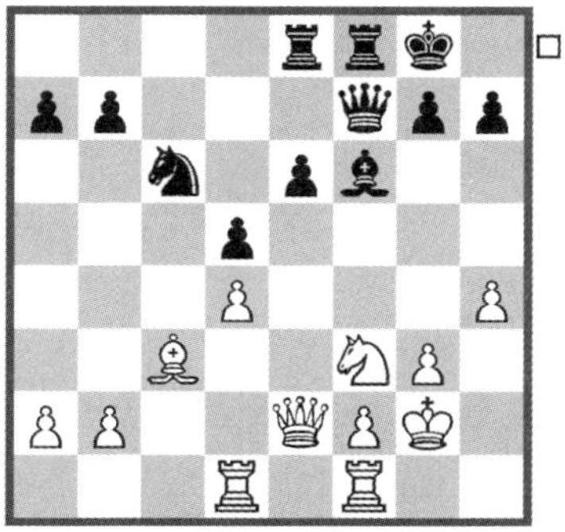

Position after: 18... ♖ce8

In the game Giri – Grandelius, chess24.com 2021, White's best continuation was the thematic rook lift:

**19. ♖d3!±**

Followed by ♖e3 as we've seen numerous times already.

## Conclusion to Chapter 5

This chapter is characterized by slower variations and more positional play, regardless of whether Black recaptures on d7 with the knight or queen. It's unlikely that a higher-rated player will play 3...♗d7 in the first instance. Even though our 'advantage' is less objective and more practical in the majority of variations, Black has to consistently deal with fairly passive and mundane positions against our Maroczy block.

In some of the subchapters, the alternative option of playing c2-c3 and d2-d4 offers welcome variety and I think I've also shown here that the road to equality is not at all easy for Black to find.

# Part III

# Rossolimo Transposition With 3...♘c6

# Various Sidelines

**1.e4 c5 2.♘f3 d6 3.♗b5+ ♘c6 4.0-0 ♗d7 5.♖e1 ♘f6 6.h3**

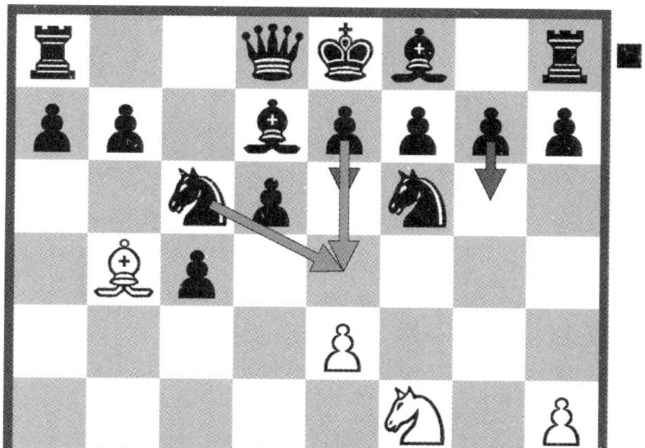

# Chapter Guide

## Chapter 6 – Various Sidelines

1.e4 c5 2.♘f3 d6 3.♗b5+ ♘c6 4.0-0 ♗d7 5.♖e1 ♘f6 6.h3

## a) 6...♘e5 7.♘xe5

**1. e4 c5 2. ♘f3 ♘c6 3. ♗b5 d6**

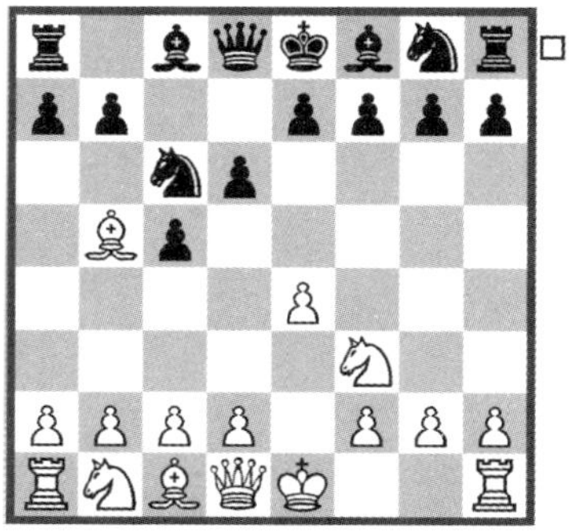

Position after: 3... d6

**4. 0-0 ♗d7 5. ♖e1 ♘f6**

In my first volume I covered this line and gave 6.c3. Although I still haven't found any problems with that move, I've also analysed 6.h3, so why not include it in this volume? :)

5... a6 6. ♗xc6 ♗xc6 7. d4 has already been covered in the first volume.

**6. h3**

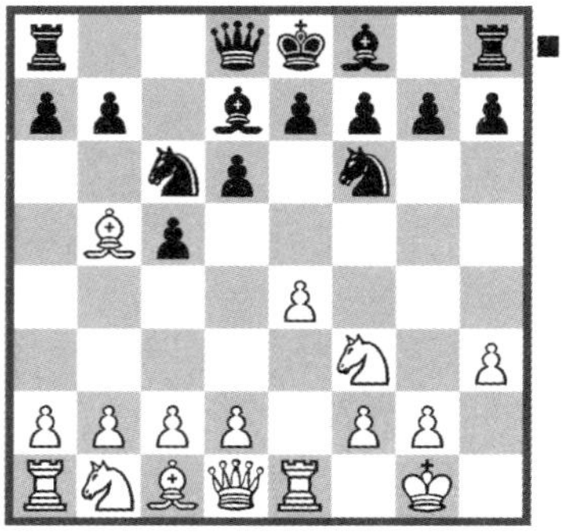

Position after: 6. h3

**6... ♘e5**

The most solid way for Black to play, trying to exchange off at least one set of minor pieces. Theory is light on the ground here, but I will give two alternatives that seem to suffice for an edge.

**A)** 6... e6 7. c3 ♘e5 8. ♗f1 ♘xf3+ 9. ♕xf3 transposes to the main line.

**B)** 6... g6 7. c3 ♘e5 is considered within the 6...g6 subchapter.

**7. ♘xe5!?**

7. ♗xd7+!? I analysed this move in great depth but couldn't find anything remotely convincing for White. I came to the realisation that it's quite prudent to refrain from exchanging off the light-squared bishops if we want to play for an advantage.

**7... ♗xb5**

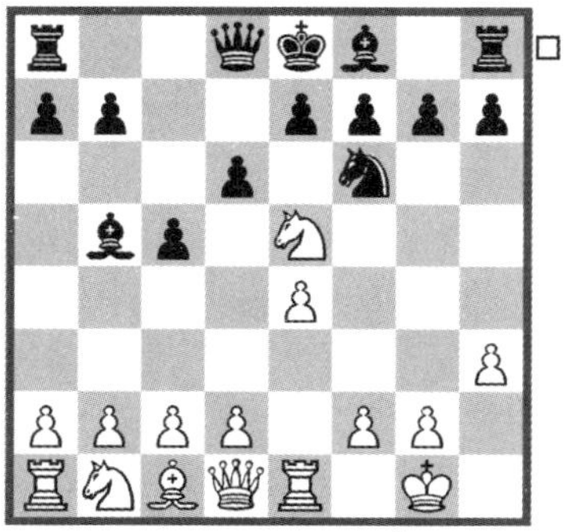

Position after: 7... ♗xb5

**8. a4!**

A fascinating idea. We've conceded the bishop-pair, but will now attempt to close the position so that our knights can dominate.

**8... ♗a6**

8... ♗d7?! 9. ♘xd7

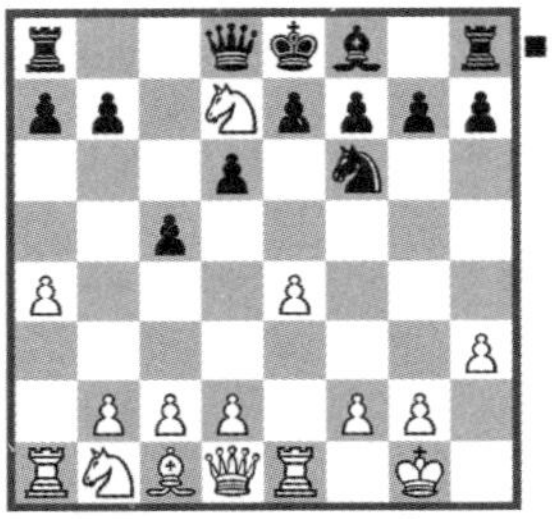

Position after: 9. ♘xd7

This time we can exchange on d7 as we have a concrete idea in mind. 9... ♕xd7 [9... ♘xd7 10. d4 cxd4 11. ♕xd4 This is basically a significantly better version of the line I give after 7. ♗xd7. 11... ♕b6 12. ♕xb6 ♘xb6 13. ♘c3 a6 14. a5 ♘d7 15. ♖a3!±] 10. d4 cxd4 11. ♗g5!

Position after: 11. ♗g5!

Black can't really stop us from capturing on f6, so may as well try to at least keep a pawn in return for the inevitable structural damage. 11... e6 [11... e5 12. c3 dxc3 13. ♗xf6! As my close friend Darragh Moran once told me, the biggest mistake people make is to quit while they're behind. cxb2 14. ♖a2 gxf6 15. ♘c3!± White has sacrificed three pawns, but the significance of this material deficit is negligible because Black is positionally lost.] 12. ♗xf6 gxf6 13. ♕xd4 ♗g7 14. ♘a3 0-0 15. ♖e3!

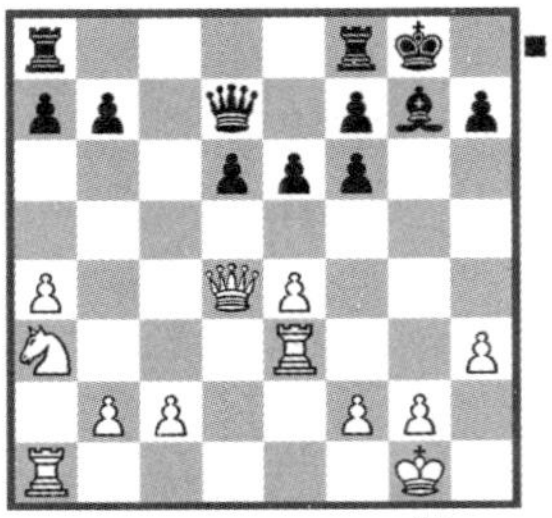

Position after: 15. ♖e3!

White is advantageous in both a positional and attacking sense. 15... ♔h8 16. ♖d1 f5 17. ♕xd6 ♕xd6 18. ♖xd6 ♗xb2 19. exf5±. White's structure is clearly better.

**9. ♘f3**

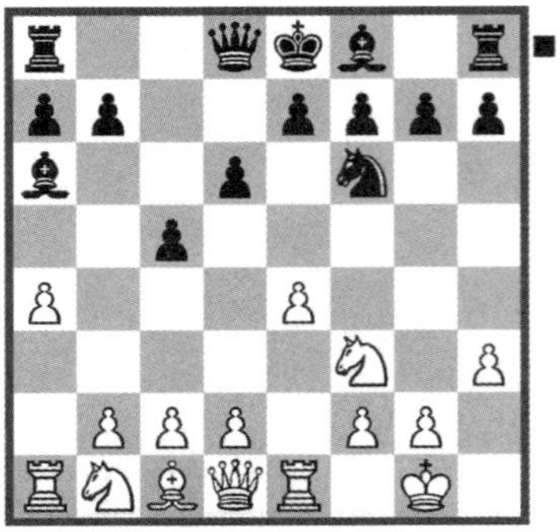

Position after: 9. ♘f3

**e5**

Seemingly Black's best option if they want to obstruct our Maroczy setup, but we can still place our pawns to hinder the prospects of Black's light-squared bishop. In the future we'll have the additional option of playing for f2-f4 ideas.

**A)** 9... g6?! We can now initiate a Maroczy structure, ordinarily playing against the light-squared bishop. 10. d4 cxd4 11. ♘xd4 ♗g7 12. b3 0-0 13. c4 b6 14. ♘c3 ♗b7 15. ♖a2!± Followed up by ♗g5 and ♖d2; our position is visibly very pleasant.

**B)** 9... e6 It makes reasonable sense for Black to play for a quick ...d6-d5 break against our potential Maroczy structure. However Black's ostracised a6-bishop renders this plan ineffective. 10. d4 cxd4 11. ♘xd4 ♗e7 12. b3

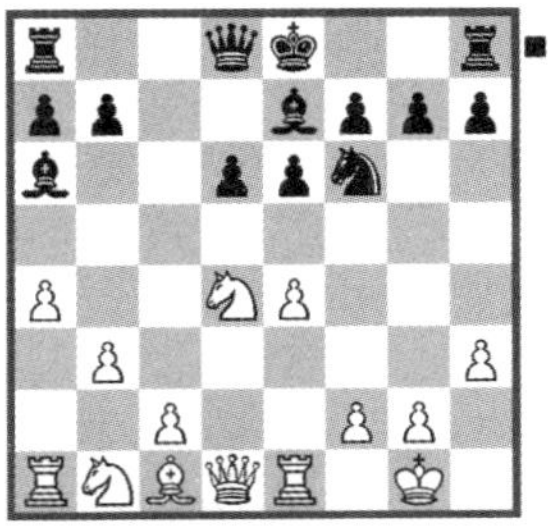

Position after: 12. b3

**B1)** 12... d5?! 13. e5 ♘e4 [13... ♘d7 14. ♕g4+–] 14. ♘d2 ♘c3 15. ♕g4 0-0 16. ♘f1→ Our pieces are well positioned to build up an initiative on the kingside.

**B2)** 12... 0-0 13. c4 d5?! 14. exd5 exd5 15. ♘f5!

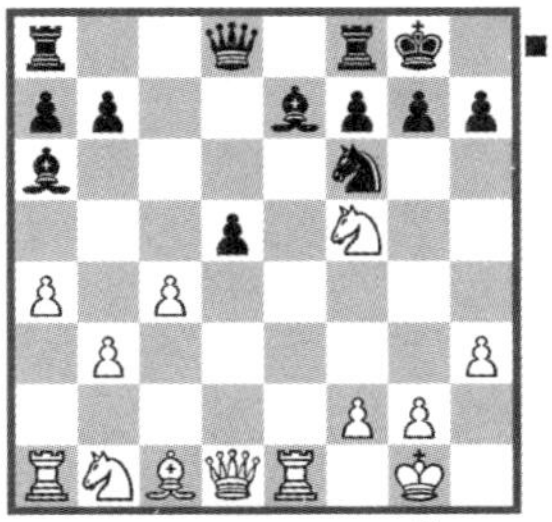

Position after: 15. ♘f5!

We wouldn't have this option if Black's bishop stood on c8 or d7. Now we have a chance to play for the initiative. 15... ♗b4 16. ♗d2 ♗xd2 17. ♕xd2 dxc4 18. ♕g5 ♘e8 19. ♘e7+ ♔h8 20. b4!

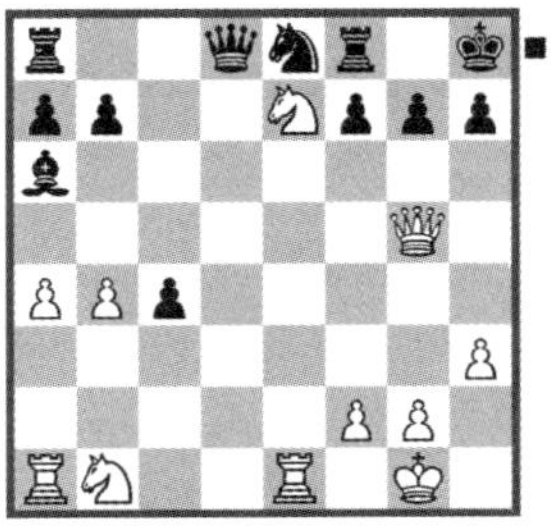

Position after: 20. b4!

We're not allowing Black's bishop to get into the game, and our active pieces are more than enough compensation for the pawn deficit. 20... ♕d4 [20... b6 21. ♘c3 h6 22. ♕h4+– followed by ♖ad1 and ♖e3 is overwhelming.] 21. ♘a3 b6 22. ♘c6 ♕f6 23. ♕xf6 ♘xf6 24. b5 ♗b7 25. ♘xc4±

**10. d3 ♗e7**

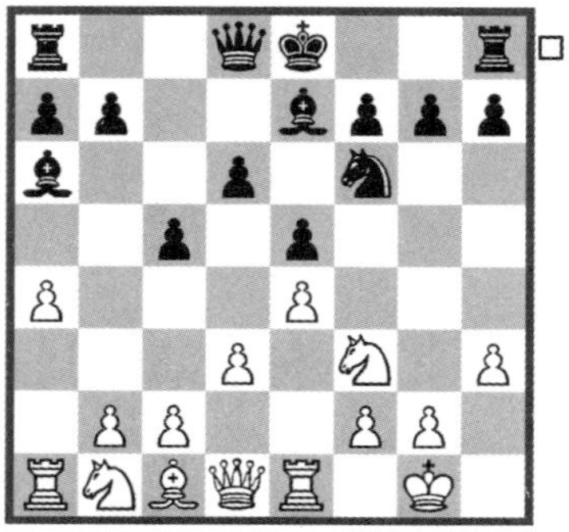

Position after: 10... ♗e7

**11. c4!**

11. ♘h4!? would force ...g7-g6, although I'm not sure how much of a difference it makes in the grand scheme of things. 11... g6 12. ♘f3 0-0 13. c4 b6 14. ♗d2 ♖e8 15. ♘c3 ♗b7 16. a5±

**11... b6 12. ♘c3 0-0 13. a5±**

The computer seems to really like this for White, although I'm not completely convinced on the actual extent of the advantage. However, I can say with some certainty that it is far more expedient to play the White side of this as Black's bishop on a6 is completely shut out from the game. We have ideas of ♘h2-f1-e3, perhaps intertwined with ♗g5-♗xf6. Finally, we can choose when to open the a-file - something which Black continuously has to watch out for.

## b) 6...♘e5 7.♗f1 ♘xf3 8.♕xf3 e6

**1. e4 c5 2. ♘f3 ♘c6 3. ♗b5 d6 4. 0-0 ♗d7 5. ♖e1 ♘f6 6. h3 ♘e5 7. ♗f1**

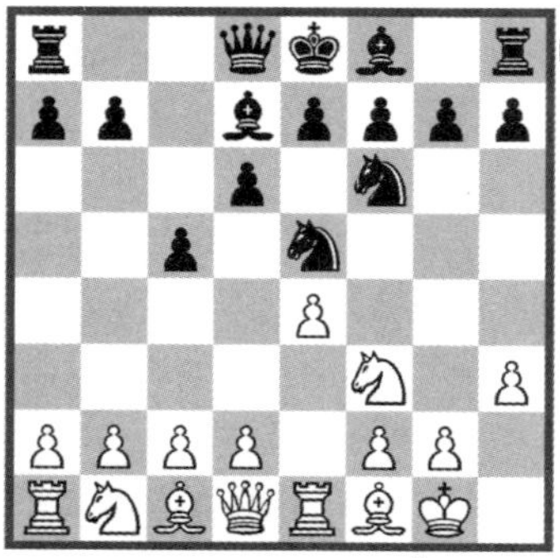

Position after: 7. ♗f1

**7... ♘xf3+!**

Black needs to capture on f3 as otherwise we will inflict doubled e-pawns. Whilst this could be positionally beneficial under specific circumstances, none of them apply here.

**A)** 7... ♗c6?! 8. ♘xe5 dxe5 9. d3

Position after: 9. d3

The e5-pawn is our target, and our next few moves will be played with the intention of maximising pressure on it. 9... e6 [9... c4 10. ♗d2! cxd3 11. cxd3 e6 12. ♗c3 ♘d7 13. ♘d2 ♗d6 14. ♘c4 ♗c7 15. ♗b4±] 10. a4

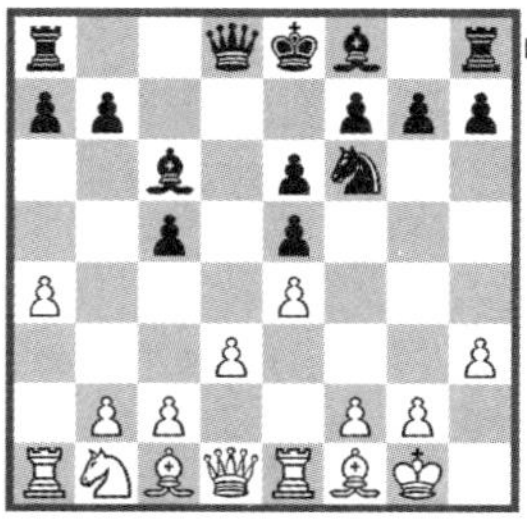

Position after: 10. a4

10... c4 [10... ♗e7 11. ♘d2 0-0 12. ♘c4 ♘d7 13. b3 ♕c7 14. ♕g4± Followed by ♗b2 and ♕g3. Black has to be careful of playing ...f7-f6, as the e6-pawn would suddenly become a weakness.] 11. ♗d2 cxd3 12. cxd3 ♗c5 13. ♗c3 ♗d4

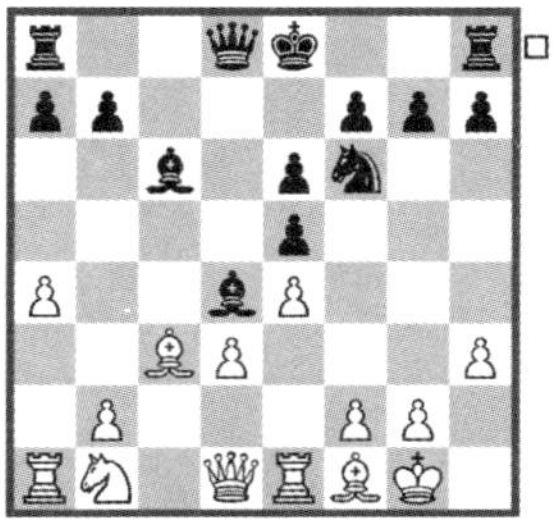

Position after: 13... ♗d4

Black has managed to justify their doubled e-pawns to a certain extent. Nevertheless, simple chess will ensure a favourable position for White. 14. ♕c2 0-0 15. ♘d2 ♖c8 16. ♖ec1 ♕d6

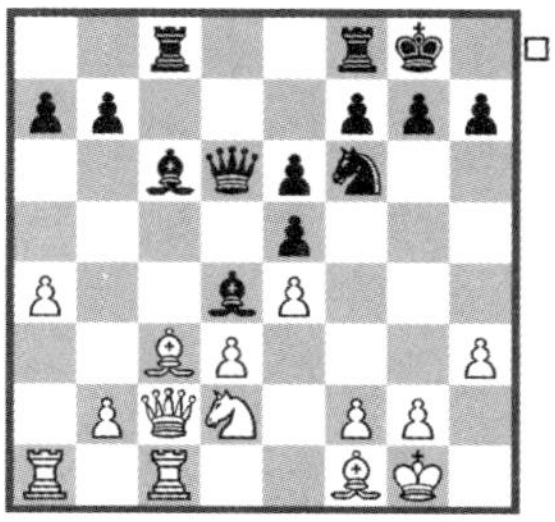

Position after: 16... ♕d6

17. ♘c4 ♕b8 18. b4± There remains plenty of scope to squeeze the opponent for the foreseeable future.

**B)** 7... e6 Invariably, it should be favourable for White if we're allowed to capture on e5. 8. ♘xe5 dxe5 9. d3 a6 10. a4

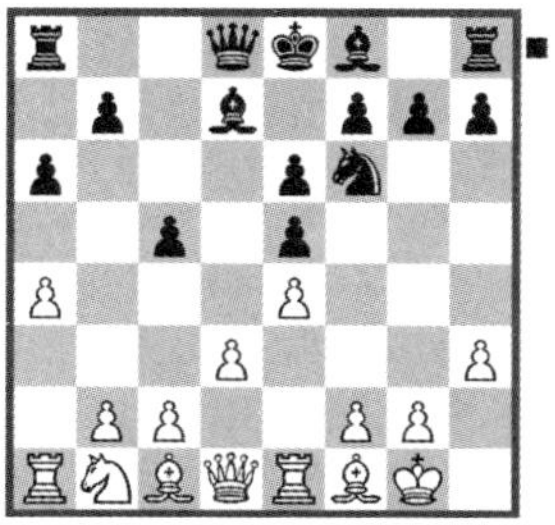

Position after: 10. a4

10... ♗d6 [10... b5?! 11. ♕f3 ♗d6 12. ♗g5 h6 13. ♗xf6 ♕xf6 14. ♕xf6 gxf6 15. axb5 ♗xb5 16. ♘c3±] 11. a5 0-0 12. ♕d2!± Our queen will go to c3, and then both Black's e5- and c5-pawns will feel the pressure after ♗e3 and ♘d2-c4.

**8. ♕xf3 e6**

**A)** 8... ♗c6 9. c3 e6 transposes to 8...e6.

**B)** 8... g5!? is probably best and I consider this separately. One reason I paid so much attention to 7.♘xe5 is because I suspect this novelty might be stronger than it looks.

**9. c3 ♗c6 10. d4**

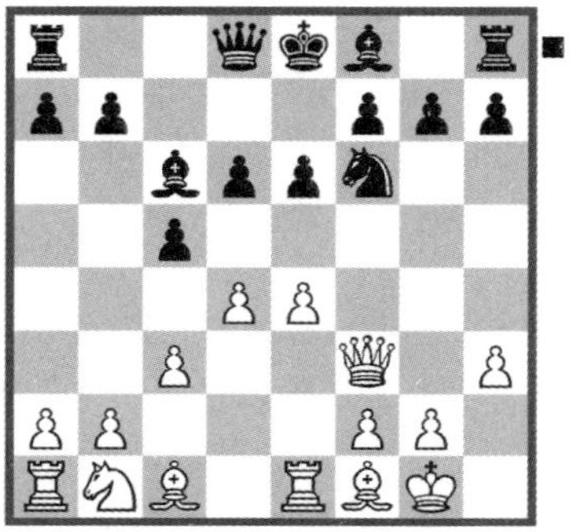

Position after: 10. d4

Although we have achieved our desired c3-d4-e4 pawn structure, Black's position is very solid. We must continue to play accurately to ensure an advantage.

**10... ♗e7**

Refraining from capturing on d4 guarantees that White can't use the c3-square for their knight. However, 10... ♗e7 has permitted us to change the pawn structure in a different way.

**A)** 10... d5 11. e5 ♘e4 12. ♗e3 cxd4 13. ♗xd4! Really important – it's always preferable to have a piece rather than a pawn on d4 in these French structures. 13... ♗c5 14. ♗xc5! ♘xc5 15. ♘d2 0-0 16. ♕e3± Followed by ♘f3-d4, and possibly f2-f4. Black lacks sufficient counterplay.

**B)** 10... cxd4 11. cxd4

**B1)** 11... ♗e7 12. ♘c3 0-0 13. ♗d3 e5 14. ♗e3

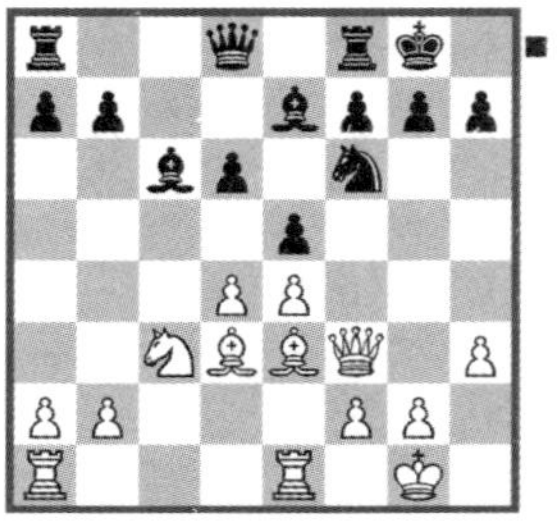

Position after: 14. ♗e3

None of Black's breaks are being permitted. 14... d5 This won't help Black's quest for equality, as our greater piece activity ensures that we maintain the initiative. 15. exd5 ♘xd5 16. ♘xd5 ♗xd5 17. ♗e4 ♗xe4 18. ♕xe4 exd4 19. ♗xd4 ♗f6 20. ♗c5 ♖e8 21. ♕xb7±. Black can't quite maintain material equality.

**B2)** 11... d5 12. e5 ♘e4 13. ♘c3

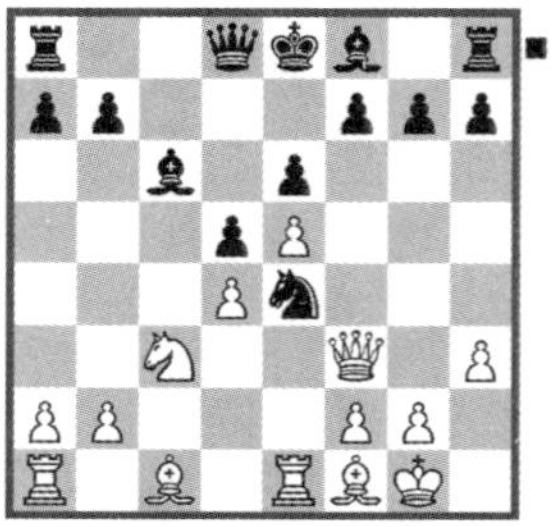

Position after: 13. ♘c3

Although we now have a pawn on d4, the difference compared to 10...d5 is that we've acquired the useful c3-square for our knight.

**B2.1)** 13... ♗e7 14. ♗d3 0-0 [14... ♘xc3 15. bxc3 0-0 16. ♕g4→] 15. ♕g4 ♔h8 16. ♘xe4 dxe4 17. ♗xe4 ♕xd4 18. ♗xc6 ♕xg4 19. hxg4 bxc6 20. ♗e3±

**B2.2)** 13... f5 14. exf6 ♕xf6 15. ♕e3± Black has had to weaken their structure in their attempt to reduce our kingside attacking possibilities.

**11. dxc5!? dxc5 12. ♘d2 0-0**

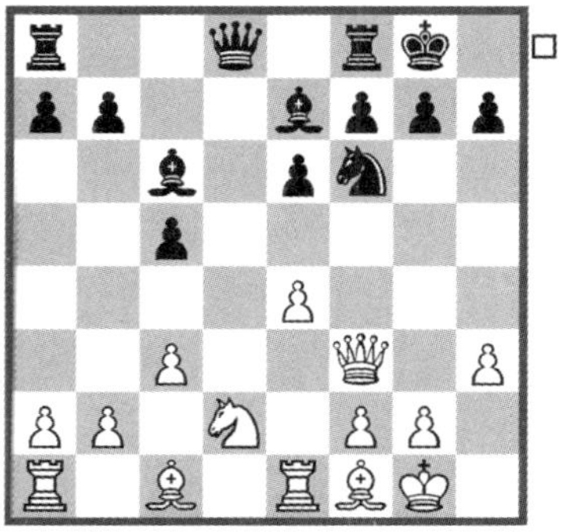

Position after: 12... 0-0

**13. ♕g3**

13. a4!? It's possible to start with this move, although we need to be aware of Black's ...♘xe4 trick which may simplify things a little too much for our liking. 13... a6 [13... ♘xe4 14. ♘xe4 f5 15. ♗c4 ♗xe4 16. ♗xe6+ ♔h8 17. ♕h5±] 14. a5 ♘xe4 15. ♘xe4 f5 16. ♗c4 ♗xe4 17. ♕d1±

**13... ♘h5**

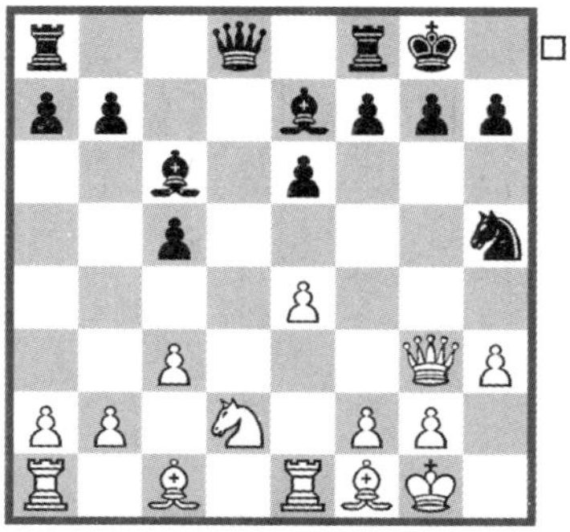

Position after: 13... ♘h5

This line was also given by Vasilios Kotronias in his book 'Beating the Anti-Sicilians', where he inferred that Black was fine. I think 'playable' is a better description of Black's position – in my opinion White has a pleasant edge.

13... ♔h8 14. e5! Here we have good attacking possibilities after 14... ♘d7 15. ♘f3 ♕c7 16. ♗f4±.

**14. ♕e3!**

14. ♕h2 was the only option given by Kotronias, but the text move feels more normal.

**14... e5**

Black should probably prevent us from playing e4-e5 ourselves.

**A)** 14... b6 15. ♘f3 ♕c7 16. e5!

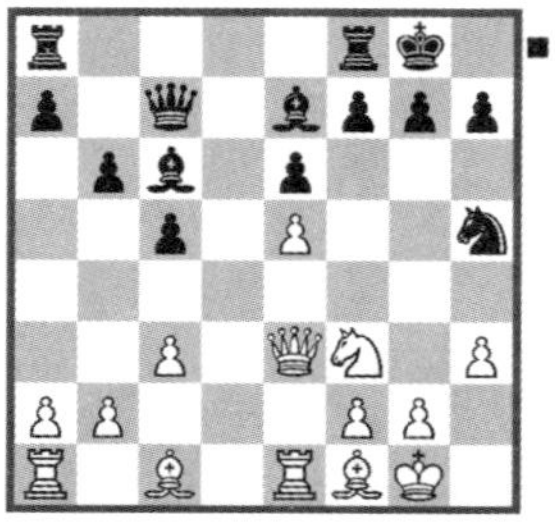

Position after: 16. e5!

Black's knight will find itself completely misplaced on h5. 16... g6 17. ♗d3 ♘g7 18. ♗e4 ♖fd8 19. g4!±

**B)** 14... ♗g5 15. ♕xc5 ♗xd2 16. ♖d1 ♘f6 17. ♖xd2 ♘xe4 18. ♖xd8± Asis Gargatagli – Baskin, Chess.com 2021.

**15. ♘c4 ♕c7 16. a4 ♘f4 17. g3 ♘e6**

Position after: 17... ♘e6

**18. h4±**

We can continue with ♕e2-g4, followed by ♘e3. Black certainly hasn't equalised yet.

## c) 6...♘e5 7.♗f1 ♘xf3 8.♕xf3 g5

**1. e4 c5 2. ♘f3 ♘c6 3. ♗b5 d6 4. 0-0 ♗d7 5. ♖e1 ♘f6 6. h3 ♘e5 7. ♗f1 ♘xf3+ 8. ♕xf3 g5!?**

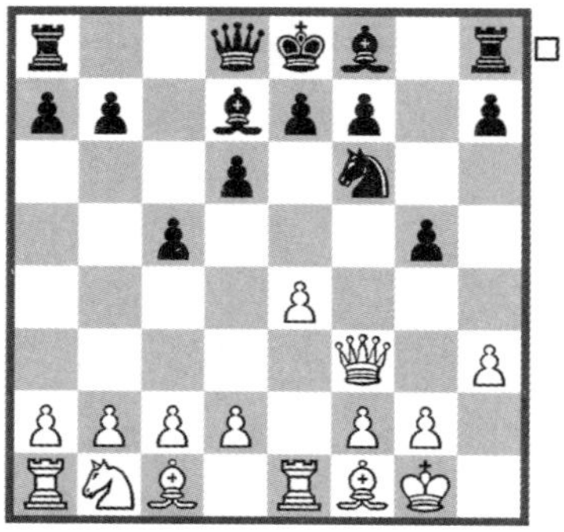

Position after: 8... g5!?

A typical way to make things unclear, and we'll look at more ...g7-g5 examples in the next pair of subchapters. For now, all we need to know is that we should almost always respond to this move with a central break.

**9. d4! g4 10. hxg4 cxd4 11. c3!**

Position after: 11. c3!

Our play is consistent in aiming to develop with tempi.

**11... ♘xg4**

11... dxc3? 12. e5! dxe5 [12... ♗c6 13. ♗b5!±] 13. ♘xc3 ♗c6 14. ♕g3 ♘d7 15. ♗e3 ♖g8 16. b4 Black doesn't have anywhere to castle and is pretty much lost. 16... a6 17. a4 b6 18. ♖ed1+–

**12. cxd4 ♗g7 13. ♖d1**

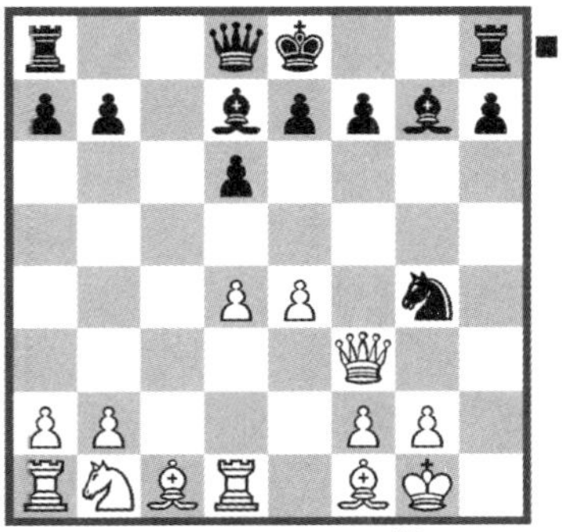

Position after: 13. ♖d1

**13... ♕b6!**

13... e5?! Here White gets a clear advantage with a couple of incisive moves. 14. ♗b5!

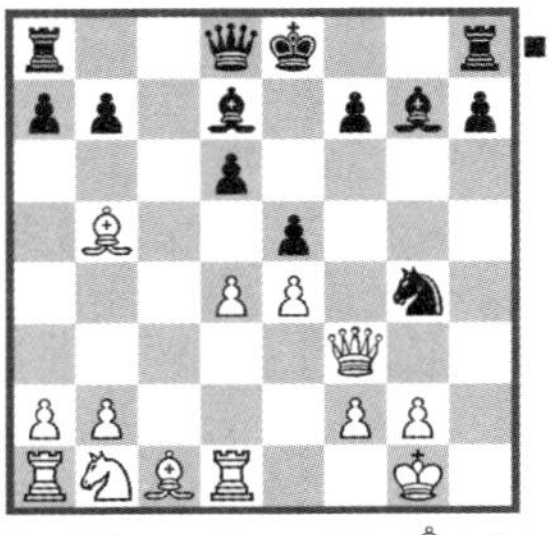

Position after: 14. ♗b5!

14... 0-0 [14... ♗xb5?! 15. ♕xg4 ♕f6 16. dxe5 dxe5 17. ♘c3 ♗c6 18. ♘d5 ♗xd5 19. ♖xd5 0-0 20. ♗e3±] 15. ♗g5!

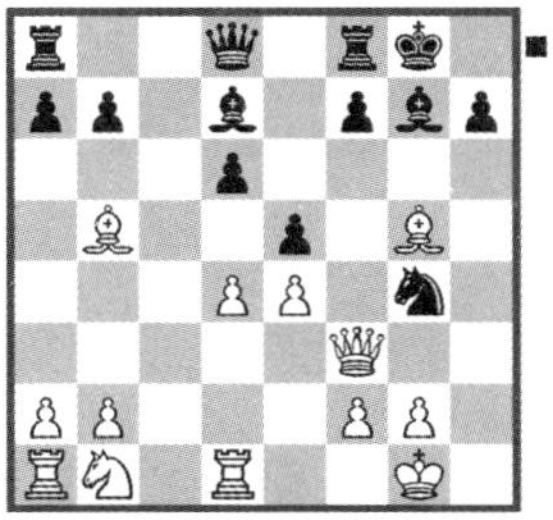

Position after: 15. ♗g5!

[15. ♗xd7 leads to complications: 15... ♕xd7 16. dxe5 f5! 17. ♖xd6 ♕c8∞]

**A)** 15... ♕xg5 16. ♗xd7 The transformation into an opposite-coloured bishop middlegame favours us, as Black's earlier ...g5-g4 advance has left behind structural holes. 16... ♘f6 17. ♗f5 exd4 18. ♖xd4

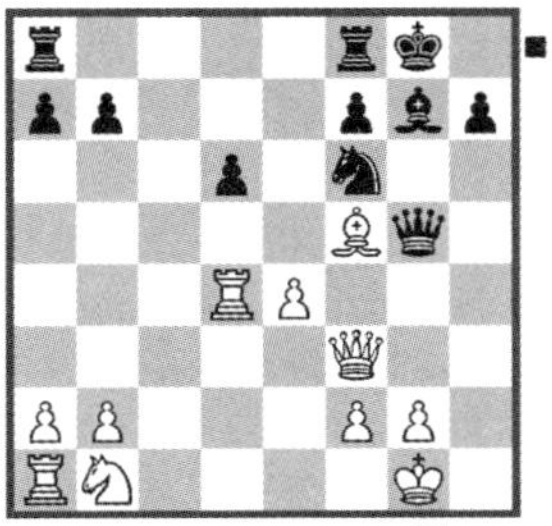

Position after: 18. ♖xd4

18... d5 [18... ♘xe4?! 19. ♖xe4 ♕c1+ 20. ♔h2 ♕xb2 21. ♖g4! ♕xa1 22. ♘c3+–] 19. ♘c3 dxe4 20. ♘xe4 ♘xe4 21. ♖xe4±

**B)** 15... f6! 16. ♗h4 ♗xb5 17. ♕xg4

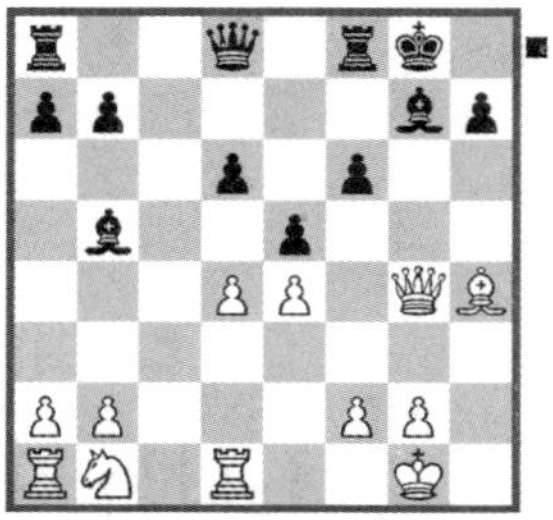

Position after: 17. ♕xg4

17... ♕c8 [17... exd4 18. ♘a3 ♗d7 19. ♕g3 ♕e8 20. ♖xd4±] 18. ♕g3 ♗e2 19. ♖e1 ♕g4 20. f3 ♕xg3 21. ♗xg3 ♗d3 22. ♖d1 ♗e2 23. ♖d2 ♗c4 24. ♘a3 ♗f7 25. b3± Once again, White's nicer structure gives us the favourable chances in this queenless middlegame.

**14. ♕d3 d5 15. ♘c3 dxe4**

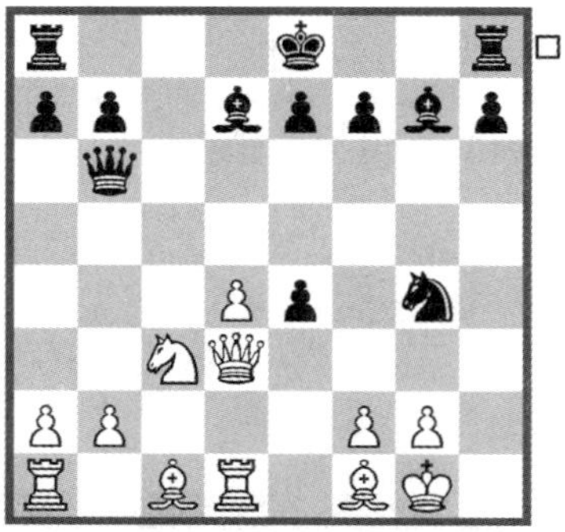

Position after: 15... dxe4

**16. ♕xe4**

White has managed to consolidate and maintain the superior pawn structure. However, with a couple of engine-like moves, Black can keep things relatively unclear.

**16... f5**

After 16... 0-0 17. ♘d5 ♕e6 18. ♘xe7+ ♔h8 19. ♕xe6 fxe6 20. f3 ♘f6 21. d5± White has good chances to press in the ending.

**17. ♕f4 ♖c8 18. a4**

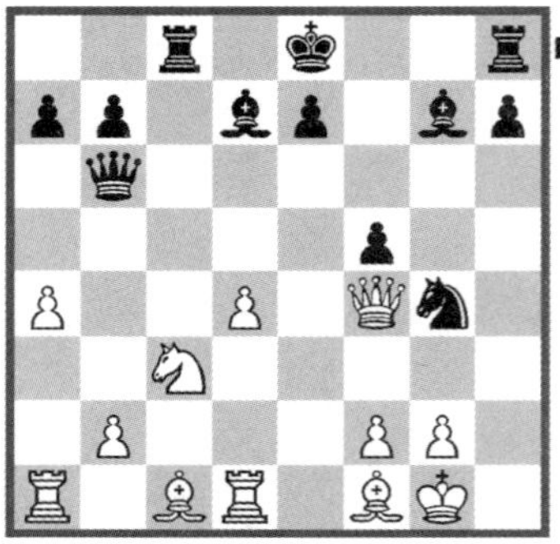

Position after: 18. a4

**18... ♗h6! 19. ♕g3 ♗xc1 20. ♖dxc1 ♕xb2**

The engine claims Black is absolutely fine, but I'd still prefer White in a practical game. Nevertheless, we have an excellent alternative in 7.♘xe5 if it's clear that your opponent is heavily booked-up.

## d) 6...e6 7.c3 d5 8.exd5 ♘xd5 9.d4 cxd4 10.♗c4 ♗e7

**1. e4 c5 2. ♘f3 ♘c6 3. ♗b5 d6 4. 0-0 ♗d7 5. ♖e1 ♘f6 6. h3 e6**

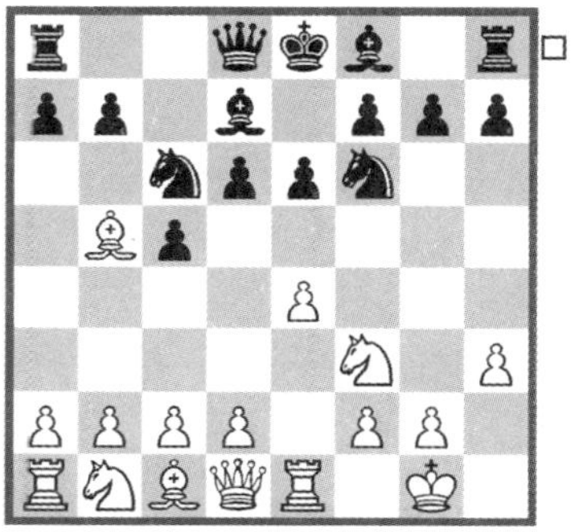

Position after: 6... e6

A popular way for Black to contest the centre is to play a quick ...e7-e6 and ...d6-d5.

6... a6 7. ♗f1 can again be inserted before embarking on roughly the same plan, and I will be looking at that next, continuing the theme from the previous pair of subchapters.

**7. c3 d5**

7... ♗e7 8. d4 cxd4 9. cxd4 d5 10. e5 ♘e4 11. ♗d3 We've reached exactly the same position as we'll encounter in the next subchapter after 6... a6, except that Black's pawn is on a7. I'm not sure who this benefits, but I don't think it makes an awful lot of difference.

**8. exd5**

8. e5 isn't possible due to 8... ♘xe5∓.

**8... ♘xd5 9. d4 cxd4**

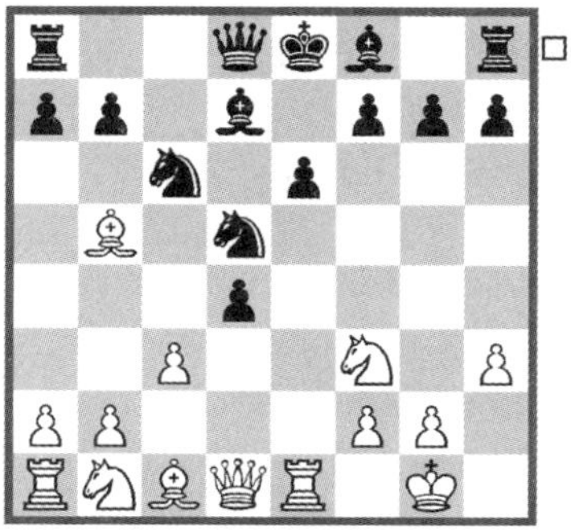

Position after: 9... cxd4

**10. ♗c4!N**

A really important move to remember, frustrating Black's attempts of stabilising a piece on d5. Here Black has two choices. They can either play ...♘b6 and capture the c3-pawn, in which case we should have excellent compensation. Or, they can simply develop normally but face a slightly inferior version of a typical IQP position.

10. cxd4 ♗d6 11. ♘c3 ♘ce7=

**10... ♗e7 11. cxd4**

11. ♗xd5 is certainly a plausible option but I'm not convinced about the extent of White's advantage after 11... exd5 12. ♘xd4 0-0 13. ♗e3±.

**11... 0-0 12. ♘c3**

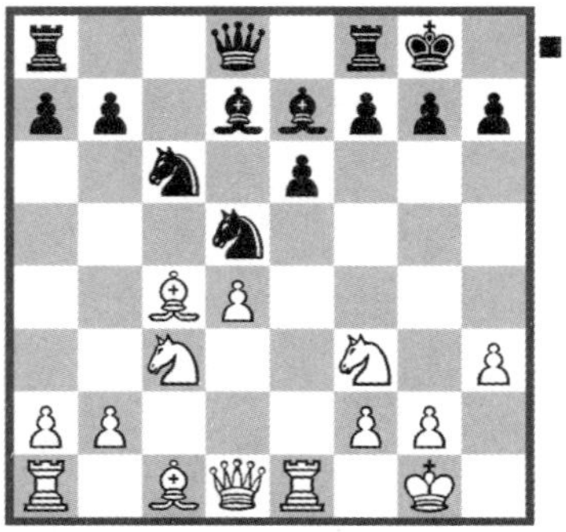

Position after: 12. ♘c3

In general, this seems a little uncomfortable for Black to play, and the following variations will illustrate various notable ideas in these IQP positions.

**12... ♘f6**

**A)** 12... ♘xc3 I feel like the position suits hanging pawns for White, as Black's kingside looks a little unprotected without an f6-knight. Of course Black still remains relatively solid. 13. bxc3 ♗f6 14. ♗d3 ♖c8 15. ♗a3 ♘e7

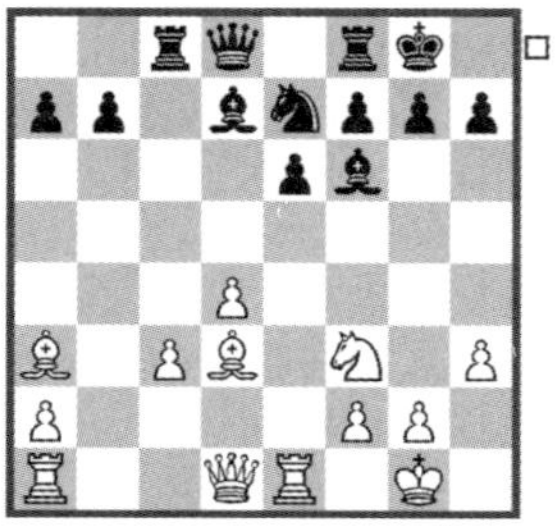

Position after: 15... ♘e7

16. ♕c2! Inducing ...g7-g6, which may further weaken Black's kingside. 16... g6 17. ♕d2 ♖e8 18. ♖ab1 ♕c7 19. c4 ♗c6 20. ♘e5↑ We have ideas of ♕f4 and even a d4-d5 push at some point. Black's position feels very dodgy.

**B)** 12... ♘cb4 13. a3 ♘xc3 14. bxc3 ♘d5 15. ♕d3

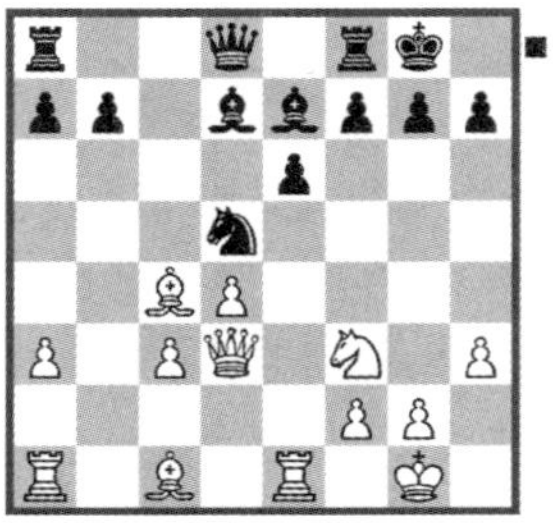

Position after: 15. ♕d3

With the Black knight on d5, we can always think about dropping our bishop back to b3 – followed by either ♗c2 or c3-c4. The rest of the variation is just an example of various ideas that we have. 15... ♖c8 16. ♗d2 ♗d6 17. ♘e5 b5 18. ♗b3 ♘b6 If the Black knight went to f6, ♗c2 followed by ♗g5 looked dangerous. 19. ♗c2 g6 20. ♗h6 ♖e8 21. ♕f3

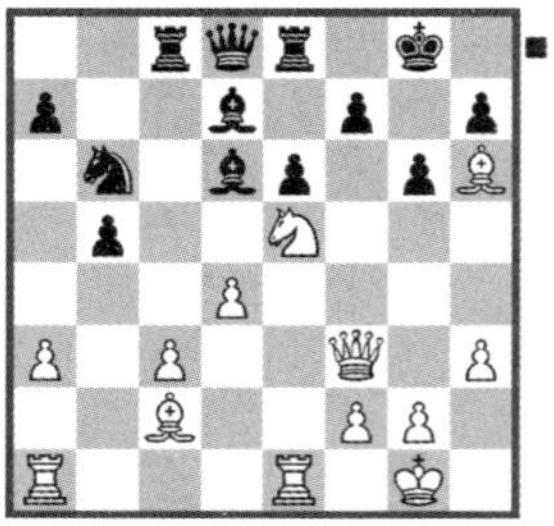

Position after: 21. ♕f3

21... ♗xe5 [21... ♕e7 22. ♖ad1↑] 22. dxe5 Now that Black has given up the dark-squared bishop, they desperately want to trade a lot of material – leading to a superior endgame. We should try our hardest to keep many pieces on the board, even if we have to sacrifice one or two pawns. This is our best chance of creating threats and building on our initiative. 22... ♕h4 23. ♕e3! ♘d5 24. ♕d2 ♖xc3 25. ♗e4 ♖ec8 26. ♖ad1↑

**C)** 12... ♗b4 13. ♗d2 ♘ce7 14. ♘xd5 ♘xd5 15. ♗xd5 ♗xd2 16. ♕xd2 exd5 17. ♖ac1± Our advantage rests on a slightly superior minor piece.

**13. ♗f4**

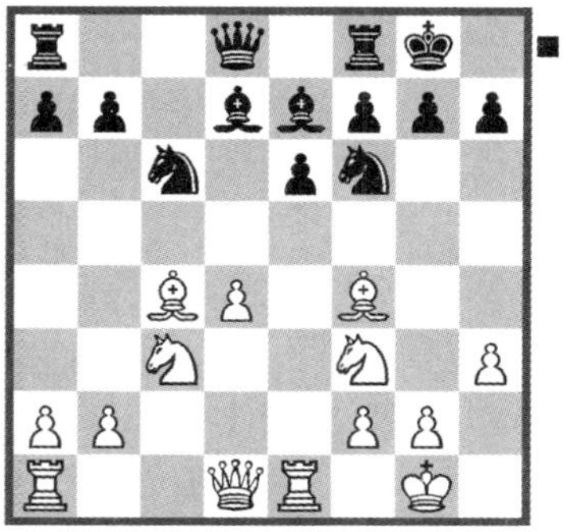
Position after: 13. ♗f4

If Black had two moves they would be ...♘cb4 and ...♗c6. Unfortunately for them, there is no time for that.

**13... ♘b4**

**A)** 13... ♘a5 14. ♗d3 ♖c8 15. ♘e5↑

**B)** 13... ♖c8 14. d5!

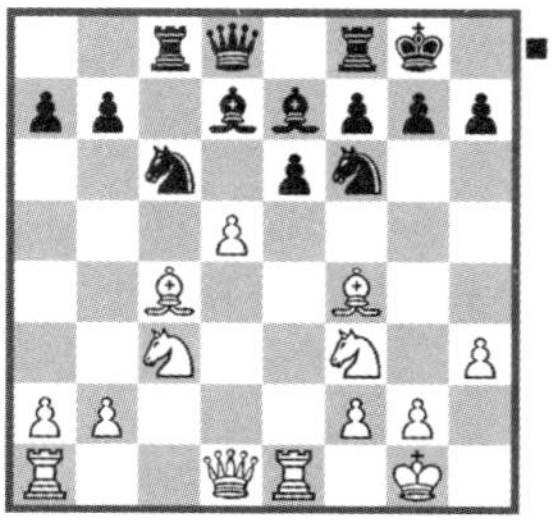
Position after: 14. d5!

A really typical break in IQP positions. We make the pawn structure symmetrical again, only with comparatively more active pieces which guarantees an initiative. 14... ♘xd5 15. ♘xd5 exd5 16. ♗xd5 ♗b4 17. ♖e2 ♕f6 18. ♗g3 ♗c5 19. ♖c1 ♗b6 20. ♖c4↑

**14. a3! ♘bd5 15. ♘xd5**

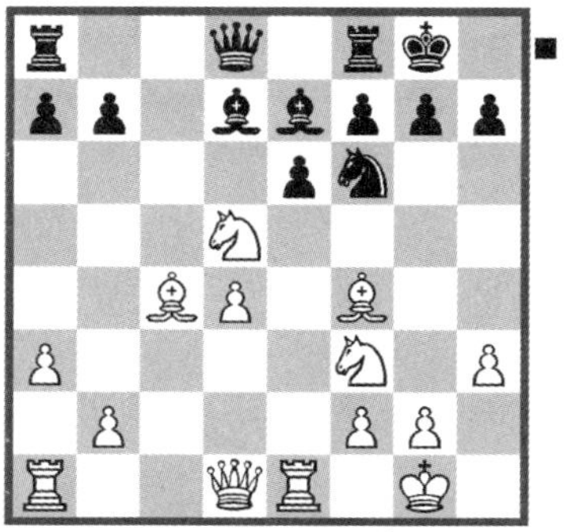
Position after: 15. ♘xd5

**15... ♘xd5**

15... exd5 16. ♗d3±

**16. ♗xd5 exd5 17. ♖c1±**

We should continue playing actively to ensure our advantage doesn't dissipate.

A future exchange of dark-squared bishops also looks beneficial for us.

## e) 6...e6 7.c3 d5 8.exd5 ♘xd5 9.d4 cxd4 10.♗c4 ♘b6

**1. e4 c5 2. ♘f3 ♘c6 3. ♗b5 d6 4. 0-0 ♗d7 5. ♖e1 ♘f6 6. h3 e6 7. c3 d5 8. exd5 ♘xd5 9. d4 cxd4 10. ♗c4!N ♘b6**

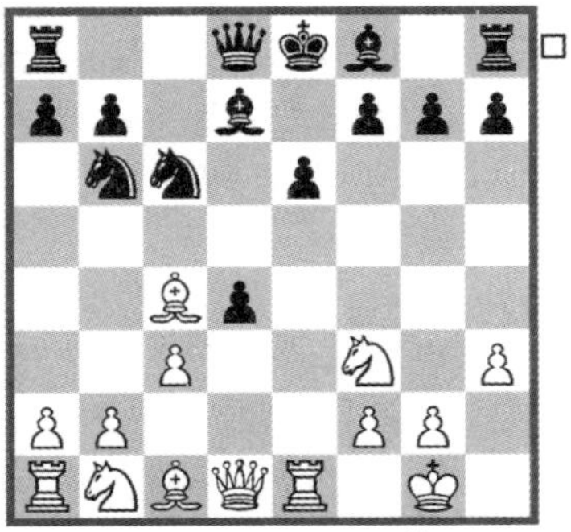

Position after: 10... ♘b6

**11. ♗b3 dxc3**

Black accepts the challenge, but now they will have to grovel in a very passive position.

**12. ♘xc3 ♗e7 13. ♕e2 0-0 14. ♗f4**

Black's pieces are confined to the queenside, whereas our plan is easy. We can bring our a1-rook into the game and continue our initiative with an attack on the kingside.

*(see diagram next column)*

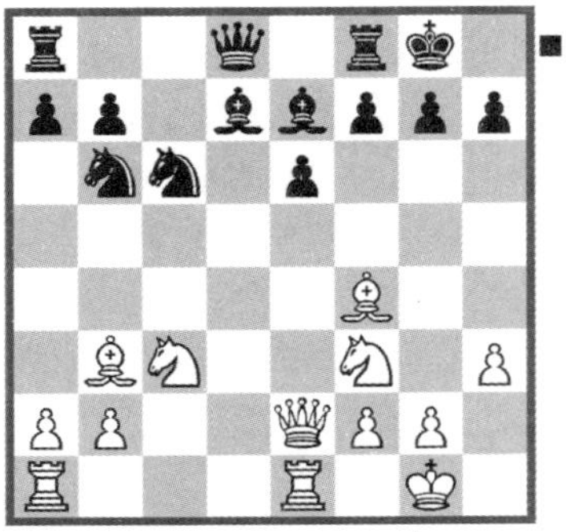

Position after: 14. ♗f4

**14... ♘a5**

After a couple of natural moves, Black again has some element of choice. Let's take the move that was tried before in correspondence as the main line.

**A)** 14... ♗b4?! Attempting to gain space and exchange pieces with this move seems very dubious to me. 15. ♖ad1 ♖e8 16. ♗c2!

Position after: 16. ♗c2!

Lining up against the h7-pawn without delay. 16... ♘d5? Critical, but not great. [After 16... g6 17. a3 ♗xc3 18. bxc3 f6 19. ♗b3 ♘d5 20. ♗xd5 exd5 21. ♕b5± White wins the pawn back and continues to press.] 17. ♗xh7+! ♔xh7 18. ♘g5+ ♔g6 [18... ♔g8 19. ♕h5+–] 19. ♕d3+ f5 20. ♕g3 ♗xc3 21. bxc3 ♔f6

Position after: 21... ♔f6

22. ♗d6! We're a piece down and don't have any immediate threats, but Black's king position is so bad (and our pieces so active) that we can afford to take our time a little bit. 22... g6 [22... b5 23. h4! ♖h8 24. ♖d3 ♖c8 25. ♗e5+ ♘xe5 26. ♕xe5+ ♔g6 27. ♖g3+–] 23. c4 ♘b6 24. ♕c3+ e5 25. h4 ♔g7 26. c5 ♘a4 27. ♕c4+–

**B)** 14... ♗f6 A more solid way to transfer the c6-knight to d5, but we'll be able to gain the bishop-pair again with ♘e4 and ♘xf6. 15. ♖ad1 ♘e7 16. ♘e4 ♘ed5 17. ♘xf6+ ♕xf6 18. ♗g5

*(see analysis diagram next column)*

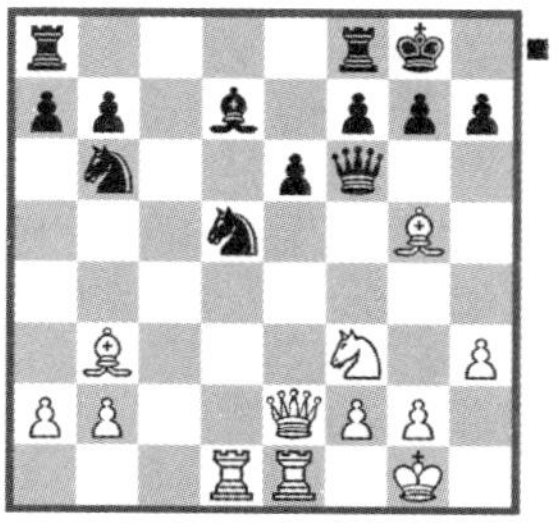

Position after: 18. ♗g5

18... ♕g6 19. ♗c2 ♗b5 Black won't lose their queen, but must defend a worse ending after 20. ♗xg6 ♗xe2 21. ♗xf7+ ♖xf7 22. ♖xe2 h6 23. ♗c1± .

**15. ♗c2 ♖c8 16. ♖ad1 ♘ac4**

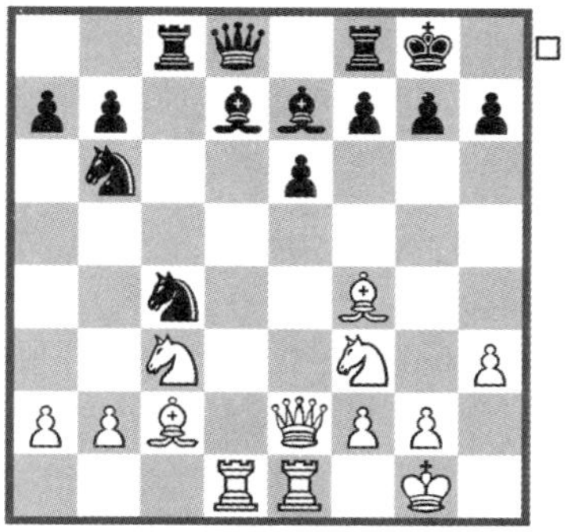

Position after: 16... ♘ac4

Reaching an interesting decision junction for White.

**17. ♗b1**

**A)** 17. ♘e5!? also kept the initiative going in Mignon – De Oliveira, ICCF email 2015.

**B)** Another nice dynamic alternative is: 17. ♘a4!?

Position after: 17. ♘a4!?

17... ♗f6 The first of a number of difficult moves Black has to find. [17... ♘xa4 18. ♗xa4 ♘d6 19. ♗b3± causes Black continuing embarrassment along the d-file.] 18. ♘xb6 ♘xb6 19. ♕e4 g6 20. ♗b3 White threatens both ♕xb7 and ♘e5. The best defense follows: 20... ♗xb2!

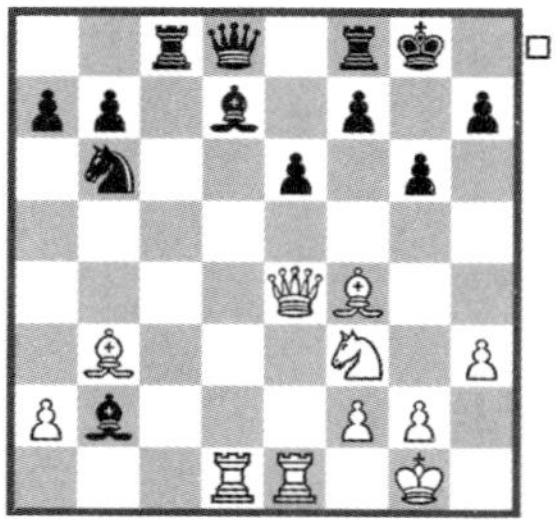

Position after: 20... ♗xb2!

21. ♘e5 ♘d5 22. ♗h6 ♗c6 23. ♖e2 ♗c3 24. ♖c2! ♘f4 25. ♕xf4 ♕xd1+ 26. ♔h2 ♗xg2 27. ♔xg2 ♕d4 28. ♕xd4 ♗xd4 29. ♗xf8 ♖xc2 30. ♗xc2 ♔xf8 31. ♘c4± and White continues to press despite Black's mostly successful handling of the position.

**17... ♗f6 18. ♗c1!**

Forced, but it's not a backward step. Our bishops are still very powerful and continue to create problems for Black. Black has a choice between giving up the f6-bishop and losing an exchange.

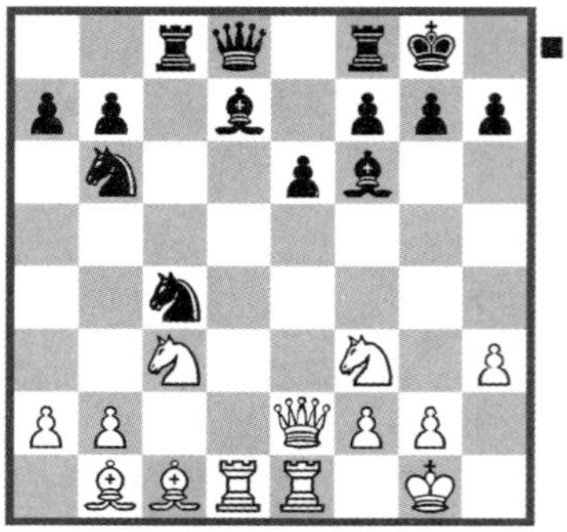

Position after: 18. ♗c1!

**18... g6**

It is more human to try and retain the bishop.

18... ♗xc3 19. ♕d3! f5 20. ♕xc3 ♘d5 21. ♕d4⩱∞ White retains good practical compensation for the pawn (+0.3).

**19. ♘e4 ♗g7 20. b3! ♘e5 21. ♘xe5 ♗xe5 22. ♗a3 ♘d5! 23. ♗xf8**

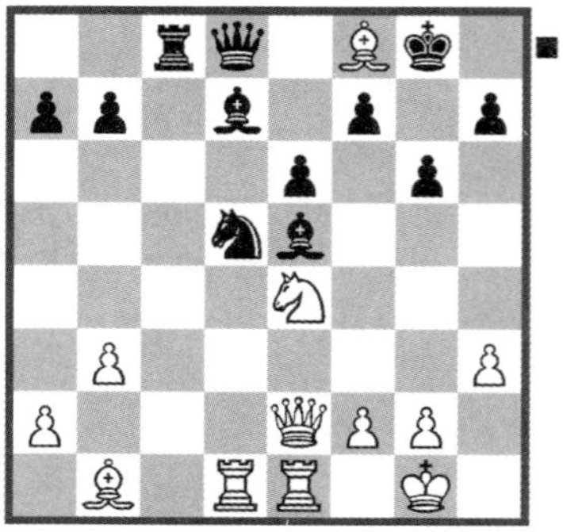

Position after: 23. ♗xf8

**23... ♕xf8±**

After a long struggle Black has obtained some measure of solidity, however I would still back the rooks in the long run.

## f) 6...e5 7.c3 ♗e7

**1. e4 c5 2. ♘f3 ♘c6 3. ♗b5 d6 4. 0-0 ♗d7 5. ♖e1 ♘f6 6. h3**

Another critical response to our attempts to control the centre is to play ...e7-e5. As always, we'll examine this move with and without the intermezzo ...a6.

**6... e5**

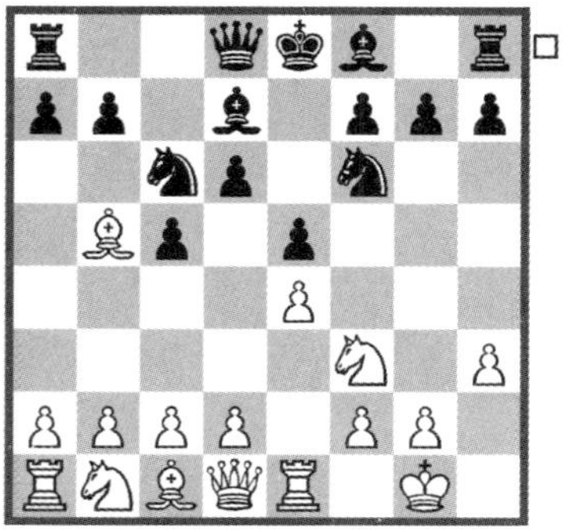

Position after: 6... e5

6... a6 7. ♗f1 e5 is considered next.

**7. c3 ♗e7 8. d4 0-0**

8... exd4 9. cxd4 cxd4 10. ♘xd4 0-0 11. ♘c3± White has a risk-free advantage.

**9. d5!**

Black's pieces will feel slightly uncoordinated after this move.

**9... ♘a5**

9... ♘b8 10. ♗d3!

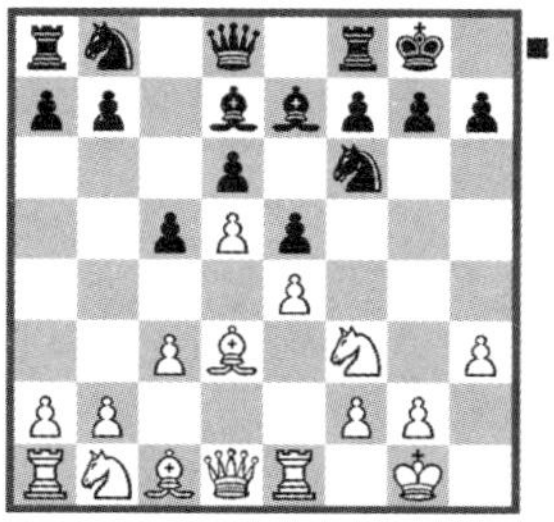

Position after: 10. ♗d3!

Swapping off light-squared bishops might seem logical, but Black's bishop on d7 is actually just hindering their own development. 10... ♘a6 [10... b5 11. a4 c4 12. ♗c2±] 11. a4 ♘e8 12. ♘bd2 ♘ac7 13. ♘c4 f5 14. exf5 ♗xf5 15. ♗xf5 ♖xf5

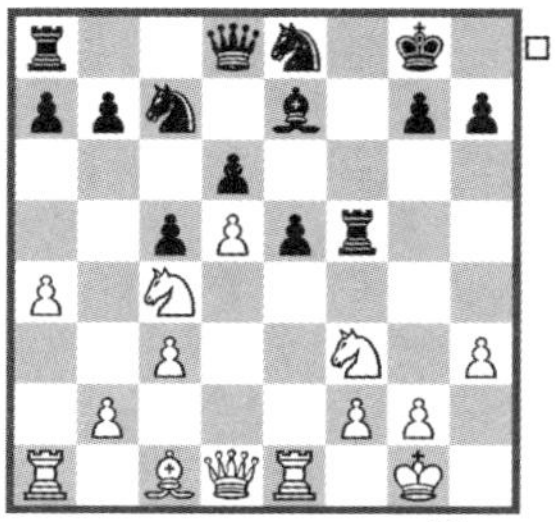

Position after: 15... ♖xf5

16. b4± We were able to trade light-squared bishops anyway, and have a positionally superior King's Indian type of position.

**10. ♗xd7**

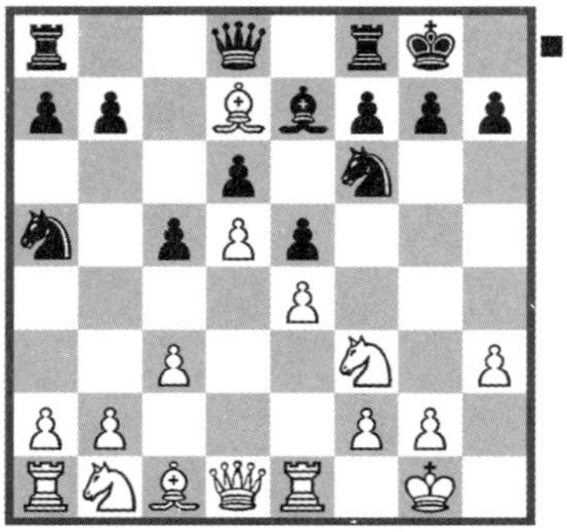

Position after: 10. ♗xd7

This time it makes sense to trade the bishops, and Black will always struggle to create anything meaningful on the kingside.

**10... ♕xd7 11. b3 b5 12. ♕c2 ♘h5 13. ♗e3**

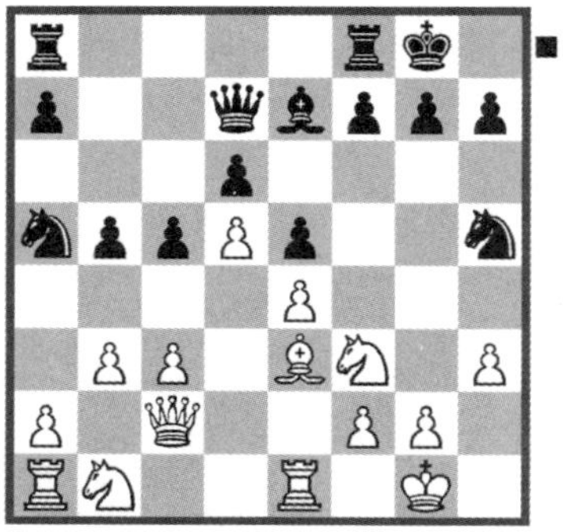

Position after: 13. ♗e3

**13... g6**

13... f5 14. exf5 ♖xf5 15. ♘bd2 ♖af8 16. c4±

**14. ♕e2!**

Hampering Black's attempts to recapture on f5 with the pawn.

**14... ♘f4 15. ♗xf4 exf4 16. ♘bd2 ♗f6 17. e5 dxe5**

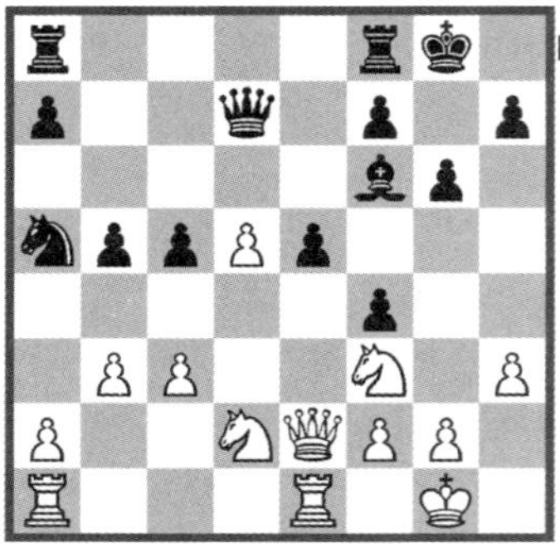

Position after: 17... dxe5

**18. ♖ad1!±**

## g) 6...e5 7.c3 ♕b6

**1. e4 c5 2. ♘f3 ♘c6 3. ♗b5 d6 4. 0-0 ♗d7 5. ♖e1 ♘f6 6. h3 e5 7. c3 ♕b6!?**

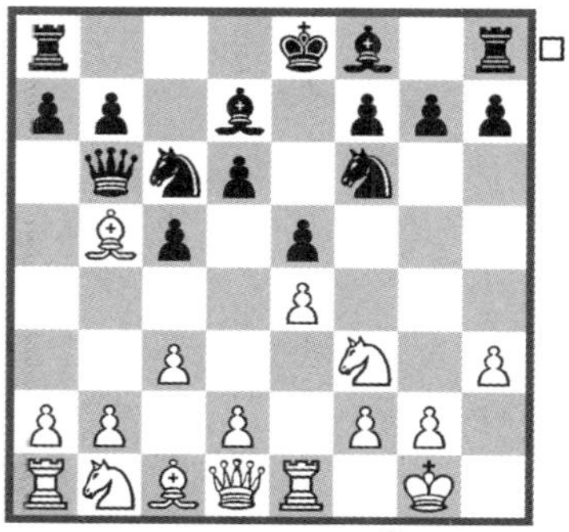

Position after: 7... ♕b6!?

This move has never been played in a practical game, but it's important to remember it because we can only achieve an advantage by playing critically.

**8. ♗xc6!**

It makes sense to capture the knight here as d2-d4 is a powerful follow-up, opening the position and capitalising on Black's lack of kingside development.

**8... ♗xc6 9. d4! cxd4 10. cxd4 ♘xe4**

10... ♗e7 is obviously non-critical, and we can just develop normally. 11. ♘c3 ♕c7 12. ♗g5 0-0 13. ♖c1 h6 14. ♗xf6 ♗xf6 15. ♘d5 ♕d8 16. ♘xf6+ ♕xf6 17. d5±

**11. ♕c2!**

Protecting the b2-pawn before we move our bishop.

**11... d5!**

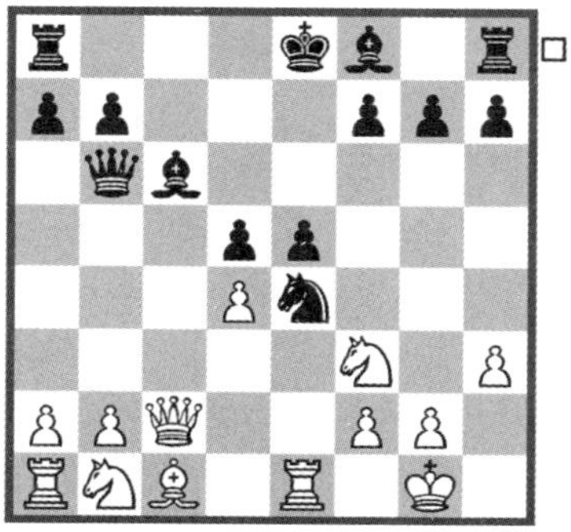

Position after: 11... d5!

11... f5?! 12. ♗e3 ♕b5 13. dxe5 dxe5 14. ♘c3 ♘xc3 15. ♕xf5!

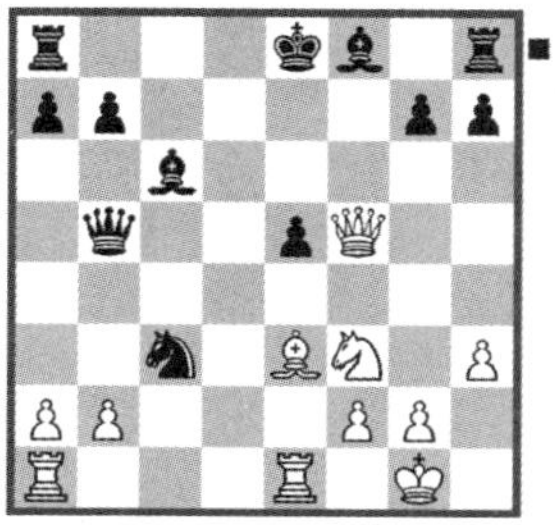

Position after: 15. ♕xf5!

Black's king will be indefensible. 15... ♗d7 16. ♕h5+ g6 17. ♕h4 ♗e7 18. ♗g5 ♗xg5 19. ♘xg5 ♘e2+ 20. ♔h2 ♗f5 21. a4 ♕a6 22. ♖ad1+–

**12. ♗e3**

At some point White needs to make a non-obvious move: after the alternative 12. ♘xe5 ♗b4 13. ♗d2 ♖c8 14. ♗xb4 ♕xb4 the only move to get an advantage is the incredible 15. ♕d2!!± reaching a pawn-up rook ending.

**12... ♗b4 13. dxe5 ♕a6 14. ♘bd2 0-0 15. a3 ♗xd2 16. ♘xd2±**

*(see diagram next column)*

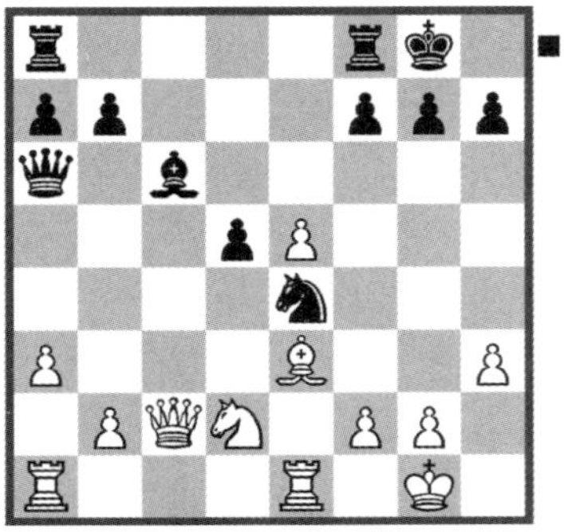

Position after: 16. ♘xd2±

Both static and dynamic factors make this opposite-coloured bishop middlegame preferable for White.

## h) 6...g6 7.c3 ♘e5

**1. e4 c5 2. ♘f3 ♘c6 3. ♗b5 d6 4. 0-0 ♗d7 5. ♖e1 ♘f6 6. h3 g6**

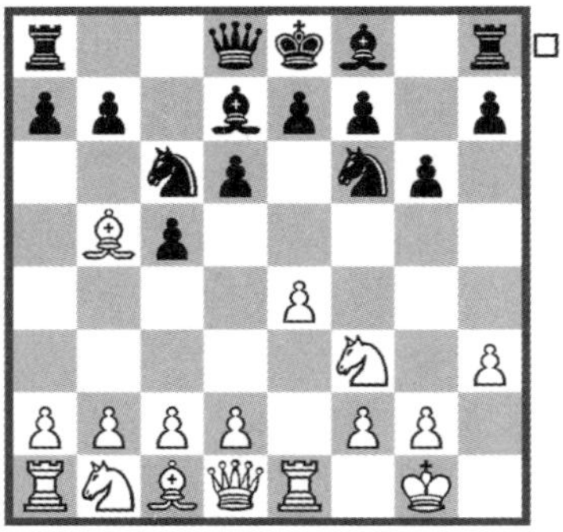

Position after: 6... g6

**7. c3 ♘e5!? 8. ♗f1 ♘xf3+ 9. ♕xf3 ♗h6**

Attempting to respond to d2-d4 by exchanging off another set of minor pieces, which in this case would favour Black.

**A)** 9... ♗g7 This is an inferior version of subchapter 1, because we always have the possibility of d4-d5. 10. d4

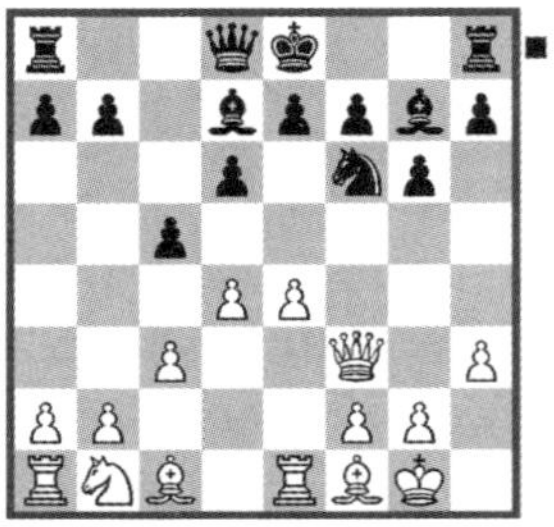

Position after: 10. d4

**A1)** 10... 0-0 11. dxc5 dxc5 12. e5 ♗c6? 13. exf6! ♗xf3 In Rozentalis – Nithander, Gothenburg 2013, White's strongest continuation was 14. fxe7! ♕d5 15. exf8=♕+ ♗xf8 16. gxf3+–.

**A2)** 10... cxd4 11. cxd4 0-0 12. ♘c3 ♗c6

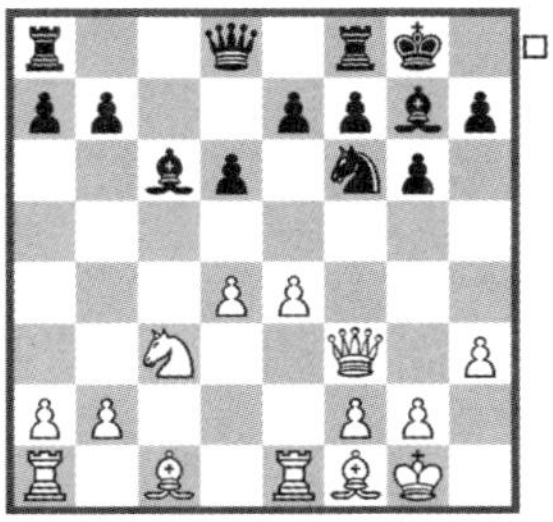
Position after: 12... ♗c6

13. d5 ♗e8 14. ♗e3 ♖c8 15. ♖ac1 ♘d7 16. ♕d1 a6 17. ♖e2± Followed by ♖ec2 – White's space advantage on the queenside suggests that we are much better here.

**A3)** 10... ♗c6 11. d5!

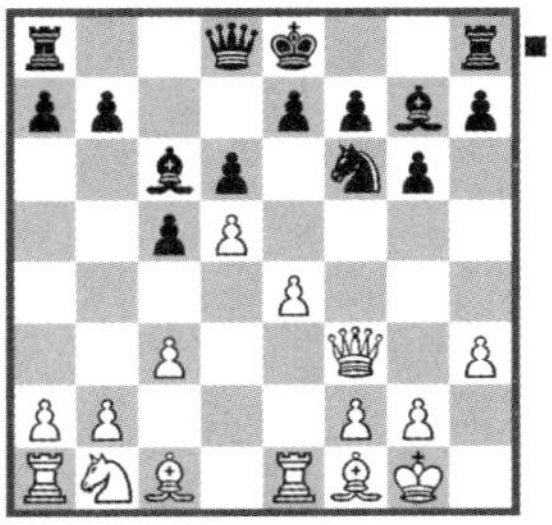
Position after: 11. d5!

11... ♗d7 12. ♗f4 0-0 13. ♘d2 Central breaks look poor for Black here, but we may as well check them to see why. 13... ♘h5 14. ♗h2 f5 [14... e5 15. dxe6 ♗xe6 16. ♖ad1 ♗e5 17. g3!+– Followed by ♕g2 and f2-f4.] 15. exf5 ♖xf5 16. ♕e3 ♖f7 [16... ♗e5 17. g3!+–] 17. ♘f3±

**B)** 9... ♕b6 10. ♘a3 ♗g7 11. ♘c4 ♕c7 12. d4 cxd4 13. cxd4 0-0

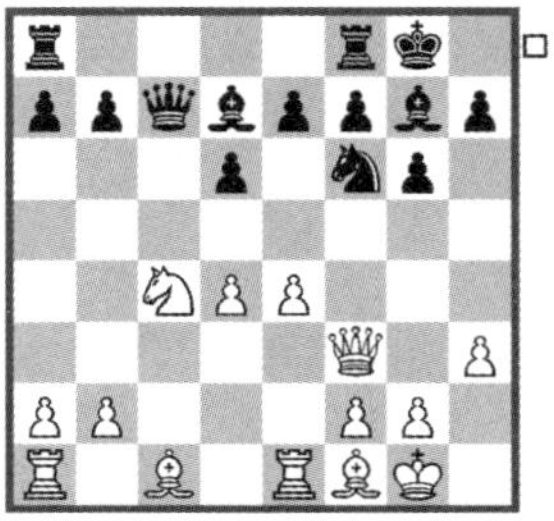
Position after: 13... 0-0

We have been following the correspondence game Mosconi – Colucci, ICCF email 2014. Here the most logical move seems to be 14. ♗d2!± which ensures that our c4-knight can go to a5 if we're hit with ...b7-b5.

**10. e5!**

We obviously don't want to entertain Black's idea.

**10... ♗c6**

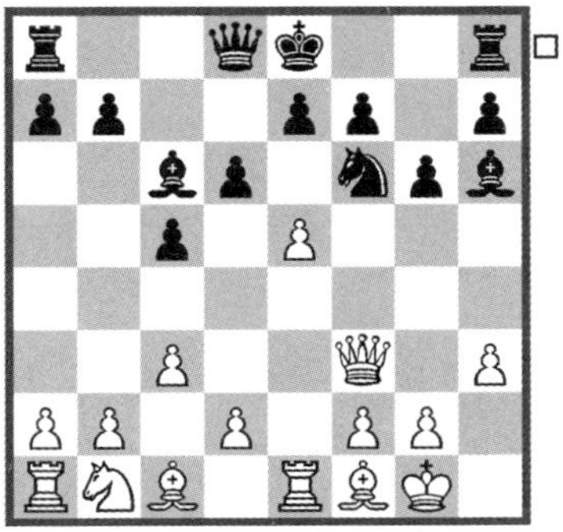
Position after: 10... ♗c6

10... dxe5 11. ♖xe5 0-0 12. ♕xb7±

**11. ♗b5! ♗xb5 12. exf6 e6 13. ♕xb7 ♖b8 14. ♕f3 ♗g5**

It looks like Black is winning their pawn back, so we need to play actively to maintain our initiative.

**15. c4!**

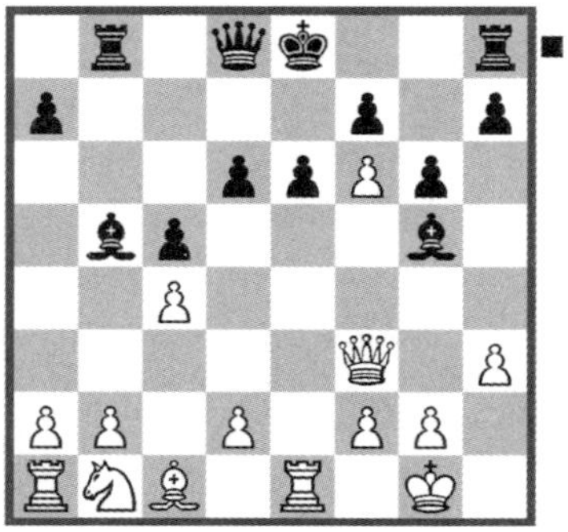

Position after: 15. c4!

**15... ♗d7**

15...♗xc4 would have been met with 16.♕g4! forking Black's bishops.

**16. d4 ♗xf6**

16... ♗xc1 17. ♖xc1 cxd4 18. c5 dxc5 19. ♕f4! ♖c8 20. ♘d2 ♕c7 21. ♕h6 ♕e5 22. ♖e1 ♕xf6 23. ♘e4 ♕e5 24. f4 ♕b8 25. ♕g7 ♖f8 26. b4!+–

**17. dxc5 dxc5 18. ♘c3 ♗d4 19. ♗e3 0-0 20. ♖ad1 e5**

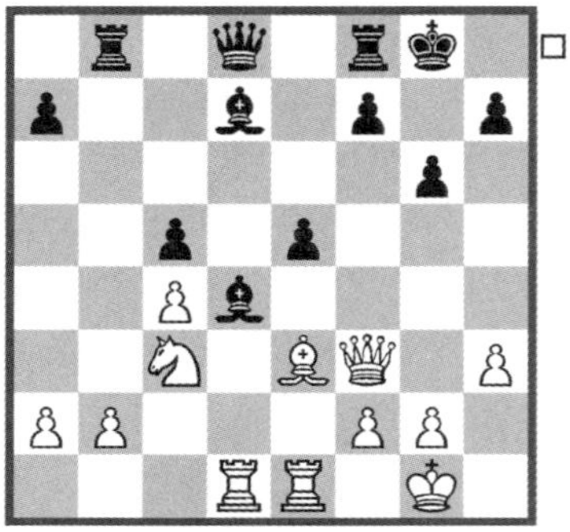

Position after: 20... e5

**21. ♘d5±**

Black was forced to concede the d5-square in order to maintain stability, which evidently hands us an advantage.

## i) 6...g6 7.c3 ♗g7

**1. e4 c5 2. ♘f3 ♘c6 3. ♗b5 d6 4. 0-0 ♗d7 5. ♖e1 ♘f6 6. h3 g6 7. c3 ♗g7**

*(see diagram opposite column)*

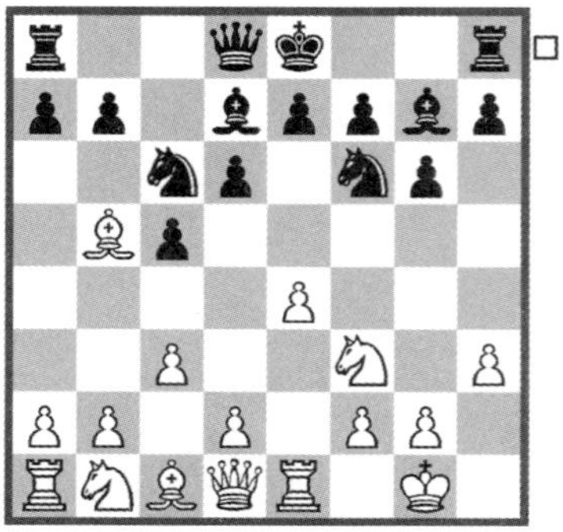

Position after: 7... ♗g7

**8. d4 0-0!**

Slightly more accurate than 8...cxd4, as we don't have the option of ♘c3 here.

8... cxd4 9. cxd4 0-0 10. ♘c3 ♖c8 [10... a6 11. ♗f1 transposes to 6...a6.] 11. ♗e3

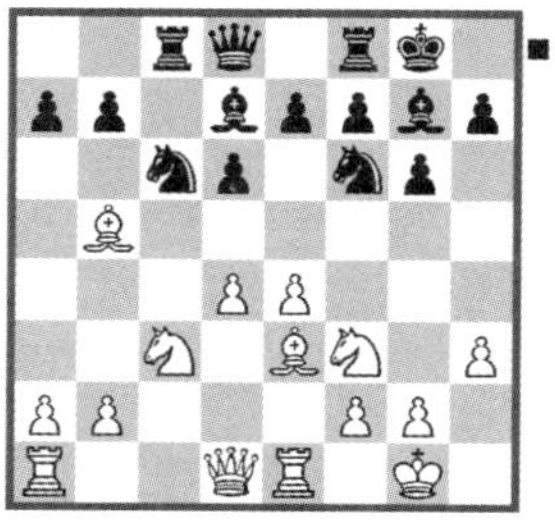

Position after: 11. ♗e3

Black doesn't really have any concrete plans, and the following variations will illustrate that any attempt to make progress will ultimately create weaknesses. 11... e6 [11... e5 12. d5 ♘a5 13. ♗d3 a6 14. ♘d2 b5 Our e4-d5 pawn structure gives rise to favourable queenside prospects for White. 15. a4 b4 16. ♘a2 ♖b8

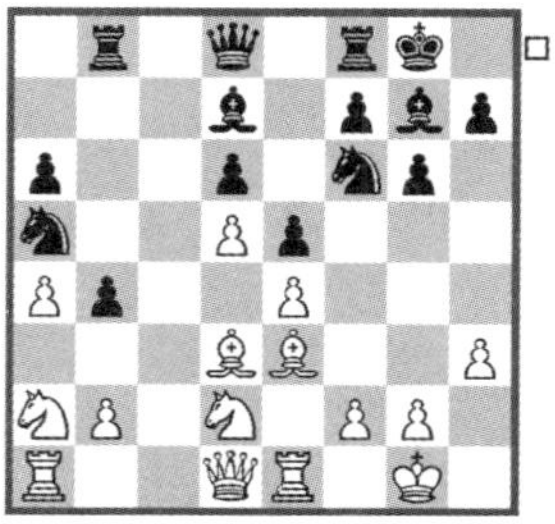

Position after: 16... ♖b8

17. ♗xa6+–; 11... a6 12. ♗f1 b5 13. a4! b4 14. ♘d5 ♘xe4 15. ♗xa6 ♖a8 16. ♗d3 ♘f6 17. ♘xf6+ ♗xf6

Position after: 17... ♗xf6

18. ♕d2±] 12. ♖c1 d5 13. e5 ♘e4 14. ♗d3 f5 15. exf6 ♘xf6 We've already encountered a few French Tarrasch-like structures, and this looks like another good version for White. 16. a3 ♘h5 17. ♘a4

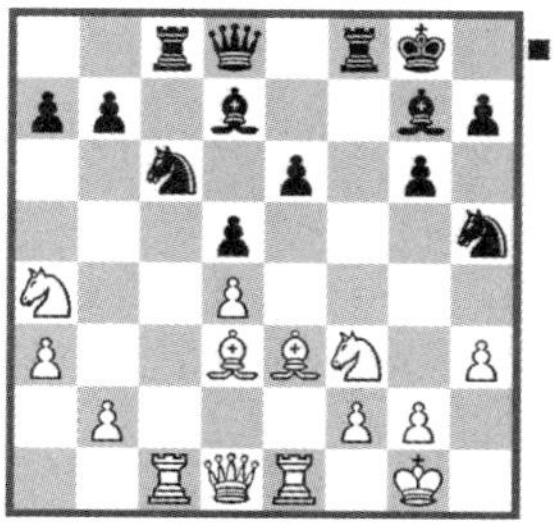

Position after: 17. ♘a4

17... b6 [17... ♖xf3 is always important to check but fails to equalise here. 18. ♕xf3 ♘xd4 19. ♕g4 e5 20. ♖xc8 ♕xc8 21. ♕d1+–] 18. ♗a6 ♖b8 19. ♗g5 ♕e8 20. ♘c3±

**9. a4!?**

We're maintaining ideas of dxc5 and d4-d5 for the moment. Meanwhile a2-a4 is always a useful move to make, as it prevents Black from gaining space on the queenside with ...b7-b5.

Position after: 9. a4!?

9. e5? is the typical reaction when Black delays capturing on d4, but it doesn't work here due to 9... dxe5 10. dxe5 ♘xe5∓.

**9... a6**

**A)** 9... ♖c8 10. dxc5! dxc5 11. e5 ♘e8 12. ♗e3

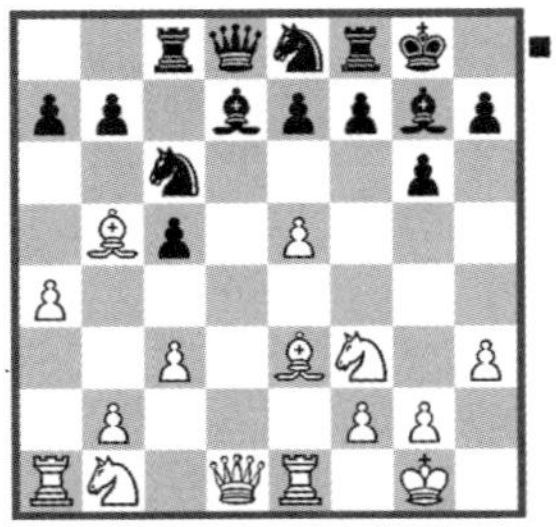

Position after: 12. ♗e3

12... b6 [12... a6 13. ♗xc6 ♗xc6 14. ♕xd8 ♖xd8 15. ♘bd2± Black faces big problems defending the c5-pawn.] 13. ♕d2 ♘c7 14. ♖d1 a6 15. ♗xa6 ♘xa6

Position after: 15... ♘xa6

16. ♕xd7 Even if we lose our e-pawn, Black's queenside pawns will be our next target and look increasingly difficult to defend. 16... ♘d4 [16... ♗xe5 17. ♕d2! ♕xd2 18. ♘fxd2±] 17. e6! fxe6 [17... ♘xe6 18. ♘a3±] 18. ♕xd8 ♘xf3+ 19. gxf3 ♖cxd8

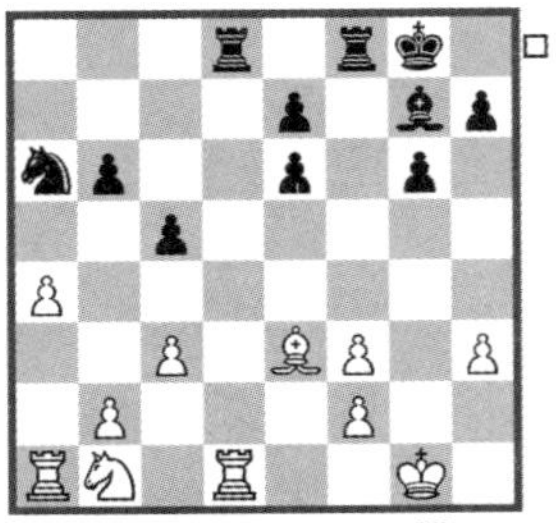

Position after: 19... ♖cxd8

20. ♖xd8 ♖xd8 21. ♘d2±

**B)** 9... e5 10. d5! In this case, exchanging light-squared bishops seems to be the best decision for thematic reasons. 10... ♘e7 11. ♗xd7 ♘xd7 12. c4! a5 13. ♖a3±

**10. ♗f1 cxd4 11. cxd4 d5 12. e5**

*(see diagram next page)*

Position after: 12. e5

**12... ♘e4**

The main downside to Black's strategy is that we can put our knight on c3. Meanwhile the g7-bishop suffers against our d4-e5 pawn structure. It's actually a favourable version of lines seen in Volume 1 (specifically the 5...♘f6 chapter.)

**13. ♘c3 ♗f5 14. ♗d3 ♘xc3 15. bxc3**

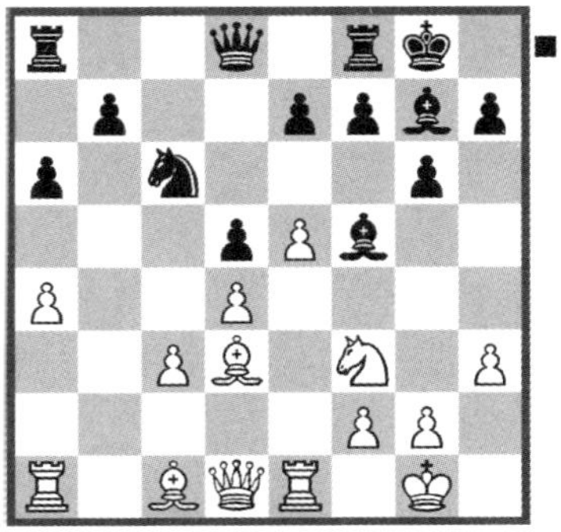

Position after: 15. bxc3

**15... ♕d7**

15... ♗xd3 16. ♕xd3 ♕d7 17. h4↑ with good prospects on both the kingside and queenside.

**16. ♗f1! f6 17. g4 ♗e6 18. exf6**

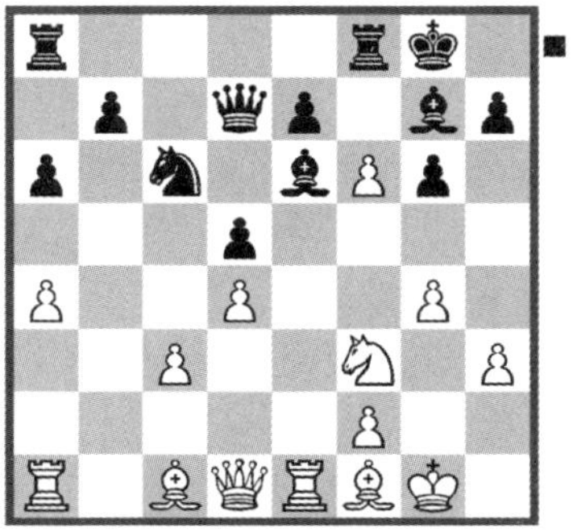

Position after: 18. exf6

**18... exf6**

18... ♗xf6 19. ♕e2 ♗f7 20. ♗f4±

**19. ♘d2±**

I'm not sure how Black will deal with our knight coming to c5.

## Conclusion to Chapter 6

Black has a number of different alternatives to 6...a6, but an underlying theme in this chapter has been the flexibility in our approach depending on how Black chooses to challenge our centre. The best example of this was subchapter e where we hinted at adopting an IQP position, only to immediately sacrifice a pawn and develop a dangerous initiative.

The next chapter continues to showcase our flexible approach in the variations following 3...♘c6 and 6.h3 – albeit only after Black elects to initially kick our bishop with 6...a6.

# 6...a6

1.e4 c5 2.♘f3 d6 3.♗b5+ ♘c6 4.0-0 ♗d7 5.♖e1 ♘f6 6.h3 a6

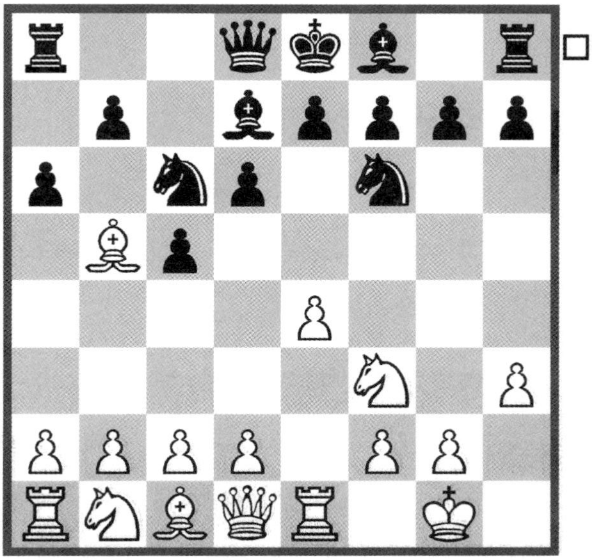

# Chapter Guide

## Chapter 7 – 6...a6

1.e4 c5 2.♘f3 d6 3.♗b5+ ♘c6 4.0-0 ♗d7 5.♖e1 ♘f6 6.h3 a6 7.♗f1

## a) Premature ...g5 tries

**1. e4 c5 2. ♘f3 ♘c6 3. ♗b5 d6 4. 0-0 ♗d7 5. ♖e1 ♘f6 6. h3 a6**

6... g5?! This immediately is not sound, as White can simply open the centre with 7. ♗xc6! ♗xc6 8. d4!

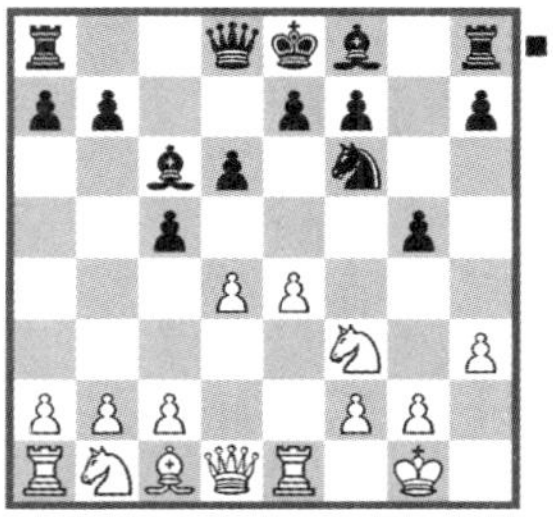

Position after: 8. d4!

8... cxd4 [8... g4 9. hxg4 ♘xg4 10. d5 ♗d7 11. ♗f4! With our pawn secured on d5, a future e4-e5 push looks like it'll be very strong. 11... ♕b6 12. ♘bd2 0-0-0 13. ♘c4 ♕a6 14. b3 h5 15. e5±] 9. ♗xg5 ♘xe4 10. ♖xe4 ♗xe4 11. ♕xd4

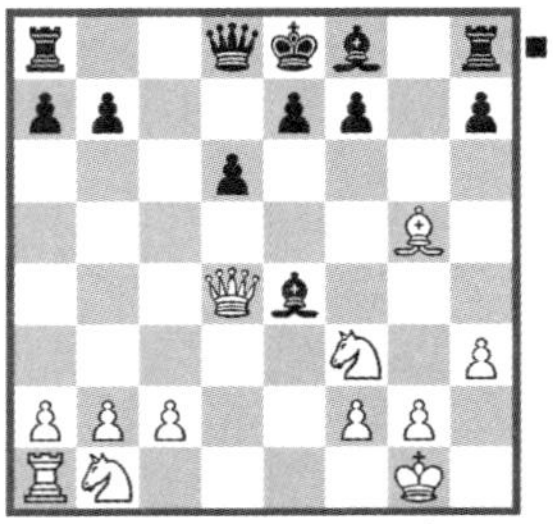

Position after: 11. ♕xd4

We'll most likely be winning Black's h-pawn along with the exchange. 11... h6 [11... ♗xf3 12. ♕xh8 ♗c6 13. ♘c3±] 12. ♗e3 ♗xf3 13. ♕xh8 ♗c6 14. ♗xh6 ♔d7 15. ♗xf8 ♕xf8 16. ♕xf8 ♖xf8 17. ♘d2±

**7. ♗f1**

In the penultimate round of the 2019 British Championships, I was helping my friend Justin 'J' Tan to prepare for his game against Simon Williams. We correctly predicted that Simon would opt for a Sicilian defence, and Justin chose 6.h3 in light of the fact that it engendered structures which would restrict Simon's attacking spirit. In analysing various lines, we humorously commented that we should probably check every possibility where Black could play ...g7-g5.

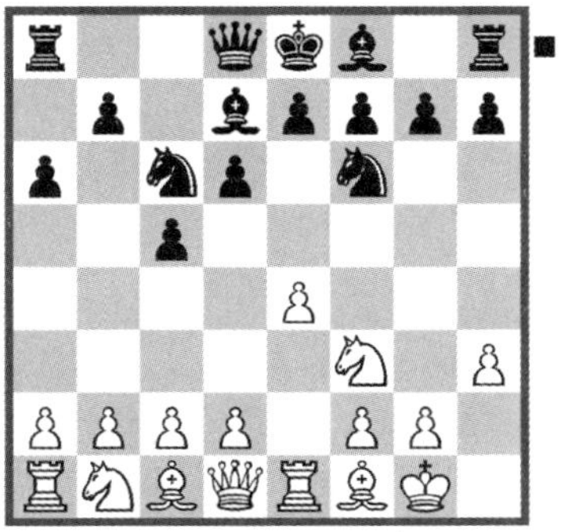

Position after: 7. ♗f1

**7... g5?!**

As luck would have it, after a mere 4 minute think Simon played the dubioustext move, and the following variations are indicative of how White should react in an effective manner.

**A)** 7... e5 8. c3 g5 In my opinion this is the best moment for Black to attempt a ...g7-g5 push as they now already have more control over the centre. We will cover this in the next subchapter.

**B)** 7... ♖g8?!

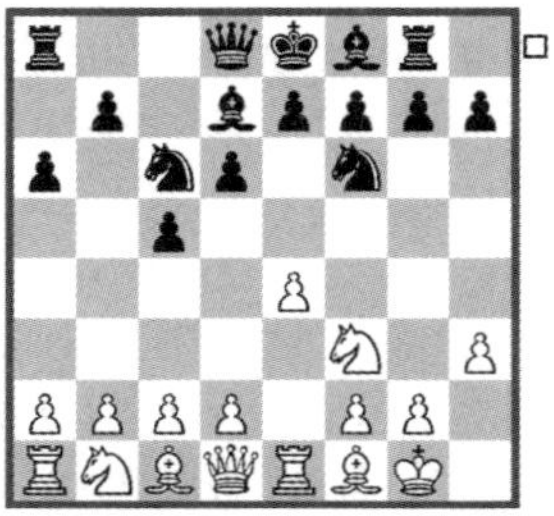

Position after: 7... ♖g8?!

**B1)** 8. d4 also gets an advantage, but White does need to play some unnatural moves along the way. 8... ♘xd4 9. ♘xd4 cxd4 10. ♕xd4 g5 11. ♘c3 g4 12. e5 dxe5 13. ♕xe5 ♗e6 14. hxg4 ♘xg4 15. ♕g3±

**B2)** 8. b4? doesn't work yet since after 8... g5 9. bxc5 g4 10. hxg4 ♗xg4 White doesn't have ♘bd2.

**B3)** 8. d3! h6 9. b4! Undermining Black's c5-pawn. The mere fact of having a central majority will ensure White has an advantage in most lines where Black doesn't accept the pawn.

Position after: 9. b4!

9... g5 [9... ♘xb4?! 10. d4!±; 9... cxb4 10. a3 b3 11. ♘bd2 bxc2 12. ♕xc2 g5 13. d4±] 10. bxc5 g4 11. hxg4 ♗xg4

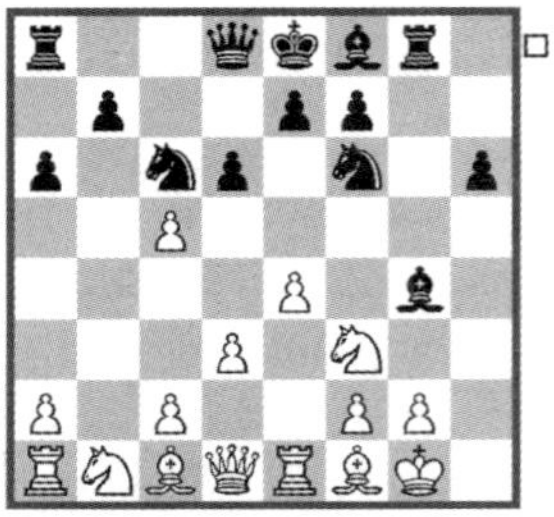

Position after: 11... ♗xg4

12. ♘bd2!± Giving back the pawn and keeping a central majority.

**8. d4! g4**

8... cxd4 9. ♗xg5 e5 10. c3 ♖g8 11. cxd4 ♗xh3 12. dxe5 ♘xe5 13. ♘xe5 ♖xg5 14. ♘f3 ♖g8 15. ♕b3+– Our rapid central play has weakened Black's king to a greater degree than our own.

**9. d5!**

*(see analysis diagram next page)*

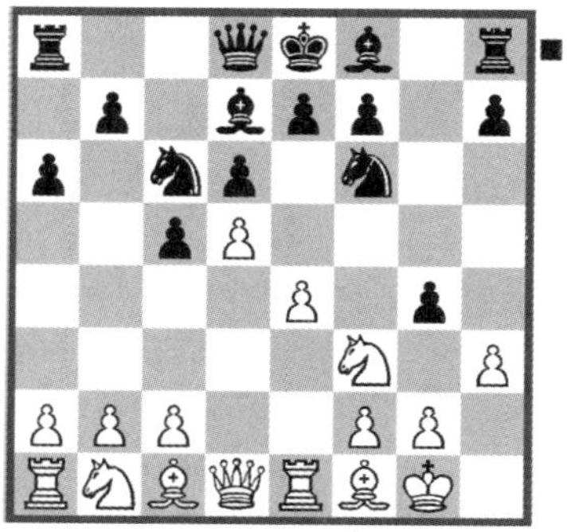

Position after: 9. d5!

**9... gxf3**

**A)** 9... ♘b8 10. e5!

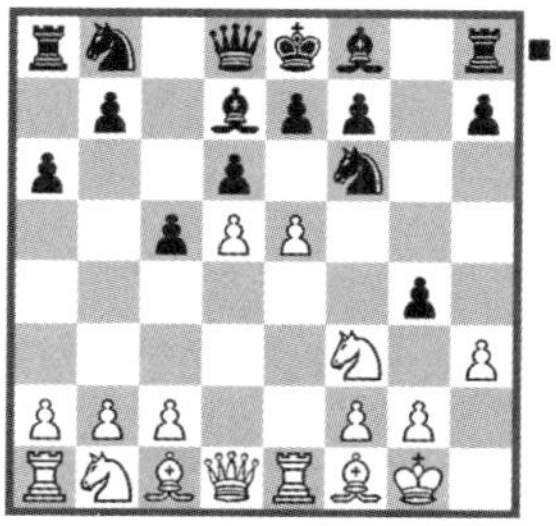

Position after: 10. e5!

10... dxe5 [10... gxf3 11. exf6 fxg2 12. ♗c4+–] 11. ♘xe5 gxh3 12. ♕f3 hxg2 13. ♗xg2 ♗g7 14. ♘c3+–

**B)** 9... ♘d4 10. ♘h2!

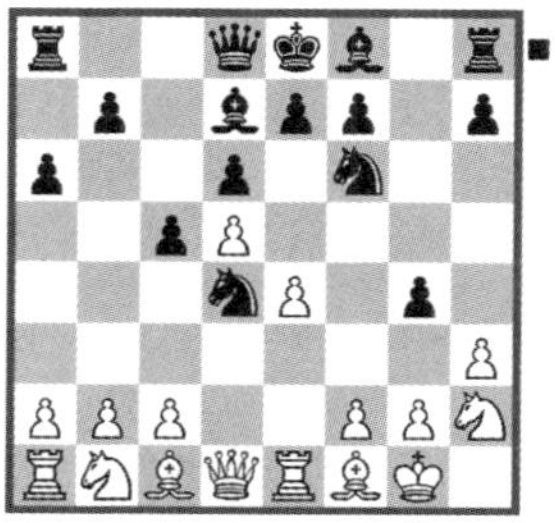

Position after: 10. ♘h2!

This time Black's knight on d4 will struggle to avoid being trapped. 10... gxh3 [10... h5 11. h4+–] 11. g3 ♖g8 12. c3 ♘b5 13. ♘d2 h5 14. a4 ♘c7 15. ♘c4 h4 16. ♕f3 As usual, our king is quite safe. Black is the one who is underdeveloped, and their king will face big problems with a forthcoming e4-e5 push.

**C)** 9... ♘e5 10. ♘xe5 dxe5 11. hxg4 ♘xg4

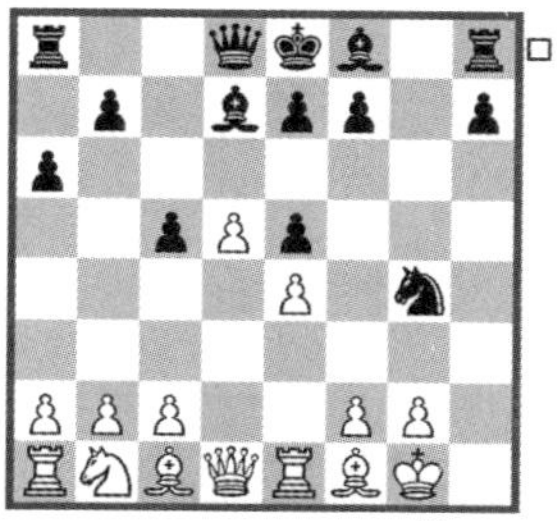

Position after: 11... ♘xg4

This might appear scary because of the open g-file, but Black's structural weaknesses should outweigh their limited attacking possibilities. The line may continue: 12. ♘d2 b5 13. a4 c4 14. ♗e2 h5 15. axb5 axb5 16. ♖xa8 ♕xa8 17. ♘f1±.

**10. dxc6 ♗xc6 11. ♕xf3 e6**

Castling queenside seems to be logical for Black – but it's easy to keep them under some pressure.

11... ♘d7 was played recently in Carlsen – Caruana, chess24.com 2020, but after 12. ♗f4 ♗g7 13. ♘c3 0-0 14.

♕h5± it's clear that White has an advantage.

**12. ♘c3 ♗e7 13. ♗f4**

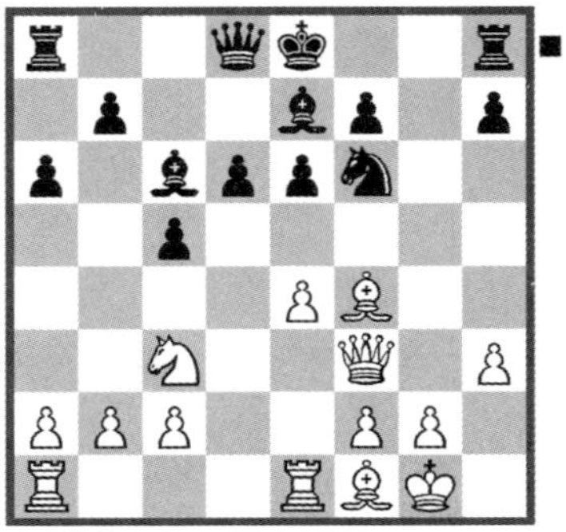

Position after: 13. ♗f4

**13... ♕c7**

**A)** 13... ♖g8 14. ♖ad1 ♖g6 15. ♕e3!± followed by e4-e5 at the right moment, perhaps with g2-g3 and ♗g2 inserted, gives White a clear advantage.

**B)** 13... b5 14. ♖ad1 ♖a7 15. ♘d5!

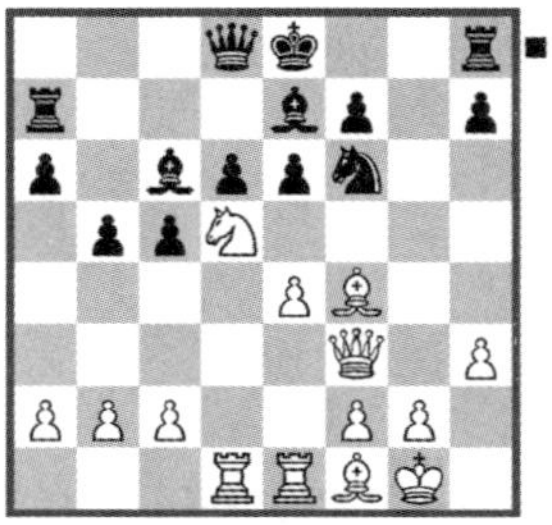

Position after: 15. ♘d5!

15... exd5 16. exd5 ♗a8 17. c4+– Another example of how to exploit Black's king. Their bishop on a8 is completely irrelevant, and we can continue to breakthrough with ideas such as b2-b4. The position is practically winning as Black's king has nowhere to go.

**14. ♖ad1 0-0-0 15. ♗g5 ♘e8 16. ♘d5!**

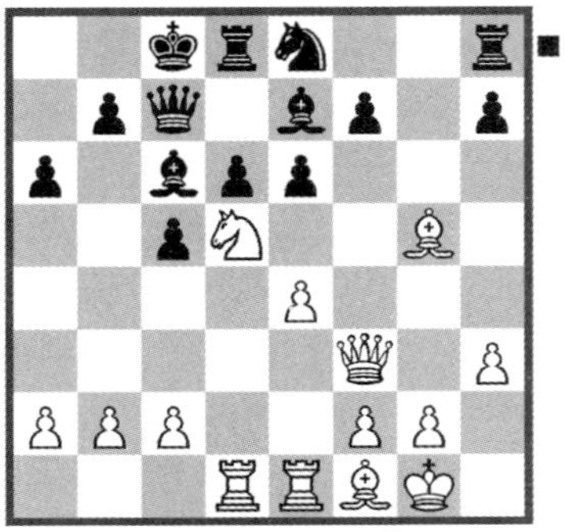

Position after: 16. ♘d5!

Very precise play from White. Black's light-squares will end up being really weak, and we shouldn't face any problems breaking through on the queenside.

**16... ♗xd5 17. ♗xe7 ♕xe7 18. exd5 e5 19. b4!**

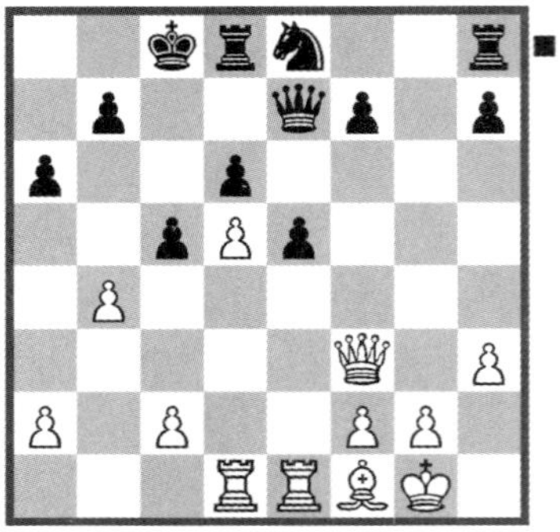

Position after: 19. b4!

**19... cxb4 20. ♖e4 ♘f6 21. ♖c4+ ♔b8 22. ♖xb4 ♘d7 23. ♗xa6 ♘c5**

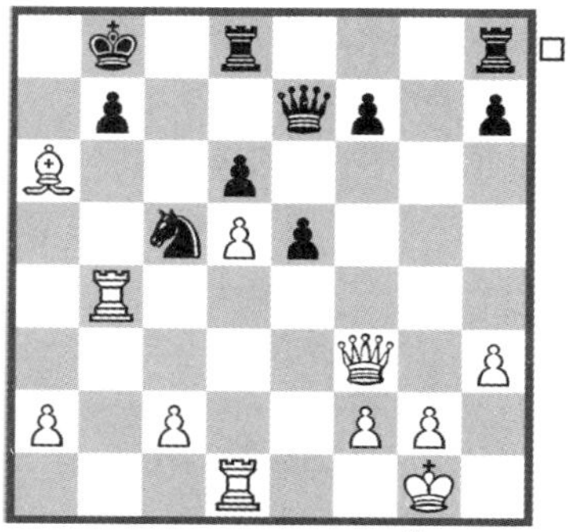

Position after: 23... ♘c5

We're still following the game Tan – Williams, Torquay 2019. Although Justin Tan went on to win the game, he missed a tactical resource which would have forced Black's resignation.

**24. ♗xb7! ♘xb7 25. ♖db1 ♖d7**

Position after: 25... ♖d7

**26. ♕a3+–**

Followed by either ♖a4 or ♕a6, when Black is getting mated.

## b) 7...e5 8.c3 g5 9.♘xg5 ♖g8 10.d4 h6 11.♘f3 ♗xh3 12.d5 ♘e7 13.♘bd2 --

**1. e4 c5 2. ♘f3 ♘c6 3. ♗b5 d6 4. 0-0 ♗d7 5. ♖e1 ♘f6 6. h3 a6 7. ♗f1 e5 8. c3 g5**

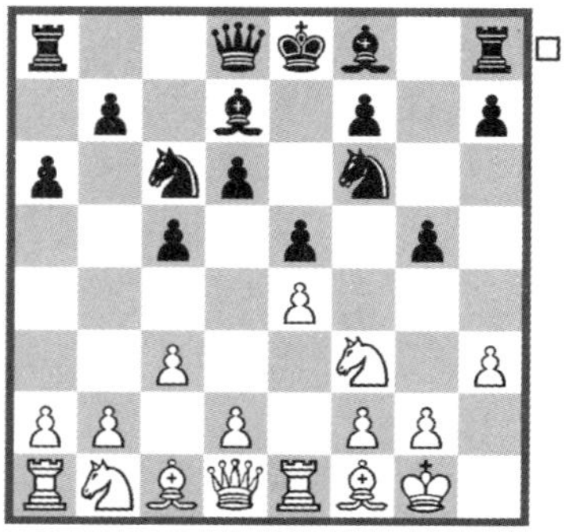

Position after: 8... g5

**9. ♘xg5**

Another valid choice is 9. d4 g4 10. hxg4 ♗xg4 11. d5 ♘e7 when we reach something quite similar to the main line: Black hasn't got the rook on the g-file, but in compensation the h-pawn isn't blocking their f8-bishop.

**9... ♖g8 10. d4 h6**

After 10... cxd4?! 11. cxd4 ♘xd4 Black will just find themselves in a positionally inferior situation, as the kingside play looks a bit limp.

*(see analysis diagram next page)*

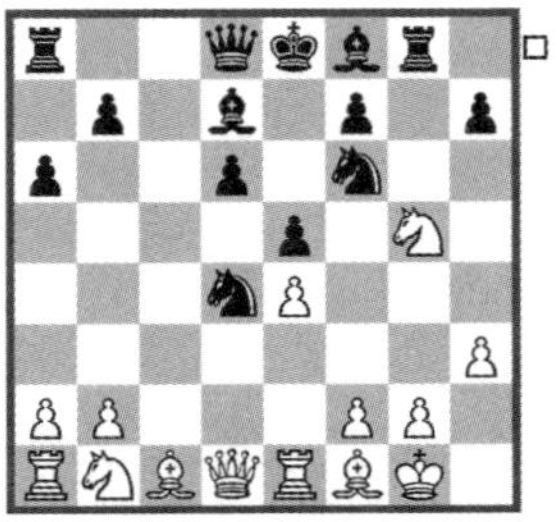
Position after: 11... ♘xd4

12. ♘c3 ♗e7 13. ♗e3 ♖c8 14. ♘f3± Black's position is starting to feel pretty suspect.

**11. ♘f3**

11. d5 gives Black the additional possibility of 11... hxg5, though this also doesn't equalise because of the light-square control that White achieves: 12. dxc6 bxc6 [12... ♗xc6 13. f3 ♗e7 14. c4±] 13. g4!

Position after: 13. g4!

Black's attack is halted, their king is stuck in the centre, and the d6-pawn is an obvious target. 13... a5 14. ♘a3 ♗e7 15. ♘c4 ♗e6 16. ♕a4 ♕c7 17. ♘e3± We can continue to command influence on the light-squares with c3-c4, ♗d2 and ♘f5. After that we have ideas of playing ♖e3-a3 targeting the weak a5-pawn.

**11... ♗xh3 12. d5 ♘e7**

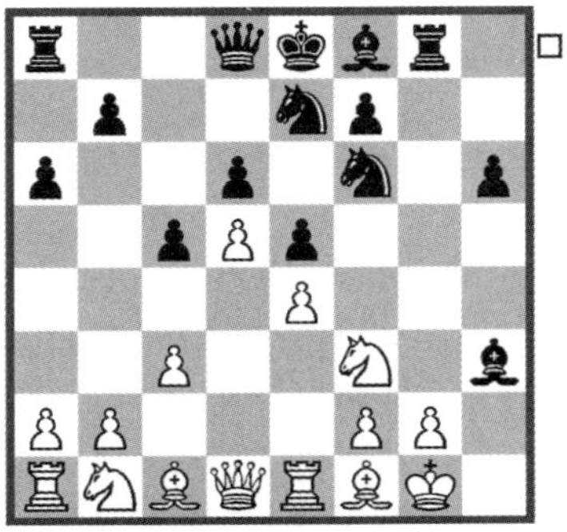
Position after: 12... ♘e7

**13. ♘bd2**

Black has achieved the desired impact of ...g7-g5, opening the g-file whilst keeping the centre closed. Despite this, the kingside attack lacks punch in many lines. Meanwhile we can switch over to probing on the queenside, safe in the knowledge that an endgame will (structurally speaking) be clearly advantageous for us.

**13... b5**

**A)** 13... ♕d7 14. ♘h2+–

**B)** 13... ♘h5? 14. ♘c4 b5

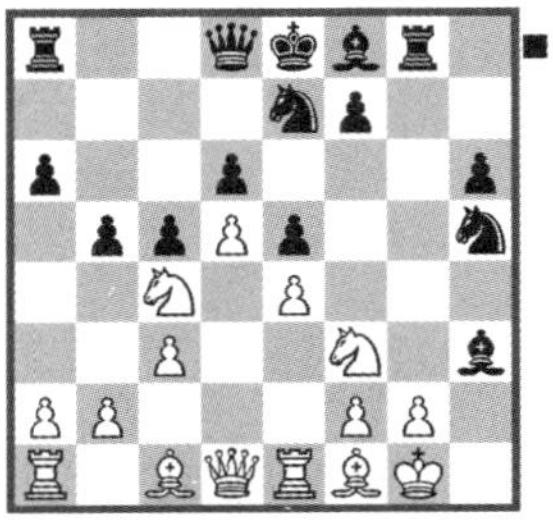
Position after: 14... b5

15. ♘cxe5! Black's scattered pieces enable us to blow open the centre with a sacrifice. It's easy to see that White is completely winning. 15... dxe5 16. ♘xe5 ♘f6 17. a4+–

**C)** 13... ♗g4?! is too early since Black's king has no flight and the f8-bishop isn't developed. 14. b4! cxb4

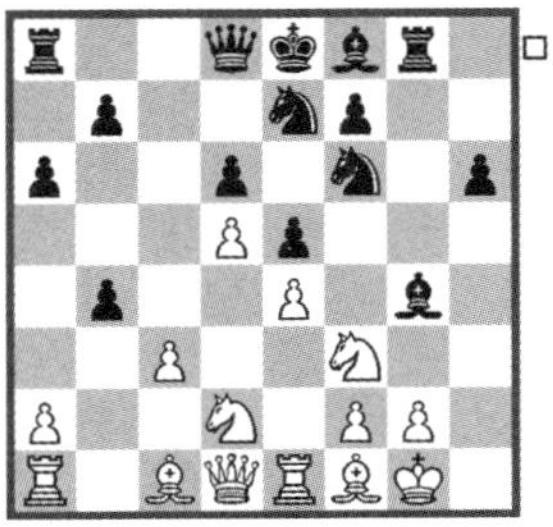
Position after: 14... cxb4

15. ♕a4+! b5 [15... ♘d7 16. cxb4 ♘g6 17. ♘h2 ♘f4 18. ♘xg4 ♖xg4 19. g3 ♕g5 20. ♕b3±] 16. ♕xb4 ♘g6 17. a4± As always, the kingside is extremely secure, whilst Black's queenside is close to collapsing.

**14. a4 ♗d7 15. ♘h4**

*(see diagram next column)*

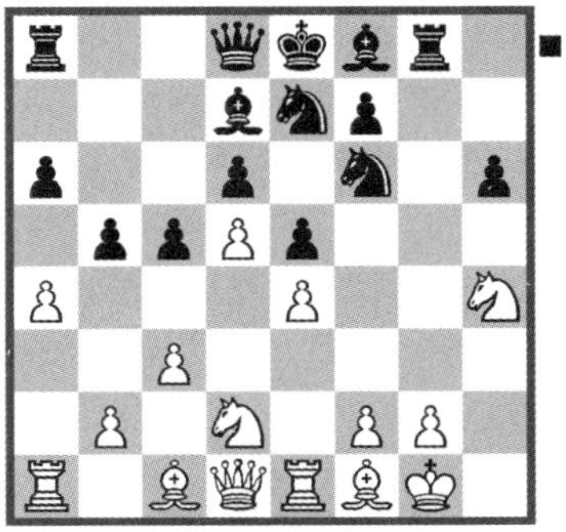
Position after: 15. ♘h4

As Black's g-pawn no longer exists, this square is a safe haven for our knight. White should now aim to trade pieces and simultaneously try to create more pawn weaknesses in Black's camp.

**15... h5 16. ♘df3!**

Straightforward development. White intends ♗g5 in many positions. The best Black can do is probably:

**16... ♘g6 17. ♘xg6**

17. ♘f5 ♘xe4 is messier.

**17... ♖xg6 18. ♘h4 ♖g4**

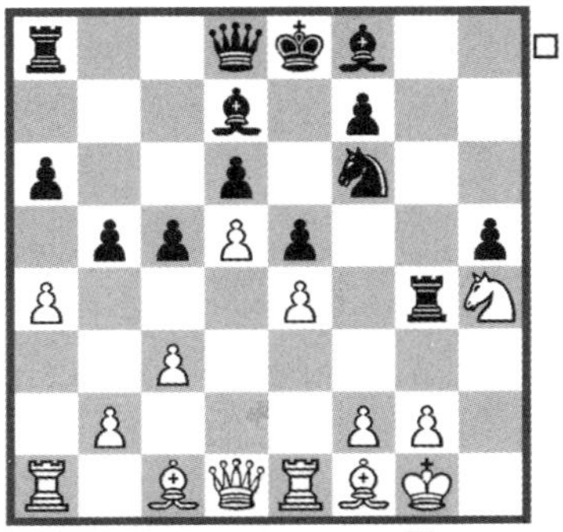
Position after: 18... ♖g4

**19. f3!±**

when Black can't take the knight, and neither do they have any realistic prospect of long-term king safety.

## c) 7...e5 8.c3 g5 9.♘xg5 ♖g8 10.d4 h6 11.♘f3 ♗xh3 12.d5 ♘e7 13.♘bd2 h5

**1. e4 c5 2. ♘f3 ♘c6 3. ♗b5 d6 4. 0-0 ♗d7 5. ♖e1 ♘f6 6. h3 a6 7. ♗f1 e5 8. c3 g5 9. ♘xg5 ♖g8 10. d4 h6 11. ♘f3 ♗xh3 12. d5 ♘e7 13. ♘bd2**

Now let's move on to Black's most critical continuation.

**13... h5!**

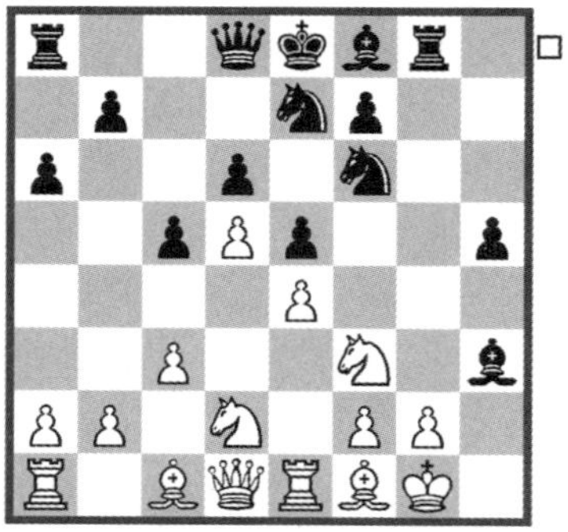

Position after: 13... h5!

Placing the bishop on h6 gives Black the most realistic shot at counterplay.

**14. ♘c4!?**

Chess is fundamentally a logical game, and this move simply aims to take away the ...♗h6 plan that Black has just created.

**A)** 14. ♘h4?! doesn't have the desired effect yet: 14... ♘g6 15. ♘xg6 ♖xg6∞ and White needs to hustle to cope with the immediate threats to the g2-pawn.

**B)** My original idea was 14. b4 cxb4 15. cxb4 [15. ♕b3!? is a funny computer idea, trying to reserve judgement on how to take back on b4.] 15... ♗h6 16. ♕b3

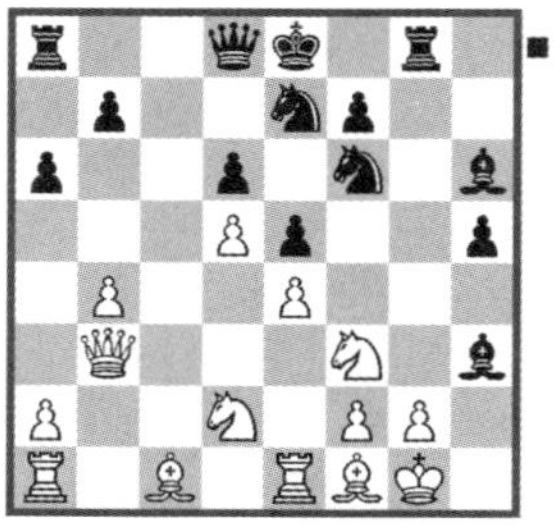

Position after: 16. ♕b3

With ideas of either a2-a4, or even b4-b5 immediately. However Black has three playable moves, of which one seems to equalise.

**B1)** The following line first needs to be checked: 16... ♗xg2!? 17. ♗xg2 ♘g6 18. b5! [18. ♔f1 ♘g4 gives Black relatively substantial pressure.] 18... axb5 19. ♕xb5+ ♔f8

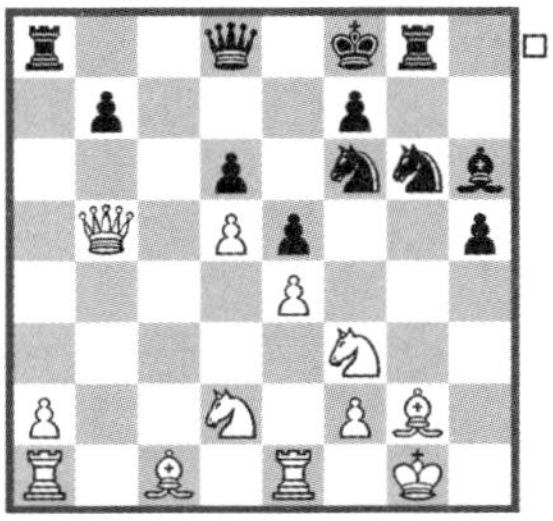
Position after: 19... ♔f8

20. a4! Still not worrying about the g-file pin since there is always ♘h4 to defend the bishop if need be. 20... ♘f4 21. ♘h4 ♘xe4 22. ♘df3 ♘c3 23. ♗xf4! Otherwise White's advantage seems to dwindle. 23... ♘xb5 24. ♗xh6+ ♔e8 25. axb5 ♖xa1 26. ♖xa1 ♖g4!

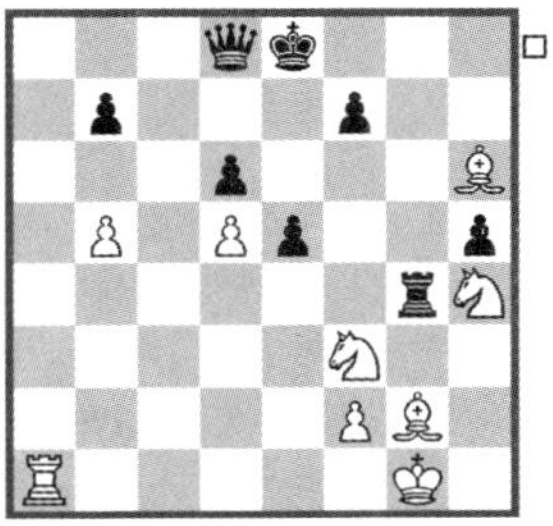
Position after: 26... ♖g4!

This resource means that Black avoids being dead lost, but of course the limit of their dreams is a draw at this point. 27. ♖e1 ♔d7 28. ♗e3 e4 29. ♘g5 ♖xg5 30. ♗xg5 ♕xg5 31. ♖xe4 ♔c7 32. ♘f3±

**B2)** Also requiring attention is 16... ♔f8!?, but after some effort I found an edge here for White: 17. ♘h4! We saw this idea in the 13...b5 note. White's knights are tripping over each other more than Black's, and at some point Black is likely to play ...♘g6. This move just sets up a trade for that eventuality. In all other cases Black seems to be doing well. 17... ♗g4 18. ♘df3 ♗xc1 19. ♖axc1±

**B3)** 16... ♗g4! 17. b5 axb5 18. ♕xb5+ ♔f8

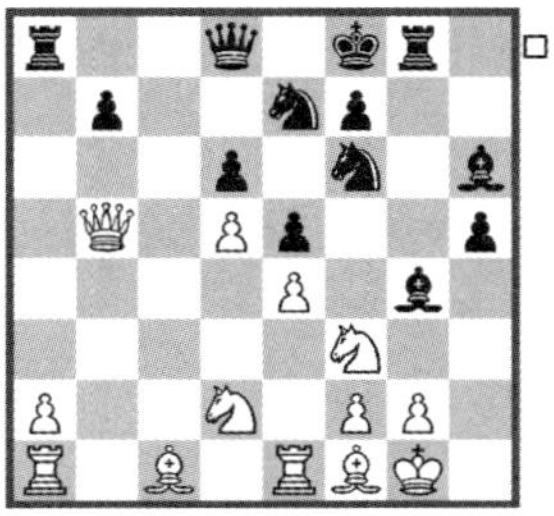
Position after: 18... ♔f8

19. a4!? ♘g6 In this messy position I'm not certain which side I'd rather have. The engine's recommendation of 20. ♕b4 can be met by the incredible pawn sacrifice 20... b5!, equalising after further complications.

**C)** The immediate attempt 14. ♘xe5?? fails: 14... dxe5 15. ♕f3 ♗xg2 16. ♗xg2 ♘g6 and White will lose the g2-bishop.

**14... b5**

Something like 14... ♗g4 15. b4 b5 16. ♘e3± is of dubious value since now the g4-square isn't secure for Black.

**15. ♘e**

15. ♘cxe5!? dxe5 16. ♘xe5∞ could be investigated, with a powerful central majority.

**15... ♘xe4**

Black more or less has to accept the challenge.

15... ♗h6 is once again possible, but with Black's b-pawn having been pulled forward White's queenside play will be faster. 16. a4!

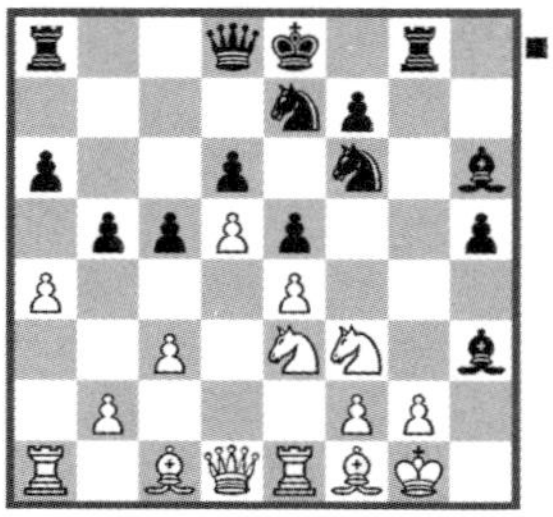

Position after: 16. a4!

16... ♘xe4 [16... ♖b8 17. axb5 axb5 18. ♘xe5! dxe5 19. ♕f3±] 17. axb5 axb5 18. ♗xb5+ ♔f8 19. ♖xa8 ♕xa8 20. ♗f1± White has a small plus in terms of king safety and structural stability.

**16. a4 ♗d7**

16... ♗h6 transposes to the last note.

**17. axb5 axb5 18. ♖xa8 ♕xa8**

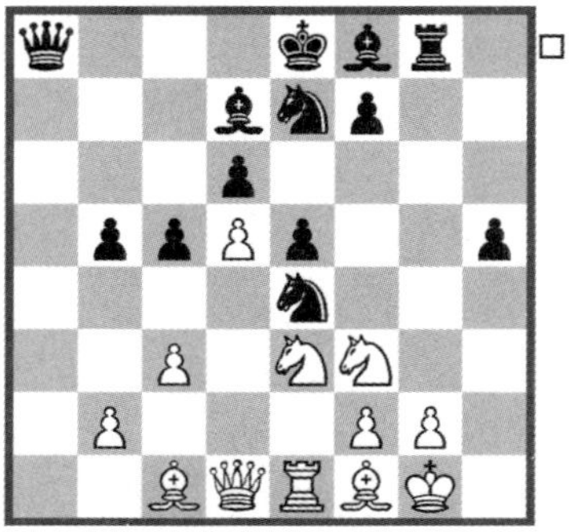

Position after: 18... ♕xa8

**19. c4±**

Black's king will remain in the centre and their kingside play has been neutralised. Due to those factors I feel comfortable ending the line here in spite of the material deficit. White can keep poking away at the centre whereas Black's position looks uncomfortable in the long term.

## d) 7...e6 8.c3 ♗e7 9.d4 cxd4 10.cxd4 d5 11.e5 ♘e4 12.♗d3 ♘b4

**1. e4 c5 2. ♘f3 ♘c6 3. ♗b5 d6 4. 0-0 ♗d7 5. ♖e1 ♘f6 6. h3 a6**

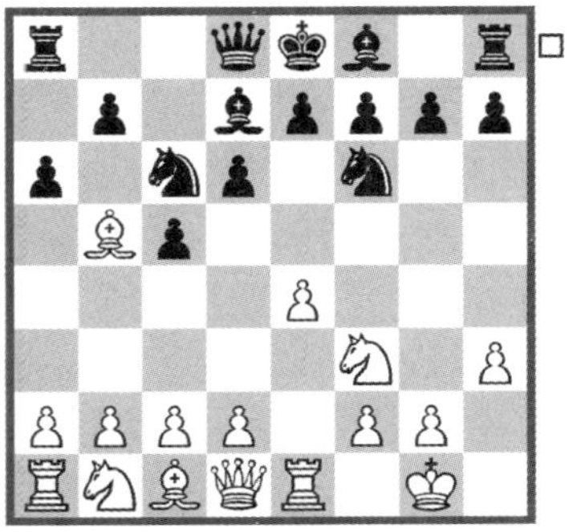

Position after: 6... a6

**7. ♗f1 e6**

The same idea as the last subchapter, though there are obviously some important differences.

**8. c3 ♗e7**

8... d5?! With our bishop on f1, we can obviously play 9. e5±.

**9. d4 cxd4 10. cxd4 d5**

The only logical way to challenge our centre.

**11. e5 ♘e4 12. ♗d3**

Here Black has two options: 1) Retreat the e4-knight, making it potentially trappable; or 2) sacrifice a pawn in the hope of gaining compensation on the light squares.

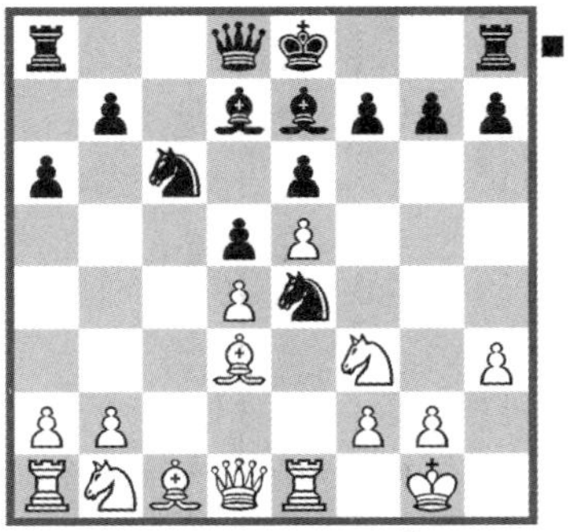

Position after: 12. ♗d3

**12... ♘b4!?**

This is of course the pawn sacrifice. After some calm play we achieve an advantage here as well.

**13. ♗xe4 dxe4 14. ♖xe4**

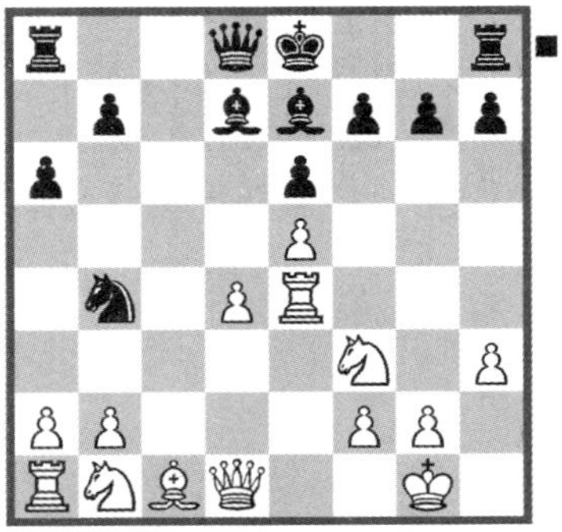

Position after: 14. ♖xe4

**14... h5!**

Black needs to control the g4-square before attacking our rook.

**A)** 14... ♗c6 15. ♖g4! ♗xf3 [Or 15... g6 16. ♗h6 ♗xf3 17. ♕xf3! ♘c2 18. ♘c3 ♘xa1 19. d5+– which looks roughly the same.] So far we're following Hamdouchi – Edouard, La Roche sur Yon 2007. White here failed to appreciate the power of taking back with the queen.

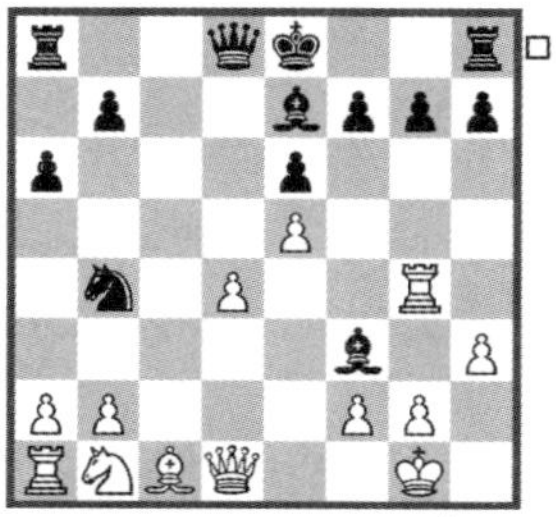

Position after: 15... ♗xf3

16. ♕xf3!N ♘c2 17. ♖xg7 ♖f8 18. ♘c3 ♘xa1 19. d5+–

**B)** 14... 0-0 15. ♖g4→ gives us a clear initiative to work with.

**15. ♘c3 ♗c6 16. ♖e1 g5**

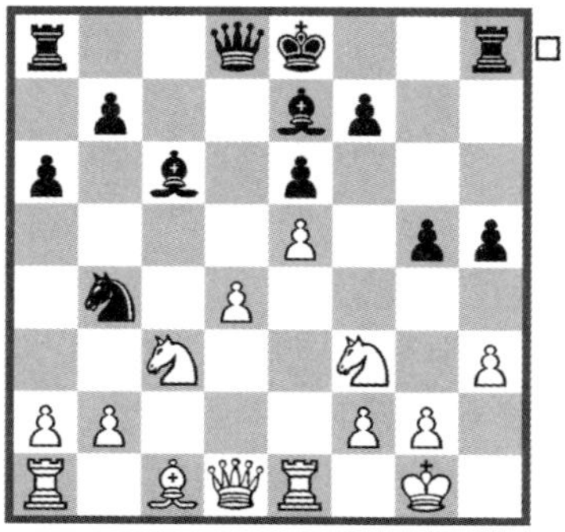

Position after: 16... g5

This may seem a bit scary, but with accurate play we can suppress Black's attack. The key here is to try and play on the dark squares with our pieces, whilst controlling the light squares with our pawns – as the following lines illustrate.

**17. a3 ♘d5 18. ♘e4**

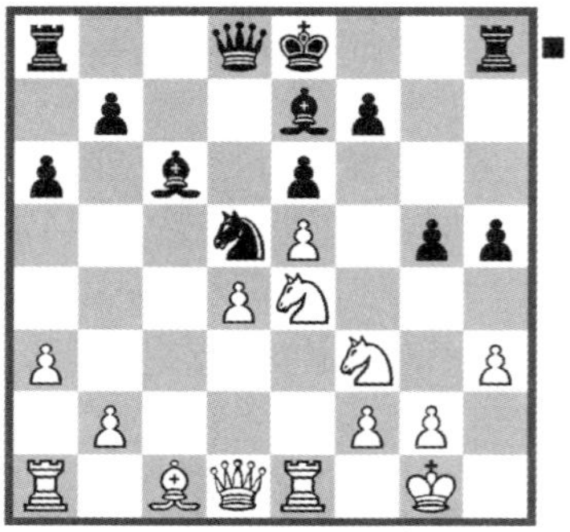

Position after: 18. ♘e4

**18... ♖g8□**

18... g4 19. ♘fg5 ♖g8 20. h4+– White is safe.

**19. ♘h2!**

19. ♘fd2 was played in Schwarz – Kurylo, ICCF email 2018, but Black managed to achieve dangerous counterplay after 19... g4 20. ♘c4 ♘b6 21. ♘cd6+ ♗xd6 22. ♘xd6+ ♔d7 23. ♘e4 ♔c7 24. ♘f6 gxh3 25. ♘xg8 ♕d5!⇆.

**19... g4 20. hxg4 hxg4 21. ♘xg4**

*(see diagram next page)*

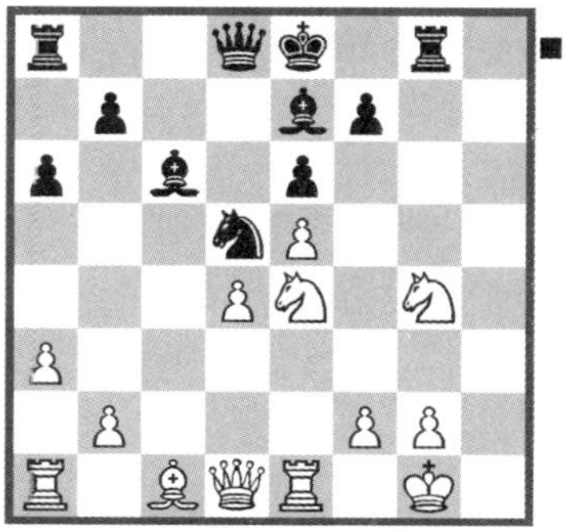

Position after: 21. ♘xg4

This knight will prove impossible to dislodge, and keeping it on g4 is a cornerstone of the policy which will deny Black full compensation.

**21... ♕b6**

21... ♖g6!? 22. f3! As I already mentioned, it's really important to maintain control of the light squares. 22... ♕b6 23. ♘c3 0-0-0 24. ♘xd5 ♖xd5 25. ♗e3 ♕xb2

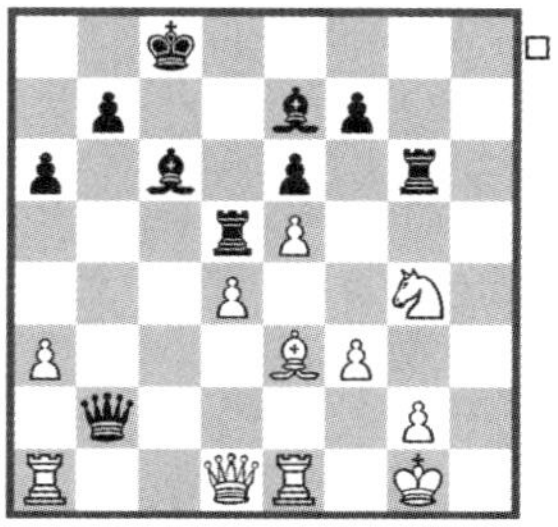

Position after: 25... ♕xb2

26. ♖e2 ♕b6 27. a4!± Invariably we are playing to restrict Black's c6-bishop. It seems difficult for Black to make any progress now.

**22. ♘ef6+! ♗xf6 23. exf6 0-0-0 24. f3!**

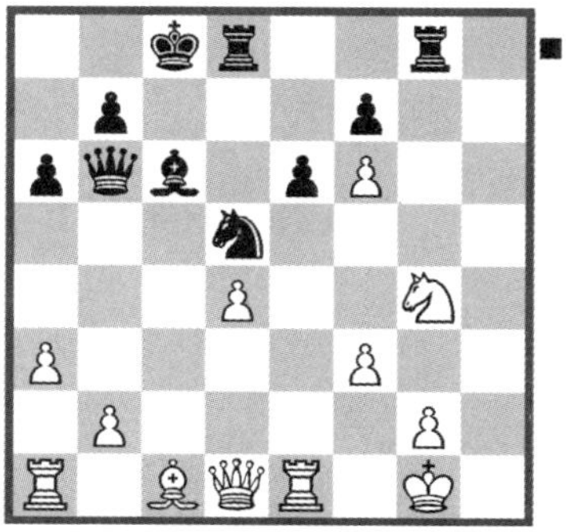

Position after: 24. f3!

In this opposite-coloured bishop middlegame, it's important to attack on the dark squares and try and control the light squares.

**24... ♕c7 25. ♗h6 ♕g3**

25... ♖xg4 Black can always sacrifice an exchange here but in general our piece activity will squash the compensation in the long run. 26. fxg4 ♘xf6 27. ♖c1 ♖g8 28. g5 ♕g3 29. d5!

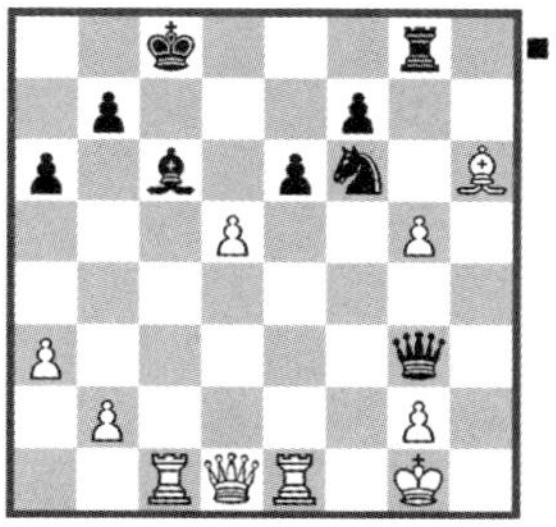

Position after: 29. d5!

29... ♘xd5 30. ♕f3 ♕xf3 31. gxf3±

**26. ♖e4 ♘xf6 27. ♗f4 ♕h4 28. ♘xf6 ♕xf6 29. ♖c1!**

*(see diagram next page)*

Position after: 29. ♖c1!

Suddenly the tables have turned and Black's king is in trouble.

**29... ♔d7 30. ♖xc6! bxc6 31. ♕b3±**

## e) 7...e6 8.c3 ♗e7 9.d4 cxd4 10.cxd4 d5 11.e5 ♘e4 12.♗d3 ♘g5

**1. e4 c5 2. ♘f3 ♘c6 3. ♗b5 d6 4. 0-0 ♗d7 5. ♖e1 ♘f6 6. h3 a6 7. ♗f1 e6 8. c3 ♗e7 9. d4 cxd4 10. cxd4 d5 11. e5 ♘e4 12. ♗d3 ♘g5**

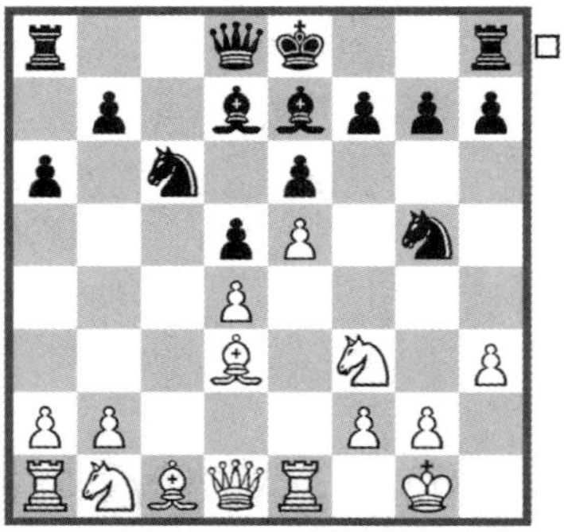

Position after: 12... ♘g5

**13. ♘h2!**

A move that comes to us courtesy of correspondence chess. The g5-knight is awkwardly placed, and we don't want to give Black the liberty of exchanging it.

**13... ♘b4**

**A)** 13... 0-0 14. ♘c3 f6 15. exf6 ♗xf6 16. ♗e3 ♖c8 17. ♘g4

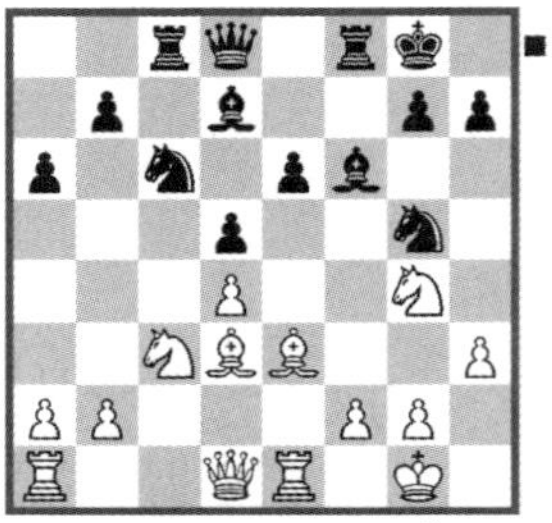

Position after: 17. ♘g4

17... ♗e7 [17... ♗xd4 18. ♗xd4 ♘xd4 19. ♗xh7+ ♘xh7 20. ♕xd4±] 18. ♖c1± It seems we've reached a better version of the lines after 13...♘b4. Our next plan can be ♘a4-c5, possibly combined with ♖e2-c2.

**B)** 13... ♘xd4? 14. h4+–

**C)** 13... f5 ends up looking much like the main line after 14. exf6 ♗xf6 15. ♘c3±.

**14. ♗f1 0-0 15. ♘c3**

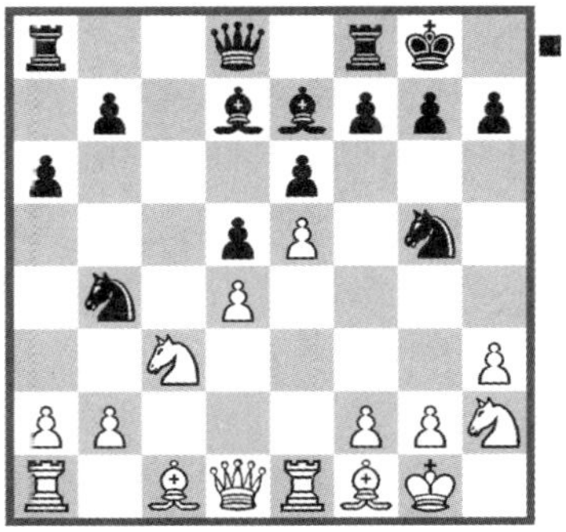

Position after: 15. ♘c3

**15... f5**

Black is forced to change the structure or else a pawn will drop.

15... ♖c8 16. a3 ♘c6 17. h4 ♘e4 18. ♘xe4 dxe4 19. ♖xe4±

**16. exf6 ♗xf6**

It's important to step back and discuss the change in structure. We've come across a few French Tarrasch-like positions in this line, but in my opinion this is arguably the best version we've had so far with White. This is mainly due to the fact that Black's dark-squared bishop and g5-knight are uncoordinated. In an ideal world for Black, the knight would be on f6 and the bishop on d6. Our d4-pawn will be protected easily by a future bishop on e3, and our knight on h2 is well placed to jump to either f3 or g4 depending on the circumstance. The knight on c3 may also jump to c5 via a4. If Black responds to this, either time will need to be wasted putting the bishop back on e7, or the queenside pawns will need to be weakened with ...b7-b6. Most significantly, the lack of a knight on f6 means that Black's kingside is also weak. By playing on both sides of the board, Black will struggle to deal with our diverse plans – and it's hard to come up with something concrete for Black either. For example an ...e6-e5 push is hard to achieve as the d5-pawn will inevitably be weak.

**17. a3 ♘c6 18. ♗e3**

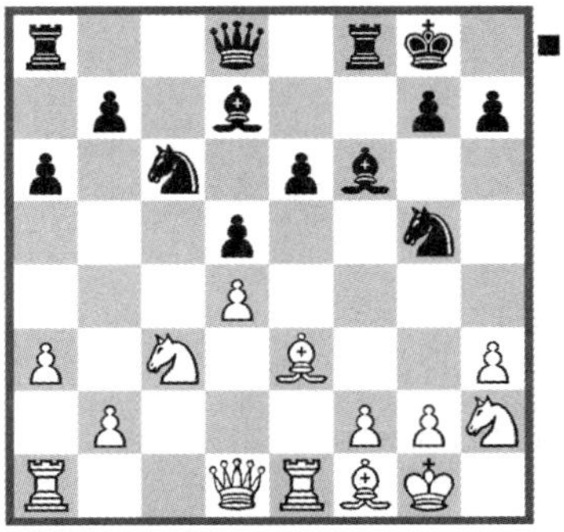

Position after: 18. ♗e3

A couple of correspondence games have reached this position.

**18... ♖c8**

18... ♘f7 19. ♘a4 ♘d6 [19... b6 is also possible but it weakens the a6-pawn and gives Black another problem to deal with. 20. ♘f3 ♘a5 21. ♗f4 ♘c4 22. ♖a2!± Followed by ♘c3 and b2-b3.] 20. ♘c5 ♗c8 21. ♖c1 ♘f5

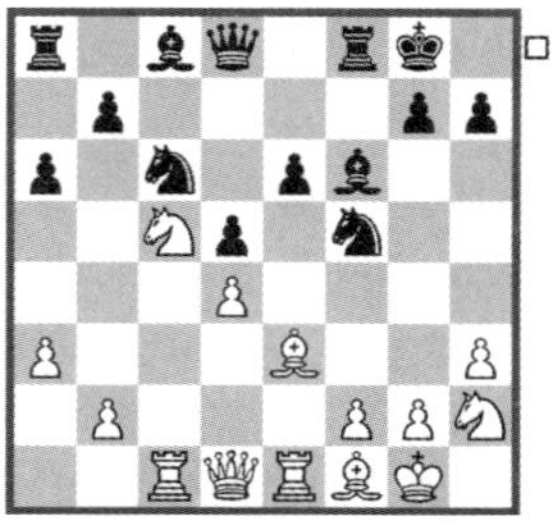

Position after: 21... ♘f5

22. ♘f3 g6 23. ♕d2± White had a comfortable advantage in Neagu – Cruzado Duenas, ICCF email 2014.

**19. ♖c1 b5**

Black's attempts to make progress will undoubtedly create weaknesses. Here again, the a6-pawn will be weak after a future a3-a4 push.

**20. ♘g4!**

This demonstrates how the knight can be useful on both f3 and g4.

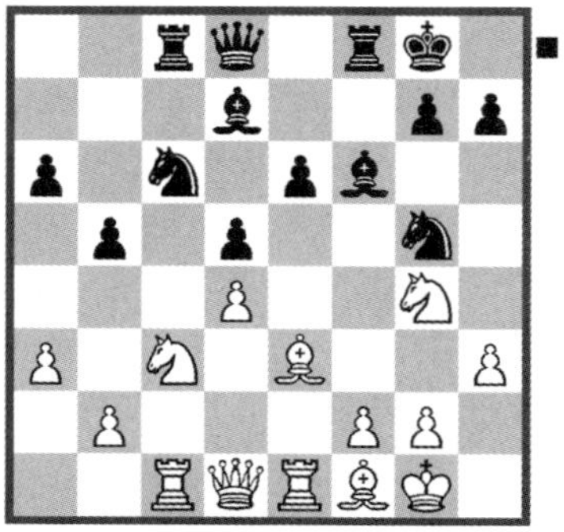

Position after: 20. ♘g4!

**20... ♘f7**

20... ♗e7 21. a4±
**21. ♘xf6+ ♕xf6 22. a4 b4 23. ♘e2 ♘d6 24. ♘g3 a5 25. ♕d2 h6**

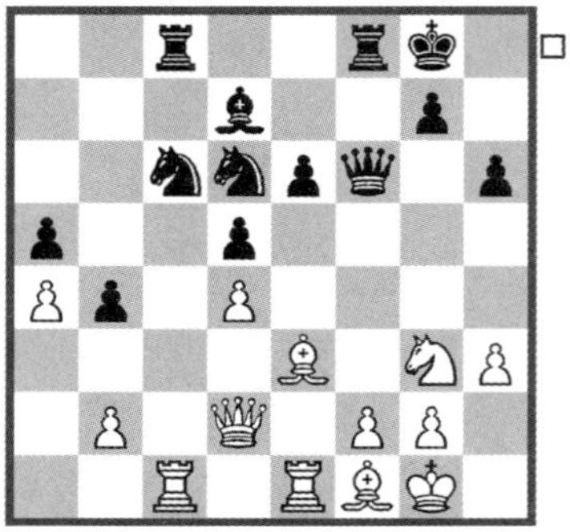

Position after: 25... h6

**26. b3±**

The bishop-pair gives us significantly better chances in the middlegame, and White converted this position into victory in Serner – Barnsley, ICCF email 2011.

## f) 7...e5 8.c3 ♗e7 9.d4 --

**1. e4 c5 2. ♘f3 ♘c6 3. ♗b5 d6 4. 0-0 ♗d7 5. ♖e1 ♘f6 6. h3 a6 7. ♗f1 e5**

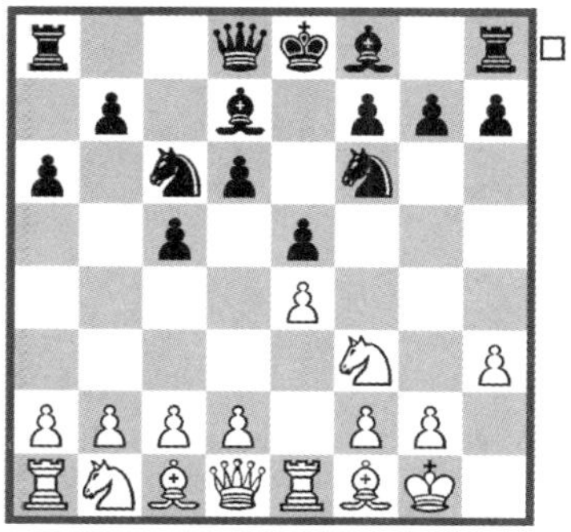

Position after: 7... e5

**8. c3 ♗e7**

This line is not really inspiring.

We have discussed the superior 8... g5 already in the fourth subchapter.

**9. d4 0-0**

9... cxd4 10. cxd4 exd4 [10... 0-0 11. d5 ♘a7 12. a4±] 11. ♘xd4

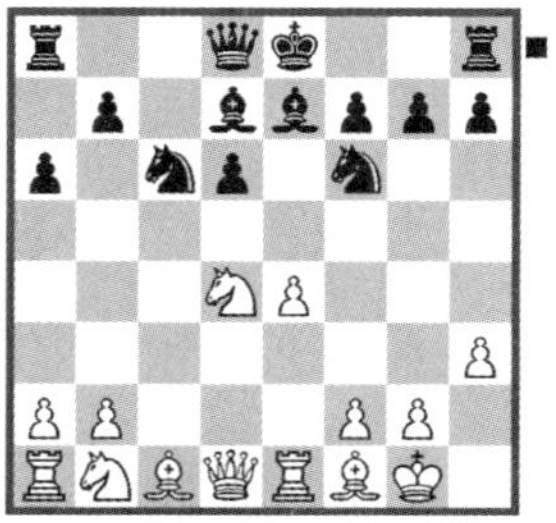

Position after: 11. ♘xd4

11... d5 Nothing else makes sense in the fight for equality. 12. exd5 ♘xd5 13. ♗c4 ♘b6 14. ♗b3 White is playing for the initiative, because if Black has a couple of free moves the game will just be completely equal. Therefore we need to ensure that we don't waste time. Also, Black has created a weakness on b6 by playing ...a7-a6, so this is something that we can try to exploit. 14... 0-0 15. ♘c3

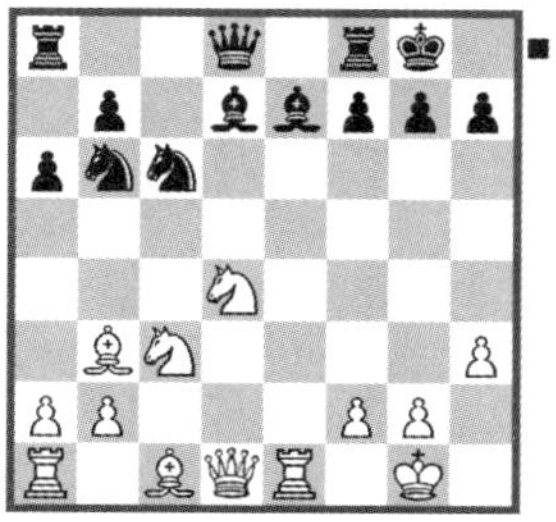

Position after: 15. ♘c3

**A)** 15... ♗f6 16. ♘xc6 ♗xc6 17. ♗e3 ♘d7 18. ♕h5 ♘e5 19. ♖ed1 ♕e7 20. ♘d5 The bishop-pair advantage should prove to be very effective here. 20... ♗xd5 21. ♗xd5±

**B)** 15... ♗c5 16. ♗e3 ♘xd4 17. ♗xd4 ♗xd4 18. ♕xd4 ♗c6 19. ♕f4! White converted his initiative to victory in Barreras Garcia – Silva, ICCF email 2011.

**C)** 15... ♘xd4 16. ♕xd4 ♗f6 17. ♕f4!

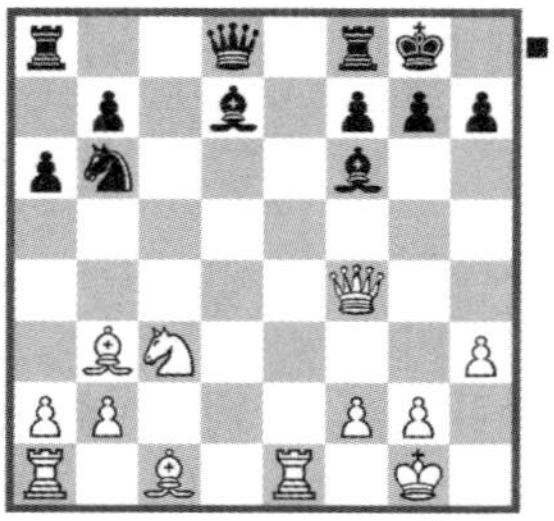

Position after: 17. ♕f4!

17... ♗c6 18. ♖d1 ♘d7 19. ♗e3 It's increasingly difficult for Black to avoid giving away the bishop-pair. 19... ♕b8 20. ♕xb8 ♖axb8 21. ♘d5±

**10. d5!**

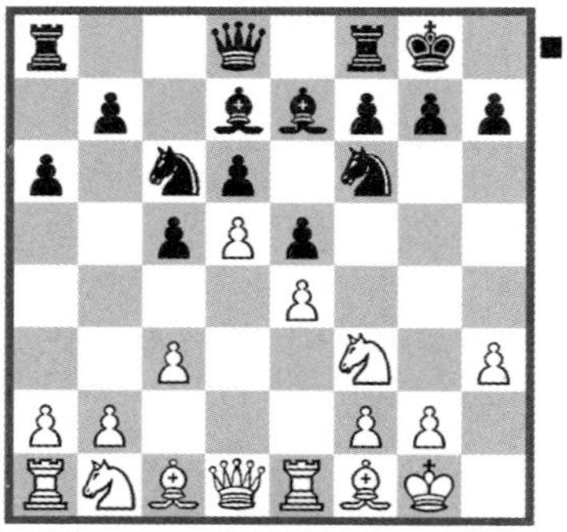

Position after: 10. d5!

We'll play in the same way as after 9...♕c7, although here Black has less choice about where to put the knight.

**10... ♘b8**

10... ♘a7 11. a4 b5 [11... ♕c7 12. a5 ♘e8 13. ♗d3 f5 14. exf5 ♗xf5 15. ♗xf5 ♖xf5 16. c4+–] 12. axb5 axb5 13. b4! cxb4 14. cxb4 ♕c7 15. ♘fd2 ♖fb8 16. ♘b3 ♘c8 17. ♘a5± Now that the a-file is successfully blocked, we can focus on invading down the c-file and occupying the c6-square. Furthermore, we also have kingside attacking possibilities with ideas such as ♖a3-g3.

**11. a4**

The main issue for Black is that all their pieces are really uncoordinated. The typical King's Indian ...f7-f5 push is Black's principal plan, but the variations illustrate that Black's queenside is far too weak for any quick kingside play to come to fruition.

**11... ♘e8 12. ♘bd2**

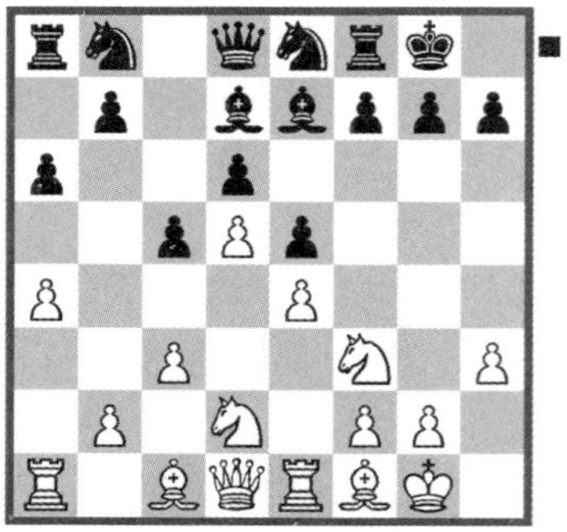

Position after: 12. ♘bd2

**12... g6**

**A)** 12... f5 13. ♕b3! b6 14. ♘xe5 dxe5 15. d6+ ♔h8 16. dxe7 ♕xe7 17. ♕xb6+–

**B)** 12... b6 13. ♗d3 f5 14. ♕b3 f4 15. ♘c4+–

**13. ♘c4 f5 14. ♗h6! ♖f7**

14... ♘g7 15. ♕b3 fxe4 16. ♘fd2 ♖a7 17. ♘xe4+–

**15. exf5**

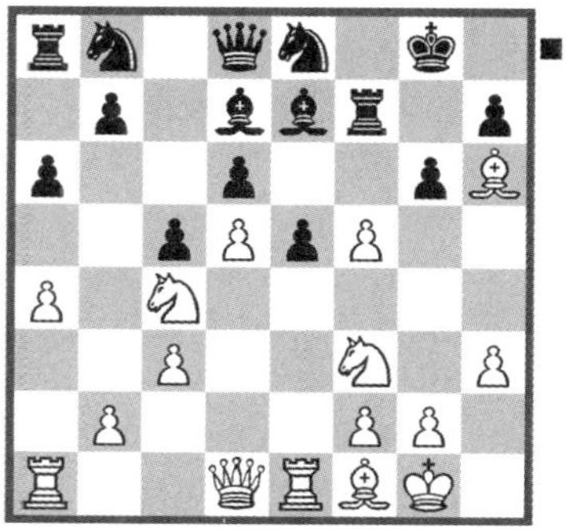

Position after: 15. exf5

**15... ♗xf5**

15... gxf5 16. ♘fxe5! dxe5 17. ♘xe5 ♖f6 18. ♗g5+–

**16. ♕d2+–**

Followed by ♘g5, and Black's position is collapsing.

## g) 7...e5 8.c3 ♗e7 9.d4 ♕c7

**1. e4 c5 2. ♘f3 ♘c6 3. ♗b5 d6 4. 0-0 ♗d7 5. ♖e1 ♘f6 6. h3 a6 7. ♗f1 e5 8. c3 ♗e7 9. d4 ♕c7**

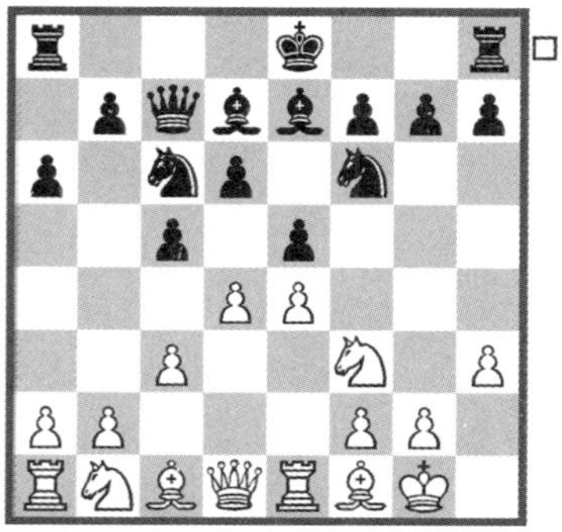

Position after: 9... ♕c7

Freeing the d8-square for the knight on c6.

**10. d5!**

Black has a choice about where to put the knight. While it's important to note the subtle differences in our responses to each alternative, I should also just say that these positions heavily favour White anyway. Black's development is nowhere near as good compared to analogous Ruy Lopez lines.

**10... ♘a5**

**A)** 10... ♘a7 11. a4 b5 [11... 0-0 12. a5 transposes to 9... 0-0.] 12. ♘h4! In this case, we can maintain queenside tension whilst simultaneously exploring kingside ventures.

*(see analysis diagram next page)*

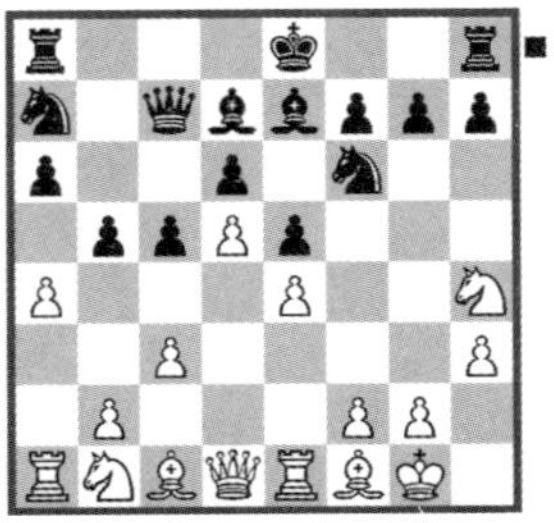

Position after: 12. ♘h4!

12... 0-0 [12... g6 13. axb5 axb5 14. ♗h6 ♗f8 15. ♕d2±] 13. ♘f5 ♗d8 [13... ♗xf5 14. exf5 c4 15. g4! h6 16. ♗g2± Followed by ♗e3, ♘d2-e4 and f2-f4. Around here Black starts to really miss the light-squared bishop.] 14. ♕f3 bxa4 15. ♗xa6 ♘b5 Black will be able to trade pieces, but our kingside play ensures that we keep an initiative. 16. ♗xb5 ♗xb5 17. b3 ♗d7 18. bxa4 ♖xa4 19. ♖xa4 ♗xa4

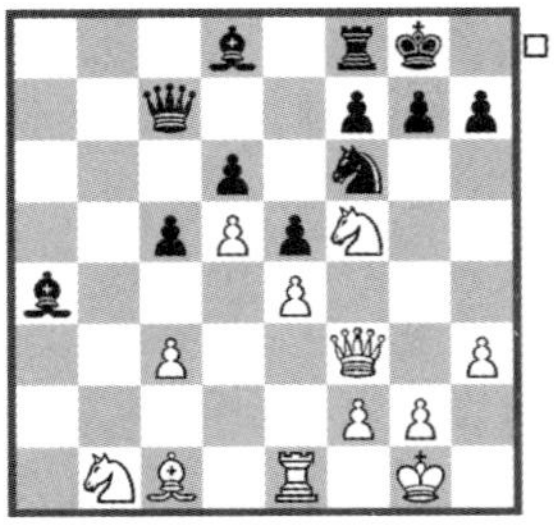

Position after: 19... ♗xa4

20. ♗h6! ♘e8 21. ♗d2± Followed by c3-c4 and ♘c3. Black's pieces are passive and it's difficult to regroup them.

**B)** 10... ♘d8?! 11. a4 Black faces the unpleasant choice between allowing us to play a4-a5, or preventing it with ...b7-b6. The latter option has the downside of creating a weakness on a6.

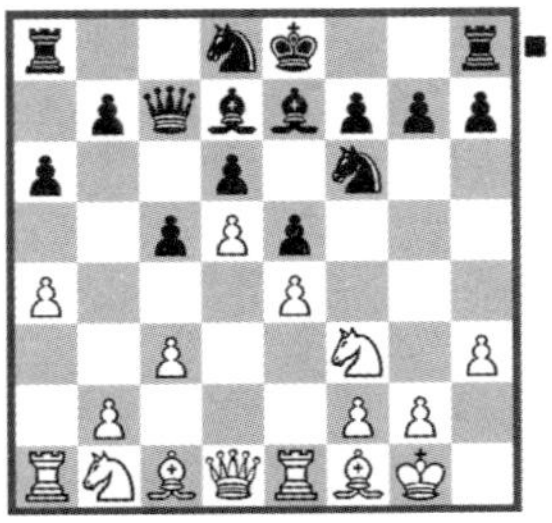

Position after: 11. a4

**B1)** 11... 0-0 Now we'll be able to fix the b7-pawn. Black's attempts at countering with ...f7-f5 should always be met with exf5 and occupation of the e4-square. 12. a5 ♘e8 13. ♘bd2

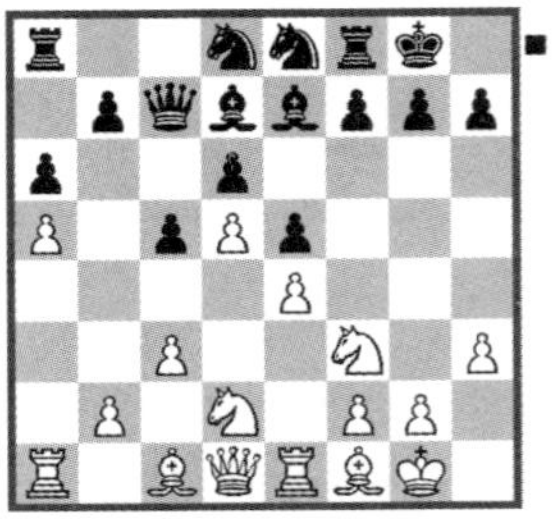

Position after: 13. ♘bd2

13... f5 [13... g6?! 14. ♘c4 f5 15. exf5 gxf5 Although Black is able to recapture with the pawn here, their minor pieces are inferior to ours. 16. ♘b6 ♖b8 17. b4!+–] 14. exf5 ♗xf5 15. ♘e4 ♘f7 16. ♘g3 ♗g6 17. c4± The logical next step would be to exchange light-squared bishops with ♗d3.

**B2)** 11... b6 12. ♘a3 0-0 13. ♗d3! ♘b7 We are following Vachier Lagrave – Ortiz Suarez, Tromso 2013. MVL chose 14.♘h2, but I would prefer the f3-knight to go to d2. 14. ♗e3

Position after: 14. ♗e3

14... b5 This is what I guess worried Maxime, but Black will suffer on the light-squares after trading the bishop on d7. [14... h6 15. ♘d2 ♘h7 16. ♕e2! ♗xa4 17. ♗xa6 ♖a7 18. b4 ♗d7 19. ♘b5 ♗xb5 20. ♕xb5+– Black is pretty much lost after we continue with either ♘c4 or ♕c6.] 15. axb5 axb5 16. ♘xb5 ♗xb5 17. ♗xb5

Position after: 17. ♗xb5

17... ♘xe4 [17... ♖xa1 18. ♕xa1 ♘xe4 19. ♕a7 ♗d8 20. ♗a6 ♘a5 21. ♕xc7 ♗xc7 22. b4 ♘b3 23. ♗c4+–] 18. ♕c2 ♘f6 19. c4 ♖fb8 20. ♘d2 g6 21. g4!± Soon we can start thinking about f2-f4 ideas.

**11. b4! cxb4 12. cxb4 ♘c4**

We are following Georgiadis – Pavlidis, Rio Achaia 2018. White should have continued the queenside pressure here with:

**13. ♕c2N ♖c8**

Position after: 13... ♖c8

**14. a4!**

We're establishing a pawn on a5 and continuing to dominate on the queenside. Black's control of the c-file is generally almost meaningless in these structures.

**14... 0-0**

**A)** 14... ♘b6 15. ♕xc7 ♖xc7 16. a5 ♘a4 [16... ♘c4 17. ♘fd2 ♘xd2 18. ♗xd2 0-0 19. ♘a3 ♖fc8 20. ♖ab1± Followed by b4-b5.] 17. ♗e3 0-0 18. ♘fd2 ♖fc8 19. ♘a3 ♖c3 20. ♖eb1± Once again with the idea of b4-b5.

**B)** 14... b5 15. ♘fd2 ♘xd2 [15... ♘b6 16. ♕xc7 ♖xc7 17. axb5 ♗xb5 18. ♗xb5+ axb5 19. ♖a6 ♘fd7 20. ♘a3± The b-pawn is lost.] 16. ♕xc7 ♖xc7 17. ♗xd2 0-0 18. ♘c3 ♖fc8 19. axb5+–

**15. a5! h6 16. ♕b3**

Our primary threat is ♖a2-c2, so Black needs to react quickly.

**16... ♗b5**

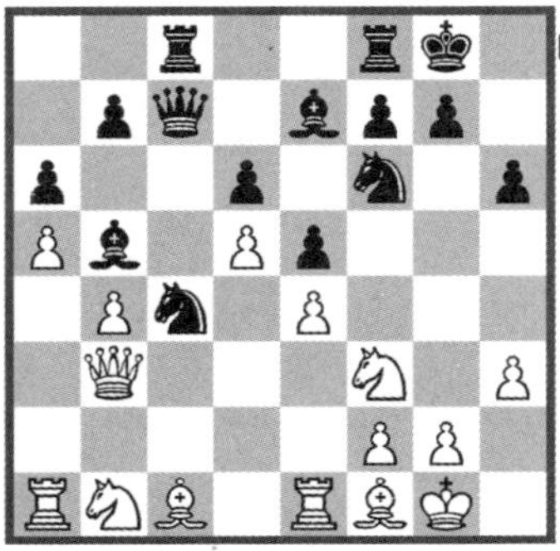
Position after: 16... ♗b5

**17. ♕a2!**

Preparing ♘c3. A sample continuation could be:

**17... ♖fd8 18. ♘c3 ♘a3 19. ♘xb5 ♘xb5 20. ♗d3 ♕c3 21. ♕b1 ♘d4 22. ♗e3 ♘c2 23. ♗xc2 ♕xc2 24. ♘d2 ♕xb1**

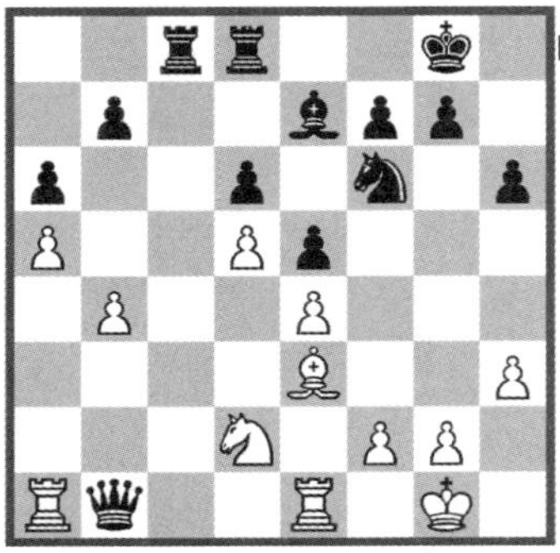
Position after: 24... ♕xb1

**25. ♖axb1±**

Black's queenside pawns will be very weak after the forthcoming b4-b5.

## h) 7...g6 8.c3 ♗g7 9.d4 cxd4 10.cxd4 0-0 11.♘c3 e5

**1. e4 c5 2. ♘f3 ♘c6 3. ♗b5 d6 4. 0-0 ♗d7 5. ♖e1 ♘f6 6. h3 a6 7. ♗f1 g6**

The text doesn't compare favourably with lines like 7... e5 .

*(see diagram opposite column)*

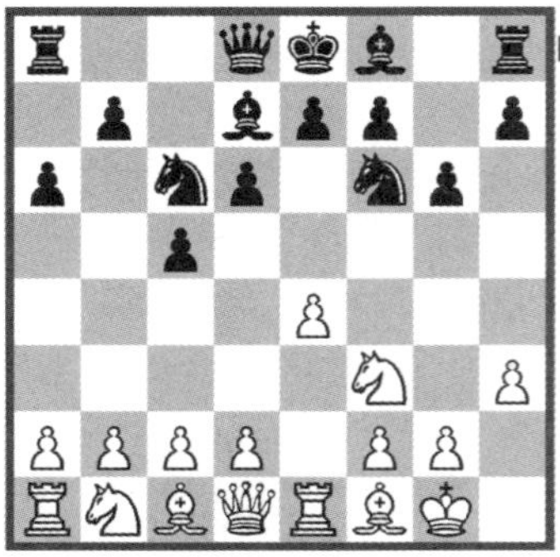
Position after: 7... g6

**8. c3**

White is already significantly better as there isn't really a way to prevent or mitigate the d4 break.

**8... ♗g7**

8... ♗h6? The attempt to exchange dark-squared bishops fails miserably. 9. d4 ♗xc1 10. ♕xc1 cxd4 11. cxd4 e5 12. d5 ♘a7 13. ♕h6+–

**9. d4 cxd4**

9... 0-0

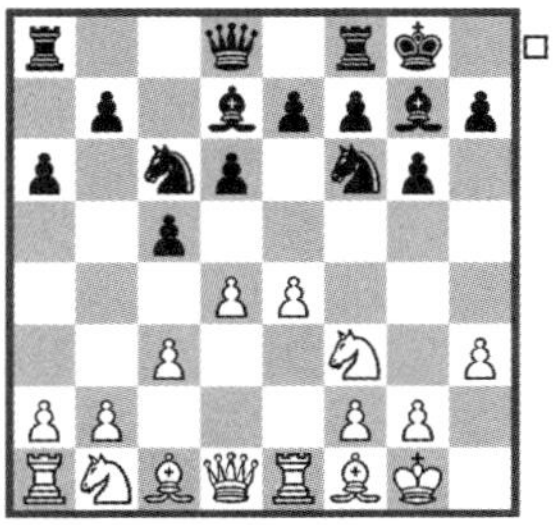

Position after: 9... 0-0

10. d5! Now that our bishop is on f1, it's the perfect opportunity to play this with a follow up of e4-e5. 10... ♘e5 [10... ♘a7 11. ♗f4 b5 12. a4!

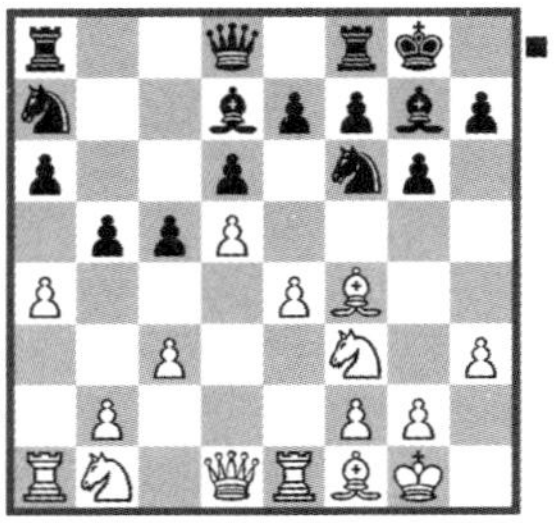

Position after: 12. a4!

12... bxa4 13. e5! ♘e8 14. c4±] 11. ♘xe5 dxe5 12. c4!

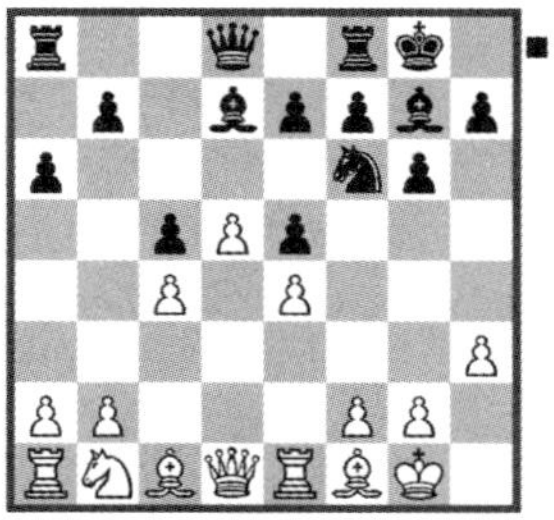

Position after: 12. c4!

12... ♘e8 [12... b6 13. a4!? a5 14. b3 ♘e8 15. ♖a2± Followed by ♖ae2, ♗b2, and at the right moment breaking through with f2-f4.] 13. b4! We need to hamper Black from achieving a solid position with a dominant knight on d6. In this case, we do so by chipping away at the c5-pawn. 13... b6 [13... cxb4 14. ♕b3 a5 15. a3! bxa3 16. c5±] 14. bxc5 bxc5 15. ♗e3 ♕c7 16. ♕c2 ♘d6 17. f3 f5 18. ♘c3± Doubling rooks on the b-file looks like a logical continuation. Black's kingside play will be limited by their weak central pawns.

**10. cxd4**

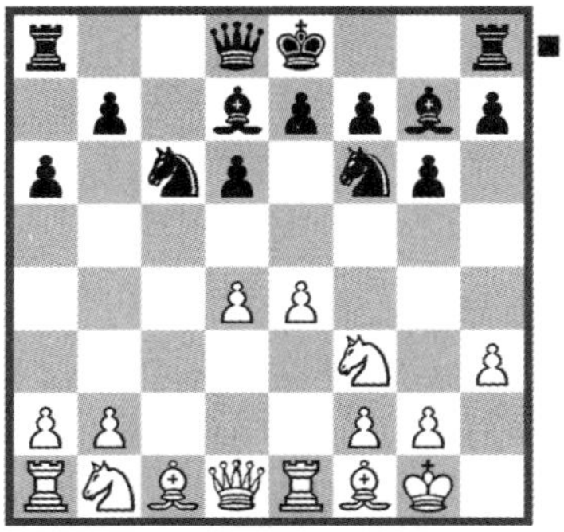

Position after: 10. cxd4

**10... 0-0**

10... d5?! should lose either a pawn or valuable time after 11. e5 ♘e4 12. ♕b3!

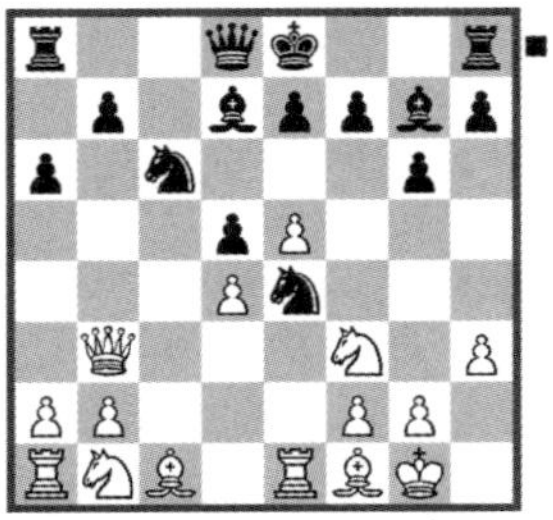

Position after: 12. ♕b3!

12... e6 [12... ♗c8 13. ♘c3!± was also extremely favourable for White in Heide – Jacobs, ICCF email 2015.] 13. ♘c3! ♘xc3 [13... f5 14. exf6 ♘xf6 15. ♘xd5+–] 14. bxc3 Black has to castle or else we'll play ♗a3. 14... 0-0 15. ♕xb7 ♘a5 16. ♕b1±

**11. ♘c3**

The biggest problem for his Black is that the d7-bishop is completely misplaced. If it were still on c8, the plan of ...b7-b5 followed by ♗b7 would make sense. Here, ...b7-b5 looks completely meaningless – but what else should Black play?

Another possibility is 11. d5 ♘e5 12. ♘xe5 dxe5 13. ♘c3± followed by normal queenside moves: a4, ♗e3, ♕b3 etc. Black can try and get some counterplay with ...f5 but White lands first in all cases.

**11... e5**

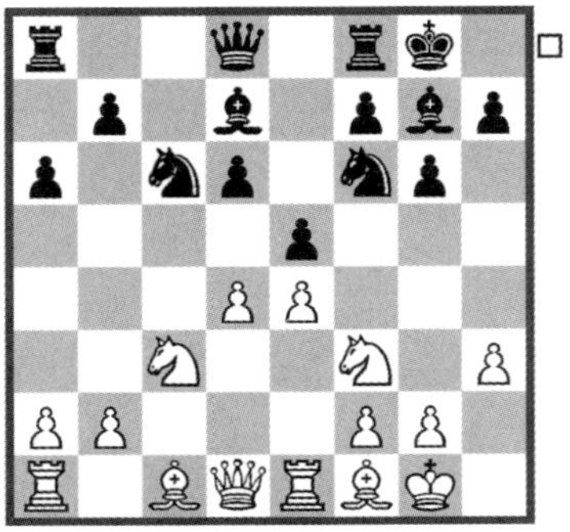

Position after: 11... e5

**12. d5!?**

12. ♗e3 exd4 13. ♘xd4 ♖e8 and even with the backward d6-pawn, Black develops some counterplay.

**12... ♘d4 13. a4 ♘xf3+ 14. ♕xf3 ♘e8**

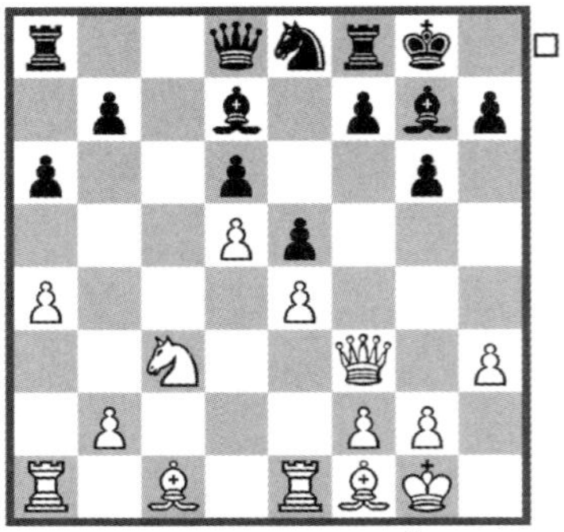

Position after: 14... ♘e8

The engine often misevaluates the KID structure, but in this case the queenside is open enough that White can just keep rolling.

**15. ♖a3 f5 16. exf5 gxf5 17. ♖b3±**

## i) 7...g6 8.c3 ♗g7 9.d4 cxd4 10.cxd4 0-0 11.♘c3 ♖c8

**1. e4 c5 2. ♘f3 ♘c6 3. ♗b5 d6 4. 0-0 ♗d7 5. ♖e1 ♘f6 6. h3 a6 7. ♗f1 g6 8. c3 ♗g7 9. d4 cxd4 10. cxd4 0-0 11. ♘c3 ♖c8**

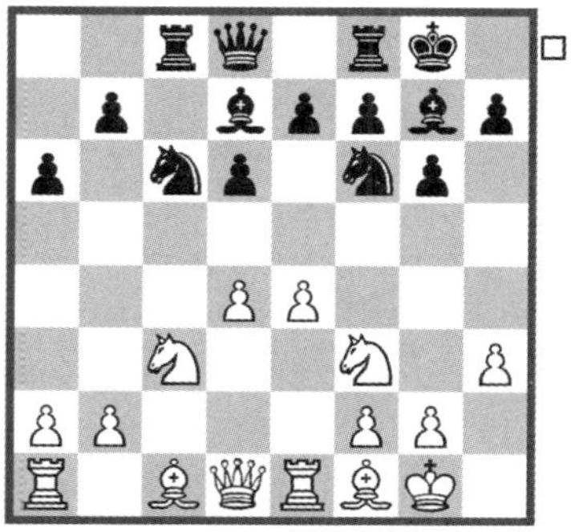

Position after: 11... ♖c8

**12. ♗e3 b5**

**A)** Here 12... e5?! will be less successful as the d4-square has been reinforced. 13. d5 White's pieces are all well-positioned to dominate on the queenside. 13... ♘a5 [13... ♘e7 14. a4!±] 14. ♘d2 b5 15. a4

Position after: 15. a4

15... ♖b8 [15... b4 16. ♘a2+–] 16. b4 ♘c4 17. ♘xc4 bxc4 18. ♖b1+–

**B)** 12... ♘a5 In Mareco – Gonzalez Zamora, Guatemala City 2020, the strongest continuation for White was 13. e5!

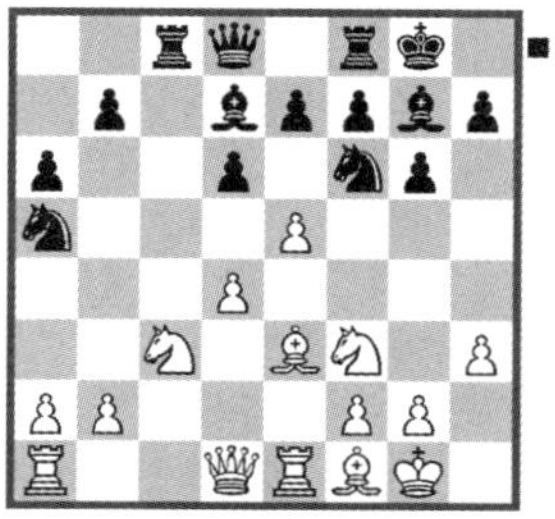

Position after: 13. e5!

13... ♘e8 14. ♕d2 ♘c4 15. ♗xc4 ♖xc4 16. ♗h6 Black will face problems on the dark squares after the exchange of the bishops. 16... ♗f5 17. ♗xg7 ♔xg7 18. ♘d5 dxe5 19. ♘e3 ♖c7 20. ♘xf5+ gxf5 21. ♖xe5±

**13. a3!**

13. a4 was also decent, but I don't see any reason to rush.

**13... e5 14. dxe5**

*(see diagram next page)*

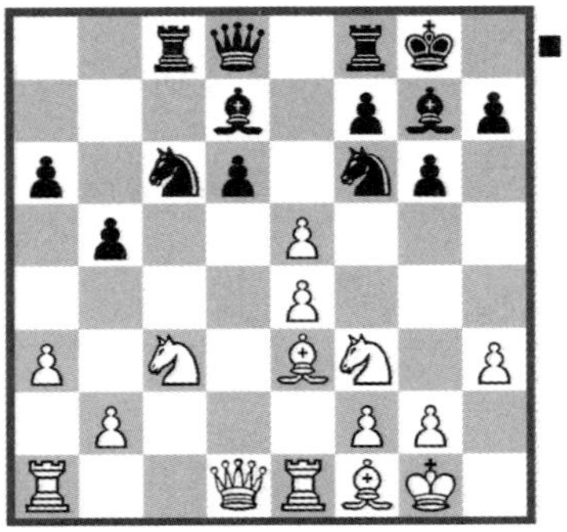

Position after: 14. dxe5

**14... ♘xe5**

14... dxe5 15. a4! b4 16. ♘d5 ♘xd5 17. ♕xd5 ♘b8 18. ♕d6+–

**15. ♕xd6 ♘xf3+ 16. gxf3±**

White is a comfortable pawn up.

## Conclusion to Chapter 7

As in the previous chapter, it's not straightforward for Black to meet our simple plan of c2-c3 and d2-d4. We can handle the wack ...g7-g5 attempts with precise play, and the transition to 'French-Advanced' type structures after 7...e6 seem to be advantageous for us too. Our approach after 7...e5 is interesting in that we adopt for an early d4-d5 advance in the style of a Ruy Lopez, where I argue that our pieces are well-placed to conquer the queenside battle.

Subchapters h) and i) seem the least threatening, as Black's development with ...g7-g6 and ...♗g7 is probably too slow to match our dynamic play In the centre.

# Part IV

# Other Sicilians Starting on Move 2

# 2...e6 - Alapin

**1.e4 c5 2.♘f3 e6 3.c3**

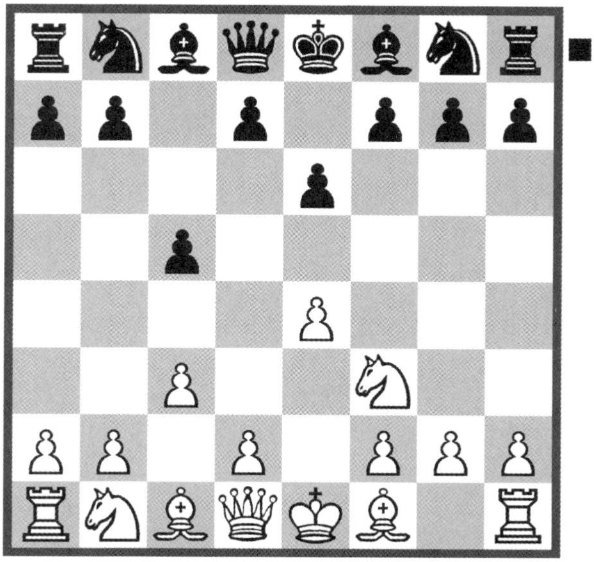

# Chapter Guide

## Chapter 8 – 2...e6 – Alapin

1.e4 c5 2.♘f3 e6 3.c3

## a) 3...d5 4.exd5 exd5

**1. e4 c5 2. ♘f3 e6**

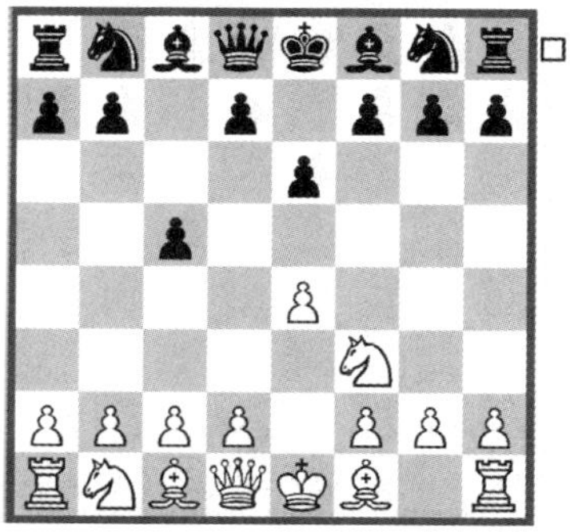

Position after: 2... e6

This move is usually designed to reach the Taimanov or Kan Sicilian. But we are not here to open the Sicilian, and I have two different recommendations: 3.c3 leads to the the Alapin Sicilian, while 3.g3 (covered in the next chapter) is more in the spirit of the King's Indian Attack.

**3. c3 d5 4. exd5 exd5**

This is slightly less popular than 4...♕xd5 – but more solid. We'll essentially be playing against an IQP. The following variations will demonstrate that our plan is very easy, and the probability of getting a long-term advantage is high.

**5. d4**

*(see diagram next column)*

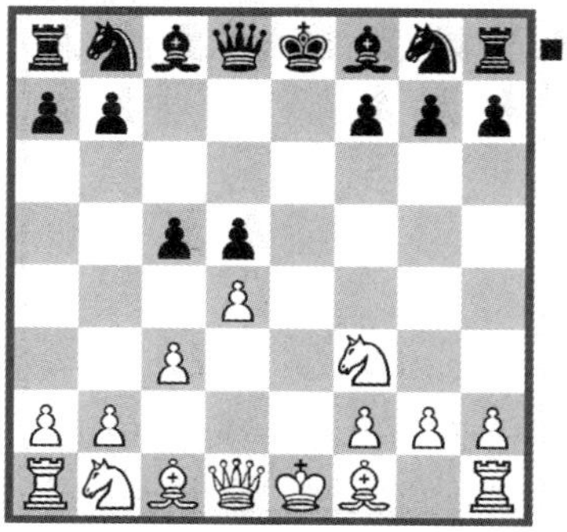

Position after: 5. d4

**♘c6**

**A)** 5... ♘f6 6. ♗b5+! Developing with tempo is rarely a bad idea.

**A1)** 6... ♘c6 7. 0-0 ♗e7 8. dxc5 The most logical move, winning a tempo as Black has already played ...♗e7. [8. ♘e5!? is also a decent option.; 8. ♕a4 c4!=∞ This is a typical theme where Black sacrifices a pawn to attain the bishop pair and a space advantage.] 8... ♗xc5 9. ♗g5

**A1.1)** 9... 0-0?! With accurate play this pawn sacrifice should be dubious for Black. 10. ♗xf6 ♕xf6 11. ♕xd5 ♗b6 12. ♘bd2 ♖d8 In Xiong – Andreikin, Chess.com 2022, the best continuation for White was the simple 13. ♕e4 ♗e6 14. ♕e2!± followed by ♖fe1, a2-a4, ♖ad1, and either ♗c4 or ♘c4.

**A1.2)** 9... ♗e6 There are several different ways to play this position with White, and it's pretty difficult to work out the small differences between each approach. In general, I think we'll always have a very slight advantage at the least, and Black will have to tread carefully to ensure the position doesn't get out of their control. 10. ♘bd2 This is the most obvious continuation, bringing the knight to b3. [10. ♕d3!? is an alternative option. It's very similar to 10.♘bd2, but we're also lining up the sneaky idea of ♗a4-c2. 10... 0-0 11. ♘bd2 ♗e7 12. ♗a4↑] 10... 0-0 11. ♘b3 ♗b6

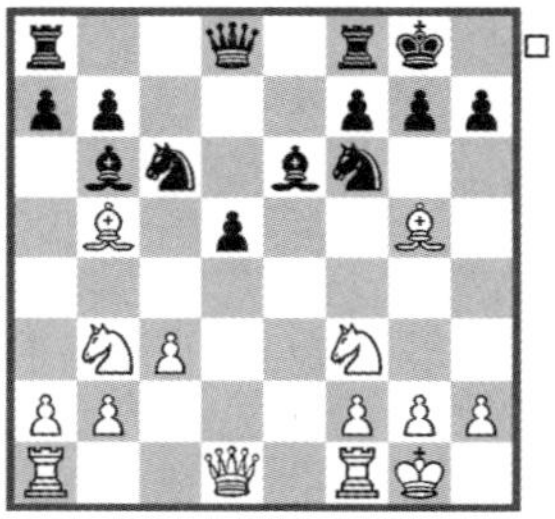

Position after: 11... ♗b6

12. ♗xc6!? [12. ♘bd4 has been the most common approach, but after 12... ♘xd4 13. ♘xd4 h6! 14. ♗e3 ♗d7 it feels like Black is consolidating.] 12... bxc6 13. ♘bd4 c5 [13... ♖c8 14. ♗h4!? h6 15. ♘e5±; 13... ♗d7?! 14. ♘e5! Black can't prevent doubled pawns. 14... ♗c7 15. ♘df3 ♖e8 16. ♘xd7 ♕xd7 17. ♗xf6 gxf6 18. ♕d2±] 14. ♘xe6 fxe6 15. c4± With a pleasant middlegame for White. The obvious follow up is to bring our rooks to the centre and put pressure on Black's pawns.

**A2)** 6... ♗d7 7. ♗xd7+

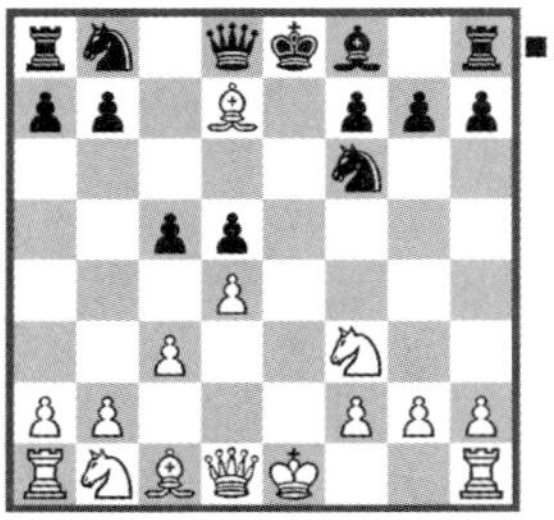

Position after: 7. ♗xd7+

7... ♘bxd7 [7... ♕xd7 is less precise as Black will lose a tempo recapturing on c5 with the bishop. 8. 0-0 ♗e7 9. dxc5 ♗xc5 10. ♖e1+ ♘e4 11. ♗e3±] 8. 0-0 ♗e7 9. dxc5 ♘xc5 [9... ♗xc5 10. ♖e1+ ♗e7 11. ♕e2±] 10. ♗e3 0-0 11. ♘bd2 The position is very simple but I think anyone would choose White here. We're basically only playing for two results. 11... ♖e8 12. ♘b3 ♘ce4 13. ♖e1± Some ideas for our following moves include h2-h3, ♘c1-d3, ♕b3, ♖ad1, ♘b4. We can slowly improve all of our pieces and increase the pressure on the d5-pawn. The position is entirely risk free.

**B)** It's probably too early to play 5... c4 6. b3 cxb3 7. axb3 ♗d6

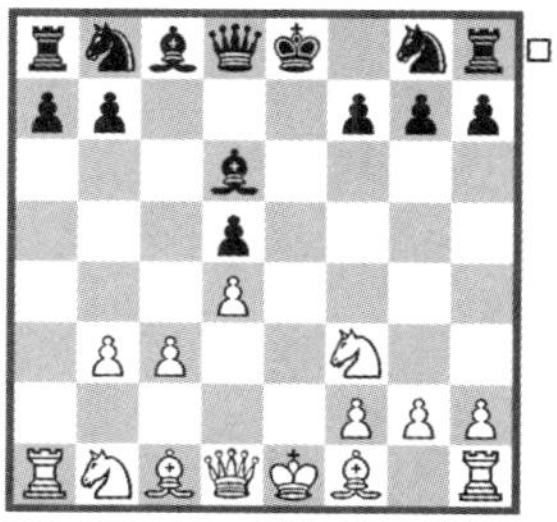
Position after: 7... ♗d6

8. ♗d3

**B1)** 8... ♘f6 9. ♕e2+! ♕e7 [9... ♗e7 10. 0-0 0-0 11. ♘e5 ♘c6 12. f4±] 10. ♕xe7+ ♗xe7 11. ♘e5± White has the better pawn structure and a very pleasant endgame. We'll probably continue with ♗a3 and ♔d2, before looking to advance our kingside pawns.

**B2)** 8... ♘e7 This has been played numerous times by Kamsky, but Black's only compensation for an inferior pawn structure is the possibility of good piece activity – which we have a clever way to prevent. 9. 0-0 0-0 10. ♘a3! Threatening ♘b5. 10... ♘bc6 11. ♘h4! The knight plays a really useful role in constraining the activity of Black's minor pieces. 11... a6 [11... ♘g6 12. ♘f5 ♗f4 13. ♘c2±] 12. ♗d2 ♘g6 13. ♘f5 ♗f4 14. ♘c2 ♗xd2 15. ♕xd2 ♕f6 16. ♘fe3 ♘f4 17. ♘e1!± Followed by g2-g3. Black will most likely capture on d3, after which we have a very pleasant advantage.

**6. ♗b5**

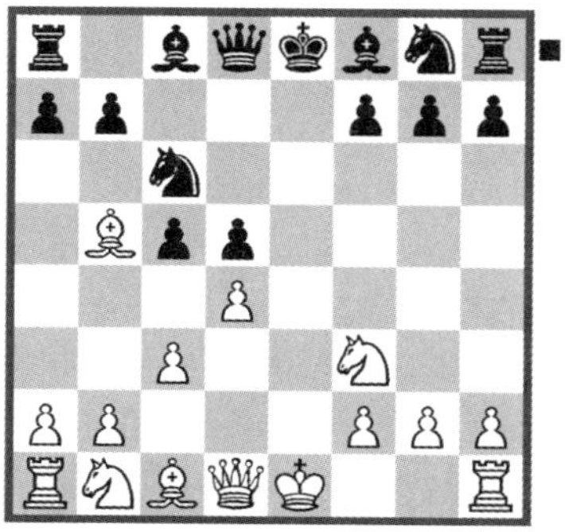
Position after: 6. ♗b5

**6... ♗d6 7. dxc5 ♗xc5 8. 0-0 ♘ge7**

The plan for White is simple – control the d4-square, complete piece development, and ideally exchange the dark-squared bishops.

8... ♘f6 transposes to 5...♘f6 6.♗b5+ ♘c6.

**9. ♘bd2 0-0 10. ♘b3**

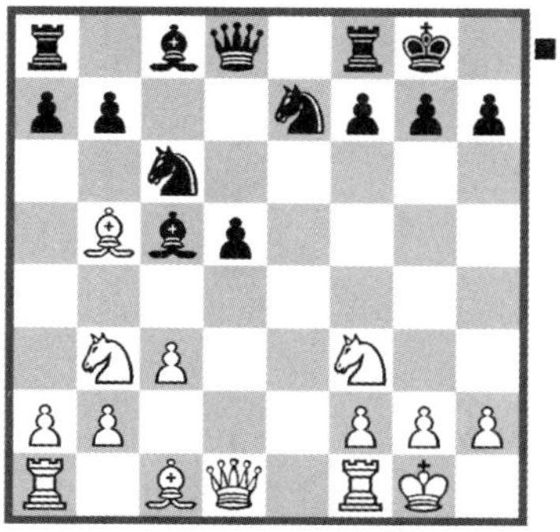
Position after: 10. ♘b3

**10... ♗b6**

10... ♗d6 Lots of different moves have been played here, but I think it makes sense to keep things simple and just develop naturally. 11. ♗e3 ♗g4 [11... ♘f5 12. ♗c5! As mentioned previously, exchanging the dark-squared bishops would be beneficial for us. 12... a6 13. ♗d3 a5 14. ♗xd6 ♘xd6 15. ♘bd4±] 12. h3 ♗h5 13. ♗e2! The bishop isn't really doing anything on b5 anymore, so it's the right time to retreat to e2. 13... ♖e8 14. ♖e1 ♕d7 15. ♘fd4

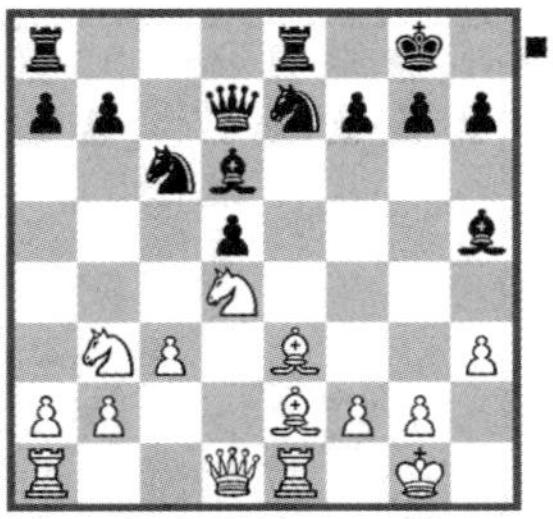

Position after: 15. ♘fd4

15... ♗xe2 [15... ♗g6 16. ♗g4! ♕d8 17. ♘c5! ♗xc5 18. ♘xc6 ♘xc6 19. ♗xc5±] 16. ♕xe2± Followed by ♖ad1, with a very comfortable position.

**11. ♖e1**

Preparing ♗e3.

**11... ♗g4**

11... ♘f5 is logical, preventing ♗e3. 12. ♗d3! The bishop stands much better on d3 than b5. Our ideas now involve ♕c2, ♗c2 and ♕d3, or simply ♗xf5 and ♗e3. 12... h6

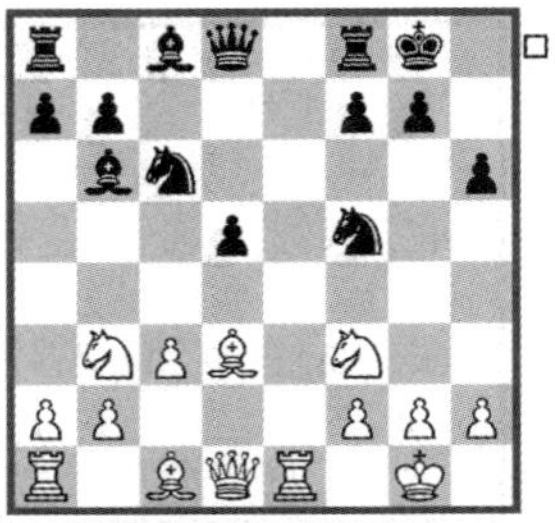

Position after: 12... h6

13. ♗c2 [13. a4!? might be even more accurate. 13... a6 14. a5 ♗a7 15. ♗xf5 ♗xf5 16. ♗e3±]

**A)** 13... ♗e6 14. ♕d3 ♕f6 [14... ♖e8 15. a4 a6 16. a5 ♗a7 17. ♗f4±] 15. ♗e3! ♗xe3 16. ♖xe3± We have achieved our goal of exchanging dark-squared bishops, and can follow up with either ♖e2 or ♖ee1, before bringing the a-rook into play.

**B)** 13... d4! The critical move. 14. ♗xf5 ♗xf5 15. ♘bxd4 ♘xd4 16. ♘xd4 ♗xd4 17. cxd4 The engine claims that the position is completely equal, but that's not entirely obvious. I think Black would struggle to go for this line without knowing the position thoroughly. In any case, we also had a completely viable alternative on move 13.

**12. h3 ♗h5 13. ♗e3**

*(see diagram next page)*

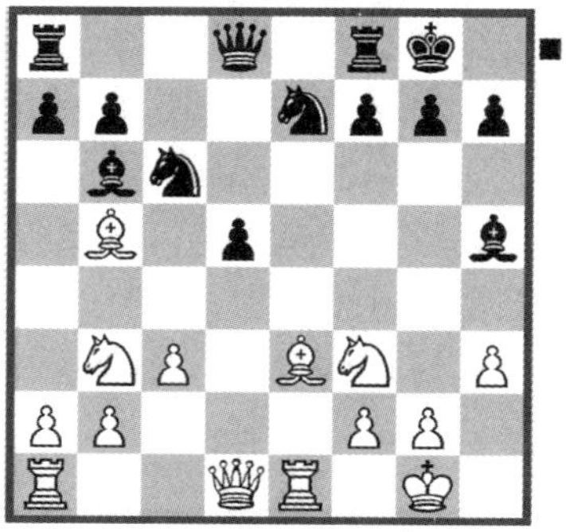

Position after: 13. ♗e3

**13... ♗xe3**

13... ♗c7?! 14. ♗c5! ♖e8 15. ♘bd4! ♘xd4 16. ♕xd4 ♘c6 17. ♗xc6 bxc6 18. ♖xe8+ ♕xe8 19. ♖e1+– Followed by ♘e5, after which Black is positionally lost.

**14. ♖xe3 ♘f5 15. ♖e1±**

We'll most likely continue with ♗e2, ♕d2, and ♖ad1. It's important to keep an eye on whether Black can push ...d5-d4. If not, we'll easily maintain a long-term advantage.

## b) 3...d5 4.exd5 ♕xd5

**1. e4 c5 2. ♘f3 e6 3. c3 d5 4. exd5 ♕xd5**

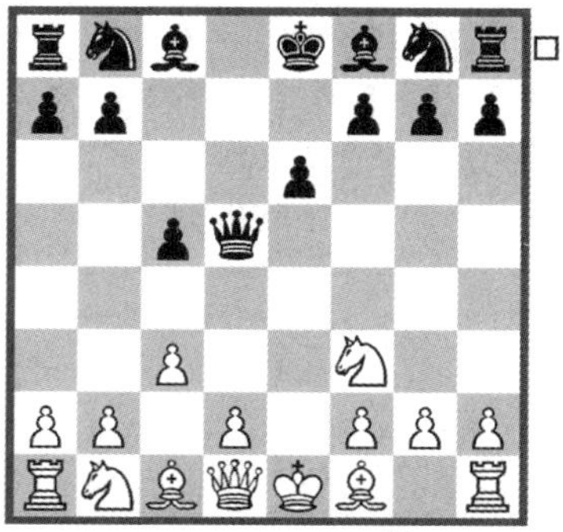

Position after: 4... ♕xd5

**5. d4 ♘f6**

5... ♘c6 6. ♘a3 Here 6... ♘f6 would transpose to the mainline, but Black has other options.

**A)** 6... cxd4 7. ♘b5! ♗d6 The only move which keeps Black fighting, but White should be much better here after a few accurate moves. [7... ♕d8 8. ♗f4+–] 8. ♗c4! ♕e4+ 9. ♗e3! ♗b8 10. ♗d3 ♕d5 11. ♘bxd4 ♗d7 12. ♕e2!± Followed by ♘b3 and 0-0-0. This is an even better version of a few lines we'll encounter after 5...♘f6.

**B)** 6... a6? This leaves a big hole on b6. 7. ♘c4 ♕d8 [7... ♖b8 8. dxc5! ♕xd1+ 9. ♔xd1 ♗xc5 10. b4! ♗xf2 11. a4+– With ideas such as b4-b5, ♘d6+, and ♖a2, Black's position is close to collapsing.] 8. ♗e3 b5 9. ♘ce5 ♘xe5 10. ♘xe5 White has a huge development advantage, and a2-a4 is coming on the next move. 10... ♕c7 11. a4 b4 12. a5!+– Clearing the way for ♕a4+ next move. White was already winning in Nihal – Martirosyan, Chess.com 2021.

**C)** 6... ♗d7 7. ♘b5 ♖c8 8. c4! ♕e4+ 9. ♗e2 ♘xd4 [9... cxd4 10. 0-0! gives White a great initiative.] 10. ♘fxd4 cxd4 11. 0-0! ♗xb5 12. ♗f3! ♕e5 13. cxb5± With a clear advantage due to the lead in development plus the bishop pair.

**D)** 6... ♕d8 The point of this prophylactic move is to be able to capture on d4 followed by ...♗xa3, without allowing an intermediary ♘b5. 7. ♗e3! Nevertheless we don't mind Black ruining our pawn structure. 7... cxd4 8. ♘xd4

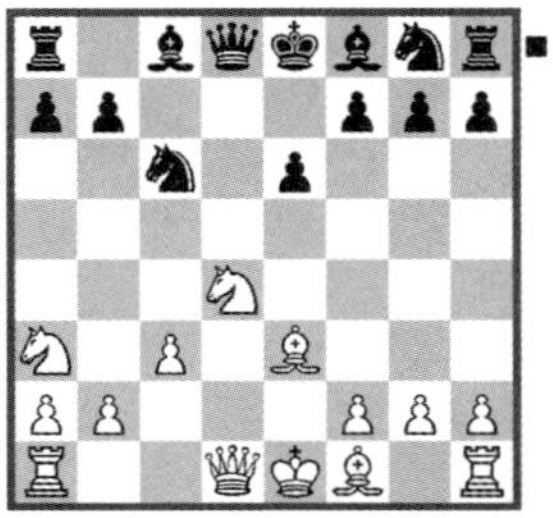
Position after: 8. ♘xd4

8... ♗xa3 [8... ♘f6 9. ♘c4±] 9. ♘xc6 ♕xd1+ 10. ♖xd1 bxc6 11. bxa3 White has a very pleasant advantage with the bishop pair. For example: 11... ♘f6 12. c4 e5 13. ♗d3± Followed by ♔d2-c3, and Black faces a tough defensive task.

**6. ♘a3**

*(see diagram next column)*

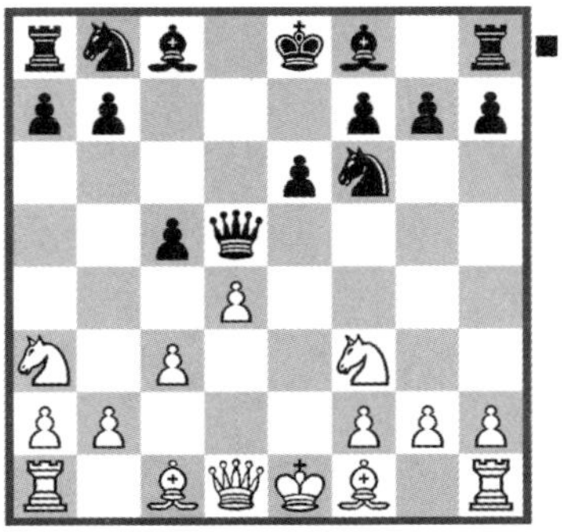
Position after: 6. ♘a3

6. ♗e2 and 6.♗e3 are the other main options, but I like the text move. The knight stands well here, potentially jumping to b5 but also enabling a future ♗c4.

**6... ♘c6**

**A)** 6... a6 is a logical option for Black, cutting out all the annoying ♘b5 possibilities. Note that it makes more sense here compared to after 5...♘c6, as Black can put their knight on d7 now. 7. ♘c4 ♘bd7 [7... ♕d8 8. ♗e2± With a nice development advantage.] 8. ♗e2 b5 Black needs to create space for the queen. [8... ♗e7 9. 0-0 0-0 10. ♘fe5!± Followed by ♗f3.]

Position after: 8... b5

**A1)** 9. ♘fd2!? is an interesting option but feels slightly overcomplicated.

**A2)** 9. ♘a5 is also possible: 9... ♗d6 [9... ♗e7 10. 0-0 0-0 11. ♘d2! ♕d6 12. ♗f3 ♖b8 13. dxc5 ♘xc5 14. ♘db3±] 10. c4! Otherwise ...♗c7 comes and Black would be fine. 10... bxc4 11. ♘xc4 0-0 12. 0-0± It feels like White has a slight pull here.

**A3)** 9. ♘e3 ♕c6 10. a4

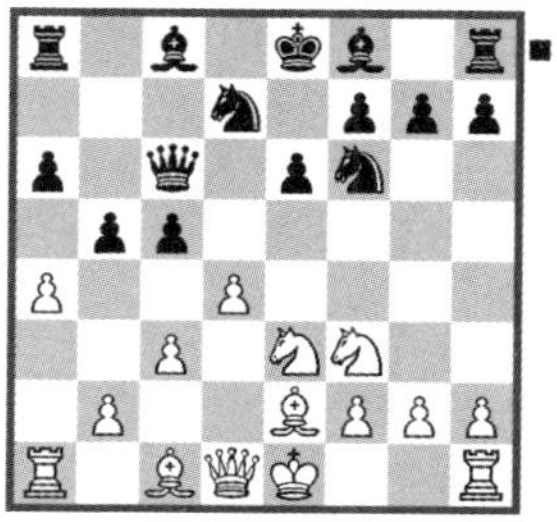

Position after: 10. a4

10... ♗b7 [10... b4?! creates too many holes on the queenside. 11. cxb4 cxb4 12. 0-0±] 11. dxc5 ♕xc5 The other alternatives were all advantageous for White. [11... ♗xc5?! 12. axb5 axb5 13. ♖xa8+ ♗xa8 14. ♘d4 ♗xd4 15. ♕xd4±; 11... ♘xc5? 12. axb5 axb5 13. ♘d4+–; 11... bxa4 12. ♕xa4 ♕xa4 13. ♖xa4 ♘xc5 14. ♖a3!±] 12. axb5 axb5 13. ♖xa8+ ♗xa8 14. ♘c2 Followed by 0-0 and ♘fd4. It's unclear whether White is better at all, but in practical terms the b5-pawn seems tough to defend and Black is the one who will have to find counterplay.

**B)** 6... ♕d8 7. ♘c4!

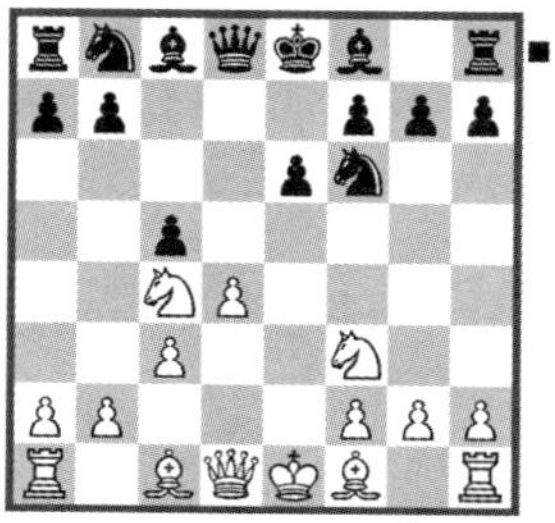

Position after: 7. ♘c4!

Black was threatening to capture on d4 followed by ...♗xa3, so it makes sense to bring the knight towards the centre. 7... ♘c6 [7... cxd4 8. ♕xd4!±] 8. ♗e3 [8. ♘ce5 is the other move played here, but I think Black is doing okay after 8... ♕c7! 9. ♗b5 ♗d6∞.] 8... ♘d5 [8... cxd4 9. ♘xd4 ♘xd4 10. ♗xd4 ♗e7 11. ♕f3 0-0 12. 0-0-0± I converted my advantage nicely in Haria – Arakhamia-Grant, Stafford 2022.] 9. ♗d3! Black has wasted a lot of time, so we don't mind allowing ...♘xe3. We can simply recapture with the pawn, opening the f-file and making it extremely dangerous for Black to castle. 9... ♗e7 [9... b5 10. ♘ce5±; 9... ♘xe3 10. fxe3 ♗e7 11. ♕c2! ♕c7 12. 0-0-0→] 10. dxc5!

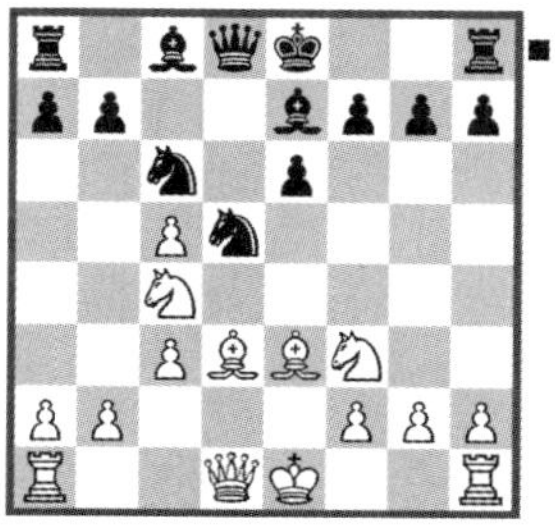

Position after: 10. dxc5!

10... ♘xe3 11. fxe3! We still opt for recapturing with the f-pawn – this structure isn't bad for White as long as Black is unable to capitalise on the perceived weaknesses around our king. 11... ♗xc5 12. ♘d4 e5 13. ♘xc6 bxc6 14. b4± Followed by ♗e4, with a pleasant edge.

**C)** 6... cxd4 7. ♘b5!

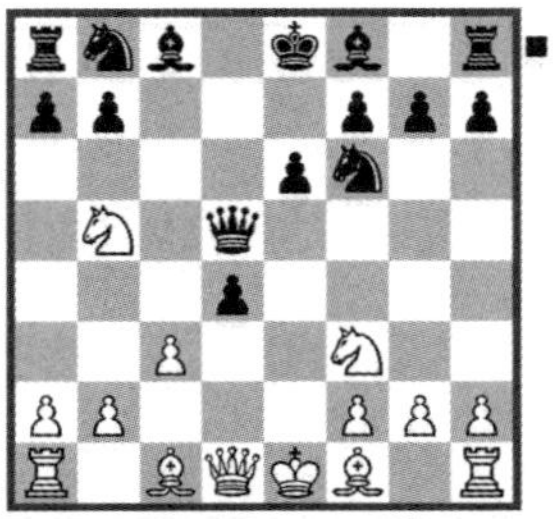

Position after: 7. ♘b5!

7... ♘a6 [7... ♕d8 8. ♕xd4!±] 8. ♘bxd4 Our pieces are pretty harmonious in this structure. We'll most likely continue with moves like ♗e2, 0-0, ♖e1 and ♗f4. A criticial option for Black is pushing ...e6-e5, which we constantly have to be aware of. However with the knight on a6 (rather than c6), it will often be difficult for Black to achieve this pawn push. [8. ♕xd4 also seems nice for White.]

**C1)** 8... ♗d7 9. ♗xa6! bxa6 10. 0-0± Followed by something like ♕e2 and ♘e5.

**C2)** 8... ♗d6 9. ♗g5! 0-0 10. ♗e2 ♘c5 11. c4 ♕e4 12. 0-0± Black's queen looks vulnerable on e4. A natural continuation is ♖e1 and ♗f1. We also have options of going for ♗xf6 and ♘b5 possibilities. In practical terms, Black's position appears very difficult to navigate.

**C3)** 8... ♗e7 9. ♗e2

**C3.1)** 9... e5 This looks logical, but Black will basically be forced to push the pawn to e4 – gifting White a few central squares. 10. ♘b5 e4 [10... ♕xd1+ 11. ♔xd1! e4 12. ♘e5 0-0 13. ♔c2±] 11. ♘fd4 0-0 12. ♗f4±

**C3.2)** 9... 0-0 10. ♗f4± With nice control – White has a simple but effective plan of 0-0, ♖e1, ♘e5 and ♗f3.

**D)** 6... ♗e7 7. ♘b5 ♘a6 8. ♗e2 0-0 9. ♗f4±

**7. ♗e3**

Position after: 7. ♗e3

Threatening to capture on c5.

**7... cxd4**

**A)** 7... ♘g4 8. ♗c4 ♕d8 [8... ♕e4 9. ♕e2 ♘xe3 10. fxe3 threatens to ruin our pawn structure, but as always we have the in-between move ♘b5 before we recapture on d4. 10... cxd4 11. ♘b5 ♖b8 12. cxd4±; 8... ♕d7 9. d5±] 9. d5 ♘xe3 10. fxe3 exd5 11. ♕xd5±

**B)** 7... a6!? 8. dxc5 ♕xd1+ 9. ♔xd1! Bringing the king to c2. 9... ♘d5 10. ♗d4 ♘xd4 11. cxd4 b6 12. cxb6 ♘xb6 13. ♘c4± Black has compensation for the pawn but I don't think it's full compensation – there's still a lot to prove.

**8. ♘b5**

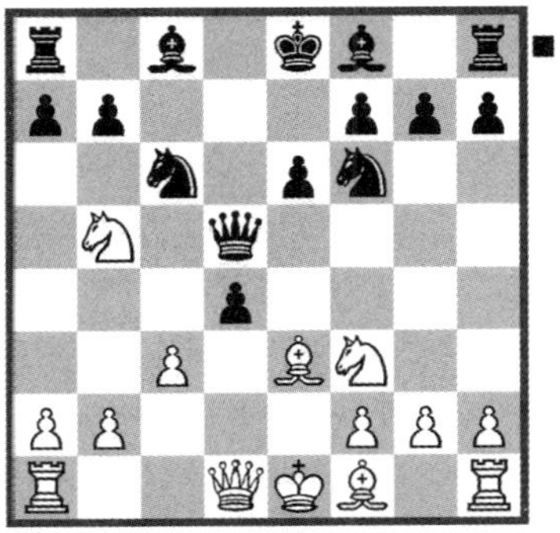

Position after: 8. ♘b5

**8... ♕d8**

8... ♕d7 The point of ♖his move is that in some lines Black can recapture on c6 with the queen – preventing their structure from getting ruined. A common theme to remember, regardless of whether the queen goes to d7 or d8, is the possibility of castling queenside and launching a kingside attack. We'll encounter this in numerous variations. 9. ♘bxd4

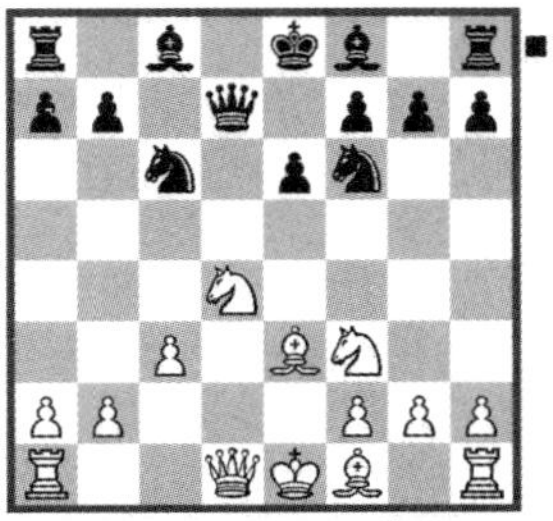

Position after: 9. ♘bxd4

**A)** 9... a6 10. ♗d3 ♗d6 11. ♕e2! [11. 0-0 ♘e7 12. ♕c2?! 0-0∞ Aronian – Caruana, Stavanger 2020.] 11... 0-0 12. 0-0-0 It's clear that White is better placed for opposite-side castling. 12... ♘e7 13. ♗g5 ♘ed5 14. ♔b1→ We have a lot of ideas – ♖he1 and ♘e5 is the more positional approach, or we can simply push the h-pawn up the board.

**B)** 9... ♗e7 10. ♗d3! Once again we want to castle queenside. 10... ♘d5 11. ♕c2! ♘xe3 12. fxe3 h6 13. 0-0-0 ♕c7 14. ♘xc6 bxc6 15. g4!± Followed by h2-h4 – and again Black faces a nervous defensive task.

**C)** 9... ♗d6 10. ♘b5! ♗b8 11. ♗c5 ♕xd1+ [11... ♘e4 12. ♗a3 a6 13. ♕a4+–] 12. ♖xd1 ♘e4 13. ♗a3 a6 14. ♘bd4± With good control – Black still needs to figure out where to put the king.

**D)** 9... ♕c7 transposes to the same move in the 8...♕d8 line.

**E)** 9... ♘d5 10. ♗d2

Position after: 10. ♗d2

While we often don't mind leaving the bishop on e3, here we have a different plan: ♘xc6, c3-c4 and ♗c3.

**E1)** 10... ♕c7 11. ♘xc6 bxc6 12. c4±

**E2)** 10... ♗d6 11. ♘xc6

**E2.1)** 11... bxc6 12. c4 ♘f6 13. ♗d3 0-0 [13... ♗xh2 14. ♗c3±; 13... e5 14. 0-0 e4 15. ♖e1 ♗xh2+ 16. ♔xh2 ♕xd3 17. ♗c3± The e-pawn is lost, and White emerges with a very pleasant edge.] 14. ♕c2 c5 15. ♗c3± Our pieces are extremely well coordinated against Black's king. We can follow up by simply castling kingside and ♖ad1 – it looks difficult for Black to survive.

**E2.2)** 11... ♕xc6 12. ♘d4 ♕b6 13. ♗b5+ ♔e7 14. ♗c4!± Black's king is extremely weak – ♕h5 or ♕g4 next look very appealing.

**E3)** 10... ♗e7 11. ♘xc6 ♕xc6 [11... bxc6 12. c4 ♘b4 13. ♘e5! ♕d4 14. ♗c3 ♕xd1+ 15. ♔xd1! ♗b7 16. a3 ♖d8+ 17. ♗d2 ♘a6 18. ♔c2±] 12. ♘e5 ♕b6 13. ♕a4+ ♔f8 14. ♘d3± Black will require a lot of time to finish their development, while we can simply play ♗e2 and 0-0, followed by something like c3-c4. In practical terms White is doing excellently.

**9. ♘bxd4**

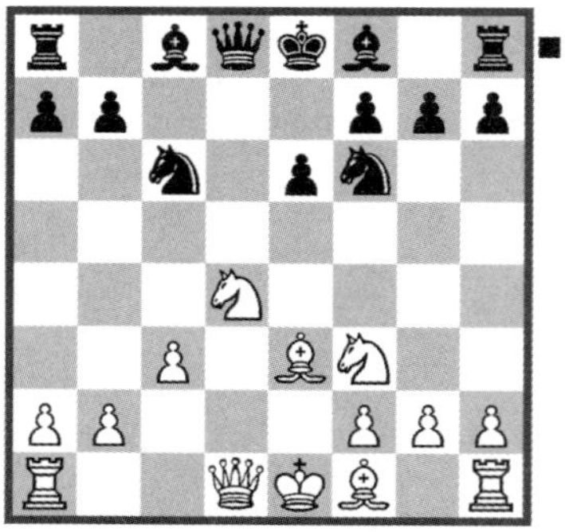
Position after: 9. ♘bxd4

**9... ♘d5**

**A)** 9... ♘xd4?! 10. ♗xd4 ♗e7 11. ♗d3 0-0 12. ♕e2 ♕a5 Preventing us from castling queenside, but now the queen will be a target when we advance our queenside pawns. 13. 0-0± Followed by a2-a4, ♗e5 and ♘d4. Black is slowly starting to get squeezed.

**B)** 9... ♕c7 10. ♕a4! Once again preparing to castle queenside.

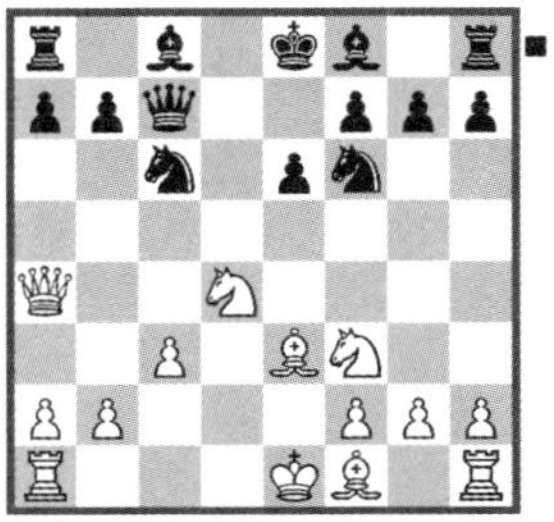
Position after: 10. ♕a4!

**B1)** 10... ♗d7 11. ♘b5 ♕d8 [11... ♕c8 12. ♗f4 ♘d5 13. ♘d6+ ♗xd6 14. ♗xd6±] 12. ♗f4 ♘d5 13. 0-0-0!± Immediately threatening ♖xd5 and ♘c7+. ♘d6+ also looks incredibly difficult to deal with. We are simply doing very well.

**B2)** 10... ♗e7 11. ♘xc6 bxc6 12. ♗f4 ♕b6 13. 0-0-0 0-0 14. ♗g3± Defending the f2-pawn. Here we have a strong positional advantage – both our pawn structure and our pieces are superior to Black's. We can continue with simple moves like ♘e5 and ♗e2.

**B3)** 10... ♘d5 11. 0-0-0!

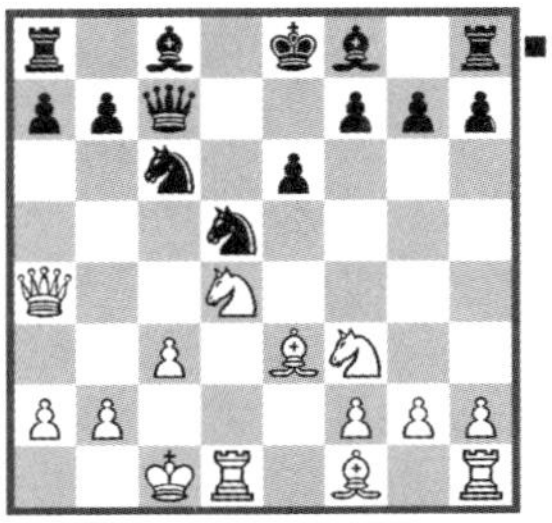
Position after: 11. 0-0-0!

11... ♘xe3 [11... ♗d7?! 12. ♘b5 This leads to a forcing line: 12... ♕d8 13. ♗g5 f6 14. ♕e4! a6 15. ♖xd5 axb5 16. ♗xb5 ♗e7 17. ♖xd7! ♕xd7 18. ♖d1 ♕c8 19. ♗e3 ♖xa2 20. ♔b1 ♖a5 21. ♗c4 ♘e5 22. ♗b3 0-0 23. ♘d4±; 11... ♗c5 12. ♘b5 ♗xe3+ 13. fxe3 ♕e7 14. e4 ♘b6 15. ♕b3±] 12. fxe3 ♗c5 13. ♘xc6! ♗xe3+ 14. ♔c2 bxc6 15. ♕e4 ♗h6 16. ♘e5± Once we recapture on c6, we will stand better. Even though Black has the bishop pair, our knight is probably the most powerful minor piece on the board.

**C)** 9... ♗d6 10. ♘b5! ♗b8 11. ♕xd8+ ♘xd8 12. 0-0-0±

**D)** 9... ♗e7 10. ♘xc6! ♕xd1+ [10... bxc6 11. ♕xd8+ ♗xd8 12. ♘e5±] 11. ♔xd1!? 11.♖xd1 also looks good for White, but I like the idea of putting the king on c2. 11... bxc6 12. ♘e5 ♗b7 13. ♔c2 ♘d5 14. ♗d2±

**10. ♘xc6 bxc6**

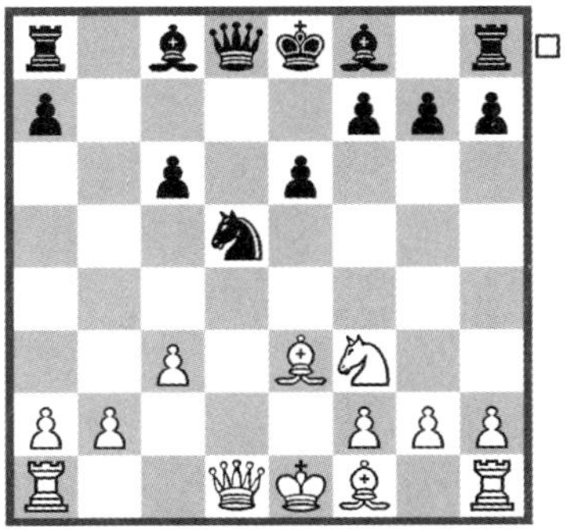
Position after: 10... bxc6

**11. ♗d2!**

The plan is simple: c3-c4, ♗c3, ♕c2 and ♗d3.

11. ♗d4 is more common but after 11... f6! 12. ♗c4 c5! we will have to trade off our dark-squared bishop – and this time there aren't really any positional benefits to doing so.

**11... ♗e7**

11... ♗b7 12. ♕c2 ♕c7 13. c4 ♘f6 14. c5!? Locking the bishop in on b7. 14... ♗e7 15. ♗e2 0-0 16. 0-0±

**12. c4 ♘b4!**

12... ♘f6 would make life extremely easy for us. 13. ♕c2 c5 [13... 0-0 14. ♗d3 ♗b7 15. 0-0 ♕c7 16. ♗c3 c5 17. ♘e5±] 14. ♘e5 ♕c7 15. ♗c3±

**13. ♕a4 ♗d7 14. c5!?**

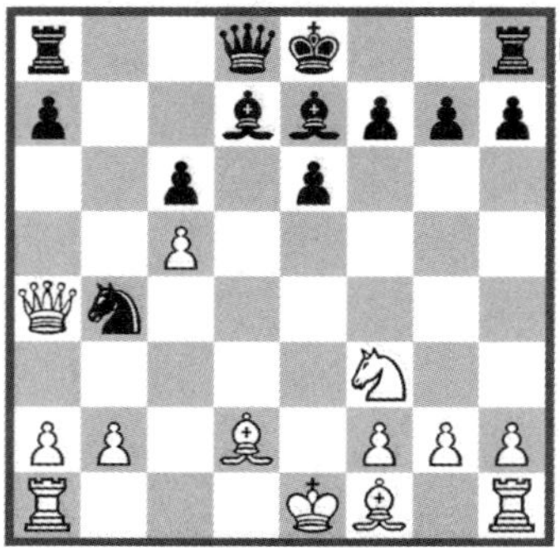

Position after: 14. c5!?

**14... a5 15. a3 ♘d5 16. ♖c1±**

It's unclear how much of an edge we actually have. The engine is hinting more towards equality, but I also think that Black has a few practical problems to solve. The a5-pawn looks like it will be a long-term weakness, and their pieces are quite passive. I think anyone would choose White here.

## c) 3...♘c6

**1. e4 c5 2. ♘f3 e6 3. c3**

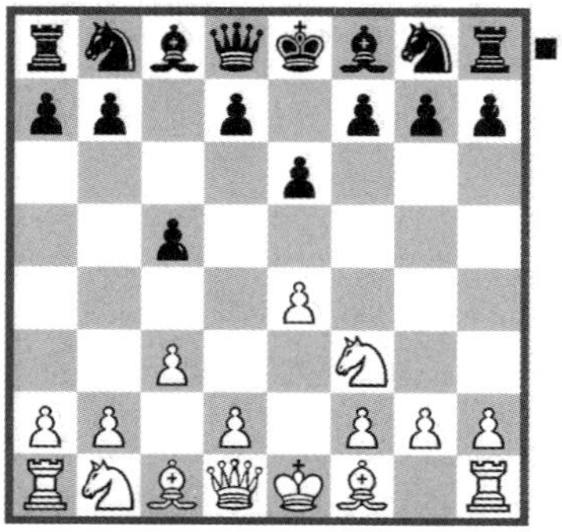

Position after: 3. c3

**3... ♘c6**

3... ♘e7 is an interesting try, but White stands better after 4. d4 cxd4 5. cxd4 d5 6. ♗d3!? [6. e5 is probably simpler to learn as it will transpose to 3...♘c6 after 6... ♘bc6.] 6... dxe4 7. ♗xe4 This would be a fairly normal position if Black's knight was able to develop to f6 instead of e7. Because of this, Black has to waste a bit of time getting their pieces developed.

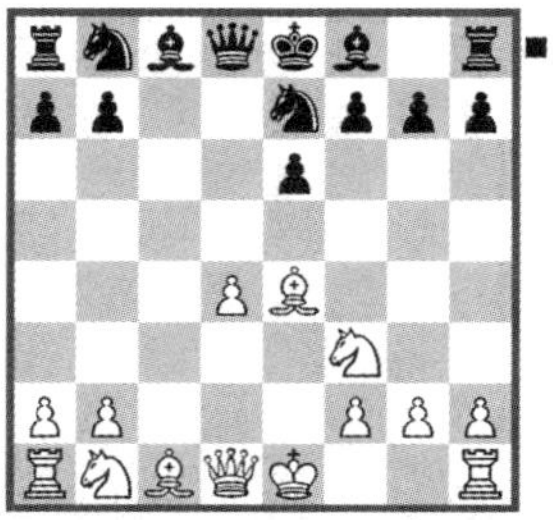

Position after: 7. ♗xe4

7... ♘d7 A better way of reorganising the Black pieces compared to 7...♘bc6. [7... ♘bc6 8. ♘c3 ♘d5 9. 0-0 ♗e7 10. a3 0-0 11. ♖e1± With a possible idea of ♗b1 and ♕d3 setting up a battery. The development advantage combined with an isolated queen's pawn structure means the position is very dangerous for Black.] 8. ♘c3 ♘f6 9. ♗c2 ♗d7 [9... ♘ed5 10. ♘e5!± Now Black can't develop the c8-bishop as we simply capture it with a great initiative.] 10. ♗g5 [10. ♘e5 is also possible here but I think Black is slightly closer to consolidating after 10... ♗c6.] 10... ♗c6 11. 0-0 ♘ed5 12. ♗a4! It's important to play actively, given that Black still hasn't castled. 12... ♗e7 13. ♘e5 Increasing the pressure on the c6-bishop. 13... ♖c8 14. ♘xd5 ♕xd5 15. ♗xc6+ bxc6 16. ♕a4 h6 17. ♗h4 0-0 18. ♕xa7± Black has to prove that there is compensation for the pawn.

**4. d4 cxd4**

4... d5 5. exd5 ♕xd5 transposes back to the previous subchapter.

**5. cxd4 d5 6. e5**

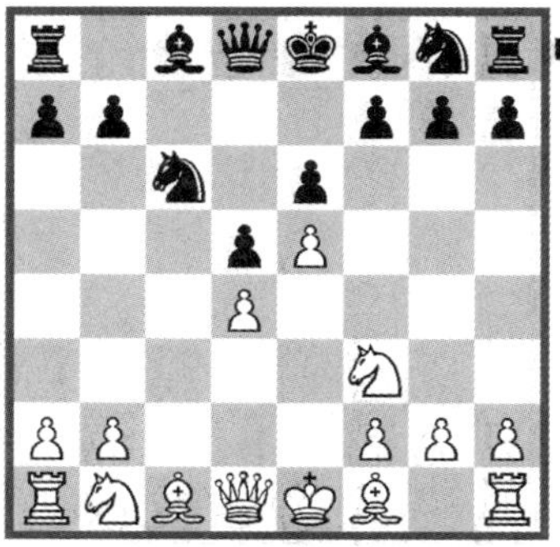

Position after: 6. e5

This is simply a good version of the French-advanced, as we have gained the c3-square for our knight. Nevertheless, it's also a fairly popular line for Black, as the plan is quite simple.

**6... ♘ge7**

The only critical move – the alternatives are simply bad.

**A)** 6... ♗b4+ is the most common move but makes no sense after 7. ♘c3± as we will simply gain tempi on queenside expansion with a2-a3 and b2-b4.

**B)** 6... ♕b6 has also been played a lot, but again after 7. ♘c3± the queen will be hit by a future ♘a4.

**7. ♘a3!?**

I did say that an advantage of this line was gaining the c3-square for our knight, but now that Black is committing to a ...♘f5 plan, I like meeting it with ♘a3-c2. The knight sits perfectly here – it protects the d4-square, enables a potential b2-b4 push, and also offers the possibility of jumping to e3.

**7... ♘f5 8. ♘c2 ♗d7**

**A)** 8... ♗e7 9. ♗d3 0-0? [9... ♗d7 would transpose back to 8...♗d7.; 9... f6 10. exf6 ♗xf6 11. ♗d2 0-0 12. ♗c3±] 10. g4!

Position after: 10. g4!

**A1)** 10... ♘h6 11. ♖g1!+– With the clever plan of ♖g3, ♔f1 and ♔g2. Black is stuck – the knight on h6 prevents them from breaking with ...f7-f6. Meanwhile we can continue improving and choose the right time to strike on the kingside.

**A2)** 10... ♘h4 11. ♘xh4 ♗xh4 12. g5! Threatening ♕h5 trapping the bishop. 12... ♗xg5 13. ♕h5 h6 14. ♖g1 ♗xc1 15. ♖xc1 ♔h8 16. ♔d2!+– The threats of ♖xg7, or simply doubling rooks on the g-file, are too much for Black to handle.

**B)** 8... ♕b6 9. ♗d3! Black obviously can't capture on d4. 9... ♗d7 transposing back to 8...♗d7.

**9. ♗d3**

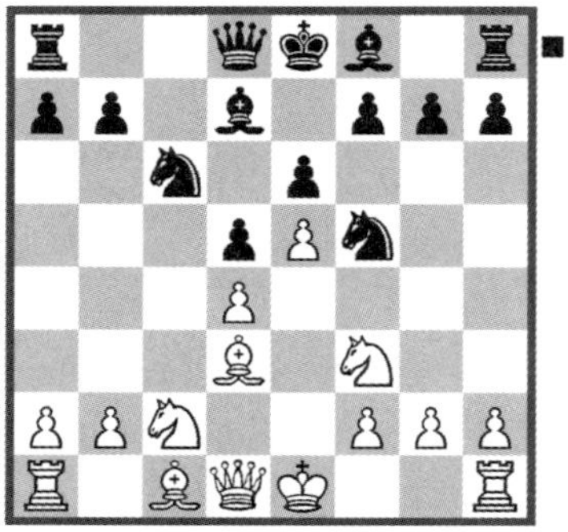

Position after: 9. ♗d3

**9... ♗e7**

9... ♕b6 10. 0-0! a5 Renewing the threat of capturing on d4, as now our b2-b4 idea won't work. [10... ♘cxd4? 11. ♘fxd4 ♘xd4 12. ♗e3 ♗c5 13. b4+–] 11. ♔h1!

**A)** 11... ♗e7 12. g4! ♘h6 [12... ♘h4 13. ♘xh4 ♗xh4 14. g5+–] 13. ♖g1±

**B)** 11... ♘cxd4 12. ♘cxd4 ♘xd4 13. ♗e3 ♗c5 14. ♖c1!+– Now the point of ♔h1 is obvious – Black can't capture on f3 with check. There's no way to prevent ♖xc5, and so Black is just lost.

**C)** 11... ♖c8 12. ♖b1!? ♘b4 [12... h6 I reached this position in the recent Olympiad. Here the best continuation is 13. g4! ♘fe7 14. ♔g2±] 13. ♘xb4

*(see analysis diagram next page)*

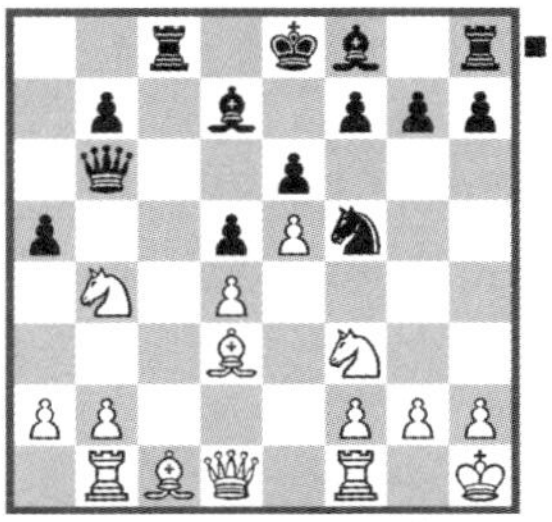

Position after: 13. ♘xb4

13... axb4 [13... ♗xb4 14. a3 ♗e7 15. g4! ♘h4 16. ♘xh4 ♗xh4 17. ♗e3± Followed by f2-f4, with a strong initiative.] 14. a4! Demonstrating the point of 12.♖b1. We will consolidate on the queenside with something like ♖a1, b2-b3 and ♗b2, before choosing the right time to play g2-g4. White converted the advantage in Guseinov – Juksta, Terme Catez 2022.

**D)** 11... h6 Black prepares ...♗e7, as after g2-g4 ♘h4 ♘xh4 ♗xh4 there is no g5 trick anymore. 12. h3!? ♗e7 13. ♗f4!

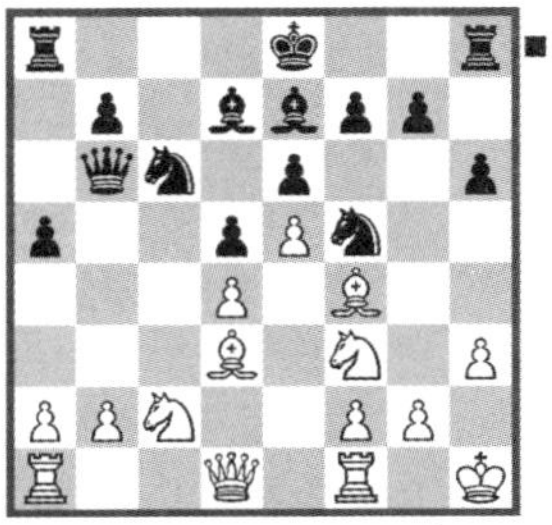

Position after: 13. ♗f4!

Black is still unable to castle here, as g2-g4 would be devastating. 13... ♘b4 [13... ♖c8 14. ♖b1±; 13... 0-0? 14. g4 ♘h4 15. ♘xh4 ♗xh4 16. g5!+–] 14. ♘xb4 axb4 15. ♗c2± It's difficult to find a viable plan for Black. Castling would lose immediately due to the threat of g2-g4, while ...f7-f6 would be too weakening. Meanwhile we can continue to slowly improve our pieces.

**10. 0-0**

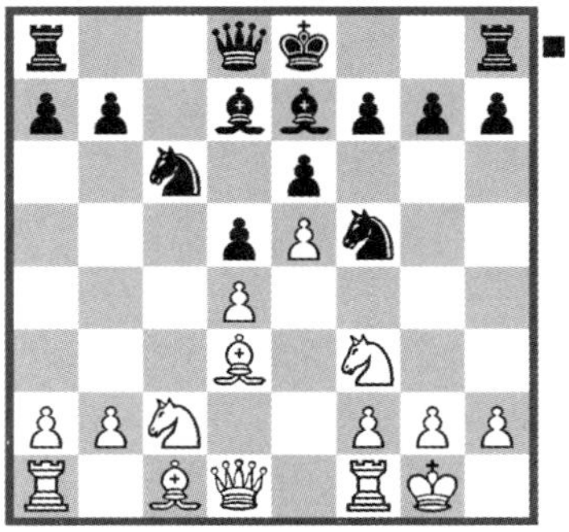

Position after: 10. 0-0

**10... 0-0**

**A)** 10... h5 Preventing g2-g4 at all costs, but it's simply too weakening. 11. b4! g5 Black needs to go active or else they'll simply get overrun on the queenside. 12. ♖b1 g4 13. ♗xf5! gxf3 [13... exf5 14. ♘fe1±] 14. ♗d3 fxg2 15. ♔xg2± Our king is perfectly safe – the opening of the g-file is probably more risky for Black, as we'll follow up with something like ♔h1 and ♖g1.

**B)** 10... ♕b6 11. g4! ♘h6 12. h3±

**11. ♗d2!**

Black's idea is to break with ...f7-f6, so the bishop will stand well on c3 after the change in pawn structure.

**11... f6 12. exf6 ♗xf6 13. ♗c3**

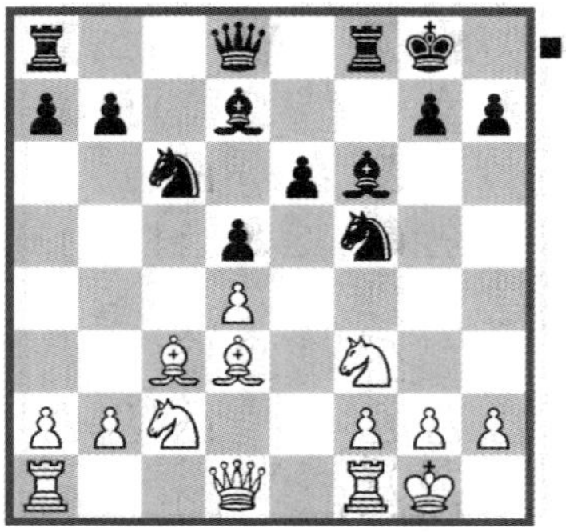

Position after: 13. ♗c3

Black is solid but worse. There are a few factors to consider: control of the e5-square, Black's weak e6-pawn, and potential counterplay down the f-file. In general Black does well in these structures when they manage to put pressure on the d4-pawn, carry out an ...e6-e5 push, and potentially sacrifice an exchange with ...♖xf3. None of these factors really apply here, meaning that White simply has a comfortable game. A sample line would follow:

**13... ♖c8**

13... ♗e8 Transferring the bishop to h5 is a logical plan, but after 14. ♕e2 ♕d6 15. ♖fe1 ♗f7 16. ♘e5!± we are doing very well.

**14. ♕e2 ♕e8 15. ♖fe1 ♕h5**

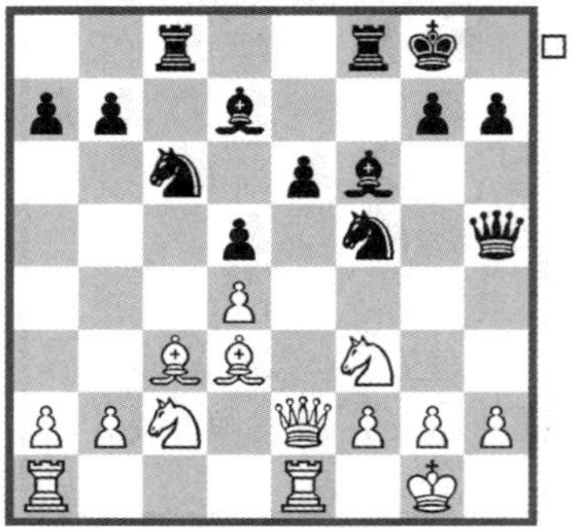

Position after: 15... ♕h5

Trying to gain some form of counter-play.

**16. ♘e3 ♘xe3 17. ♕xe3 ♗e7 18. ♗e2±**

We can continue slowly improving our pieces. Black has managed to open up the f-file but still struggles for adequate counterplay.

## d) 3...♘f6 4.e5 ♘d5 5.d4 cxd4 6.cxd4 b6

**1. e4 c5 2. ♘f3 e6 3. c3 ♘f6 4. e5 ♘d5 5. d4 cxd4 6. cxd4**

*(see diagram next page)*

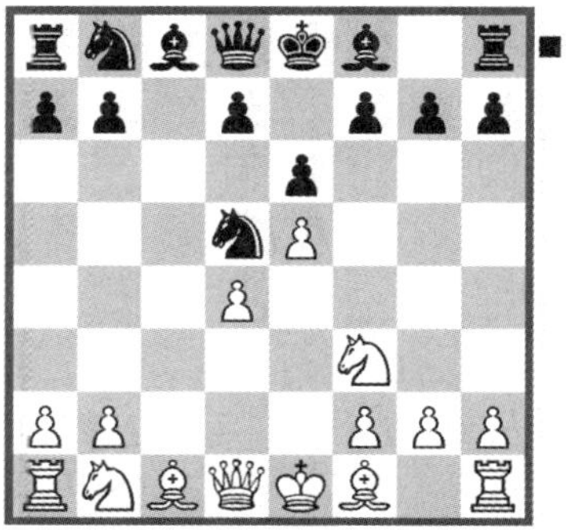

Position after: 6. cxd4

**6... b6**

6... ♗b4+ doesn't make any sense, as the bishop will be kicked back with a2-a3. 7. ♘bd2 0-0 8. a3 ♗xd2+ [8... ♗e7 9. ♗d3±] 9. ♗xd2±

**7. ♗d2!?**

A rare but interesting move. The point is simple – to play ♘c3 and recapture with the bishop. We retain the bishop on f1 for the moment in order to meet 7...♗a6 with 8.h4.

**7... ♗b7**

**A)** 7... ♗e7 8. ♘c3 ♘xc3 9. ♗xc3 ♗b7 transposes to 7...♗b7.

**B)** 7... ♗a6 8. h4! As Black is wasting time trying to trade light-squared bishops, we should immediately play for the initiative. The idea is simply to advance the h-pawn as far as possible and then follow up with ♖h3-g3. 8... ♗xf1 9. ♔xf1

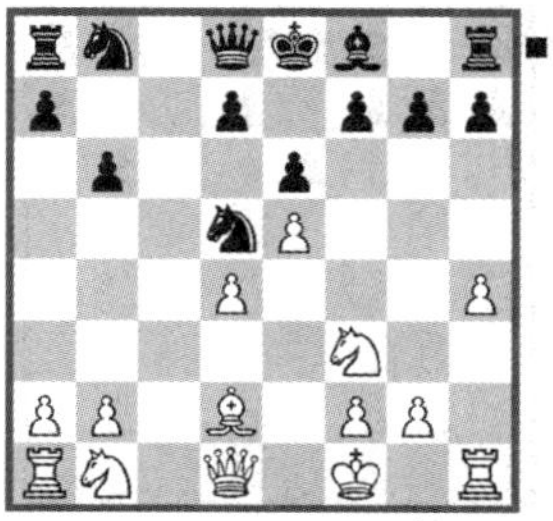

Position after: 9. ♔xf1

9... ♗e7 [9... ♘c6 10. ♘c3 ♘xc3 11. ♗xc3 ♘e7 Black plans to meet ♖h3-g3 with ...♘d5 and ...♖c8, but we can go for a different line of attack. 12. ♘g5! h6 13. ♕h5 g6 14. ♘e4 ♘d5 15. ♕f3±] 10. ♘c3 ♘xc3 11. ♗xc3 d6 12. d5! This leads to the following forcing line: [12. h5 also looks very strong.] 12... dxe5 13. ♘xe5 ♕xd5 14. ♕e2! 0-0 15. h5 ♖d8 16. ♖h3 ♘c6 17. ♘xc6 ♕xc6 18. ♖g3 f6 19. ♕g4 ♗f8 20. ♗xf6 ♖d7 21. ♖d1± Black will struggle to survive here.

**8. ♘c3**

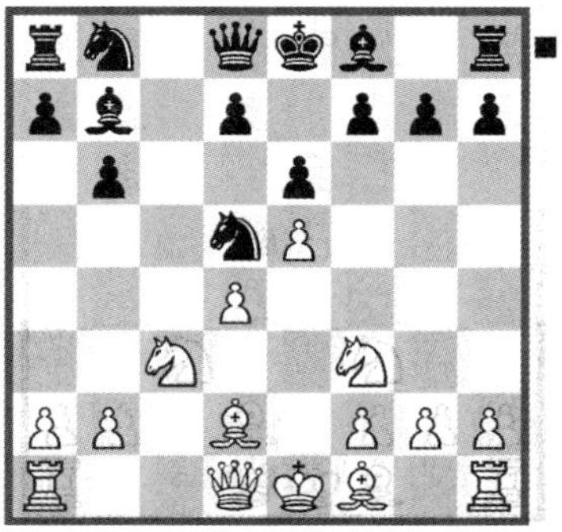

Position after: 8. ♘c3

**8... ♘xc3**

8... ♗e7 Here we'll examine why it's dangerous for Black to delay capturing on c3. 9. ♗d3

**A)** 9... 0-0 10. ♖c1!

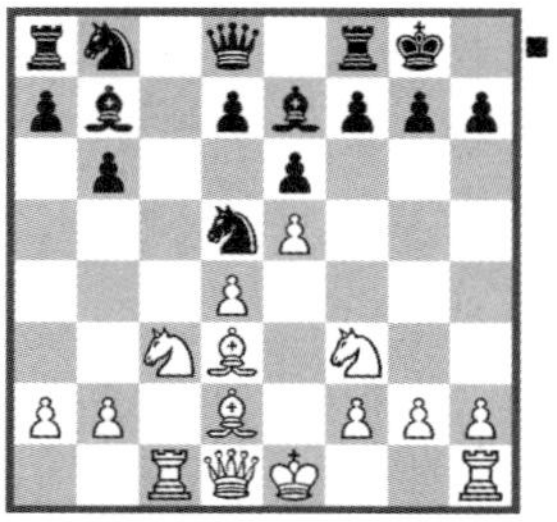

Position after: 10. ♖c1!

Threatening ♗b1 and ♕c2, which is surprisingly difficult to prevent. If we induce ...g7-g6, then h4-h5 will be extremely worrisome for Black.

**A1)** 10... ♘xc3 11. ♖xc3 ♘c6 12. h4 h6 13. ♕e2± Black is forced to play ...f7-f5 to prevent ♕e4 – which is simply a worse version of 10...f5.

**A2)** 10... d6 11. ♘xd5 ♗xd5 12. h4 h6 [12... dxe5 13. ♗xh7+! ♔xh7 14. ♘g5+ ♔g8 15. ♕h5 ♗e4 16. ♘xe4 ♘d7 17. dxe5±] 13. ♖h3+– Followed by either ♖g3, or ♗b1 and ♕d3. It's simply too much for Black to deal with.

**B)** 9... d6 10. ♗b5+! ♘d7 11. exd6 ♗xd6 12. ♘e4 ♗c7 13. ♘e5± Black is forced to give up their dark-squared bishop, after which we have a sizeable advantage.

**9. ♗xc3**

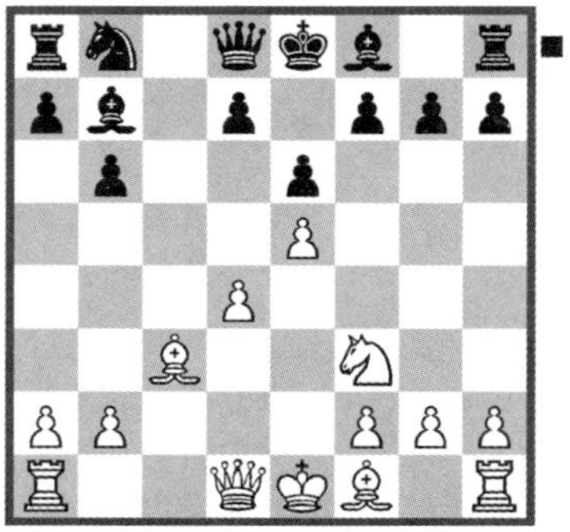

Position after: 9. ♗xc3

**9... ♗e7**

**A)** 9... d6?! 10. ♗c4! We want to push d4-d5. 10... ♕c7 [10... ♘d7 11. d5±] 11. ♕e2 ♗e7 12. d5! ♗xd5 13. ♗xd5 exd5 14. 0-0 0-0 15. e6!± White has a comfortable advantage – Black can't prevent us from recapturing the d5-pawn.

**B)** 9... ♘a6 10. a3 ♘c7 11. ♗d3 f5!? An engine idea – Stockfish doesn't want to play a passive game, and immediately seeks counterplay. [11... ♗e7 would transpose to 9...♗e7 10... ♘a6.] 12. exf6

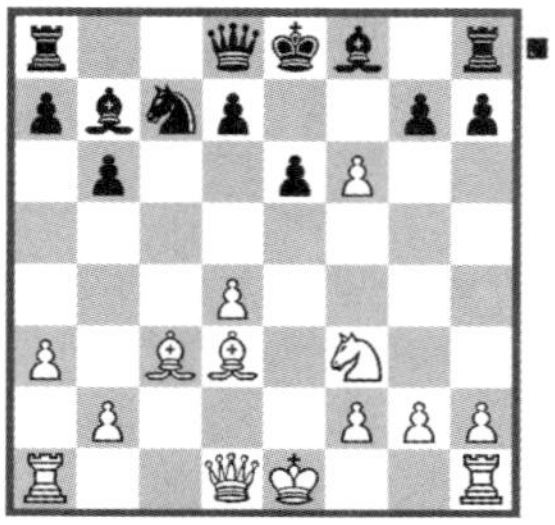

Position after: 12. exf6

12... gxf6 [12... ♕xf6 13. d5 ♕h6 14. dxe6 ♕xe6+ 15. ♕e2±] 13. 0-0 ♕e7 Black's plan is simple – castle queenside and load up on the g-file with ...♕g7 and ...♖g8. In response, it makes sense to trade off the light-squared bishops. 14. ♖e1 ♕g7 15. ♗e4 ♗xe4 16. ♖xe4↑ Stockfish still claims that Black is doing okay but in practical terms I disagree. Black's king will never be safe, and there doesn't seem to be much of a threat to our own king. We can continue with ♕a4 and ♖ae1. It feels like Black's play is much too artificial.

**10. ♗d3**

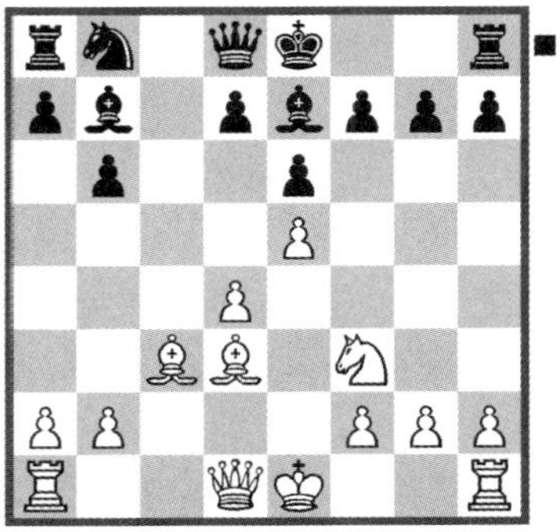

Position after: 10. ♗d3

**10... d6**

**A)** 10... 0-0?! 11. h4! f5 [11... h6 12. ♗c2 ♗a6 13. ♗b1!+–] 12. exf6 ♖xf6 [12... ♗xf6 13. ♗xh7++–] 13. d5± Black is forced to sacrifice an exchange, while their king remains weak.

**B)** 10... ♘a6 As with 9... ♘a6, Black threatens to annoy us with ...♘b4. 11. a3 ♘c7 12. h4! Once again the h-pawn advance works well. 12... d6 13. ♖h3! dxe5 14. ♘xe5 0-0 15. ♕c2 h6 16. ♕e2!→ Followed by ♕h5 and ♖g3. In practical terms, Black will have to do well to survive our attack.

**11. ♕e2 ♘d7**

11... 0-0 12. h4 h6 13. ♖h3 A common theme whenever Black castles – our attack is very strong. 13... ♘d7 14. ♗c2!→ White was clearly on top but unfortunately blew the game in S.Lee – C. O'Donnell, Budapest 2021.

**12. h4!**

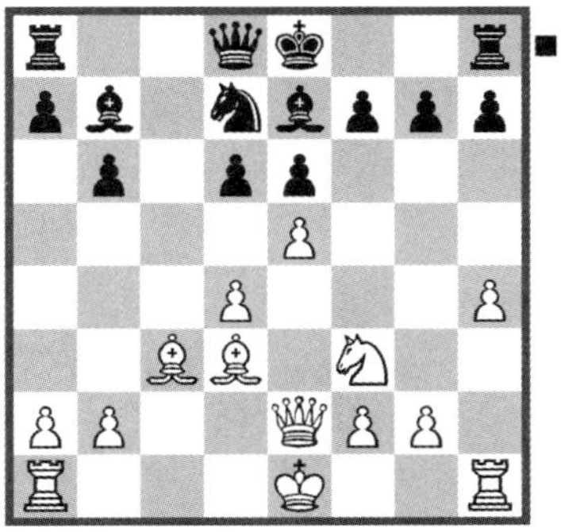

Position after: 12. h4!

**12... ♕c7!**

If we continue with ♖h3 then Black will simply queenside castle.

12... dxe5 13. dxe5 ♕c7 14. 0-0 is similar to the mainline.

**13. 0-0**

This is the simplest option – the h-pawn

is still a useful asset even if we don't have the option of ♖h3.

**13... dxe5**

13... ♖c8 14. ♗b5! 0-0 15. ♗b4! ♘b8 16. ♖ac1 ♕d8 17. ♖xc8 ♗xc8 18. ♗d3±

**14. dxe5 0-0**

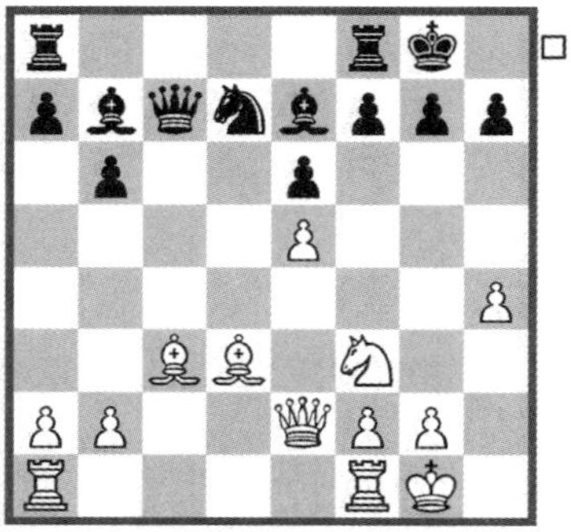

Position after: 14... 0-0

Obviously it's much safer for Black to castle now compared to when we had the ♖h3-g3 idea. Nevertheless, I still think we have good attacking chances.

**15. ♖fe1**

A useful move to safeguard the e5-pawn.

**15... ♘c5 16. ♗c2 ♕c6 17. ♕c4!→**

Now that our f3-knight can't move, we need to find another way to re-route the queen to the kingside. I don't think there's any point in analysing this further – it just seems like White has a very promising attack.

## e) 3...♘f6 4.e5 ♘d5 5.d4 cxd4 6.cxd4 d6 7.♗c4 ♗e7 8.0-0 0-0 9.♕e2 --

**1. e4 c5 2. ♘f3 e6 3. c3 ♘f6 4. e5 ♘d5 5. d4 cxd4 6. cxd4**

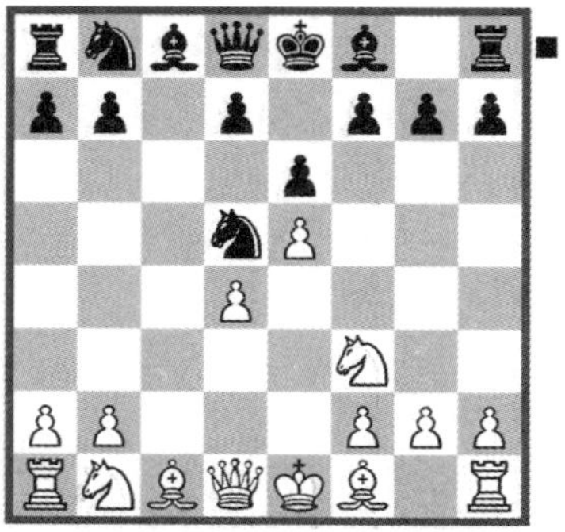

Position after: 6. cxd4

**6... d6**

6... ♘c6 This will likely transpose to the mainline as Black will push ...d7-d6 at some point. 7. ♗c4 ♗e7 8. 0-0 0-0?! [8... d6 transposes to 6...d6.] 9. ♘c3! ♘xc3 10. bxc3 d6 11. ♕c2!± Followed by ♗d3. This is an even better version of the positions we'll encounter after 6...d6.

**7. ♗c4 ♗e7**

7... ♘b6 has been played quite a few times but isn't a particularly great move. 8. ♗d3! An important guideline to remember is that ♗d3 is the correct response to ... ♘b6 in most positions. 8... ♘c6 9. 0-0

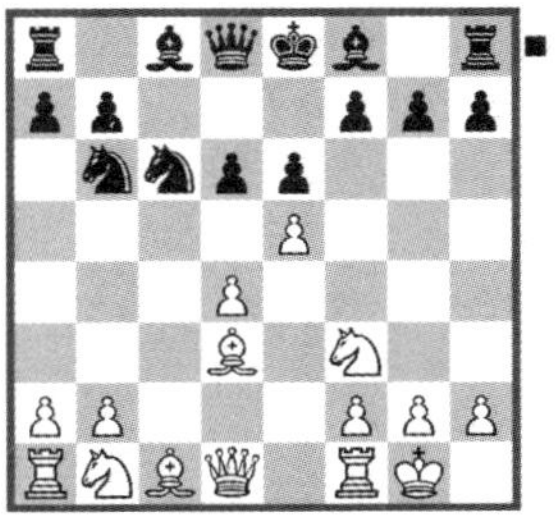

Position after: 9. 0-0

**A)** 9... dxe5 10. dxe5 ♘b4 11. ♗e4 ♕xd1 12. ♖xd1

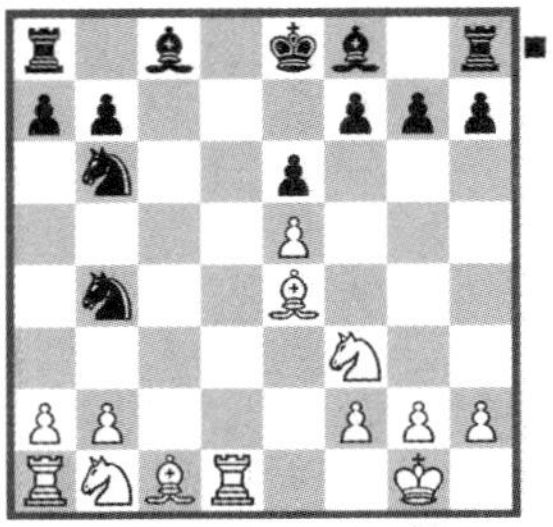

Position after: 12. ♖xd1

**A1)** 12... ♗d7 This position was reached in Caruana – Andreikin, Chess.com 2022. Here White missed the chance to play 13. ♗xb7!, as after 13... ♘c2 14. ♗xa8 ♘xa8 15. ♗e3! White will win the a1-knight. Surprisingly, the position has been reached around 10 times, but not once has 10.♗e3 been played.

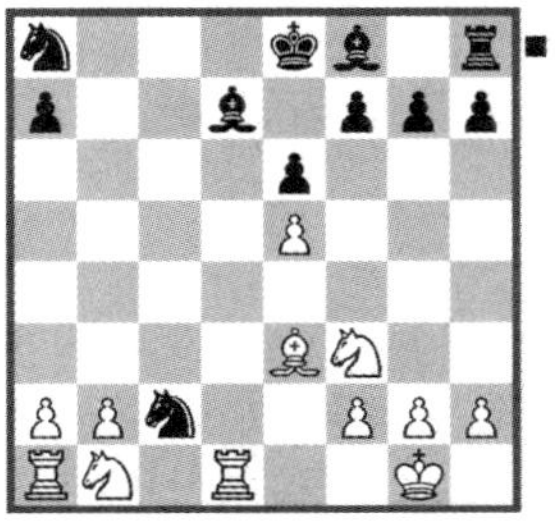

Position after: 15. ♗e3!

15... ♘xa1 16. ♘e1! ♘b6 17. ♘d2 f6 18. ♖xa1! ♔f7 [18... fxe5 19. ♘e4+– This gives White total domination.] 19. ♘e4 ♗e7 20. ♖c1 ♘d5 21. ♗c5±

**A2)** 12... ♘4d5 13. a4!

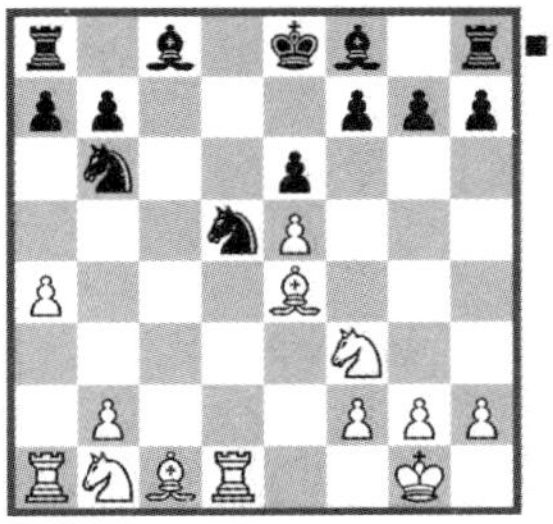

Position after: 13. a4!

Black has the difficult choice between conceding the b5-square with 13...a5, or allowing us to push a4-a5 and kick the b6-knight away. 13... a5 [13... ♗d7 14. ♘c3! ♖c8 15. a5 ♘xc3 16. bxc3 ♘d5 17. ♗xd5 Despite conceding the bishop pair, I'm confident White retains an edge in the following line: 17... exd5 18. ♗e3 ♗c5 19. ♗xc5 ♖xc5 20. ♖db1±] 14. ♘c3 ♗e7 15. ♘xd5 ♘xd5 16. ♗xd5 exd5 17. ♖xd5 ♗e6 18. ♖d1± It's not at all clear that Black has full compensation for the pawn.

**B)** 9... ♗e7 It's a bit dangerous for Black to castle here, as our pieces are all lining up against their king. 10. ♘c3 0-0 11. ♕c2! g6 12. ♕e2±

**C)** 9... ♘b4 10. ♗e4 d5 11. ♗d3

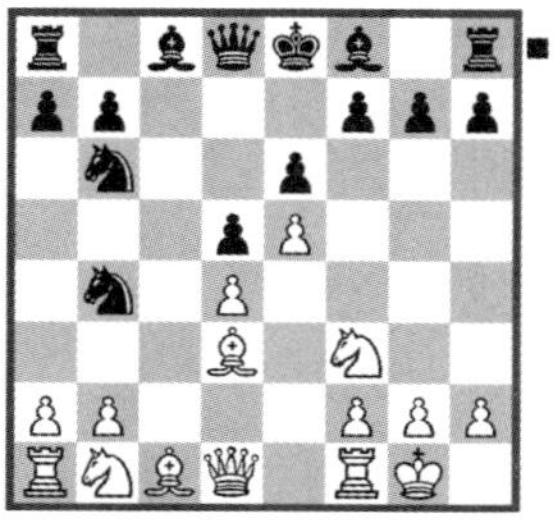

Position after: 11. ♗d3

11... ♘xd3 Black has achieved their task of capturing our light-squared bishop, but in doing so has closed the position with ...d7-d5. This is beneficial for us, as Black's bishop pair will struggle to become effective. [11... ♗d7 12. ♘c3 ♘xd3 13. ♕xd3 transposes to 11...♘xd3.; 11... ♗e7 12. ♘c3 Black has nothing better than to capture on d3, which again transposes back to 11...♘xd3.] 12. ♕xd3

**C1)** 12... ♗e7 13. ♘c3 ♗d7 [13... 0-0 14. h4→] 14. a4 a5 15. b3 This transposes to 12...♗d7.

**C2)** 12... ♗d7 13. b3!? Preventing Black from meeting 13.♘c3 with 13...♘a4. 13... ♖c8 [13... ♗e7 14. a4! a5 15. ♘c3 ♘c8 16. h4!± Black is very passive here.] 14. ♘c3 ♗e7 15. ♗d2 0-0 16. ♘e2 ♘a8 17. h4! ♗xh4 18. g4!+– This is a really cool way to start a kingside attack, and White was already winning in Lintchevski – Rublevsky, Cheliabinsk 2022.

**8. 0-0 0-0 9. ♕e2**

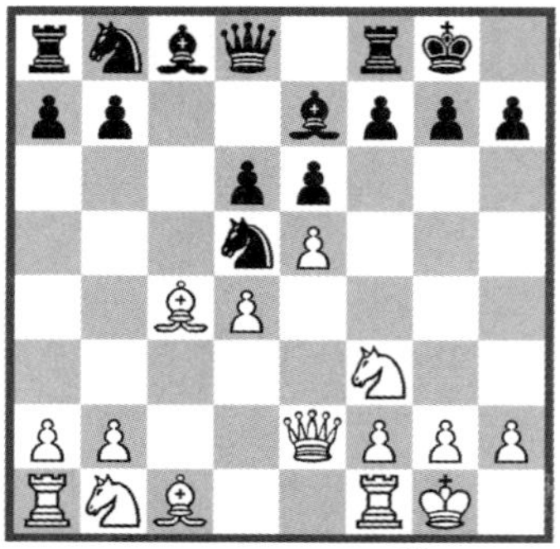

Position after: 9. ♕e2

**9... b6**

This has been played in quite a few high-level games, but it's fairly easy for White to get a pleasant position.

**A)** 9... dxe5?! The open d-file suits White more than Black. 10. dxe5 ♘c6 11. ♖d1±

**B)** 9... a6 This move is quite rare, although it's one of Stockfish's top choices and has been played recently in a couple of high-level games. The point is obvious – Black wants to gain space on the queenside with ...b7-b5 (and gain a favourable version of 9...b6). 10. ♘c3 I don't see any reason to play differently from the mainline after 9...♘c6, as essentially Black has wasted a bit of time with ...a7-a6. 10... ♘xc3 [10... dxe5 11. ♘xe5! ♘c6 12. ♘xc6 bxc6 13. ♖d1 a5 14. ♘a4± Marbourg – Sanchez Carol, ICCF email 2017.] 11. bxc3 b5 12. ♗d3 It feels like Black needs to be slightly careful about their king here. 12... ♗b7

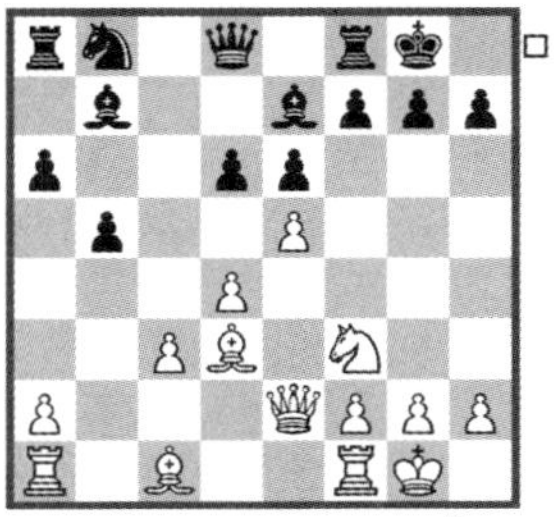

Position after: 12... ♗b7

13. exd6

**B1)** 13... ♗xd6?! 14. ♘g5! g6 [14... h6 15. ♘xe6 ♕h4 16. ♗f4!±] 15. a4!± With good play on both sides of the board. One idea here is to transfer our queen to the h-file via g4.

**B2)** 13... ♕xd6 14. a4 There are also less concrete options such as 14.♖e1 and 14.♖b1. The text move is quite testing, as Black has to find a series of only moves. 14... b4! Or else Black would be much worse. 15. cxb4 ♘c6 16. ♗e4 [16. ♕e4!? f5! 17. ♕e2 ♘xb4 18. ♗c4 ♗e4!∞] 16... ♖fb8! 17. ♗d2 ♘xd4 18. ♘xd4 ♕xd4 19. ♗xb7 ♖xb7 20. ♖fd1± We still have a slight edge due to the outside passed pawn. If this isn't to your taste, the alternatives on move 14 might be more preferable.

**10. ♖d1!**

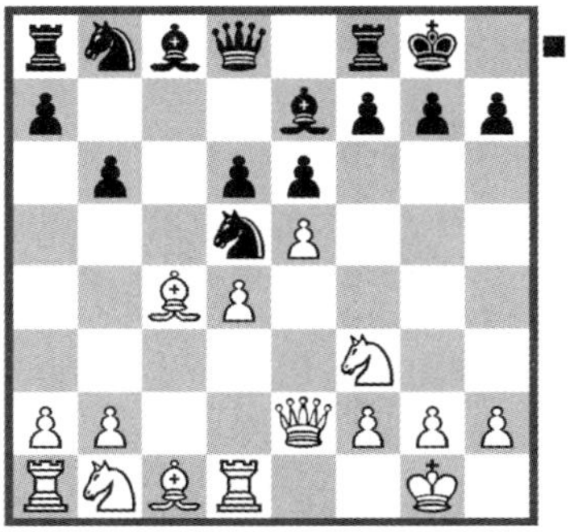

Position after: 10. ♖d1!

10.♘c3 wouldn't make any sense as Black's knight can develop to d7 instead of c6.

**10... ♗b7**

10... ♘c6!? Trying to tempt us into 11.♘c3, after which Black gets an improved version of the mainline. 11. a3! However we need to stay consistent with our new plan – finding the right time to capture on d5. 11.a3 enables us to meet ...♘a5 with ♗a2. 11... ♗b7 [11... ♘a5 12. ♗a2±; 11... dxe5 12. dxe5 ♗b7 13. ♗xd5 exd5 14. ♘c3 transposes to 11...♗b7.] 12. ♗xd5! exd5 13. ♘c3 dxe5 14. dxe5 d4 15. ♗e3

*(see analysis diagram next page)*

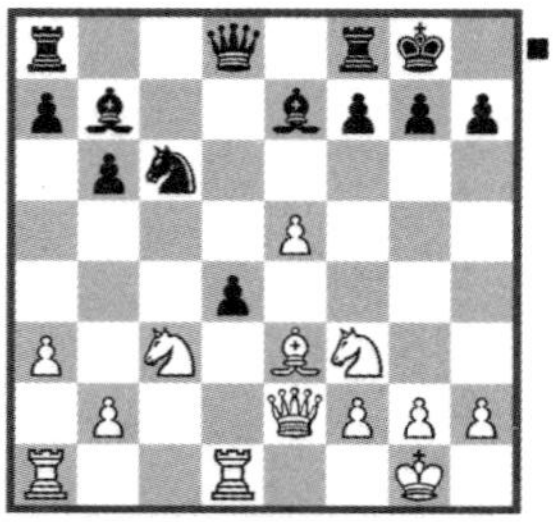

Position after: 15. ♗e3

15... ♕c8 [15... ♗c5 16. b4 This leads to a forcing line: 16... ♕e8! 17. ♘xd4 ♘xd4 18. ♗xd4 ♕c6 19. ♘e4 ♕xe4 20. ♕xe4 ♗xe4 21. bxc5 bxc5 22. ♗xc5± The game is still very far from a draw.] 16. ♗xd4 ♕e6 17. ♘b5 ♘xd4 18. ♖xd4± Black has some compensation in the form of the bishop pair, but it's certainly not enough.

**11. ♗xd5!**

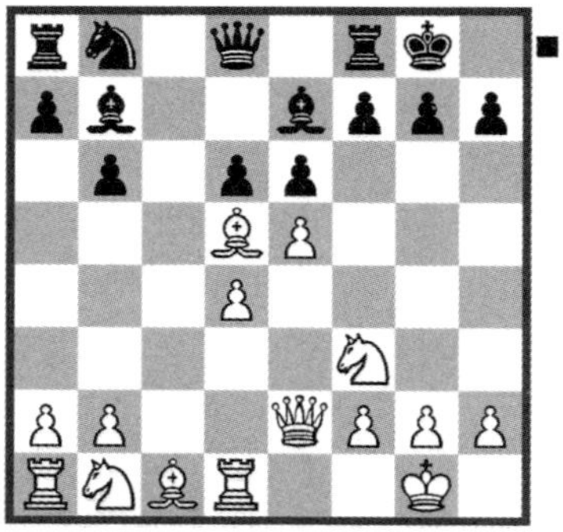

Position after: 11. ♗xd5!

**11... exd5**

11... ♗xd5 12. ♘c3

**A)** 12... ♗xf3?! 13. ♕xf3 d5 On first glance the trade of light-squared bishops looks beneficial for Black. But they're simply too underdeveloped, and we can immediately go for a kingside attack. 14. ♕g4!

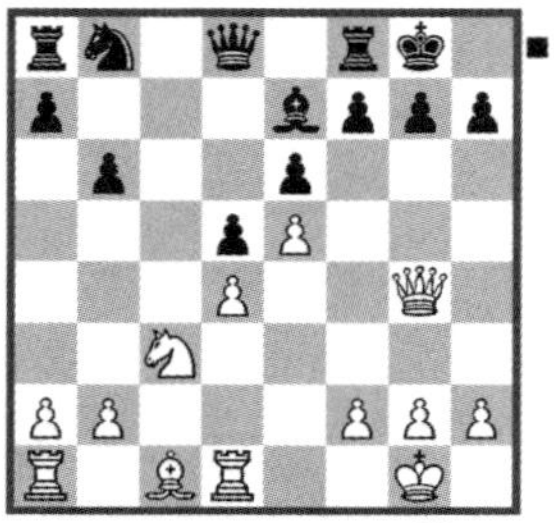

Position after: 14. ♕g4!

14... f5 [14... ♔h8 15. ♗f4→ Followed by ♖d3.] 15. ♕f3!± Now we can continue with ♘e2, g2-g3 and h2-h4. The e6-pawn is a permanent weakness, meaning we have a large long-term positional advantage.

**B)** 12... ♗b7 13. d5! Despite the position liquidating, we'll definitely end up with at least a small advantage. 13... exd5 14. ♘xd5 ♘d7 15. e6 ♘c5 16. exf7+ ♖xf7 17. ♘xe7+ [17. b4 is also probably quite good: 17... ♘a4 18. ♕c2 ♗f6 19. ♘xf6+ ♕xf6 20. ♘g5 ♕f5 21. ♕xf5 ♖xf5 22. ♖xd6±] 17... ♕xe7 18. ♕xe7 ♖xe7 19. ♘d4±

**C)** 12... ♘c6 13. ♘xd5 exd5 14. e6±

**D)** 12... ♕d7 13. ♘g5! Threatening ♘xd5 and e5-e6. 13... ♕b7 [13... ♘c6 14. ♘xd5 exd5 15. e6 fxe6 16. ♕xe6+ ♕xe6 17. ♘xe6 ♖fc8 18. ♘f4 ♗f6 19. ♗e3 ♘e7 20. ♖ac1±] 14. ♕d3! ♗xg5 15. ♗xg5

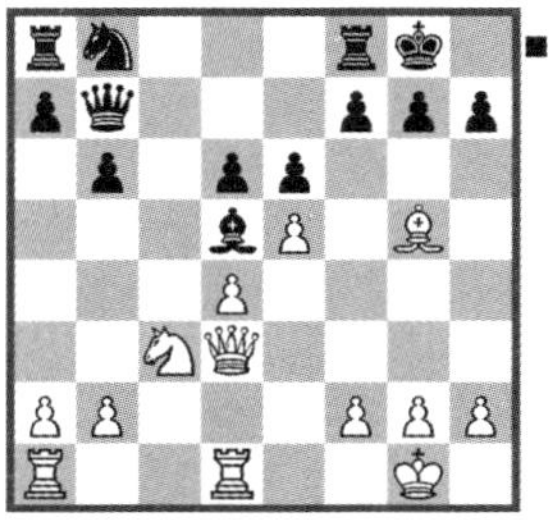

Position after: 15. ♗xg5

15... dxe5 [15... ♗xg2? 16. ♕g3 ♗e4 17. d5! ♗g6 18. exd6+–; 15... h6 16. ♗h4 ♗xg2 17. ♕g3 ♗e4 18. d5±] 16. dxe5 ♗xg2 This is obviously the critical test. Otherwise we will just continue ♕g3 with a strong position. 17. ♕g3 ♗e4 18. ♘b5! ♗g6 19. ♘d6 ♕d7 20. ♖ac1± Total domination. It's probably worthwhile analysing this a bit further, but I can safely stop here and say that this is a dream position for White.

**12. ♘c3**

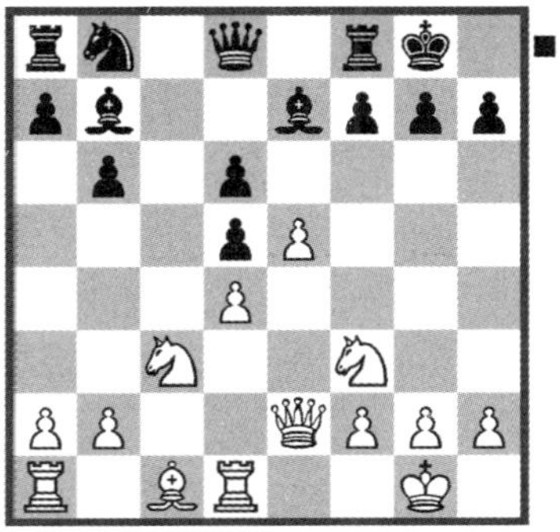

Position after: 12. ♘c3

**12... ♘a6**

12... ♘d7 13. e6 fxe6 14. ♕xe6+ ♖f7 15. ♖e1!±

**13. ♗e3!?**

Surprisingly this move is a novelty. I don't think there is a huge difference between ♗e3 compared with the more popular 13.♘b5 and 13.♗f4. However, the point of the text move is simple: if Black ever captures on e5, we will capture back with the d-pawn, ensuring that we have maximum control over the d4-square. If Black delays capturing on e5 they'll most likely start to feel more and more suffocated. The computer evaluation for all three moves is between 0.2 and 0.3. This is understandable – Black is solid, with no obvious weaknesses, but White has a space advantage and better development. In general this position simply seems very pleasant for us, and I will just present a few sample variations too avoid over-complicating a simple position.

**13... ♘c7 14. ♕d3!**

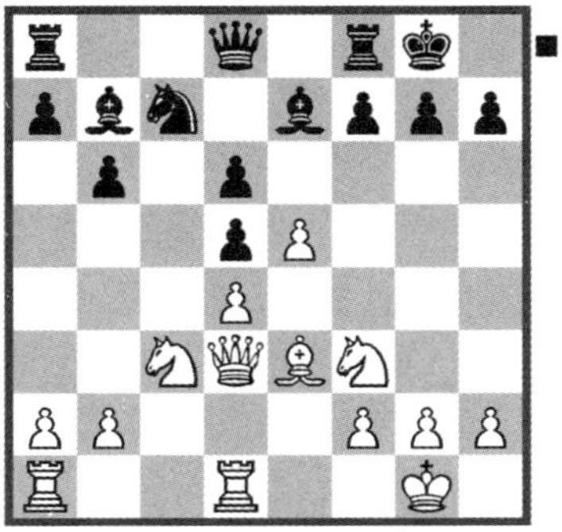

Position after: 14. ♕d3!

Setting up ideas of ♕f5 and ♘g5.

**14... ♖c8**

14... ♘e6 15. ♕b5!? Re-routing the queen to b3. 15... ♘c7 16. ♕b3 ♕d7 17. a4±

**15. h3**

15. ♖e1 followed by ♖ad1 also looks good and sensible.

**15... ♖e8**

**A)** 15... ♕d7 16. ♗g5!±

**B)** 15... ♘e6 16. ♘b5! a6 17. ♘xd6 ♗xd6 18. exd6 ♕xd6 19. ♖e1± White has the better minor pieces. One idea here is ♗d2 and ♘h4-f5.

**16. ♕f5!? ♘e6 17. a3!±**

Preventing the sequence ...dxe5 dxe5 ♗b4. Black will probably be tempted to push ...g6, which isn't objectively bad but might later prove to be slightly weakening. I think White has a small edge here.

## f) 3...♘f6 4.e5 ♘d5 5.d4 cxd4 6.cxd4 d6 7.♗c4 ♗e7 8.0-0 0-0 9.♕e2 ♘c6

**1. e4 c5 2. ♘f3 e6 3. c3 ♘f6 4. e5 ♘d5 5. d4 cxd4 6. cxd4 d6 7. ♗c4 ♗e7 8. 0-0 0-0 9. ♕e2**

Position after: 9. ♕e2

**9... ♘c6**

9... ♗d7 also gives White a good version of 'hanging pawns' after 10. ♘c3 ♘xc3 11. bxc3 ♗c6 12. exd6 ♗xd6 13. ♘e5±.

**10. ♘c3!**

White accepts a worsened pawn structure in order to gain strong attacking chances.

**10... ♘xc3**

**A)** 10... dxe5 11. dxe5 ♘xc3 12. bxc3 transposes to 10...♘xc3.

**B)** 10... ♘b6? 11. ♗d3 dxe5 12. dxe5±

**11. bxc3**

*(see diagram next page)*

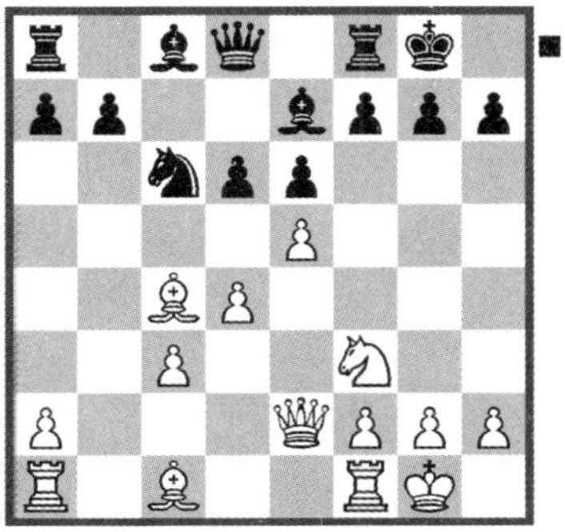

Position after: 11. bxc3

**11... dxe5**

11... ♕c7 12. exd6! ♗xd6 13. ♗d3± This is a good version of the typical 'hanging pawns' structure. At some point we'll go ♕e4, forcing Black to make a concession on the kingside. Alongside this, we can simply finish development with ♖e1 and ♗d2, whilst also considering the pawn pushes h2-h4 and c3-c4. Black's position seems a bit passive.

**12. dxe5 b6**

**A)** 12... ♕a5 This is the most common move for Black but it seems too greedy to think they can get away with capturing on c3. 13. ♗d3! No need to defend the pawn – instead we reposition our pieces to threaten Black's king.

**A1)** 13... ♕xc3 14. ♗d2 ♕a3 15. ♖fc1! ♖d8 16. ♖c3 ♕b2 17. ♕d1!± Threatening ♖b3. Black will either have to give up material or waste time retreating the queen to c7, which would allow us to simply get on with advancing the h-pawn down the board.

**A2)** 13... ♖d8 14. ♖b1!

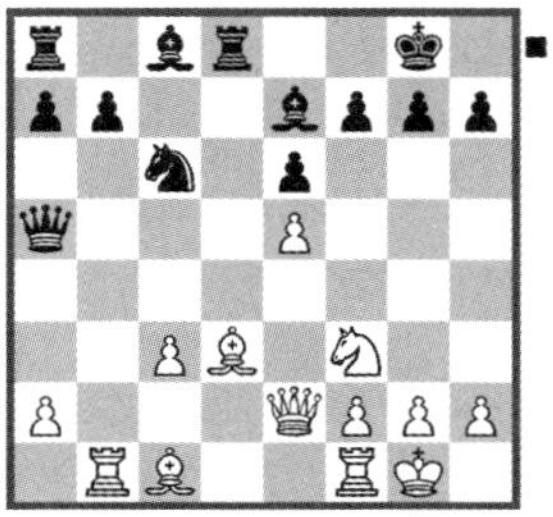

Position after: 14. ♖b1!

Planning to meet ...♕xc3 with ♖b3. 14... g6 In Matlakov – Mchedlishvili, Tornelo INT 2021, White should have kept the initiative going with the following line: [14... b6 15. ♘g5! ♗xg5 16. ♗xg5± Black is forced to capture on d3, after which we're simply an exchange up.] 15. h4! b6 16. ♗b5! ♗b7 17. ♕e4 ♖ac8 18. ♗g5 ♗xg5 19. ♘xg5 a6 20. ♗xc6 ♗xc6 21. ♕f4 ♖f8 22. ♖b4!→

**B)** 12... ♕c7 13. ♖e1 Here Black doesn't have a good move apart from 13...b6, which transposes back to 12...b6. For example after 13... ♖d8, 14.♕e4 is already very strong for us.

**13. ♗d3!**

The bishop isn't doing anything on c4, so it makes sense to reposition it.

*(see diagram next page)*

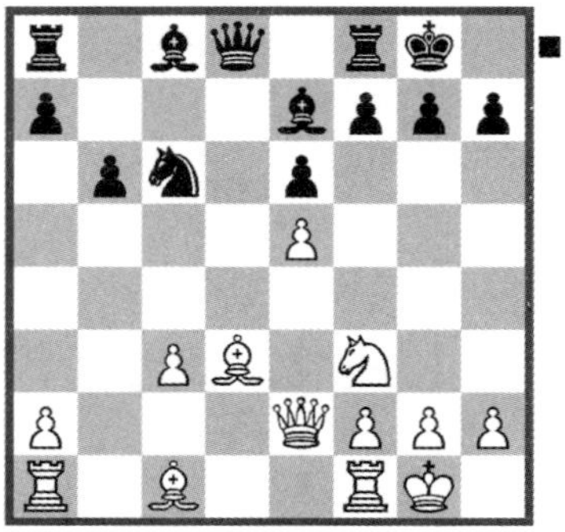

Position after: 13. ♗d3!

**13... ♕c7!**

13... ♗b7?! is too slow – Black's f8-rook needs to get to d8 as soon as possible in order to create counterplay. 14. ♕e4 g6 15. ♗h6

**A)** 15... ♘a5 16. ♕e3 ♗c5? [16... ♖e8 17. ♗b5 ♗c6 18. ♗xc6 ♘xc6 19. h4±] 17. ♕f4 ♗xf3 18. ♕xf3 ♖e8 19. ♗b5+– Narva – Harikrishna, Chess.com 2019.

**B)** 15... ♖e8 16. ♖ad1 ♕c7 17. ♕f4± Followed by h2-h4, ♖fe1, and ♘g5 – Black will be forced to trade off their dark-squared bishop.

**14. ♖e1!**

The e5-pawn is both a strength and a weakness – we need to ensure it is adequately protected before playing ♘g5.

14. ♕e4 g6 15. ♗h6 ♖d8⇆

**14... ♗b7**

14... ♖d8 15. ♗c2! [The immediate 15. ♘g5 would allow 15... ♕xe5!=.] 15... ♗b7 16. ♘g5!

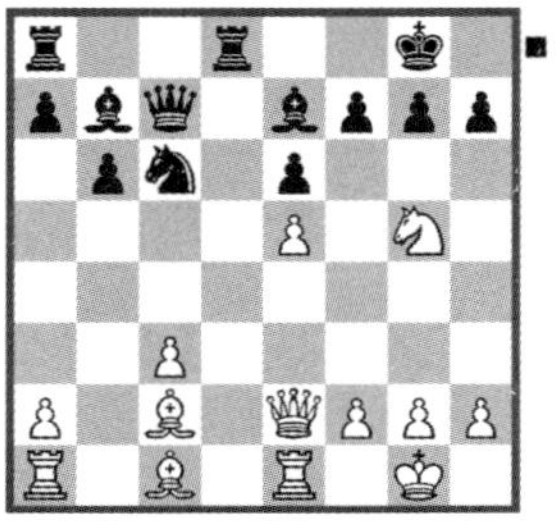

Position after: 16. ♘g5!

16... g6 [16... ♗xg5? 17. ♗xg5 ♘e7 18. ♕h5+– This is just winning for White. An important factor is that ♗xd8 attacks the queen in certain lines.] 17. ♕g4!

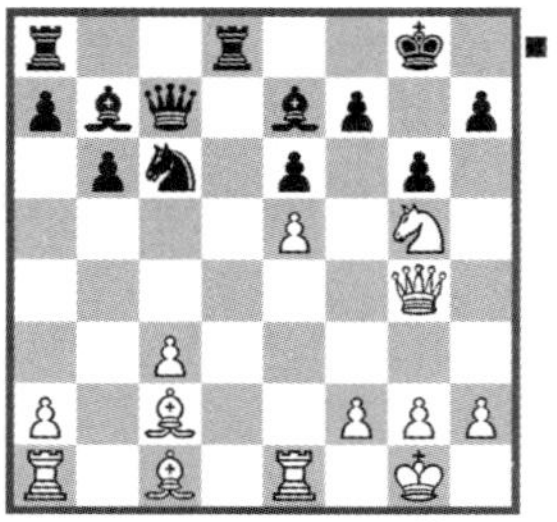

Position after: 17. ♕g4!

**A)** 17... ♘xe5?! 18. ♕h3 ♗xg5 [18... h5 is the obvious defence but here there's a nice line to win the exchange: 19. ♘xe6! ♕d7 20. ♗g5! ♗xg5 21. ♖xe5 ♗f6 22. ♘xd8 ♖xd8 23. ♕xd7 ♖xd7 24. ♖e2±] 19. ♗xg5 ♖d5 20. ♗f4! Threatening ♗e4. 20... ♖c5 21. ♕h4! Black is basically forced to give up the exchange now. 21... ♖f8 22. ♗h6 ♘d7 23. ♗xf8 ♘xf8 24. ♖ad1±

**B)** 17... ♖d5 Once again Black is forced to sacrifice an exchange in order to ward off our attack. This is probably the best version of it they can get. 18. ♗b3

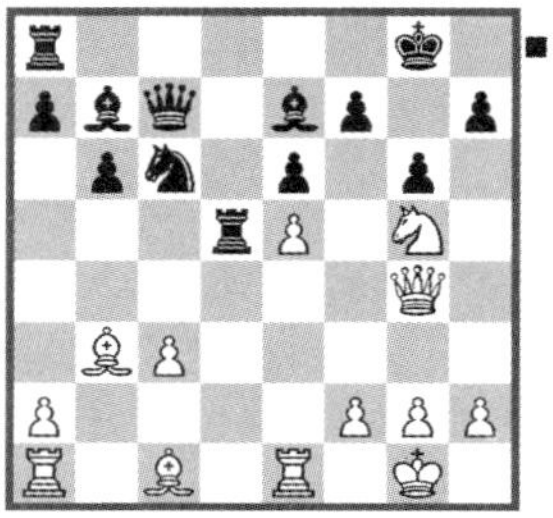

Position after: 18. ♗b3

**B1)** 18... ♖xe5 is slightly inaccurate due to the following line: 19. ♗f4 h5 20. ♗xe5! [20. ♕g3 transposes to 18...h5.] 20... ♕xe5 [20... ♘xe5 21. ♘xe6! ♕c6 22. ♕h3 ♘g4 23. ♕f3! ♗h4 24. ♕xc6 ♗xf2+ 25. ♔h1 ♗xc6 26. ♖e2±] 21. ♖xe5 hxg4 22. ♘xf7! ♘xe5 23. ♘xe5± With good chances in the ending.

**B2)** 18... h5! 19. ♕g3 ♖xe5 20. ♗f4 ♖xg5 [20... ♗xg5?! 21. ♗xe5 ♘xe5 22. ♕xg5±] 21. ♗xc7 ♖xg3 22. hxg3± We are an exchange up but Black is very solid. However we are clearly only playing for two results – and it's absolutely nowhere near a draw yet. We'll most likely follow with something like ♖ad1, ♗d6 and c3-c4. Ideally we want to open another file and trade a pair of bishops. In doing so, there will be more squares to penetrate with our rooks.

**15. ♘g5!**

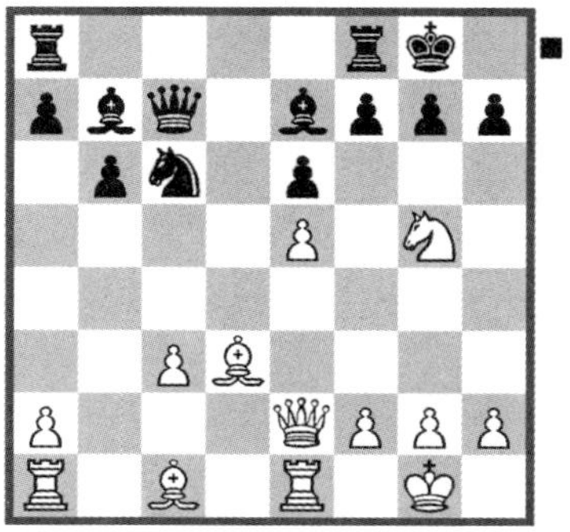

Position after: 15. ♘g5!

**15... ♗xg5**

15... g6 16. ♘xh7! would win a clean pawn – Black is simply lost if they recapture. 16... ♖fd8 17. ♘f6+ ♗xf6 18. exf6±

**16. ♗xg5 ♘e7**

The more practical option – Black brings the knight round to defend the king.

16... ♘xe5 is possible but leads to a worse ending for Black: 17. ♕xe5 ♕xe5 18. ♖xe5 f6 19. ♖xe6 fxg5 20. ♗c4! Re-routing the bishop to b3. 20... ♖ac8! [20... ♔h8 is the only move that has been played here, but after 21. ♖e7! ♗c6 22. f3± White is dominating.] 21. ♗b3 ♗a6 22. ♖xb6+ ♗c4 23. ♖b7 ♖f7 24. ♖xf7 ♔xf7 25. ♖c1± I guess that Black can probably hold this with accurate defence, but the defence doesn't seem obvious at all.

**17. ♕h5 ♘g6**

17... h6? 18. ♗xh6 gxh6 19. ♕xh6 ♘g6 20. ♖e3+–

**18. ♖e3!**

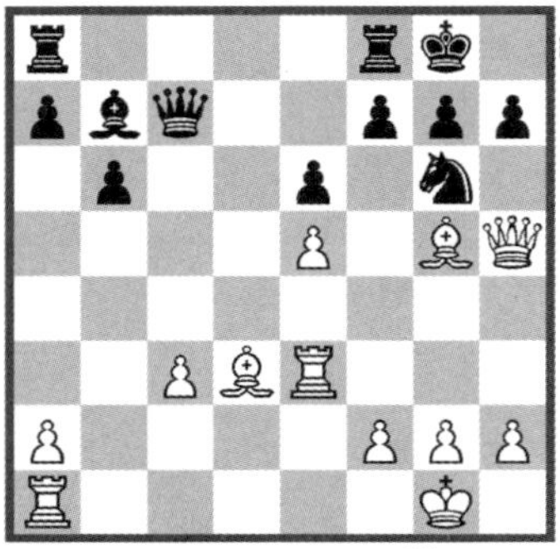

Position after: 18. ♖e3!

Black is forced to sacrifice their queen in order to prevent a crushing attack.

**18... ♕xc3**

18... ♕c6 19. ♗e4 ♕xe4 20. ♖xe4 ♗xe4 21. ♕e2! An important move in this variation – White is simply winning due to the h-pawn push. 21... ♗c6 22. h4 h6 23. h5 hxg5 24. hxg6 fxg6 25. ♖d1+– There will be no fortress for the Black king here.

**19. ♖d1 ♕c6 20. ♗e4 ♕xe4 21. ♖xe4 ♗xe4 22. h4! ♗d5 23. ♖d4!**

Bringing all our resources to the attack.

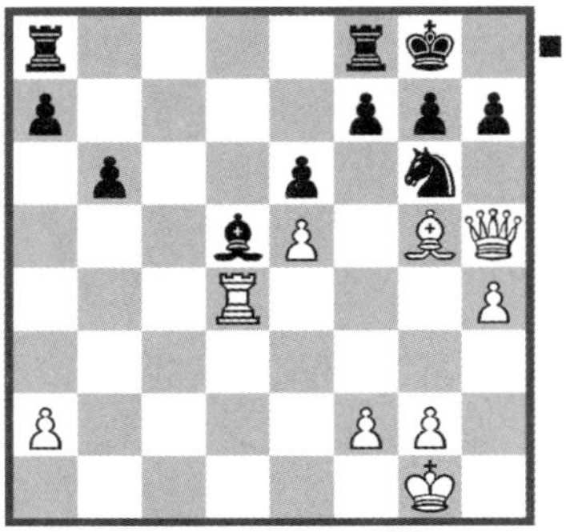

Position after: 23. ♖d4!

**23... ♖ac8**

23... h6? 24. ♗xh6 gxh6 25. ♕xh6+–

**24. ♕e2 h6 25. ♗f6!**

The point of 23.♖d4.

**25... gxf6 26. exf6 ♔h7 27. h5 ♖g8 28. ♕d3 ♔h8 29. hxg6 ♖xg6 30. f3**

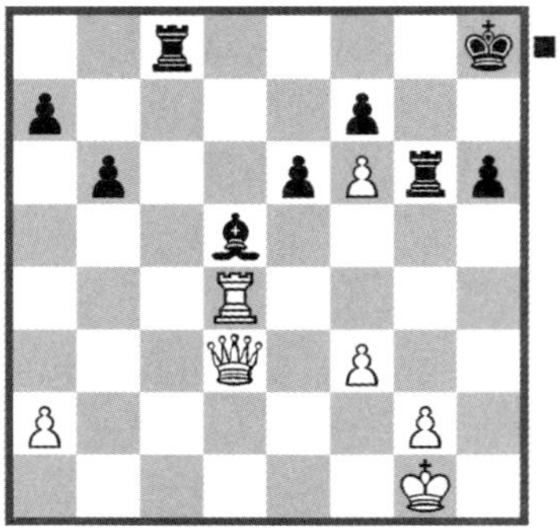

Position after: 30. f3

**30... ♖cg8!**

The only move for Black to maintain relative equality.

30... ♖xf6 31. ♖g4 ♖g8 In Marbourg – Zavrazhnov, ICCF email 2017, the best continuation for White was 32. ♕d4! ♖xg4 33. ♕xf6+ ♖g7 34. ♕xh6+ ♔g8 35. ♕d2± with good winning chances.

**31. g4 ♖c8!=**

Bringing the rook to c5. There is still potential for White to press with moves like ♖f4 and ♕a3-e7, so Black definitely isn't out of the woods yet. But according to the engine, the position is finally a firm 0.00, demonstrating that Black has adequate compensation for the material deficit here.

## *Conclusion to Chapter 8*

The Alapin Sicilian is a great example of how a 'timid' move like 3.c3 can even more dangerous than many Open Sicilians.

I want to highlight two subchapters in particular: subchapter b), where we can capitalize on Black's early ...♕xd5 by rapidly developing and gaining tempi against the queen. It's important to realise that we consistently have the option of castling queenside to increase our initiative.

Subchapter d) is also noteworthy because of the variety of our attacking ideas – exemplified with moves like h2-h4 and ♖h3. Even in the final and arguably most critical subchapter, Black only achieves a draw by navigating down a narrow and extremely dangerous path.

# 2...e6 – King's Indian Attack

1.e4 c5 2.♘f3 e6 3.g3

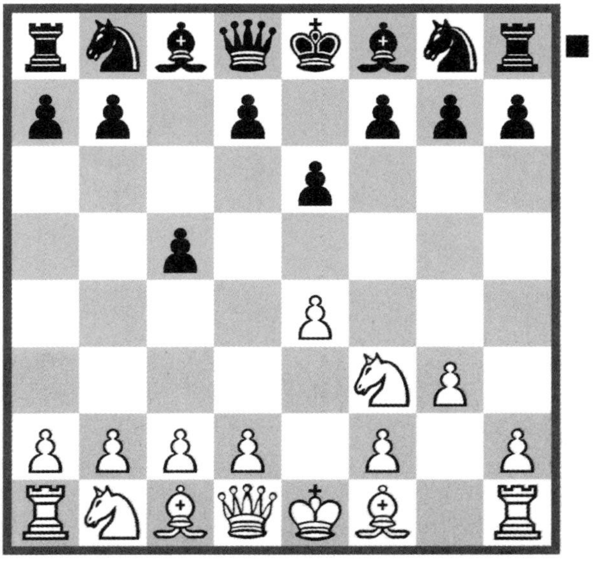

# Chapter Guide

## Chapter 9 – 2...e6 – King's Indian Attack

1.e4 c5 2.♘f3 e3 3.g3

## a) 3...--

**1. e4 c5 2. ♘f3 e6 3. g3**

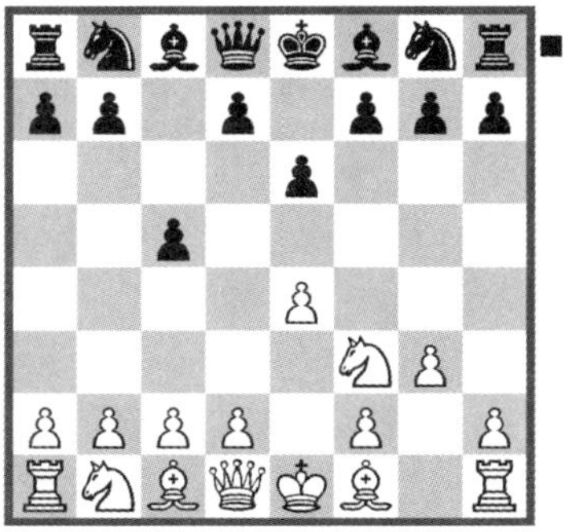

Position after: 3. g3

Now let's have a look at another interesting try which has become quite popular against 2...e6. The basic idea is that our bishop on g2 is supports our c2-c3 and d2-d4 plan, but is also effective in acting against Black's queenside development.

**3... ♘f6**

**A)** 3... a6 The plan of ...a7-a6 and ...b7-b5 is quite dubious here, as Black will always face problems along the h1-a8 diagonal. 4. ♗g2! [4. d4?! cxd4 5. ♘xd4 d5! This looks okay for Black.] 4... b5 5. d4! Now Black doesn't have the ...d7-d5 break, so it's the right time to open the centre.

*(see analysis diagram next column)*

Position after: 5. d4!

**A1)** 5... ♗b7 6. d5!

**A1.1)** 6... ♘f6 7. 0-0! ♘xe4 [7... exd5 8. e5 ♘e4 9. ♘h4!+– White is already crushing here. We'll follow up with a2-a4, and then start hacking away at Black's centre. Our development advantage will prove to be decisive.] 8. ♘h4! ♗xd5 9. ♖e1± Winning a piece, after which Black has very little compensation.

**A1.2)** 6... exd5 7. exd5 d6 Otherwise we will advance d5-d6. 8. 0-0 ♗e7 9. ♖e1 ♘f6 10. ♗g5 Planning to meet 10... 0-0 with 11.♕e2. 10... ♘bd7 11. ♕e2 ♔f8 Black is winning the d5-pawn, but their position is pretty much lost in every other department. 12. c4! bxc4 13. ♘a3±

**A2)** 5... cxd4 6. ♘xd4 ♗b7 7. 0-0

*(see analysis diagram next page)*

Position after: 7. 0-0

The engine already gives an evaluation of around 0.70. The reason is simple: an open position favours the side-with a lead in development. Black's construction of pawns on a6 and b5 is vulnerable and will be hit with an a2-a4 break. Finally, a common theme here is the ♘c3-d5 sacrifice, further opening the position and continuing to cramp Black's pieces. On a side note, the position is a transposition to the dubious sideline: 1.e4 c5 2.♘f3 e6 3.d4 cxd4 4.♘xd4 a6 5.g3 b5?!. I will just give a few sample variations to show how easy the position is to play with White.

**A2.1)** 7... ♕c7 8. ♘c3

**A2.1a)** 8... d6 9. a4 b4 10. ♘d5! exd5 11. exd5 ♗e7 12. ♖e1± White has too many threats for Black to survive. Even if there is nothing concrete, something simple like ♗f4 followed by c2-c3 and ♖c1 will be devastating; the material deficit means nothing when Black's pieces are as bad as they are.

**A2.1b)** 8... ♘c6 9. a4 b4 10. ♘d5! exd5 11. exd5

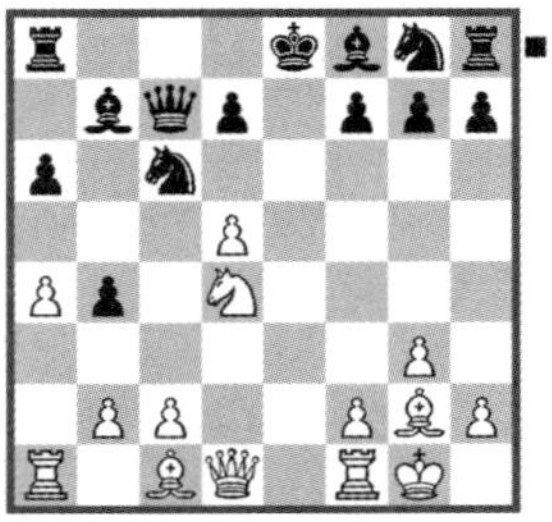

Position after: 11. exd5

11... ♘e5 [11... ♘xd4 12. ♕xd4 d6 13. ♖e1+ ♘e7 14. ♕xb4+–] 12. ♖e1 f6 This leads to the following forcing line, but Black didn't have anything better. 13. f4 ♗c5 14. fxe5 fxe5 15. d6! ♕xd6 16. ♗xb7 ♗xd4+ 17. ♗e3 ♗xe3+ 18. ♖xe3 ♕xd1+ 19. ♖xd1+–

**A2.2)** 7... ♘c6 Here the ♘c3-d5 ideas aren't as effective, so we should simply continue developing. 8. a4 b4 9. ♗e3 We already have a great position – Black has incurred a few weaknesses. 9... ♘f6 10. e5! ♘d5 11. ♗xd5 exd5 12. ♘d2±

**A2.3)** 7... ♘f6 8. ♖e1

Position after: 8. ♖e1

**A2.3a)** 8... ♘c6? 9. e5! ♘d5 10. ♗xd5 exd5 11. ♘f5+–

**A2.3b)** 8... ♕c7? 9. ♘c3 d6 This is a transposition from a few different lines, but the best move has rarely been played here. [9... b4 10. ♘d5! exd5 11. exd5+ ♔d8 12. ♘b3!+– Followed by developing the c1-bishop and opening up the c-file with c2-c3.] 10. ♘d5! exd5 11. exd5+ ♔d8 12. a4 b4 13. c3+– The computer already gives a solid evaluation of +6, so I think it's a good point to stop.

**A2.3c)** 8... ♗c5 9. ♘b3 ♗a7 10. e5! ♘d5 [10... ♗xg2 11. exf6 ♗b7 12. fxg7 ♖g8 13. ♗e3 ♕c7 14. ♗xa7 ♕c6 15. f3 ♖xa7 16. a4!±] 11. ♗xd5!? ♗xd5 12. ♘c3± Followed by ♘e4 and/or ♕g4.

**A2.3d)** 8... d6 9. a4 b4 10. c3!

Position after: 10. c3!

It makes sense to open the position, as Black is still lagging behind in development. For example, the natural looking 10... ♗e7? would be a blunder on account of 11. e5! winning material. 10... d5 The only logical way to defend the b4-pawn without opening the c-file. 11. ♘d2! ♘c6 [11... ♗e7 12. e5 ♘fd7 13. cxb4 ♗xb4 14. ♕g4 ♗f8 15. ♘c4!+–] 12. ♘xe6! fxe6 13. exd5 ♘e7 14. d6+– White regains the piece and is just winning.

**B)** 3... d6 Preparing ...♘f6. 4. ♗g2

Position after: 4. ♗g2

4... ♘f6 [4... ♘c6 5. 0-0 ♘f6 6. ♖e1 ♗e7 7. d4 cxd4 8. ♘xd4± Followed by c2-c4 and ♘c3, this is simply an improved version of the final subchapter.] 5. e5! I think this is the simplest way to play – Black has to be very precise to achieve equality.
5... dxe5 6. ♘xe5

**B1)** 6... ♗d6 7. ♘c4 ♗c7 8. b3 0-0 9. ♗b2 ♘bd7 10. 0-0 ♖b8 11. a4± Frostick – Marwitz, Dresden 2018.

**B2)** 6... ♘bd7 7. ♘c4N ♗e7 8. 0-0 0-0 9. a4 ♘b6 10. d3!±

**B3)** 6... ♕c7! 7. d4!

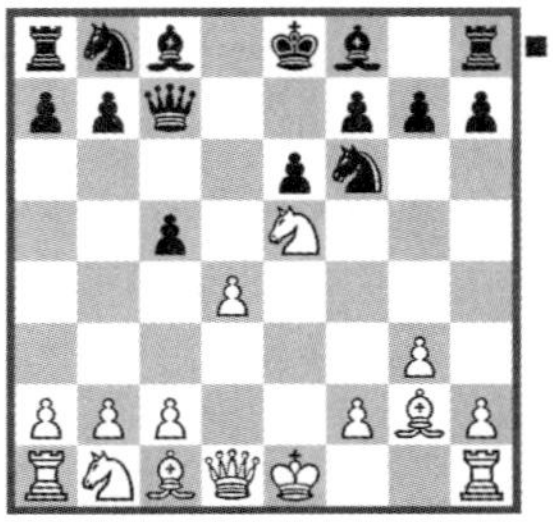

Position after: 7. d4!

**B3.1)** 7... cxd4 is very similar but gives us an extra option on move 9. 8. ♕xd4 ♘bd7 9. ♘d3!? [9. ♘c4 transposes back to 7...♘bd7.] 9... ♕xc2! Black should accept the pawn sacrifice. [9... ♗d6 10. ♕c3!±] 10. 0-0 ♗c5! 11. ♘xc5 ♕xc5 12. ♗e3 ♕xd4 13. ♗xd4 0-0 14. ♘c3⩱∞ I like White's chances here. We're basically just playing for two results and Black's position seems really passive.

**B3.2)** 7... ♘bd7! 8. ♘c4 [8. 0-0!? cxd4 9. ♘f3 e5 10. c3!⩱∞ also looks like a perfectly viable attempt to create problems for Black.] 8... cxd4 [8... ♘b6 9. ♘ba3 ♕d8 10. ♕e2! cxd4 11. 0-0↑ Followed by ♖d1 and ♗f4.] 9. ♕xd4 ♗c5 10. ♗f4! e5! A necessary pawn sacrifice. [10... ♗xd4 11. ♗xc7 ♘d5 12. ♗xd5 exd5 13. ♘d6+ ♔f8 14. c3±] 11. ♗xe5 ♘xe5 12. ♕xe5+ ♕xe5+ 13. ♘xe5 The engine suggests an evaluation between 0.10 and 0.20, but Black still needs to prove compensation for the pawn. For example:

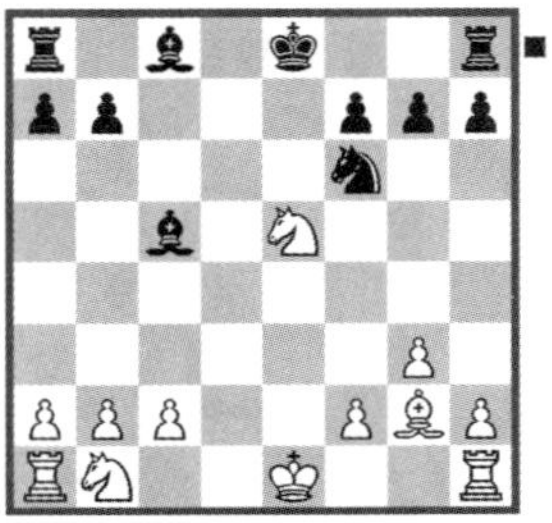

Position after: 13. ♘xe5

13... ♗d4 [13... ♗f5?! 14. ♘d2! 0-0-0 15. 0-0-0±] 14. ♘d3 0-0 15. 0-0 ♗f5 16. ♘d2 Followed by ♘c4 or ♘b3, and the game is still far away from a draw.

**C)** 3... g6 This is strange, considering Black just pushed ...e7-e6 on the previous move. 4. d4!

Position after: 4. d4!

A good moment to transition into an Open Sicilian type of position. 4... cxd4 5. ♘xd4 ♗g7 6. ♗g2 ♘e7 7. 0-0 ♘bc6 8. ♗e3 0-0 9. ♘c3 [9. c4?! d5=] 9... a6 [9... d5 10. exd5 ♘xd5 11. ♘xd5 exd5 12. ♖e1±] 10. ♘xc6! ♘xc6 11. f4± With a big advantage.

**4. e5**

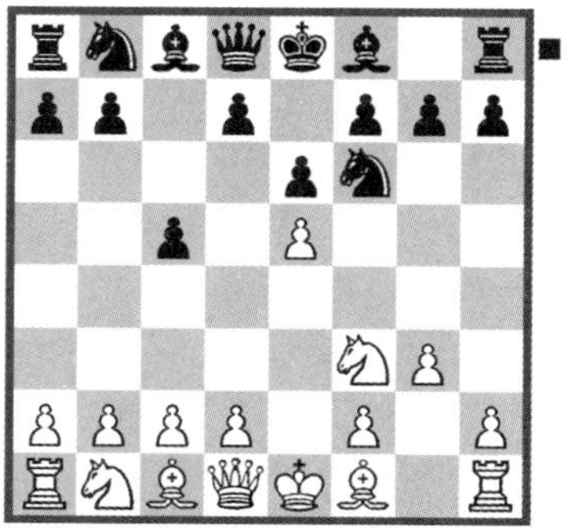
Position after: 4. e5

**4... ♘d5**

4... ♘g4!? 5. c3!N The point is to ensure that the e5-pawn is well protected, after which Black's knight on g4 looks out of place. 5... ♘c6 6. d4 cxd4 7. cxd4 d6 8. ♗h3!

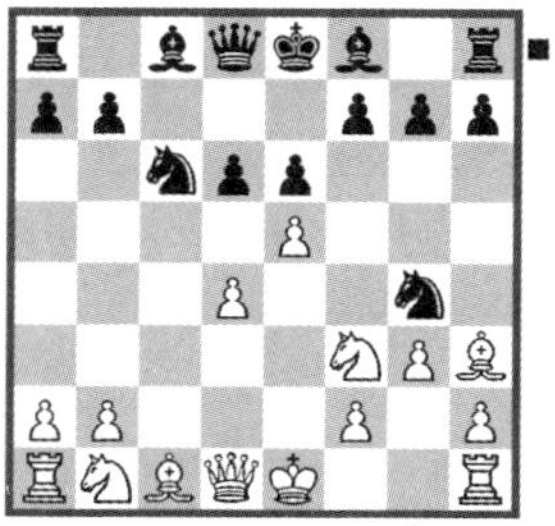
Position after: 8. ♗h3!

**A)** 8... ♘h6 is suboptimal, as the knight isn't really able to jump to the f5-square here. 9. exd6 ♗xd6 [9... ♕xd6 10. ♘c3± ♘f5? 11. ♗xf5 exf5 12. 0-0 Followed by d4-d5, and Black's position is collapsing.] 10. ♗xh6! gxh6 11. ♘c3±

**B)** 8... h5 9. exd6 ♗xd6 10. 0-0± Now that Black has played ...h7-h5, it makes castling safely a little more difficult. It's safe to say that White has a small advantage here.

**5. ♗g2**

Whenever Black plays ...d7-d6, it suits us to open the position with d2-d4.

**5... ♘c6**

5... d6 6. 0-0 dxe5 7. ♘xe5 ♗d6 8. d4!

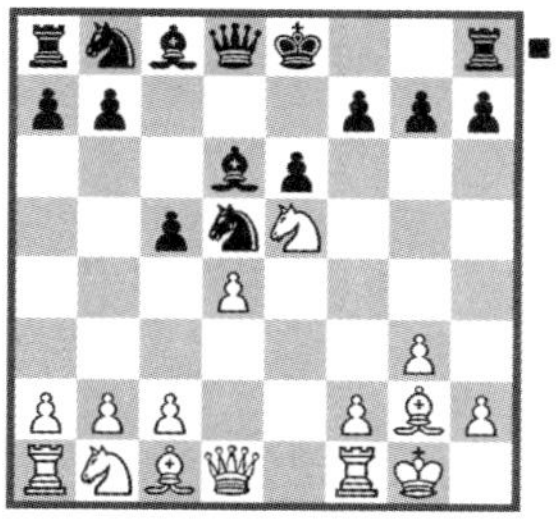
Position after: 8. d4!

8... 0-0 [8... cxd4 9. ♕xd4 0-0 10. c4 ♘b4 11. ♖d1!±] 9. b3!? Not the only option, but I like the idea of maintaining tension in the centre and simply continuing to develop our pieces. A sample line could follow: 9... cxd4 10. ♕xd4 ♕c7 11. ♗b2 f6 12. ♘d3± Followed by either ♘a3 or ♕e4.

**6. 0-0**

*(see diagram next page)*

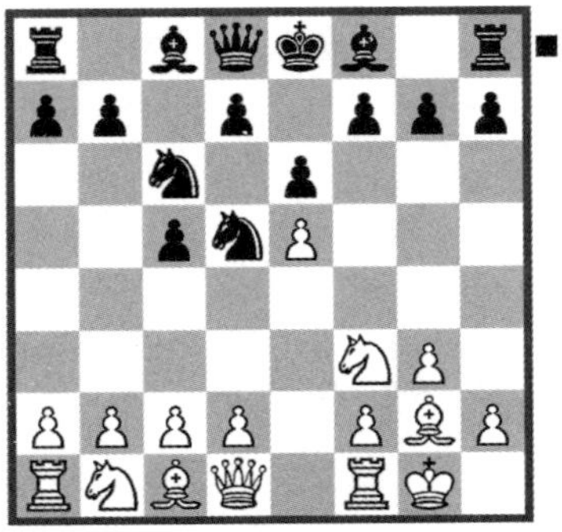

Position after: 6. 0-0

**6... ♗e7**

6... d6 7. d4!

**A)** 7... dxe5 8. ♘xe5! ♘xd4 [8... cxd4 9. ♘xc6 bxc6 10. ♕xd4±] 9. c3 ♘c6 10. ♘xc6 bxc6 11. c4 ♘e7 12. ♘c3+– Black is a pawn up but positionally lost.

**B)** 7... cxd4 8. exd6 ♗xd6 9. ♘xd4± Once again, opening the centre has benefited us. We are ahead in development, and will continue with c2-c4 and ♘c3.

**7. c4!**

There's no reason to continue delaying opening the position.

**7... ♘b6**

7... ♘db4 8. d4 ♘xd4 9. ♘xd4 cxd4 10. ♕g4! Forcing a concession.

*(see analysis diagram next column)*

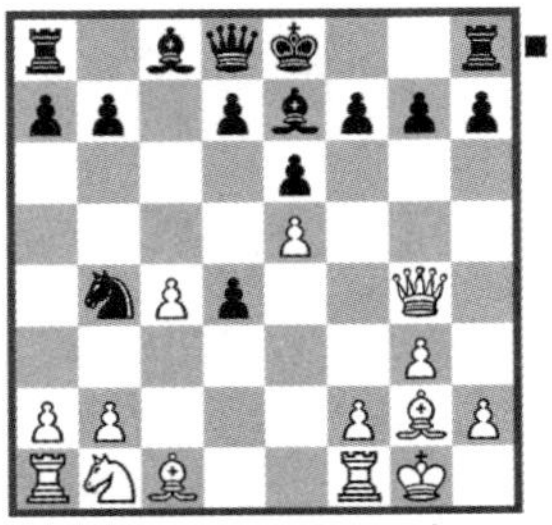

Position after: 10. ♕g4!

10... ♔f8 [10... ♗f8 11. ♘a3±; 10... g6 11. ♘a3±] 11. ♘a3 ♘c6 12. ♘b5 d6 13. exd6 ♗xd6 14. ♘xd6 ♕xd6 15. ♕h5! The bishop pair is hugely beneficial here, as illustrated by 15... e5 16. b4!±.

**8. b3**

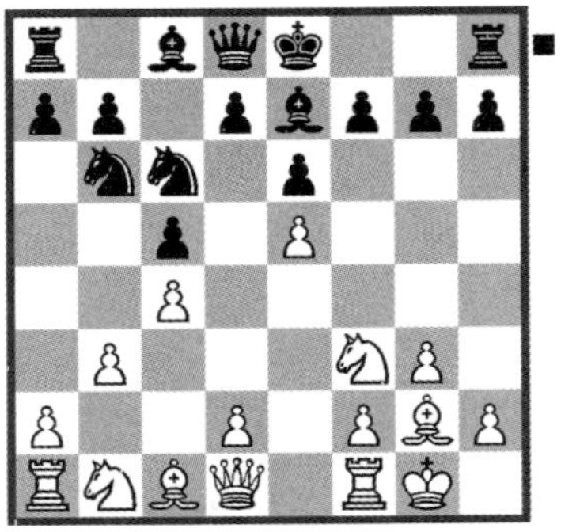

Position after: 8. b3

**8... 0-0**

8... d5 9. exd6

**A)** 9... ♗xd6 10. d4 0-0 11. ♘c3!± [11. ♗b2? cxd4 12. ♘xd4 ♗e5! is an important equaliser which we shouldn't allow.]

**B)** 9... ♕xd6 10. ♘c3 0-0 11. ♗b2 e5 [11... ♖d8 12. ♕e1! With ideas of ♖d1, ♕e3, and eventually achieving d2-d4.] 12. a4!± Black doesn't have a good way to deal with the advance of the a-pawn.

**9. ♗a3!**

Attempting to avoid a transposition to the line 8...d5 9. exd6 ♗xd6 10.d4 0-0 11.♗b2?.

**9... f6**

9... d6 10. exd6 ♗xd6 11. d4 ♕e7 12. ♗b2!⩲ Now the annoying 12...cxd4 13.♘xd4 ♗e5 obviously doesn't work anymore.

**10. d4! cxd4 11. ♘xd4**

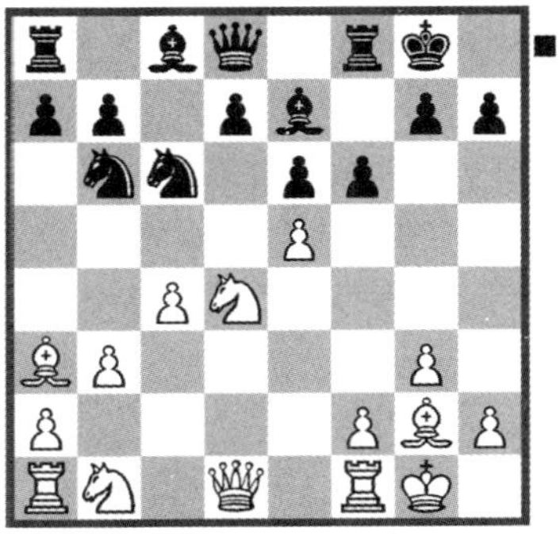
Position after: 11. ♘xd4

White emerges much better in all variations:

**11... ♘xe5**

**A)** 11... ♗xa3 12. ♘xa3

**A1)** 12... fxe5 13. ♘xc6 dxc6 [13... bxc6 14. ♕d6 ♕f6 15. ♖ae1+– ] 14. ♕e2±

**A2)** 12... ♘xe5 13. ♖e1!

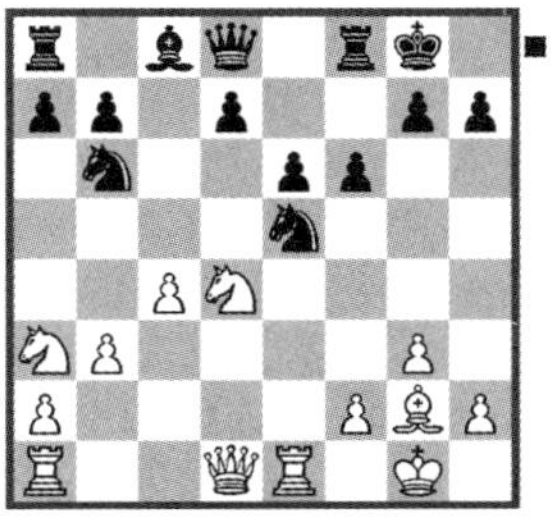
Position after: 13. ♖e1!

The two big issues for Black are their dark-squared weaknesses, and inability to complete queenside development. 13... a6 14. f4 ♘f7 15. c5 ♘d5 16. ♘c4+–

**B)** 11... ♘xd4 12. ♗xe7 ♕xe7 13. ♕xd4+–

**12. ♖e1 ♖b8 13. ♗xe7 ♕xe7 14. ♘c3±**

Probably followed by ♕d2 and ♖ad1 – White is dominating.

## b) 3...b6

**1. e4 c5 2. ♘f3 e6 3. g3 b6**

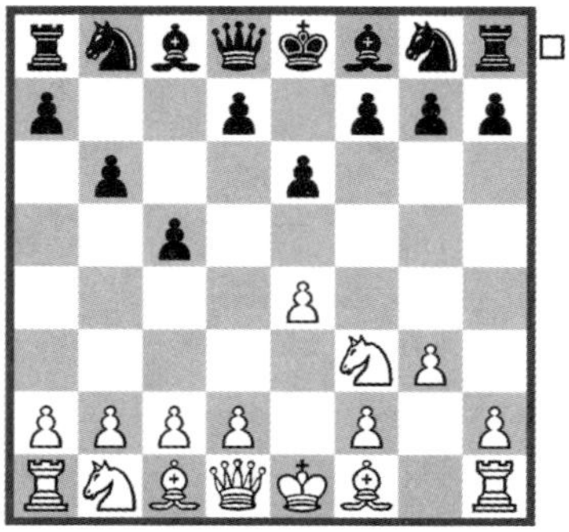
Position after: 3... b6

**4. d4!**

Another excellent moment to open the position. As demonstrated in the lines after 3...a6, Black will face big problems along the h1-a8 diagonal.

**4... cxd4**

4... ♗b7 5. d5! ♘f6 6. ♘c3 exd5 7. exd5 ♗e7 8.♗g2 is logical and good, but even better is the wild 8. g4!

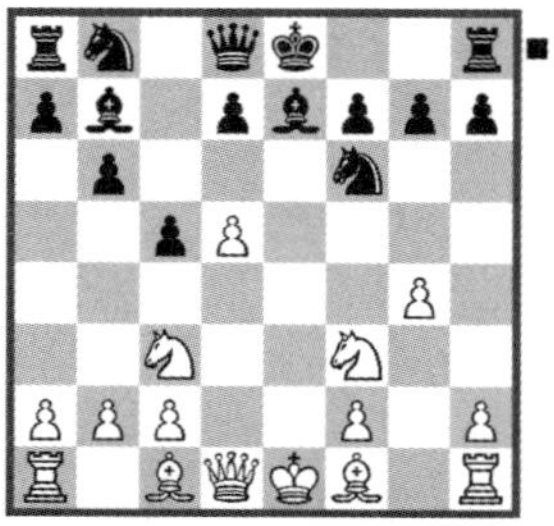
Position after: 8. g4!

8... 0-0 [8... ♘xg4 9. ♖g1+–; 8... h6 9. ♖g1+–] 9. g5 ♘e8 10. ♗f4± Followed by ♕d2 and 0-0-0.

**5. ♘xd4 ♗b7**

5... d5? 6. ♗b5+ ♗d7 7. exd5± and Black is already seriously struggling not to lose a pawn. It's easy to see the difference between this position and the line with 3...a6 4.d4?! cxd4 5. ♘xd4 d5!.

**6. ♗g2 ♘f6**

6... ♘c6 7. ♘b5! d6 8. ♗f4

Position after: 8. ♗f4

8... e5 [8... ♘e5?! 9. ♕d4!± Threatening to capture on d6.] 9. ♗e3 a6 10. ♘5c3 ♘f6 11. ♘d2± This is just a great Sicilian Sveshnikov for White.

**7. ♘c3**

The position looks relatively normal, but Black already needs to be extremely careful.

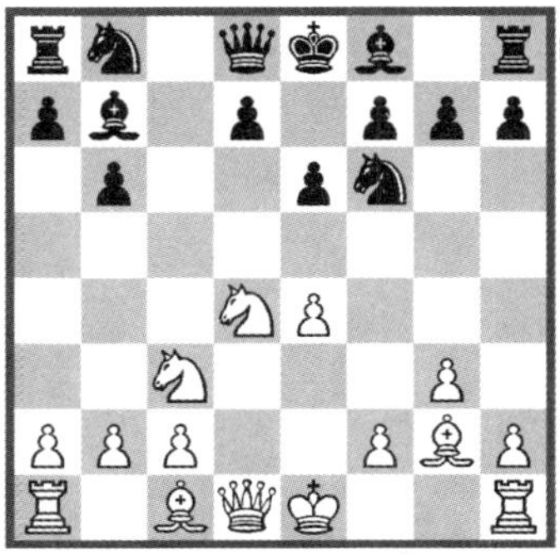
Position after: 7. ♘c3

**7... ♗b4?!**

**A)** 7... a6?! Attempting to set up a Hedgehog structure, but it's too slow and the following variations will show a recurrence of the themes after 3...a6. 8. 0-0 d6 9. ♖e1 ♕c7 [9... ♗e7? 10. e5 dxe5 11. ♗xb7 ♖a7 12. ♗c6++–; 9... ♘bd7? 10. e5 ♗xg2 11. exf6 ♗b7 12. ♘xe6! fxe6 13. ♖xe6+ ♔f7 14. fxg7 ♗xg7 15. ♖xd6+–; 9... ♕c8 10. ♘d5! ♘bd7 11. ♗g5 h6 12. ♗xf6 gxf6 13. ♕h5+–] 10. ♘d5!

Position after: 10. ♘d5!

White is already completely winning. 10... exd5 [10... ♘xd5 11. exd5 e5 12. ♖e3!+– Followed by ♖c3.] 11. exd5+ ♔d8 12. ♗g5 ♘bd7 13. ♘c6+! ♗xc6 14. dxc6 ♘c5 15. ♗xf6+ gxf6 16. ♗d5!+– With total domination. We will just slowly improve our pieces and Black has nothing to do.

**B)** 7... ♘c6 8. e5! This leads to a forced line with a nice advantage for White. 8... ♘xd4 9. ♗xb7 ♕b8 10. ♕xd4 ♕xb7 11. 0-0 ♗c5 12. ♕h4 ♘d5 13. ♕e4! ♕c6 14. ♘xd5 exd5 15. ♕d3±

**C)** 7... d6 Playing without ...a7-a6 doesn't solve any of Black's problems. I'll just show a few sample variations as it's all very similar to the previous lines. 8. 0-0 ♘bd7 [8... ♗e7? 9. e5! ♗xg2 10. exf6 ♗xf1 11. fxe7 ♕xe7 12. ♔xf1+– Zivkovic – Rodic, Obrenovac 2010.] 9. ♖e1 ♕c7 10. ♗g5!

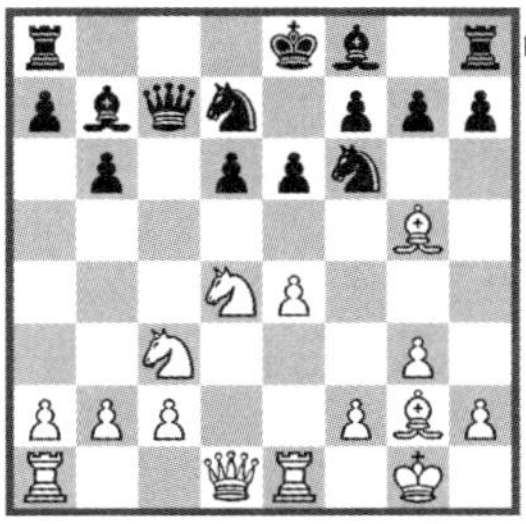
Position after: 10. ♗g5!

Threatening ♘d5.

**C1)** 10... h6 11. ♘cb5! ♕c8 [11... ♕b8 12. ♗xf6 ♘xf6 13. e5 dxe5 14. ♘c6+–] 12. ♗f4 ♘e5 13. ♘f5! exf5 14. exf5+–

**C2)** 10... ♗e7 11. ♘cb5! ♕b8 [11... ♕c8 12. ♘f5! exf5 13. exf5+–] 12. ♗xf6 ♘xf6 [12... ♗xf6 13. e5!

♗xe5 14. ♗xb7 ♕xb7 15. ♖xe5+–; 12... gxf6 13. ♕h5+–] 13. e5 dxe5 14. ♘c6! ♗xc6 15. ♗xc6+ ♔f8 16. ♗xa8 ♕xa8 17. ♖xe5+–

**C3)** 10... ♖d8 The only move which doesn't lose immediately, but White still has a great position. 11. ♘d5! exd5 12. exd5+ ♘e5 13. ♗xf6 gxf6 14. ♕h5!± We can play f2-f4 at our leisure to pick up the piece.

**D)** 7... d5?! 8. ♗g5 ♗e7 9. exd5 ♘xd5 10. ♗xe7 ♕xe7 11. ♘xd5 ♗xd5 12. ♗xd5 exd5+ 13. ♕e2±

**8. 0-0!**

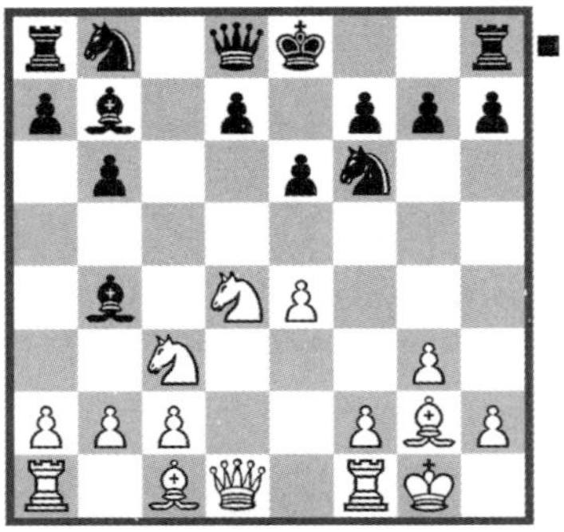

Position after: 8. 0-0!

**8... ♗xc3**

Capturing the pawn is just bad for Black, but there aren't any better alternatives.

**A)** 8... 0-0 9. ♗g5±

**B)** 8... d6 9. ♗g5! Threatening to capture on f6 and then follow up with ♕h5. 9... ♘bd7 10. ♘cb5! 0-0 11. c3 ♗c5 12. b4 ♗xd4 13. cxd4±

**9. bxc3 ♗xe4**

**A)** 9... ♘xe4 10. ♕g4 0-0 11. ♗xe4 f5 12. ♗xb7! fxg4 13. ♗xa8+–

**B)** 9... 0-0 10. ♗g5±

**10. ♗xe4 ♘xe4 11. ♕g4**

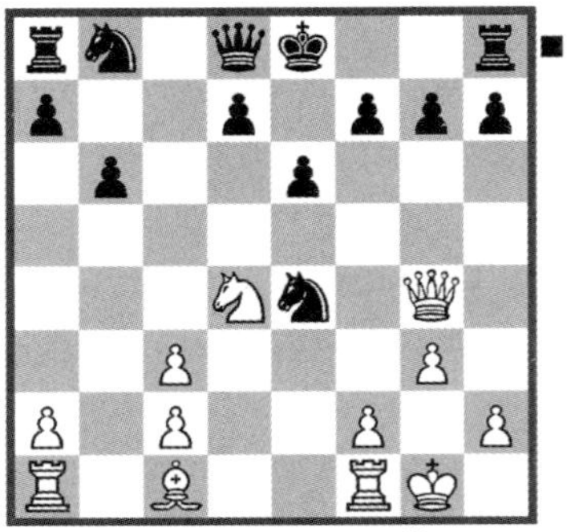

Position after: 11. ♕g4

**11... f5?**

11... ♘f6 12. ♕xg7 ♖g8 13. ♕h6 ♖g6 14. ♕e3 ♘c6 15. ♘xc6 dxc6 16. c4+– Black has too many weaknesses to survive.

**12. ♕xg7 ♕f6 13. ♘xe6!**

The critical strike.

**13... dxe6 14. ♕b7**

*(see diagram next page)*

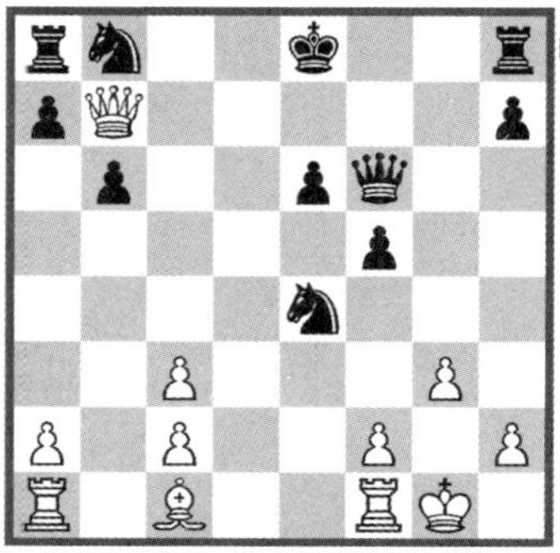

Position after: 14. ♕b7

**14... ♕e7**

14... ♕xc3 15. ♕xa8 ♕xa1 16. ♕xb8+ ♔f7 17. ♕xa7++– Breder – Gheorghiu, Switzerland 2016.

**15. ♕c8+ ♕d8 16. ♕xe6+ ♕e7 17. ♕c8+ ♕d8 18. ♕xf5+–**

I won a nice game in Haria – Bosboom, Struga 2021.

## c) 3...d5 4.exd5 exd5 5.d4 cxd4

**1. e4 c5 2. ♘f3 e6 3. g3 d5**

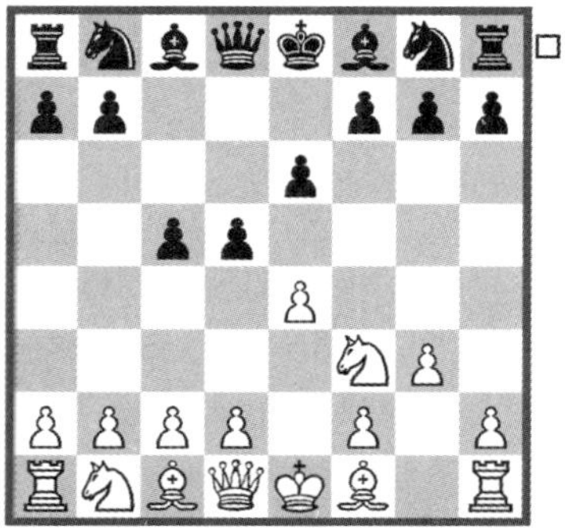

Position after: 3... d5

**4. exd5 exd5**

4... ♕xd5 This recapture enables White to achieve a comfortable edge. The point is that we will control the e5-square, and our bishop stands very well on g2 to support future queenside play. 5. ♘c3 ♕d8 6. d4 ♘f6 [6... cxd4 7. ♘xd4 ♘f6 8. ♗g2 e5 9. ♕e2! The critical idea in this line. 9... ♕xd4 10. ♘b5±] 7. ♗g5!

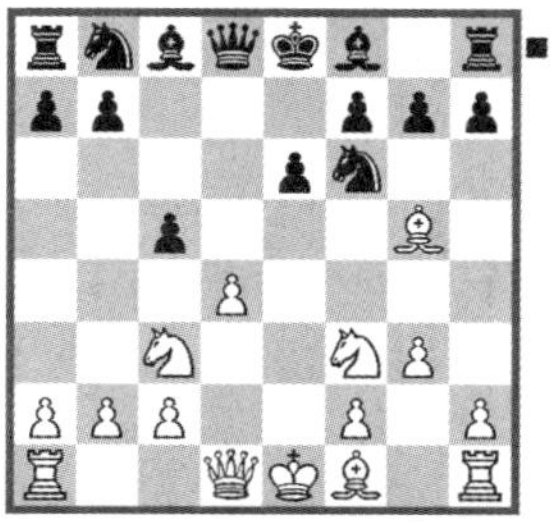

Position after: 7. ♗g5!

7... ♘c6 [7... h6 8. ♗xf6 ♕xf6 9. ♗b5+ ♗d7 10. ♘e5! Maintaining the tension. Black can't afford to capture on b5. 10... ♗c6 11. 0-0 a6 12. ♗a4! b5 13. ♖e1!+– Followed by d4-d5 and White is crashing through.; 7... ♗e7 8. dxc5 0-0 9. ♗g2 ♗xc5 10. ♕e2± Followed by 0-0 and ♖ad1 with very easy play.] 8. ♗b5!? ♕b6 [8... a6 9. ♗xc6+ bxc6 10. dxc5 ♕xd1+ 11. ♖xd1 ♗xc5 12. ♘e4±; 8... ♗e7 9. dxc5 0-0 10. ♕e2 ♗xc5 11. ♘e4 ♗e7 12. ♗xc6 bxc6 13. ♘xf6+ ♗xf6 14. ♗xf6 ♕xf6 15. 0-0-0±] 9. a4 cxd4 10. ♕xd4 ♕xd4 11. ♘xd4 ♗d7 12. ♘xc6 bxc6 13.

♗c4± Castling queenside makes sense here, perhaps after first protecting the f2-pawn. Black's inferior pawn structure grants us a nice plus.

**5. d4 cxd4!?**

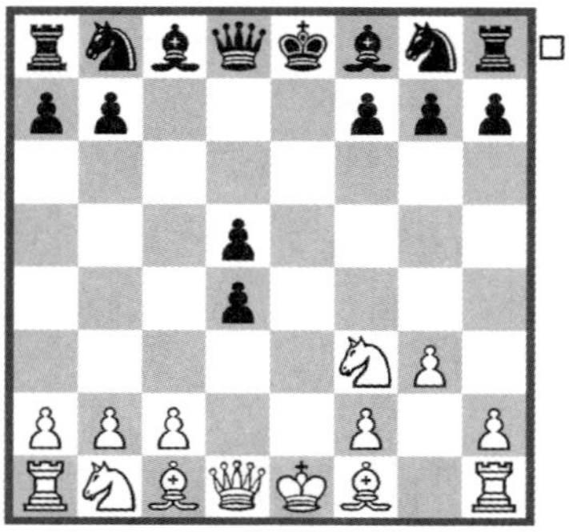

Position after: 5... cxd4!?

The immediate capture on d4 has been quite popular recently. Black's plan is to continue developing with ...♘c6 and ...♗c5, increasing pressure on the d4-square and gaining piece activity in exchange for the isolated queen's pawn on d5.

**6. ♘xd4 ♘c6 7. ♗g2**

7. ♘c3!? This is an interesting attempt to play against Black's ...♗c5 idea.

Position after: 7. ♘c3!?

**A)** 7... ♗c5?! would be a mistake here as White can respond with 8. ♗e3! The point is that with the bishop still on f1, 8... ♘xd4 9.♗xd4 ♕e7+ is simply met with 10.♗e2 – which would not be possible after the more natural 7.♗g2. 8... ♗b4 9. ♕d2 ♘ge7 10. a3 ♗a5 11. ♗g2±

**B)** 7... ♘f6! 8. ♗g2

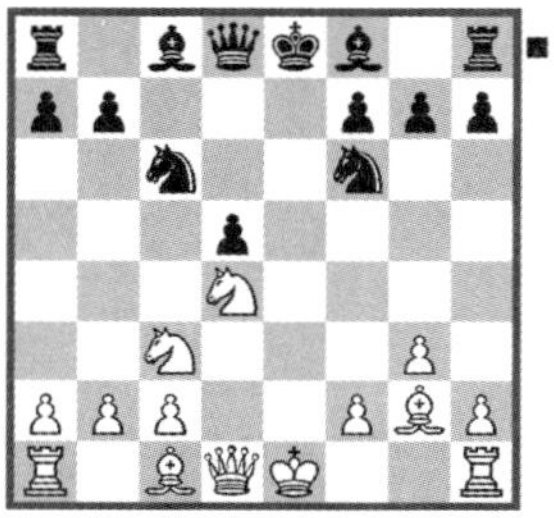

Position after: 8. ♗g2

**B1)** 8... ♗c5 9. ♕e2+! ♗e7 Trading queens would give White a great position, so Black must retreat. 10. ♗e3 0-0 11. 0-0 It's possible to stop here and claim White has a nice position, but there are a few important ideas to be aware of.

Position after: 11. 0-0

**B1.1)** 11... ♗g4 12. ♕b5! A great square for the queen. 12... a6

[12... ♕d7 Black will regain the pawn, but the resulting endgame is advantageous for us: 13. ♘xd5 ♘xd5 14. ♕xd5 ♕xd5 15. ♗xd5 ♘xd4 16. ♗xd4 ♖fd8 17. c4 ♗f3 18. ♖fe1 ♗xd5 19. cxd5 ♗f8 20. ♖ad1! ♖xd5 21. ♗e3±] 13. ♘xc6! This is the point behind 12.♕b5, leading to the following forcing line: 13... axb5 14. ♘xd8 ♖fxd8 15. h3 d4 16. ♗xd4 ♖xd4 17. hxg4 b4 18. ♗xb7! ♖b8 19. ♘e2 ♖d2 20. ♗f3± I think White has very good chances to convert this edge into a full point.

**B1.2)** 11... ♗b4! Putting the bishop on a more active square and opening the e-file for the f8-rook. 12. ♕b5!

Position after: 12. ♕b5!

Once again the queen stands very well on b5.

**B1.2a)** 12... ♗xc3 13. bxc3 ♘e4 [13... a6 Here 14. ♘xc6 transposes to 12...a6, but potentially stronger is 14. ♕c5!?±.] 14. ♘xc6 bxc6 15. ♕xc6 ♗e6 16. ♖fe1! ♕c8 Black's best option is to head for an opposite-coloured bishop + rook ending, but we'll still retain good practical chances there. 17. ♕xc8 ♖fxc8 18. ♗xe4 dxe4 19. ♗d4±

**B1.2b)** 12... a6 13. ♘xc6 axb5 14. ♘xd8 ♗xc3 15. bxc3 ♖xd8 16. ♖fb1 ♗d7 [16... ♘e4 17. ♖xb5 ♘xc3 18. ♖b3 ♖xa2 19. ♖xa2 ♘xa2 20. c3± Black will have to return the d-pawn in order to save the knight.] 17. c4!± Black is still yet to fully equalise.

**B2)** 8... ♕b6 9. ♘b3 d4 10. ♘e2 ♗b4+ 11. c3 dxc3 12. bxc3 ♗e7 13. 0-0 0-0 14. ♗e3± Followed by something like ♘ed4 and ♖e1, with good pressure on Black's queenside.

**B3)** 8... ♗g4! The only way to achieve equality. 9. ♘de2

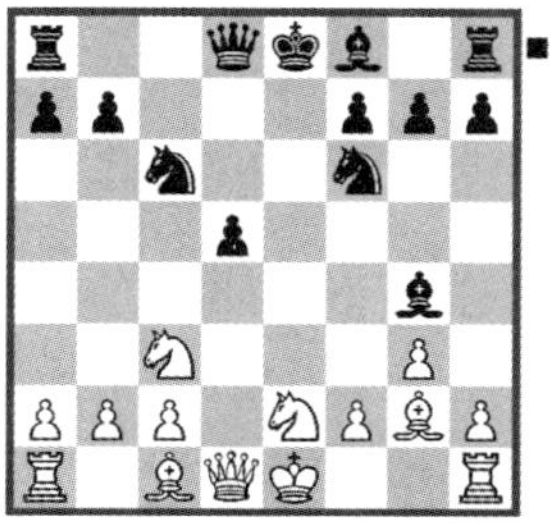

Position after: 9. ♘de2

**B3.1)** 9... ♗c5 has also been played a few times, but I quite like White's chances in the following line: 10. 0-0 0-0 11. ♗g5 d4 [11...

♘d4 is the other way to defend the d5-pawn, but after 12. h3 ♘f3+ 13. ♗xf3 ♗xf3 14. ♕d3 ♗xe2 15. ♘xe2± White is comfortable.] 12. ♘e4 ♗e7 13. ♗xf6 ♗xf6 14. h3 ♗f5 15. ♘f4 The engine suggests that the position is completely equal, but practically speaking I feel like White's knights have enough scope to cause a few problems. In the long term, Black's isolated pawn will probably be more of a weakness than a strength too.

**B3.2)** 9... ♗b4 10. h3 ♗xc3+ It makes sense for Black to double our pawns whilst they still have the opportunity to do so. 11. bxc3

Position after: 11. bxc3

**B3.2a)** 11... ♗e6 12. ♖b1 0-0 13. ♘f4↑

**B3.2b)** 11... ♗h5 In So – Gledura, Saint Louis 2022, I preferred the immediate 12. ♖b1! ♕e7 [12... ♕a5 13. g4 ♗g6 14. 0-0 0-0 15. ♖xb7 ♕xa2 16. ♗g5 ♘e4 17. ♗e3±; 12... 0-0 13. g4! ♗g6 14. ♖xb7±] 13. ♖b3! threatening ♗a3. 13... ♕xe2+ 14. ♕xe2+ ♗xe2 15. ♔xe2 0-0-0 16. f3!

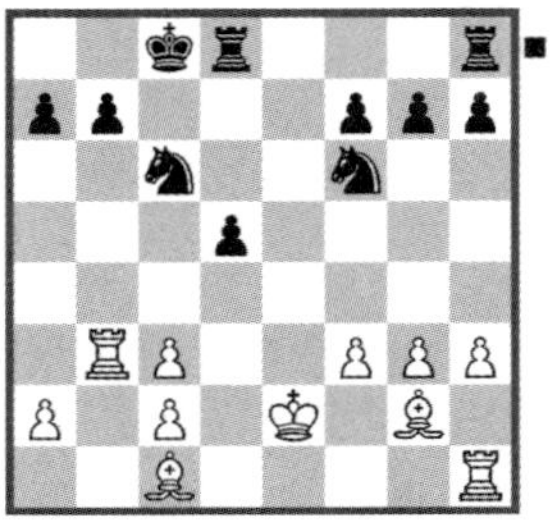

Position after: 16. f3!

Enabling the king to come to f2. 16... d4 Black needs to continue playing actively, otherwise our bishop pair will start to dominate. 17. ♔f2 ♘d5 18. cxd4 ♘xd4 19. ♖d3 ♘b4 20. ♖c3+ ♘dc6 21. ♖c4 ♘xa2 22. ♗e3⩱∞ We're a pawn down, but with excellent compensation. For example, the forthcoming f3-f4 and ♖b1 looks quite dangerous for Black.

**B3.2c)** 11... ♗f5! Probably the most accurate retreat, aiming to neutralise the g2-bishop with ...♗e4 at some point. 12. ♖b1 0-0 [12... ♗e4 13. f3 ♗g6 14. ♖xb7 0-0 15. 0-0∞ This looks double-edged, but again I prefer the potential of White's position. We have the bishop pair and at some point our pawns will start advancing on the kingside.] 13. 0-0 b6 14. g4!? ♗e4 15. f3 ♗g6 16. ♘f4↑ With ideas of h3-h4. Again we're not better, but there's plenty of play in the position and it feels like our pieces have lots of potential to cause Black problems.

**7... ♗c5**

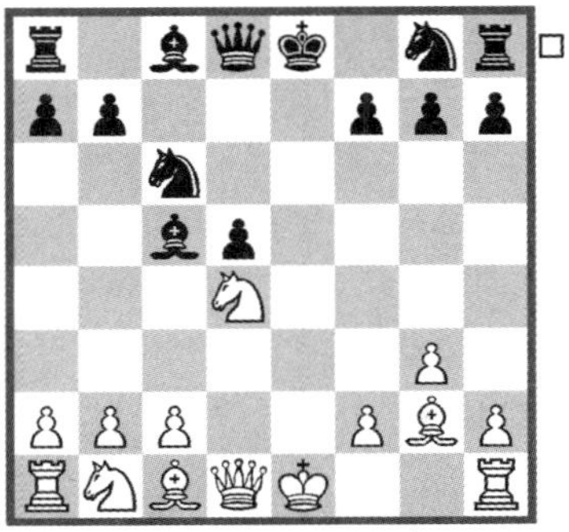
Position after: 7... ♗c5

**8. ♘b3!**

**A)** The following game is an example of how quickly things can go wrong for White here: 8. ♘xc6 bxc6 9. 0-0 ♘f6 10. c4?! [10. ♖e1+ ♗e6 11. ♘c3 0-0 12. ♘a4 ♗e7 13. ♗e3 ♘d7=] 10... 0-0 11. cxd5? ♗a6! 12. ♖e1 cxd5 13. ♘c3 ♕b6

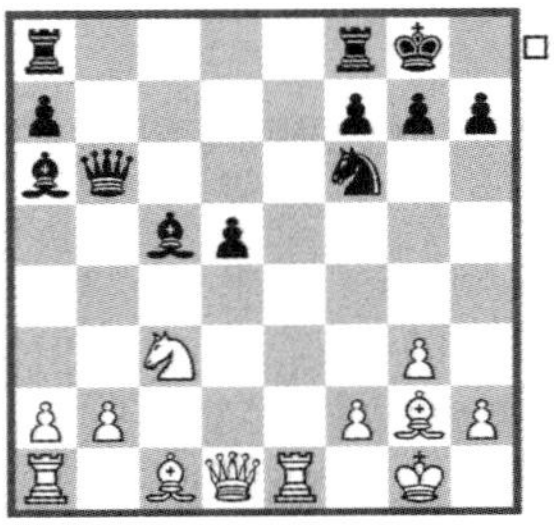
Position after: 13... ♕b6

14. ♗e3?? [14. ♕c2 ♖ac8↑] 14... d4 15. ♘a4 dxe3! 16. ♘xb6 exf2+ 17. ♔h1 fxe1=♕+ 18. ♕xe1 ♗xb6–+ McShane – Lagarde 2021.

**B)** 8. ♗e3?! ♘xd4 9. ♗xd4 ♕e7+∓

**8... ♕e7+!**

Black must prevent us from castling.

8... ♗b6 is too slow: 9. 0-0

**A)** 9... ♘f6 10. ♗g5 h6 11. ♗xf6 ♕xf6 12. ♘c3 0-0 13. a4!

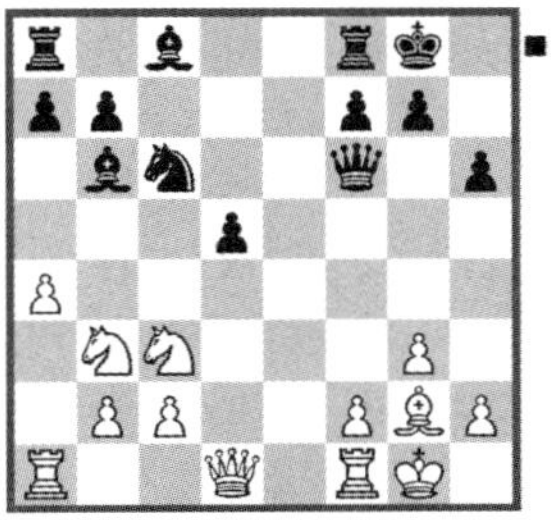
Position after: 13. a4!

A useful intermediate move before we consider capturing on d5. 13... d4 [13... ♘a5 14. ♘xd5 ♕xb2 15. ♘xa5 ♗xa5 16. c4!± The knight on d5 is extremely powerful. We'll follow up with ♖b1, and Black's pieces are highly uncoordinated.] 14. ♘d5 ♕d8 15. ♖e1 ♗e6 A typical idea in Tarrasch positions is to sacrifice the d4-pawn in return for good piece activity, but here Black has very little compensation. 16. ♘xb6 axb6 17. ♗xc6 bxc6 18. ♘xd4±

**B)** 9... ♘ge7 10. ♘c3 0-0

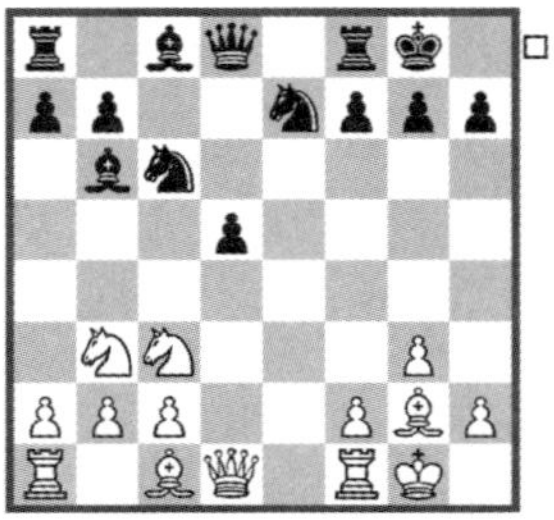

Position after: 10... 0-0

11. ♘a4! [11. ♘xd5 doesn't gain an advantage as Black is very active. 11... ♘xd5 12. ♗xd5 ♘b4 13. ♗f3 ♗f5⇆] 11... ♗c7 [11... d4 12. ♗g5! f6 The only way to defend the d4-pawn. 13. ♗d2± With ideas of ♖e1 and ♘bc5 coming, White's position looks really appealing.] 12. ♗e3± Again there's no point analysing anything more – White just has a comfortable edge.

**9. ♕e2**

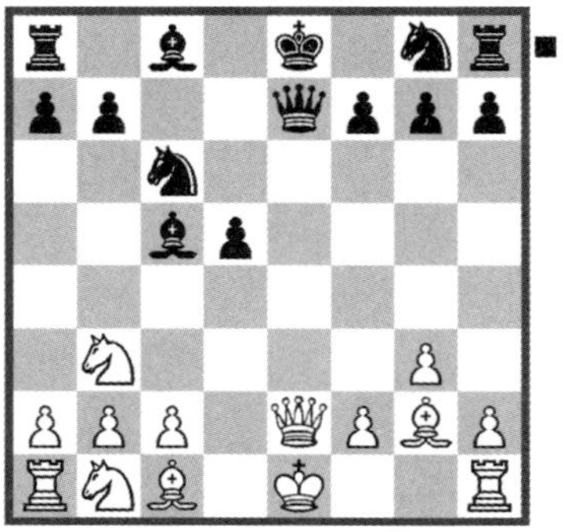

Position after: 9. ♕e2

Now Black has a choice about whether to immediately capture on e2, or first retreat the c5-bishop.

**9... ♕xe2+**

**A)** 9... ♗b6 10. ♗e3! [10. ♘c3?! ♘b4!∓ Adams – Vidit, Tornelo INT 2021.] 10... ♗xe3 11. ♕xe3 ♕xe3+ 12. fxe3

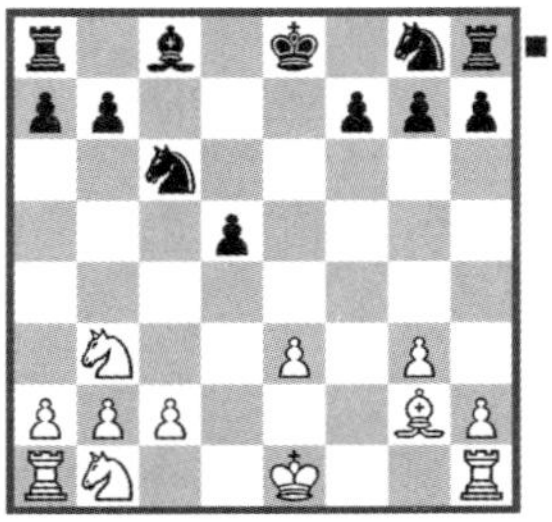

Position after: 12. fxe3

I'm not claiming that White is better here, but the position feels easier to play for us. The pawn on e3 is useful in controlling the d4-square, and Black will experience ongoing pressure against their d5-pawn. 12... ♗e6 13. ♘c3 ♘f6 14. 0-0-0 0-0-0 15. h3! Preventing ...♘g4 and threatening to push g3-g4. 15... h5 16. ♘d4 We have various options here, for example, doubling rooks on the d-file and playing ♘d4-e2-f4 to increase the pressure on d5.

**B)** 9... ♗e6 has been the most common move but White is clearly better after 10. 0-0 ♘f6 11. ♗g5 ♗b6 12. ♘c3±.

**10. ♔xe2 ♗b6 11. ♘c3**

*(see diagram next page)*

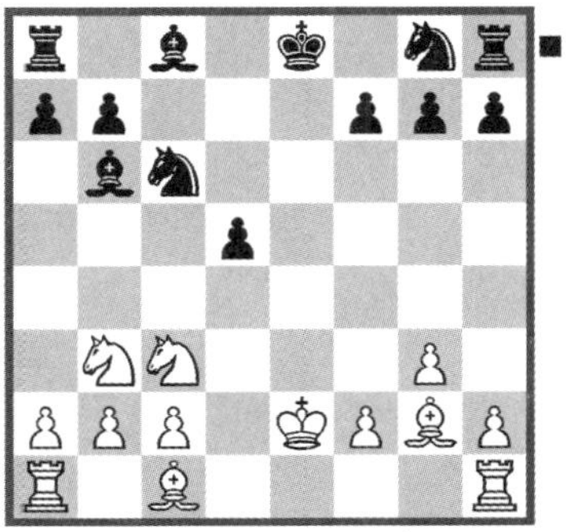

Position after: 11. ♘c3

**11... ♗g4+!**

**A)** 11... ♘f6 12. ♗g5 [12. ♗xd5? ♘b4–+ There is no ♗e4 here, in contrast to the line after 11...♘ge7.] 12... ♗g4+ 13. ♔f1! White has good practical chances in the following line: 13... d4 14. ♗xf6 gxf6 15. ♘d5 0-0-0 16. ♘c1!±

**B)** 11... ♘ge7 12. ♗xd5! ♘xd5 13. ♘xd5 0-0 14. ♗e3±

**12. ♗f3**

12. f3!? ♗e6 13. ♘a4 ♗c7 14. ♘ac5 ♗f5! Black should be fine after this move. [14... ♗c8 15. ♗e3±] 15. ♘xb7 ♗xc2 16. ♗e3 ♘ge7 17. ♖hc1 ♗xb3 18. axb3 0-0=

**12... ♗xf3+ 13. ♔xf3 ♘ge7**

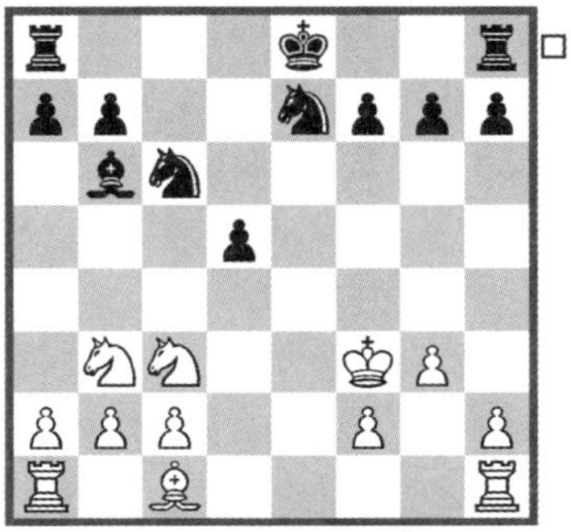

Position after: 13... ♘ge7

There are several ways to play this position with White, but I prefer just continuing to develop naturally:

**14. ♗f4 0-0-0 15. ♖ad1 d4 16. ♘b5 ♘f5 17. a4±**

An important manoeuvre here is ♘c1-d3 at the right moment.

## d) 3...d5 4.exd5 exd5 5.d4 ♘f6

**1. e4 c5 2. ♘f3 e6 3. g3 d5 4. exd5 exd5 5. d4 ♘f6**

In this subchapter we'll examine Black's strategy of prioriting kingside development and castling.

**6. ♗g2**

*(see diagram next page)*

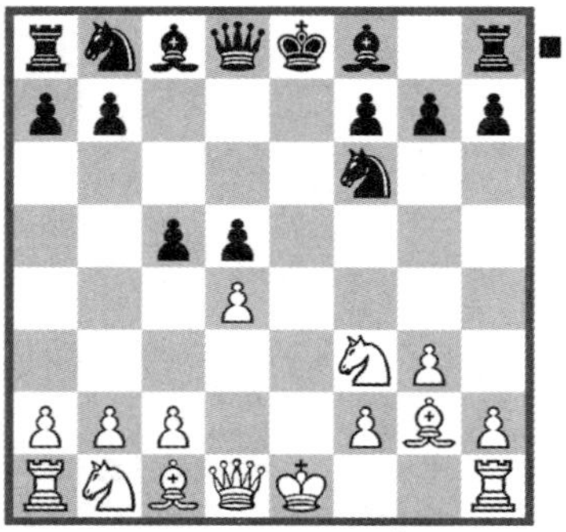

Position after: 6. ♗g2

**6... ♗e7**

**A)** 6... ♕e7+? 7. ♗e3 ♘g4 8. 0-0! A typical pawn sacrifice. 8... ♘xe3 9. fxe3 ♘c6 Black can't capture on e3, but now their queen just looks stupid on e7. [9... ♕xe3+? 10. ♔h1 ♗e7 11. c4!+–] 10. c4! dxc4 11. d5! Not the only option, but probably the most straightforward. 11... ♘e5 12. ♘xe5 ♕xe5 13. ♘a3

Position after: 13. ♘a3

13... ♗d6 [13... ♕b8 Martynov – Krejci, Pardubice 2015. 14. ♕f3!+–] 14. ♘xc4 ♕e7 15. e4! Threatening e4-e5. 15... ♗e5 [15... 0-0? 16. e5 ♗xe5 17. d6 ♕g5 18. ♘xe5 ♕xe5 19. d7+–] 16. ♘xe5 ♕xe5 17. ♕c2± White is dominating, and will win the c5-pawn. For example, 17...b6 is met with 18.b4!.

**B)** 6... ♗d6!? A rare move, but it is the engine's top choice. The bishop feels more natural on e7, from where it guards against a potential ♗g5 pin on the f6-knight. 7. 0-0 0-0 8. ♘c3 h6 It seems necessary for Black to prevent ♗g5. [8... ♘c6 9. dxc5 ♗xc5 10. a3 would simply transpose to 6...♗e7.; 8... cxd4 9. ♘xd4±] 9. ♗e3 c4

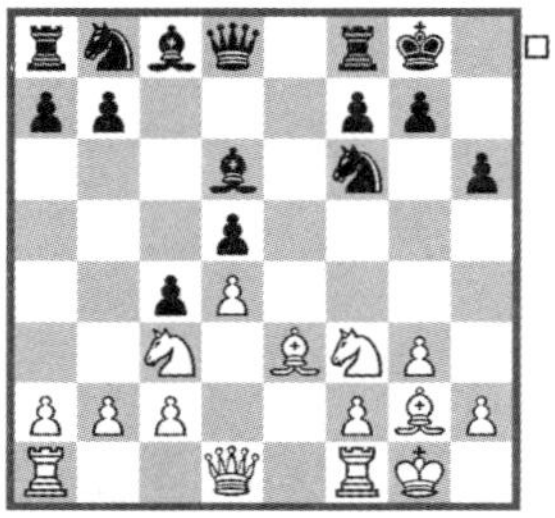

Position after: 9... c4

Capturing on d4 appears to give White a very healthy position, so it makes sense for Black to push ...c5-c4. 10. ♘e5 A natural response. One idea now is to push f2-f4 and even g3-g4 if possible. 10... ♗b4! Defending the d5-pawn. [10... ♗c7 11. f4 ♘c6 12. g4!± ♘xe5 An attempt to grab the pawn on g4 doesn't work, but it's the only line that is worth checking. 13. fxe5 ♗xg4 14. ♗f3 ♗xf3 15. ♕xf3 ♘e4 16. ♘xe4 dxe4 17. ♕g4!+– It's unlikely that Black will survive on the kingside.] 11. f4!? [11. ♘a4 is also logical, aiming for b2-b3: 11... ♘c6 12. b3 cxb3 13. axb3 ♖e8 14. c3 ♗d6 15. ♘xc6 bxc6= However, Black seems really solid here.] 11... ♘c6 12. g4!

*(see analysis diagram next page)*

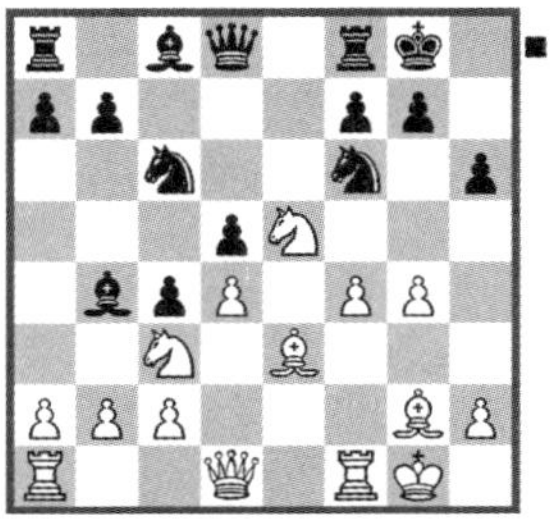
Position after: 12. g4!

This active approach forces Black to find some accurate moves. 12... ♗xc3! 13. bxc3 ♕a5 14. ♕d2 Again we don't care about losing the g-pawn. 14... ♗xg4 [14... ♘e4 15. ♗xe4 dxe4 16. ♘xc6 bxc6 17. f5→] 15. f5!

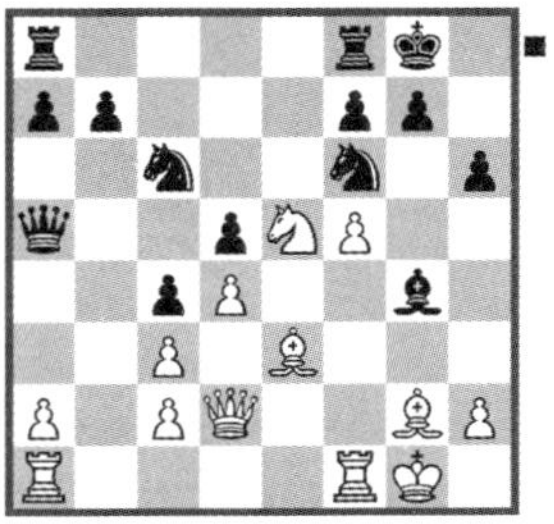
Position after: 15. f5!

**B1)** 15... ♘xe5 leads to a forcing line: 16. dxe5 ♘e4 17. ♕e1 ♕xc3 18. ♖f4! ♕xe1+ 19. ♖xe1 ♗h5 20. ♖h4 g6 21. ♗xe4 dxe4 22. ♗xh6 ♖fd8 23. ♗g5 ♖d4 24. fxg6 fxg6 25. c3 ♖d5 26. ♖hxe4± White is pressing in this endgame.

**B2)** 15... ♖fe8 16. ♗xh6

**B2.1)** 16... ♘xe5 17. ♕g5 The difference compared to 15...♖ae8 is that Black doesn't have ...♘g6 here, as there is no rook on f8 to cover the f7-pawn. 17... ♘h5 18. ♗xg7 ♘xg7 19. f6 ♘g6 20. ♕xg4 ♕xc3 21. fxg7→ The assault on Black's king will continue, for example with ♔h1 and h2-h4.

**B2.2)** 16... gxh6 17. ♘xg4! ♘xg4 18. ♖f4 ♘f6 19. ♖h4 Black needs to be very careful here to survive. 19... ♔f8! 20. ♖xh6 ♘g8 21. ♖h8

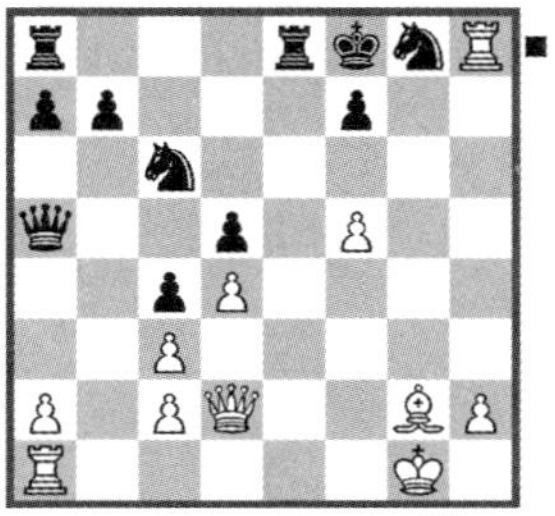
Position after: 21. ♖h8

**B2.2a)** 21... f6 22. ♗f3!→

**B2.2b)** 21... ♔e7 22. ♖b1! ♖ab8 23. ♖h7 ♔d7 [23... ♖f8 24. ♕e3+ ♔d8 25. f6! ♕c7 26. ♕f3!+– Followed by ♖h5.] 24. ♖xf7+ ♖e7 25. ♖xe7+ ♘cxe7 26. f6!+– With ♕f4 or ♕g5 coming next, Black is lost.

**B2.2c)** 21... ♔g7 22. ♖h3!+–

**B2.2d)** 21... ♕d8! 22. ♕h6+ ♔e7 23. ♕g7 ♘f6 [23... ♖f8 is less logical: 24. ♔h1! Followed by f5-f6, and White continues pressing.] 24. ♖e1+ ♘e4 25. ♖xe8+ ♕xe8 26. ♗xe4 ♔d8 27. ♖b1 ♕xe4 28. ♖xb7 ♕e1+ 29.

♔g2 ♕d2+=

**B3)** 15... ♖ae8

**B3.1)** 16. ♘xc6!? We can also start with this. 16... bxc6 17. ♗xh6 ♔h7! [17... gxh6 transposes to 16.♗xh6 gxh6?.; 17... ♔h8 18. ♗xg7+ is also the same.] 18. ♗xg7 ♔xg7 19. ♕g5+ ♔h7 20. ♕xf6 ♕d8 21. ♕xd8 ♖xd8= Despite the pawn deficit, it seems that Black is just fine here.

**B3.2)** 16. ♗xh6! ♘xe5! [16... gxh6? 17. ♘xc6 bxc6 18. ♕xh6 ♕d8 19. ♔h1 Threatening ♖g1. 19... ♘h5 20. f6 ♖e6 21. ♕g5+ ♔h8 22. ♕xg4 ♘xf6 23. ♕h3+! ♘h7 24. ♖xf7 ♖xf7 25. ♕xe6±] 17. ♕g5 ♘g6 18. fxg6 ♕xc3! 19. ♗xg7 ♕xd4+ 20. ♔h1 ♔xg7 21. gxf7+ ♔xf7 22. c3! ♕xc3 23. ♕xg4 ♔e7!

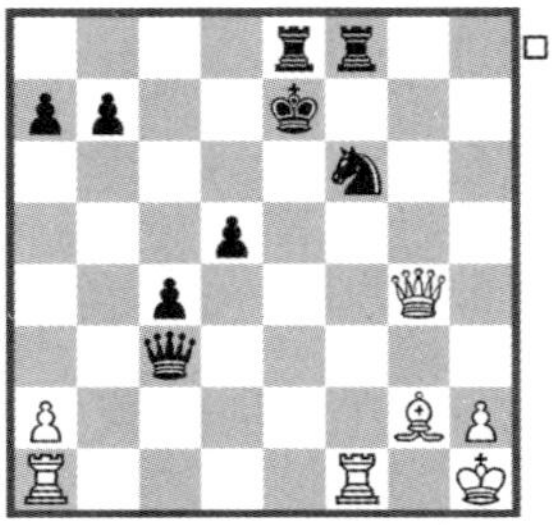

Position after: 23... ♔e7!

Black has had to find a large number of only moves to reach this position, and for that their reward is likely going to be a draw via perpetual check. For example: 24. ♕g7+ ♔d6 25. ♕xb7 ♘e4! Otherwise ♖ad1 would be lethal. 26. ♕a6+ ♔c7 27. ♕xa7+ ♔c6 28. ♕a6+ ♔c7=

**7. 0-0**

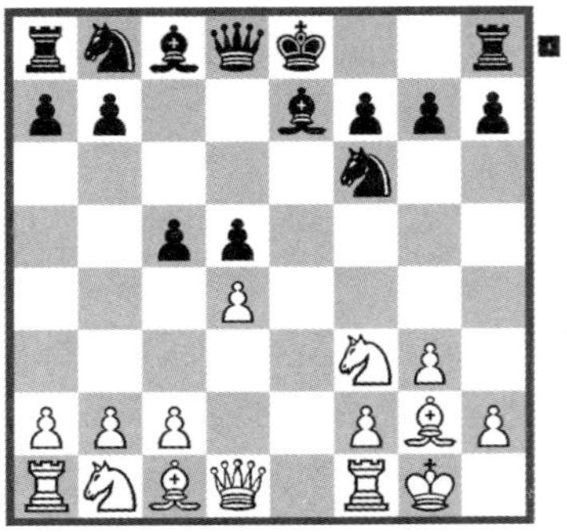

Position after: 7. 0-0

On first glance, the position looks highly favourable for White. Black has basically committed to an IQP structure, while our pieces are all well placed to capitalise on that. With our fianchettoed bishop, Black's hopes of gaining counterplay via a kingside assault are extremely remote. Nevertheless, Black is also extremely solid with no obvious weaknesses. The following variations will demonstrate that we need to be extremely accurate in order to gain hopes of attaining an advantage.

**7... 0-0 8. ♘c3**

8. dxc5 is most popular, but Black has a clever order of moves to get a very satisfactory position: 8... ♗xc5

*(see analysis diagram next page)*

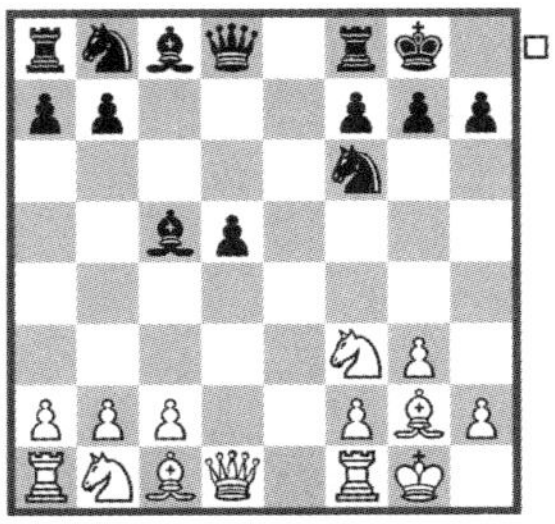

Position after: 8... ♗xc5

**A)** 9. ♗g5 is probably best, but I'm not optimistic about White's chances after 9... ♘c6 10. ♘c3 d4 11. ♗xf6 ♕xf6 12. ♘d5 [12. ♘e4 ♕e7 13. ♘xc5 ♕xc5 14. ♘e1 ♗f5=] 12... ♕d8 13. ♘d2 ♗e6 14. ♘f4 ♗f5=. Of course this position is definitely playable – I just preferred the lines after 8.♘c3.

**B)** 9. ♘c3 h6! Black postpones developing the queenside knight to c6 to secure their dark-squared bishop's position first. 10. a3 a5! I couldn't find anything convincing for White in this position. 11. ♘a4 [11. ♗f4 ♘c6 12. ♕d3 a4! 13. ♖ad1 ♖a5⇆] 11... ♗a7 12. c4!? dxc4 13. ♕xd8 ♖xd8 14. ♘e5 ♘c6! 15. ♘xc4 ♗g4= Black is active and certainly not any worse.

**8... ♘c6**

8... h6 9. ♗e3! This avoids a transposition to 8.dxc5. 9... cxd4 [9... c4 10. a3!± followed by ♘e5 is an improved version of the positions we encountered after 6...♗d6.; 9... ♘g4 10. dxc5! ♘xe3 11. fxe3 ♗xc5 12. ♘d4 ♗e6 13. ♘xe6 fxe6 14. ♖xf8+ ♕xf8 15. ♕g4!± Next will come ♗h3, when White is dominating.]

**9. dxc5**

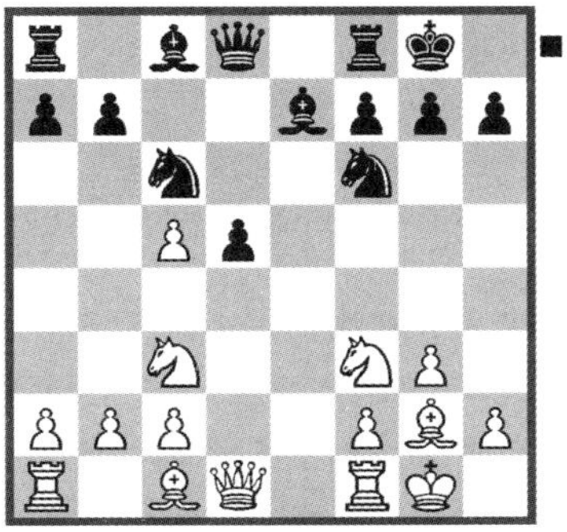

Position after: 9. dxc5

9. ♗e3 ♘g4 10. ♗f4 ♗e6 seems alright for Black, although it's definitely another playable line for us.

**9... ♗xc5**

By far the most popular choice, but doesn't seem to completely equalise.

9... d4 Allowing this move is the one drawback of playing 8.♘c3 before 9.dxc5, but I believe we can still get an advantage here with accurate play. 10. ♘a4 ♕a5 [10... ♗g4 11. h3 ♗h5 12. c3! Changing the pawn structure, but in doing so our pieces suddenly become really active. 12... dxc3 13. bxc3 ♕a5 14. ♕b3 ♖ad8 15. ♘d2! ♗e2 16. ♖e1 ♗b5 17. ♘b2 ♗xc5 18. ♘bc4 ♕a6 19. ♖b1±; 10... ♖e8 11. a3 ♗f5 12. b4 b5 13. ♘b2 a5 14. ♗d2 axb4 15. ♗xb4 ♘d5 16. ♕d2±] 11. b3 ♗xc5 12. a3! Preparing to capture on c5 and push b3-b4.

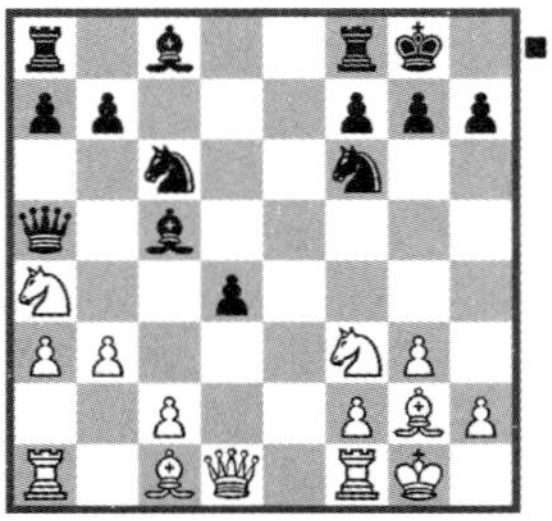

Position after: 12. a3!

**A)** 12... ♗e7 13. ♘xd4±

**B)** 12... ♗d6 13. c3!± Winning a pawn. [13. ♘xd4?! ♘xd4 14. ♕xd4 ♗e5∞]

**C)** 12... ♖d8 13. ♘xc5 ♕xc5 14. b4 ♕h5 The engine believes that Black is active enough to have basically equalised, but I still prefer to have the bishop pair. [14... ♕b5 15. ♕d3!±] 15. ♖e1 a5 [15... ♗g4 16. ♕d3 ♗f5 17. ♕b5 ♖ab8 18. ♗f4 a6 19. ♕c5 ♖d5 20. ♕c4 ♖bd8 21. ♗g5±] 16. ♗b2!

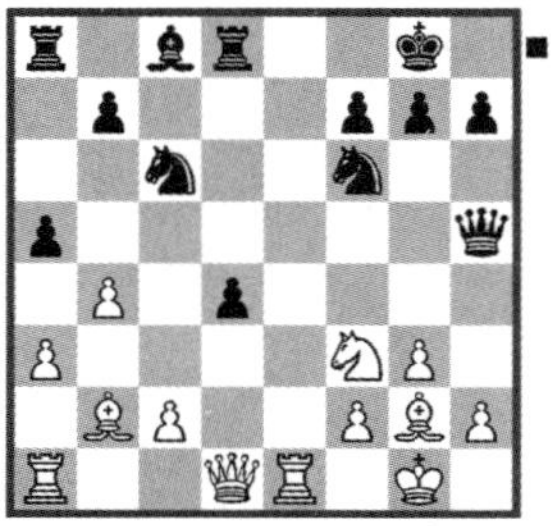

Position after: 16. ♗b2!

16... ♗g4! [16... axb4 17. axb4 ♖xa1 18. ♕xa1 ♘xb4 19. ♘xd4±] 17. h3 ♗xf3 18. ♗xf3 ♕f5 19. ♕d3 ♕xd3 20. cxd3 axb4 21. axb4 ♘xb4 22. ♖xa8 ♖xa8 23. ♗xb7 ♖b8 24. ♖a1 ♘xd3 25. ♗xd4± White can continue to press here, even if the result is likely to be a draw.

**10. a3!**

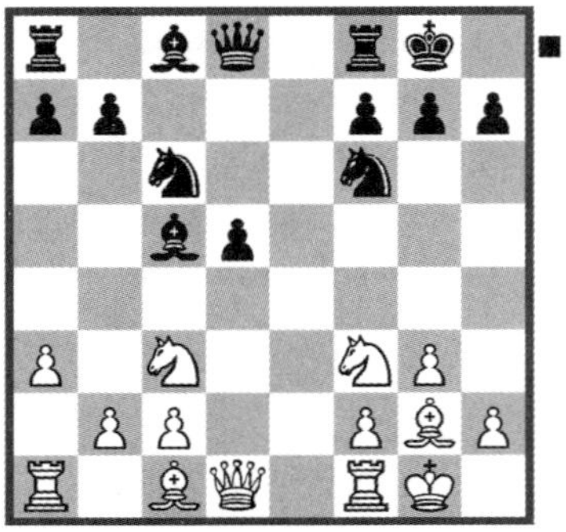

Position after: 10. a3!

**10... h6**

The most popular move, although now we'll get b2-b4 in and start to assert dominance.

**A)** 10... a5 This is generally Black's best response to the a2-a3 push, but most players would be nervous about creating such a weakness on b5. 11. ♗g5

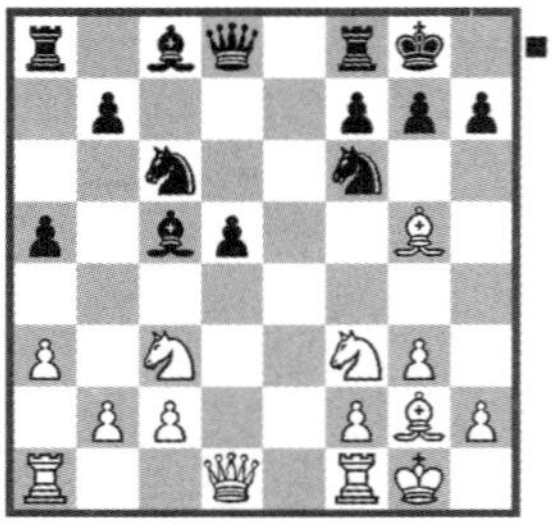

Position after: 11. ♗g5

**A1)** 11... ♗e6 is the most natural choice. 12. ♖b1! Threatening to capture on f6 and then d5. 12... ♗e7 13. ♖e1 ♕d7 14. ♘e2 h6 15. ♗xf6 ♗xf6 16. ♘f4 ♖fe8 17. h4!?± Followed by ♕d2 and a b2-b4 push at the right moment, with nice play on both sides of the board.

**A2)** 11... d4 12. ♗xf6 ♕xf6 13. ♘e4 ♕e7 14. ♘e1!± The knight will sit well on d3, after which we can continue to improve with moves like ♕d2 and ♖e1.

**A3)** 11... a4!? 12. ♕d3!

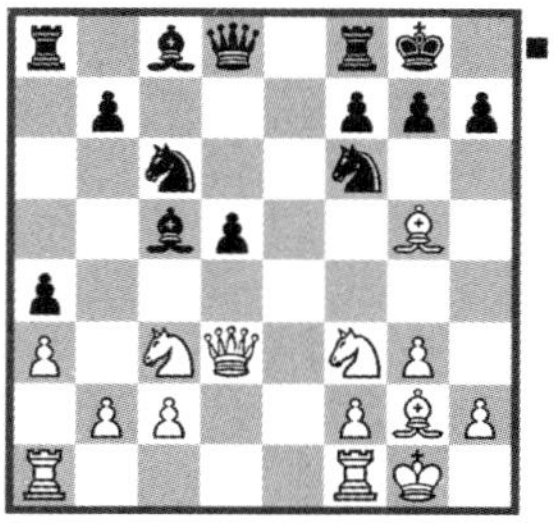

Position after: 12. ♕d3!

12... d4 [12... ♗e6 13. ♗xf6 ♕xf6 14. ♘xd5 ♗xd5 15. ♕xd5 ♖a5 16. ♕a2±] 13. ♗xf6 ♕xf6 14. ♘e4 ♕e7 15. ♖fe1± White's pieces are more active here. An interesting idea at the right moment would be to open the position with c2-c3.

**B)** 10... a6 11. b4 ♗a7 12. ♗g5 ♗e6 13. ♗xf6 ♕xf6 14. ♘xd5 ♗xd5 15. ♕xd5± Zvjaginsev – Yudin, Cheliabinsk 2018.

**C)** 10... ♖e8 11. b4 ♗f8 [11... ♗b6 12. ♘a4 ♗c7 13. ♗b2±; 11... d4 12. ♘a4 ♗f8 13. ♗b2 ♗g4 14. h3 ♗h5 15. g4 ♗g6 16. ♘xd4 ♘xd4 17. ♕xd4± Indjic – Kobalia, Moscow 2019.] 12. ♗g5 ♗e7 13. ♕d3 h6 14. ♗xf6 ♗xf6 15. ♖ad1±

**11. b4 ♗b6**

11... ♗e7 12. ♕d3! White is doing well. A sample line follows: 12... ♗e6 13. ♗b2 ♕d7 14. ♖ad1 ♖fe8 15. ♘e2±

**12. ♘a4!**

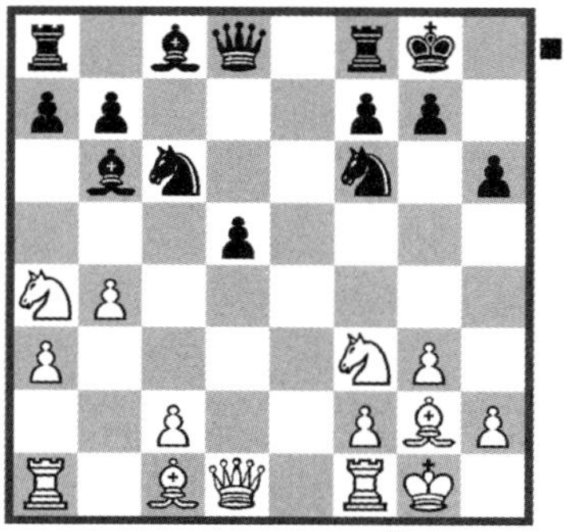

Position after: 12. ♘a4!

**12... ♗c7**

12... ♗f5 13. ♗b2 ♖e8 14. ♘xb6 axb6 15. ♖e1±

**13. ♗b2 ♗g4 14. ♖e1 ♘e4? 15. c4!+–**

White was already winning in Zvjaginsev – Kobalia, Khanty – Mansiysk 2013, while the Black alternatives on move 14 wouldn't have changed the fact that White was already doing very well there.

## e) 3...d5 4.exd5 exd5 5.d4 ♘c6

**1. e4 c5 2. ♘f3 e6 3. g3 d5 4. exd5 exd5 5. d4 ♘c6**

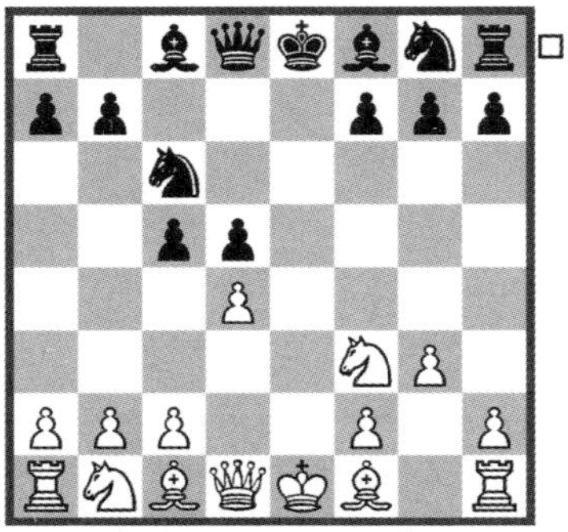

Position after: 5... ♘c6

**6. ♗g2 ♗g4**

Attempting to force us to capture on c5, in which case Black's dark-squared bishop can recapture the c5-pawn in one move, thereby avoiding any waste of tempo.

6... cxd4 7. 0-0! [7. ♘xd4 would transpose to 5...cxd4, but we have an even better option.] 7... ♗c5 The critical line to check, but it's easy to see that we regain the pawn with an advantage. [7... ♗g4 8. ♖e1+ transposes to 6...♗g4.; 7... ♘f6 8. ♘xd4 ♗e7 9. ♘c3 0-0 10. h3±] 8. ♘bd2 ♗b6 9. ♖e1+ ♘ge7 10. ♘b3 ♗g4 [10... 0-0 11. ♘fxd4±] 11. ♕d3! 0-0 12. ♘bxd4±

**7. 0-0!**

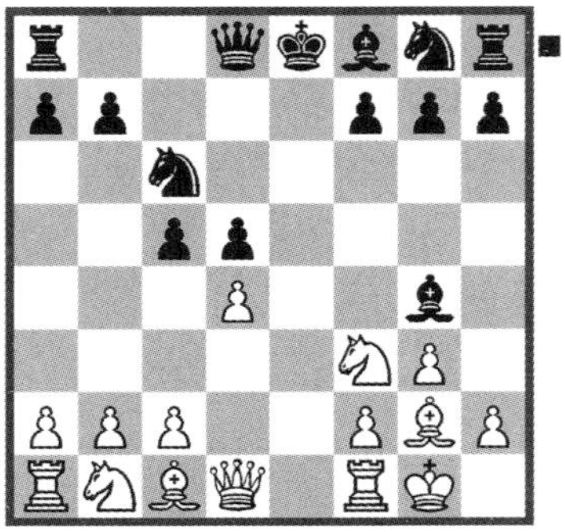

Position after: 7. 0-0!

**7... cxd4**

**A)** 7... ♘xd4 8. ♕e1+ ♗e7 [8... ♘e6?! 9. ♘e5 ♗f5 10. c4±; 8... ♘e7 9. ♘xd4 cxd4 10. ♘d2 ♗e6 11. ♘f3 ♘f5 12. ♗g5! ♗e7 13. ♗xe7 ♕xe7 14. ♕e5±] 9. ♘xd4 cxd4 10. ♕e5! A typical idea in this line to recapture the pawn immediately. 10... ♘f6 11. ♕xd4 0-0 12. ♘c3±

**B)** 7... ♘f6 8. ♖e1+ ♗e7 9. dxc5 0-0 10. h3 ♗h5 [Black can only recapture the pawn by giving up their bishop pair: 10... ♗xf3 11. ♕xf3 ♗xc5 12. ♘c3 d4 13. ♘e2±] 11. g4 ♗g6 12. ♗e3 ♘e4 13. ♘c3 ♘xc3 14. bxc3 ♗e4 15. ♘d4±

**8. ♘bd2!**

*(see diagram next page)*

8. ♕d3 also looks good but there's no point learning two separate lines here.

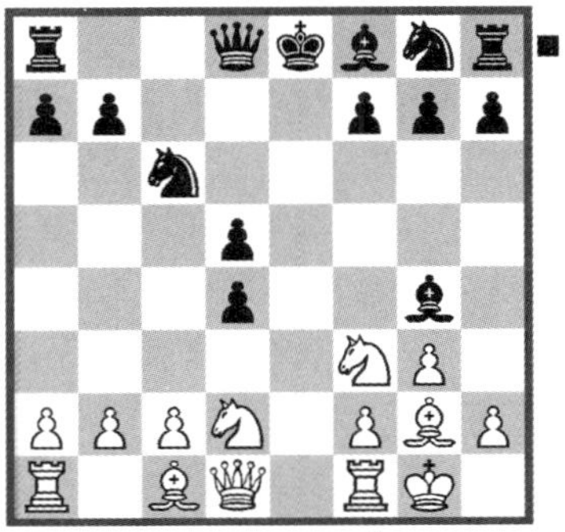

Position after: 8. ♘bd2!

**8... ♗e7!?**

Planning to protect the d4-pawn with ...♗f6 followed by ...♘ge7. However Black's set up feels a bit weird to me.

**A)** 8... ♘f6 9. ♘b3

**A1)** 9... ♗xf3?! It doesn't make sense for Black to try and keep the d4-pawn. 10. ♗xf3 ♕b6 11. a4!

Position after: 11. a4!

**A1.1)** 11... a5?! 12. ♕e2+ ♗e7 13. ♕b5 ♕xb5 14. axb5 ♘e5 15. ♗g2±

**A1.2)** 11... a6 12. a5 ♕a7 13. ♖a4!±

**A1.3)** 11... ♗b4?! 12. a5! ♕c7 [12... ♗xa5?? 13. ♘xa5 ♘xa5 14. ♕e1++–; 12... ♘xa5?? 13. ♘xa5 ♗xa5 14. c3+–] 13. ♘xd4±

**A1.4)** 11... ♗e7 12. a5 ♕b4 13. ♗d2 ♕d6 14. a6 b6 15. ♗f4+–

**A2)** 9... ♗e7 10. ♘bxd4 0-0 11. ♗e3± With a comfortable position.

**B)** 8... ♕b6?! 9. ♖e1+ ♗e7 10. h3 ♗xf3 [10... ♗h5?! 11. c4! dxc3 12. bxc3+– Followed by some combination of ♗a3, ♖b1, c3-c4, and Black can't survive.] 11. ♘xf3 ♘f6 12. ♘e5!± Black will struggle to castle. In the meantime, we can either advance the a-pawn, or keep developing naturally with something like ♗f4.

**C)** 8... ♗c5 The most logical move, but it doesn't prevent White from getting a comfortable game. 9. ♘b3

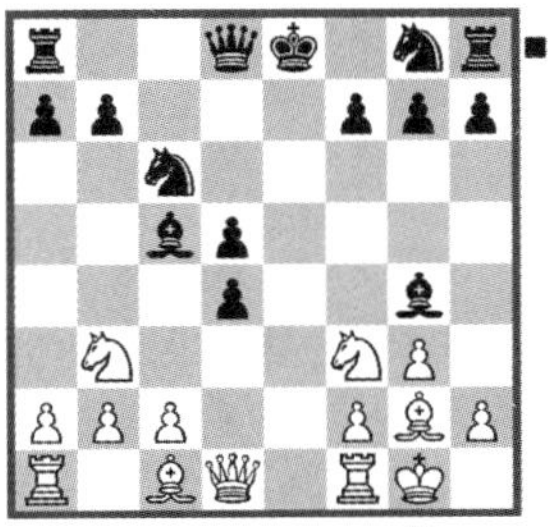

Position after: 9. ♘b3

9... ♗b6 [9... b6!? is a weird engine suggestion, and after 10. h3 ♗xf3 11. ♕xf3 ♘ge7 12. c4! White is doing great. For example: 12... dxc4 13. ♘xc5 bxc5 14. ♕g4 0-0 15. ♗h6± Winning an exchange.] 10. ♖e1+N ♘ge7 11. ♕d3 0-0 [11... ♗xf3 12. ♕xf3 0-0 13. ♗d2± White has great compensation for the sacrificed pawn.] 12. ♘fxd4± Followed by either a2-a4 or the simple c2-c3 and ♗e3.

**9. ♘b3 ♗f6 10. ♕d3!**

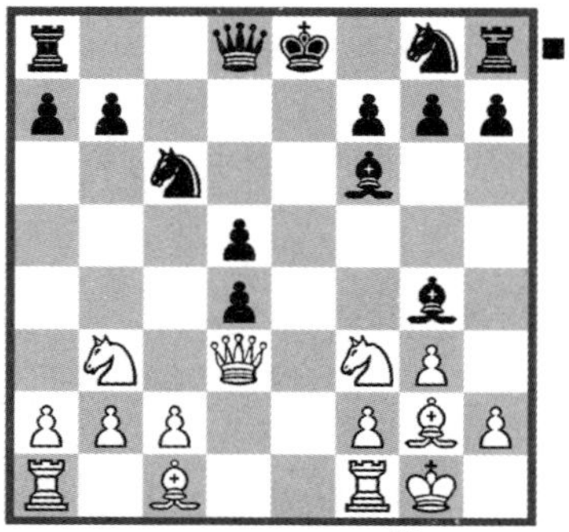

Position after: 10. ♕d3!

**10... ♗xf3**

**A)** 10... ♘ge7 11. ♘bxd4 0-0 12. h3 ♗h5 13. ♗e3±

**B)** 10... ♕b6 11. ♖e1+ ♘ge7 12. ♗g5! ♗xg5 13. ♘xg5

**B1)** 13... h6 14. ♘f3 ♗xf3 15. ♗xf3 0-0 16. ♖ad1± Threatening ♘xd4. If Black defends the e7-knight with one of their rooks, we can continue slowly with something like ♖e2. Eventually one of the d-pawns will fall, after which Black is still struggling for equality.

**B2)** 13... ♖d8 14. h4!?

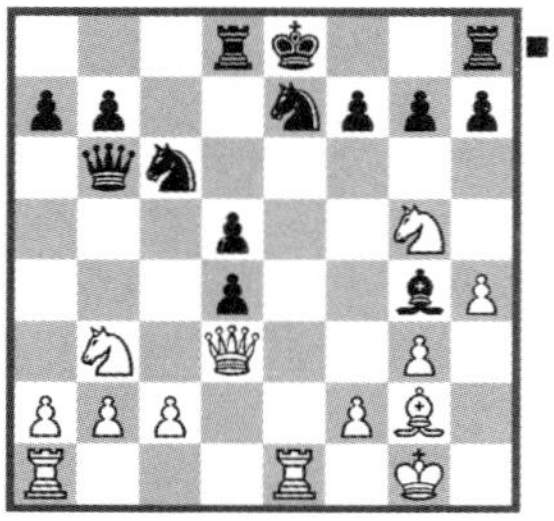

Position after: 14. h4!?

Slightly improving our position and provoking ...h7-h6 before dropping our knight back to f3. 14... h6 15. ♘f3 ♗xf3 16. ♗xf3 0-0 17. ♖e2± The same principle applies: we continue improving slowly, and Black will lose the d4-pawn at some point.

**11. ♕xf3 ♘ge7 12. ♘c5!**

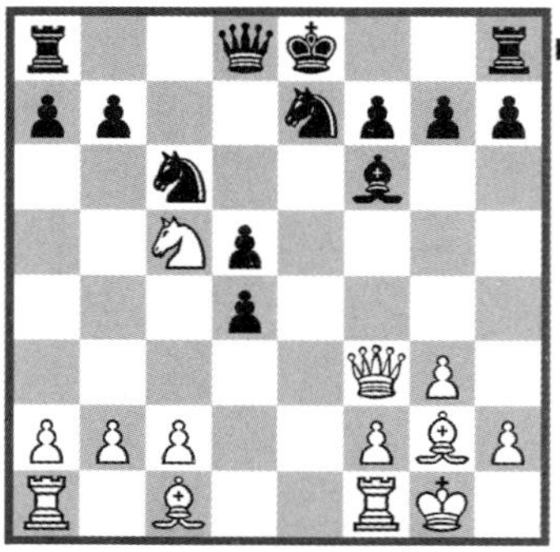

Position after: 12. ♘c5!

Capturing the d4-pawn seems a bit unrealistic, so we switch plans and focus on improving our pieces instead. The knight is heading back to d3.

**12... ♕b6 13. ♘d3 ♘b4**

13... 0-0 14. ♗d2 ♘e5 15. ♘xe5 ♗xe5 16. ♖fe1 ♘c6 17. b4±

**14. ♗d2! ♘xd3 15. cxd3**

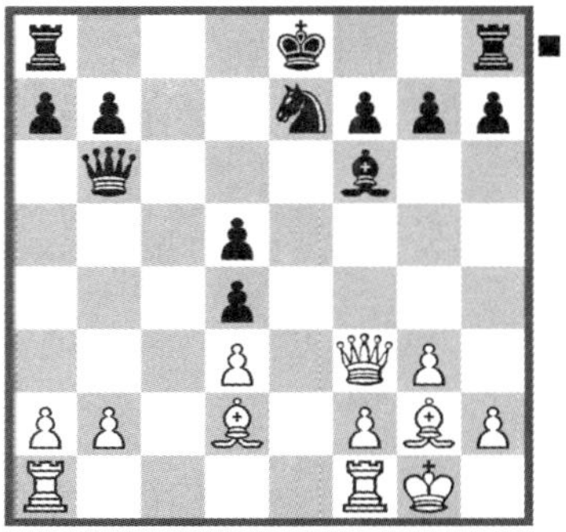

Position after: 15. cxd3

**15... ♕xb2**

15... 0-0 16. b4±

**16. ♕e2 0-0 17. ♖fb1 ♕c2 18. ♖xb7±** Black's poor minor pieces make this position practically difficult for them.

## f) 3...♘c6 4.♗g2 ♘f6 5.♘c3 d5 6.exd5 exd5 7.d4 ♗g4 8.0-0 & 8.h3 cxd4 9.hxg4

**1. e4 c5 2. ♘f3 e6 3. g3 ♘c6 4. ♗g2 ♘f6 5. ♘c3!?**

Instead 5.♕e2 is the most common move, but I prefer waiting to see Black's set up before deciding where to place my queen.

**5... d5**

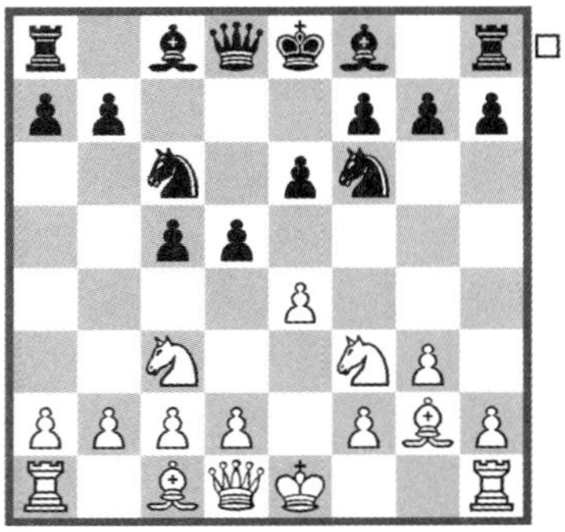

Position after: 5... d5

**6. exd5 exd5**

6... ♘xd5 7. 0-0 Preparing to capture on d5 and push d2-d4. 7... ♗e7 [7... ♘xc3 8. dxc3! Transitioning into an excellent queenless middlegame position. 8... ♕xd1 9. ♖xd1 f6 10. ♗e3 e5 11. ♘d2 ♗g4 12. ♖e1±; 7... ♘f6

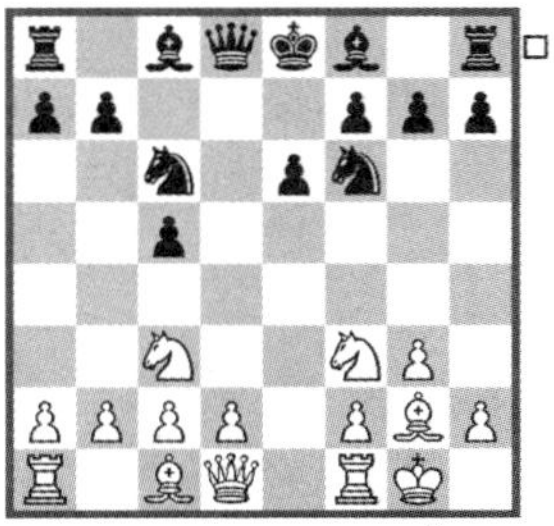

Position after: 7... ♘f6

8. d3 ♗e7 9. ♘d2 0-0 10. ♘c4± Followed by ♗d2, a2-a4, and ♖e1. Black's queenside will start to come under pressure.] **8. ♘xd5 exd5** [8... ♕xd5 This is risky for Black – the queen will suddenly become a big target. 9. d4! ♘xd4

10. ♘xd4 ♕xd4 11. ♕e2 0-0 12. ♖d1 ♕b4 13. ♗f4! ♕xb2 14. ♖ab1 ♕a3 15. ♗e5!↑ White is completely dominating. Some ideas now include ♗e4 and h2-h4.] 9. d4

Position after: 9. d4

Now Black most likely has no better choice than to accept the fact that they will have to defend a slightly worse position with an isolated pawn. 9... c4 There are a few ways to play here, but Stockfish comes up with a really wack idea which I want to show: 10. ♘e1!? 0-0 11. ♗f3 ♗e6 12. ♘g2± Followed by c2-c3 and ♗f4. The knight on g2 is well placed to either support the bishop on f4 or jump to e3.

**7. d4**

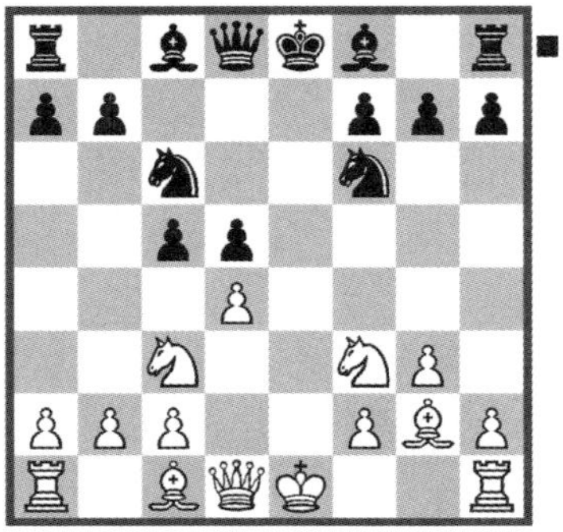

Position after: 7. d4

**7... ♗g4**

The most critical way of playing.

7... cxd4 8. ♘xd4 ♗g4 transposes to the 2nd subchapter after 7.♘c3!?.

**8. h3!**

8. 0-0!? ♘xd4

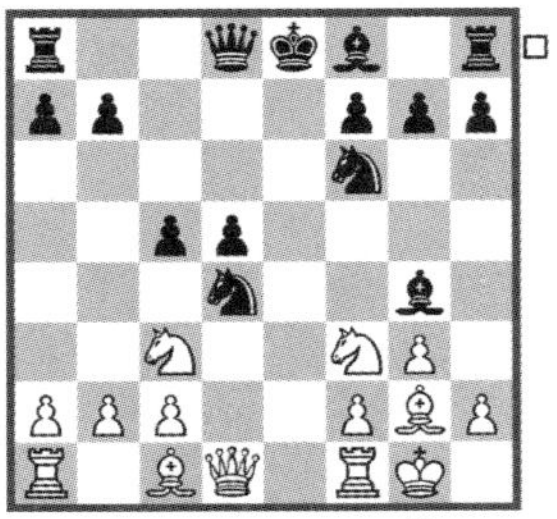

Position after: 8... ♘xd4

[8... cxd4 will likely lead to the following forcing line: 9. ♖e1+ ♗e7 10. ♘b5 0-0 11. ♘bxd4 ♗c5 12. ♗e3 ♕b6 13. ♘xc6! bxc6 14. ♗xc5 ♕xc5 15. ♕d4 ♕xd4 16. ♘xd4 ♗d7 17. c4± Chadaev – Novikov, Dagomys 2010.] 9. ♕e1+

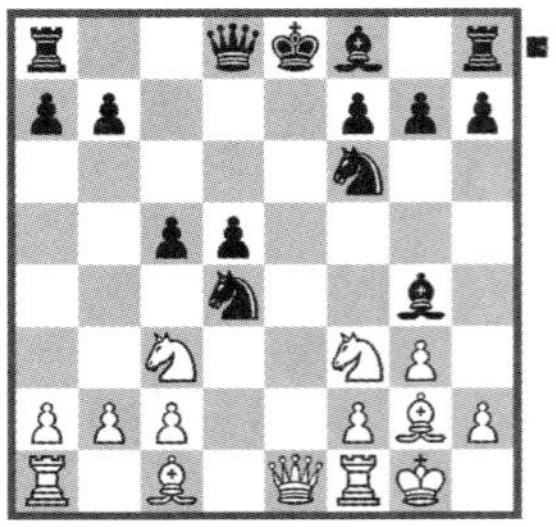

Position after: 9. ♕e1+

**A)** 9... ♗e6 10. ♘xd4 cxd4 11. ♘e2

**A1)** 11... ♗c5 12. b4! ♗b6 13. a4 a5 14. ♘f4 ♕d7 The most accurate defence as Black also eyeballs the a4-pawn. [14... ♕c8?! 15. bxa5 ♗xa5 16. ♗d2 ♗xd2 17. ♕xd2 0-0 18. ♕xd4±] 15. ♗h3 0-0 16. ♘xe6 ♖fe8 17. ♘f4 ♖xe1 18. ♗xd7

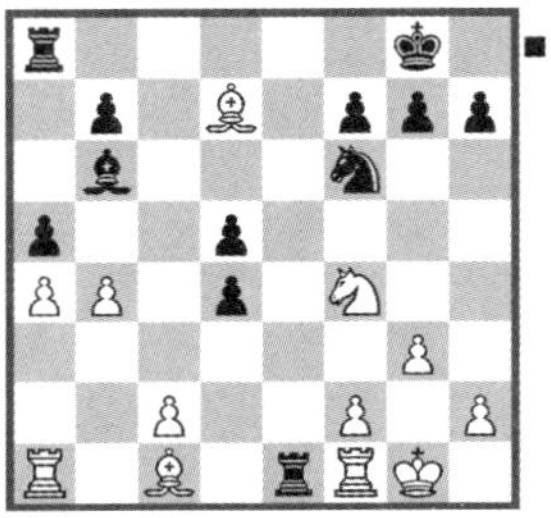

Position after: 18. ♗xd7

18... ♖xf1+ 19. ♔xf1 ♘xd7 20. ♖b1 White is still pressing here, despite the engine's reluctance to claim an advantage.

**A2)** 11... ♕b6 12. ♗f4! ♗b4 [12... ♗c5?! 13. ♗e5 0-0 14. ♗xf6 gxf6 15. ♘f4±] 13. ♕d1 ♗c5 14. ♗e5 ♗g4 15. ♗xd4±

**B)** 9... ♘e6?! This defensive retreat runs into immediate trouble. 10. ♘e5 ♗f5 11. ♗g5!

**B1)** 11... d4 12. ♗xb7 ♗e7 [12... dxc3 13. ♗c6+ ♔e7 14. ♖d1+–] 13. ♘c6 ♕d7 14. ♘xe7+– Wittmann – Heinatz, Wuerttemberg 2009.

**B2)** 11... ♗e7 12. ♗xf6 ♗xf6 13. ♘xd5 0-0 14. c3±

**C)** 9... ♗e7! Black's best way to equalise. 10. ♘xd4 cxd4 11. ♘e2 ♗xe2! Leading to quite an easy equalising setup. [11... d3 also looks fine for Black: 12. cxd3 0-0 13. h3 ♗f5 14. ♕d1 ♗c5=; 11... ♕b6 is also completely viable – I was unable to find anything here either, but it's still playable for White after something like 12. a4!?.] 12. ♕xe2 0-0 13. ♕e5!

Position after: 13. ♕e5!

13... ♗c5 [13... ♖c8 14. ♕xd4 ♖xc2 15. ♕xa7 ♘g4 16. ♗e3 ♘xe3 17. ♕xe3 ♖xb2 18. ♖ad1=] 14. ♗g5 ♖e8 15. ♕f5 ♕d7 16. ♕xd7 ♘xd7 17. ♗xd5 ♖e5 18. ♗xb7 ♖b8 19. ♗c6 ♖xg5 20. ♗xd7=

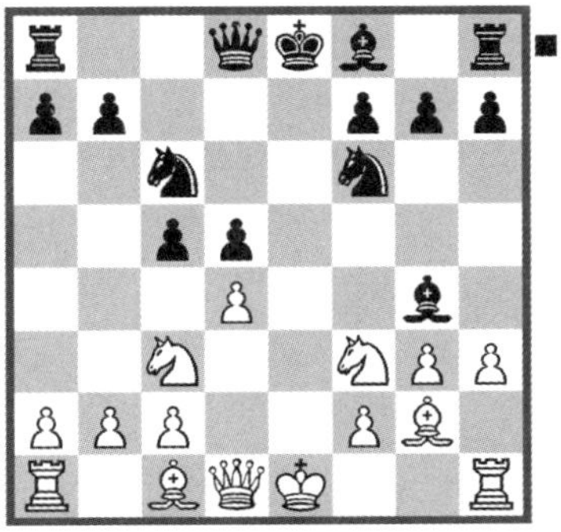

Position after: 8. h3!

**8... cxd4**

**A)** 8... ♕e7+!?N An interesting move which forces White to move the king. However since Black's queen is blocking the further development of their own pieces, it's still an advantageous situation for White. 9. ♔f1 [9. ♘e2? ♗xf3 10. ♗xf3 ♘xd4∓]

Position after: 9. ♔f1

**A1)** 9... ♗xf3 10. ♗xf3 ♘xd4 [10... cxd4 11. ♘b5 ♕d7 12. ♗f4 ♖c8 13. ♘xd4±] 11. ♘xd5 ♘xd5 12. ♗xd5 0-0-0 13. c4± ♖xd5?! 14. cxd5 ♕d7 15. ♗e3 ♕xd5 16. ♖g1±

**A2)** 9... ♗e6 10. ♗e3 c4 [10... cxd4 11. ♘xd4 ♕d7 12. ♔g1 ♗d6 13. ♕d2 0-0 14. ♔h2 With an edge for White. We can easily improve the positioning of our pieces, while the weakness of the isolated pawn on d5 isn't disappearing any time soon.] 11. ♘e5± White will manually castle with ♔g1-h2. Other ideas include ♘e2-f4 or even a possible ♘g4 at some point.

**B)** 8... ♗xf3?! By far the most popular choice, but objectively a poor one. 9. ♕xf3

Position after: 9. ♕xf3

**B1)** 9... cxd4 leads almost by force to an endgame where White retains excellent winning chances. 10. ♘xd5 ♘xd5 11. ♕xd5 ♗b4+ 12. ♗d2

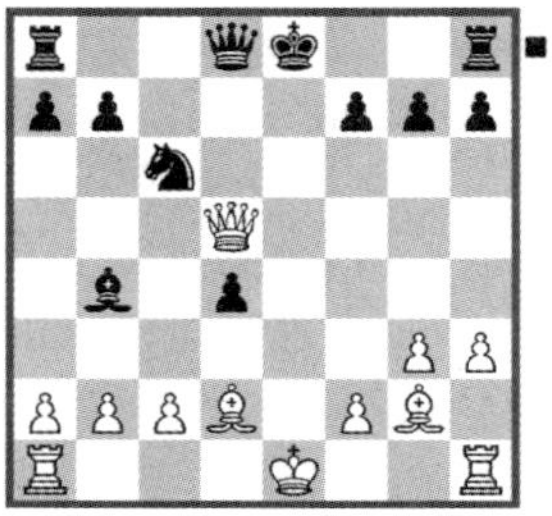
Position after: 12. ♗d2

12... ♕e7+ [12... ♕b6 13. ♕e4+! ♗e7 14. 0-0 0-0 15. ♖ab1 ♖ac8 16. b4!± I was already dominating in Haria – Arvola, Terme Catez 2021.] 13. ♕e4 ♕xe4+ 14. ♗xe4 ♗xd2+ 15. ♔xd2 0-0-0 16. ♖he1± White won a nice game in Lu – Cuhendi, Tashkent 2016.

**B2)** 9... ♕e7+N 10. ♔f1 0-0-0 11. dxc5! ♕xc5 12. ♗g5 d4 13. ♗xf6 gxf6 14. ♘d5±

**B3)** 9... ♘xd4 10. ♕d3 ♗e7 [10... ♕e7+?! 11. ♗e3 0-0-0 12. 0-0-0+–] 11. 0-0 0-0

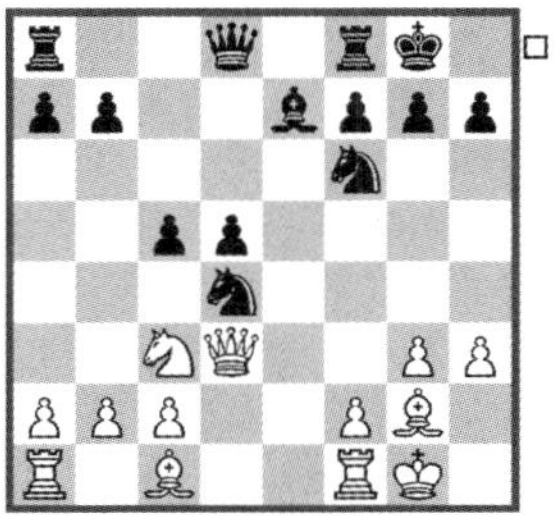

Position after: 11... 0-0

12. ♗g5 The simplest choice – White regains the sacrificed pawn with some interest. 12... ♘c6 13. ♗xf6 ♗xf6 14. ♘xd5± Gu – Munguntuul, Riadh 2017.

**C)** 8... ♗h5?!N 9. g4 ♗g6 10. 0-0 cxd4 11. ♘xd4 ♗e7 12. ♗e3±

**9. hxg4!?**

9. ♘xd5!? is analysed in the next subchapter.

**9... dxc3**

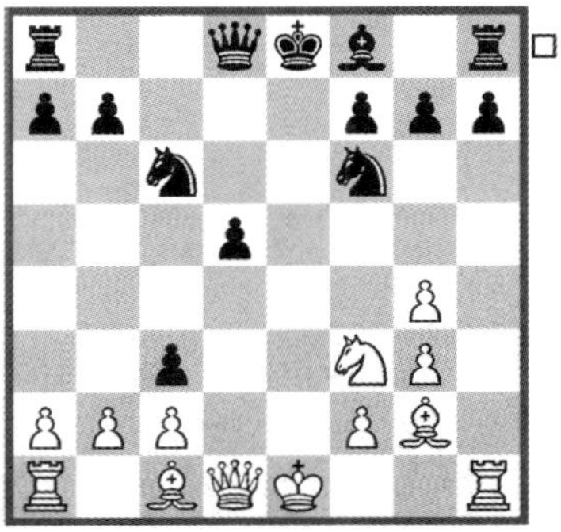

Position after: 9... dxc3

**10. bxc3**

10. ♘d4 ♗c5⇆

**10... ♗c5!**

Black needs to play actively and prioritise king safety in order to secure equality.

**A)** 10... ♘xg4 11. 0-0! The knight is poorly placed on g4. We now have several ideas: ♖b1, c3-c4, and ♘d4/♘h4. 11... ♗e7 [11... ♗c5 12. ♘d4 ♘f6 13. ♖e1+ ♔f8 14. ♖b1± is just dangerous for Black.] 12. ♖b1 0-0 13. ♖xb7±

**B)** 10... ♕a5?! 11. 0-0±

**C)** 10... ♗e7 11. ♘d2! With the idea of pushing g4-g5. 11... ♕a5 12. 0-0 h6 13. c4! dxc4 14. ♖b1 ♕a6 15. ♕e2 ♖c8 16. ♖d1↑

**11. ♘d4! ♘e4!**

11... 0-0?! 12. g5 ♘e4 13. ♕h5 h6 14. ♗xe4 ♖e8 15. ♗e3 ♖xe4 16. ♔f1→

**12. ♗xe4**

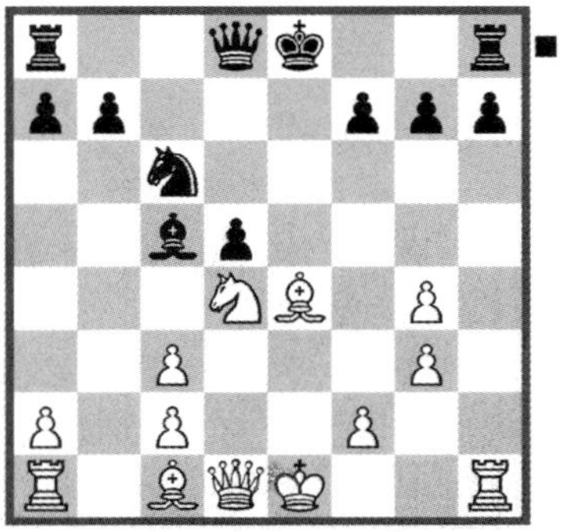

Position after: 12. ♗xe4

**12... ♗xd4!**

**A)** 12... dxe4 leads to a slightly worse ending for Black. 13. ♘xc6 bxc6 14. ♕xd8+ ♖xd8 15. ♖h5! ♖d5 16. ♖b1⩲

**B)** 12... ♕e7?! Attempting to keep the queens on will harm Black. 13. 0-0 dxe4 14. ♘f5 ♕e5 15. ♖b1 b6 16. ♗f4 ♕f6 17. ♖e1 0-0 18. ♖xe4 ♕xc3 19. ♗d2 ♕f6 20. ♕f3±

**13. cxd4 dxe4 14. ♗e3 0-0 15. ♔f1∞**

The computer suggests an evaluation of 0.00, but all hope is not lost. White still has several interesting plans, for example ♖b1-b5-h5, or g4-g5 and ♕h5. It's easy to see Black getting outplayed here.

## g) 3...♘c6 4.♗g2 ♘f6 5.♘c3 d5 6.exd5 exd5 7.d4 ♗g4 8.h3 cxd4 9.♘xd5

**1. e4 c5 2. ♘f3 e6 3. g3 ♘c6 4. ♗g2 ♘f6 5. ♘c3!? d5 6. exd5 exd5 7. d4 ♗g4 8. h3!? cxd4! 9. ♘xd5!?**

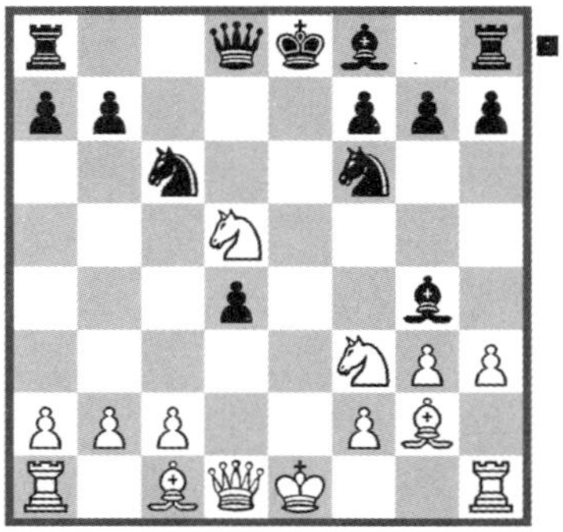

Position after: 9. ♘xd5!?

**9... ♕xd5**

9... ♗e6 I think White keeps a small edge here. 10. ♘f4!? [10. ♘xf6+ ♕xf6 11. 0-0 h6 12. ♗f4 ♖d8 13. ♘e1⩲] 10... ♗c4 11. ♘d3⩲

**10. hxg4 ♕c4!**

The only way for Black to equalise.

**A)** 10... ♘xg4 11. 0-0 Threatening to capture on d4.

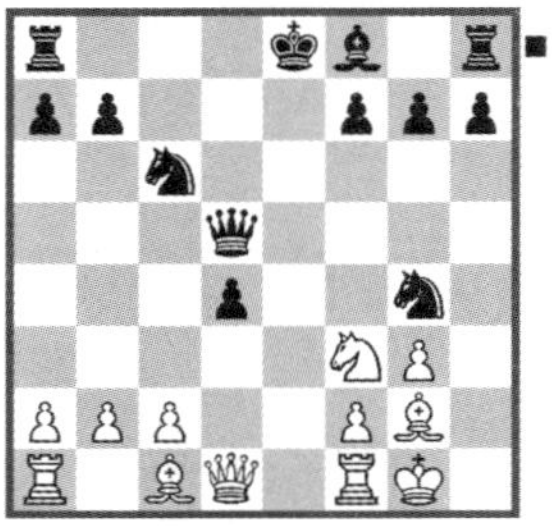

Position after: 11. 0-0

**A1)** 11... ♕h5? 12. ♖e1+ ♗e7 13. ♘h4! ♔f8 [13... 0-0 14. ♗f3 f5 15. ♗xc6 ♗xh4 16. ♗d5+ ♔h8 17. gxh4 ♕xh4 18. ♕f3+–] 14. ♗f3 f5 15. ♕d3 ♗xh4 16. gxh4± Followed by ♗f4.

**A2)** 11... ♕d7 The only move. 12. c3!

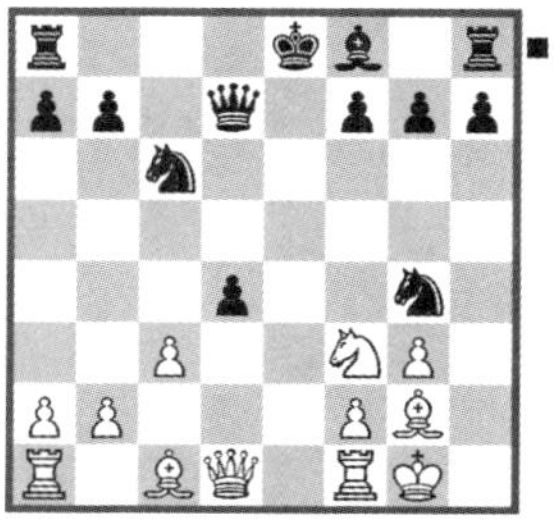

Position after: 12. c3!

12... d3 [12... dxc3 13. ♕xd7+ ♔xd7 14. bxc3± Despite being a pawn down, White is dominating with ♖b1 and ♗f4 coming next.] 13. ♘d4! ♘xd4 14. cxd4 ♗e7 [14... ♕xd4? 15. ♗xb7+–] 15. ♕xd3 0-0 16. ♗f4± White has a nice edge with the bishop pair and passed d-pawn.

**B)** 10... ♕e6+ weakens Black's king more than our own. 11. ♔f1 ♘xg4

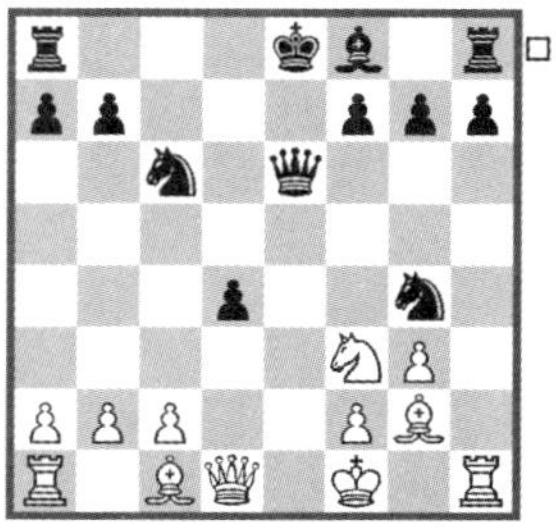

Position after: 11... ♘xg4

12. ♗f4!± Followed by ♕d3 and ♖e1.

**C)** 10... ♕e4+? 11. ♔f1 ♕xg4 12. ♖h4 ♕d7 13. ♘xd4+–

**D)** 10... ♗b4+ 11. ♔f1 ♕c4+ [11... ♘xg4 12. ♕d3!± With multiple threats in mind. Black is unlikely to survive.] 12. ♔g1 ♘xg4

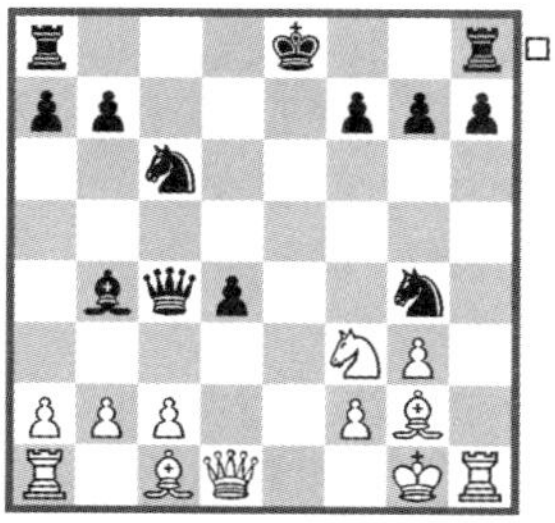

Position after: 12... ♘xg4

13. ♗f4 Castling is still too dangerous for Black due to ♘g5 coming. [13. b3 ♕c5 14. ♘xd4!±] 13... ♖d8 14. ♖h5! g6 15. ♗f1 ♕e6 16. ♘g5 ♕c8 17. ♖xh7 ♖xh7 18. ♘xh7±

**11. b3!?**

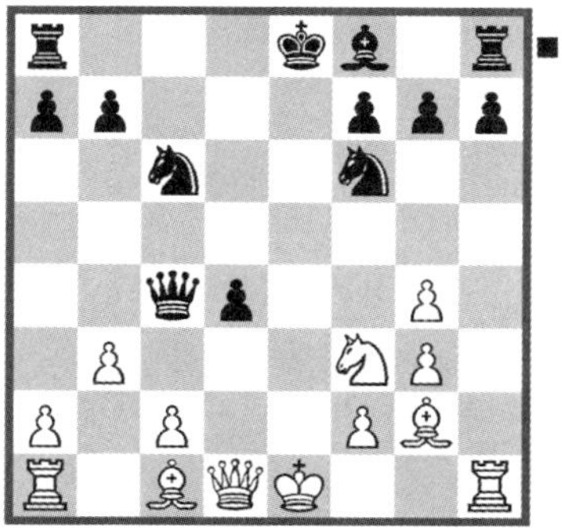

Position after: 11. b3!?

I think this is the trickiest way to play for an edge.

**11... ♗b4+!**

11... ♕a6?! 12. ♕e2+ ♕xe2+ 13. ♔xe2 ♘xg4 14. ♗b2

**A)** 14... 0-0-0 15. ♖ad1 h5! [15... ♗c5 16. ♖h5±] 16. ♘xd4 ♗a3! Let's be honest, who would find

Black's previous two moves? 17. ♗xa3 ♘xd4+ 18. ♔f1± White still has nice practical chances with the bishop pair.

**B)** 14... ♗c5

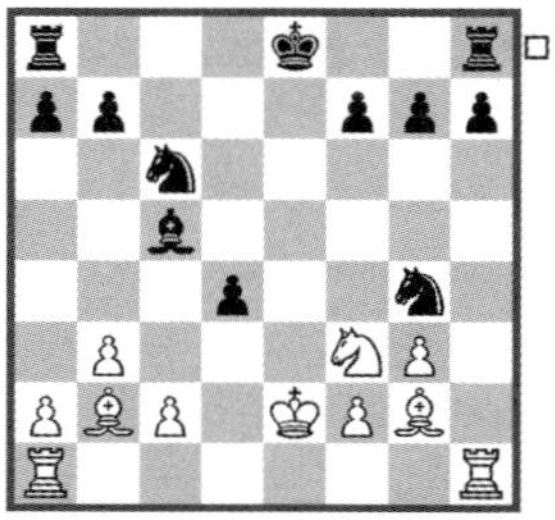

Position after: 14... ♗c5

**B1)** 15. ♖ad1 0-0! [15... d3+ 16. cxd3 ♘xf2 17. ♖c1±] 16. ♘xd4 ♖fe8+ 17. ♔f1 ♘xd4 18. ♗xd4 ♖ad8 19. c3=

**B2)** 15. ♖h5!? ♗b6 16. ♖d1!?

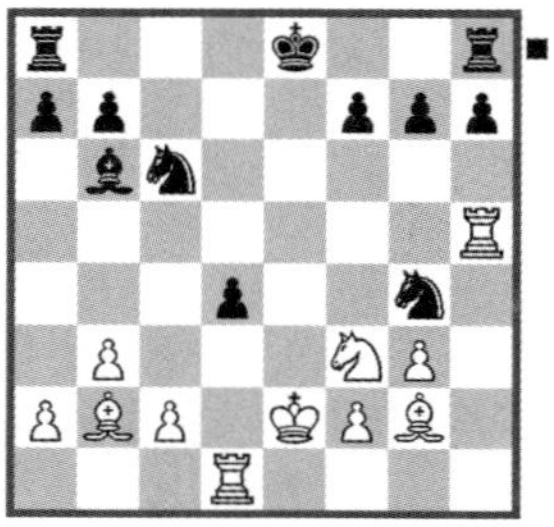

Position after: 16. ♖d1!?

[16. ♖g5 h5∞] 16... d3+ [16... 0-0 17. ♘xd4 ♖fe8+ 18. ♔f1 ♖ad8 19. ♖d5 ♖xd5 20. ♗xd5 ♖d8 21. c4±] 17. cxd3 ♘xf2 18. ♖f1 ♘g4 19. ♘h4 0-0 20. ♗e4→

**12. ♗d2**

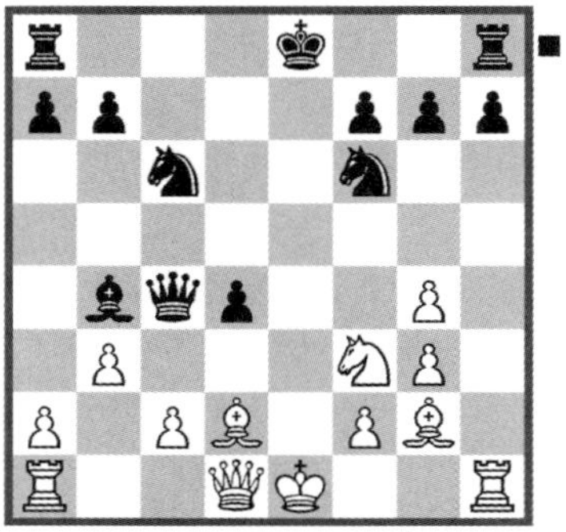

Position after: 12. ♗d2

**12... ♕a6**

12... ♗xd2+ 13. ♕xd2 ♕e6+ 14. ♔f1 0-0 15. g5 ♘e4 16. ♕d3 ♘b4 17. ♘xd4!±

**13. ♗xb4! ♘xb4**

13... 0-0-0 is an imaginative attempt but doesn't quite work: 14. ♕d3 ♕xd3 15. cxd3 ♘xb4 16. g5! ♘g4 [16... ♘xd3+ 17. ♔d2 ♘e4+ 18. ♔xd3 ♘xf2+ 19. ♔d2 ♘xh1 20. ♖xh1±] 17. 0-0!± Followed by ♖fd1.

**14. ♕e2+ ♕xe2+ 15. ♔xe2**

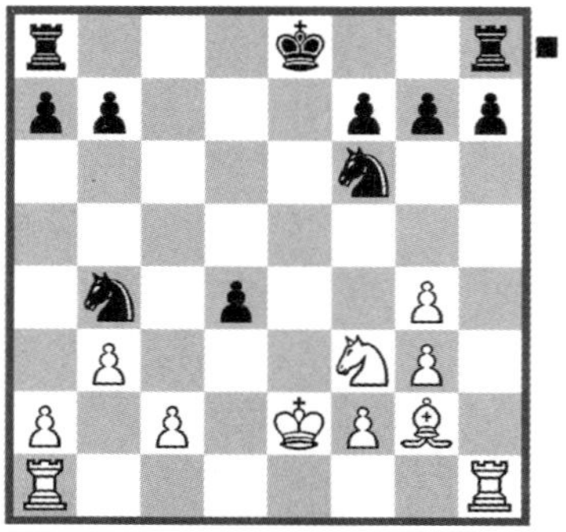

Position after: 15. ♔xe2

Setting another small trap.

**15... 0-0-0!**

15... ♘xc2?! 16. g5! ♘d5 [16... ♘e4 17. ♖ac1 ♖d8 18. ♔d3 ♘xf2+ 19. ♔xc2 ♘xh1 20. ♖e1+! ♔d7 21. ♖xh1±] 17. ♖ac1 d3+ [17... ♘db4 18. ♘e5±] 18. ♔d2!± Followed by ♖h4 and ♗f1. Black's pieces are slightly tied up.

**16. ♖hd1**

The engine gives an evaluation of 0.00 in multiple lines, but I don't think it's completely simple for Black. Note that a few of my '+/=' assessments aren't objective ones, but rather that White is the only one playing for anything.

**16... d3+**

Perhaps safest for Black.

**A)** 16... ♘c6 17. g5 ♘e4 18. ♔f1 h6 19. gxh6 ♖xh6 20. ♖e1 f5 21. ♘h4±

**B)** 16... ♖he8+ 17. ♔f1 ♔b8 [17... ♘xc2?! 18. ♖ac1 d3 19. ♘e1 ♔b8 20. ♘xd3 ♘d4 21. g5 ♘g4 22. ♗h3 f5 23. gxf6 ♘xf6

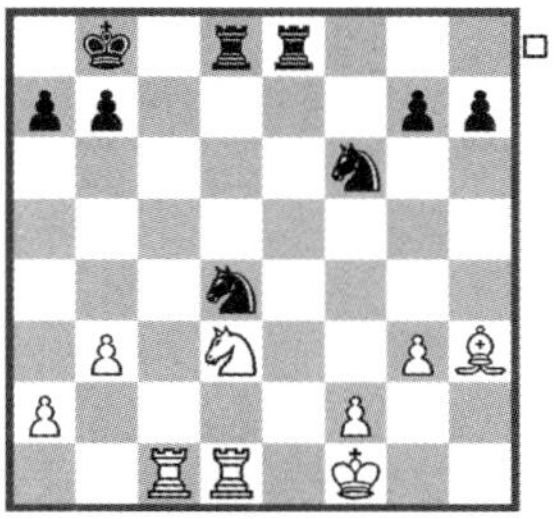

Position after: 23... ♘xf6

24. ♘c5±] 18. ♘xd4 ♖xd4 19. ♖xd4 ♘xc2 20. ♖ad1 ♘xd4 21. g5!? ♖d8! 22. gxf6 gxf6 23. ♖e1=

**17. cxd3 ♖he8+ 18. ♔f1 ♘xd3 19. ♘e1**

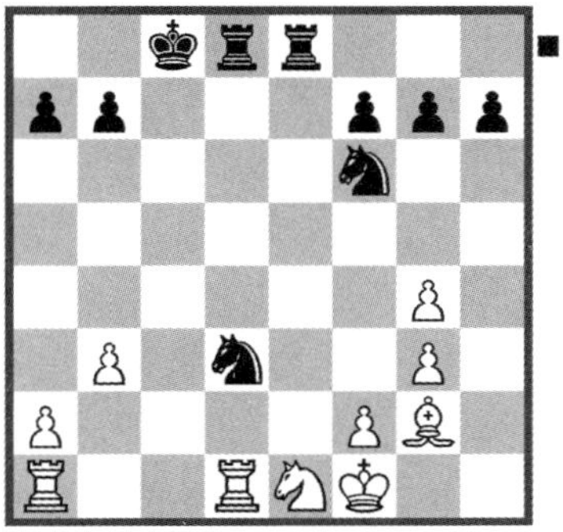

Position after: 19. ♘e1

**19... ♘xe1 20. ♖ac1+ ♔b8 21. ♖xd8+ ♖xd8 22. ♖xe1 h6 23. ♖e7 ♖d7 24. ♖xd7 ♘xd7 25. f4±**

Black should hold this with reasonable play.

## h) 3...♘c6 4.♗g2 ♘f6 5.♘c3 d6

**1. e4 c5 2. ♘f3 e6 3. g3 ♘c6 4. ♗g2 ♘f6 5. ♘c3 d6**

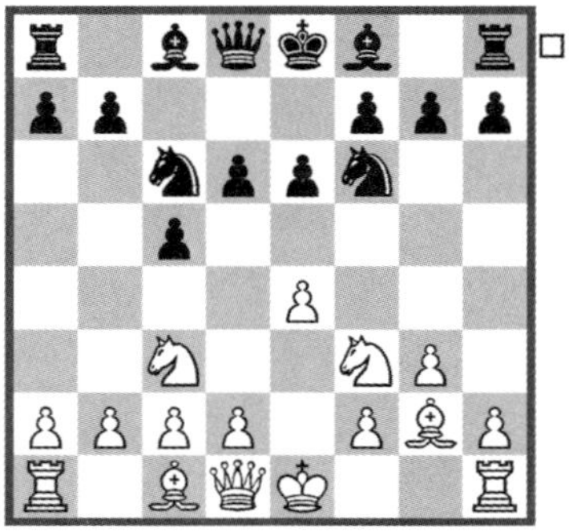

Position after: 5... d6

Black refrains from the theoretical lines after 5...d5. This is by no means inferior, and will likely transpose to a Taimanov if we push d2-d4.

**6. 0-0 ♗e7 7. d4**

I couldn't find anything better than transitioning to an Open Sicilian position.

**7... cxd4 8. ♘xd4 0-0 9. ♘ce2!?**

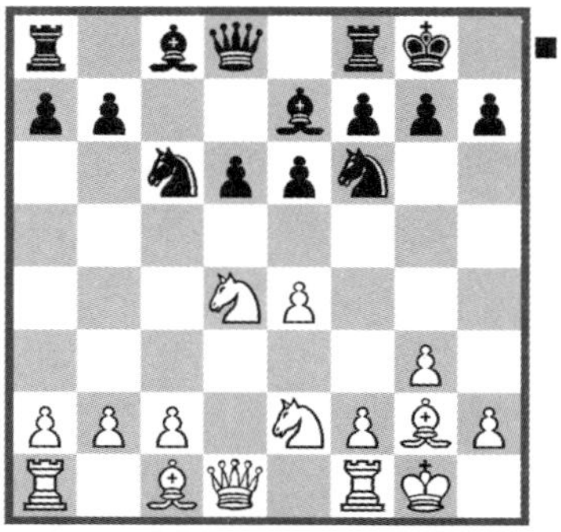

Position after: 9. ♘ce2!?

Boris Avrukh recommended this to me, and I think it's an interesting concept. The point is to push c2-c4 and gain further control of the centre. It may be difficult for Black to handle, especially if they're not familiar with the idea.

9. ♗e3 is the mainline.

**9... e5!?**

I think this is Black's best, but it's a very commital move to make.

**A)** 9... ♕c7 10. b3

**A1)** 10... ♗d7?! 11. ♘b5!

Position after: 11. ♘b5!

**A1.1)** 11... ♕b6 12. c4 d5 13. exd5 exd5 14. cxd5 ♕xb5 15. dxc6 bxc6 [15... ♗xc6 16. ♘d4±] 16. ♗b2±

**A1.2)** 11... ♕b8 12. ♗a3! ♘b4 [12... d5 13. exd5 exd5 14. ♗b2±] 13. ♗xb4 ♗xb5 14. c4 ♗c6 In Zagar – Sajn, Slovenia 2002, the best continuation for White was 15. ♕d3!±

followed by ♘d4 and ♖fd1, with a comfortable advantage.

**A2)** 10... a6 11. c4

Position after: 11. c4

**A2.1)** 11... ♗d7 12. ♗b2 ♖ac8 13. ♖c1 ♕b8 14. a4! This move should only be made when absolutely necessary. In this case I feel it is, as we don't really want Black to be able to break with ...b7-b5. 14... ♖fe8 [14... ♖fd8 15. ♖e1±] 15. ♕d3! Keeping an eye on the b5-square. [15. ♕d2 e5 16. ♘f5 b5⇆] 15... ♘b4 16. ♕d2 d5 17. cxd5 exd5 18. ♖xc8 ♖xc8 19. e5 ♘e4 20. ♗xe4 dxe4 21. e6! fxe6 22. ♘f5 exf5 23. ♕xd7↑ Winning the f-pawn and maintaining a strong advantage.

**A2.2)** 11... ♖d8 12. ♗b2 ♗d7 13. ♖c1 ♖ac8 14. h3 ♕b8 15. a4 transposes to 9...♗d7.

**A3)** 10... ♖d8 11. ♗b2 d5 12. exd5 ♘xd5 13. c4 ♘f6 14. ♕e1!±

**B)** 9... ♗d7 10. c4 a6

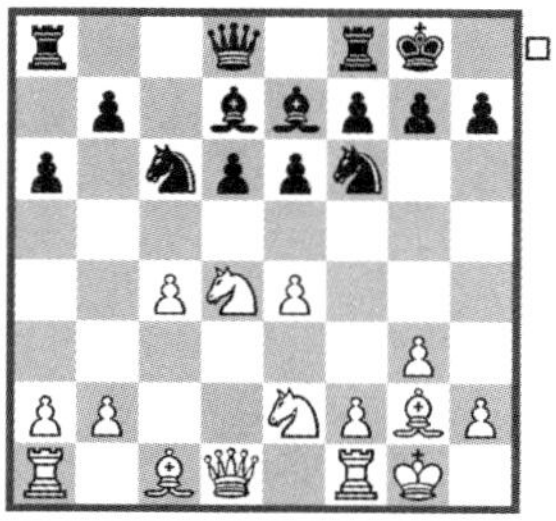
Position after: 10... a6

11. a4 [11. b3 is another option, but after 11... b5 12. cxb5 ♘xd4 13. ♘xd4 axb5 I think Black was doing fine in Felgaer – Nielsen, Lugo 2007.] 11... ♕c7 [11... ♖e8 12. b3±] 12. b3

Position after: 12. b3

**B1)** 12... ♖ad8 13. ♗b2 ♗c8 14. ♕d2±

**B2)** 12... ♖fd8 13. ♗e3N ♗e8 [13... ♘g4 14. ♗d2± Followed by h2-h3 and either ♗e3 or ♗c3.] 14. ♖c1 ♘g4 [14... d5? 15. exd5 exd5 16. c5±] 15. ♗d2 ♘ge5 16. ♗c3 ♘d7 17. h3 ♗f6 18. ♔h2 ♘xd4 19. ♗xd4±

**B3)** 12... ♘xd4 13. ♘xd4 ♗c6 14. ♕e2± Makarian – Praggnanandhaa, Lichess.org 2020.

**C)** 9... a6 10. c4 ♖b8 11. ♘xc6!?N

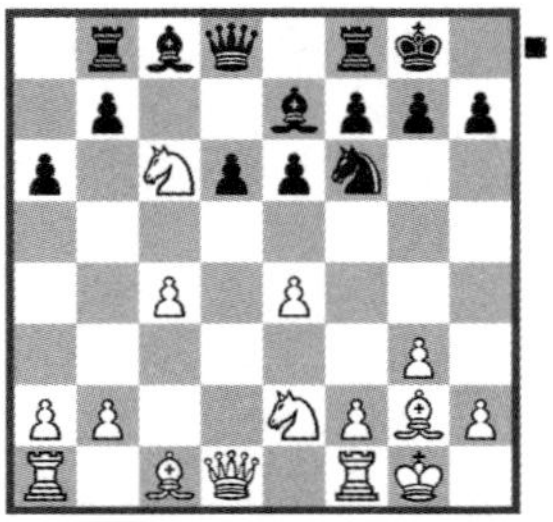

Position after: 11. ♘xc6!?N

11.b3 was also possible, but I think it's useful to see the various structures which benefit us. 11... bxc6 12. b3 c5 [12... ♗b7 13. ♗b2±] 13. ♗b2 ♗b7 14. ♕d3 ♕c7 15. ♖ad1 ♖bd8 16. h3 ♗c6 17. ♘c3± Followed by ♔h2, ♖d2, and f2-f4.

**D)** 9... d5?! This push is quite logical but fails to achieve equality. 10. exd5 ♘xd4 [10... ♘xd5? 11. ♘xc6 bxc6 12. c4 ♘b4 13. a3 ♘d3 Zaksaite – Budylina, Yerevan 1999. 14. ♗e3±] 11. ♘xd4 ♘xd5 [11... exd5 12. c3±] 12. c4 ♘f6 13. b3 a6 Van Riemsdijk – Bailey, Queenstown 2006. 14. ♘f3±

**10. ♘b5**

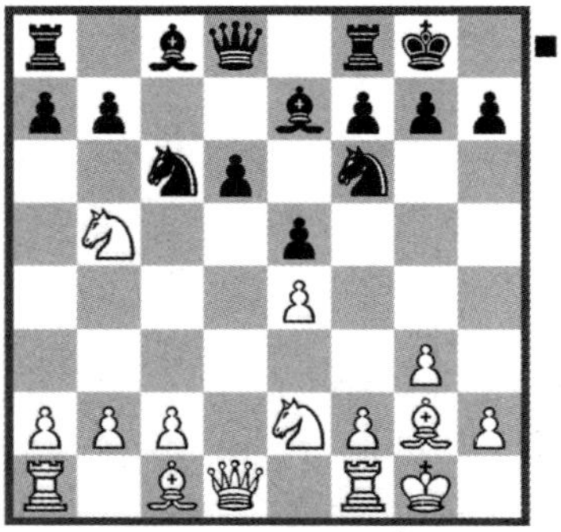

Position after: 10. ♘b5

10. ♘f5!? ♗xf5 11. exf5 ♕c8 12. c4 ♕xf5 13. ♘c3 ♕g6 14. ♗d2!⩱ I think White has good compensation here, although it may not be anything more than that.

**10... h6**

There are several options for White here. The main plan revolves around the d5-square and playing on the queenside with moves like a2-a4. However, we can also consider h2-h3, g3-g4 and ♘g3 under the right circumstances.

10... a6 11. ♘bc3 b5 12. b3!? Preparing ♘d5. [12. ♗g5 ♖b8 13. b3 h6 14. ♗xf6 ♗xf6 15. ♘d5 ♗e6=; 12. ♘d5 ♘xd5 13. exd5 ♘a5∞] 12... h6 [12... ♗e6 13. ♘d5±] 13. a4 ♖b8 14. axb5 axb5 15. ♘d5 ♘xd5 16. exd5 ♘b4 17. c3 ♘a6 18. b4 ♘c7 19. ♗e3 The game remains complex, although I prefer White. For example: 19... f5 20. f4 e4 21. g4 ♗b7 22. ♖a7! ♘xd5 23. ♗d4↑ Black's position feels slightly fragile here.

**11. h3**

11. c4 allows a quick break: 11... ♗e6 12. b3 a6 13. ♘bc3 b5! 14. cxb5 axb5 15. ♘xb5 d5∞

**11... a6 12. ♘bc3 b5 13. ♗e3 ♕c7**

This position was reached in Popovic – Ivic, Ruma 2017. Obviously there are many options for both sides, but a possible sample line follows:

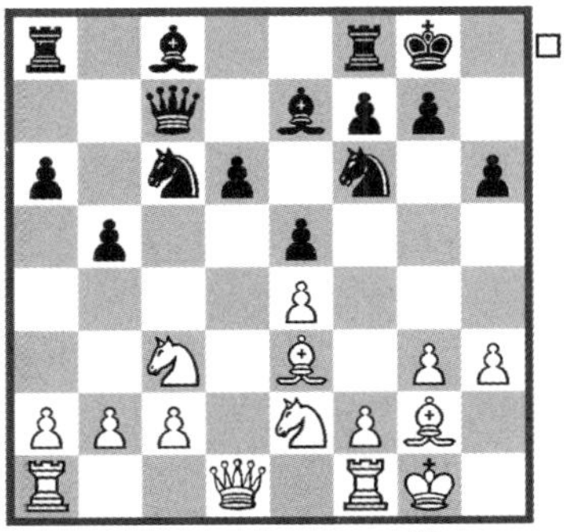

Position after: 13... ♕c7

**14. ♕d2N ♘a5 15. b3 ♗d7 16. a4 ♖fc8 17. ♖a2 ♘b7 18. axb5 axb5**

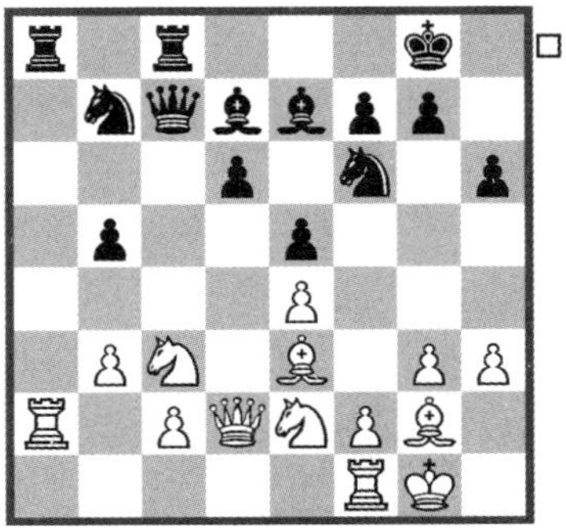

Position after: 18... axb5

**19. ♖fa1 ♖xa2 20. ♖xa2 ♘c5 21. g4±**

With ♘d5 or ♘g3 coming next.

## *Conclusion to Chapter 9*

3.g3 looks like a perfectly reasonable alternative to 3.c3. I think it's a really underrated option to stick our light-squared bishop on g2. The first two subchapters indicate that Black can be close to losing if they try to meet our fianchetto with quick queenside development.

On the other hand, the ...d7-d5 central break – as in subchapters c-g) – are either positionally risky or lead to murky waters after our cool 8.h3 idea. Black's most solid option is clearly to react cautiously as in subchapter h, but even here I have recommended the creative 9.♘ce2 which will stray away from any theoretical battlegrounds and offer good chances for an edge.

# 10

# 2...g6 3.c4 – Accelerated Dragon

1.e4 c5 2.♘f3 g6 3.c4

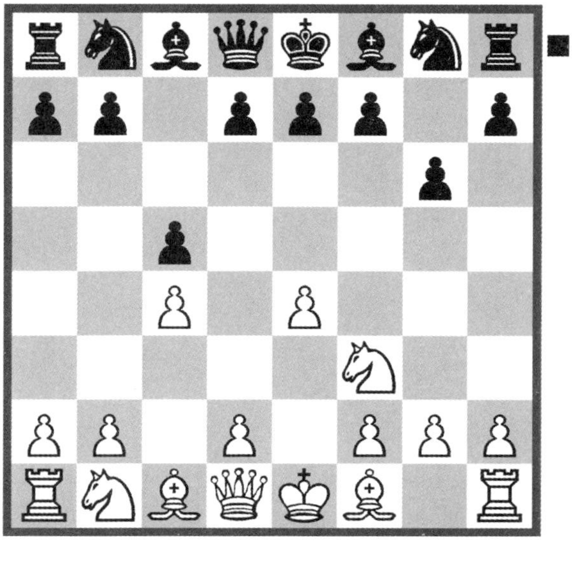

# Chapter Guide

## Chapter 10 – 2...g6 – Accelerated Dragon

1.e4 c5 2.♘f3 g6 3.c4

# a) 3...♗g7

**1. e4 c5 2. ♘f3 g6**

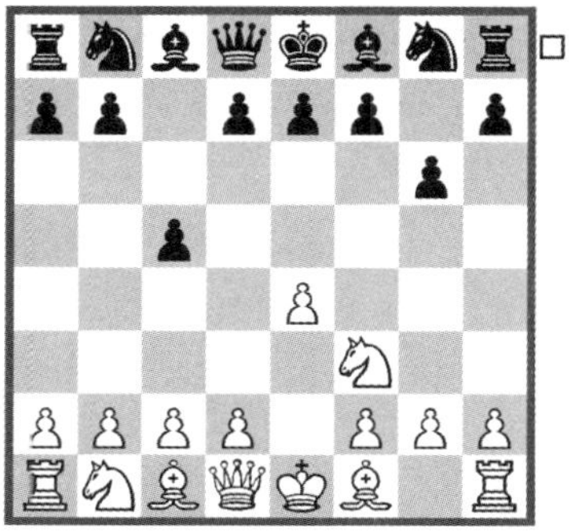

Position after: 2... g6

**3. c4**

3. d4 gives Black the option of 3... cxd4 4. ♘xd4 ♘f6 5. ♘c3 d6 transposing to a standard Dragon – which doesn't fit with our repertoire.

**3... ♗g7**

This will usually transpose to the lines after 3...♘c6, but there are a few less critical options to be aware of too. There have been lots of different move-order attempts by Black – I'll try to cover them all.

3... d6 Black aims to meet d2-d4 with ...♗g4 at the earliest opportunity. 4. d4 ♗g4 5. dxc5! We've already seen a few times that this is the typical response.

*(see analysis diagram next column)*

Position after: 5. dxc5!

5... dxc5 6. ♕xd8+ ♔xd8 7. ♘e5! ♗e6 8. ♘c3 ♗g7 We've been following Miles – Ljubojevic, Tilburg 1985. Here I like 9. f4!? attempting to shut out the g7-bishop. For example: 9... ♘d7 [9... ♗xe5 10. fxe5 ♘c6 11. ♗f4±] 10. ♘f3! h6 Otherwise ♘g5 will be played. 11. ♗d2+– Followed by something like 0-0-0 and e4-e5. White is clearly dominating.

**4. d4**

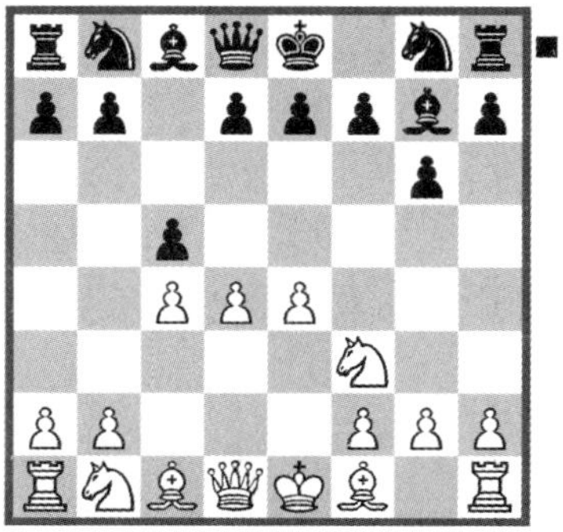

Position after: 4. d4

**4... d6**

**A)** 4... cxd4 5. ♘xd4 ♕b6 [5... ♘f6 6.

♘c3 0-0 7. ♗e2 will again transpose back to 3...♘c6 – I couldn't find any independent options for Black here.] 6. ♘b5! Tempting Black into the weakening ...a7-a6, and to be honest it's difficult to come up with another response for them. 6... a6 [6... ♕d8 is the engine's suggestion but we'll just continue developing with 7. ♗e2 d6 8. ♘1c3 and most likely transpose to a favourable version of the mainlines after 3... ♘c6.] 7. ♗e3

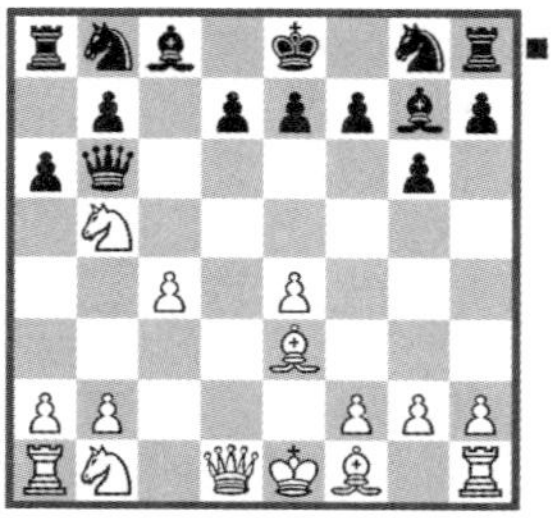
Position after: 7. ♗e3

**A1)** 7... ♕d8 8. ♘5c3! Threatening to immediately jump into d5 and exploit the hole on b6. 8... d6 9. ♘d5 ♘d7 10. ♘bc3± The position is again very awkward for Black. They really don't want to have to play ...e7-e6 and create further weaknesses, but it seems hard to avoid that move forever.

**A2)** 7... ♕a5+ 8. ♘5c3 ♘f6 9. ♘d2 d6 10. ♗e2 0-0 11. 0-0± Again this seems favourable compared to the mainlines after 3... ♘c6, as Black has wasted a lot of time jumping around with the queen. We'll continue with moves like ♘b3, ♕d2, and ♖ac1.

**B)** 4... ♕a5+ 5. ♘c3 ♘c6 Every other move will transpose to a line covered elsewhere in this chapter. 6. d5 ♘d4 7. ♗d2!

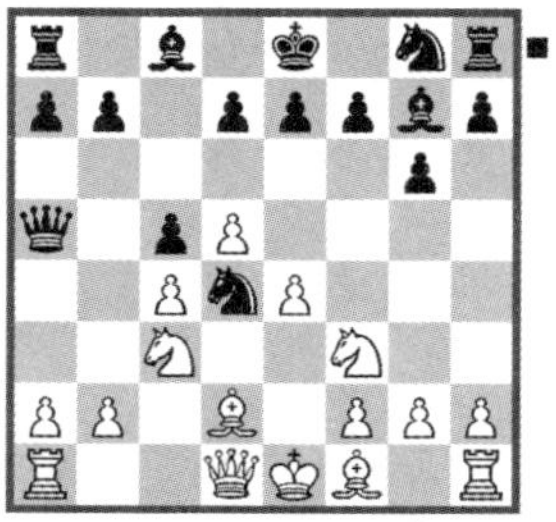
Position after: 7. ♗d2!

White already has a big advantage thanks to the central control and the fact that Black's queen on a5 is poorly placed.

**B1)** 7... d6 8. ♘xd4 cxd4 9. ♘b5 ♕d8 [9... ♕b6 In Svane – Nakamura, Chess.com 2020, White was just winning with the thematic 10. c5! dxc5 11. ♕a4!+– followed by ♗a5 and ♘c7.] 10. ♗b4! Simply threatening ♘xd4. 10... ♘f6 11. e5! ♘e4 [11... dxe5 12. d6!+–] 12. ♕xd4 f5 13. f4+–

**B2)** 7... ♘xf3+ 8. ♕xf3 d6 9. ♗e2! This move is better than the more common 9. ♗d3 because the d3-square is best suited for our queen instead. The bishop on e2 is useful to cover the g4- and h5-squares, either of which Black's f6-knight may want to jump after we push f2-f4. 9... ♘f6 10. ♕d3 0-0 11. 0-0± We will probably play a2-a4 next to prevent any queenside counterplay, before either f2-f4 or even potentially ♖ab1 and b2-b4.

**C)** 4... ♘c6 5. dxc5! Black will waste time recapturing the pawn with ...♕a5 and ...♕xc5, after which the queen will be misplaced and we'll continue developing with tempi. 5... ♕a5+ 6. ♗d2 ♕xc5 7. ♘c3 ♘f6 8. ♗e2 0-0 9. 0-0± White was clearly better in Neiksans – Chirila, Saint Louis 2019. A logical plan would involve moves like h2-h3, ♕c1, ♖d1, and ♗e3/♗h6.

**5. ♘c3!**

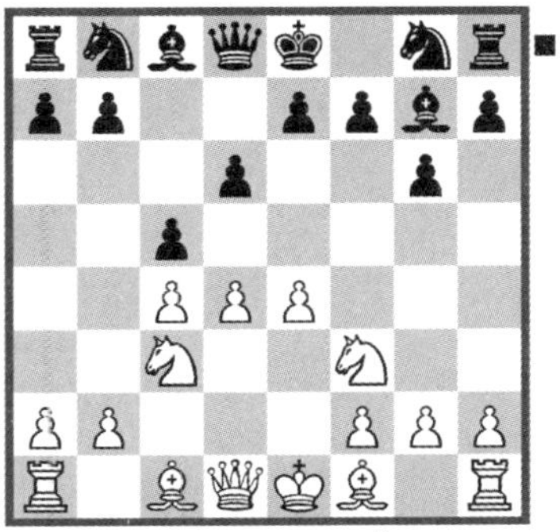

Position after: 5. ♘c3!

5. d5 is the computer's suggestion but it also gives Black what they want. It's definitely an option to explore, but for now 5.♘c3 is the easier path to learn.

**5... ♘c6**

**A)** 5... ♗g4 6. dxc5! I think this is the simplest route to an advantage. 6... dxc5 [6... ♗xf3 7. gxf3! Insisting on trading queens. 7... dxc5 8. ♕xd8+ ♔xd8 9. ♗e3 This transposes to 6...dxc5.] 7. ♕xd8+ ♔xd8 8. ♗e3

Position after: 8. ♗e3

**A1)** 8... b6 9. 0-0-0+± Followed by either ♔c2 or e4-e5. White has a comfortable advantage.

**A2)** 8... ♗xc3+ We don't actually mind the doubled pawns here. Black will likely play ...b7-b6 soon to defend the c5-pawn, after which we can utilise the open b-file by pushing our a-pawn. 9. bxc3 b6 10. ♘e5! ♗e6 11. a4±

**A3)** 8... ♗xf3 9. gxf3 ♗d4 [9... b6 10. 0-0-0+ ♔c8 11. f4+– Followed by e4-e5.] 10. 0-0-0 ♘c6 11. ♘b5 e5 12. f4

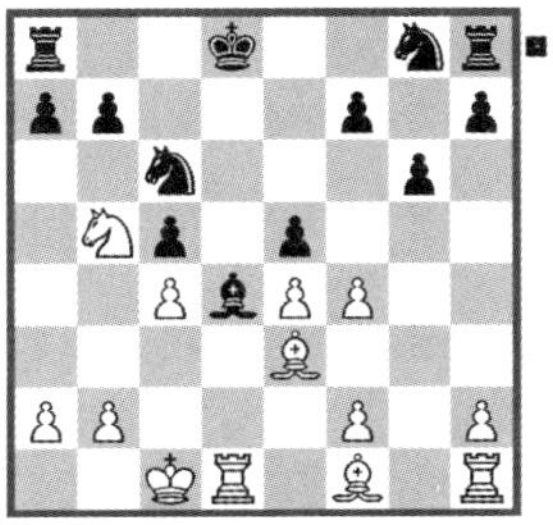

Position after: 12. f4

Getting rid of the doubled pawns.

12... ♔e7 [12... f6 13. fxe5 fxe5 14. h4+–] 13. ♗xd4 exd4 14. ♘c7!± With the idea of ♘d5+ and h2-h4.

**B)** 5... cxd4 6. ♘xd4 ♘c6 [6... ♘f6 7. ♗e2 will also transpose to the mainline arising after 3...♘c6, as Black can't avoid playing ...♘c6 at some point here.] 7. ♗e3 transposes to the mainline after 3...♘c6.

**C)** 5... ♕a5 6. ♗e2 Again I think we should keep our workload simple. 6.d5 is probably the best move objectively, but it seems unnecessary to complicate things for such a rare sideline.

**C1)** 6... ♘f6 7. 0-0 and Black will capture on d4, transposing to a normal Marcozy position.

**C2)** 6... ♘c6 7. d5! ♘d4 8. 0-0 ♗g4 The only critical move. Instead capturing immediately on f3 or e2 would give us a great position. 9. ♘xd4 cxd4 10. ♗xg4! dxc3 11. bxc3± Although Black has some activity, our bishop pair combined with the open b-file gives us the much better prospects.

**C3)** 6... ♗g4 7. dxc5!

The simplest route to an advantage. 7... dxc5 [7... ♕xc5 8. ♕b3!±; 7... ♗xc3+ 8. bxc3 ♕xc5 9. ♖b1± Despite our weakened pawn structure, the position is still extremely favourable for us. The dark squares are always going to be a problem for Black here.] 8. ♕b3! ♗xf3 9. ♗xf3 ♘c6 10. e5! It makes sense to open the position, given we have the bishop pair. 10... ♕c7 11. 0-0! ♗xe5 12. ♖e1!± It looks too dangerous for Black to capture on h2, but it also seems difficult for their king to get castled. It's important to note that ...♘d4 is always met by ♘d5.

**6. d5!**

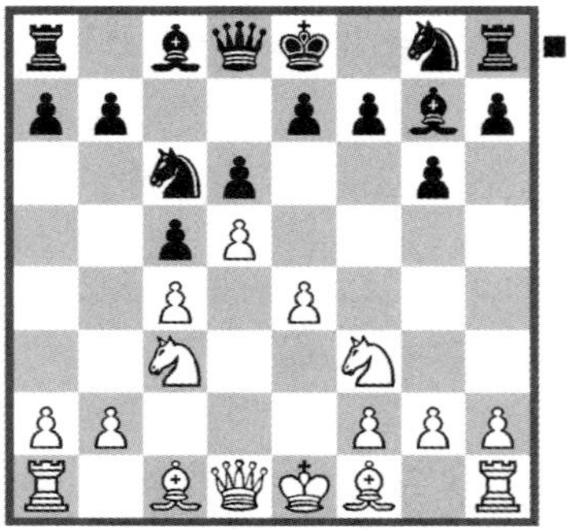

Position after: 6. d5!

Finally we push the d-pawn, gaining a tempo by hitting the c6-knight. It makes sense to push d4-d5 as Black will most likely attempt to exchange the c6-knight for our f3-knight. This exchange is beneficial for us, as it would enable our kingside pawns to roll forward with ease in the near future.

**6... ♘d4**

6... ♘e5 7. ♘xe5 ♗xe5 8. ♗d3

*(see analysis diagram next page)*

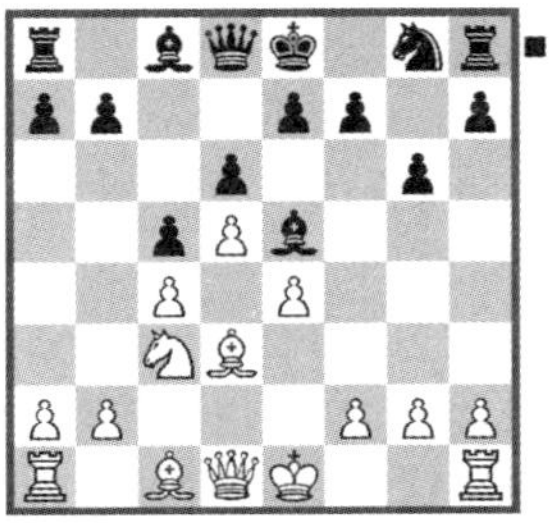

Position after: 8. ♗d3

Black's bishop seems misplaced on e5. It's an easy target for an f2-f4 push in the near future. The bishop will have to either drop back to g7 or capture on c3, with neither option looking particularly satisfactory.

**A)** 8... ♗xc3+ 9. bxc3 e5 10. f4! [10. 0-0?! g5!∞ We can't allow this option, or else Black suddenly has a good position.] 10... ♕h4+ 11. g3 ♕e7 12. fxe5 dxe5 13. h3!± Followed by ♗e3, ♕f3, and perhaps g3-g4. White's king has the option to castle on either side of the board, or even to stay in the centre with ♔d2.

**B)** 8... ♗g7 9. 0-0 ♘f6 [9... e6 is rarely played so early, but I wanted to check what to do if Black puts the knight on e7. 10. dxe6!? ♗xe6 11. ♕e1! Preparing f2-f4 and ♕g3. 11... ♘e7 12. f4± Immediately threatening f4-f5. This looks really scary for Black.] 10. h3 0-0 In Hawkins – Fernandez, London 2016, White should have finished development with something like:

*(see analysis diagram next column)*

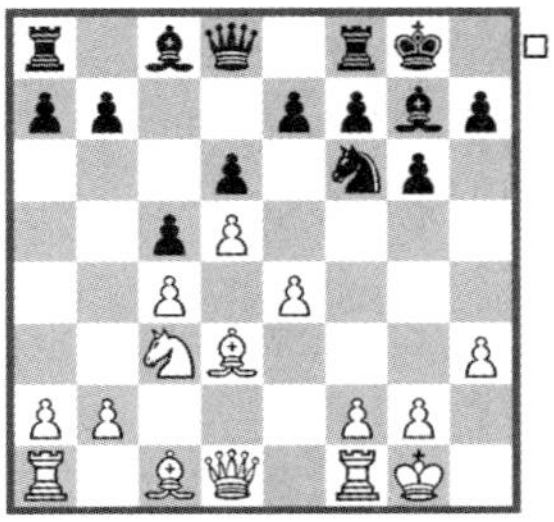

Position after: 10... 0-0

11. ♗g5!?± followed by ♕d2, before considering the f2-f4 push. Black's position is incredibly passive.

**7. ♘xd4 cxd4**

7... ♗xd4 Black has the same problem here as after 6...♘e5, namely that the bishop is misplaced. 8. ♗d3 There's nothing better than either ...♗g7 or ...♗xc3, transposing to 6... ♘e5.

**8. ♘b5**

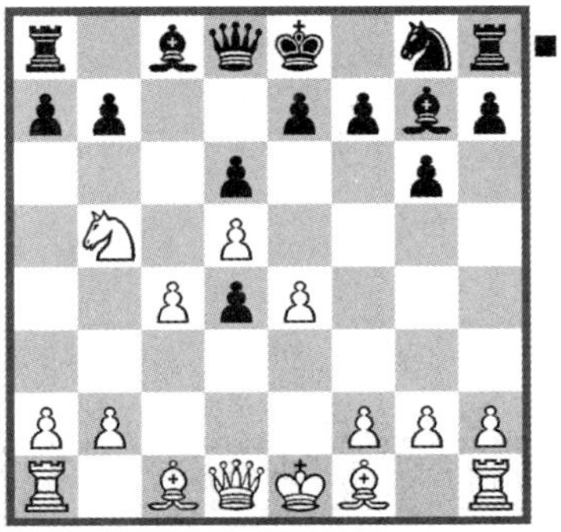

Position after: 8. ♘b5

**8... ♕b6**

Nearly always played, but we have a nice shot here:

8... ♘f6 is the engine's suggestion, but there isn't enough compensation for the pawn. 9. ♕xd4 0-0 10. ♗e2 a6 11. ♘c3 The only critical test is if Black immediately plays dynamically and tries to open the position: 11... e6 12. ♕d3 exd5 13. cxd5 b5 14. a3!± Followed by 0-0, when White is basically just a pawn up.

**9. c5!**

Black is close to losing on the queenside.

**9... dxc5**

9... ♕xc5 10. ♗d2+– Followed by ♖c1. White was already completely winning in Emms – Villiers, London 2022.

**10. ♗f4 ♔f8 11. ♖c1**

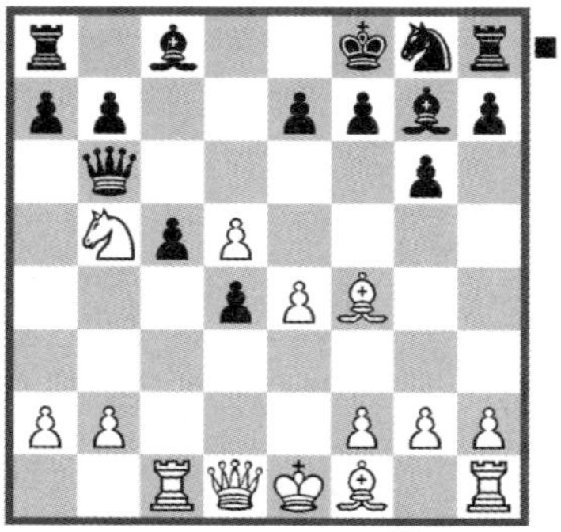

Position after: 11. ♖c1

**11... a6**

11... ♘f6 12. ♗c7 ♕a6 13. ♗d3!+– Followed by 0-0, and it looks impossible for Black to complete development.

**12. ♗c7**

The following line is important to remember:

**12... ♕f6 13. ♘a3 b5! 14. ♗d3!**

14. ♖xc5 d3! gives Black good counterplay.

**14... c4 15. ♗xc4! bxc4 16. ♘xc4**

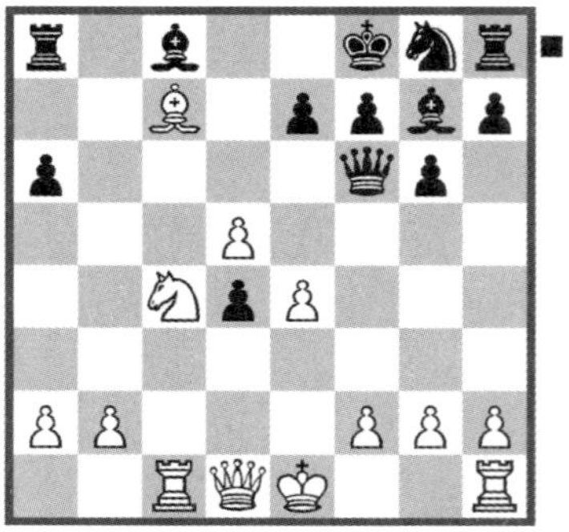

Position after: 16. ♘xc4

Followed by 0-0 and f2-f4. Actually, it's probably worth checking a couple more moves.

**16... ♗h6 17. 0-0!±**

Sacrificing another exchange. Even though we're a rook down, Black is close to lost.

## b) 3...♘c6 4.d4 cxd4 5.♘xd4 ♗g7 6.♗e3 ♕b6

**1. e4 c5 2. ♘f3 g6 3. c4 ♘c6**

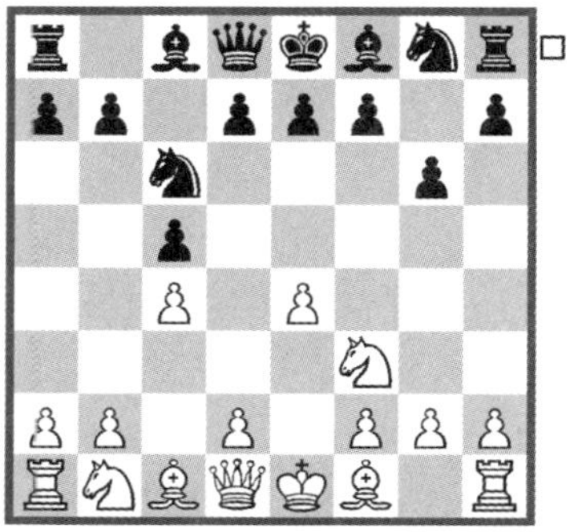

Position after: 3... ♘c6

**4. d4 cxd4 5. ♘xd4**

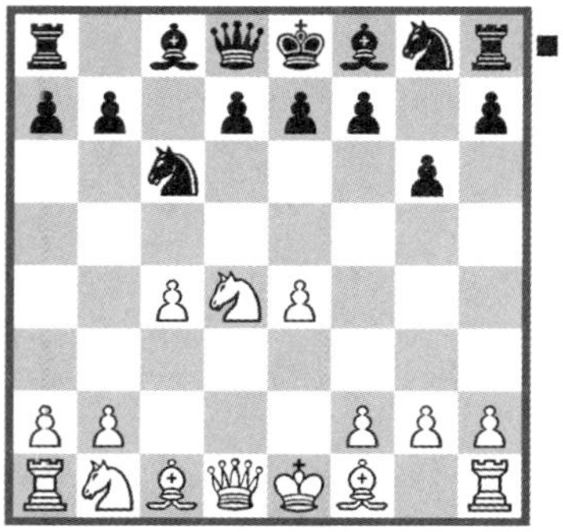

Position after: 5. ♘xd4

In the chapter 'Moscow 3...♘d7 4. 0-0 ♘f6 with 6...b6', I explained our plans in the Hedgehog structure. The difference with the Maroczy structure is that here Black fianchettoes their bishop on g7, compared to the Hedgehog where ...e7-e6 and ...♗e7 are played. There are a few important things to note: We don't need to be particularly cautious about allowing the ...d7-d5 or ...d6-d5 central break. It's easier for Black to attempt to trade pieces in order to alleviate the space problem, as the d6-pawn will never be too weak (because ... e7-e6 is rarely played). Because of this, a typical idea for us is to place a knight on d5. If Black captures on d5, we can consider both exd5 and cxd5, depending on the position. Both of these recaptures have the potential to transform the position favourably for us. Alongside placing a knight on d5, White should consider expanding on the kingside with f2-f4, placing the rooks on the central lines, and pushing either f4-f5 or e4-e5. Meanwhile, Black's main prospects revolve around pressuring our queenside pawns with moves like ...a7-a5-a4, ...♕a5-b4, ...♘f6-d7-c5, and ...♗e6. After re-routing the f6-knight, Black will also be considering the ...f7-f5 break. Discussing these ideas should make it slightly easier to understand the recommendations in this chapter. The main thing to note is that White should try to keep pieces on the board unless we can transform the structure and reach a favourable late middlegame/endgame.

**5... ♗g7**

**A)** 5... ♗h6?! It's dubious for Black to exchange the dark-squared bishops so early. 6. ♗xh6 ♘xh6 7. ♘c3 0-0 The best way to capitalise on Black's premature exchange is by castling queenside and attacking their king: 8. f3 d6 9. ♕d2 ♔g7 10. 0-0-0± Followed by h2-h4, etc.

**B)** 5... ♘f6 It's important to consider both 5...♘f6 and 5...♗g7 here, as there are some slight differences. In particular, with 5...♘f6 Black will capture on d4 before we've played ♗e3, thereby forcing us to recapture with the queen. 6. ♘c3

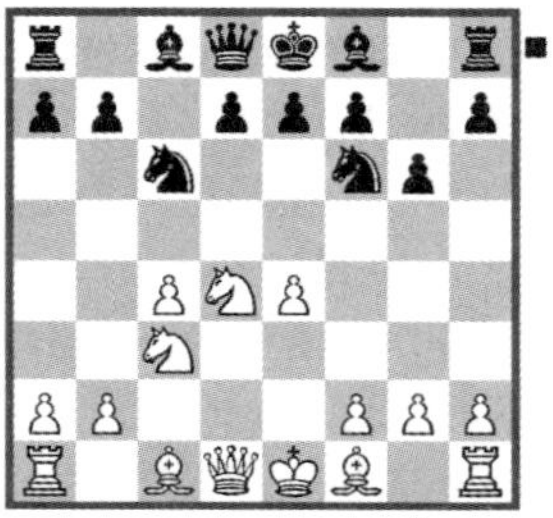

Position after: 6. ♘c3

6... d6 [6... ♘xd4 7. ♕xd4 d6 8. ♗e3 ♗g7 transposes to 5...d6.] 7. ♗e2 [7. f3 is the alternative, preventing any possibility of ...♘g4, but I thought Black was doing okay in the following line: 7... ♗g7 8. ♗e3 0-0 9. ♗e2 ♘h5!?] 7... ♘xd4 8. ♕xd4 ♗g7 9. ♗e3 0-0 Black is threatening ...♘g4 so we need to make a decision about where to retreat the queen. 10. ♕d3! Much less common than 10.♕d2, but there is a point to the more 'unnatural' queen retreat. In general we want to keep the queens on the board. Black is planning to play ...♕a5, so therefore placing the queen on d3 avoids a pin and potential exchange if our c3-knight moves.

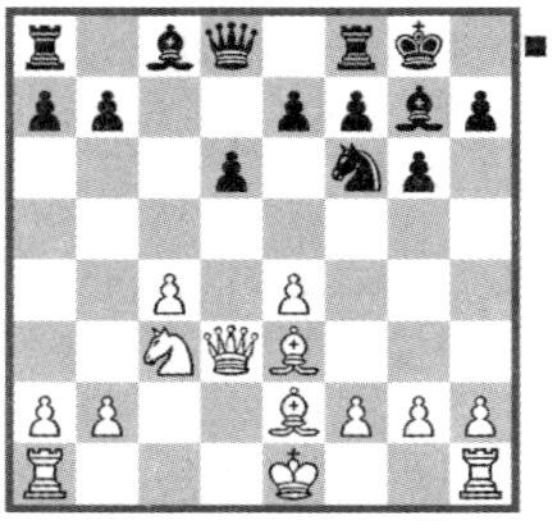

Position after: 10. ♕d3!

**B1)** 10... a5 A typical idea in these structures. Black plans to advance their pawn to a4 before manoeuvering their pieces to the queenside. 11. 0-0 a4 12. ♗d4! Ensuring that ...♘d7 will be met by an exchange of dark-squared bishops. 12... ♕a5 13. f4! In the corresponding position with the queen on d2, Black would have the tactical shot ...♘xe4!. This is one example of why it's more beneficial to have the White queen on d3. 13... ♗g4 [13... ♗e6 14. ♖ad1 ♖fc8 15. b3 axb3 16. axb3 ♗d7 17. e5!+– White was already winning in the game Bellahcene – Gabuzyan, Krasnaya Polyana 2021.] 14. ♖ad1 ♗xe2 15. ♕xe2 a3 This leads to the following forcing line:

*(see analysis diagram next page)*

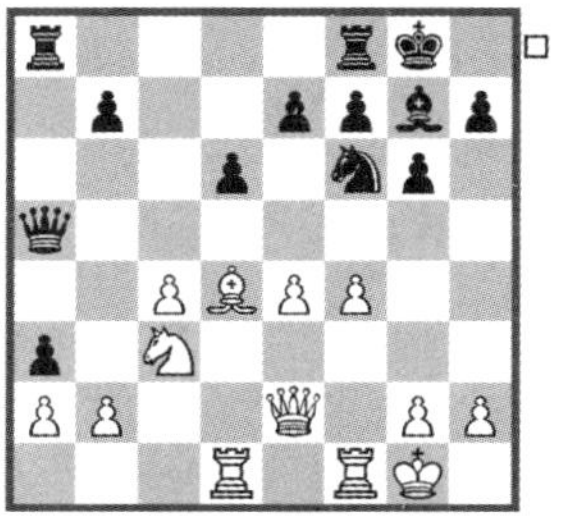

Position after: 15... a3

16. e5! dxe5 17. fxe5 ♘d7 18. b4! ♕xb4 19. ♘d5 ♕a5 In Perez Ponsa – Fiorito, Villa Martelli 2021, the best continuation was 20. ♘xe7+ ♔h8 21. ♘d5 ♖ac8 22. h3↑ with a strong initiative.

**B2)** 10... ♘g4 11. ♗xg4 ♗xg4 12. 0-0± Followed by ♗d4. Our c3-knight will dominate Black's light-squared bishop in this Maroczy structure.

**B3)** 10... ♗d7 Black aims for an ...a7-a6 and ...b7-b5 break. 11. ♖d1! Threatening c4-c5. 11... ♕a5 12. 0-0 a6 13. a3± The break ...b7-b5 is still met with c4-c5. Meanwhile we can continue with ♗d4 next, while ♘d5 is always an option to consider.

**B4)** 10... ♗e6 11. ♗d4! Black most likely planned ...♘d7 next, so this way we ensure the exchange of bishops. 11... ♘d7 [11... ♕a5 12. 0-0 ♖fc8 13. b3 and Black had nothing better than 13... ♘d7 in Niemann – Sindarov, Riga 2021, which is similar to the positions after 11...♘d7.] 12. ♗xg7 ♔xg7 13. 0-0 ♕a5

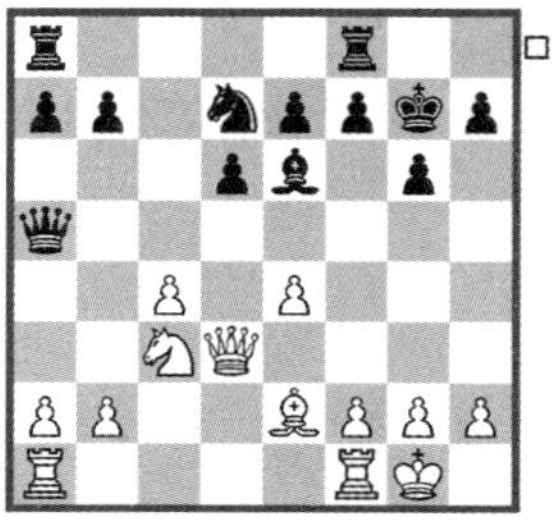

Position after: 13... ♕a5

Black's plan revolves around breaking on the queenside with ... b7-b5, so we need to prepare against this. 14. b3 a6 15. h3 ♖ab8 16. a4± We can follow with ♖ab1 and ♖fd1 before continuing to improve our position, for example with ♕e3 and ♘d5.

**6. ♗e3**

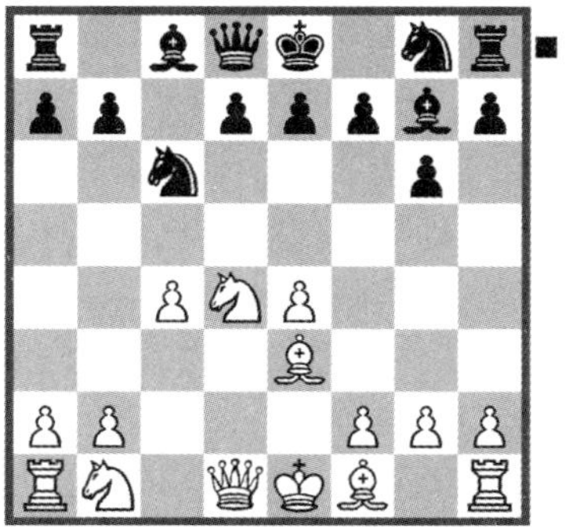

Position after: 6. ♗e3

**6... ♕b6!?**

Quickly forcing our knight to either b3 or b5. This has been played numerous times recently, in particular by Jahongir Vakhidov and Nordirbek Abdusattorov. Vakhidov deeply prepared this for the 2021 World Cup where he eliminated Leinier Dominguez Perez –

demonstrating that it's a line we need to take seriously. It has most likely replaced 6... ♘f6 as the main move here, although I'll still leave 6...♘f6 as my mainline considering it's been played over 19,000 times more than 6...♕b6.

6... ♘h6?! is another dubious sideline where Black aims for a quick ...f7-f5. 7. h3! Controlling the knight and potentially threatening ♕d2. 7... f5 [7... 0-0 8. ♕d2 ♘xd4 9. ♗xd4 ♗xd4 10. ♕xd4± Followed by ♘c3 and 0-0-0.] 8. exf5 ♘xf5 9. ♘xf5 ♕a5+ The point of the variation, but all Black has succeeded in is creating some positional weaknesses. 10. ♘c3!

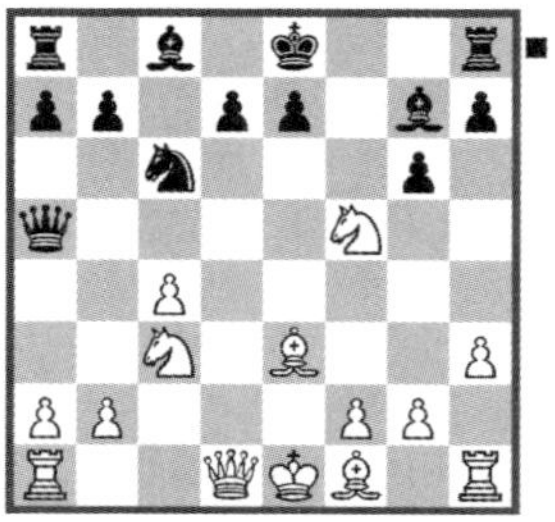

Position after: 10. ♘c3!

10... ♕xf5 [10... ♗xc3+ 11. bxc3 gxf5 Richter – Narkun, ICCF email 2020. 12. ♗e2 0-0 13. f4!+– Followed by ♔f2. Black's king is too weak to survive the power of our bishop pair.] 11. ♗d3 ♕a5 12. 0-0+– Simply followed by something like ♗e4, ♕d2, and ♖ad1. Black's position is just too weak here.

**7. ♘b5!?**

7.♘b3 is the alternative and definitely something to explore. However after lengthy analysis, I really quite like our plan of dropping the b5-knight back to c3 and developing the b1-knight to d2 – it feels like we have more control over Black's counterplay, and our knights will be well placed to support the b2-b4 and f2-f4 pawn advances.

**7... ♕a5+**

7... ♕d8 will most likely transpose back to 6...♘f6 after 8. ♘1c3 ♘f6 [8... a6? 9. ♘d5+–] 9. ♗e2 [9. ♘d4 already transposes back, but it might be a good idea to force ...a7-a6.] 9... 0-0 10. 0-0 d6 11. h3 a6 12. ♘d4±.

**8. ♘5c3!**

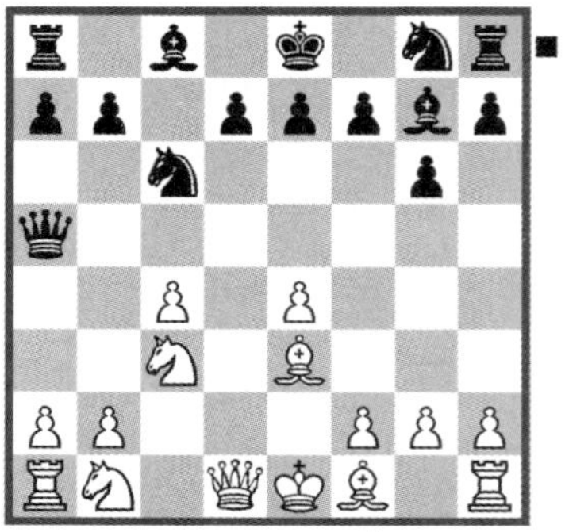

Position after: 8. ♘5c3!

8. ♘1c3 is more common but I prefer a knight on d2 rather than d4.

**8... d6**

The critical line is where Black delays

...♘f6, in order to prevent our b1-knight from jumping to d2.

**A)** 8... ♕b4!? 9. ♕c2! [9. ♕d2 was played in Kamsky – Abdusattorov, Biel 2022, but I'd rather leave the d2-square open for the knight to jump to.] 9... d6 10. ♘d2

**A1)** 10... ♗xc3 11. bxc3 ♕a5 12. c5! A clever pawn sacrifice to open the position and exploit Black's dark-squared weaknesses. 12... dxc5 13. ♗f4 ♘f6 14. ♘c4 ♕d8 15. ♗e2± White has fantastic compensation here – in practical terms it looks horrible to defend with Black.

**A2)** 10... ♕a5 Preparing ...♗xc3. 11. ♖c1!

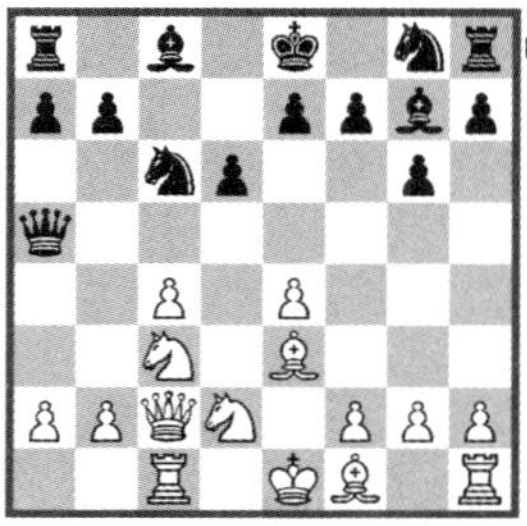

Position after: 11. ♖c1!

11... ♘f6 12. ♘b3 ♕d8 13. h3± Followed by ♗e2 and 0-0 with a standard Maroczy position – except that Black has wasted a fair amount of time with their queen.

**B)** 8... ♘f6 The most common move but fairly uncritical, as now we can just develop normally. 9. ♘d2 0-0 10. ♗e2 d6 11. 0-0 ♗e6 [11... ♘d7 12. ♘b3 ♕d8 Ruck – Mamedov, Skopje 2018. 13. ♕c2!± Followed by ♖ad1 and ♘d5, after which the queen can slip back to b1 if needed.] 12.a3 was played in Nepomniachtchi – Abdusattorov, Chess.com 2022, but I prefer 12. ♖c1, aiming for ♘d5 next.

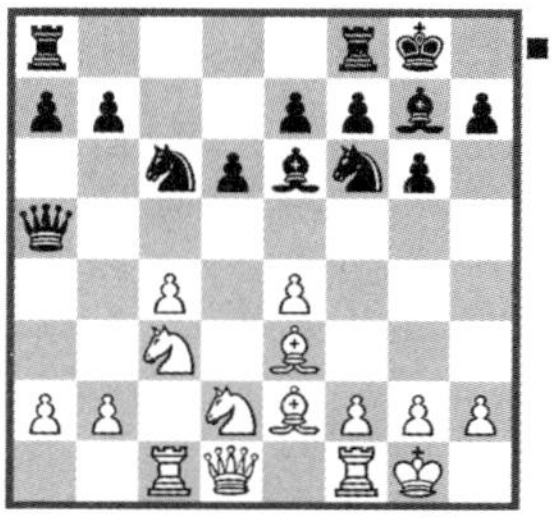

Position after: 12. ♖c1

Now f2-f4 will always be met with ...♘g4, so we should focus more on achieving the ♘d5 jump. [12... ♖fc8 13. f4!± This is always on the cards under the right circumstances, and it makes a lot of sense now that Black has played ...♖fc8.] 13. a3 ♖fc8 14. ♘d5 ♗xd5 15. exd5!± We'll relocate the d2-knight to b3 or even b1, before pushing f2-f4. The change in pawn structure is beneficial for White as we have good control over the central squares. In particular, the bishop pair prevents Black from achieving any counterplay.

**9. ♗e2 ♕b4**

A typical idea to try and disrupt our queenside development.

9... ♘h6 is given by the engine, with the idea of pushing ...f7-f5 and recapturing with the knight. However I don't see a way for Black to completely equalise in the following line: 10. 0-0 f5 11. ♕c1! 11... ♘g4 12. ♗d2 0-0 13. ♘d5 ♕d8 14. exf5 [14. ♘bc3 immediately is also possible but the position gets a bit unclear after 14... ♘d4 15. ♗xg4 fxg4∞.] 14... ♗xf5 15. ♘bc3 ♘d4 16. ♗xg4 ♗xg4 17. f3 ♗e6 18. ♗h6

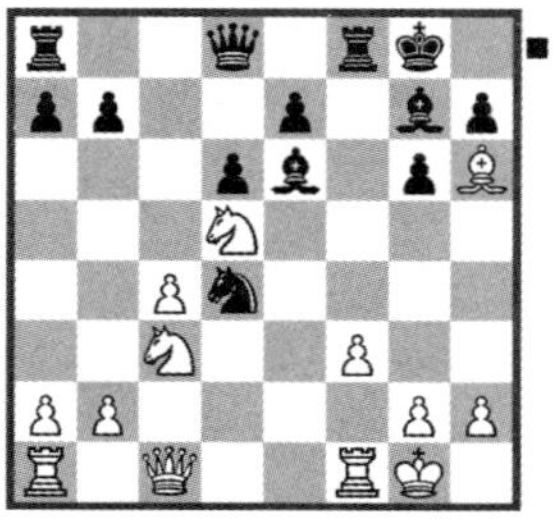

Position after: 18. ♗h6

It's important to exchange bishops – now Black has no counterplay. 18... ♗xh6 19. ♕xh6 ♗xd5 20. ♘xd5 ♘f5 21. ♕d2 e6 22. ♘f4 ♕b6+ 23. ♖f2±

**10. ♕c1**

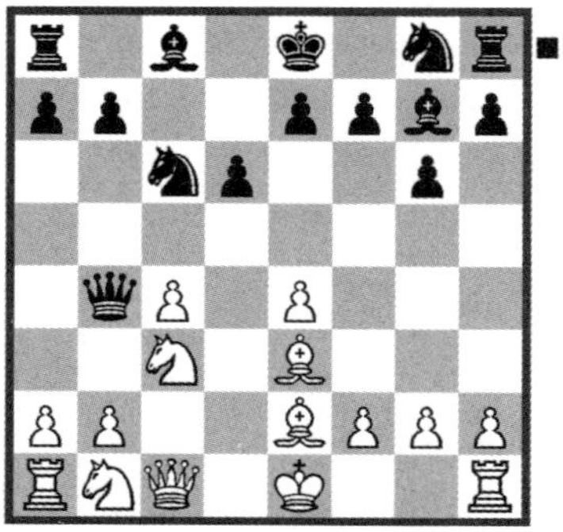

Position after: 10. ♕c1

Once again I prefer to leave the d2-square open for the b1-knight.

**10... ♗d4!?**

Capitalising on the drawback of our queen leaving the d-file.

10... ♘f6 11. 0-0 0-0 12. a3 ♕a5 13. ♕d1!± Followed by either ♘d2 and ♖c1, or the inventive ♖a2 and b2-b3. After both options, we'll consider pushing f2-f4 and perhaps b2-b4.

**11. 0-0**

11. ♗d2 ♘f6 12. ♘a3 ♕c5 13. 0-0 In Vitiugov – Abdusattorov, Chess.com 2022, Black could have equalised with 13... ♗g4! 14. ♕d1 ♗xe2 15. ♕xe2 ♕h5!=.

**11... ♘f6**

It's important to note that Black can't really grab the pawn with 11... ♗xe3 12. ♕xe3 ♕xb2 because White gets a dangerous initiative after 13. ♘b5!

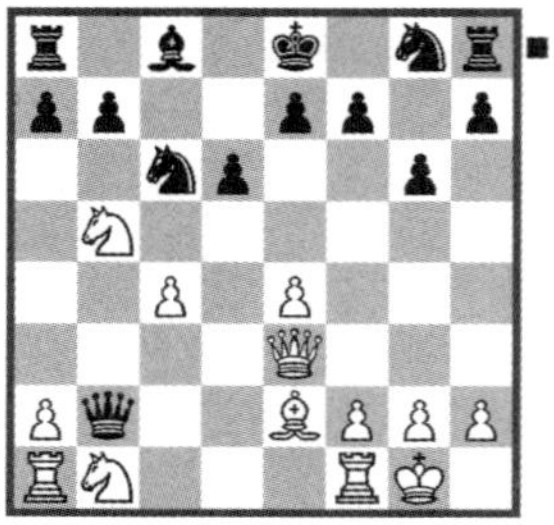

Position after: 13. ♘b5!

13... ♕xa1 [13... ♖b8 14. ♘1c3 ♕b4 15. ♖ab1 ♕c5 16. ♕c1!+– Followed by either ♘c7+ or ♖d1, and it seems difficult for Black to survive. The queen in particular looks short of squares.] 14. ♘1c3 ♕b2 15. ♖b1 ♕xb1+ 16. ♘xb1 ♔f8 17. ♘1c3± White has the good side of the material imbalance. Our pieces are all active and it will take time for Black's rooks to connect. We can increase the pressure with moves like ♘d5, ♕c3, and f2-f4.

**12. ♘a3**

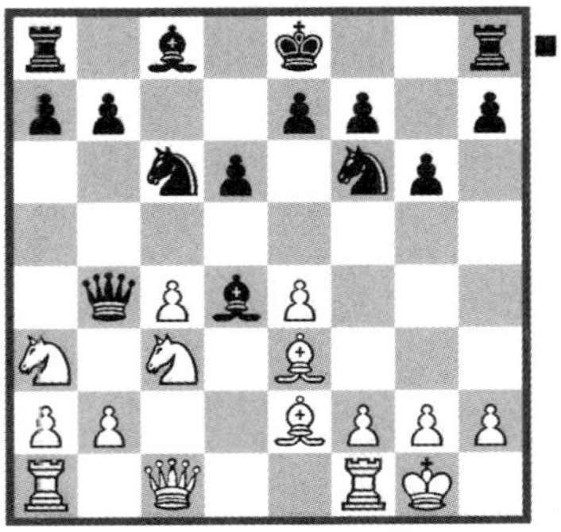

Position after: 12. ♘a3

One of the only times we allow our pawns to be doubled, as our initiative will be strong due to Black's queen being misplaced.

**12... ♗xc3**

12... ♗xe3 13. ♕xe3 0-0 14. ♕d2±

**13. bxc3 ♕a5 14. f3 0-0 15. ♖b1!**

A sample line continues:

**15... ♘d7 16. f4!? ♘f6 17. ♖b5 ♕d8 18. ♕c2→**

Followed by ♖g5.

## c) 3...♘c6 4.d4 cxd4 5.♘xd4 ♗g7 6.♗e3 ♘f6

**1. e4 c5 2. ♘f3 g6 3. c4 ♘c6 4. d4 cxd4 5. ♘xd4 ♗g7 6. ♗e3 ♘f6**

*(see diagram opposite column)*

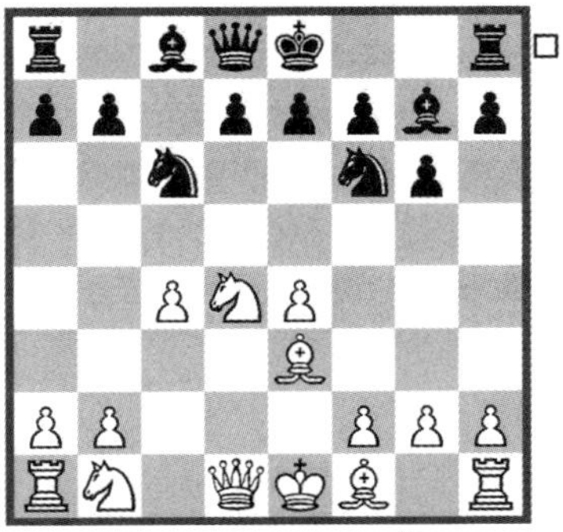

Position after: 6... ♘f6

**7. ♘c3 0-0**

**A)** 7... ♘g4?! This used to be very common, and is quite logical based on Black's aim of exchanging pieces. However without the f6-knight, Black will be devoid of counterplay associated with the ...♘d7-♘c5 manoeuvre. 8. ♕xg4 ♘xd4 9. ♕d1!

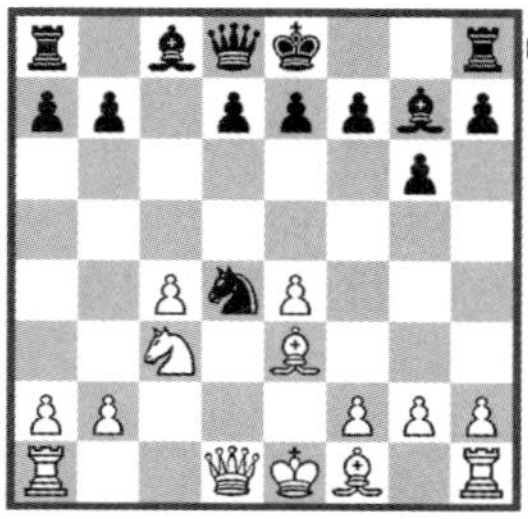

Position after: 9. ♕d1!

Necessary, as Black threatened both ...d7-d5 and ...♘c2+.

**A1)** 9... ♘c6 Here it makes sense to complete development before pushing f2-f4. 10. ♕d2 d6 11. ♗e2 There are a few different options for Black here but it doesn't make sense to explore all of them deeply – our plan is the same against everything. A sample line continues: 11... ♕a5 12. ♖c1 0-0 13. 0-0 ♗e6 14. b3 ♖ac8 15. f4! After consolidating, we can expand on the kingside.

*(see analysis diagram next column)*

Position after: 15. f4!

**A1.1)** 15... ♖fd8 is the other less commital move, but after 16. ♗f3± it's difficult to understand what Black is doing. Meanwhile we have several ways to improve – ♖fd1, ♔h1, h2-h3, before potentially g2-g4 or even an immediate f4-f5/e4-e5.

**A1.2)** 15... f5 16. exf5 ♗xf5 17. ♗f3± Exchanging our e-pawn for Black's f-pawn is always beneficial for us. With our pawn on f4 and bishop on f3, we control the board, while Black's central pawns are clear targets.

**A2)** 9... e5!? 10. ♗d3 0-0 11. 0-0 d6 There are plenty of good moves for White, but simplest is just 12. ♕d2 ♗e6 13. b3 a6 14. ♖ab1!.

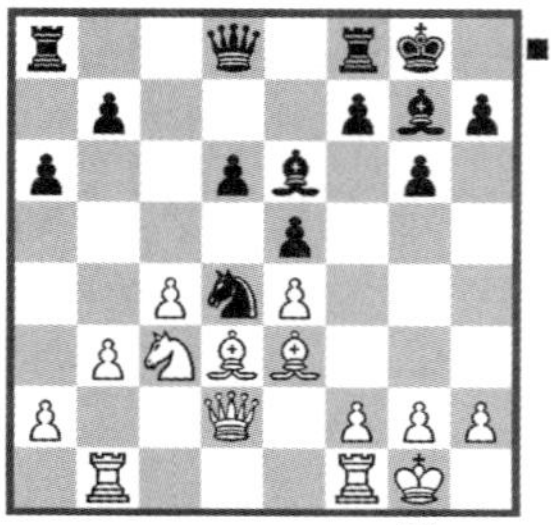

Position after: 14. ♖ab1!

We want to push a2-a4 at the right moment, to stop any queenside counterplay. 14... ♖c8 15. a4 ♕a5 16. ♖fd1± With control of the b5-square, the next plan is to kick the d4-knight away with ♘e2. This can be prepared with moves like ♕b2 and ♗f1.

**A3)** 9... ♘e6 The point of this retreat is that the knight is well placed to jump to c5. 10. ♖c1! We shouldn't allow Black to double our pawns. There are four moves played here so I'll quickly cover all of them, although none are particularly independent of the others.

**A3.1)** 10... ♕a5 11. ♗e2 b6 12. ♕d5! Transforming the pawn structure to our benefit. 12... ♕xd5 [12... ♖b8!? 13. ♕xa5 bxa5 14. b3 ♗d4 15. ♗xd4 ♘xd4 16. ♘b5! White converted the advantage in Smeets – Finegold, Al Ain 2012.] 13. cxd5 ♘d4 14. ♗c4 f5 15. f3± With the idea of ♔d2-d3.

**A3.2)** 10... 0-0 11. ♗e2 b6 12. 0-0 ♗b7 13. ♕d2 If Black plays ...♘c5 we'll continue with f2-f3 before trying to prepare a b2-b4 break. The only other critical continuation is 13... f5, but as we know, exchanging our e-pawn for Black's f-pawn is quite beneficial for White. 14. exf5 gxf5 15. ♘d5!± Followed by f2-f4 and b2-b4, controlling both sides of the board.

**A3.3)** 10... d6 11. ♗e2 0-0 12. 0-0 ♗d7 13. b3 [13. b4 immediately is also good, but I'd rather not allow Black counterplay with 13... a5.] 13... ♘c5 [13... ♗c6 14. b4! Now we can meet ...a7-a5 with b4-b5 followed by ♘a4. 14... b6 15. a3± Followed by ♕d2. Black is very passive and ...a7-a5 is always difficult to achieve due to the weakness on b6.] 14. ♗f3 a5 15. ♕e2± Followed by ♖fd1, and ♘d5 at the right moment. Once again Black is very passive and we can just slowly improve.

**B)** 7... d6 8. ♗e2 will transpose back to 7... 0-0.

**8. ♗e2**

Reaching the standard Maroczy position. Black has several interpretations of this position, so we'll cover a broad range of lines that have been tried.

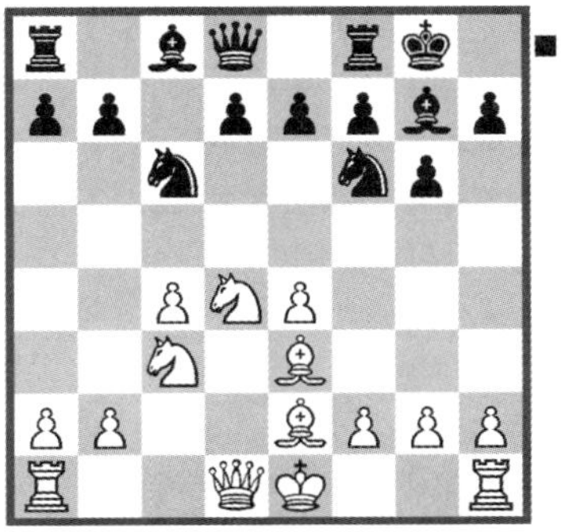

Position after: 8. ♗e2

**8... d6**

8... b6 is slightly inferior because with this fianchetto, Black's only feasible pawn break is ...d7-d5 which is very hard to achieve. 9. 0-0 ♗b7 10. f3

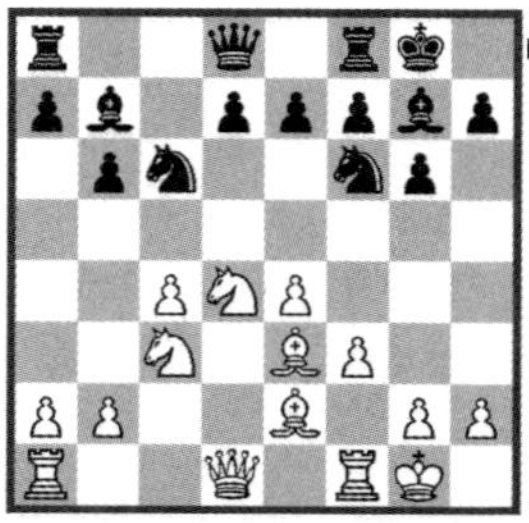

Position after: 10. f3

**A)** 10... d6 11. ♕d2 ♘d7 12. ♘c2!± White was clearly better in Tomashevsky – Inarkiev, Dubai 2014. Black lacks a plan, whereas we will play ♖ad1 followed by either ♗h6 or f3-f4.

**B)** 10... ♘h5 Threatening ...♘f4. 11. ♘db5!? d6 12. ♕d2 a6 13. ♘a3! Rerouting to c2, after which Black's knight is misplaced on h5. 13... ♘f6 14. ♘c2±

**C)** 10... ♕b8 11. ♕d2 ♖d8 Black prepares ...e7-e6 and ...d7-d5, but we have a good reaction: 12. ♘db5! d6 13. ♘d5!± Followed by ♗h6, and Black is extremely passive.

**D)** 10... e6 11. ♘db5! d5 This sequence has been played quite a few times, but doesn't come close to equalising: 12. cxd5 exd5 13. exd5 ♘b4 14. d6 ♘fd5 15. ♗f2!

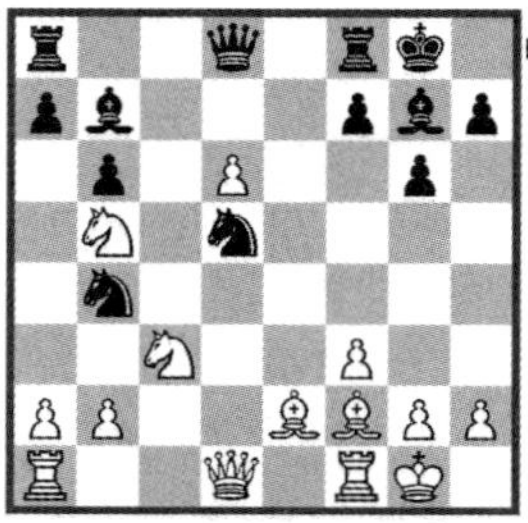

Position after: 15. ♗f2!

Black won't be able to win back the pawn, for example: 15... ♘f4 [15... a6 16. ♘c7! ♘xc7 17. ♗xb6 ♕d7 18. ♗xc7 ♗xc3 19. bxc3 ♘d5 20. ♗a5 ♕xd6 21. ♕d4+–] 16. ♗g3 ♘h5 17. f4! ♘xg3 18. hxg3+–

**E)** 10... ♘xd4 11. ♗xd4 d6 This is just an inferior version of the mainline after 8...d6 – the b7-bishop is useless against our f3-e4 pawn construction. 12. ♕d2 ♘d7 [12... ♖c8 13. ♖ac1±] 13. ♗xg7 ♔xg7 14. ♖ac1± Followed by ♖fd1, and b2-b4 or h2-h4.

**9. 0-0**

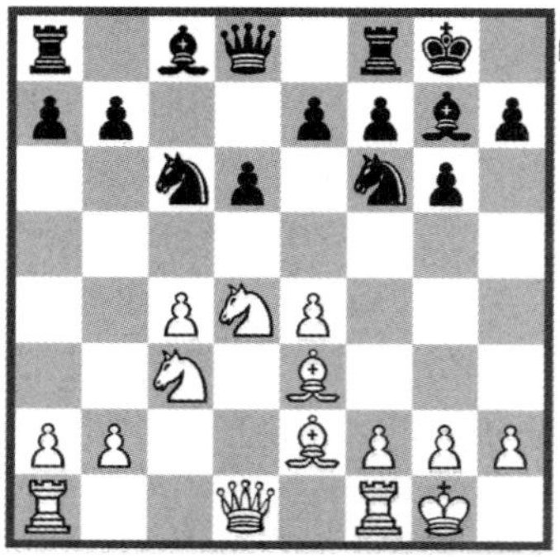

Position after: 9. 0-0

**9... ♗d7**

**A)** 9... ♘xd4 10. ♗xd4 ♗e6 [10... ♗d7 11. h3 transposes to 9...♗d7.; 10... b6 11. ♕d3! ♗b7 12. ♖ad1± Followed by ♖fe1 and ♗f1, with excellent control.] 11. f4! ♖c8 12. b3 ♕a5 This position has been reached in several high-level games. The best continuation looks to be 13. ♖b1!± threatening f4-f5. We can still continue to prepare the push, for example with ♔h1 and ♕d3, depending on Black's responses.

**B)** 9... a6 10. h3 will also transpose to 9...♗d7.

**C)** 9... ♘d7 10. ♖b1!? A typical improvement of the rook, where it supports both b2-b3 or even b2-b4. 10... ♘c5 [10... ♘xd4 11. ♗xd4 ♗xd4 12. ♕xd4 ♕b6 13. ♕d2 ♘f6 14. ♖fe1± Again White has excellent control.] 11. ♕d2 ♘xd4 12. ♗xd4 a5 This position was reached in Anand – Morovic Fernandez, Novi Sad 1990. Here White should switch their attention to the kingside:13. ♖bd1!± followed by f2-f4.

**10. h3!**

Position after: 10. h3!

I want to cover the g4-square and it feels less weakening to do it this way compared to f2-f3. Also, importantly, it leaves the f3-square open for the d4-knight to drop back to.

**10... ♘xd4**

**A)** 10... a5 11. ♘db5! a4 Shchekachev – Maghsoodloo, Europe Echecs INT 2020. Here we can ignore Black's queenside expansion and play on the other side of the board with 12. f4!. For example: 12... a3 13. b3 ♘b4 14. ♕d2± I don't really know what Black has achieved by pushing the pawn to a3.

**B)** 10... a6 11. ♘f3!? [11. ♕c2 is also possible although it gives Black the option of 11... ♘d5!?.] 11... ♖c8 12. ♖c1 ♕a5 13. ♕d3 transposing to 10...♖c8.

**11. ♗xd4 ♗c6 12. ♕c2**

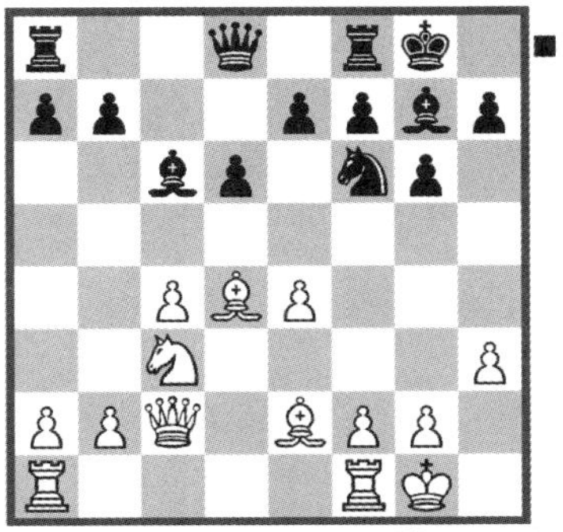

Position after: 12. ♕c2

**12... a5**

It's logical for Black to prevent us from expanding with b2-b4.

12... ♘d7 13. ♗xg7 As usual this exchange is quite advantageous for White. 13... ♔xg7 14. b4!? b6 15. ♖ad1± Followed by f2-f4, with a very comfortable advantage. The push ...a7-a5 can always be met with a2-a3.

**13. b3**

13. ♖ad1 is much more common, but the engine seems to think that Black is not too much worse if they react appropriately:

**A)** 13... ♘d7 14. ♗xg7 ♔xg7 15. ♗g4!± Followed by either capturing on d7, or pushing c4-c5.
**B)** 13... ♕c7 14. ♘d5! ♗xd5 15. exd5

Position after: 15. exd5

15... ♘d7 [15... b5 16. c5 dxc5 17. ♕xc5 ♖fc8 18. ♕xc7 ♖xc7 19. ♗xb5±] 16. ♗xg7 ♔xg7 I reached this position in Haria – Aabling Thomsen, Reykjavik 2019. White is doing well because Black's king is quite weak – we should continue by activating our rooks and then pushing some kingside pawns. A sample line continues: 17. b3 ♖fe8 18. ♕b2+ ♔g8 19. ♖d4± Followed by h2-h4.

**C)** 13... a4 14. c5 ♕a5 15. cxd6 exd6 16. a3±. However, this also strikes me as a very decent position for us.

**13... ♘d7 14. ♗xg7 ♔xg7 15. ♖ad1**

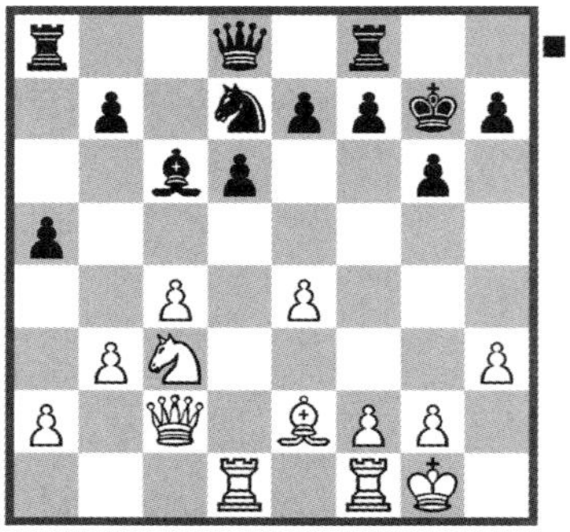

Position after: 15. ♖ad1

With a similar position to ones we've already seen before – White should continue activating their pieces before pushing either the f- or h-pawn.

**15... ♕b6 16. ♕b2 ♔g8 17. ♘d5 ♗xd5 18. exd5±**

Followed by ♖d4.

## Conclusion to Chapter 10

I hope readers will forgive me for daring to analyse Open Sicilian theory in an Anti-Sicilian book. However, when the engine suggested that White should have an advantage after three moves, I was naturally inclined to analyse the Accelerated Dragon in more depth. It's clear that Black players don't pay attention to engine evaluations in this variation, rather focusing on the dynamic advantages of the early fianchetto.

Nevertheless, the knowledge that we've gained in Maroczy structures in both Volume 1 and this book will be extremely helpful in understanding our general plans and ideas. For those who find Open Sicilian theory unacceptable, the next chapter presents a more Anti-Sicilian response to 2...g6.

# 2...g6 3.c3 – Alapin Dragon

**1.e4 c5 2.♘f3 g6 3.c3**

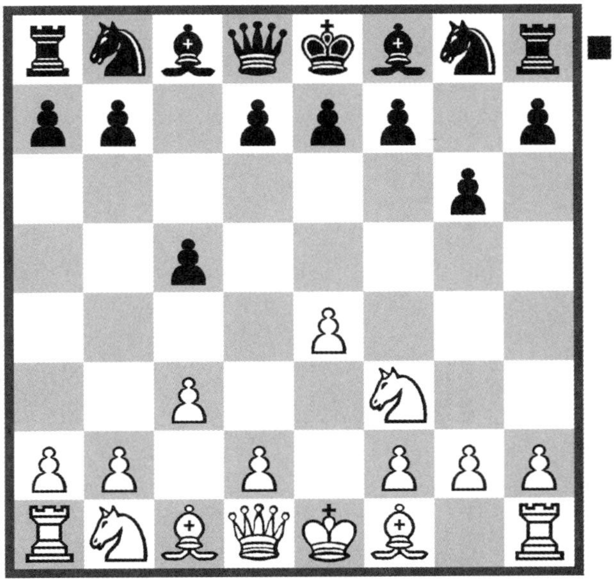

# Chapter Guide

## Chapter 11 – 2...g6 3.c3 – Alapin Dragon

1.e4 c5 2.♘f3 g6 3.c3

## a) 3...♗g7

**1. e4 c5 2. ♘f3 g6 3. c3**

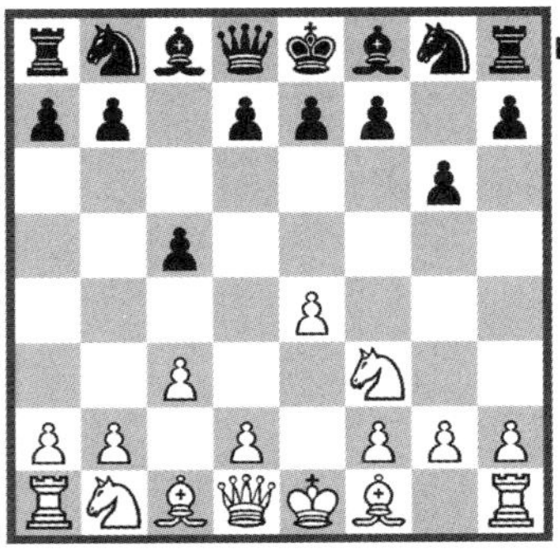
Position after: 3. c3

This is a simpler alternative to 3.c4, but I don't think it reduces White's chances of gaining an advantage out of the opening. It's clear that Black will counter our plan with a quick ...d7-d5 push – the question is whether they'll play this on move 3 or move 4.

**3... ♗g7?!**

It seems weird to say that such a natural move is dubious – but the point is obvious once explained. Black's only way to achieve equality is to challenge our centre with ...d7-d5. By playing 3...♗g7 first, it forces Black to capture on d4 before playing ...d7-d5. This gives us substantially improved versions of the lines we'll encounter after 3...d5 4.e5, for two reasons. Firstly, our b1-knight is able to develop to c3. Secondly, and perhaps more significantly, Black has 'wasted' a move with ...♗g7. This might seem confusing but it is important to understand that g7 may not be a good square for the Black bishop. This will become more apparent in the mainline after 3...d5 4.e5. To put it simply, Black's dark-squared bishop is very poorly placed against our future d4-e5 pawn chain.

**4. d4 cxd4**

**A)** 4... d5? just loses a pawn after 5. dxc5 dxe4 6. ♕xd8+ ♔xd8 7. ♘g5+–.

**B)** 4... ♕c7 has also been played but White has a comfortable advantage after something simple like 5. ♗d3

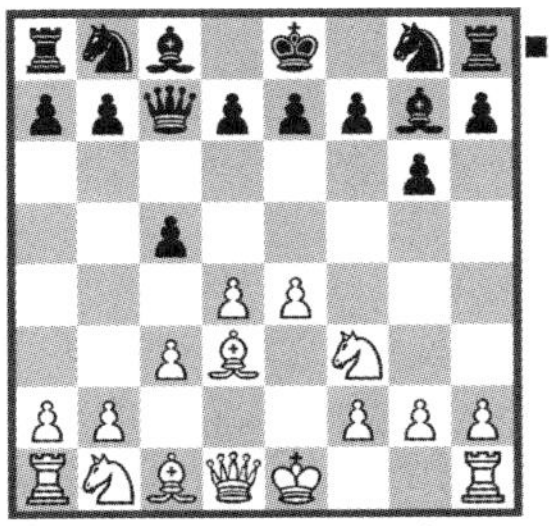
Position after: 5. ♗d3

**B1)** 5... d5!? is probably important to check. 6. exd5 ♘f6 7. c4! cxd4 8. ♘xd4 ♘xd5 9. cxd5 ♗xd4 10. 0-0 Black has recaptured the pawn but their position looks fragile. Castling is impossible for the moment, enabling us to develop a dangerous initiative. 10... ♗g7 11. ♘c3 0-0 12. ♖e1+– Followed by something like ♗e3, ♕f3, and either ♖ac1 or ♖ad1. I don't know how Black will complete development.

**B2)** 5... d6 6. 0-0 ♘f6 7. h3 0-0 8. a4 a6 9. ♖e1 b6 10. ♘a3±

**5. cxd4**

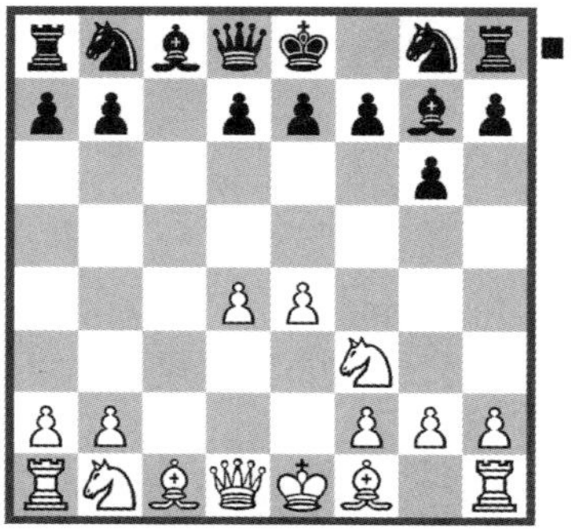
Position after: 5. cxd4

**5... d5**

5... d6 is just very passive. 6. ♘c3 ♘c6 [6... ♘f6 7. ♗b5+ ♗d7 8. e5! dxe5 9. dxe5 ♘g4 10. ♗f4 ♕b6 11. ♕e2 ♗xb5 12. ♘xb5± Black's knight on g4 will get kicked with a timely h2-h3.] 7. d5! ♘e5 8. ♘xe5 ♗xe5 The space advantage is beneficial for White, and Black's bishop will have to spend further time relocating from e5. A sample line here is: 9. ♗e3 ♗g7 10. ♗d3 ♘f6 11. 0-0 0-0 12. h3± We can consider f2-f4, or just play more slowly with ♖e1, a2-a4, ♕b3 etc.

**6. e5**

*(see diagram next column)*

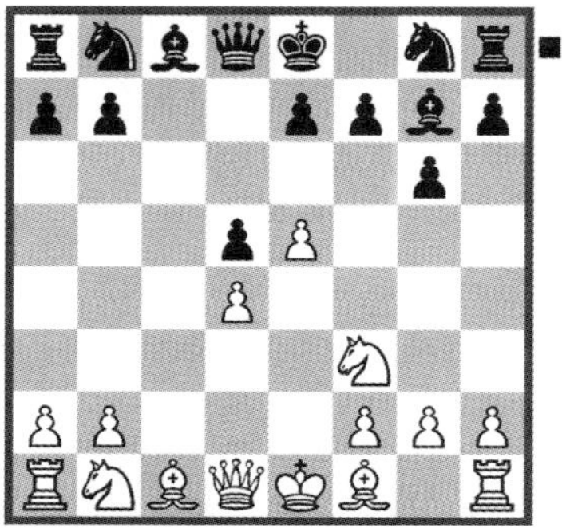
Position after: 6. e5

The positions we'll encounter in this variation, and also the positions in the mainline with 3...d5 4.e5, are very similar to those in the first volume of this series in the line 1. e4 c5 2. ♘f3 ♘c6 3.♗b5 g6 4. 0-0 ♗g7 5. c3 ♘f6 6.♖e1 0-0 7.d4 d5 8.e5 ♘e4. The predominant reason why I like this structure for White is because Black's dark-squared bishop is hemmed in by our d4-e5 pawn chain. Similar to the aforementioned chapter from volume 1, we'll be looking to play ♗b5+ and potentially force the sequence ♗xc6 dxc6, acquring a positional advantage on the queenside due to Black's weak c6-pawn and our new outpost on c5. Even if Black avoids this concession, queenside play is still attractive due to the open c-file. We're not limited to the queenside either – a potential h-pawn push in the future looks appealing too. Black's main plan will be to break in the centre with ...f7-f6 but I'll demonstrate a few effective ways of reacting to this break. I'll keep analysis fairly brief in this section as there aren't too many concrete variations – it's more important to focus on the various plans I've outlined. For simplicity, it makes sense to play ♗b5 on the next move unless Black directly prevents it.

**6... ♗g4**

**A)** 6... a6 Only the fourth most common move, but I think it's very sensible. Black prevents us from developing with a tempo and avoids any unwanted positional concessions. 7. ♗e2 I also considered 7.♗d3 and 7.h3, but this seems simplest. The bishop prevents the pin after a potential ...♗g4, and also stands well in case the f-file opens after Black plays ...f7-f6. 7... ♘c6 8. 0-0

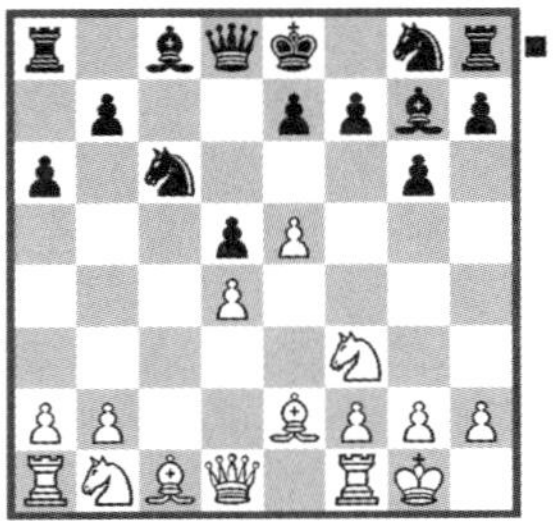

Position after: 8. 0-0

8... ♗g4 [8... ♘h6 9. h3 0-0 10. ♘c3 f6 11. exf6 exf6 12. ♖e1± The d5-pawn will be a constant problem for Black. We can also consider ideas like ♕b3 and ♘a4-b6.] 9. ♘bd2! We want to recapture on f3 with our d2-knight. 9... e6 10. h3 ♗xf3 11. ♘xf3 ♘ge7 12. ♗d3! Planning to meet ...♘f5 with ♗xf5. 12... 0-0 13. ♗e3 f6 14. exf6 ♖xf6 15. ♖c1± White has a comfortable advantage.

**B)** 6... ♘h6 7. ♗b5+!

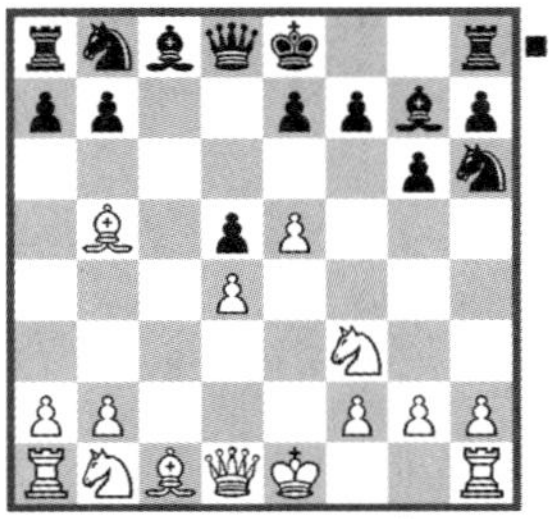

Position after: 7. ♗b5+!

**B1)** 7... ♘c6 8. h3! It's probably wise to hold off on capturing on c6 for now, as we don't want to allow Black to get active with a future ...♗a6. 8... 0-0 9. 0-0 f6 In Carlsen – Nakamura, chess24.com 2021, it was better to keep developing with 10. ♘c3!, after which 10... ♘f7 11. exf6 exf6 12. ♖e1± gives a clear advantage for White. Black is very passive and we can re-route our light squared bishop to either b3 or c2, followed by ideas of h4-h5 or queenside expansion.

**B2)** 7... ♗d7 8. ♗xd7+ ♕xd7 9. ♘c3 0-0 10. 0-0 ♘c6 11. ♖e1± Black has avoided weakening their queenside but they still face the same issue of an inactive dark-squared bishop and a space disadvantage.

**C)** 6... ♘c6 7. ♗b5

*(see analysis diagram next page)*

Position after: 7. ♗b5

7... ♗d7 [7... ♕a5+ seems ineffective as our knight was probably heading to c3 anyway. 8. ♘c3 ♗g4 9. ♗d2! Threatening ♘xd5. 9... ♖c8 10. a4! ♕d8 11. h3±] 8. ♘c3 a6 9. ♗xc6! It's even good to capture on c6 here, as the following line will show: 9... ♗xc6 10. 0-0 e6 11. a4! Restricting Black's light-squared bishop. 11... ♘e7 12. b3 0-0 13. ♘e2!± The plan is ♘g3, ♗a3, ♕d3 and h4-h5. Black's bishop pair is useless here.

**7. ♗b5+**

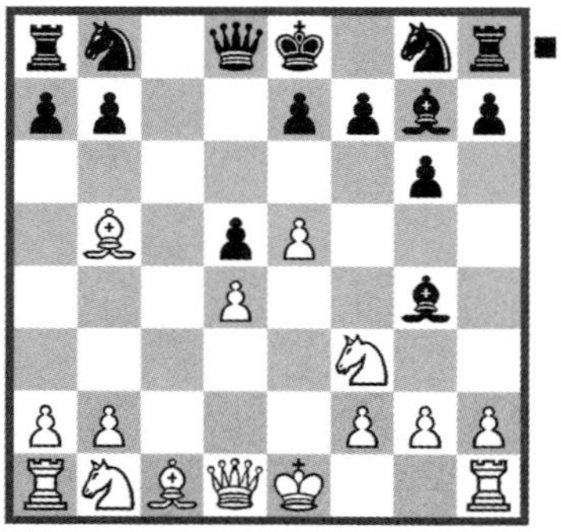

Position after: 7. ♗b5+

**7... ♘d7**

7... ♘c6 8. ♗xc6+! bxc6 9. ♘bd2 f6 [9... ♘h6 10. 0-0 0-0 11. h3 ♗xf3 12. ♘xf3± Followed by ♗f4 and ♖c1 – White has great control over the position.] 10. 0-0! fxe5 11. dxe5 ♘h6 12. h3 ♗xf3 13. ♘xf3 0-0 14. ♗e3± The bishop is heading for c5. Black's position might appear quite reasonable, but the c6-pawn is a big weakness and we'll continue with something like ♗c5, ♕a4, b2-b4, ♖fe1 and ♖ac1.

**8. ♘bd2!**

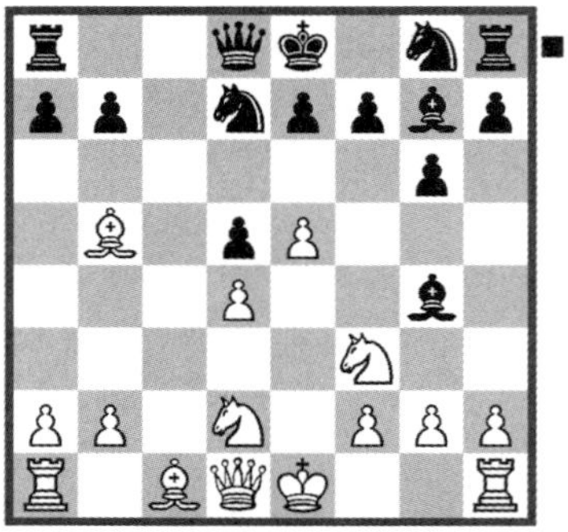

Position after: 8. ♘bd2!

I like the idea of putting the knight on b3, and we also gain the option of recapturing on f3 with the knight if we so desire.

**8... e6 9. 0-0 a6 10. ♗e2 ♘e7 11. h3 ♗xf3 12. ♘xf3±**

White has good prospects on both the queenside and the kingside. If Black ever breaks in the centre with ...f7-f6, White's bishop pair will only increase in their significance.

## b) 3...♘f6

**1. e4 c5 2. ♘f3 g6 3. c3 ♘f6**

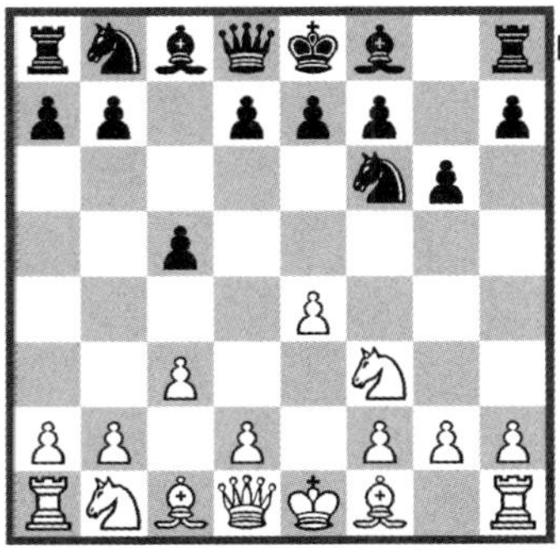

Position after: 3... ♘f6

This has also been tried, but it looks like Black is putting themselves in a dangerous situation.

**4. e5 ♘d5 5. d4 cxd4 6. ♕xd4!**

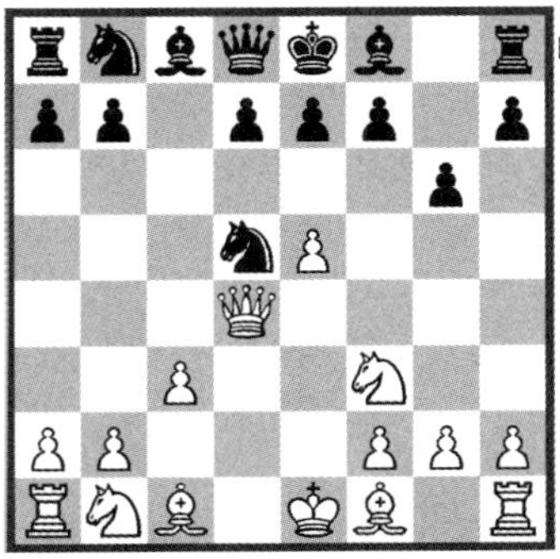

Position after: 6. ♕xd4!

Forcing Black to move the knight again.

**6... ♘c7**

**A)** 6... e6 looks very strange, for example: 7. c4 ♘c6 8. ♕e4 ♘de7 [8... f5 9. ♕e2! ♘de7 10. ♗f4 ♗g7 11. ♘c3± Black has weakened their position immensely. One plan for White is to push h4-h5.] 9. ♘c3 ♗g7 10. ♗f4 0-0 11. ♗e2 b6 12. ♗g5!± Enabling our queen to slide to f4, getting out of a potential discovered attack on the a8-h1 diagonal. White once again has excellent control.

**B)** 6... ♘b6 This feels slightly inferior to 6...♘c7 as the knight doesn't have as many squares to jump to, and it also hinders the b7-pawn from moving. 7. ♘a3

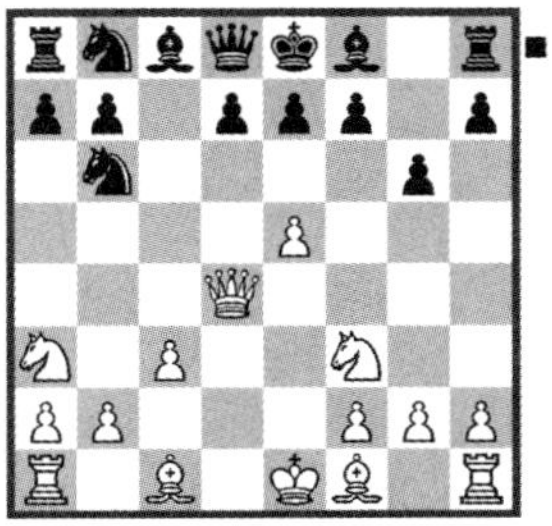

Position after: 7. ♘a3

There are quite a few good moves for White here, but it's logical to just continue developing. The knight is looking to jump to either b5 or c4 in the near future.

**B1)** 7... ♘c6 8. ♕h4 h6 Preventing ♗h6, but Black will now face problems getting castled. [8... ♗g7 9. ♗h6 0-0 10. 0-0-0 d5 11. ♗xg7 ♔xg7 12. ♗d3→ With a strong attack coming on the kingside.] 9. ♗f4 If Black continues with 9...♗g7, it's difficult to find a good move after 10. 0-0-0. So it's logical for them to attempt to exchange queens instead. 9... ♘d5 10. ♗g3 e6 11. ♕xd8+ ♘xd8 12. ♘b5 a6 13. ♘d6+ ♗xd6 14. exd6± With excellent control – there are lots of holes in Black's position.

**B2)** 7... ♗g7 8. ♕h4!

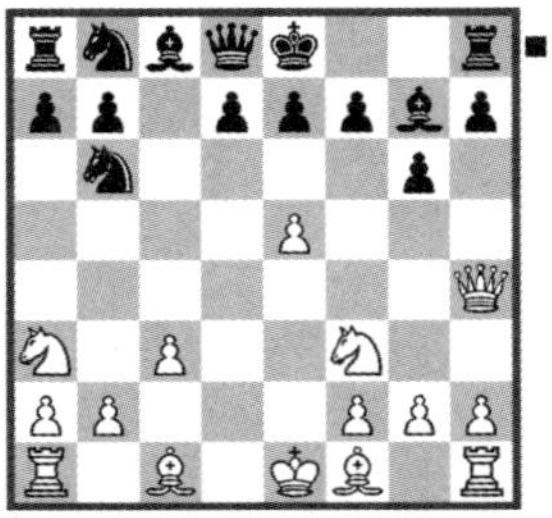
Position after: 8. ♕h4!

Anticipating either ...d7-d6 or ...d7-d5, and lining up ♗h6.

**B2.1)** 8... d5 9. exd6 ♕xd6 10. ♘b5! ♕c6 [10... ♕e6+ 11. ♗e2 ♘a6 12. 0-0!+– and White has a winning initiative as Black is unable to castle.] 11. ♗e2 Again there are several good options, but this is the easiest. Black's pieces are misplaced whereas ours are working extremely well. 11... h6 [11... 0-0 12. ♗h6!± Followed by 0-0 and bringing our rooks to the centre.] It's always logical for Black to try and prevent ♗h6, but after 12. ♘fd4! ♕d7 13. ♕g3 ♘a6 14. h4! 0-0 15. h5 g5 16. f4!+– we are simply breaking through on the kingside. Remember, we always have the option to castle queenside.

**B2.2)** 8... h6 9. ♗f4!

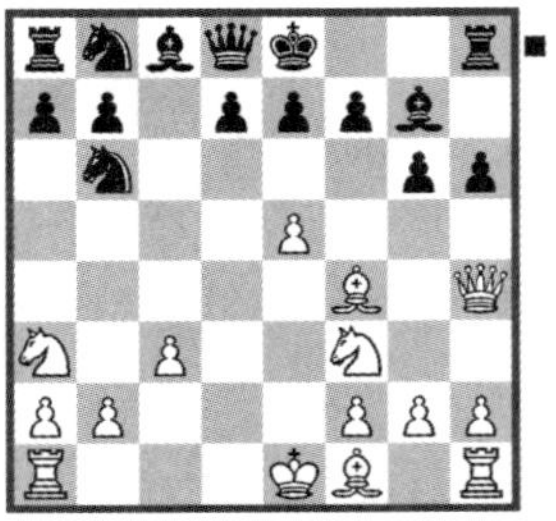
Position after: 9. ♗f4!

Planning to castle queenside. Black needs to play actively or else they'll simply be lost, as castling isn't an option.

**B2.2a)** 9... g5 10. ♕g3 0-0 11. ♗e3 Followed by 0-0-0, and it becomes clear that Black has compromised their kingside too much. There is one critical line to know here: 11... ♘d5 12. ♘c4 f5 13. ♗xg5! The only move for an advantage – but White is just winning now. 13... hxg5 14. 0-0-0! ♘c7 15. ♘xg5 Threatening ♕h4. 15... ♕e8 16. f4!+– The piece deficit means nothing – we have two pawns and a strong attack. We can even continue slowly, with moves like ♗d3, ♘e3 and ♕f2, planning a g2-g4 break.

**B2.2b)** 9... d5!? 10. exd6 g5! 11. ♕g3 0-0 12. ♗e3 f5 Black doesn't want to capture on d6 as it would give us a great position after 0-0-0 (or ♕xd6 followed by 0-0-0), so it's logical to continue creating threats. 13. ♗xb6 axb6 14. ♗c4+ ♔h8 [14... ♔h7 15. 0-0-0 f4 is just lost after 16. ♘xg5+ hxg5 17. ♕xg5+–.] 15. ♘e5!

Position after: 15. ♘e5!

Turning the tables. Now it's Black who has to deal with our threats. 15... ♕e8 16. ♕e3! Planning to capture on f7. 16... exd6 17. ♘f7+! ♔h7 18. 0-0-0! ♕xe3+ 19. fxe3 ♗xc3 20. ♘xd6

**B2.2b1)** 20... ♗b4 21. ♘c2 ♗xd6 22. ♖xd6 ♘c6 23. h4 g4 24. ♘d4±

**B2.2b2)** 20... ♗d7 21. bxc3 ♖xa3 22. ♗b3± Our pieces are extremely active and Black will struggle to prevent the loss of at least a pawn here. We're likely to follow up with some combination of h2-h4 and ♖hf1.

**B2.2b3)** 20... ♗g7 21. ♖hf1! f4 22. exf4 ♗g4 23. ♖de1 gxf4 24. ♘e8!

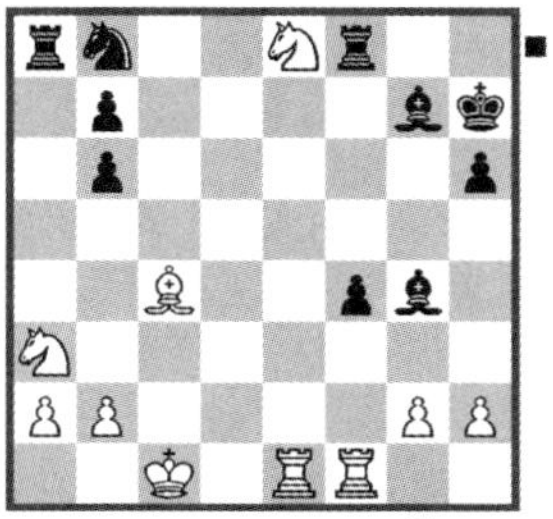

Position after: 24. ♘e8!

Our main plan now is to pick off the f4-pawn. 24... ♗d4 25. ♘c2 ♘c6 26. ♘xd4 ♘xd4 27. ♖e4!+– Even if Black manages to save the f-pawn, the queenside pawns are bound to fall.

**7. ♕h4!**

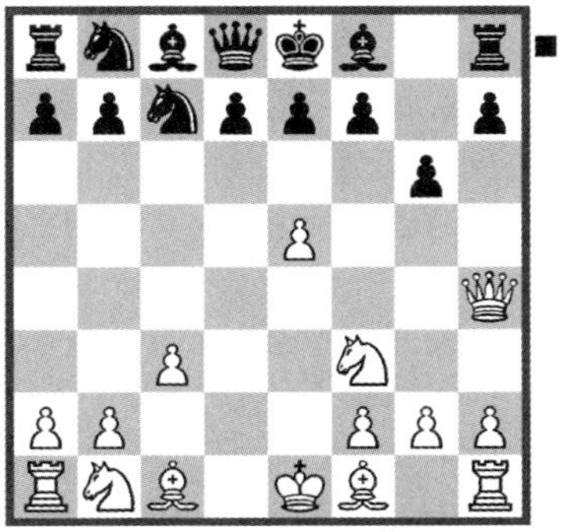

Position after: 7. ♕h4!

From the variations that we examined after 6...♘b6, it's obvious that our queen belongs on this square, so we may as well do it immediately. Bringing our knight to a3 is less logical here as the b5-square is unavailable. Instead we'll capitalise on the fact that Black doesn't control the c4-square – by bringing our f1-bishop there and launching an attack against the Black king.

**7... ♘c6**

7... h6 has also been played but Black will run into the usual problem of finding it difficult to get castled. For example: 8. ♗c4 ♘c6 9. 0-0 ♗g7 10. ♖e1 b5 11. ♗d3! 11.♗b3 This isn't too bad for Black but our position is nice and flexible. Here we can aim for a quick f4-f5. 11... ♖b8 12. ♘a3

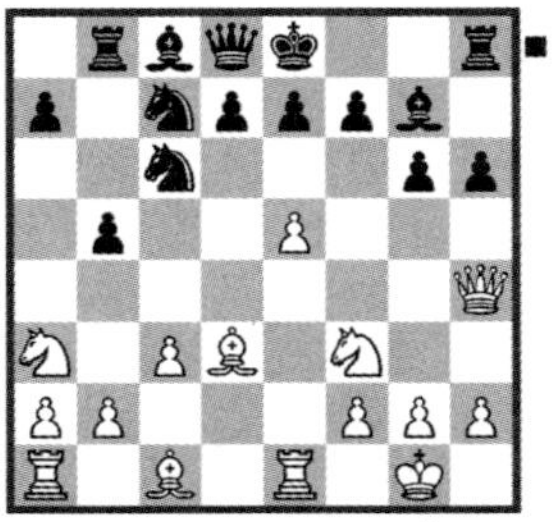
Position after: 12. ♘a3

12... a6 [12... b4 13. cxb4 ♘xb4 14. ♗f1± is also good for White. Our knight will jump to c4, and Black's position looks increasingly difficult to play.] 13. ♕g3!± Followed by ♘h4 and f2-f4 with a clear advantage.

**8. ♗c4**

*(see diagram next column)*

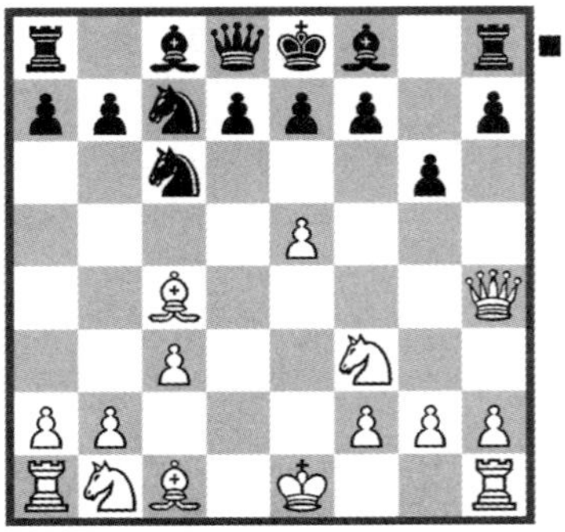
Position after: 8. ♗c4

**8... b5**

It makes sense for Black to develop on the queenside first, as the other alternatives don't look very appealing.

**A)** 8... ♗g7 9. ♗h6!± is already clearly great for White.

**B)** 8... d5 9. exd6 ♕xd6 [9... exd6 10. ♕xd8+ ♘xd8 11. 0-0± Followed by ♖e1/d1, ♗e3, ♘bd2, and White has very comfortable play in this queenless middlegame.] 10. 0-0

Position after: 10. 0-0

**B1)** 10... ♗g7 11. ♘bd2 The big problem for Black is that castling is suicidal on account of moves like ♘e4,

♗h6, and ♘fg5 coming in rapidly. Black's king won't be able to survive the onslaught. Instead, the only alternative is to try something like 11... ♕f6 but after 12. ♕g3± it's extremely unclear how Black will unravel. The engine recommends 12... ♕d6, but in that case we have an improved version of the queenless middlegame that we saw in the line after 9...exd6.

**B2)** 10... ♗e6 In Chigaev – Iturrizaga Bonelli, Chess.com 2017, White would have been completely dominating after 11. ♘bd2 ♗xc4 12. ♘xc4 ♕d5 13. ♖e1 ♘e6 14. ♘g5!±. Black has to make some kind of concession in order to complete development.

**9. ♗b3 ♗b7**

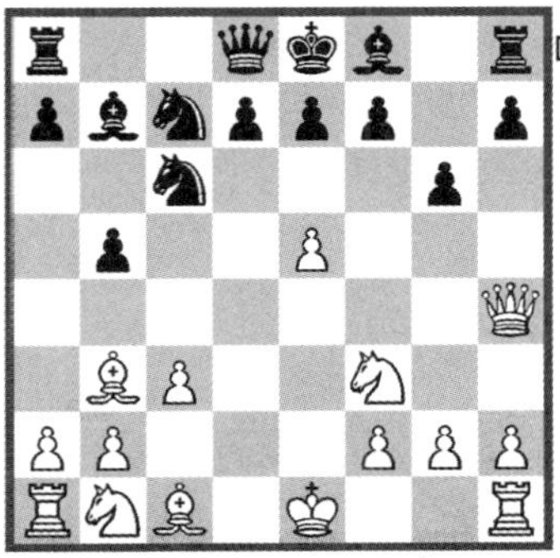

Position after: 9... ♗b7

**10. 0-0**

10. ♗h6 seems logical but allows 10... e6! and after something like 11. ♕f4 ♗xh6 12. ♕xh6 ♘e7! Black has decent counterplay.

**10... h6**

10... ♘a5 is also possible but after the simple 11. ♗d1!± we can carry on developing as normal and Black's knight on a5 is more misplaced than our bishop on d1, which even has the option of rerouting to e2.

**11. ♖e1 ♗g7 12. a4**

It's always useful throwing in this move.

**12... a6 13. ♕g3!**

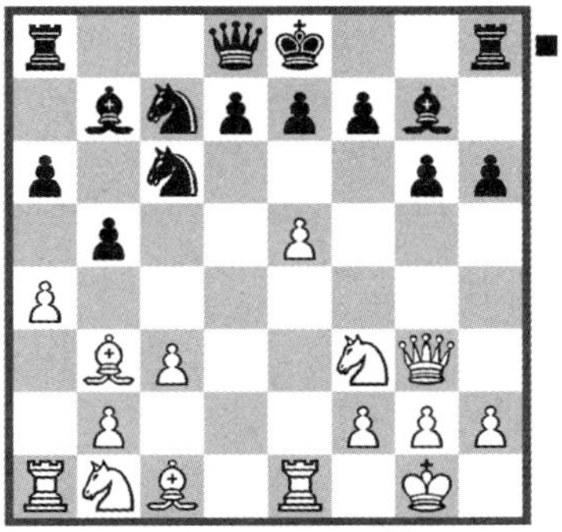

Position after: 13. ♕g3!

Preventing Black from castling.

**13... ♘e6 14. ♘bd2 ♕c7 15. h4! h5 16. ♗xe6! dxe6 17. ♘e4±**

Followed by ♗f4, with a very pleasant advantage for White.

## c) 3...d5 4.exd5

**1. e4 c5 2. ♘f3 g6 3. c3 d5**

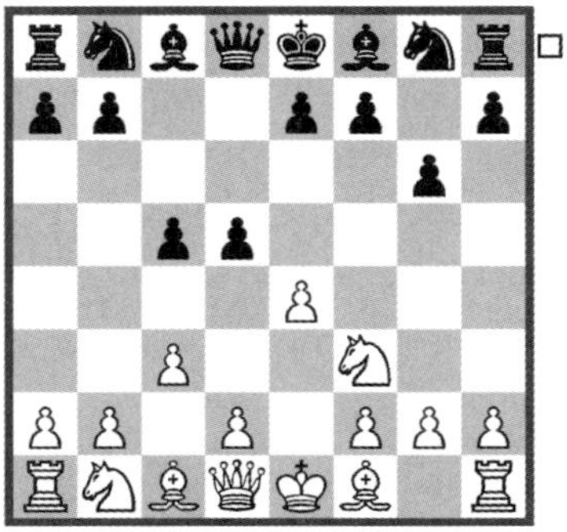

Position after: 3... d5

**4. exd5**

This offers White good chances of an advantage.

4. e5 will be our mainline, analysed in the next subchapter.

**4... ♕xd5 5. d4 ♗g7**

**A)** 5... cxd4 is clearly inferior as we gain the c3-square for our knight to jump to. 6. cxd4 ♗g7 7. ♘c3

Position after: 7. ♘c3

7... ♕a5 8. ♗b5+! ♗d7 9. ♗xd7+ ♘xd7 10. 0-0 ♘gf6 11. ♖e1 Black has to waste time protecting the e-pawn, enabling us to develop a nice initiative. For example: 11... ♘d5 [11... ♕d8 12. ♕a4 0-0 13. ♕b4± seems to win a pawn.] 12. ♗d2 ♘xc3 13. bxc3! ♘b6 14. h4! ♕d5 15. a4!± Followed by ♖b1-b5. Black still can't castle.

**B)** 5... ♘f6?! 6. ♕b3! ♗g7 7. ♗c4 ♕e4+ 8. ♗e3 0-0 9. 0-0↑

**6. ♘bd2!**

This is a rare move but the point is clever. We aim to recapture on d4 with the f3-knight, and then move the d2-knight to f3. At the same time, we are immediately threatening to play ♗c4 now.

6. ♘a3 is the most common move but I couldn't find anything in either of the following variations: 6... cxd4

Position after: 6... cxd4

7. ♘b5 [7. ♗c4 ♕e4+ 8. ♗e3 ♘h6 9. cxd4 0-0 10. 0-0 ♗g4∞] 7... ♘a6 8. ♘bxd4 ♘f6 9. ♗b5+ ♗d7 10. ♗xa6 bxa6 11. 0-0 0-0 12. ♖e1 ♖fe8 13. ♘e5∞ Nihal – Mamedov, Chess.com 2022.

**6... cxd4**

6... ♘f6 7. ♗c4

**A)** 7... ♕h5 8. 0-0 0-0 9. h3 ♘c6 10. ♘b3 cxd4 11. ♘fxd4± White definitely has a small edge here. After exchanging queens we can start to think about playing on the queenside, for example with a2-a4 and ♗e3/♗f4. It's difficult to find a good plan for Black.

**B)** 7... ♕d8? 8. dxc5 ♕c7 9. b4±

**C)** 7... ♕d6 8. ♘b3 cxd4 9. ♕xd4! Once again the queen exchange will cause Black some problems. I will provide some sample variations here: 9... ♕xd4 [9... ♗e6 10. ♕xd6 exd6 11. ♗e2±] 10. ♘bxd4 0-0 11. 0-0 ♗d7 [11... ♘bd7 12. ♖e1 e6 13. a4±] 12. ♘e5 ♗e8 [12... ♘c6 13. ♘xd7 ♘xd7 14. ♘b3±] 13. ♖e1 e6 14. ♗f4 ♘h5 15. ♗d2 ♘d7 16. ♘ef3± Black's pieces are very awkwardly placed. We have a clever idea here of ♗f1, g2-g3 and ♗g2, though we should also consider pushing some pawns on the queenside.

**7. ♗c4!**

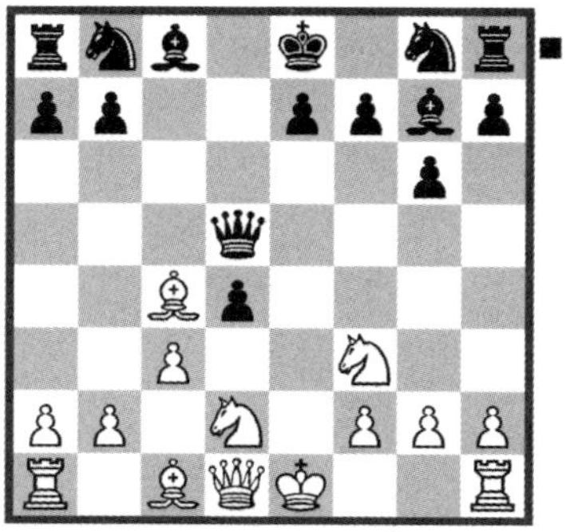

Position after: 7. ♗c4!

**7... ♕d8**

**A)** 7... ♕a5 8. ♘xd4 ♘f6 9. 0-0 0-0 10. ♕e2± We'll continue developing with ♘2f3, and Black's queen looks misplaced on a5.

**B)** 7... ♕d6 is just bad as we gain further tempi hitting the Black queen. 8. ♘e4 ♕b6 9. 0-0! dxc3 10. ♗e3 ♕c7 11. ♕b3 e6 12. ♗d4+–

**C)** 7... ♕h5 8. 0-0!

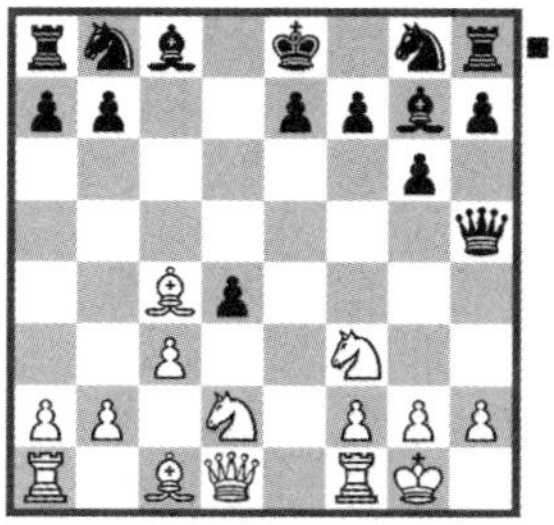

Position after: 8. 0-0!

**C1)** 8... ♘c6 9. ♕b3 ♘h6 10. ♘xd4 ♘xd4 11. cxd4 Black can't capture on d4 here due to ♘f3 followed by ♗xh6. 11... 0-0 12. h3! Preventing the h6-knight from moving to either f5 or g4. 12... ♗xd4 [12... g5 13. g4! ♘xg4 14. ♗e2 ♗xd4 15. ♕f3!+–] 13. ♖e1± With a strong initiative.

**C2)** 8... dxc3 9. ♘e4 cxb2 [9... ♘c6 10. ♕b3 e6 11. bxc3+– Black is completely lost, especially with ♗a3 and ♘d6+ coming next.] 10. ♗xf7+! ♔xf7 11. ♕b3+ ♔f8 12. ♘eg5+–

**D)** 7... ♕c5 8. ♕b3! ♘h6 9. ♘e4 ♕b6 10. ♘xd4 0-0 11. 0-0 White has great control over the centre. A sample line follows: 11... ♘f5 12. ♘xf5 ♗xf5 13. ♘g3 ♗d7 14. ♖e1 ♘c6 15. ♕xb6 axb6 16. ♗e3 ♘a5 17. ♗f1 b5 18. ♗c5± It's unclear how much compensation Black has for the pawn.

**8. ♘xd4**

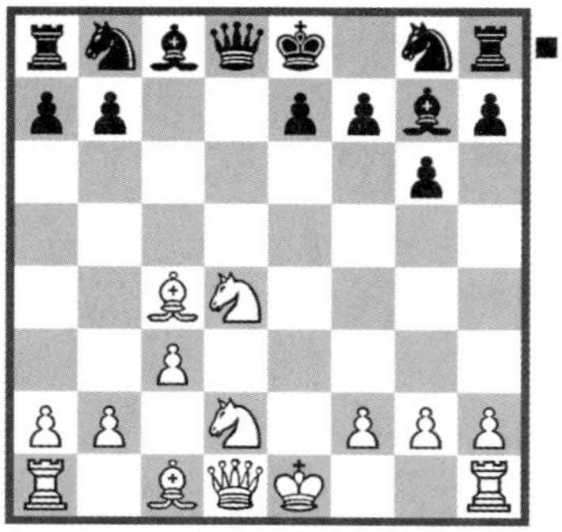

Position after: 8. ♘xd4

**8... ♘f6**

8... ♗xd4? is way too risky. 9. cxd4 ♕xd4 10. 0-0 ♘f6 11. ♕a4+ ♕d7 12. ♕b3 0-0 13. ♘f3+– Followed by either ♘e5 or ♗h6.

**9. 0-0 0-0 10. ♘2f3**

Black is definitely solid, but I still believe that White has a small edge due to our more active pieces.

**10... ♘bd7**

10... ♕c7 11. ♕e2

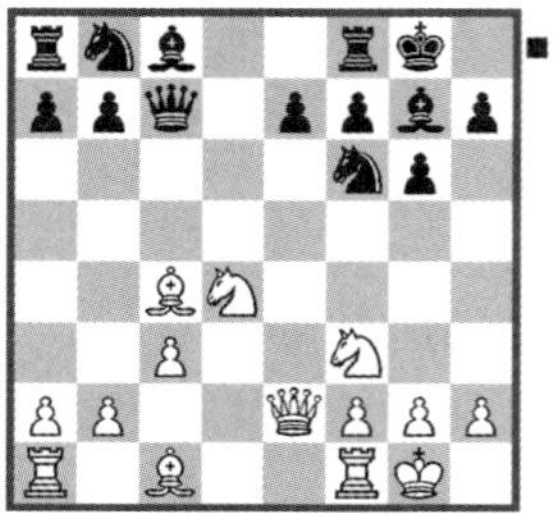

Position after: 11. ♕e2

11... ♗g4 [11... ♘c6 12. ♘xc6 ♕xc6 13. h3± We can continue with ♘e5 and ♗f4 before bringing our rooks to the centre.] 12. h3 ♗xf3 13. ♘xf3± Black has consolidated but has given up the bishop pair in doing so. We have a comfortable advantage here.

**11. ♖e1 a6 12. ♘g5!**

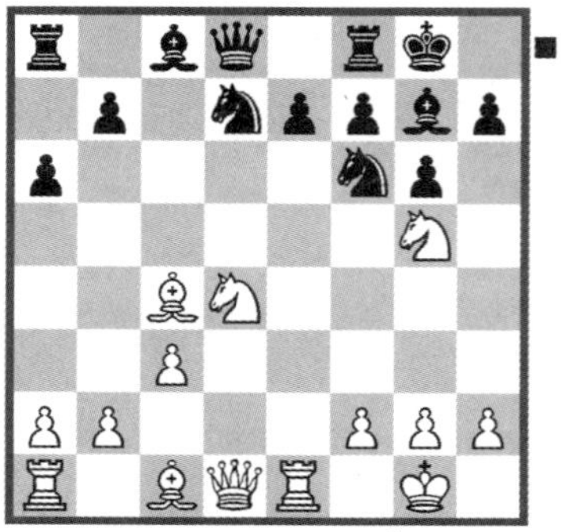

Position after: 12. ♘g5!

Threatening ♕b3.

**12... ♘b6 13. ♗b3 ♘bd5 14. ♘gf3!±**

Black's knight is surprisingly worse on d5 than on d7. We can continue with either ♗g5 or ♘e5, with the pawn push a2-a4 being another appealing option.

## d) 3...d5 4.e5

**1. e4 c5 2. ♘f3 g6 3. c3 d5 4. e5!?**

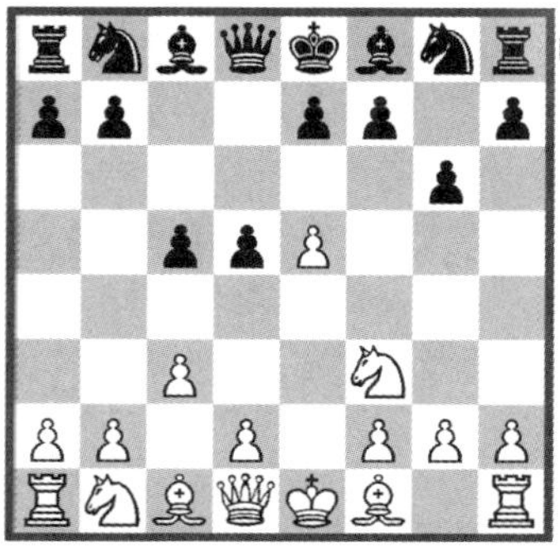

Position after: 4. e5!?

This seems like a strange way to force the desired d4-e5 pawn structure, but it's not easy for Black to deal with. The same principles that I described in the line after 3... ♗g7 apply here and are useful in understanding Black's best way to continue. I think it makes sense for Black to delay playing ...♗g7 for as long as possible. For example, continuing with ...♗g4, ...♘c6 and ...e7-e6 offers the dark-squared bishop the possibility of developing to e7 (presumably after either ...♘h6-f5 or ...♘ge7-f5). The other option for Black is to play an early ...a7-a6, preventing any possibility of us playing ♗b5+. If Black does develop the bishop to g7 in this line, this should be followed up with active play involving ...f7-f6, directly playing against our central stronghold. I think it makes sense to focus on plans and themes rather than too many concrete variations (particularly as there could be quite a few transpositions), although I will specify when it's important to remember individual moves. From White's perspective, our aim is to achieve strong positional control depending on Black's choice of development. The lines that I analyse will hopefully demonstrate that we have good chances of achieving an advantage.

**4... ♗g4**

**A)** 4... ♘c6 5. ♗b5 There are only two logical independent continuations for Black that we haven't analysed in a separate variation. 5... ♕b6 [5... ♗d7 6. ♗xc6! Important to note that Black was threatening ...♘xe5. 6... ♗xc6 7. d4 cxd4 8. ♘xd4! 8.cxd4 is also good, but recapturing with the knight is a strong positional move. 8... ♗g7 9. ♕e2 ♕c7 10. ♗f4 e6 11. 0-0±; 5... ♗g4 transposes to 4...♗g4.] 6. ♗xc6+

*(see analysis diagram next page)*

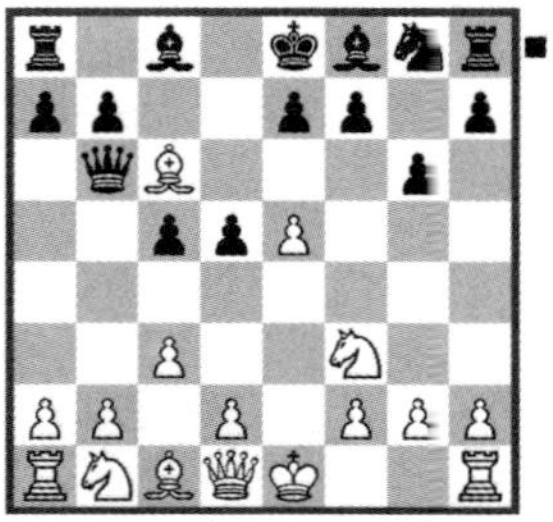
Position after: 6. ♗xc6+

**A1)** 6... bxc6 7. 0-0

**A1.1)** 7... ♘h6 8. d4 ♗g7 9. h3 0-0 10. ♖e1 a5 Kobalia – Gutenev, Sochi 2018. [10... f6 11. dxc5 ♕xc5 12. b4 ♕b6 13. exf6 exf6 14. ♗e3±] 11. b3! A clever idea in response to Black's plan of pushing the a-pawn. 11... a4 12. dxc5 ♕xc5 13. ♗e3 ♕a5 14. b4±

**A1.2)** 7... ♗g4 8. d3

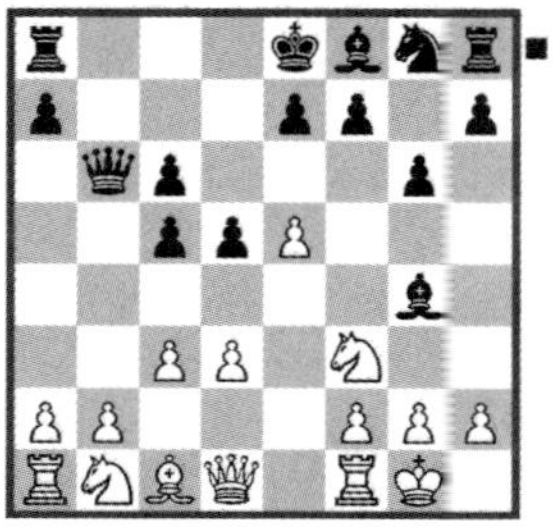
Position after: 8. d3

8.d4 isn't possible as Black can capture on f3, but we are still doing well. Black's doubled c-pawns are going to be a future weakness. A sample continuation is: 8... ♗g7 9. ♖e1 ♗xf3 Otherwise we'll play ♘bd2 and be able to recapture with the knight. 10. ♕xf3 e6 11. ♘d2 a5 12. ♕e2 ♘e7 13. ♘f3 0-0 14. ♖b1± There are many plans available to us but an interesting one is to play g2-g4 next and slowly build a kingside attack.

**A2)** 6... ♕xc6 7. 0-0

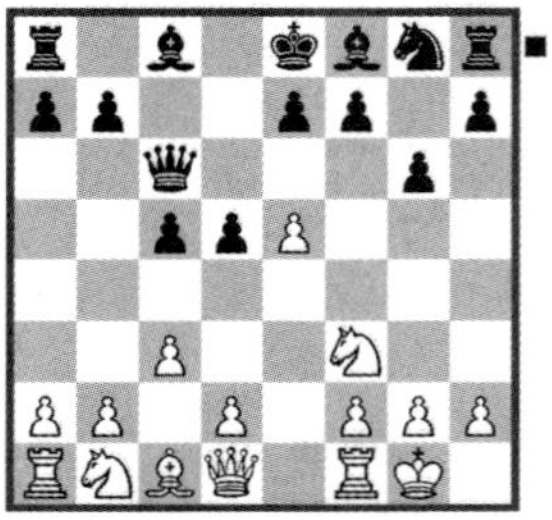
Position after: 7. 0-0

**A2.1)** 7... ♗f5 is also logical, and I think a good response is 8. d3!± with the idea of expanding on the queenside with a2-a4 and b2-b4. If Black does play ...♗g4, we can always switch plans again and play ♘bd2 and d3-d4.

**A2.2)** 7... ♗g4 8. d4 cxd4 [8... ♗g7 9. ♘bd2±; 8... e6 9. dxc5! ♗xc5 10. ♘bd2± Followed by ♘b3-d4.] 9. cxd4 e6 10. h3 ♗xf3 11. ♕xf3 ♗g7 12. ♖d1!

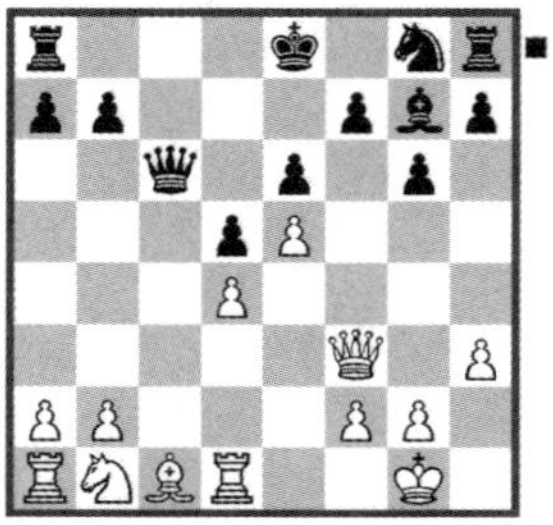
Position after: 12. ♖d1!

The point becomes clear after Black's next move. 12... ♘e7 13. ♗g5! Now 13...♘f5 is met with 14.g4. 13... ♕d7 14. ♘c3⩲ Followed by ♖ac1, and White has a small edge due to the space advantage and Black's poor bishop on g7. We can try to exchange dark-squared bishops at the right moment and play for a kingside attack.

**B)** 4... a6 5. d4

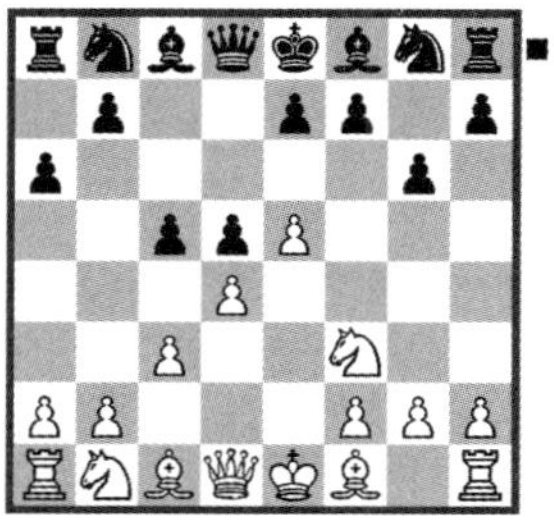

Position after: 5. d4

**B1)** 5... f6 6. g3! A nice response to ...f7-f6 if we haven't yet moved our light-squared bishop. The fianchetto structure works well now that the position is opening up. 6... ♘c6 7. ♗g2 cxd4 8. cxd4 ♗g4 9. 0-0! ♗g7 [9... fxe5 10. dxe5 ♘xe5 11. ♕d4!+–] 10. ♗f4!

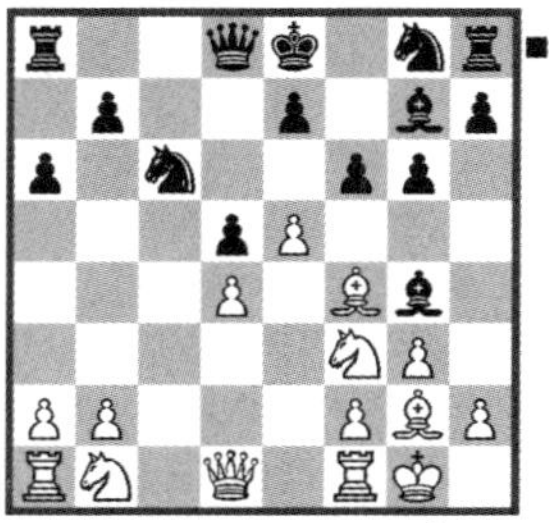

Position after: 10. ♗f4!

10... ♗xf3 [10... fxe5 11. dxe5 ♘xe5 12. ♗xe5 ♗xe5 13. ♕a4+ ♗d7 14. ♕b3± Followed by ♘c3 with a dangerous initiative.] 11. exf6! A clever intermediate move. 11... ♗xf6 [11... ♘xf6 12. ♗xf3⩲] 12. ♗xf3 ♘xd4 13. ♖e1! ♘xf3+ 14. ♕xf3 ♗xb2 15. ♘c3 ♗xa1 [15... ♘f6 16. ♖ab1 ♗xc3 17. ♕xc3 0-0 18. ♖xb7±] 16. ♘xd5!+– Followed by either ♖xa1 or ♘c7+. White is crushing.

**B2)** 5... ♘c6 6. ♗e2

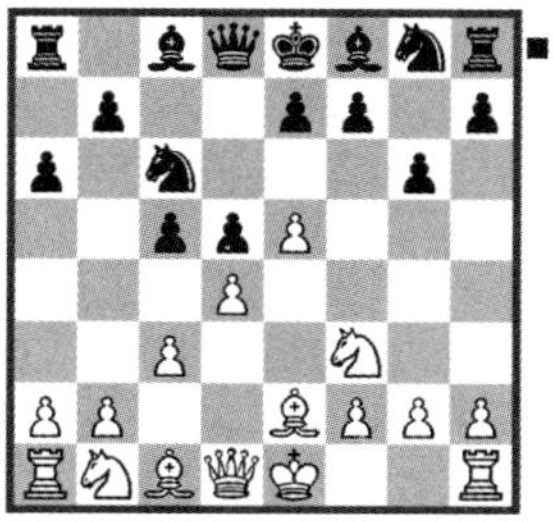

Position after: 6. ♗e2

**B2.1)** 6... f6 7. 0-0! fxe5?! It's too early to open the position – Black needs to develop their kingside first. [7... ♗g7 transposes to 6...♗g7.] 8. ♘xe5 ♗g7 [8... ♘xe5 9. dxe5 ♗g7 10. f4 e6 11. ♗e3 b6 12. b4!±; 8... cxd4 9. ♘xc6 bxc6 10. ♕xd4 ♘f6 11. ♗f4± Followed by ♗f4 and ♘e5 – Black has already incurred lots of weaknesses.] 9. ♘xc6 bxc6 10. dxc5± It looks like we're just a pawn up.

**B2.2)** 6... ♗g7 7. 0-0

Position after: 7. 0-0

**B2.2a)** 7... ♗g4 I'll use this variation to show why it's bad for Black to put the bishop on g7 and not follow up with a quick ...f7-f6 break. 8. ♘bd2 e6 9. h3 ♗xf3 10. ♘xf3 ♘ge7 11. b4! Not the only move, but it's clear that Black is passive and we can start to dominate on both sides of the board. 11... cxb4 12. cxb4↑ The main problem for Black is that their g7-bishop is out of the game, and our bishop pair will start to dominate as the position opens up.

**B2.2b)** 7... cxd4 8. cxd4 f6

Position after: 8... f6

Black attempts to break in the centre without sacrificing a pawn, but there's a big difference compared to 7...f6, as we can now play 9. ♘c3! fxe5 10. dxe5 e6 [10... ♘xe5 11. ♕xd5!+–] 11. ♘a4!± followed by ♗e3 or ♗f4.

**B2.2c)** 7... f6 This has been played four times by Jahongir Vakhidov. Black sacrifices a pawn to get active play, so we need to ensure that we're accurate in order to achieve an advantage. 8. exf6 I think it's logical to accept the pawn sacrifice. Even though Black will gain central control and active play, we remain solid. After all, a pawn is a pawn. 8... ♘xf6 9. dxc5

Position after: 9. dxc5

9... 0-0 [9... e5 10. ♗g5 Followed by ♘bd2, this will likely transpose to 9... 0-0.] 10. ♗g5! The most logical square to develop the bishop to. It would be more vulnerable on f4 or e3. Black is clearly intending to push ...e7-e5, so the bishop stands well on g5.

Position after: 10. ♗g5!

**B2.2c1)** 10... ♘e4 11. ♗e3 Now we retreat to e3, as the bishop can't be hit with ...♘g4. 11... e5 12. ♘bd2 ♘f6 13. ♖e1! Prophylaxis against ...d5-d4-d3. 13... h6! Preventing our idea of c3-c4 followed by ♗g5. [13... ♗e6 14. c4! d4 15. ♗g5± Followed by ♗f1 or ♗d3, with good control.] 14. ♘f1 ♗e6 15. h3

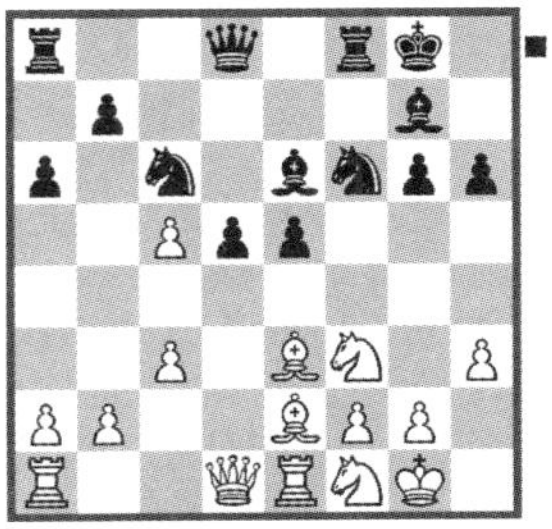

Position after: 15. h3

15... ♘h5 [15... ♕d7 16. ♘g3 ♖ad8 17. ♕d2 g5 18. ♖ad1± We can continue to manoeuvre about and improve our pieces, for example with ♕c2 and ♘h2.] 16. ♘1h2! Clearing the f1-square for our light-squared bishop. 16... ♘f4 17. ♗f1± Followed by ♕d2, ♖ad1 etc.

**B2.2c2)** 10... h6 11. ♗xf6 ♗xf6 12. ♕b3 e5 13. ♘bd2± Followed by ♖ad1 with annoying pressure against Black's d5-pawn.

**B2.2c3)** 10... e5 11. c4!?

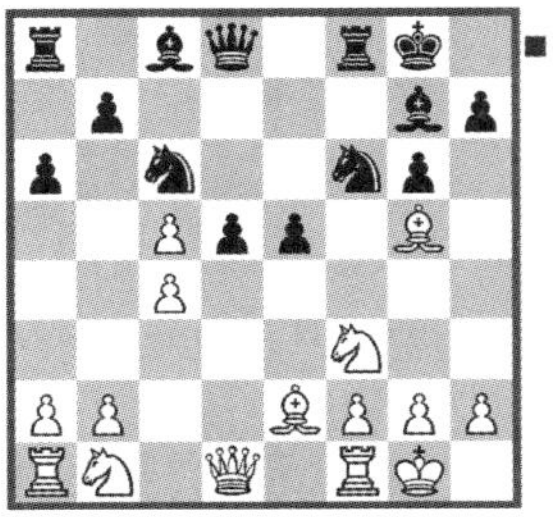

Position after: 11. c4!?

A good moment to play this move, as our bishop isn't on e3 so can't be hit by ...d5-d4 (in contrast to the line after 10...♘e4). 11... d4 12. ♘fd2! ♗f5 13. ♗f3 ♕e7?! [13... ♕d7 stepping out of the pin is more accurate, but I still like White after 14. ♗xf6 ♗xf6 15. ♘e4 ♗e7 16. a3±. Black will recapture the pawn at some point but their light squares are likely going to be a weakness.] In Piorun – Vakhidov, Jerusalem 2022, White's best continuation was 14. ♘e4 ♗xe4 15. ♗xe4 ♕xc5 16. ♗xf6 ♗xf6 17. ♘d2± with great control due to having the superior pawn structure and better minor pieces.

**C)** 4... ♗g7 5. d4

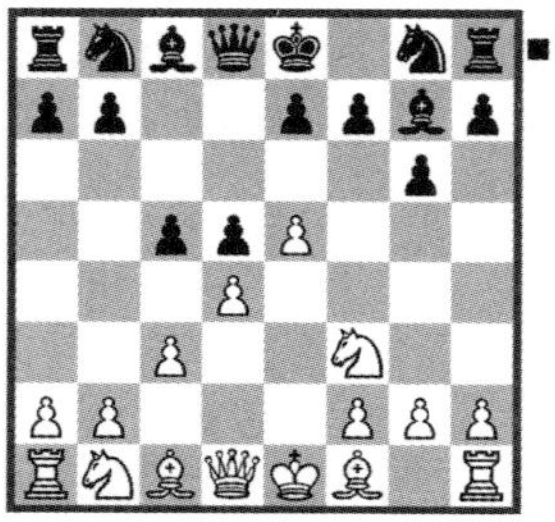
Position after: 5. d4

**C1)** 5... ♘c6 This variation again demonstrates that Black shouldn't put the bishop on g7 without quickly breaking with ...f7-f6. 6. ♗b5

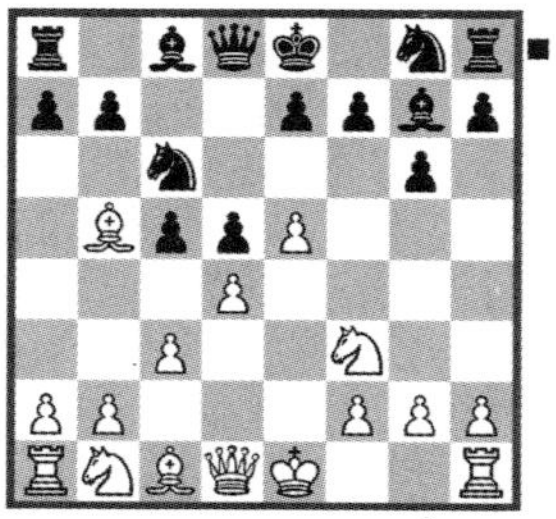
Position after: 6. ♗b5

6... ♕b6 [6... cxd4 7. cxd4 ♕b6 8. ♘c3 e6 9. ♗xc6+ ♕xc6 Meier – Kovalenko, chess24.com 2020. 10. a4! Threatening ♘b5. 10... a6 11. 0-0± Followed by ♗d2, ♕b3 and h2-h4. Black will struggle to deal with our queenside and kingside control.] 7. ♗xc6+ ♕xc6 8. dxc5! Not the only move, but I like to use the d4-square for a minor piece where possible. 8... ♗g4 9. ♘bd2 e6 10. 0-0 ♗xf3 11. ♘xf3 ♕xc5 12. ♖e1±

**C2)** 5... f6 6. ♗b5+! ♗d7 7. ♕e2!

*(see analysis diagram next column)*

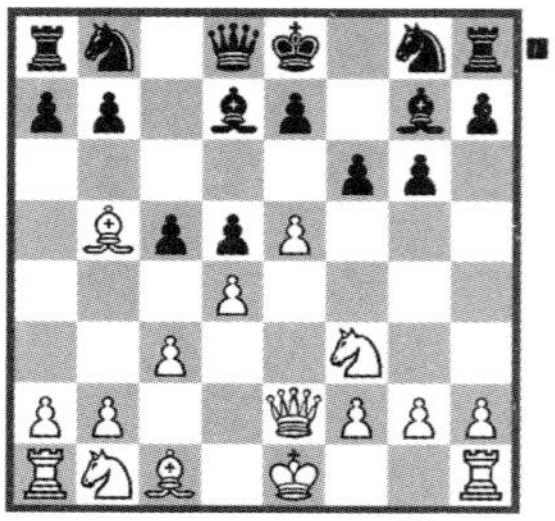
Position after: 7. ♕e2!

Black is too weak on the light-squares. For example: 7... ♕b6 8. a4 fxe5 9. ♘xe5 cxd4 10. ♘xd7 ♘xd7 11. a5! ♕c7 12. a6! dxc3 13. 0-0± With a massive position. It's almost impossible for Black to survive as their position is close to collapsing.

**D)** 4... d4!? This is not as bad as it looks. Black is directly preventing us from pushing d2-d4, but consequently weakens their own d-pawn. However, we need to respond accurately in order to capitalise. 5. ♗b5+ ♗d7 6. a4!

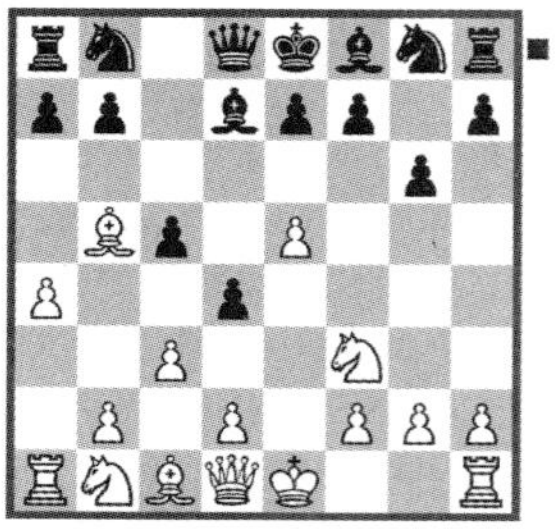
Position after: 6. a4!

Very clever. Black doesn't want to capture on a4 as it opens the a-file and denies their knight the c6-square. 6... ♘c6 [6... a6 7. ♗xd7+ ♘xd7 8. ♘a3 ♗g7 9. ♕e2 ♘h6 10. 0-0± Followed by d2-d3 with great domination, particularly on the light-squares. Black's pieces are suffering from inactivity.] 7. 0-0 ♗g7 8. ♖e1 a6 9. ♗xc6! It doesn't seem natural to give up the bishop pair, but the closed position suits our knights. 9... ♗xc6 10. cxd4 cxd4 11. d3± Followed by ♗f4 and ♘bd2 with an edge.

**5. ♗b5+**

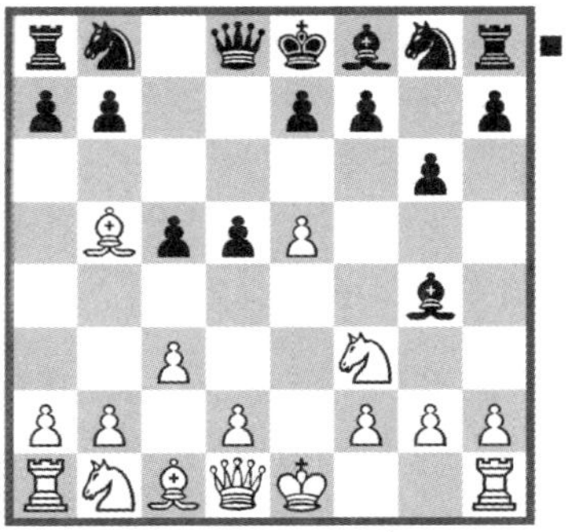

Position after: 5. ♗b5+

This check is usually good if we're offered the opportunity to play it.

**5... ♘c6**

5... ♘d7 is logical if Black wants to avoid potentially getting doubled pawns. 6. d4 a6 7. ♗a4 e6 8. 0-0 b5 9. ♗c2 ♘e7 Now that Black has expanded on the queenside, it makes sense for us to play on the kingside. For example: 10. ♘bd2 ♗g7 11. ♖e1 0-0 12. h3 ♗f5 13. ♗xf5 ♘xf5 14. ♘f1→ Followed by ♘e3 or ♗g5. White's play is easy and looks dangerous.

**6. 0-0**

I also considered 6. ♗xc6!? but I think Black is just wasting time if they try to further protect the c6-knight.

**6... ♘h6**

6... ♖c8 7. d4 cxd4 8. cxd4

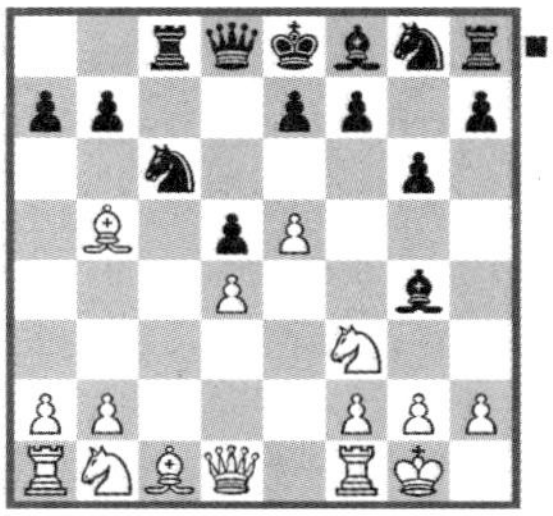

Position after: 8. cxd4

8... ♕b6 [8... e6 9. ♘bd2! a6 10. ♗xc6+ ♖xc6 11. ♘b3! The other point of ♘bd2 (aside from wanting to recapture on f3 with the knight). 11... ♘h6 12. ♗d2 ♘f5 13. h3 ♗xf3 14. ♕xf3± Followed by ♖ac1.] 9. ♗xc6+ ♖xc6 10. ♘bd2 Again the knight wants to jump to b3, from where it stands well protecting the queenside and enabling our c1-bishop to develop. 10... ♗f5! Planning to meet ♘b3 with ...♗c2. [10... e6 11. ♘b3 ♗g7 12. h3 ♗xf3 13. ♕xf3 ♘e7 14. ♗g5±] 11. ♕e2 ♗c2 12. ♘b1! Switching plans again, which works because Black has wasted time with their bishop. 12... ♗e4 13. ♘g5 ♗f5 14. ♘c3±

**7. d4**

*(see diagram next page)*

Position after: 7. d4

**7... ♗xf3**

7... cxd4 We can recapture on d4 and transpose to 7...♗xf3, but there's something even stronger here. 8. ♕a4! ♕c8 9. ♘xd4 ♗d7 10. ♖e1± With good control over the position.

**8. ♕xf3 cxd4 9. cxd4 ♘f5 10. ♕d3 e6**

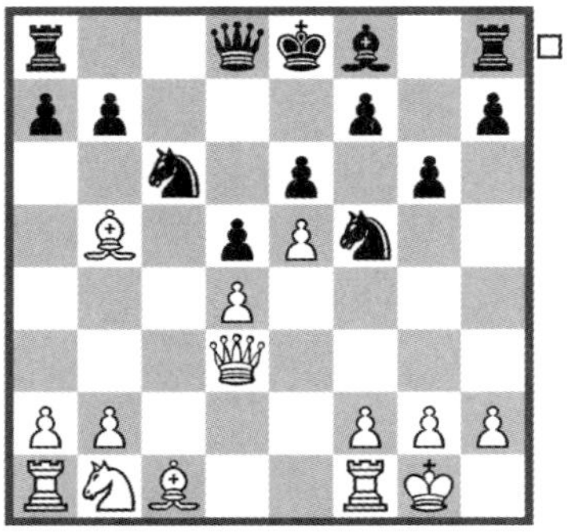

Position after: 10... e6

Black remains solid. This variation is a good example of how they are better off delaying the development of their dark-squared bishop. However, I still believe that White has a small edge.

**11. ♘d2 ♗e7 12. ♘b3 h5 13. ♗d2 ♔f8 14. ♖fc1±**

Black definitely hasn't completely equalised yet.

## Conclusion to Chapter 11

3.c3 is a simpler approach to Black's Accelerated Dragon, but by no means reduces our chance of achieving an advantage out of the opening. Black's dark-squared bishop consistently remains a passenger throughout the variations we've analysed.

In my opinion, the most critical line is in subchapter d) after 4...a6 where Black sacrifices a pawn to free their bishop of inactivity – but if such a drastic solution is required, it clearly shows that 3.c3 is a testing line in itself.

# O'Kelly & Nimzowitsch Variations

1.e4 c5 2.♘f3

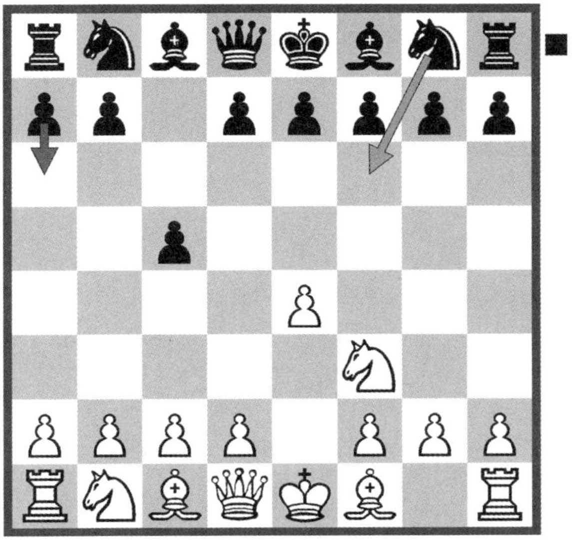

# Chapter Guide

## Chapter 12 – O'Kelly & Nimzowitsch Variations

1.e4 c5 2.♘f3

## a) 2...a6 3.g3

**1. e4 c5 2. ♘f3 a6**

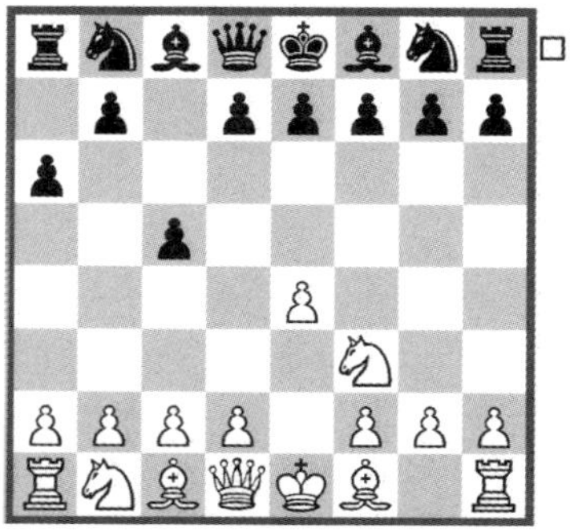

Position after: 2... a6

A common sideline, aiming to meet 3.d4 with 3...cxd4 4. ♘xd4 ♘f6 5.♘c3 e5, after which the b5-square is importantly covered.

**3. g3!?**

Let's start with this logical and underrated option before moving on to my main recommendation. The point is that our g2-bishop will be well placed against the likely ...b7-b5 push. I'll provide a few sample lines for the reader to get a better feel for the ideas. The positions are familiar to the chapter 3.g3 against 2...e6.

**3... ♘c6**

**A)** 3... b5 4. ♗g2 ♗b7 5. ♕e2 e6 6. 0-0

*(see analysis diagram next column)*

Position after: 6. 0-0

6... ♘f6 [6... d6 7. ♖d1!± Lining up the d2-d4 push. Also, it's difficult for Black to deal with the incoming a2-a4. Combined with our development advantage, this position looks practically horrible to defend.] 7. e5 ♘d5 8. ♘c3!± Aiming for ♘e4. White won a nice game in Svidler – Zhukova, Caleta 2017.

**B)** 3... d6 is a common reaction by Najdorf players. However, I don't think Black equalises here: 4. ♗g2

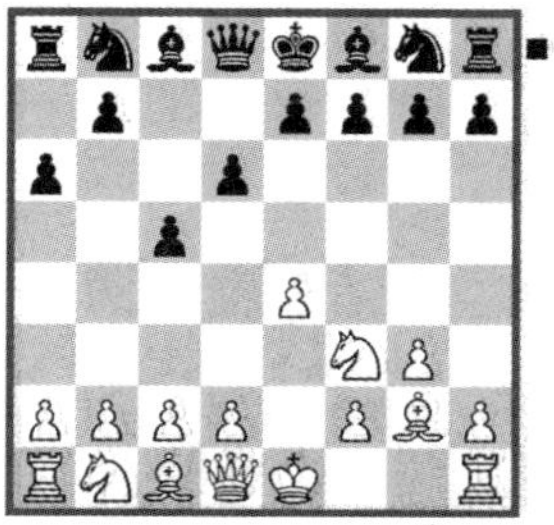

Position after: 4. ♗g2

**B1)** 4... g6 5. 0-0 ♗g7 6. c3±

**B2)** 4... ♘c6 5. c3 ♘f6 6. d4!

*(see analysis diagram next page)*

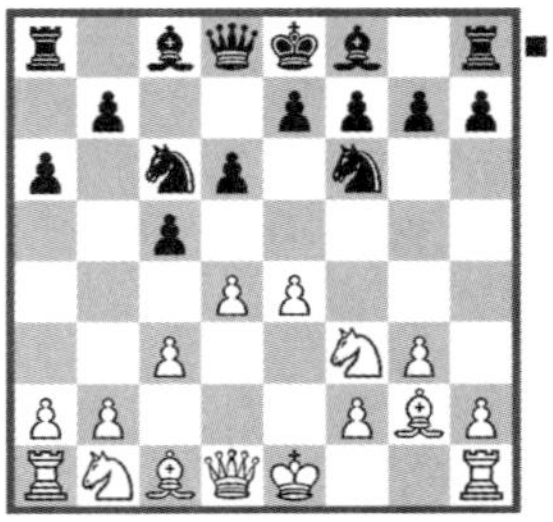

Position after: 6. d4!

The e4-pawn isn't hanging as we have the classic d4-d5 and ♕a4+ trick. 6... cxd4 7. cxd4 d5 [7... ♘xe4 8. d5 ♕a5+ 9. ♘fd2!+–; 7... ♗g4 8. 0-0 e5 9. d5 ♘d4 10. ♗e3±] 8. exd5 [8. e5 is also good but 8.exd5 is simpler to learn.] 8... ♘xd5 9. 0-0 e6 10. ♘c3±

**B3)** 4... ♘f6 5. e5! dxe5 [5... ♘fd7 6. exd6 e5 7. d4! cxd4 8. 0-0 ♗xd6 9. c3±] 6. ♘xe5

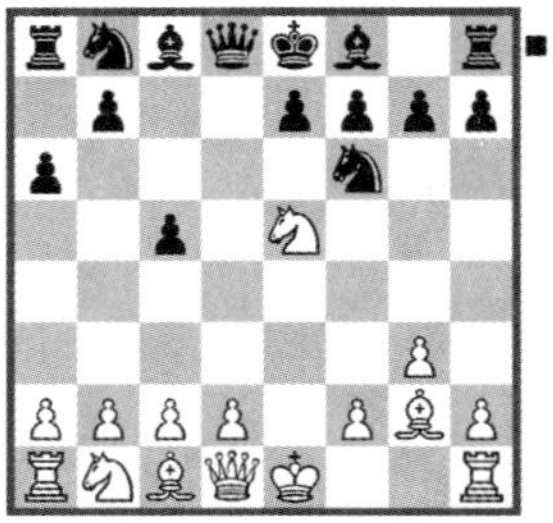

Position after: 6. ♘xe5

White is doing well regardless of how Black chooses to develop the f8-bishop. 6... g6 [6... e6 7. 0-0 ♗e7 8. a4±] 7. 0-0 ♗g7 8. ♖e1 ♘bd7 9. ♘c4 ♘b6 10. ♘xb6 ♕xb6 11. ♕f3± Followed by d2-d3 and a2-a4, with good pressure on Black's queenside.

**C)** 3... d5?! 4. exd5 ♕xd5 5. ♘c3! ♕e6+ 6. ♗e2 ♘f6 7. 0-0± Followed by ♖e1. Our bishop can easily relocate to the h1-a8 diagonal if needed, but the d2-d4 break already looks dangerous considering Black's lack of development.

**D)** 3... e6 will transpose to the chapter 2...e6 3.g3.

**4. ♗g2**

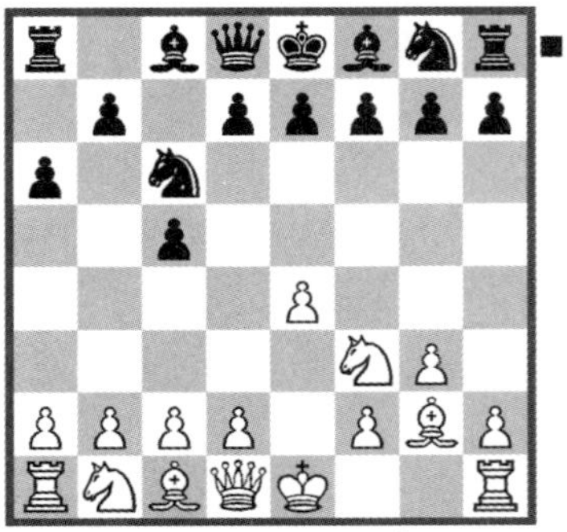

Position after: 4. ♗g2

**4... ♘f6**

**A)** 4... g6 Black aims to get control of the d4-square, but we are faster. 5. c3! [5. 0-0?! ♗g7 6. ♖e1 e5∞ Shankland – Moradiabadi, Saint Louis 2022.]

**A1)** 5... d5 is a typical response, but our bishop on g2 is well placed for this break: 6. exd5 ♕xd5 7. d4 cxd4 8. cxd4 ♗g4 9. ♘c3 ♕c4 Black's only critical option, but it leads to the following forcing line: 10. d5! ♗xf3 11. ♗xf3 ♘d4 12. d6! ♘xf3+ 13. ♕xf3 ♗g7 14. ♗f4± Followed by castling queenside. Black's king is much weaker than ours.

**A2)** 5... ♗g7 6. d4 cxd4 7. cxd4 d6

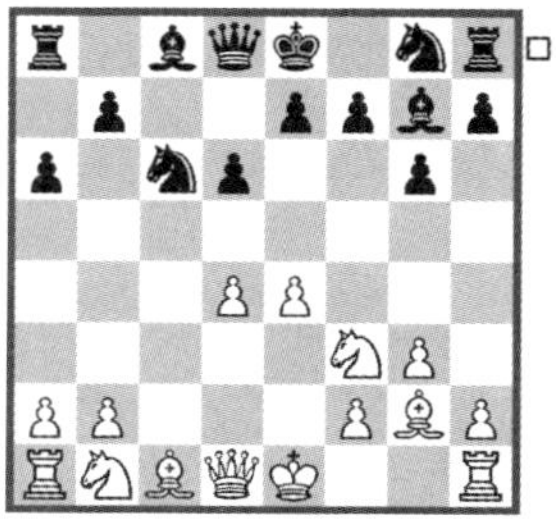

Position after: 7... d6

In Paravyan – Balakrishnan, Chess.com 2021, White's best continuation was 8. d5! ♘e5 9. ♘xe5 ♗xe5 10. 0-0± followed by ♘c3, ♗e3, ♕d2 etc.

**B)** 4... d6 is also met with 5. c3 where White has a comfortable advantage, e.g. 5... ♘f6 6. d4 cxd4 7. cxd4 ♗g4 8. 0-0 e5 9. d5 ♘d4 10. ♗e3⩲.

**5. e5 ♘g4 6. c3!**

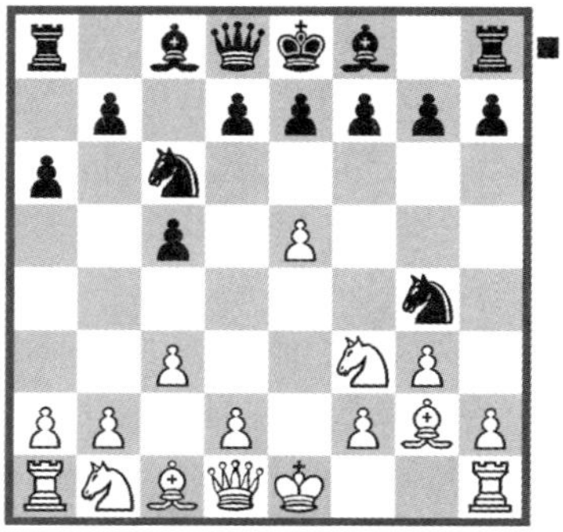

Position after: 6. c3!

This pawn sacrifice is the only way to achieve an advantage.

**6... d6**

6... ♘gxe5 7. ♘xe5 ♘xe5 8. d4 We'll gain a few tempi on the knight as we build our initiative. 8... cxd4 [8... ♘c6 9. d5 ♘e5 10. f4 ♘c4 11. ♕e2 ♘d6 12. 0-0± Black has a big problem with completing development. For example, 12...g6 is met with 13.f5!.] 9. cxd4

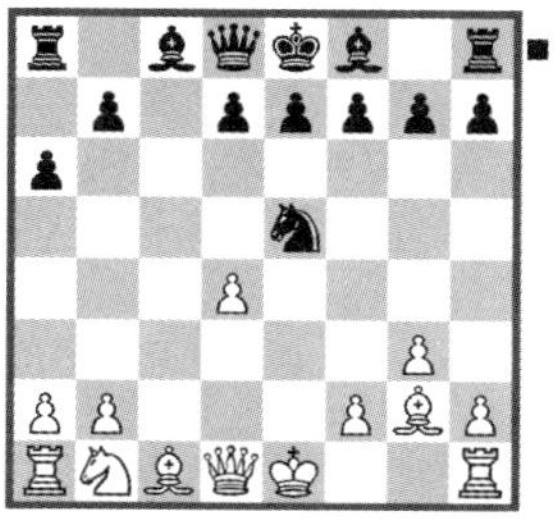

Position after: 9. cxd4

9... ♘g6 [9... ♘c6 10. d5 ♘e5 11. f4 ♘c4 12. ♕d3 ♘d6 13. ♗e3± Again, it's difficult for Black to complete development.] 10. h4! e6 11. d5!↑ With a strong initiative. It makes sense to castle queenside, after first developing with ♘c3, ♕d3 and ♗d2, for example.

**7. exd6**

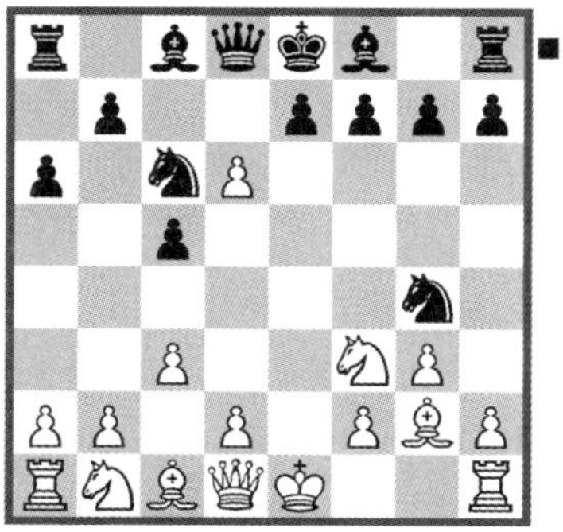

Position after: 7. exd6

**7... e5**

7... exd6 8. 0-0 ♗e7 9. d4 d5 Or else we'll push d4-d5. 10. dxc5 ♗xc5 11. h3 ♘f6 12. ♖e1+ ♗e6 13. ♘bd2±

**8. d4! cxd4**

8... exd4 9. ♕e2+ ♗e6 10. ♘g5 ♕xd6 11. 0-0

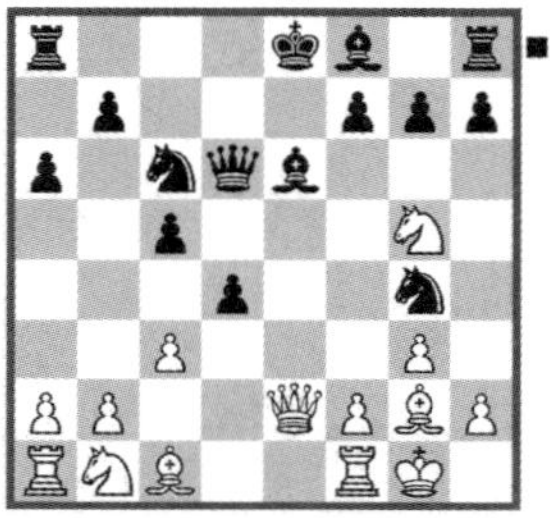

Position after: 11. 0-0

Note that it's more important to keep playing actively rather than attempting to recapture any material. 11... ♗e7 12. ♗f4 ♕d7 13. ♘xe6 ♕xe6 14. ♖e1! ♕xe2 15. ♖xe2 ♔d7 16. h3 ♘f6 17. cxd4 cxd4 [17... ♘xd4 18. ♖d2±] 18. ♘d2± White is still a pawn down but has excellent compensation, and the d4-pawn will soon be won.

**9. h3! ♘f6 10. cxd4 ♗xd6 11. dxe5 ♘xe5 12. 0-0**

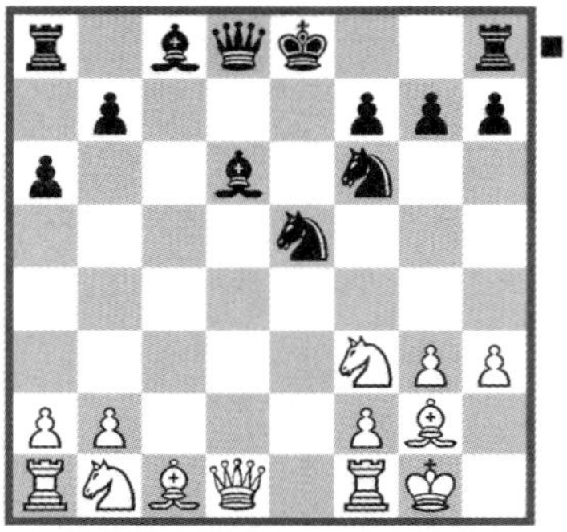

Position after: 12. 0-0

**12... 0-0 13. ♘c3±**

With a nice initiative. It's difficult for Black's queenside to complete development.

## b) 2...a6 3.c3 e6 & 3...♘f6

**1. e4 c5 2. ♘f3 a6 3. c3**

This is my choice – based on the fact that it's easiest to learn and understand, and ties in well with our choice of 3.c3 against 2...e6.

*(see diagram opposite column)*

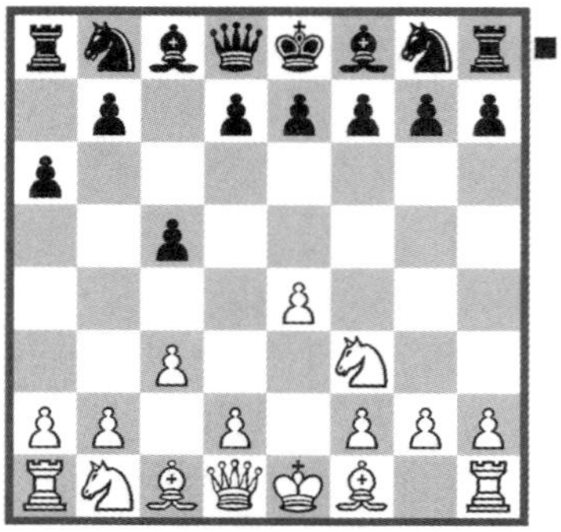

Position after: 3. c3

**3... e6**

3... ♘f6 Rarely played, but it's important to know how to gain an advantage here. It's similar to the Alapin structure except that Black hasn't committed to ...e7-e6 yet. We should play as actively as possible to capitalise on Black's lack of development. 4. e5 ♘d5 5. d4 cxd4 6. ♗c4!

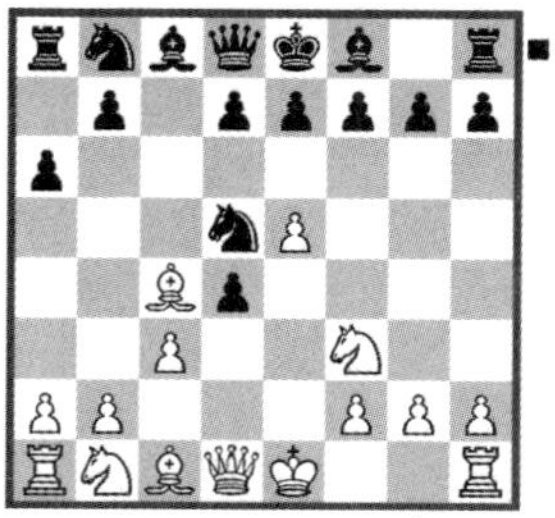

Position after: 6. ♗c4!

**A)** 6... e6 7. 0-0! ♘c6 [7... dxc3? 8. ♗xd5 cxb2 9. ♗xb2 exd5 10. ♘c3+–] 8. cxd4 d6 9. ♕e2 ♗e7 10. ♘c3 ♘xc3 11. bxc3± This is a favourable version of the positions encountered in the final subchapter of the section on the Alapin.

**B)** 6... ♘b6 7. ♗b3 Our plan is to wait for Black to commit to ...e7-e6 before we recapture on d4, which just transposes to an Alapin except that Black has wasted time on the useless ...a7-a6.

**B1)** 7... e6 8. cxd4 ♘c6 9. 0-0 d6 10. ♕e2 d5 11. ♘c3 ♗e7 12. ♗c2 ♗d7 13. a3±

**B2)** 7... dxc3? 8. ♘g5! e6 9. ♕h5 ♕e7 10. ♘xc3+– Followed by ♘ge4.

**B3)** 7... ♘c6 8. 0-0! d5 9. exd6 e6 10. cxd4 ♗xd6 11. ♘c3 0-0 12. ♖e1± This is a good IQP position, especially as Black's knight has moved from f6 to b6. Now we can focus our pieces on Black's kingside, for example with ♗c2, ♕d3, and ♘e5.

**B4)** 7... d5 8. exd6 ♕xd6 9. 0-0!

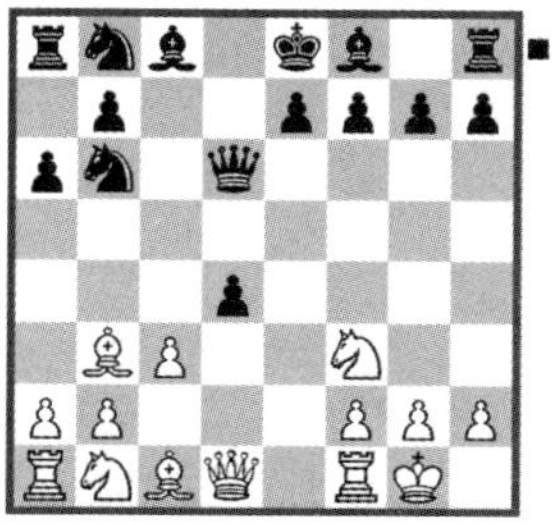

Position after: 9. 0-0!

9... ♘c6 [9... dxc3 10. ♘g5 still works, e.g. 10... e6 11. ♕f3 ♕e7 12. ♘xc3+–with a crushing lead in development.] 10. cxd4 e6 11. ♘c3 ♗e7 12. ♖e1 0-0 13. h4!± With a strong attack incoming.

**4. d4 d5 5. e5**

This is a favourable version of the French advanced for White, as Black has wasted time on ...a7-a6.

*(see diagram next page)*

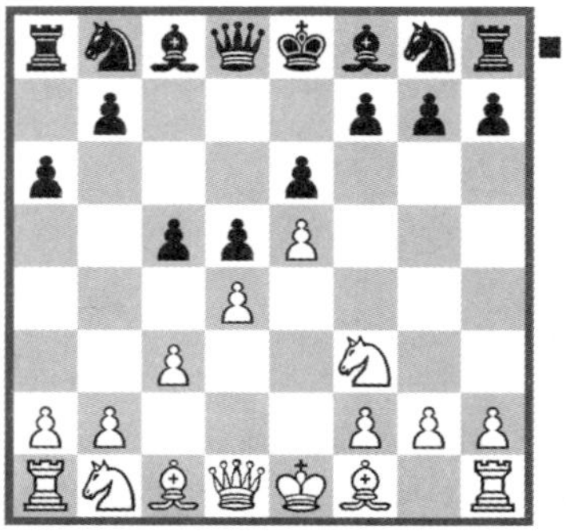

Position after: 5. e5

**5... ♗d7**

Black aims to make use of their ...a7-a6 move by quickly trading the light-squared bishops with ...♗b5.

5... ♘c6 There aren't any particularly critical lines here. I will just give a short summary of the standard variations and explain how to reach an advantage. 6. ♗d3

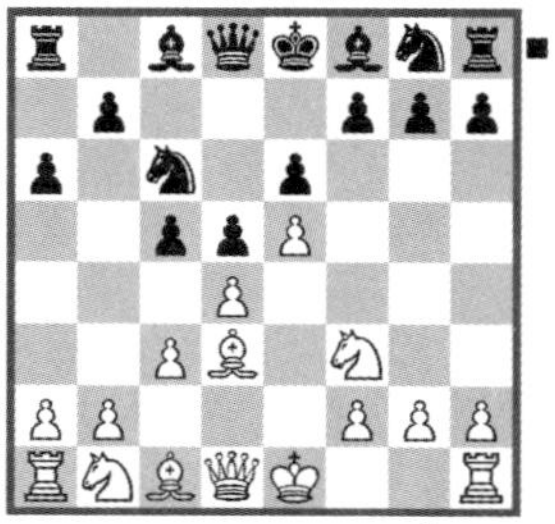

Position after: 6. ♗d3

**A)** 6... ♕b6 7. dxc5! ♗xc5 8. 0-0 ♕c7 9. ♗f4 ♘ge7 10. ♗g3 ♘g6 11. ♖e1±

**B)** 6... cxd4 7. cxd4 ♘ge7 This is similar to the Alapin chapter on 3...♘c6. However, because Black has wasted time on ...a7-a6, we don't need to defend the d-pawn with ♘a3-c2. 8. ♘c3 ♘f5 9. ♗c2!± The point is that 9...♕b6 would lose the d5-pawn.

**C)** 6... ♗d7 7. a3!

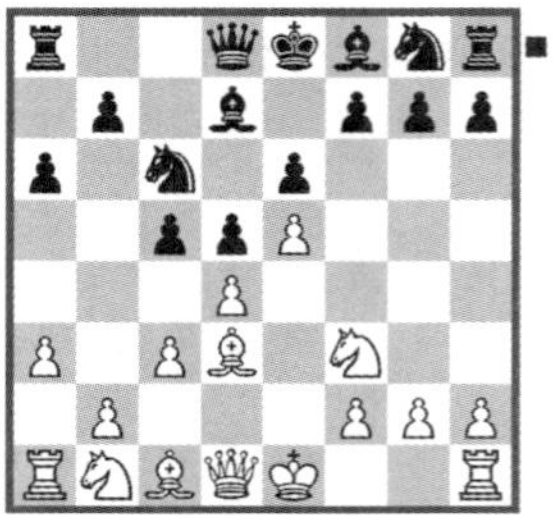

Position after: 7. a3!

Attempting to expand on the queenside with b2-b4. Black has several ways to play here but none of them seem to equalise.

**C1)** 7... ♘h6 8. 0-0 ♘f5 transposes to 7... ♘ge7 as we will see now.

**C2)** 7... ♘ge7 8. 0-0

**C2.1)** 8... cxd4 9. cxd4 ♘f5 10. ♗xf5! This capture makes sense considering Black has played ...♗d7, since now ...♗e6 will require another tempo to be wasted. 10... exf5 11. ♘c3 ♗e6 12. ♘e2! ♗e7 13. ♗d2 h6 14. ♕b3± Followed by ♘e1-d3. White has good control over the position.

**C2.2)** 8... ♘f5 9. ♖e1

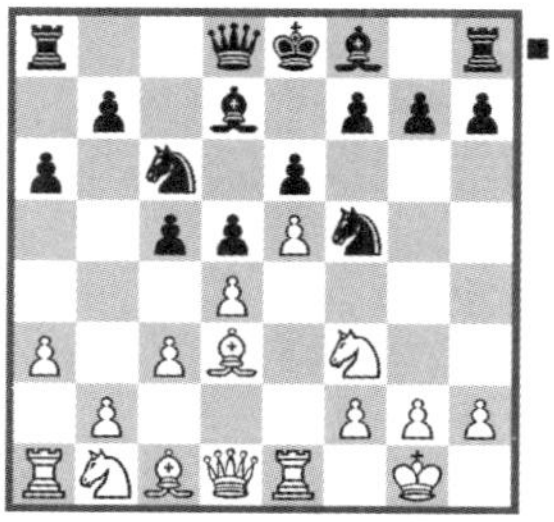

Position after: 9. ♖e1

This is the best available option, considering we don't have the possibility of capturing on f5 followed by ♘c3 here. 9... cxd4 [9... ♗e7 10. dxc5 ♗xc5 11. ♘bd2± White has plenty of ideas here, for example b2-b4 and c3-c4, or ♘f1-g3.] 10. ♗xf5 exf5 11. ♘xd4 ♘xd4 12. ♕xd4±

**C3)** 7... ♖c8 ties in to Black's strategy of focusing on the queenside. 8. b4 cxd4 9. cxd4 ♕b6 10. ♗e3! ♘a7 11. ♕d2 ♗b5 Black manages to exchange the light-squared bishops, but I still think White has an advantage after 12. ♘c3 ♗xd3 13. ♕xd3 ♕c6 14. ♖c1±.

**C4)** 7... ♕b6 8. ♗c2! The pawn on a3 is very useful in covering the b4-square. 8... ♖c8 [8... ♘ge7 9. dxc5 ♕xc5 10. 0-0 ♘g6 11. ♖e1± Followed by ♘bd2, and White was doing well in Pingin – Zvjaginsev, Khanty – Mansiysk 2020.] 9. dxc5! It makes sense to prevent the c-file from completely opening. 9... ♗xc5 10. 0-0 ♕c7 11. ♗f4± Followed by ♘bd2.

**6. ♗d3**

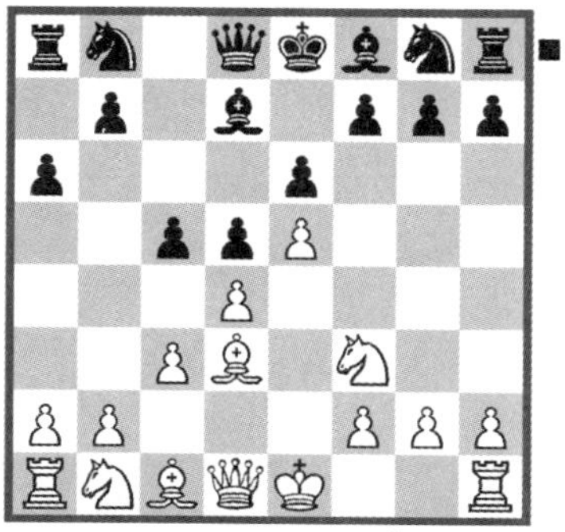

Position after: 6. ♗d3

**6... cxd4**

**A)** 6... ♗b5?! 7. ♗xb5+ axb5 8. dxc5! ♗xc5 9. b4 ♗b6 and now in Lagno – Hou, Chess.com 2020, White could have simply won a pawn with 10. ♘a3!±.

**B)** 6... ♕b6 7. 0-0 ♗b5 8. dxc5 ♗xc5 9. b4 ♗e7 10. ♗e3+–

**7. cxd4 ♗b5 8. ♗c2!**

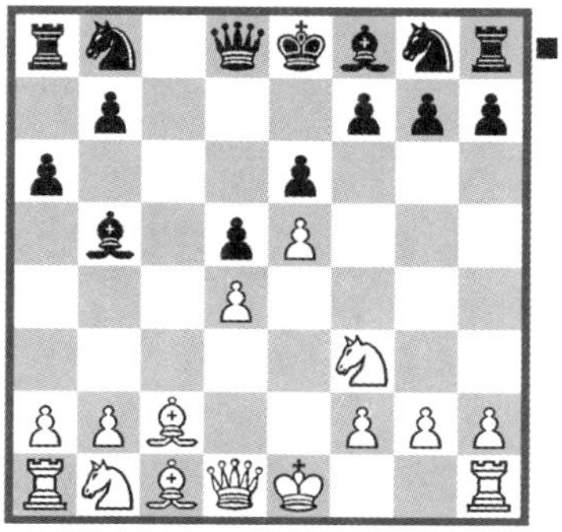

Position after: 8. ♗c2!

Black only prevents us from castling temporarily.

**8... ♗b4+**

8... a5 9. ♘c3 ♗a6 10. ♘e2±
**9. ♗d2 a5 10. ♘c3 ♗a6 11. ♘e2±**

Followed by 0-0, and White has an excellent position.

## c) 2...a6 3.c3 d5

**1. e4 c5 2. ♘f3 a6 3. c3 d5**

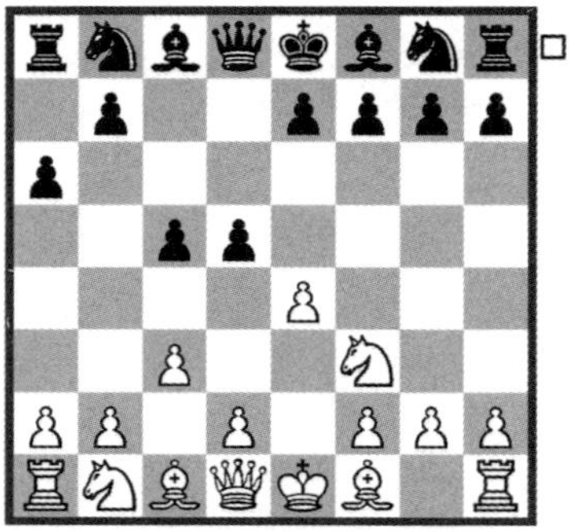
Position after: 3... d5

**4. exd5 ♕xd5**

4... ♘f6 has also been tried, but after 5. ♕a4+! it looks difficult for Black to recapture the pawn.

**A)** 5... ♘bd7 6. c4! b5

Position after: 6... b5

The only testing line, but with accurate play we keep a comfortable advantage. 7. cxb5 g6 [7... ♘xd5 8. ♘c3 ♘b4 9. d4±] 8. bxa6! ♘xd5 9. ♘c3 ♘b4 10. d4 ♗xa6 11. ♗xa6 ♖xa6 12. ♕d1± Followed by 0-0.

**B)** 5... ♕d7 6. ♕xd7+ ♗xd7 7. c4±

**C)** 5... ♗d7 6. ♕b3 ♗c8 [6... b5 7. a4 e6 8. axb5 exd5 9. d4±] 7. c4 e6 8. ♘c3 exd5 9. ♘xd5 ♘xd5 10. cxd5± Followed by ♗e2 and d2-d4. It's not clear how Black will win the pawn back.

**5. d4**

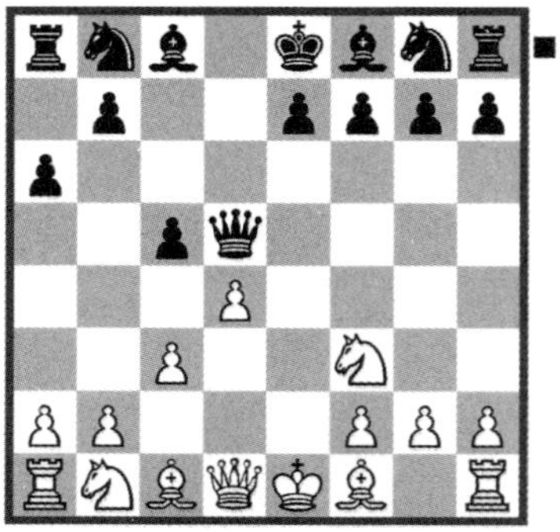
Position after: 5. d4

The reason why I think 3. c3 is easiest to learn against 2...a6 is because it corresponds closely to the Alapin line with 3...d5 4...♕xd5. It's likely that Black will play ...e7-e6 at some point here.

**5... ♘f6**

**A)** 5... ♗g4 is logical, attempting to capitalise on the fact that Black has delayed ... e7-e6. However, the bishop is actually misplaced on this square. 6. ♗e2 e6 7. h3 ♗h5 It's possible to simply castle here, but I like the dynamic option considering that Black has yet to develop their kingside. [7... ♗f5 8. 0-0 ♘f6 9. ♘bd2!± Followed by ♘c4, and Black's position looks suspect.] 8. c4! ♕d8 9. d5!

Position after: 9. d5!

9... exd5 [9... ♘f6 10. ♘c3 exd5 11. g4! ♗g6 12. cxd5 ♗d6 This transposes to 9...exd5.] 10. cxd5 ♗d6 11. ♘c3 ♘f6 [11... ♘e7 doesn't make Black's life any easier: 12. g4! ♗g6 13. h4 h6 14. h5 ♗h7 15. ♗d3 ♗xd3 16. ♕xd3 ♘d7 17. ♗e3± Followed by 0-0-0.] 12. g4! In general this advance is very strong because we always retain the option to castle queenside. 12... ♗g6 13. g5! ♘g8 [13... ♘fd7 14. h4 ♗h5 15. ♘d2+–] 14. h4 ♘d7 15. h5 ♗f5 16. ♗d3± With another strong initiative.

**B)** 5... e6 6. ♗e3 Threatening to capture on d4. 6... cxd4 would transpose to the mainline after 5...♘f6, but we can check the alternatives:

**B1)** 6... b6 7. c4! ♕d8 8. ♘c3 ♘f6 9. d5! exd5 10. ♘xd5 ♘xd5 11. ♕xd5 ♕xd5 12. cxd5± Followed by 0-0-0 and ♘d2, with a strong initiative.

**B2)** 6... ♘f6 Black doesn't have enough compensation for the pawn in the following line: 7. dxc5 ♕xd1+ 8. ♔xd1 ♘c6 9. ♘bd2 ♘d5 10. ♗d4 ♘xd4 11. cxd4 b6 12. cxb6 ♘xb6 13. ♗d3±

**B3)** 6... ♘d7 7. c4 ♕d6 8. ♘c3 ♘gf6 9. ♗e2 b6 10. 0-0 ♗b7

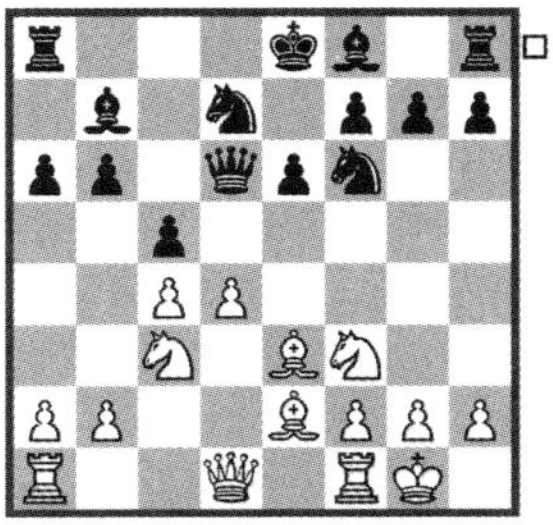

Position after: 10... ♗b7

We have been following Giri – Artemiev, Chess.com 2020. Here the best continuation for White is 11. dxc5! ♘xc5 [11... bxc5 12. ♕xd6 ♗xd6 13. ♘d2± White has a nice edge here due to the superior pawn structure. A logical continuation is ♖ad1, f2-f4, and ♗f3.] 12. b4! ♘cd7 13. ♕xd6 ♗xd6 14. ♖ab1±.

**6. ♗e3**

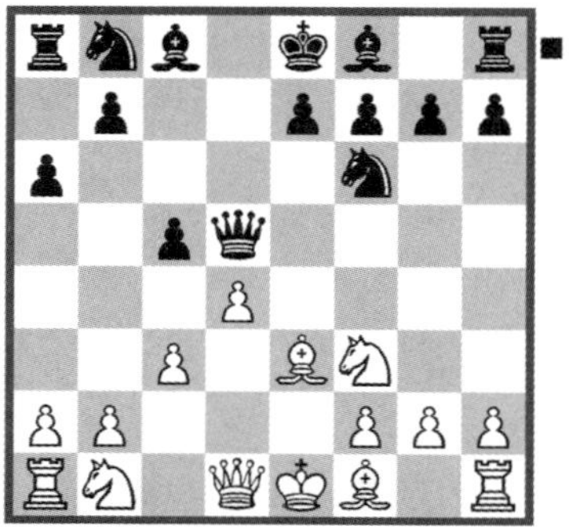

Position after: 6. ♗e3

The fact that Black has played ...a7-a6 instead of ...e7-e6 means that ♘a3 here isn't as effective, since the b5-square is already covered. Rather, the text move forces Black to capture on d4, after which we can develop the b1-knight to its optimal c3-square and apply central pressure.

**6... cxd4**

There aren't any alternatives which don't lose material.

**7. cxd4 e6**

7... ♗g4 In general this move is bad – the bishop is often important in defending Black's queenside, particularly the b7-pawn. 8. ♘c3 ♕d7 9. ♗e2 e6 10. ♕b3!± Threatening ♘e5. Black probably has to capture on f3, after which our advantage is clear.

**8. ♘c3**

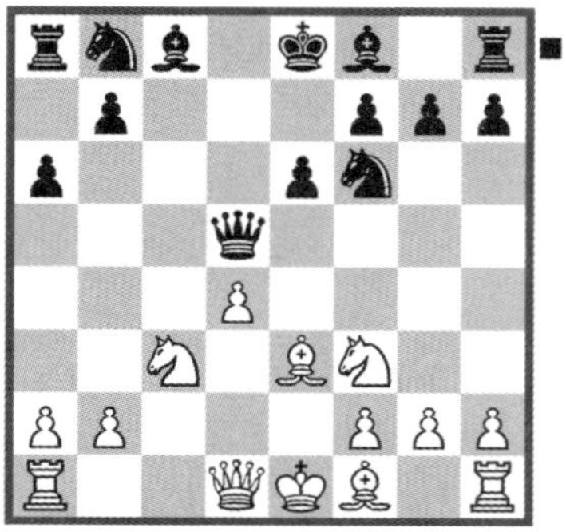

Position after: 8. ♘c3

Our plan is the same regardless of where Black puts the queen. We'll continue with ♗d3, 0-0, and finish development while always considering either ♘e5 or ♘e4. There's not much theory here so I won't make the variations too detailed. It is more important to gain a feel for how to continue playing dynamically with an IQP.

**8... ♕d8**

8... ♕d6 More popular than 8...♕d8, although it feels like the queen is a target here. 9. ♗d3

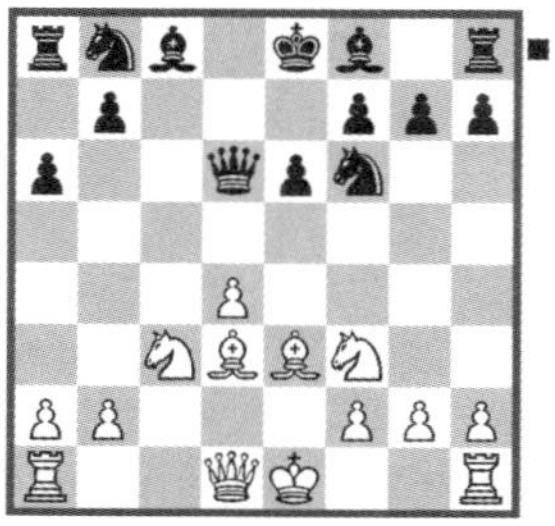

Position after: 9. ♗d3

**A)** 9... ♘c6 10. 0-0 ♗e7 11. ♘e4!? It's logical to exchange these knights – in essence we're removing a defender of Black's king. 11... ♘xe4 12. ♗xe4 ♘b4 13. ♘e5! 0-0 [13... ♘d5 14. ♕h5! g6 15. ♕f3+– Black is forced to make another concession and we'll follow up with ♘c4 and ♗xd5, after which their position is basically lost.] 14. ♖e1 ♘d5 15. ♕d3 ♘f6 16. ♖ac1± Black has managed to bring the knight to f6, but we have excellent piece activity and retain a strong initiative.

**B)** 9... ♗e7 10. 0-0 0-0 11. ♖c1

Position after: 11. ♖c1

[11. ♘e4?! is too early, as Black can play 11... ♘xe4 12. ♗xe4 ♘d7!∞, bringing another knight to f6.]

**B1)** 11... ♘bd7 12. ♖e1 b5 13. ♘e4! The typical reaction against ...b7-b5. The following line is one example of how we can keep increasing the pressure on Black's position. 13... ♕b8 14. ♗g5 ♗b7 15. ♘e5! ♕d8 16. ♘c5!

Position after: 16. ♘c5!

16... ♗xc5 [16... ♗d5 17. ♘cxd7 ♘xd7 18. ♕h5 g6 19. ♘xg6 hxg6 20. ♗xg6 fxg6 21. ♕xg6+ ♔h8 22. ♖c3 ♗xg5 23. ♖h3+ ♗h4 24. ♕h6+ ♔g8 25. ♖xh4 ♕xh4 26. ♕xh4±] 17. ♗xf6 ♘xf6 18. dxc5±

**B2)** 11... ♘c6 12. ♖e1 ♘b4 13. ♗b1 ♘bd5 14. ♗g5 ♗d7 15. ♘e5↑ We can continue to ramp up the pressure with ♕d3 and h2-h4. This doesn't look like an easy position for Black to handle.

**9. ♗d3**

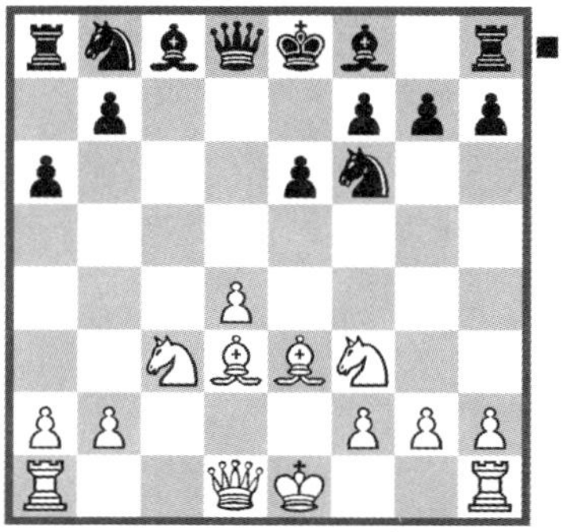
Position after: 9. ♗d3

As Black is definitely castling kingside, this is the best place for the bishop to eye up the h7-square.

**9... ♘c6**

**A)** 9... b6 10. ♕a4+! Disrupting Black's queenside development.

**A1)** 10... ♘bd7 11. d5! A typical sacrifice, opening the position and enabling our queen to switch over to the kingside once Black has castled. 11... exd5 12. 0-0 ♗b7 13. ♖fe1 ♗e7 14. ♗g5 0-0 15. ♕h4→ With a strong attack – there are plenty of sacrifices on the cards. ♗xh7 is the immediate threat, and 15... h6 can be met with 16. ♗xh6!.

**A2)** 10... ♗d7 11. ♕b3 ♘c6 12. 0-0 ♗e7 13. ♖ad1± Black is very passive. Meanwhile we have ideas like d4-d5 and ♘e5 incoming.

**B)** 9... b5 10. a4! b4 11. ♘e4 ♗b7 12. ♘xf6+

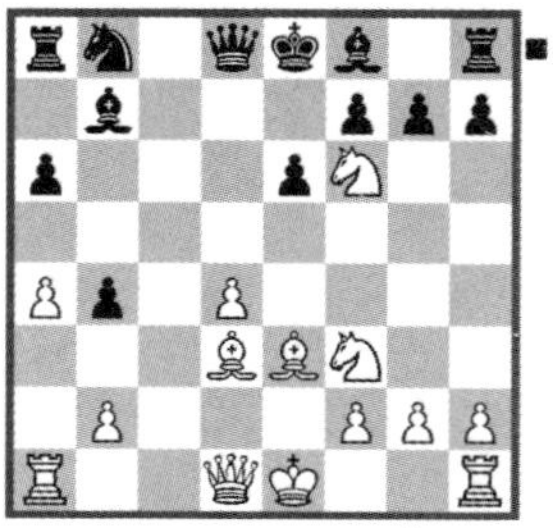

Position after: 12. ♘xf6+

12... gxf6 [12... ♕xf6? loses the queen after 13. ♗g5 ♗xf3 14. ♕c1+–.] 13. 0-0 White has an excellent position. It's not clear where Black's king is going – the only line to check is 13... ♖g8 14. ♖e1 ♕d5 but here we have the important 15. ♔f1!± followed by ♖c1 and ♗c4.

**10. a3!**

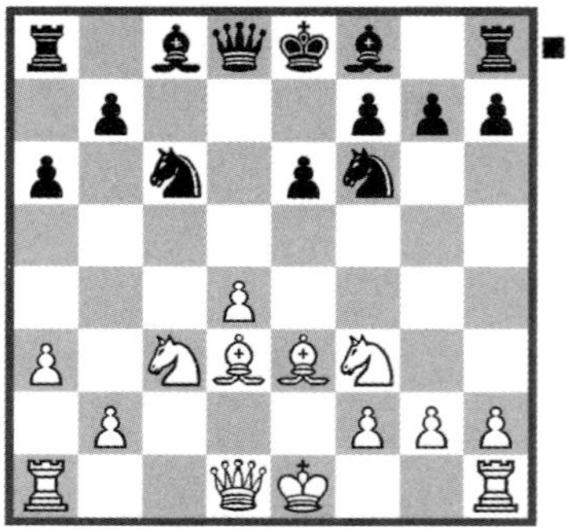

Position after: 10. a3!

I don't really want to allow ...♘b4.

**10... ♗e7 11. 0-0 0-0 12. ♕c2!±**

This looks like the best place for the queen. We'll continue with ♖ad1 and ♖fe1, before considering moves like ♘e5, d4-d5, ♗g5, or ♘e4. White has a comfortable edge and pleasant prospects for the future.

## d) 2...♘f6 – Nimzowitsch Variation

**1. e4 c5 2. ♘f3 ♘f6**

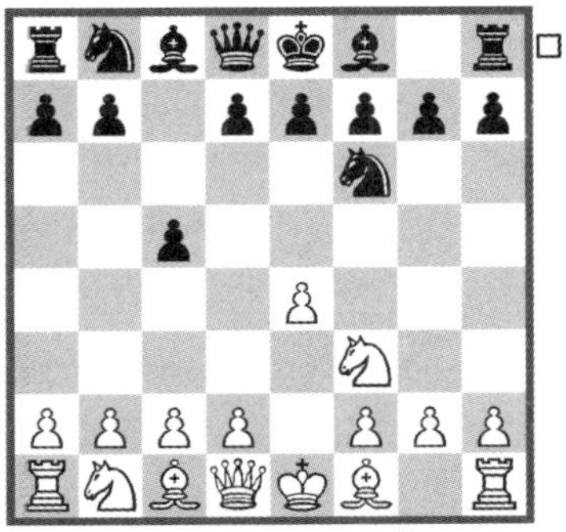

Position after: 2... ♘f6

This is a popular variation in rapid or blitz chess, aiming to catch us out and avoid heavy theoretical lines. I don't think it's necessary to know a huge amount here, so I won't delve too deeply with my analysis.

**3. e5**

3. ♘c3 is the alternative option, but doesn't fit with our repertoire as Black could respond 3... d6 bringing us towards a Najdorf.

**3... ♘d5 4. ♘c3!**

Black has two main options here, namely 4...e6 or 4...♘xc3, but it's worth briefly considering the other knight jumps too.

*(see diagram next column)*

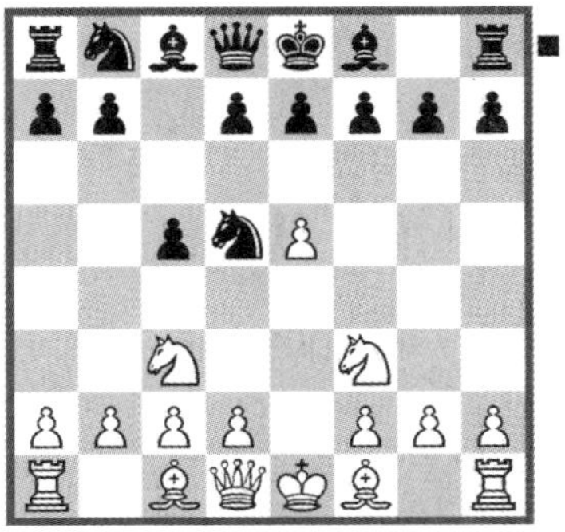

Position after: 4. ♘c3!

**4... e6**

**A)** 4... ♘b4? 5. d4! cxd4 6. ♘xd4 ♘8c6 7. a3! ♘xd4

Position after: 7... ♘xd4

Black obviously didn't want to retreat to a6, but now the d4-knight can be chased around the board. 8. axb4 ♘c6 9. b5! ♘xe5 10. f4 ♘g6 11. f5 ♘e5 12. ♗f4 d6 13. b6! The final blow – ♘d5 next will be crushing. 13... ♕xb6 14. ♘d5 ♕d8 15. ♗xe5 dxe5 16. ♗b5+ ♗d7 17. ♕e2! ♗c6 18. ♕xe5+– Most likely followed by 0-0-0, when Black can probably resign.

**B)** 4... ♘c7?! 5. d4 cxd4 6. ♕xd4! ♘c6 7. ♕h4

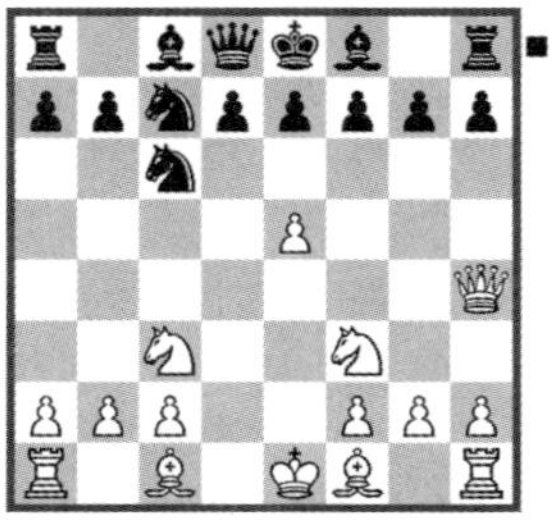
Position after: 7. ♕h4

The queen is well placed here to support a kingside attack after we develop our c1-bishop and castle queenside. 7... d5 8. exd6 exd6 Necessary, but the queen trade doesn't reduce our advantage. [8... ♕xd6 9. ♗f4 ♕e6+ 10. ♗e2+– Followed by castling on either side and putting a rook on e1. Black won't be able to survive as our pieces are too active.] 9. ♕xd8+ ♘xd8 10. ♗e3± Followed by 0-0-0 with a big advantage.

**C)** 4... ♘xc3 5. dxc3 ♘c6 6. ♗f4 This line has been tested in several top-level games, albeit at shorter time controls. However engines nowadays have shown that White's advantage is quite large. The most common plan is simply to push the h-pawn and acquire even more space.

**C1)** 6... d5 7. exd6 exd6 8. ♕d2 d5 9. 0-0-0 ♗e6 10. ♘g5±

**C2)** 6... e6 7. h4! h6 8. h5 b6 9. ♕d3!± Followed by ♘d2 and ♘e4. White will also obviously castle queenside.

**C3)** 6... ♕b6 Black aims to force a queenside concession before completing their development, but this doesn't really bother us. 7. b3 ♕c7 8. h4! We embark on the same plan as shown after 6...♕c7. 8... b6 9. ♗g3 e6 10. h5 h6 11. ♗d3 ♗b7 12. ♕e2 0-0-0 13. 0-0-0 d5

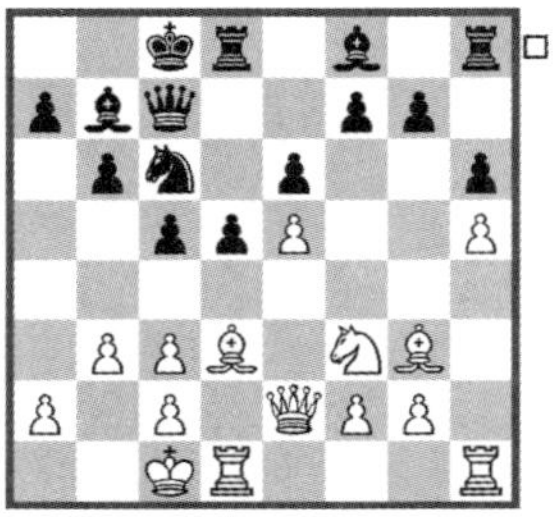
Position after: 13... d5

Black must make this break, but we still keep a large advantage with accurate play. 14. exd6 ♗xd6 15. ♖h3!± The big issue for Black is that their kingside pawns will be big weaknesses in the long term.

**C4)** 6... ♕c7 7. h4! e6 8. h5 h6 [8... f6 9. ♕e2 d6 10. exd6 ♗xd6 11. ♗xd6 ♕xd6 12. ♕e3± Followed by ♘d2 and ♘e4.] 9. ♕d3!± I like this plan. We'll continue with ♘d2, before potentially opting to castle queenside.

**5. ♘e4!?**

*(see diagram next page)*

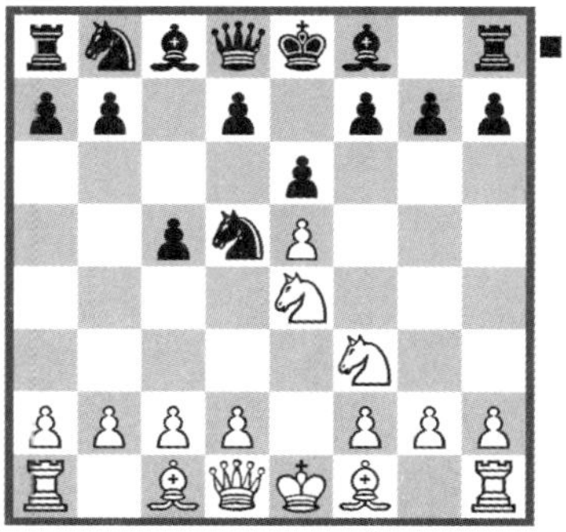

Position after: 5. ♘e4!?

Planning to kick the d5-knight away with c2-c4.

5. ♘xd5 is the other possibility, and also looks good for White: 5... exd5 6. d4 ♘c6 7. dxc5 ♗xc5 8. ♕xd5 ♕b6 [8... d6 The more solid option, although White has an advantage here too. 9. exd6 ♕b6 10. ♕e4+! ♗e6 11. ♕h4 ♗xd6 12. ♗e2± Followed by 0-0. Black is yet to prove full compensation for the pawn.] 9. ♗c4! ♗xf2+ 10. ♔e2 0-0 11. ♖f1 ♗c5 12. ♘g5 ♘d4+ [12... ♘xe5 leads to an advantageous ending for White after 13. ♘xf7 ♘xf7 14. ♖xf7 ♕e6+ 15. ♕xe6 dxe6 16. ♖xf8+ ♔xf8 17. ♗g5±.] 13. ♔d1 ♘e6 14. ♘e4 d6 [14... ♗e7 15. ♘d6!±] 15. exd6 ♖d8 In Karjakin – Mamedyarov, chess24.com 2021, White was just winning after 16. ♕h5 ♗xd6 17. ♗d3+–.

**5... f5**

5... ♘c6 6. c4!

*(see analysis diagram next column)*

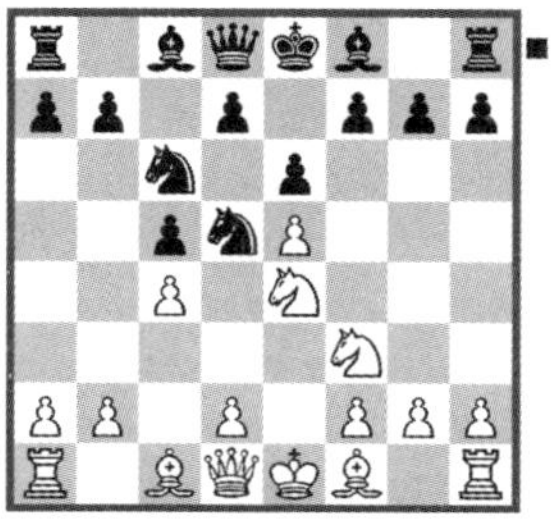

Position after: 6. c4!

**A)** 6... f5 is rarely played but is important to know about. 7. cxd5 fxe4 8. dxc6 exf3 9. ♕xf3 dxc6 10. ♗e2

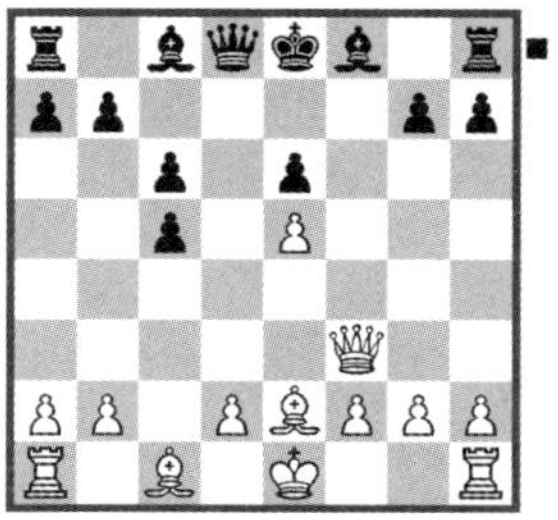

Position after: 10. ♗e2

The big problem for Black is their awful pawn structure. If we can prevent Black from getting their pieces active, we will just be positionally winning. 10... ♗e7 [10... ♕d4 11. ♕c3 ♕e4 12. f3 ♕d4 13. b3± Followed by ♗b2.] 11. d3 ♕d4 12. ♕g3! ♕b4+ [12... g6 13. 0-0±] 13. ♔d1! A surprising direction, but the king will stand well on c2. For example: 13... g6 14. ♔c2 ♗d7 15. ♗e3 0-0-0 16. ♖ac1± Followed by ♔b1, before probing on the kingside with h2-h4.

**B)** 6... ♘c7 7. ♘d6+! ♗xd6 8. exd6 ♘a6 9. d4 cxd4 10. a3!

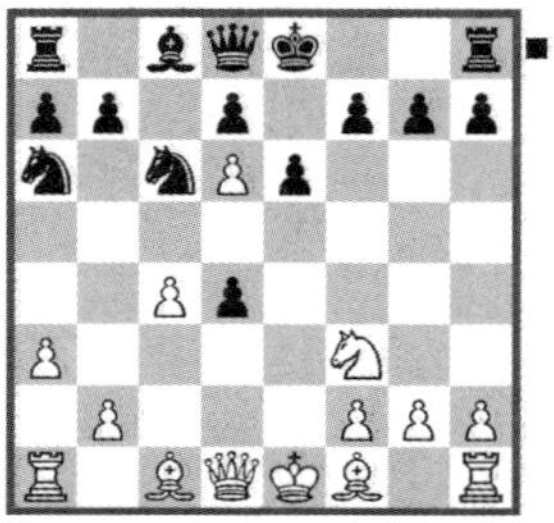
Position after: 10. a3!

Dominating on the dark squares. We don't mind sacrificing a pawn – for example, 10...e5 is met with 11.b4. The other critical line follows: 10... ♘c5 11. b4 ♘e4 12. ♗d3 ♘xd6 13. c5 ♘f5 14. 0-0 0-0 15. ♗xf5 exf5 16. b5 ♘e7 17. ♕xd4± With total dominance.

**C)** 6... ♘b6 7. d4 cxd4 8. ♘d6+! Once again it's logical to sacrifice a pawn, as Black will be positionally lost. 8... ♗xd6 9. exd6 e5 10. ♗d3 0-0 11. 0-0+–

**6. ♘c3!**

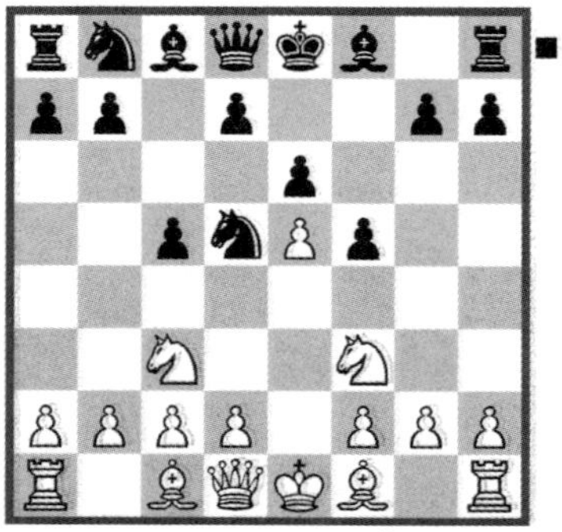
Position after: 6. ♘c3!

The concept behind our play is that Black has weakened their position by pushing ...f7-f5, and that concession is worth us losing two tempi for.

**6... ♘c6**

**A)** 6... ♘xc3 7. dxc3 ♘c6 8. ♗f4 b6 There are many ways to play this position, but the most direct is: [8... ♕b6 9. ♕c1 ♕c7 10. h4 a6 11. a4 b6 12. h5 ♗b7 13. ♗e2 ♗e7 14. ♕e3±] 9. h4! ♗b7 10. ♖h3 ♕c7 11. ♕e2 ♗e7 12. ♘g5 g6 13. h5± White won a nice game in Deac – Krastev, Reykjavik 2021.

**B)** 6... ♘e7 7. ♘b5! ♘g6 8. b3 Once again preparing a pawn sacrifice. 8... a6 9. ♘d6+ ♗xd6 10. exd6 ♕b6 11. ♗b2 0-0 12. h4!

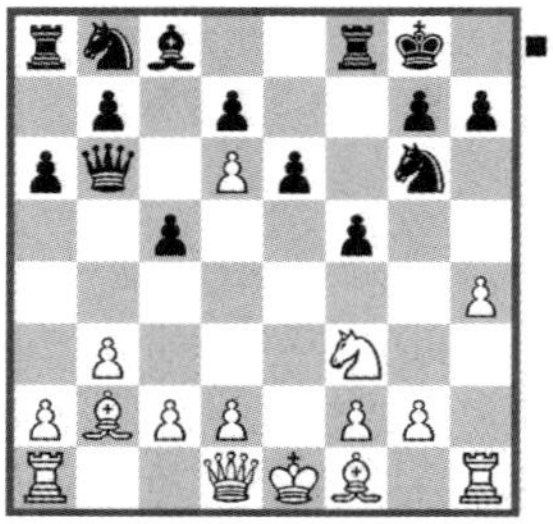
Position after: 12. h4!

12... ♕xd6 13. h5 ♘e7 [13... ♘h8 14. ♖g1! ♘c6 15. g4→] 14. h6 g6 In Giri – Le, Chess.com 2020, White would have had a big advantage after the logical 15. d4! cxd4 16. ♗xd4 ♘bc6 17. ♗g7 ♕xd1+ 18. ♖xd1 ♖e8 19. c4±.

**7. ♘xd5 exd5 8. d4**

*(see diagram next page)*

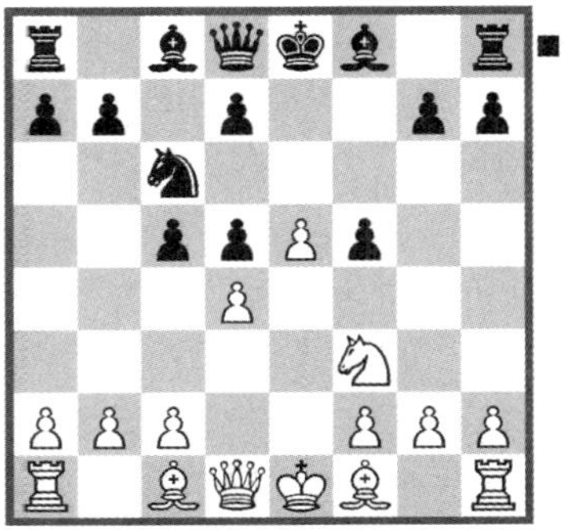
Position after: 8. d4

This line is the clearest demonstration that Black's ...f7-f5 push has created a significant weakness.

**8... d6 9. ♗f4 cxd4 10. exd6 ♗xd6 11. ♗xd6 ♕xd6 12. ♕d2±**

Followed by 0-0-0 and recapturing on d4.

## *Conclusion to Chapter 12*

It's logical to conclude this series with the O'Kelly and Nimzowitsch sidelines because the structures that we've encountered in this chapter correspond closely to lines from both this book and Volume 1. For example, 2...a6 3.g3 is very similar to our chapter on the Kings Indian Attack, whilst the variations after 2...a6 3.c3 often relate to the Alapin chapter.

Against the Nimzowitsch, the idea of playing d2-d4 followed by Qxd4 and a quick Qh4 reminds me of the Rossolimo line 3...g6 4.♗xc6 bxc6 5.0-0 ♗g7 6.♖e1 ♘f6 from Volume 1. These similarities sum up our approach across both volumes in consistently interlinking themes and integrating an 'Anti-Sicilian style'.

As I've repeated many times, the theory in this book will become outdated but the interconnected ideas will always remain and ensure that readers will be able to respond to any future developments in the Anti-Sicilian.

# www.thinkerspublishing.com

# SPRING 2023

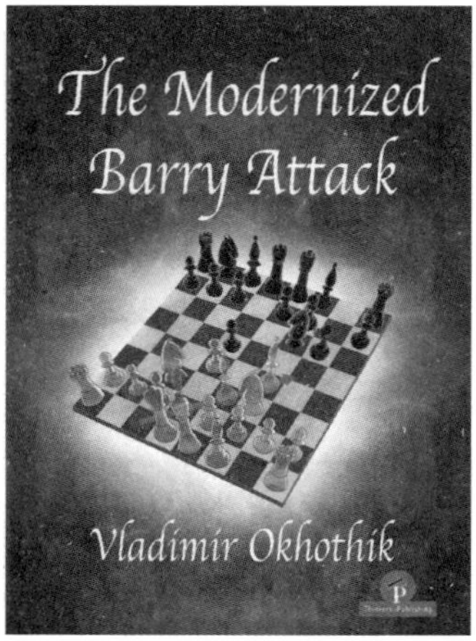

www.thinkerspublishing.com

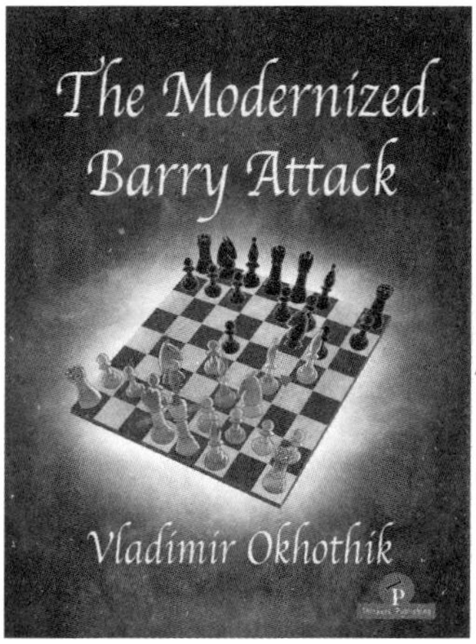